ELIHU BURRITT LIBRARY
CENTRAL CONNECTICUT STATE UNIVERSITY
NEW BRITAIN, CONNECTICUT 06050

Dictionary of the modern politics of Japan

The politics of Japan are less widely reported than the Japanese economy. Most people are aware of the economic 'miracle' following the Second World War, whereby Japan became the second largest economy in the world after the United States, and the economic stagnation of the early 1990s is also well known. But it is difficult to make sense of these phenomena without a knowledge of the political system and the ways in which it works in practice. Containing an Introductory essay, a section on Theories of Japanese politics, and around 250 A-Z entries, the *Dictionary of the Modern Politics of Japan* remedies this imbalance and answers the need for an accessible work of reference bringing together information and authoritative analysis on all aspects of the politics of Japan and the Japanese political system.

Written by a leading academic authority and commentator on the domestic and international politics of Japan, the Dictionary provides comprehensive coverage of:

- prime ministers, party leaders and important politicians;
- political parties and other political bodies;
- agencies of central government and the judicial and electoral systems;
- political crises, episodes and scandals;
- influential interest groups, such as those representing industry, commerce, the professions, agriculture, consumers, women, etc;
- the constitution and constitutional issues, including the peace clause; and
- areas of government policy.

Including a full and annotated bibliography to guide the user to further reading, the entries are thoroughly cross-referenced and indexed, and are supplemented with maps, graphs and tables, to ensure that the *Dictionary of the Modern Politics of Japan* is essential reading for all scholars and students of the politics and international relations of Japan. It is also destined to become a vital resource for journalists, diplomats and others with an interest in the region.

J.A.A. Stockwin is Director of the Nissan Institute of Japanese Studies at the University of Oxford, Professorial Fellow at St Antony's College, Oxford, and Nissan Professor of Modern Japanese Studies. Among his many publications he is the author of *The Japanese Socialist Party and Neutralism* (1968) and *Governing Japan: Divided Politics in a Major Economy* (1999). He is the co-author of *Dynamic and Immobilist Politics in Japan* (1988) and the translator of Junji Banno's *The Establishment of the Japanese Constitutional System* (1992), also published by Routledge, and is the general editor of the acclaimed Routledge/Nissan Institute Japanese Studies Series.

Dictionary of the modern politics of Japan

J.A.A. Stockwin

LONDON AND NEW YORK

CCSU Reference
Ref JQ1605 S86 2003
Stockwin, J. A. A. (James
Arthur Ainscow)

First published 2003
by RoutledgeCurzon
11 New Fetter Lane, London EC4P 4EE

Simultaneously published in the USA and Canada
by RoutledgeCurzon
29 West 35th Street, New York, NY 10001

RoutledgeCurzon is an imprint of the Taylor & Francis Group
© 2003 J.A.A. Stockwin

Typeset in Times by Taylor & Francis Books Ltd
Printed and bound in Great Britain by
TJ International Ltd, Padstow, Cornwall

All rights reserved. No part of this book may be reprinted or
reproduced or utilised in any form or by any electronic,
mechanical, or other means, now known or hereafter
invented, including photocopying and recording, or in any
information storage or retrieval system, without permission in
writing from the publishers.

British Library Cataloguing in Publication Data
A catalogue record for this book is available from the British Library

Library of Congress Cataloging in Publication Data
A catalog record for this book has been requested

ISBN 0–415–15170–8

TO RUPERT

'Who sows a field, or trains a flower,
Or plants a tree, is more than all'

Contents

List of Tables	viii	ENTRIES A–Z	1–258
Preface	x		
Introductory essay	xii	Bibliography	259
Theories of Japanese politics	xxii	Japanese bibliography	271
Maps	xxxviii, xxxix	Index	273

Tables

Tables

1	Types of attitude exhibited by theorists	xxii
2	Characteristics of Japanese politics identified by theorists	xxiii
3	Former and new ministries and agencies	4
4	Results of the 1990 elections in the first district of Fukushima	52
5	Allocation of seats to the 11 regions	53
6	Renewed seats in two consecutive elections	54
7	Distribution of prefectural members	55
8	Votes for party and votes for candidates, House of Councillors PR constituency, July 2001 elections	56
9	House of Councillors elections, 20 April 1947	60
10	House of Councillors elections, 4 June 1950	61
11	House of Councillors elections, 24 April 1953	61
12	House of Councillors elections, 8 July 1956	62
13	House of Councillors elections, 2 June 1959	62
14	House of Councillors elections, 1 July 1962	63
15	House of Councillors elections, 15 July 1965	63
16	House of Councillors elections, 13 June 1968	63
17	House of Councillors elections, 27 June 1971	64
18	House of Councillors elections, 7 July 1974	64
19	House of Councillors elections, 10 July 1977	65
20	House of Councillors elections, 22 June 1980	65
21	House of Councillors elections, 26 June 1983	66
22	House of Councillors elections, 6 July 1986	66
23	House of Councillors elections, 23 July 1989	67
24	House of Councillors elections, 26 July 1992	68
25	House of Councillors elections, 23 July 1995	69
26	House of Councillors elections, 12 July 1998	69
27	House of Councillors elections, 29 July 2001	70
28	Elections for the House of Representatives, 1946–55	72
29	Elections for the House of Representatives, 1958–76	74
30	Elections for the House of Representatives, 1979–93	75

31	Elections for the House of Representatives, 1996 and 2000	77
32	Length of prime ministerial tenure	211
33	Average length of tenure	212
34	Eleven separate *zoku*	241
35	Turnout rates for general elections to the House of Representatives	254

Preface

The idea of this *Dictionary* was generated in the mid-1990s in discussion with Gordon Smith at Routledge, and subsequently with other editors. At that time, the politics of Japan appeared to have entered a period of change, and possibly of radical reform, but like any such process, the facts were often obscure and capable of various interpretations. Suddenly, the old predictabilities of Japanese politics seemed to have been turned on their head, and confusion reigned. I had taught regular courses on the subject at the Australian National University in Canberra between 1964 and 1981, and at the University of Oxford from 1982 into the new Millennium. One of the most persistent demands from my students was for a book that would serve as a factual database of the subject. They had textbooks providing a general overview and monographs that went into great detail about some narrow topic. But books of reference in English were either too broad (on Japan in general) or too narrow and dated (for instance on political parties). A *Dictionary* might supplement these and fulfil a real need.

For various reasons the project was delayed, but the increasingly confused, and confusing, nature of Japanese politics made the need for a comprehensive *Dictionary of the Modern Politics of Japan* more, rather than less, urgent. My University gave me a welcome period of sabbatical leave for two terms from January 2002, and this enabled me to complete the project.

Japan remains the second largest economy in the world, after the United States, and it has a massive economic presence in Asia. Even though Japanese now talk of the period from the early 1990s to the early 2000s as the 'lost decade', in which effective systemic reform has been shirked, and powerful vested interests have been tamely protected, the Japanese economy remains massive and crucial in regional and global terms. It may eventually be overtaken by the dynamic economy of the People's Republic of China, but such a process will be counted in decades rather than years. Much hinges on whether Japan can put its own house in order in the immediate period ahead.

The experience of Japan with constitutional government goes back to 1889, and with democratic government to the late 1940s. No Asian country, apart from India, has such a long experience of democracy as Japan. Some have contested the quality of Japanese democracy, and have argued that it is overlaid with authoritarian values and practices. But others have even hinted that Japanese politics is *too* democratic, in the sense that the central authorities lack sufficient power to overcome obstruction from a plurality of entrenched interests well represented within Government. However this may be, the politics of Japan provides political scientists with a fascinating example of a mature democratic system in a political culture that differs markedly from those based on the Judaeo-Christian tradition. Many are the observers of Japanese politics who have based their analyses on Western models and theories, only to see these upset by their failure to understand that, in significant ways, the Japanese play their politics to a different tune. On the other hand, the tune is not incomprehensible to a Western ear (even if a few Japanese think it is). It just requires some hard study, a period of familiarisation and enough flexibility of mind to adjust expectations. I hope that this *Dictionary* may help readers make such adjustments and become familiar with what I have come to believe is one of the most fascinating political systems in the world.

I should like to thank Frances Parkes for setting me off on the right course in my final attempt to come to grips with this project; Dominic Shryane for dealing with the entries as I sent them in (and giving me much excellent advice in the process); Tony Nixon for copy editing; and Vanessa Winch for steering the manuscript through its final stages. My colleagues at the Nissan Institute of Japanese Studies and at St Antony's College in Oxford have provided an atmosphere of enquiry and critical judgement. Other colleagues in Britain, Australia, Japan, the United States, Canada, France, Germany, Israel, Korea, Singapore and elsewhere have led me into new lines of research, sometimes through conferences and often through exchanges of ideas in e-mails. My graduate students have been a constant source of inspiration, and I can think of few better ways of staying on track with one's own research than teaching highly motivated graduate students. Meanwhile, undergraduate students have taught me much about how to teach Japanese politics to those who, in most cases, are starting from scratch. And what would I do without the beautiful pottery that my wife Audrey continues to create, part of whose inspiration derives from the pottery of Japan?

Japanese names are given in the original order, with surname first, followed by personal name. A macron (horizontal line) over a vowel in a Japanese word indicates that the length in pronunciation is doubled.

On 15 February 2003 a pound sterling was worth 194.5 yen, a euro was worth 130.2 yen and a US dollar was worth 120.6 yen. [Alternatively: On 15 February 2003 £stg1=¥194.5, 1€=¥130.2, and $US1=¥120.6.]

Introductory essay

Japan is various things, and may be described in various ways. It is an island country, located in the Pacific Ocean some way to the east of the Eurasian land-mass. It is a mountainous country, with a mere 15 per cent of the land area reasonably flat. The population is very large. Even though Japan's total land area is 151 per cent of that of the United Kingdom, and 68 per cent of that of France, the number of people living in Japan exceeds that of the UK and France combined, and is more than twice that of either. In 2002 the population was approximately 126 million. It is also, however, a rapidly ageing population, which is expected to cease growing somewhere around 2007, and then start gradually declining. These geographic and demographic factors have led to extreme concentration of population along the Pacific coast, from the Kantō region, centred on Tokyo, in the east, through the Kansai region, centred on Osaka, to the cities of northern Kyūshū in the west. This massing of people along the coastal strip has caused problems of over-crowding and environmental pollution, but has facilitated efficient transport and other infrastructure links. It also makes it easy to centralise Government and other functions. Depending on definition, Japan's Pacific coastal strip may well be the most densely populated area of land in the world. But it functions remarkably smoothly.

Japan is a resource-poor country. Most raw materials and fuels for industry have to be imported. Food is the one essential resource that Japan has the capacity to produce in adequate quantities, but in practice a high proportion of food is now imported, the main exceptions being rice and fish. But Japan possesses one resource in great abundance: a highly educated and motivated workforce. To produce such a valuable resource has required enormous organisational effort, both to train people in the right skills and to indoctrinate them in the right attitudes. The Japanese term *kin'yoku*, which literally means 'forbidding desire', and may be roughly translated as 'asceticism', is relevant here.

Japan is a relatively homogeneous country, so far as its people are concerned. Perhaps more accurately, people think they are homogeneous, and some social engineering over the past century and a half has been required to bring this about. A single language predominates, and today there is no significant linguistic divide. Religious groups are many and various, old and new, but with a few exceptions (one of which is important) the idea of religious tolerance prevails [*see also* RELIGION AND POLITICS]. Different regions compete with each other for their share of tax revenue, Government subsidies and capital investment, but they do not threaten to fight each other. Broadly speaking, one part of urban Japan looks much like most other parts of urban Japan. For the most part people also look similar, and by comparison with much of Europe and North America, immigration has been kept to low levels. (This is despite a pressing need in some parts of the economy for labour prepared to undertake jobs Japanese are now disinclined to take on.) There is a strong sense of Japanese identity, and of difference from the outside world, though this last has been mitigated somewhat by the mass tourism and mass communications of the past three decades. Governments have, by and large, been concerned to reinforce a sense of national identity, through the education system and by other means. Even when promoting 'internationalisation' (*kokusaika*), as in the 1980s, their hidden agenda seems to involve identity.

Again speaking in broad terms, Japan is reticent in international affairs, punching 'below its weight' and seeking to maintain a low profile. Despite some evolution of a higher profile over the past decade or more, Japan seems rarely to be noticed in international affairs, except on some economic issues. This is connected with the constitutional pacifism that has influenced much of the electorate over several decades, with suspicions of Japanese intentions still held by some of her neighbours, and, perhaps most importantly, with the closeness of the security and economic relationship with the United States. By comparison with Europe (and even North America), Japanese formal multilateral links with her own region are rather weak. There has been, it is true, a certain shift towards emphasis on regional institutions over the past decade, but the bilateral relationship with the United States frequently inhibits this [*see also* SOUTH-EAST ASIA, RELATIONS WITH; UNITED STATES, RELATIONS WITH]. The contrast with Japanese foreign policy before 1945 could hardly be greater.

Finally, Japan is a conservative country. It may perhaps be described as a place whose people exhibit a tolerance for authority that exceeds that of other comparable lands, but where the institutions of democracy based on popular sovereignty are generally accepted. The acceptance of authority is far from absolute. A distinguished (and rather conservative) economist once told the present writer: 'Even we will riot, if sufficiently provoked.' But the idea that those in charge are most likely to be of superior intelligence and dedication seems more widespread than elsewhere. How far this is connected with the Confucian inheritance that Japan shares with other East Asian peoples, how far with long-standing social structures, and how far with pragmatic response to experience of Government, is a matter for speculation. In any case, the many policy failures of the past few years have clearly dented the credibility of Government (any Government), though the most evident manifestation of this is a growth in political apathy. There is indeed a paradox here, namely that acceptance of authority does not automatically translate into strong or decisive leadership. Under the current democratic Constitution, as under its authoritarian predecessor, many hard nodules of power (especially veto power) have emerged, compromising the ability of Government to act. This is the basis of the unfolding political drama that we have been witnessing in Japan over the past decade. Checks and balances of this kind may have beneficial effects in terms of political stability and the acceptability of Government, but their impact when drastic action is needed may also be detrimental.

Politics and the political system before 1945

Between the early seventeenth and mid-nineteenth centuries, Japan was almost (but not quite) a closed society. The Edo period, when Japan as a whole was under the control of the Tokugawa Shoguns (military rulers), was a time when the country, its people and its institutions were, in a sense, frozen in time. Except in so far as a Dutch trading post on an island in Nagasaki bay, and some tenuous links with China, afforded a window on the outside world, Japan missed out on the developments taking place in Europe, including the early stages of the industrial revolution. Japan under the Tokugawas was both centrally controlled and decentralised. Over 200 feudal domains substantially ran their own affairs, but were subject to various forms of interference from Edo (now Tokyo), with a view to neutralising any potential challenges to its authority.

A rigid class system prevailed, in which *samurai* (warriors) were at the top, followed by farmers (the largest class), artisans and merchants. In the virtual absence of wars to fight, the principal function of *samurai* changed from that of warriors to that of domain administrators. They learned valuable administrative skills and were important in promoting the spread of education. The merchants, though the lowest of the four main classes, and in defiance of attempts by the regime to prevent the development of commerce and internal trade, amassed great wealth, which by the mid-nineteenth century contrasted with the relative poverty of many *samurai*. The finances of the regime had become fragile, but it could have continued to limp along for some more decades, had it not been for foreign pressure to open Japan to trade. Between the appearance off Edo Bay of US Commodore Perry's 'black ships' in 1853 and the overthrow of the Tokugawa Shogunate in 1868, the country went through a turbulent and chaotic period.

What happened in 1868 is known in Japanese as *Meiji ishin*, usually translated as 'Meiji Restoration', though 'Meiji Renewal' would be more accurate. The EMPEROR (*Tennō*) (see EMPEROR AND POLITICS) was moved from seclusion and powerlessness in Kyōto to Edo (renamed Tokyo, or 'Eastern Capital'), and became the source of legitimacy for the new Meiji regime. ('Meiji' was the Emperor's era name.) The new Government was extraordinarily capable, ambitious and – though the word is seldom used in this context – revolutionary. Two words perhaps best sum up the nature of its ambitions: 'nation-building' and 'modernisation'. In the years before and after 1868 the revolutionary leaders had received some graphic illustrations of the military and industrial superiority of the Western powers. They soon became realistically aware that the only way of avoiding semi-colonial status was to embark on a crash programme of development, with heavy emphasis on the creation of modern armed forces. The British, French, Germans, Americans and others became tutors in fields of endeavour, such as establishing a modern legal system, building an educational infrastructure and creating an army and navy. A conscript army was recruited, with the old *samurai* monopoly of the right to bear arms abolished. In 1877, less than a decade after the *Meiji ishin*, the new army defeated a major revolt based in one of the former domains. By 1895 it was strong enough to win a war against China, and a mere decade after that Japan startled the world by defeating a European power, Russia. That being the age of imperialism, Japan began to acquire colonies, Taiwan in 1895 and Korea in 1910.

During the early years of the Meiji period, Japan was governed through a series of *ad hoc* administrative arrangements, to suit the convenience of the small group of oligarchs that had engineered the change of regime. But by the 1880s the business of governing had become sufficiently complicated that more formal arrangements were plainly required. A constitution was also a badge of a modern state, and therefore was needed to impress the Western powers, which had imposed 'unequal treaties' on Japan. Much of the 1880s was spent studying modern constitutions, with key leaders taking advice from constitutional specialists in Europe. What emerged was a constitution based on Prussian models rather than the more liberal models available in Britain and France. The Meiji Constitution of 1889 signalled the defeat of those political leaders associated with the Popular Rights Movement, who were more liberally inclined. In the ascendancy were those who were determined that the new constitution should enshrine the principle of executive dominance, with popular representation mediated through a Parliament whose powers would be strictly limited and confined.

The Emperor (*Tennō*) was placed at the centre of the Constitution, with reverential language used to refer to him. But how far he was expected to wield actual political power was left ambiguous. The separation of actual from nominal power-holders was a deep-seated tradition, and from some perspectives the position of the Emperor seemed more like that of a constitutional monarch on the British model than that of an autocratic ruler. On the other hand, the Emperor under the 1889 Constitution was gradually transformed from a legitimising symbol for the regime into a semi-religious focus of national loyalty. Duties rather than rights were emphasised in the Constitution, and these came to be promoted in terms of loyalty owed to the Emperor.

The politics of the first decade under the 1889 Constitution were particularly crucial. Of the two houses of the Parliament (*gikai*, Diet), only one, the House of Representatives, was elective. In the 1890s there was a highly restrictive property qualification for the vote, so that the House essentially represented rural landlords and wealthy urban businessmen. (The franchise was gradually expanded, so that by 1925 it included all males over the age of 25.) Although those who drafted the Constitution expected the House of Representatives to be little more than a sounding board for opinion at large, it quickly proved that it could hold up Government business by rejecting the Government's budget. Even though a provision of the Constitution provided that, if the budget were rejected, the Government could carry on with the budget of the previous year, this was of little use to governments intent on increasing expenditure (and thus taxation) on armaments and similar purposes. Through much of the 1890s, therefore, there was a stand-off between the 'popular parties' in the House of Representatives and the Government itself, which was, of course, outside Parliament. The ability to frustrate the Government, however, did not mean that the popular parties could govern in their own right, and a brief experiment with party rule in 1898 was a failure. For one thing, the non-elected and conservative House of Peers had equal rights with the House of Representatives and could over-ride its initiatives.

The Government tried various stratagems, including electoral manipulation, in order to break the logjam. Nothing worked until the foundation by one of the oligarchs, Itō Hirobumi, of a new political party, the *Seiyūkai*, in 1900. Positions in the new party were offered to leaders of the 'popular parties', allowing them to make the transition from an oppositional role to a position where they could exercise some genuine power. The *Seiyūkai* went on to organise a network of local associations, based largely on local notabilities, so that by the 1920s it was a party fully functioning at grass roots level. Other parties of rather similar structure also emerged, and by the 1920s the appearance, at least, was of two-party alternation. This was the period of so-called 'Taishō Democracy' (from the era name of the Emperor Taishō, 1912–26), in which, for a few years following the First World War, governments were composed mainly of party members, and dependent on the confidence of Parliament. (The norm was for 'transcendental' governments, neither responsible to Parliament nor principally composed of party members.)

In the early years of the twentieth century the ultimate string-pullers of the political system were a small group of men called the *genrō* (elders), who were the last survivors of the Meiji leadership. By dint of their prestige, political connections and skill, they were able to provide co-ordination and direction, even though their position was entirely outside the Constitution. By the 1920s, however, they were a dying breed, with no effective mechanism being provided to replace them. During the late 1920s and the 1930s, only one of them, Saionji Kinmochi, was left. He was a man of patrician but liberal instincts, but lacking many of the sharp political skills of his predecessors. He advised the Emperor to avoid entering the political arena (as the Emperor was occasionally inclined to do), so as not to compromise his political neutrality.

For a variety of reasons, economic, political and international, the party-and-Parliament-centred politics of the 1920s were not sustained in the harsher environment of the 1930s. The so-called 'Manchurian Incident' of October 1931 marked a key stage in Japan's increasing involvement in China – a highly troubled country at that time. It also marked a trend of insubordination to the civilian power on the part of the armed forces. The take-over of Manchuria was engineered by army units without having first obtained permission from Tokyo, creating a *fait accompli* that the civilian Government had to accept. According to accepted conventions of the 1889 Constitution, the Chiefs-of-Staff of the armed forces had privileged access to the Emperor (meaning, in practice, his advisers) on matters of military concern. Moreover, two essential members of Cabinet, the Minister for War (in charge of the army) and the Minister of the Navy, were expected to be senior officers of the most senior rank. The fact that they were serving officers meant that they were subject to military discipline, so that they had no choice to withdraw from Cabinet should their superiors deem the current Cabinet unacceptable. This happened repeatedly during the 1930s, with the result that governments became increasingly subordinate to service interests. With the beginning of full-scale war in China in 1937, Japan gradually became bogged down in a quagmire that has been compared to the US experience, 30 years later, in Vietnam. The effects on Japanese politics were profound. Industry became more and more mobilised for the production of munitions, and Government became increasingly repressive. In 1940 all existing political parties were merged into a single party, known, significantly, as the Imperial Rule Assistance Association (*Taisei yokusankai*), and other functional groups were incorporated into State-run associations.

In December 1941, the Japanese air force destroyed the US fleet stationed at Pearl Harbour in Hawai'i.

A new political revolution

Japan surrendered on 15 August 1945, a date that has been described as 'Japan's longest day'. Faced with a divided Cabinet – some in favour of surrender and others proposing to fight to the finish – the Emperor was asked to decide, and came down in favour of surrender. His surrender broadcast to the nation, couched in archaic court language that ordinary people found hard to understand, was the first time that most of his subjects had heard the sound of his voice. Had the decision been taken ten days earlier, the atomic bombing of Hiroshima and Nagasaki might have been avoided, and the Soviet invasion of Japanese territories on the mainland and in the islands might never have taken place. The Allies insisted on unconditional surrender, but on the point that most concerned Japan's leaders – the survival of the Emperor and the Emperor system – a compromise was later negotiated, whereby the Emperor was retained, but stripped of most of his assets and nearly all of his influence.

Introductory essay

The Allied Occupation of Japan was in most of its aspects a US operation. Its aims were ambitious, being no less than the democratisation and demilitarisation of Japan. It was led by an ambitious and supremely self-confident man, General Douglas MacArthur, who had pre-war experience of Asia and had fought the Japanese in the Philippines and elsewhere. The Japanese reputation for fanatical behaviour in battle was such that at the beginning of the Occupation many of its participants were genuinely surprised that they met virtually no resistance.

The Occupation lasted from September 1945 to April 1952. Its approach was not entirely consistent from start to finish. In the earlier stages (up to 1948–9) radical programmes of reform were initiated, based on the determination to change for all time the ideology and practice of Japanese politics and Government. Moreover, these reforms extended to the organisation of the economy, and to socially vital areas such as family law. Many of those Americans devising and implementing reform were inspired by the ideals of Roosevelt's New Deal in the 1930s. This was the period in which the new Constitution was introduced (see CONSTITUTION OF 1946), with its demotion of the Emperor to 'Symbol of the State', introduction of an advanced set of human rights, and of the 'peace clause'. During the later stages (1949–52) priorities changed under the impact of worsening relations between the United States and the USSR, and the start of what came to be called the 'Cold War'. In October 1949 the Chinese Communist Party gained control of the Chinese mainland, leaving Chiang Kai Shek and his forces to retreat to their island redoubt of Taiwan. In June 1950 war broke out in Korea, lasting until a truce was signed in 1953. In these circumstances, a main imperative for the United States became to recruit Japan as a Cold War ally, and to promote her economic recovery. This meant moving US support from relatively left-wing and liberal political forces that had been favoured early in the Occupation, towards more conservative elements in the later stages. These changes mirrored shifts occurring in Japanese politics itself, and we may mark as the key turning point the victory of the Democratic Liberal Party (*Minshu jiyūtō*) led by YOSHIDA SHIGERU in January 1949.

There are various ways in which the reforms of the Occupation might be categorised. We favour a categorisation emphasising three distinct, though overlapping, aims.

The first of these was to simplify and unify lines of responsibility and accountability in Government. According to many observers (including some who influenced Occupation thinking), a principal problem with pre-war politics was that nobody was clearly or consistently in charge. There was a partial vacuum of power at the very centre of the system in that the Emperor, broadly speaking, reigned but did not rule. This meant that politics was a matter of different elites jockeying for power in a system that did not make clear which of them was supposed to prevail. The most extreme manifestation of this was the so-called 'dual Government' phenomenon, whereby the military had a great deal of power outside the normal channels of political responsibility. Thus the Government in Tokyo was unable to prevent the unauthorised take-over of Manchuria by elements of the armed forces in 1931. To solve this deficit of responsibility and accountability, the Americans, surprisingly perhaps, sought to shape Japanese political institutions, not on a Washington model of separation of powers, but rather on a Westminster model of substantial fusion of the powers of executive and legislature. The basic political relationships that emerged from the Occupation were that the electorate elected a Parliament, from which a Cabinet was selected (normally composed exclusively of members of the majority party or coalition of parties). The Cabinet was headed by a Prime

Minister (technically elected by Parliament but nearly always being the head of the majority party). Nearly all members of Cabinet headed a Government ministry or agency (sometimes more than one). This, on paper at least, is very close to the British system and distant from the American. A closely related point is that the Emperor was converted essentially into a constitutional monarch on the British model.

The second category of reform was that designed to broaden the scope of participation in politics and bring politics much more into the open. Women were given the vote for the first time, and the voting age was reduced from 25 to 20. A wide range of new freedoms were introduced, including freedom of assembly, in connection with which previous restrictions on the organisation of left-wing parties, labour unions and so on were lifted. Even the JAPAN COMMUNIST PARTY (JCP) became a legal party for the first time and succeeded in electing members of Parliament. (On the other hand those seen as too closely connected with the previous regime were subjected to a purge edict, and excluded from public life for an indefinite period.) Under this same category may also be placed a series of reforms seeking to break up what were seen as excessive concentrations of power. Measures were put in train to break up the large industrial combines, or *zaibatsu*, while landlords were almost entirely removed from agriculture. The Home Ministry was broken up, as part of the goal of promoting deconcentration of power to the localities. Central control of the police and education was also broken up, and power over these functions dispersed locally.

The third category was that of demilitarisation – important in US eyes because Japan was widely regarded as a society organised for the pursuit of militarist aims. The Imperial Armed Forces were quickly disbanded and troops located overseas repatriated. Though largely forgotten today, this was indeed a huge operation placing great strain on a devastated society and economy. Article 9, the 'peace clause' of the new Constitution was designed to enshrine a pacifist principle into the Japanese polity, and it proved far more durable than possibly even MacArthur envisaged. In 2002 it remains unamended in a Constitution that remains entirely unamended. This, of course, is not to say that reality has not evolved in various ways despite article 9. Other measures to reinforce the message of article 9 were introduced, for instance the provision that members of Cabinet must be civilians.

The formation of the '1955 political system'

What emerged from the Occupation was a political system rather different in certain ways from what had been envisaged. This should not, however, surprise us, since no formal obligation was placed upon Japan in the San Francisco Peace Treaty or in any other document that the reforms of the Occupation must be retained. In part, the differences resulted from the change of course in Occupation policy towards the end of the 1940s. Japanese Governments of the late Occupation and early post-Occupation periods succeeded in reversing some reforms, in particular the decentralisation of control over the police and education. Governments of the middle and late 1950s were intent on rewriting the 1946 Constitution, which they regarded as having been imposed on Japan under duress, but in this they failed. The Americans themselves reinforced conservative forces in Japanese politics by bringing in the 'Dodge Line' economic reforms to curb inflation and stimulate economic growth, in 1949. They backed this up by a purge of Communists and suspected Communists in 1950. They sought Japanese rearmament on a massive scale in the early 1950s, but in this they partially failed because of the far-sighted resistance of the Prime Minister of the time, Yoshida Shigeru.

Another factor that was crucial in steering the shape of the system away from the model set up in the late 1940s was the continued resilience of the Government bureaucracy, heir to long traditions of central bureaucratic influence. Here the inability of the Americans to curb the power of Government officials, because they needed their services in the introduction and implementation of reforms, was a key factor. Another was the fact that Yoshida, himself a former official of Government, brought numbers of able former officials into politics, grooming several future Prime Ministers.

A third factor was the eventual success – surely surprising to observers of Japanese conservative politics of mutual back stabbing in the early 1950s – in uniting the various conservative groups into a single party in November 1955. It is arguable that November 1955 is the most significant date in Japanese politics since the Occupation. The LIBERAL DEMOCRATIC PARTY (LDP), formed at that point, and expected to disintegrate in short order, went on to form every government for 37 years on the basis of majorities in the HOUSE OF REPRESENTATIVES. In 1993 it was excluded from power for about nine months, but then returned as the strongest party in a shifting series of coalition Governments.

Fourth, the other side of the coin of conservative dominance was the permanent opposition status for the parties of opposition, including the JAPAN SOCIALIST PARTY (JSP). The failure of the JSP to modernise and broaden its appeal in the early 1960s is a crucial element in the understanding of the course taken by Japanese politics in the period since the war. The 1959 Bad Godesberg Congress of the West German Social Democratic Party, creating a modern progressive party, lacked its counterpart in the JSP at that time. On the other hand, it is equally important to realise that opposition parties (including especially the JSP) were able to exercise substantial veto-power over certain kinds of policy (most significantly blocking revision of the Constitution) until the 1990s.

Fifth, a change of Prime Minister in 1960, from KISHI NOBUSUKE to IKEDA HAYATO, as a result of the political drama that developed over revision of the Japan-US Security Treaty, resulted in a fundamental change of political direction. Instead of Kishi's politically charged campaigns against the Constitution and other elements in the Occupation settlement, Ikeda played his politics cool and concentrated on economic issues at a time when economic growth was already an easily experienced reality. Even if these policies were later to result in Japanese being dubbed 'economic animals' by some foreign observers, the advantages in terms of political stability and economic prosperity were evident.

The sixth element in the model that emerged was the ability of the LDP, Governments, ministries and dominant industrial firms, to co-operate in a highly productive and dynamic fashion in the promotion of rapid industrial growth. Even though the sobriquet 'Japan, Incorporated' was a rather crass journalistic cliché containing a great deal of exaggeration and over-simplification, it has to be admitted that there were substantial elements of corporatism in the way the system operated in the 1960s.

The seventh part of the picture was the remarkably loose, at times cantankerous, but at the same time flexible internal structure that developed in the LDP itself. Personal factionalism, rooted in social norms and long political traditions, became a trademark of that party. To a limited extent factions (*habatsu*) became 'parties within a party' (see FACTIONS WITHIN POLITICAL PARTIES), although that metaphor should not be taken too far because no faction of the LDP ever contested an election under its own label. But factionalism was one part of a system in which electioneering was carried out on a highly personalised basis. Candidates campaigned on the basis of personality and connections more than of party and policy platform. Here again, the point should not be exaggerated, and it depends on the standard of comparison chosen. But by contrast with British elections, Japanese elections were centred to a startling degree on candidates and their personal machines (*kōenkai*). To some extent this resulted from an electoral system that pitted candidates from the same party against each other in the same electoral district, but even when the Lower House electoral system was reformed to eliminate this feature in 1994, the personal and machine-based character of electioneering persisted.

Finally, we come to a particular problem of the Japanese political system (though also of other such systems), namely how to deal with rising expectations from the electorate. In the early post-war decades Japanese Government and industry was astonishingly successful in promoting economic growth. The 15-year period between 1958 and 1973 is one of the most astonishing in the annals of mankind, for creating sustained economic growth of around 10 per cent per annum on average. Japan in the mid-1970s was a radically different place, in many senses, from Japan in the mid-1950s. The standard of living of ordinary people had been transformed. They were experiencing greater opportunities, with greater disposable income, than they had ever known before. And, yet, throughout this decade and a half the proportion of the total vote gathered by the LDP at Lower House elections steadily declined. Even if this was a product of rapid urbanisation and the loss of tight (and conservative) rural linkages, rather than disillusionment with policy, plainly the LDP base of support was narrowing. The perception that the ruling party might lose its parliamentary majority led TANAKA KAKUEI, Prime Minister between 1972 and 1974, to promote increased welfare spending and the spread of development to the remoter regions, with a view to picking up new sources of support. As Calder has argued in his book, *Crisis and Compensation*, a syndrome emerged whereby a particular interest caused a crisis, and the Government reacted to it by policies of compensation. This tended to solve short-term problems, but risked storing up trouble for the future, especially as the compensation element was often administered more on the basis of cronyism and personal linkages than was wise, or acceptable to public opinion.

Between the 1970s and the 1990s, this syndrome persisted, although the 1980s saw some impressive attempts to maintain fiscal rectitude. By the early1990s the last bastion of persistent opposition to the LDP – LABOUR UNIONS – were in the process of being tempted into the charmed circle of those to whom benefits were given. What was involved here was what the present writer has called the 'ripples in the pond' effect. When a stone is thrown into a pond, ripples flow outward from the point of impact. Eventually, if the stone is large enough, the ripples reach to the further extremities of the pond. Instead of mainstream (*shuryūha*) competing with anti-mainstream (*hanshuryūha*), nearly everyone is brought into a co-operative general mainstream (*sōshuryūha*). This phenomenon was seen graphically in elections of local chief executives from the early 1980s, since it was found to be more beneficial to belong to a general mainstream and have access to the resources consequently available, than to remain on the outside, a lonely opposition voice.

The politics of economic stagnation and political fluidity

From the early 1990s (some would date the changes from the LDP defeat in the House of Councillors elections of 1989), the sand began to shift under the feet of the apparently impregnable political establishment based on the LDP. Part of the reason for this was the long-term effects of the final factor of the previous section: the 'ripples in the pond' effect. In 1990–1 there was a massive economic shake-out based on the collapse of an asset

Introductory essay

bubble (land prices had reached ludicrous levels), leaving the banking sector saddled with enormous sums owed to it that its debtors could never repay. Such, however, was the complexity of linkages within the politico-economic system that it proved extraordinarily difficult to administer the harsh medicine necessary to unravel the debt crisis. The effect on public confidence also became serious, and a deflationary situation developed, in which savings levels – always high – rose even further, and consumers could not be persuaded to spend enough to promote an economic recovery.

Meanwhile, the party political core of the 1955 system began to unravel, though, after the brief experiment with opposition party politics in 1993–4, it did not unravel far enough to create any real possibility of alternative Government. The LDP, from its return to power, in coalition under a Socialist Prime Minister, in June 1994, has presided over a series of shifting coalition Governments, always remaining much the largest element in each. Between June 1994 and August 2002 there have been five Prime Ministers, all but the first of them from the LDP. The present Prime Minister, KOIZUMI JUNICHIRŌ, at the time of his election in April 2001, seemed likely to break the mould of politics, since he owed his position more to impressive levels of popularity in the electorate at large, rather than to being acceptable to faction bosses of the LDP. But as Prime Minister he has had a stony furrow to plough, and has experienced many frustrations.

When we contemplate the difficulties experienced by Koizumi, the most popular of recent Prime Ministers, in exercising firm leadership, we come back to the effects of the many checks and balances existing within the system. These checks and balances, however, have been put there less by design than by the cumulative effect of political deals worked out over many years. As Aurelia George Mulgan argues, the 'Westminster model' upon which the Japanese political system is supposed to be based, has been drastically modified by the semi-independent decision-making power of LDP committees and by powerful ministries of the Government bureaucracy. Whereas a British Prime Minister commanding a comfortable majority in Parliament is likely to control Cabinet and Parliament relatively easily, and mainly needs to worry about winning the next general election, for the Japanese Prime Minister things are much more difficult. He has to contend with many hard nodules of power that have been created in a rather *ad hoc* manner over the years, and needs to negotiate every policy initiative to which he is committed.

This is hardly a benign scenario, considering the magnitude of the tasks of reform needed to set the Japanese economy once again on a firm footing. The one bright element in the picture, however, is that some progress has been made since the late 1990s in reforming the structure of the Government bureaucracy, and in strengthening the powers of the Prime Minister. Whether these reforms will prove sufficient remains to be seen.

In the opinion of the present writer, the most serious defect of the Japanese political system since the 1950s is its inability to bring about clear changes of Government. The advantage of a system that permits (not necessarily at every election, but with reasonable regularity) a substitution in power of one party or parties for another is that it becomes so much easier to shake out and get rid of the hard nodules of power. These normally emerge in an atmosphere of cronyism and easy familiarity that will inevitably accompany any Government that has been in power for a very long period of time. This is not so much a question of Japanese cultural exceptionalism as a universal characteristic of political interaction. We put this forward as the central structural problem currently facing the Japanese political system.

Theories of Japanese politics

The emergence of Japan from the ashes of defeat in 1945 to become the world's second largest economy has excited enormous interest from economists, but also from historians, and specialists in politics, international relations, sociology, social anthropology, criminology, law and other academic disciplines. Although many such observers have been primarily Japan-specialists, trying to understand what happens in Japan for its own sake, a substantial number have endeavoured to place Japan in a comparative context, to test existing theories against Japanese data, and generate new theories to be tested elsewhere, based on Japanese experience. Not all creators of theory have, strictly speaking, been academics. Some journalists and others have made significant contributions to the formation of theory from their experience of Japan.

This essay will necessarily be schematic and selective. From a vast compass of writing we shall concentrate on those items that seem most relevant to certain themes we consider especially important. It is true that there are differences between Japanese and non-Japanese approaches, but to sort these out is hardly practicable in the space available. In the more recent period, in any case, there is so much collaborative work between Japanese and non-Japanese specialists that the differences are less significant that they possibly once were. (In the earlier post-war period many Japanese theorists were influenced by Marxism, but non-Japanese theorists very much less so.)

A bewildering variety of approaches to the understanding of Japanese politics may be found in the literature. There is no simple way of categorising them, but the following two tables may be helpful. They are organised in terms of pairs of opposites.

Table 1 categorises theoretical approaches in terms of their underlying attitudes towards the subject. Here there is often a sharp divide between the attitudes expressed in the left hand and right hand columns of the table.

Table 1 Types of attitude exhibited by theorists

Positive, favourable	Negative, critical
Japan as a model to emulate	Japan as a model to correct
Right	Left
Japan as a contributor	Japan as a threat
Universalist	Culturalist

The correlation between the items in the left hand column is imperfect, as is that between items in the right hand column. Nevertheless, they do correlate to some extent.

While all the pairs in Table 2 are opposites, the relationships between the various pairs are complicated, and it should not be assumed that all the items in the left hand column represent approved phenomena and those in the right hand column ones that are disapproved. For instance, the break in historical continuity that occurred during the Allied Occupation may be regarded positively by an enthusiast for democracy, but with disdain by a supporter of 'traditional values'. A statist orientation was lauded by many observers during the 'economic miracle' period of the 1960s, but decried in favour of a market orientation (occasionally by the same people) during the economically stagnant 1990s and 2000s. Post-modern elements in contemporary Japanese society may not be to the liking of those who want Japan to be an exemplar of rapid economic growth, but may be preferred by those who enjoy the rather zany sophistication of Japanese cities in the twenty-first century.

We now progress to an examination of selected theories themselves. We shall do this more or less chronologically. From the previous discussion it will be realised that the relationships between them are multi-dimensional. Some of the 'theories' are in fact pairs of opposites.

Table 2 Characteristics of Japanese politics identified by theorists

Historical continuity	Historical discontinuity
Democratic norms and practices	Authoritarian norms and practices
Egalitarian norms and practices	Hierarchical norms and practices
Market orientation	Statist orientation
Dynamic policy-making	Immobilist policy-making
Modernising, industrial society	Post-modern, post-industrial society
Functioning, sophisticated system	Dysfunctional, unworkable system

Popular democracy versus traditional values and a system centred on the Emperor

Very understandably, the principal concern of those observing Japanese politics between 1945 and the early 1960s was the success or otherwise of the Occupation experiment with introducing the institutions, norms and practices of popular democracy. Observers were exercised by two overlapping questions:

First, could democracy be successfully introduced in a non-Western society? An azalea needs a lime-free soil to thrive. Could democracy thrive in soil to which it was not suited? In terms of the final item of Table 1 above, those who had faith in the success of the democratising experiment were universalists, whereas those who doubted that the cultural divide could be bridged to make it work were culturalists. Scalapino, in his seminal work on pre-war politics, was plainly a universalist by conviction, but appreciative of cultural barriers. Significantly, his book was entitled *Democracy and the Party Movement in Prewar Japan: The Failure of the First Attempt*. An early analysis of post-war politics, in which universalism is more or less assumed, is by Quigley and Turner (1956), whereas a more sceptical, culturalist view (especially in relation to the CONSTITUTION OF 1946) is provided by Kawai (1960). The work of Ward inclined towards universalism, though he regarded the success of Japanese democracy as 'unexpected' (1978, p. 206), whereas that of Ike (by implication at least) is rather more culturalist (1957). A much more recent work by Dower (1999) emphasises the arbitrary nature of parts of the Occupation exercise, but delivers a not unfavourable verdict on the Occupation as a whole.

The second question related to the inconsistencies in Occupation policy over time. Early Occupation policy had been liberal, even left wing, and certainly inspired by the New Deal of the 1930s. Later Occupation policy turned decisively to the right, partly under Cold War pressures, and this was reinforced by a partial 'reverse course', pursued by Japanese Governments in the 1950s. A consequence of this was to dig a deep gulf between a Marxist-influenced left wing and a revisionist-reactionary right wing. This gulf profoundly marked the debate within Japan itself about the nature of the new political system throughout the 1950s and into the 1960s. Crucially, the middle ground in the debate – those championing parliamentary democracy and genuine parliamentary debate – was weakened. Instead, the debate polarised between those (on the right) seeking a reversion to more authoritarian forms of rule, and those (on the left) pursuing 'parliamentarism plus', in other words reliance on strikes, mass demonstrations and the like. In terms of Table 1 above, the divide between right and left was salient. After the 1960 crisis, both sides stepped back from the brink, and more moderate analyses began to be listened to.

Pro-US versus neutralist and pacifist approaches

At the same time as confrontation raged between left and right over the new political system, the Peace Constitution exercised a profound influence on the debate. In significant senses the divide between neutralism and pacifism on the one hand, and pro-Americanism on the other hand, turned into the central issue of competitive party politics. The international context of this was the Cold War. The domestic context was the party political confrontation between the LIBERAL DEMOCRATIC PARTY (LDP) and the JAPAN SOCIALIST PARTY (JSP). It was, however, more complex than this suggests, because some aspects of pacifism penetrated also into parts of the LDP and other Establishment and semi-establishment bodies.

This ultimately led to what we may term a 'stand-off' on constitutional matters (including DEFENCE policy, much affected by the Constitution as obstacle), between constitutional revisionists and defenders. The result has been that defence policy has come to be seen as an example of rearmament by stealth, on the one side, and as a prime example of immobilist politics, on the other. In a curious fashion, however, immobilism and rearmament by stealth are seen as going along together, in the sense that lack of decisive leadership – no doubt deriving from structural factors – leads to decisions being made 'underground', without proper scrutiny and certainly not in a democratic manner.

Theories of collective irresponsibility

This leads on to one of the most influential theories of Japanese political behaviour to emerge in the post-war period, that of the political scientist and historian, Maruyama Masao, who argued that pre-war politics – and by implication post-war politics as well – was permeated by collective irresponsibility. This meant that nobody was ultimately in charge, and that accountability within the system was lacking. Rather, there were concentrations of power within various parts of the system, but they were highly competitive with each other, and no institution or individual leader existed with enough power to pull them all together. A particularly corrosive aspect of this phenomenon in the 1930s had been military insubordination in relation to civilian Government – the phenomenon of so-called 'dual Government'.

Variations on Maruyama's theme of collective irresponsibility recurred in later attempts to make sense of post-war politics. Despite the fact that the Occupation had concentrated on simplifying and unifying lines of authority and accountability within the political system, continuing problems with accountability struck later writers as highly significant. Van Wolferen, for instance (1989), wrote of a System 'where the buck just keeps circulating', and where nobody appeared to be in charge.

Modernisation theories

It is in no way surprising that the 15-year period of economic transformation from 1958 to 1973 should have been the focus of much literature seeking new ways of understanding such an unprecedented phenomenon. The 1960s also happened to be a period in which large-scale decolonisation was taking place, with many new states emerging (as well as old states with new governments interested in development) in Africa, Asia and elsewhere. Therefore the spectacular Japanese economic successes seemed likely to be an enlightening model from which lessons could be learned by newly decolonised states.

Books by Almond and Coleman, Almond and Verba, Lucien Pye and many others produced innovative frameworks for the understanding of economic development, as well as political and social modernisation. Many of these writers were American, and their intellectual roots could be traced back to Max Weber, with the sociologist Talcott Parsons as a kind of intermediary. To an extent the development of modernisation theory constituted an intellectual challenge to Marxism. A major exercise in this approach was contained in a series of books published by Princeton University Press during the 1960s. Ward (1968) used 'political modernisation' and 'political development' interchangeably. He gave four prerequisites for a modern political system: (1) shared nationalism, at least among the ruling elite; (2) enough stability and security to permit sustained governmental planning and action; (3) political leaders chosen according to achievement rather than status: and (4) a political elite attuned to change, with Government seen as an appropriate agency to achieve change. In addition, he considered four further conditions as important criteria for such a system: (5) expanding involvement and action by Government; (6) increasing popular involvement with the political system, though not necessarily with its decision-making aspects; (7) increasing functional differentiation in Government; and (8) an increasingly secular, impersonal and rationalised system of governmental decision-making.

Several things may be noted about this list. First, it is evolutionary, not revolutionary. Second, it is statist to a degree that was to become unfashionable in later decades. Government functions were expected to expand, and encroach on the private sector. Third, though it is not anti-democratic, democratic norms are not greatly emphasised. Ordinary people are supposed to be involved in the political system, 'but not necessarily with its decision-making aspects'. Some authoritarian, even totalitarian, systems were regarded as modernising, and thus comparable with modernising systems that happened to be democratic. Finally, functional differentiation was taken very seriously by the modernisation theorists. It seems reasonable to derive this from US notions of separation of powers.

For the modernisation theorists, Japan was a scintillating example of how a non-Western state could modernise. Naturally, they tended to concentrate on the late nineteenth and early twentieth centuries, when Japan was in the early phases of her modernising trajectory, and therefore reasonably comparable with newly independent states of the 1960s, even though the global environment had changed. They tended to play down the manifestly undemocratic nature of the pre-war regime, and even implied that too early introduction of democratic forms and practices would have risked slowing down economic and political modernisation (see Ward, 1963). It is also probably fair to comment that the modernisation theorists had rather little of significance to say about the period 1931–45.

So far as the post-war system was concerned, they were naturally impressed with the 'economic miracle', which was happening as they wrote. This appeared to show that the road to modernity could be traversed rapidly, provided that the right sorts of institution and incentives were put into place. On the other hand, they had problems with the manifest lack of clear functional differentiation between what to them should have been separate parts of the system, and with the continued Japanese reliance in political and economic life on personal relationships (*kankei*), rather than impersonal relationships based on contract and legal rules.

Essentially, the modernisation theorists believed (in terms of Table 2 above) that Japan had created a modernising, industrial society through dynamic policy-making in a functioning, sophisticated system. Japan therefore (in terms of Table 1) was a model to emulate, not a model to correct, and this was so because the Japanese elite for a century had been convinced modernisers.

Post-Marxist society

In his 1967 book on the JAPAN COMMUNIST PARTY (JCP), Scalapino argued that, to all intents and purposes, Japan had become a 'post-Marxist society'. This argument was of a piece with the commitment, manifest in his earlier works, to democratic development for Japan, and a hostility to extremes of both left and right on the grounds that they threatened democratic Government. His primary concern with democracy makes it difficult to categorise him as a modernisation theorist, but his perception of democracy was of a rather conservative kind, and, as the Vietnam War developed, increasingly concerned with the integrity of the United States-led alliance against Communist states.

His 'post-Marxist society' idea was challenged in 1968 by Stockwin, who pointed out that the JCP, reduced to near extinction in the 1950s, was now rapidly gaining support from those who had been economic victims of the 'economic miracle' – a trend that was to continue well into the 1970s. He also argued that various forms of Marxist argumentation still permeated much of the non-Communist left, so that the idea of a linear progression away from Marxism towards Western-style liberal democratic politics was hardly justified by what was actually happening on the ground.

Ironically, Scalapino's argument would have been far more appropriate for the 1990s, following the collapse of both the Soviet Union and the Japanese 'economic miracle', when the old left found itself greatly reduced in influence.

New Left theories

The Vietnam War exercised a powerful influence on political thinking in the United States and elsewhere, including Japan. In these circumstances, 'New Left' thinking came to prominence. In the case of Japan, it focused on the negative aspects of rapid economic growth, most notably environmental degradation, reduction in the quality of life for substantial minorities, ruthless employment practices, subordination of women, cramped and poor quality housing, inadequate or non-existent town planning and neglect of social infrastructure and SOCIAL WELFARE provision.

In general, the emergence of the 'New Left' in the early 1970s constituted a direct challenge to the modernisation theorists. Whereas the latter tended to brush aside the kinds of problem mentioned in the previous paragraph as incidental by-products of the supreme task of expanding the wealth available ultimately to all, New Left thinkers were more concerned with the victims. Like the modernisation theorists, they wrote extensively about Japan before 1945, but unlike them they did not neglect the 1930s and early 1940s. Unlike 'universalist' democratic theorists such as Scalapino, they took a much more pessimistic view of the prospects for real democracy in Japan, pointing to deep social and political structures that militated against the formation of a true democracy with guarantees of accountability and effective popular participation. They were highly critical of the conservative Establishment in contemporary Japan, and its subordination to the global strategy of the United States.

The flagship of the New Left in the 1970s was the journal *Bulletin of Concerned Asian Scholars*. The title is significant, because it suggests a stepping down from cold academic objectivity into a commitment to causes of human welfare. These were *intellectuels engagés*, but most of them were far from being dogmatic or hard-line Marxists. A surprising number of them were historians, and in terms of Table 2 above they believed in the underlying continuity of modern Japanese history, rather than discontinuity brought about by external intervention. At least two of them, John Dower and Herbert Bix, went on to publish major works on Japanese history in later decades.

'Middle mass' versus 'class society'

In the 1970s the issue of equality in Japanese society began to attract attention. Some modernisation theorists had argued, with statistics, that economic development had brought about an egalitarian trend in Japanese society, rather than the other way round. On the other hand, some on the left pointed to structural inequalities in employment systems and between types of firm.

An example of the first is Murakami Yasusuke, who in the 1970s popularised the concept of 'middle mass' (1982). Having noticed that in public opinion polls very high proportions of those polled identified themselves as 'middle class', he suggested that Japan had created mass society, but the 'mass' was middle class, rather than, according to the classic formulation, working class. Thus 'middle mass'. Years later Kinmonth challenged the notion of a uniformly middle-class (or 'middle-mass') society, arguing that this was more perception than reality.

A 'class society' model was put forward in 1983 by Steven, who, arguing from an avowedly Marxist standpoint, held that there was a potent class divide in Japanese society. This was between those (almost all male) with permanent contracts in the larger firms, and enjoying generous fringe benefits, and employees of smaller firms, with more tenuous security and little in the way of fringe benefits. Casual employees of large and smaller firms also fell into the latter category. A considerable proportion of these were women. So far as public opinion polls on class identification were concerned, they were evidence of false consciousness rather than of objective reality.

Japan as a model, Japan as number one

In 1979 the American scholar Ezra Vogel published a provocative book entitled *Japan as Number One*. The book could be regarded as directed at a US, rather than a Japanese, audience, although it sold many more copies in Japanese translation, than in the US edition. Vogel was concerned with US demoralisation in the aftermath of the Vietnam War, and with what he saw as defects in the US politico-economic system at the time he wrote. By contrast, Japan, in his view, could show the way ahead in terms of many of its systems in place, including even, surprisingly, those concerned with social welfare. To some extent, Vogel was using Japan as stick to pummel Americans out of depression and complacency. He even commended Japan for having a single police emergency number, thus giving the present writer the new and surprising information that different US states actually have different police emergency numbers. Japan was hardly the only example of virtue in this respect.

Vogel's book was a slightly extreme example of a wider genre, that of Japan as a model from which lessons could be learned elsewhere. We have already seen that the modernisation theorists regarded Japan as a model of development for newly emerged states in Asia, Africa and elsewhere. But by the 1970s there was already a substantial literature that argued for Japan as a model in relation also to the developed world. Indeed, perhaps the earliest example was *Japanese Factory*, published by James Abegglen in 1958. In it, Abegglen argued that the Japanese system of permanent employment contracts for much of the workforce fostered loyalty to the firm, whereas free firing and hiring systems, prevalent in Western countries, detracted from such loyalty and commitment, to the detriment of quality and productivity. In a series of studies during the 1960s, the London *Economist* lauded Japanese economic development, and the decision-making structures that had made it possible. The best known of these is *Consider Japan* (1963). Ronald Dore, in his book, *British Factory Japanese Factory* (1973), compared work and employment practices in British and Japanese factories, concluding that most aspects of Japanese practice were substantially more effective than those prevailing in Britain. This book marked a turning point in Dore's thinking about Japan, and was followed by such works as *Taking Japan Seriously* (1987). Another area where Japanese practice was seen as worth emulating was that of education, where international comparisons indicated exceptionally high levels of attainment by Japanese schoolchildren, especially in mathematics [*see also* EDUCATION AND POLITICS].

It was less common to find the political system, narrowly defined, presented as a model worthy of emulation, though this depended on the standards against which it was judged. If the standards were those of participatory democracy, transparency and accountability, then the system was often found wanting, but if the standards were continuity of policy and purposeful action, then observers were more frequently impressed, at least before the 1990s.

Cultural uniqueness and its critics, consensus versus conflict

A number of works appeared during the 1970s seeking to explain much that took place in Japan in terms of cultural uniqueness. In the English-speaking world the most influential book in this genre was *Japanese Society*, by the Japanese anthropologist, Nakane Chie (1970). Her model of vertically structured social relations, with weak horizontal linkages, became a key point of reference for much writing about Japan in that period. So far as politics was concerned, it appeared to explain aspects of factionalism within political parties (see FACTIONS WITHIN POLITICAL PARTIES). If, for instance, you could succeed in attracting a political leader to your side, then his followers would automatically come over to your side as well. In so far as this was correct, it suggested a markedly different form of political interaction, either from one based on individual autonomy, or from one emphasising the primacy of horizontal (say, social class-based) interactions.

From the end of the 1970s, cultural theories – and Nakane in particular – faced challenges from various sources. Two sociologists based in Australia, Ross Mouer and Sugimoto Yoshio, argued in a series of publications that much cultural school writing was based on anecdotal evidence rather than on scientific methodology, and that patterns of interaction in Japanese society were far more varied than the narrow viewpoint of Nakane and others would suggest. In particular, they (and others) focused on the relationship between consensus and conflict. Some culturalists tended to present consensus, or the search for consensus, as the fundamental force in society, whereas Mouer and Sugimoto sought to revive interest in conflict. On the other hand, it could be argued that consensus and conflict were two sides of the same coin, in that the formation of a consensus would hardly be necessary unless there were at least incipient conflict preceding it. It could even be argued that a society placing great emphasis on mechanisms for the creation of consensus must be especially prone to conflict. In the United States, Krauss, Rohlen and Steinhoff (1984) embarked on a rather similar exercise of 'placing' conflict into an understanding of Japanese social patterns.

The same set of issues was approached from a very different intellectual perspective, but with not dissimilar conclusions, by Peter Dale, in his book *The Myth of Japanese Uniqueness* (1986). Sharing an Australian background with Mouer and Sugimoto, he was, unlike them, trained as a classicist, and had a thorough grounding in the main European literary cultures, as well as those of China and Japan. In his book he set himself the task of tracing the origins and credentials of *nihonjinron*, a pervasive genre of Japanese writing that sought answers to the question 'What does it mean to be Japanese?' He found that much of the genre was based on tenuous intellectual credentials, made spurious dichotomies between Japanese and Western ways of thinking, and was often served up as an excuse for Japanese to work to their own exclusive rules. His research showed that practitioners of *nihonjinron* endlessly produced variations on a limited set of themes and propositions. Much of this he was able to trace back to right-wing German stereotypes current in the first four decades of the twentieth century.

Not surprisingly, the book proved highly controversial, and evoked furious rebuttal from some quarters in Japan and elsewhere. Although now somewhat dated, because *nihonjinron* itself is now far less important than it was in the 1970s and 1980s, it remains one of the most significant works to emerge from the Japan studies literature in recent years.

Theories of Japanese politics

Japan Incorporated

The 'economic miracle' of the 1960s naturally gave birth to a small industry of attempts to explain it. One of these that attained particularly wide currency was 'Japan Incorporated'. The coinage, which may have been invented by James Abegglen, likened the Japanese politico-economic system to that of a large corporate firm, with shareholders, managers and employees. It was not entirely original, because the same metaphor had been applied by Tucker to the Soviet Union at about the same period. But it implied that the Japanese system was corporate rather than pluralist. Specifically, single-party dominance ensured continuity of direction, the power of the bureaucracy guaranteed continuity of managerial ethos, and big business provided the entrepreneurial dynamic. The employees, according to the theory, did more or less what they were told.

The problem with 'Japan, Inc.' was that it became a journalistic cliché, ignoring significant detail since it was so much easier to rely on a broad formula for understanding. In its day, however, it had a certain positive role, in that it focused attention on the relative co-ordination of purpose that informed the Japanese politico-economic system in the era of rapid economic growth.

Creative conservatism

In 1982 T.J. Pempel published *Policy and Politics in Japan*, subtitled *Creative Conservatism*. Essentially the book was a reflection on the adaptability shown by the LDP in the 1970s, faced by successive external 'shocks' and a chronic decline in the level of its electoral support. He showed how, first under TANAKA and later under other leaders, the party had managed to turn around the electoral situation in its favour by appealing to social groups that had previously been outside its orbit. Pempel later published *Uncommon Democracies* (1990) comparing single-party dominance in Japan with that in Italy, Sweden and (though it had come to an end) Israel. His essential message was that a long-term ruling party can stay in power so long as it is flexible enough to reach out continuously to new social groups.

Bureaucratic dominance and the developmental State

In 1982 Chalmers Johnson published his book, *MITI and the Japanese Miracle*, which became perhaps the most quoted book on Japanese political economy of the past 30 years. Johnson was a strong believer in the historical continuity thesis, specifically the continuity of experience from the 1920s and 1930s into the post-war period and beyond. He saw the whole period as a learning experience in which some spectacular mistakes were made, particularly in the late 1930s and early 1940s. But he writes:

> The effectiveness of the Japanese state in the economic realm is to be explained in the first instance by its priorities. For more than 50 years the Japanese state has given its first priority to economic development.... the consistency and continuity of its top priority generated a learning process that made the state much more effective during the second half of the period than the first.
>
> (p. 305)

In Johnson's opinion, the fact that economic development was made top priority over a long period stemmed from situational imperatives, including 'late development, a lack of natural resources, a large population, the need to trade, and the constraints of the international balance of payments' (p. 307). The fact, however, that it was given top priority meant that the State geared its organisational structure single-mindedly towards the tasks of developing the economy as rapidly as possible. This meant, in particular, concentrating central power in the bureaucracy and ensuring that politics, Government and big business walked hand in hand. How this was done through the instrument of the MINISTRY OF INTERNATIONAL TRADE AND INDUSTRY (MITI) is the subject of the book. In his analysis, MITI used its powers to influence the direction of the economy through a mixture of formal controls and informal pressure. But given that economic development (not social welfare, environmental control or other purposes) was the top priority, MITI performed its directing role essentially in a 'market-conforming' manner.

The book raises a host of fascinating issues, and has inevitably received much criticism from sceptics. Johnson has been accused (not least, by some MITI officials themselves) of exaggerating the role of MITI. Since the period covered by his book ended in 1975, some critics have argued that he extrapolated from the extraordinary circumstances of a particular period to make generalisations that were much less applicable to later periods, when the role of MITI had diminished, or changed in character. Some have argued that in general he tended to overstate the bureaucratic input into policy and understate the political input. Nevertheless, he responded vigorously to critics and continued to defend his views in numerous fora. Undoubtedly his book helped shape the debate about the Japanese political economy from the early 1980s onwards.

1980s revisionism

By the 1980s, the size of the Japanese economy had reached the point where the economic power of Japan could no longer be ignored. Japanese investment in the United States had become substantial, and Americans increasingly accused Japan of pursuing a highly unbalanced trading policy – of exporting huge quantities of manufactured goods to the United States, but importing very little in exchange. The yen was evidently undervalued, and, though this was corrected by the Plaza Accords in 1985, Japanese industry was able to survive this and continued to create a tsunami of exports. The late 1980s were punctuated by a series of acrimonious trade disputes between the United States and Japan [see also UNITED STATES, RELATIONS WITH].

In these circumstances the benign 'learn from Japan' approach of Vogel gave way to an altogether more worried and bad-tempered set of theorising about Japan. Towards the end of the decade the press were speaking of a 'gang of four', constituting a US school of criticism of the Japanese political economy. The four were three Americans, Chalmers Johnson, Clyde Prestowitz, whose book, *Trading Places* (1988), was a sharp analysis of Japanese trading policies, and James Fallows, as well as a Dutchman long resident in Japan, Karel van Wolferen. To some extent the 'gang of four' was a media creation, since each of the four concerned had distinct and separate analyses of the Japanese system. But what they had in common was a conviction that it was misleading and even dangerous to regard the way the Japanese political economy worked as similar to that of Western models, such as the United States.

Van Wolferen's 1989 book, *The Enigma of Japanese Power*, probably had the greatest impact of all the writings in this category, in part because of his gift for memorable phrases. The Japanese System of political economy was like a 'headless chicken' or a 'truncated pyramid', with nobody ultimately in charge. Whereas President Truman had insisted that 'the buck stops here', in Japan 'the buck just keeps on circulating'. But, according to van Wolferen, that did not mean that nothing got done. Rather, there was a System (capital S) that was potentially dangerous, since it had neither pilot nor brakes. In one sense at least, his analysis contrasted with that of Johnson. Whereas for Johnson the dominance of a developmentally inclined bureaucracy meant that the Japanese political economy was controlled by a central agency with a clear purpose, for van Wolferen there was nobody ultimately in charge at all, and yet the System kept rolling according to some kind of internal logic.

The Enigma of Japanese Power is vulnerable to the criticism that his analysis is essentially closed. If the System works in the way he portrays it, it is difficult to see how it could ever be changed. The book also lacks a rigorous comparative dimension. There are many systems of political economy around the world (not entirely excluding the United States) where the ultimate real (as distinct from formal) responsibility for decisions is far from clear. But the book makes a key contribution in demonstrating the importance of probing beneath the surface of events to a deeper structure of power relationships below.

One of the less enlightening themes running through some, at least, of the writings of the 1980s revisionists was the concept of the 'Chrysanthemum Club'. This was the idea that anyone who spoke or wrote favourably about Japan was in some way selling out to the Japanese machine. The idea gained considerable currency in the United States and elsewhere for a number of years. Perhaps its most extreme manifestation is to be found in Michael Crichton's depressingly unpleasant novel, *The Rising Sun*, whose author makes specific acknowledgement to the revisionist writers. No doubt some high-profile academics and others had compromised their objectivity by coming too close to the Japanese establishment, and this merited forthright criticism. But some writers of the period (not, for the most part, the four principals) were inclined to lump together anyone who had good things to say about any aspect of Japan under the common rubric of the 'Chrysanthemum Club'. Such undiscriminating treatment smacked of conspiracy theory and even paranoia.

Japan as an exception to the End of History

In 1990, when the Soviet Union was approaching its demise, the US writer, Francis Fukuyama, wrote his book *The End of History and the Last Man*, which made a big impact and was on the best-seller lists. Whatever may have been the intention of the author, what most readers took from it was the notion that from now on there would be only one system of political economy worth taking note of, the free market liberal democratic system of which the United States was the leading exemplar. This idea gelled with a short-lived US triumphalism at having 'won' the Cold War.

Fukuyama's view was challenged by David Williams in his book, *Japan beyond the End of History* (1994). The argument of the book is complex, but the essential point is that Japan represents a theoretically and practically distinct system of political economy, which can be traced back to the precepts of the nineteenth-century German writer, Friedrich List. List was a developmentalist, who believed that the State had a crucial role to play in the promotion of development. Japan, in Williams's view, had a regime based more on the principles of Listian statist developmentalism than on free market economics. This, he believed, was why Japan constituted a refutation of the 'End of History' argument.

In one sense, Williams's argument has much in common with the views of the 1980s revisionists. He maintained that the Japanese system of political economy was fundamentally different from that of the United States. But he parted from them in seeing it in positive terms, as a distinct model deserving of respect and emulation, rather than dismissing it as aberrant or dangerous. Perhaps in this respect, he has more in common with Johnson than with the other revisionists, since, although Johnson moved to a highly critical stance in respect of Japan in the late 1980s, his earlier writings provide evidence of a far more positive appreciation of the Japanese model, and a critical view of the impact of classical economics on thinking in the United States.

Williams was unlucky in his timing, because the long Japanese recession of the 1990s and beyond made the Listian model seem less interesting to outside observers.

Rational choice

A challenge to the revisionists (especially Johnson) emerged in the early 1990s with the publication of *Japan's Political Marketplace*, by Ramseyer and Rosenbluth. Their thinking was profoundly influenced by the currently fashionable rational choice theory, and by a sub-branch of it, principal-agent theory. The book covers several aspects of Japanese political economy, but the one most widely noticed was their analysis of relations between politicians and bureaucrats. Working on the assumption that LDP politicians are the principals and Government officials their agents, they turn on its head the previously dominant view that Government officials run Japan. To take one particular aspect of the relationship, they interpret the role of ex-bureaucrats who have become LDP parliamentarians, not as infiltration of the LDP by the bureaucracy, but a mechanism whereby the LDP can influence and control the BUREAUCRACY. Similarly the AMAKUDARI phenomenon is regarded by them as a case of 'postponed income', whereby officials are kept on modest salaries during their careers in their ministries, but their political loyalty is ensured by the prospect of fat salaries after they have 'retired'.

Their position was thus almost diametrically opposed to that of Johnson, for whom the bureaucracy was always dominant. Johnson was inclined to dismiss much rational choice theory as a case of a priori reasoning significantly influenced by US assumptions about political economy. In terms of our earlier discussion (see Table 1) the controversy developed strong overtones of culturalism versus universalism.

During the 1990s rational choice theorists made a contribution to the understanding of electoral behaviour and the implications of different ELECTION SYSTEMS. Principal among them were Cox and Rosenbluth.

Patterned pluralism

Some of the theories we have already examined tend to rely on one particular factor or set of factors as an explanatory variable. The theories we shall now more briefly discuss attempt to capture the complexity of politics in Japan by emphasising combinations of factors that, separately, might appear to point in different directions. One example is the concept of 'patterned pluralism' put forward by Muramatsu and Krauss (1987). They describe it as follows:

> Patterned pluralism is pluralistic in fundamental ways: influence is widely distributed, not concentrated; interest groups have many points of access to the policymaking process; and although interest groups are definitely tied to the government, there are elements of autonomy and conflict in the relationship. We are not dealing here with classical pluralism in which policy was merely the outcome of open-ended, competitive lobbying by pressure groups on a relatively weak government. Rather, the patterned pluralist government is strong, interest groups sometimes have cooperative relations with the government and with each other, and lobbying is not open-ended because interest groups usually are almost constantly allied with the same parties and bureaucratic agencies.
>
> (p. 537)

Muramatsu and Krauss emphasise the importance of long-term LDP rule, and insist that, while Government is not weak, 'it is *penetrated* by interest groups and political parties'. They describe the LDP as a 'pragmatic, catchall party at least partially responsive to a wide variety of sometimes competing social interests' (p. 538). It will be evident that this formula not only emphasises complexity, but also implies a sceptical attitude towards claims either of long-term intentionality or of absence of central direction.

Bureaucrat-led, mass-inclusionary pluralism

This is the formulation of Inoguchi, in various writings of the 1990s, and is similar in its emphasis to that of Muramatsu and Krauss. Once again, the strong State is emphasised, in the shape of a system where Government officials have a leading role. But the mass of the population is included in the political system through many types of linkage, and politics is pluralistic rather than elitist or hierarchical.

Dynamism together with immobilism

This was the theme of a book by Stockwin, Rix, George, Horne, Itō and Collick published in 1988, entitled *Dynamic and Immobilist Politics in Japan*. The starting point of the analysis was the apparent paradox that certain areas of policy in certain historical circumstances were dealt with in expeditious and innovative ways, whereas other areas of policy seemed bogged down and resistant to change. They suggested that this could be explained through an authority maintenance model, according to which one party remains in power over a very long period and judges policy initiatives on the basis of how far they serve to keep their regime in power. This was not incompatible with dynamic developmentalism, nor with a considerable degree of pluralism. But the determination of the ruling regime to maintain its power meant that many areas of policy, where the regime was beholden to vested interests of various kinds, led to what could well be described as immobilism.

To some extent, this analysis anticipated the problems of the 1990s and beyond, when ambitious programmes of reform in circumstances of economic stagnation were repeatedly obstructed by the influence of vested interests that the LDP had long relied on to keep itself in power.

Crisis and compensation

A somewhat analogous approach was taken by Kent Calder, in his book, *Crisis and Compensation*, also published in 1988. Calder maintained that 'circles of compensation' characterise the Japanese political process. He writes:

> Japanese politics... operates largely in terms of institutionalized networks of players engaged in special reciprocal relationships of obligation and reward with public authority.... Government provides benefits to private sector participants, in return for their consistent political support.
>
> (p. 25)

He argues that accommodation between Government and its opponents 'occurs at crucial junctures when either the continuance of a given administration's tenure in office is perceived to be severely threatened or internal political unrest seriously impairs its international credibility' (p. 25). Thus the end result over the long term tends to be an expansion of the veto power of vested interests over Government.

Economic stagnation and political instability from the early 1990s has tarnished the lustre of the Japanese model, so that the impetus to theorise about it has declined. On the other hand, there have been many interesting developments deserving theoretical treatment. The following questions arise, among others: Why did what appeared to be a winning formula for achieving economic growth and prosperity up to the 1980s appear to have failed – or not to have prevented severe economic problems – from the early 1990s?

Was it essential to embark on radical reshaping of the politico-economic system in order to cope with the difficult economic situation? Why, once reform was proposed and attempted, did it prove so difficult to put into practice? Might reform have been achieved more effectively and quickly had the LDP remained out of office instead of returning to office in 1994? What have been the consequences of LDP-centred coalition Government since 1994, and is the LDP really weaker than it was up to the early 1990s? Why has the party system returned to something very like its shape before 1993, despite great instability and change in the mid-1990s? How far is the Government bureaucracy actually weakened by the ADMINISTRATIVE REORGANISATION that took place in January 2001 and related reforms? How far is the office of PRIME MINISTER enhanced by these and associated reforms? Are governments in the early 2000s any less beholden to myriad vested interests than they were before? Has the shape of the politico-economic system significantly changed, and, if so, is that change for the better?

Relational and contract-based transactions

Though most commentators express themselves in favour of reform, there are some who believe some features of the existing system may be valuable and worth retaining. Dore, for instance, argues for retention of some 'relational', as distinct from contract-based, transactions within the politico-economic system, on the ground that inter-personal understanding gained over a long period is likely to be a better guarantee of reliability than a written contract. Dore's view is vulnerable to the criticism that much of the bank indebtedness problems of the past decade have resulted from a softly-softly approach by Government owing to long-standing 'relational' ties. Nevertheless, we should not assume that relational transactions are necessarily a bad thing in Japan or anywhere else, since in many situations it helps greatly to have a close knowledge of the people you have to deal with.

Redistributive regulated party rule

Jean-Marie Bouissou and Paolo Pombeni, in a fascinating comparison of the political systems of Japan and Italy (2001), argue that in each country a dominant party has presided over a system of sharing the fruits of economic growth among what they call 'historically closed sectors' of society, as well as among the political parties themselves, whether those parties be in coalition with the dominant party or not. To this they give the designation 'redistributive regulated party-rule'. Although the systems they describe plainly differ greatly from that in the United Kingdom, for instance, they are inclined to regard them favourably for having contributed both to economic growth and – by sharing out benefits – to social cohesion. There is an obvious link with Dore's view here.

An 'unWestminster' model

It has normally been assumed that the basic structure of the Japanese political system is essentially that of the Westminster model. In this model the Prime Minister and CABINET are able to exercise almost exclusive policy-making power so long as the Government party or parties maintain a majority in Parliament and stay united. The model also holds that the legislature controls the executive, in other words that policy decided in Cabinet and endorsed by Parliament is automatically executed by the Government ministries. Aurelia George Mulgan challenges the model in relation to Japan, holding that in the Japanese case it breaks down in at least two respects. First, much decision-making takes place in internal committees of the LDP. Second, even though politicians have encroached on bureaucratic powers in recent years, Government officials still exercise substantially more power, especially of initiating and preparing legislation, than would be the norm in a Westminster system. She examines the experience of the Koizumi Government and argues that the frustrations faced by its reformist programmes stem essentially from these two competing sources of power. She further argues that the recent attempts to enhance prime ministerial powers by the creation of a CABINET OFFICE and the installation of deputy ministers increase the risk of serious clashes between prime ministerial power and traditional power structures in the ruling party and the Government ministries.

Further reading

Abegglen (1958)
Calder (1988)
Cox and Rosenbluth (1995)
Dale (1986)
Dore (1973)
—— (1987)
Dower (1999)
Economist (1963)
George Mulgan (2002)

Ike (1957)
Inoguchi (1983)
Johnson (1982)
Kawai (1960)
Kinmonth (1985)
Krauss *et al.* (1984)
Maruyama (1963)
Mouer and Sugimoto (1986)
Murakami (1982)
Muramatsu and Krauss (1987)
Nakane (1970)
Pempel (1982)
—— (1990)
Prestowitz (1988)
Quigley and Turner (1956)
Ramseyer and Rosenbluth (1993)
Scalapino (1962)
—— (1967)
Steven (1983)
Stockwin (1968)
Stockwin *et al.* (1988)
Van Wolferen (1989)
Vogel, Ezra (1979)
Ward (1963)
—— (ed.) (1968)
—— (1978)
Williams, David (1994)

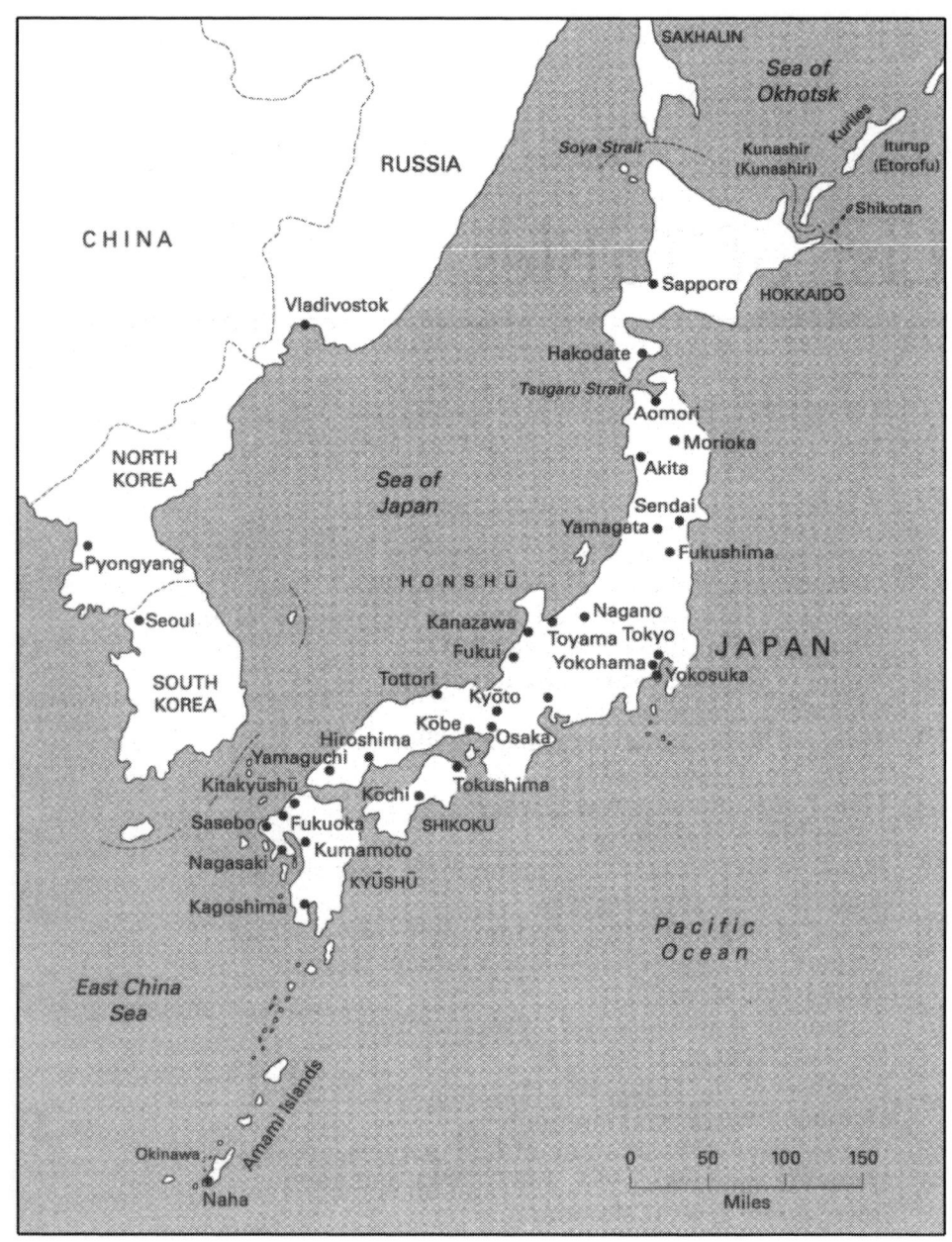

The maps were first published in *Governing Japan* © J.A.A. Stockwin 1975, 1982, 1999. Reproduced by permission of Blackwell Publishing.

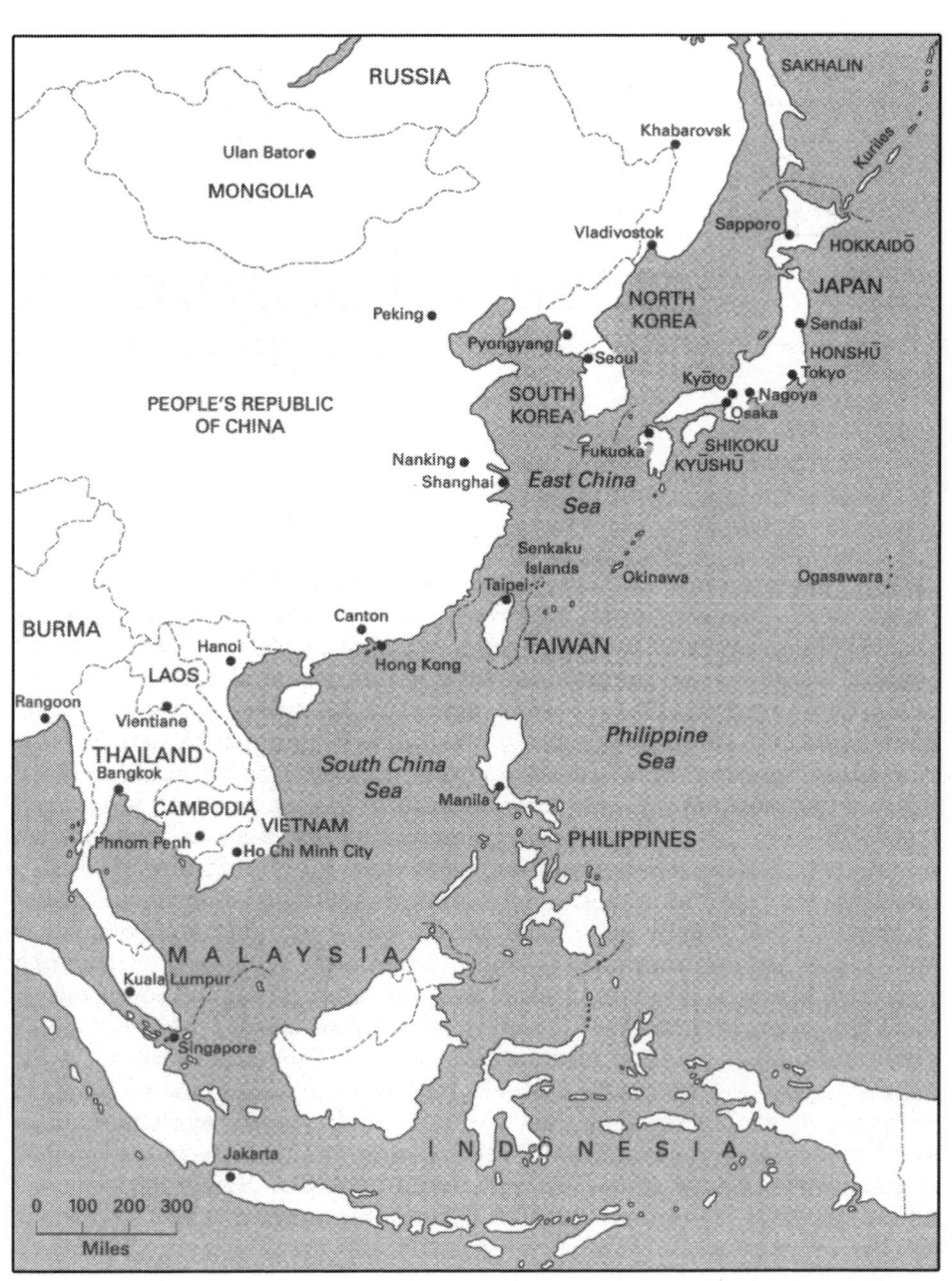

Abe Shintarō Son-in-law of KISHI NOBUSUKE, Abe in 1986 took over what had been the Kishi faction from FUKUDA TAKEO, and was one of four principal faction leaders in the LIBERAL DEMOCRATIC PARTY (LDP) from then until his death in 1991.

Born in Yamaguchi in 1924, he graduated from Tokyo University and became a journalist soon after the war. In 1958 he was first elected to the HOUSE OF REPRESENTATIVES for a Yamaguchi constituency. His first Cabinet position was that of Agriculture Minister in the MIKI Government (1974–6). He then became Chief Cabinet Secretary in the Government of his faction leader, Fukuda, in 1977–8. He was later Minister of Trade and Industry under SUZUKI in 1981–2. In November 1982 he entered the primary elections for the LDP presidency and came third out of four candidates, with a mere 8.28 per cent of the vote. NAKASONE YASUHIRO, however, the victor in that contest, made him Foreign Minister, a post in which he remained between November 1982 and July 1986. As Foreign Minister to a Prime Minister dedicated to activism on the world stage, Abe made many international trips; he was in frequent touch with world leaders such as President Reagan and Margaret Thatcher. He also explored the implications of the emergence of the Gorbachev regime in the USSR.

He served at various times in senior party positions, including that of Secretary-General. Like other faction leaders, he was implicated in the RECRUIT SCANDAL of 1989.

At about this time he became ill with cancer and died in May 1991.

Further reading
Curtis (1988)

administrative guidance (Gyōsei shidō) The practice of administrative guidance has been a controversial method of bureaucratic control that used to be a central method in the management of the economy. By some, it has been criticised as undemocratic interference in the sovereignty of the people's elected representatives in Parliament. Others have seen it as one of the key instruments of the Japanese economic 'miracle'. Foreign governments and businesses have pilloried it as an obstacle to free trade.

In fact, administrative guidance was a product of the particular circumstances of the 1960s, and has declined greatly in importance since the 1980s. From the late 1940s until the early 1960s the Japanese economy was essentially an administered economy. Government – meaning for the most part Government ministries – had at their disposal a comprehensive range of legal controls affecting much of what industry was able to do. If a firm wanted to move into a new area of manufacture, was reluctant to merge with another firm, needed foreign exchange, or could be accused of 'dumping' in foreign markets, it was liable to regulatory action sanctioned by law. The same went for 'excessive competition' in an industry, something not normally well regarded by Government officials. By the early 1960s, however, Japan was embarking on a range of liberalising measures – in part owing to international pressure – and these threatened the integrity of bureaucratic control. The MINISTRY OF INTERNATIONAL TRADE AND INDUSTRY (MITI, *Tsūsanshō*) put great pressure on politicians to pass a Special Measures Law, designed in particular to protect designated industries. This, however, failed to attain sufficient LIBERAL DEMOCRATIC PARTY (LDP) support, and was aborted in 1963. In the opinion of Chalmers Johnson it was this failure, and the fear of MITI officials that their ability to influence industrial decisions and the direction of the economy would disappear, which led to the emergence of administrative guidance as a primary instrument of policy.

The essence of administrative guidance was that it was informal and extra-legal, but that its efficacy depended on a combination of continuous networking and implied sanctions. In addition, at the time when the practice was at its height, Japanese society lacked a culture fiercely defensive of individual autonomy and rights, such as would have severely inhibited attempts to apply it in most Western countries. It is at least arguable that a culture privileging conformity over rugged independence facilitated the promotion of administrative guidance. MITI, the key ministry in this regard, used it to promote mergers and strengthen the competitiveness of new industries that needed to establish their competitiveness in the international market-place. As foreign interests frequently pointed out, bureaucratic regulation – most often informal and opaque – also conspired to minimise foreign penetration of the domestic Japanese market.

Okimoto argues that for administrative guidance to work, several conditions need to be fulfilled. The industry concerned should contain few firms and they should be used to interacting with each other. There should be a market-leader. The market should be rather concentrated. The industry should have reached a mature stage in its life cycle. There should be a strong industrial association, a history of dependence on MITI, and common problems affecting the whole industry. He points out that the newer industries of the 1980s, such as computer software, hardly at all fulfilled these conditions, though administrative guidance was still used in relation to international trade and the administered decline of sunset industries.

In the early 2000s, administrative guidance is not entirely dead. Since the early 1990s attacks on the kind of 'regulatory state' philosophy that it implies have become intense. It is widely felt that administrative guidance is hardly appropriate for a mature economy, and the difficulties experienced by the economy in recent years tend to be placed at the door of over-regulation and networks that are instruments of regulation. The instinct of government officials to persuade, pressure, cajole and sanction remains, but the spheres in which such actions are effective have narrowed.

Further reading
Inoguchi and Okimoto (1988)
Johnson (1982)
Okimoto (1989)
Yamamura and Yasuba (eds) (1987)

Administrative Management Agency After earlier *ad hoc* arrangements, this agency was set up during the Allied Occupation in 1948 in order to provide guidance and control over the public service as a whole. It became an external agency of the PRIME MINISTER'S OFFICE (*Sōrifu*, originally *Sōrichō*), with a Minister of State as its Director. It consisted of the Director's Secretariat, an Administrative Control Bureau (*Gyōsei kanrikyoku*) and an Administrative Inspection Bureau (*Gyōsei kansatsukyoku*). Although it was not generally regarded as a major Government body, it could on occasion provide a useful political springboard for its Director. NAKASONE YASUHIRO, as its Director between 1980 and 1982, used it to organise the Second Ad Hoc Administrative Reform Commission (*Dai niji Rinchō*), which reported during his own period as Prime Minister from 1982.

In 1984, as a result of a recommendation of the *Dai niji Rinchō*, the Administrative Management Agency became the MANAGEMENT AND CO-ORDINATION AGENCY (*Sōmuchō*), which also inherited a few functions from elsewhere.

administrative reorganisation, January 2001
In December 1997 a report commissioned by the HASHIMOTO Government recommended a

drastic reorganisation of Japanese Government ministries and agencies. This meant in particular a substantial reduction in their number through amalgamations of existing bodies. Given the extraordinary stability of the administrative structure since the Occupation period (and, in the cases of some ministries, back to the Meiji period), the reform appeared surprisingly radical.

On 6 January 2001 the number of ministries and agencies was drastically cut back, creating a number of super-ministries. The broad purposes of the reform were, first, to attack what had come to be known as 'vertical administration', whereby rather narrowly based administrative organs jealously protected their turf and developed projects that often overlapped with those of other organs regarded as their competitors. Amalgamation was expected to facilitate co-operative relationships within broad functional areas of the bureaucracy. Second, the reform was designed to make political control of the public service easier to implement. Third, it was expected to help create a more lean and efficient administrative culture. And a final purpose was to promote transparency and policy review – rather weak elements of the system up to that point.

In tabular form, the changes may be portrayed as on Table 3.

Several aspects of this reorganisation are worth noting. First, three ministries survived without amalgamation or change of name. These are the MINISTRY OF JUSTICE, MINISTRY OF FOREIGN AFFAIRS and MINISTRY OF AGRICULTURE, FORESTRY AND FISHERIES. Second, the MINISTRY OF FINANCE suffered a change of name in Japanese (the English translation is the same) that was a psychological blow given the long history of its cherished name, *Okurashō*. By contrast, the ENVIRONMENT AGENCY found its status upgraded to that of ministry.

Third, amalgamation of four ministries and agencies (including the MINISTRY OF TRANSPORT and the MINISTRY OF CONSTRUCTION) into the MINISTRY OF LAND, INFRASTRUCTURE AND TRANSPORT was designed to produce a co-ordinated approach to all aspects of transport infrastructure. The joining of the MINISTRY OF LABOUR and the MINISTRY OF HEALTH AND WELFARE was supposed to link employment policy with welfare policy. The creation of the MINISTRY OF EDUCATION, CULTURE, SPORTS, SCIENCE AND TECHNOLOGY produced a linkage with obvious policy implications. It was rather less obvious why MINISTRY OF POSTS AND TELECOMMUNICATIONS, the MANAGEMENT AND CO-ORDINATION AGENCY (now called Public Management) and MINISTRY OF HOME AFFAIRS (local government) should have been put together in one super-ministry.

Fourth, the creation of the CABINET OFFICE, with various administrative bodies responsible to it, was part of a broader attempt to strengthen the powers of the PRIME MINISTER. Finally, all the ministries and agencies in the new structure were under pressure to cut costs and pare down their functions, rationalising overlapping functions wherever possible.

Administrative Vice-Minister (jimu jikan)

The Administrative Vice-Minister is the most senior official in a ministry or agency of government. It is not to be confused with the Political Vice-Minister (*Seimu jikan*), which is a junior ministerial position filled by a politician.

Normally, the Administrative Vice-Minister is in effect chosen within the ministry from among the most senior cohort of officials. Until recent reforms that have made the system less predictable, those entering the ministry in a particular year rose by seniority at the same pace as each other, until they reached senior echelons, when opportunities narrowed, and at the very top level only one position remained, that of Administrative Vice-Minister. Typically, though not always, all other members of his cohort resign when one of them attains the top position. Some of these are then found *amakudari* positions. In recent years there have been some well-publicised examples of interference by the minister in top personnel appointments, including appointments to the position of Administrative Vice-Minister. This tends to cause great controversy and is intensely resented within the ministry or agency.

Koh found that over 80 per cent of those appointed Administrative Vice-Minister in the 12 ministries of the national government between 1981 and 1987 had graduated in Law, with Economics the runner-up on just over 11 per cent. Well over 80 per cent of them were

Table 3 Former and new ministries and agencies

Former structure	New structure
Ministry of Posts and Telecommunications (*Yūseishō*) Management and Co-ordination Agency (*Sōmuchō*) Ministry of Home Affairs (Ministry of Local Autonomy) (*Jichishō*)	Ministry of Public Management, Home Affairs, Posts and Telecommunications (*Sōmushō*)
Ministry of Justice (MOJ, *Hōmushō*)	Ministry of Justice (MOJ *Hōmushō*)
Ministry of Foreign Affairs (MFA, *Gaimushō*)	Ministry of Foreign Affairs (MFA *Gaimushō*)
Ministry of Finance (MOF, *Ōkurashō*)	Ministry of Finance (MOF *Zaimushō*)
Ministry of Education (MOE, *Monbushō*) Science and Technology Agency (*Kagakugijutsuchō*)	Ministry of Education, Culture, Sports, Science and Technology (*Monbukagakushō*)
Ministry of Labour (*Rōdōshō*) Ministry of Health and Welfare (*Kōseishō*)	Ministry of Health, Labour and Welfare (*Kōseirōdōshō*) [Some functions move to the Ministry of the Environment – see below]
Ministry of Agriculture, Forestry and Fisheries (MAFF, *Nōrinsuisanshō*)	Ministry of Agriculture, Forestry and Fisheries (MAFF, *Nōrinsuisanshō*)
Ministry of International Trade and Industry (MITI, *Tsūshōsangyōshō, Tsūsanshō*)	Ministry of Economy, Trade and Industry (METI, *Keizaisangyōshō*) [some functions move to the Ministry of the Environment – see below]
Hokkaidō Development Agency (*Hokkaidō Kaihatsuchō*) Ministry of Transport (*Unyūshō*) Ministry of Construction (*Kensetsushō*) National Land Agency (*Kokudochō*)	Ministry of Land, Infrastructure and Transport (*Kokudokōtsūshō*)
Environment Agency (*Kankyōchō*)	Ministry of the Environment (*Kankyōshō*) [some functions from the Ministry of Welfare and some from MITI – see above]
Cabinet Secretariat (*Naikaku Kanbō*)	Cabinet Secretariat (*Naikaku Kanbō*)

Former structure	New structure
Prime Minister's Office (*Sōrifu*) Economic Planning Agency (EPA, *Keizaikikakuchō*) Okinawa Development Agency (*Okinawa Kaihatsuchō*)	Cabinet Office (*Naikakufu*)
	Financial Services (*Kinyūchō*)
Defence Agency (*Bōeichō*)	Defence Agency (*Bōeichō*) [responsible to the Cabinet Office]
National Public Safety Commission (*Kokka kōan iinkai*)	National Public Safety Commission (*Kokka kōan iinkai*) [responsible to the Cabinet Office]

Source: *Yomiuri Nenkan*, 2002, p. 178, and Japanese Government Internet sites.

graduates of Tokyo University, and of these an overwhelming majority were graduates of its Faculty of Law. In nearly all ministries those achieving the top position were *jimukan* (generalists) as distinct from *gikan* (technical officials). The only exception among the 12 ministries of the pre-2001 system was the MINISTRY OF CONSTRUCTION (*Kensetsushō*), where the position of Administrative Vice-Minister alternated between *jimukan* and *gikan*.

The Conference of Administrative Vice-Ministers (*Jimu jikan kaigi*) has been widely regarded as a key decision-making body of government. It consists of the *jimu jikan* in all ministries and agencies, as well as one or two other top officials not actually enjoying the same title. Its meetings precede those of Cabinet, and its function is to 'pre-digest' issues and reach decisions to be put for final decision to Cabinet itself. If this means that Cabinet meetings are often perfunctory, there is evidence that even the *Jimu jikan kaigi* essentially ratifies decisions that have been negotiated beforehand in **nemawashi** exercises between ministries and agencies, no doubt with some political input as well.

Reforms since the late 1990s designed to increase political input into decision-making has complicated, and perhaps slightly weakened, the role of the Administrative Vice-Minister and of the *Jimu jikan kaigi*. The ending of the practice whereby government officials could speak on behalf of ministers in Parliament, and the introduction of Deputy Ministers (*Fukudaijin* and *Seimukan*), as well as the creation of the CABINET OFFICE (*Naikakufu*) in January 2001, were designed to mitigate the dominance of top officials in the decision-making process. How far these reforms will have the desired effect remains to be seen.

Further reading
Johnson (1982)
Koh (1989)

Africa, relations with Relations with Africa have never been a major part of Japan's relations with the outside world as a whole. Nevertheless, in recent years Japan has had significant relations with a number of African countries.

For the most part, sub-Saharan Africa has not been an attractive location for Japanese foreign direct investment, and it has attracted only a relatively small proportion of Japan's overseas development aid budget, the bulk of which has traditionally gone to other Asian countries. Ampiah has shown, however, that for many years Japan was notably strategic in its policies towards Africa. From a national interest point of view, trade with South Africa was of major importance to Japan, since South Africa was an important source of several raw materials vital to Japanese industry but difficult to obtain elsewhere. Interestingly enough,

Japan was able to maintain reasonable trading levels with South Africa under the Apartheid regime and still avoid the kinds of criticism that were regularly meted out to other advanced countries seeking to do the same thing in the face of sanctions. This was also despite the fact that Japanese voting patterns at the United Nations were highly discrepant from those of states taking a clear anti-Apartheid stance, especially on matters relating to sanctions.

A key to this may be found in Ampiah's analysis of Japanese policy towards frontline states during the Apartheid years, notably Tanzania, where the extent of Japan's commitment was much greater than could be justified in terms of economic interest. His conclusion is that Japan was strategically cultivating the frontline states with a view to easing pressure to reduce trade with South Africa. This is consistent with the great concern felt by Japanese authorities about access to key raw materials, of which South Africa happened to be a major supplier. It suggests that the strategic dimension to Japanese foreign economic policy is strong and that resources diplomacy is actively pursued. Ampiah suggests also that African opinion tended to be favourably disposed towards Japan because it had never been a colonial power in Africa.

Since the ending of Apartheid in South Africa, Japan has consolidated its links with that country, and in a modest way has been developing economic relationships with other parts of the continent. As Japan's role in international organisations increases, so indirectly does its role in aspects of African affairs.

Further reading
Ampiah (1997)
Johnson (1982)
Koh (1989)
Morikawa (1984)
Rix (1993)

Agricultural Politics and the Agricultural Co-operative Association (Nōgyō kyōdō kumiai, Nōkyō) There is no doubt that the agricultural interest has been enabled to 'punch above its weight' in Japanese politics since the war. Japan is not the only country in the world where agriculture has been able to exercise an influence on policy-making disproportionate both to the number of active farmers and to the weight of farming in the total economy. But it must be very close to the top of the list.

In population terms, Japan up to the Second World War was still to a very large extent an agricultural country. The prevalence of landlord–tenant relationships in many parts of the country had created social and economic tensions that manifested themselves in radical politics in several areas. One of the most important reforms of the Allied Occupation of Japan from 1945 was the Land Reform, which had as its principal aim the elimination of landlordism. It was almost wholly successful in this aim, creating a uniform class of small farmers and a virtual absence of large farms (except in the northern island of Hokkaidō).

One effect of this was to remove, for the most part, radical left-wing organisations, such as farmers' unions (Nōmin kumiai), from agricultural politics. Henceforth, the bulk of farmers accepted conservative values and were supporters of the LIBERAL DEMOCRATIC PARTY (LDP). The importance of farmers in sustaining the LDP in power after its formation in 1955 is difficult to overestimate. The conservative influence went far beyond the ranks of farmers proper, to encompass the whole local economy sustaining the activities of agriculture.

This became even more important politically because the post-war electoral laws lacked effective means of regularly adjusting electoral district boundaries so as to reflect population distribution accurately. The district boundaries were drawn after the war when the rural population was more than 40 per cent of the total. The spectacular growth of manufacturing industry from the late 1950s caused a massive migration from the countryside to the big cities, such as Tokyo, Yokohama, Osaka and Nagoya. But any resultant adjustment to electoral district boundaries came very late and was wholly inadequate to ensure equitable representation. This meant that by the 1970s some rural districts were over-represented by a factor of as much as four-to-one by comparison with some big-city districts. Since these were agricultural districts returning mostly LDP parliamentarians, agriculture was supporting, in a crucial sense, the stability of LDP government. Not surprisingly, in a reciprocal fashion, the LDP exerted itself to develop policies that were highly protective of the interests of farmers. Essentially this was the state of affairs from the late 1950s until around the late 1980s.

The economics of agriculture has for most of the period since the war been based more on corporatist than on market-based principles. In the words of Aurelia George Mulgan: 'Interest group penetration of political institutions is counterbalanced by bureaucratic penetration of interest groups through corporatist modes of interaction, with varying degrees of state sponsorship and interest group capture' (p. 646).

There are many interest groups operating in the agricultural sector, but the most important and wide-ranging of them has been the Agriculture Co-operative Association (Nōgyō kyōdō kumiai, or Nōkyō). Founded originally in 1947, it quickly outpaced all others in its centrality. According to George Mulgan, the organisation of Nōkyō,

> in its totality, comprises a massive and highly complex grouping with a multitude of organisational offshoots. It brings together a collection of several thousand separately-constituted agricultural cooperative organisations that are independent in organisational set-up and internal decision-making structures, but highly interdependent in the flow of goods, services and finance.

The Nōkyō in its totality is a statutory body based on a defined legal framework. Locally, there are general co-operatives (sōgō nōkyō) and specialist co-operatives (senmon nōkyō), several thousand of each. They are also federated at sub-prefectural level into federations with different functions (for instance, provision of credit, marketing and purchasing). These in turn link in with federations at national level. They are the National Federation of Agricultural Co-operatives (Zennō), which deals largely with purchasing and marketing, the National Mutual Aid Nokyo Federation (Zenkyōren), and the Nōrinchūkin, which is a banking institution. The national level of the specialist co-operatives includes numerous bodies, and deals with particular product categories. At the apex of the organisation is the National Central Union of Agricultural Co-operatives, known as Zenchū, to which the prefectural central unions (chūōkai) are answerable. The Zenchū is legally entitled to make representations to government on matters of policy.

After its establishment in 1947 the Nōkyō was quickly mobilised to help distribute scarce food supplies, and was employed as a kind of external organisation of the Ministry of Agriculture and Forestry to help administer the Food Control Law (Shokuryō kanri hō, Shokkan hō). This was the instrument (now abolished) whereby the Ministry controlled prices of rice and other foodstuffs to the farmer and to the consumer. It was turned into a powerful method whereby the farmer could be paid a guaranteed price for his produce, at the expense of the consumer, who had to pay inflated prices for food.

As can be seen from the above highly simplified description, the Nōkyō has been an almost infinitely complex organisation, and is exceedingly difficult to categorise, in its totality, according to function. Indeed, it may be seen as having three main functions, each of which one might expect to be performed by different institutions. First of all, it is an interest group (or pressure group), able to exercise effective pressure on Government in the interests of farmers. Second, its banking, insurance, marketing and purchasing functions (as well as many others) give it a structure reminiscent of a large conglomerate firm. And, third, it has performed significant administrative functions on behalf of Government, becoming in the early post-war years virtually incorporated into the structure of the Ministry of Agriculture and Forestry.

Inevitably, as farming has declined both absolutely and as a proportion of total economic activity, so the political clout of agriculture has also declined. The change in the electoral system for the House of Representatives in 1994 removed some (but by no means all) of the bias in the system in favour of the rural areas. Most rural areas have developed urban characteristics, and the numbers of those engaged in full-time farming is very small (though part-time farming remains quite popular). The Hosokawa Government took Japan into the World Trade Organization in 1993–4, opening up the domestic rice market, for the first time, to rice imports. The Food Control system was radically reshaped in the 1990s, and the role of *Nōkyō* in its administration downgraded. Market forces have been allowed into agriculture as never before.

Nevertheless, agriculture continues to receive unexpectedly high degrees of protection and subsidy. Huge sums were paid by Government to compensate rice farmers for the lifting of the ban on rice imports in 1994. Then in 1998 rice imports were moved from a quota to a tariff system, but the tariff was set at an extremely high rate. The politics of corporatism and special interests, applied to agriculture over several decades, may well have harmed the interests of farmers in the long term by depriving them of incentives to increase productivity. Indeed many social, political and even cultural factors have entered into the equation, with rice grown in Japan being accorded spiritual status in some quarters. Leaving aside the issue of failure to give a good deal to consumers, even the aim of national food security has hardly been achieved by corporatist policies, since the bulk of food consumed in Japan is now in any case imported.

Further reading
Calder (1988)
Donnelly, in Pempel (ed.) (1977)
Dore (1959)
George Mulgan (2000)
——, in Heenan (ed.) (1998)
Waswo (1996)

All-Japan Council of Private Sector Trade Unions (Zen Nihon minkan rōdō kumiai kyōgikai, Zenmin rōkyō) This was a rather loose organisation of 41 industrial unions, accounting for some 4,250,000 workers, formed in December 1982, and aiming at eventual unification of the labour movement. It represented a widening feeling that the splits in the labour union movement that had occurred in the 1950s were of diminishing relevance in the 1980s, and that unification ought to be possible. It engaged in a range of policy studies to this end. It did not supersede existing national union centres, but its efforts were rewarded when these centres (federations) were dissolved over the period between 1987 and 1989, and the JAPANESE TRADE UNION COUNCIL (*Rengō*) replaced them.

All-Japan Council of Teachers' and Staff Unions (Zen Nihon Kyōshokuin Keimeikai, Zenkyō) With the final establishment of the JAPANESE TRADE UNION COUNCIL (JTU, *Rengō*) in 1989, a group of unionists belonging to the JAPAN TEACHERS' UNION (*Nikkyōso*) broke away and formed their own union, *Zenkyō*, launched in November of the same year. They objected to the 'accomodationist' approach to Government and employers favoured by the new national centre, and created their own union in order to pursue policy aims more traditionally favoured by the JTU. On its formation, *Zenkyō* affiliated with the NATIONAL LABOUR UNION ALLIANCE (*Zenrōren*), the national union centre set up in opposition to *Rengō*. Links with the JAPAN COMMUNIST PARTY have been marked, and the union faces the accusation of Communist domination.

With Japan's teachers divided between two divergent unions, *Zenkyō* was the smaller and weaker of the two. Nevertheless, regional patterns varied greatly, and in some prefectures (Aomori, Saitama, Tokyo, Shiga, Kyōto, Nara, Wakayama and Kōchi) more teachers belonged to *Zenkyō* in 1992 than to *Nikkyōso* (Aspinall, pp 60–1). At national level, however, the influence of *Zenkyō* was slight.

The principal issues on which the union has campaigned are, first and foremost, the traditional one of peace and anti-militarism. It also opposes curriculum control by the MINISTRY OF EDUCATION (and its successor), singing the *Kimigayo* anthem and flying the *Hinomaru* flag in schools, and campaigns vigorously for more money for education. It considers social class divisions as important. *Zenkyō* also favours the time-honoured methods of demonstration and petition.

Further reading
Aspinall (2001)
Hood (2001)

All-Japan General Federation of Labour Unions (Nihon rōdō kumiai sōdōmei, Sōdōmei) The *Sōdōmei* labour union federation was launched in August 1946. It was based on a pre-war union tradition originating in the *Yūaikai* (Friendly Society) around the time of the First World War, and a later union federation, also called *Sōdōmei*. This tradition included elements derived from Christian ideas of charity, as well as the ideal of co-operation between management and labour. It did not rule out the strike weapon, but strongly opposed the kinds of confrontational unionism favoured by the CONGRESS OF INDUSTRIAL UNIONS (*Sanbetsu kaigi*) and other left-wing union groups. Organisationally, it was based on enterprise unions, which, being in close and constant touch with the management of their firms, tended to favour negotiation over confrontation.

The prime mover in the foundation of *Sōdōmei* was the right-of-centre union leader, Matsuoka Komakichi, who had been the most recent Chairman of the pre-war *Sōdōmei*. During 1946 the issue arose of a united union front, including both of the major federations, but this idea was quickly rejected by the *Sōdōmei* leadership in the face of Communist attempts to control the general strike scheduled for 1 February 1947, but banned by General MacArthur. Not only the left-wing *Sanbetsu kaigi*, but also the more conservative *Sōdōmei*, were affected by the Democratisation Leagues (*Mindō*) that were exercising a powerful influence in the labour movement at this time.

When the GENERAL COUNCIL OF JAPANESE TRADE UNIONS (*Sōhyō*) was founded in November 1950, the decision was made to dissolve the Federation. One faction, however, disputed the decision, and re-established *Sōdōmei* in June 1951. In April 1954, following the politically leftward shift that had taken place in *Sōhyō* under the leadership of Takano Minoru in 1953, a group of right-of-centre unions defected from *Sōhyō* and formed a new federation called the ALL-JAPAN TRADE UNION CONGRESS (*Zenrō kaigi*). A much truncated *Sōdōmei* remained in existence until 1964, when it merged with *Zenrō kaigi* and other groups to form the Japan Confederation of Labour (*Dōmei*), which became the main federation of economically oriented private-sector unionism.

Further reading
Cole *et al*. (1966)
Levine (1958)

All-Japan Trade Union Congress (Zen Nihon rōdō kumiai kaigi, Zenrō kaigi) *Zenrō kaigi* was a labour union national centre formed in April 1954 by right-of-centre unions defecting from the GENERAL COUNCIL OF JAPANESE TRADE UNIONS (*Sōhyō*), after the leadership of the latter had shifted policies towards the extreme left. Its most important constituent industrial unions were the Japan Federation of Textile Industry Workers' Unions (*Zensen dōmei*) and the Japan Seamen's Union (*Nihon kaiin kumiai*). It represented unions in the private sector, professed economic unionism, concentrating on wages and conditions of workers (rather than political campaigns), and was happy to affiliate with the International Congress of Free Trade Unions. It maintained political connections with the right wing of the JAPAN SOCIALIST PARTY in the 1950s and, after its formation in 1960, with the DEMOCRATIC SOCIALIST PARTY. Its affiliated unions accounted for a membership that remained stable at around one and a half million.

In 1962 it merged with the ALL-JAPAN GENERAL FEDERATION OF LABOUR UNIONS (*Sōdōmei*) and other groups to form *Dōmei kaigi*, and in 1964 effected a complete merger with the formation of the Japan Confederation of Labour (*Dōmei*).

Further reading
Cole *et al*. (1966)
Levine (1958)
Masumi (1995)

amakudari (descent from heaven, parachuting) In many countries it is not unknown for former Government officials, after retirement, to find senior (and lucrative) positions with companies or other organisations in the private sector. This is referred to in the United States as 'parachuting'. Generally speaking, this practice is frowned upon because of its potential for corrupt relationships. For instance, if an official from a Government agency responsible for land planning policy is 'parachuted' onto the board of management of a construction company, the danger is that he would divulge confidential information of benefit to the company. For this reason, such movement of post-retirement officials is carefully regulated in most Western countries, with, at the very least, a prescribed period after the official's retirement in which he may not join an organisation in the private sector.

In Japan, the practice is known as *amakudari*, which literally, and ironically, translates as 'descending from heaven'. Obviously, the idea behind the term is that officials are members of a bureaucratic elite, who deign to float down into a private company. Although regulations relating to *amakudari* exist, they are lightly policed, and every year several hundred senior officials of the national government 'descend from heaven' in this way. Not surprisingly, it has been subjected to widespread criticism, especially from those wishing to reduce bureaucratic influence in decision-making.

It is controversial, however, how far *amakudari* results from 'pull' factors (firms wishing to gain privileged access to official information and expertise by employing former officials), and how far from 'push' factors (ministries wishing to find lucrative employment for their former officials to reward them for loyal service at low pay; Ramseyer and Rosenbluth analyse this in terms of 'postponed income'). There is evidence that some firms are reluctant to take on former officials because of the extra financial burden involved. Ulrike Schaede argues that a complex mixture of 'pull' and 'push' factors are involved, and that the phenomenon of *amakudari* ought to be seen in terms of communication mechanisms throughout the structure of decision-making.

A variant of *amakudari* is *yokosuberi* (side slip). Technically, this means that a Government official moves to a position in a Government corporation, or similar entity, thus remaining within the public sector. Unlike *amakudari* proper, the same person can move more than once between different Government instrumentalities. As the name implies, moving to another part of the public sector does not have the same vertical connotations as moving from the public to the private sector. In common parlance, however, what is technically *yokosuberi* is often referred to as *amakudari*.

Although the term *amakudari* is not used in the political context, an analogy may be drawn with Government officials who retire early from their ministries and stand for election, typically on the LIBERAL DEMOCRATIC PARTY (LDP) ticket. This always used to be regarded as a case of bureaucratic infiltration of the LDP, but some observers have more recently suggested that the resultant communication patterns may be two-way rather than unidirectional. This would reflect the gradual enhancement of political over bureaucratic power.

Moreover the changing function of *amakudari* in its strict sense appears to reflect the greatly strengthened position of the private sector by comparison with public BUREAUCRACY in recent years. What is interesting, however, is that the practice has not died out, despite the intense criticism to which it has been subjected. The lesson would seem to be that the maintenance of stable communication channels continues to be given high priority.

Further reading

Koh (1989)
Nakano (1998)
Ramseyer and Rosenbluth (1993)
Schaede (1995)
Stockwin (1999)

Asanuma Inejirō One of the most colourful of Socialist leaders, Asanuma, born in 1898, was briefly influenced by Communism in the early 1920s, was important in farmers' unions and various left-wing parties of the late 1920s and was elected to the Tokyo Municipal Assembly. In the 1930s he was a central figure in the Socialist Masses Party and the nationalist-inclined 'Japan Labour faction' (together with KAWAKAMI JŌTARŌ), being elected to Parliament in the 1936 and 1937 elections. He was an official of the Imperial Rule Assistance Association from 1940. After the war he was active in the JAPAN SOCIALIST PARTY (JSP), and, when that party split in 1951 over the peace settlement, he became Secretary-General of the Right Socialist Party, though his views were well to the left of the NISHIO group within that party. When the Socialists were reunited in October 1955, Asanuma became the JSP Secretary-General, a position he retained until

March 1960, when he became party chairman, beating his patron Kawakami for the position.

On 12 October 1960, while making a speech at a televised election debate between the three principal parties, he was fatally stabbed by a 17-year-old former member of an ultra-rightist mini-party and son of a Self-Defence Forces officer [see also extremist movements (right)]. What probably sealed his fate was the remark he made while on a JSP delegation to the PRC in March 1959 that 'American imperialism is the common enemy of the peoples of Japan and China'. Even though his original statement was apparently qualified in ways that were obscured in press reports, it reflected the leftward trend in the JSP during the late 1950s that split the party again in 1959–60. This episode was ironic in the sense that Asanuma was known less for his intellectual commitment than for his energetic warm-hearted populism – earning him his nickname of 'human steam engine' (*ningen kikansha*).

Further reading
Cole et al. (1966)
Stockwin (1968)
Totten (1966)

Ashida Hitoshi A native of Kyōto, born in 1887, Ashida entered the MINISTRY OF FOREIGN AFFAIRS after graduating from Tokyo Imperial University in 1912, but resigned in 1932 in protest against a foreign policy that had permitted the Manchurian Incident. In the same year he was elected to the House of Representatives for the *Seiyūkai*, and thenceforth criticised the militarisation of politics. In the 1930s he was President of the English-language *Japan Times*, where he expressed liberal views, and having earned a doctorate in Law in 1929, he also taught at Keio University. During the war he was politically marginalised.

After the defeat he was active in Liberal Party politics, and was Minister for Health and Welfare in the SHIDEHARA Cabinet of 1945–6. Most significantly, in 1946 he participated in the Lower House committee discussing the drafting of a new Constitution, and is credited with introducing two extra clauses whose implicit purpose was to modify the absolute ban on armed forces contained in the original draft (see CONSTITUTION OF 1946). Early in 1947 he defected from the Liberal Party and founded the Japan Democratic Party (*Nihon Minshutō*), taking his party into the KATAYAMA coalition Cabinet formed in May, where he served as Deputy Prime Minister and Foreign Minister. When that Cabinet collapsed in March 1948, he took over as Prime Minister in a Cabinet containing the same three parties as before. Operating at a time of hyper-inflation, the Ashida Cabinet had a rough passage, and faced dissent within its ranks from left-wing Socialists, two of whom had been appointed to ministerial positions. Also facing trouble from public-sector unions, the Cabinet, backed by General MacArthur, passed legislation curbing the union rights of public-sector workers. The Ashida Cabinet resigned in October 1948, mired in the SHŌWA DENKŌ SCANDAL [see also conservative parties, 1945–55].

Ashida continued to be active in politics, joined the Liberal Democratic Party when it was formed in 1955, and was made a party counsellor. He was the author of several books and had one of the sharpest minds in the politics of his time. He died in 1959.

Further reading
Masumi (1985)

Asukata Ichio Asukata Ichio was a radical member of the JAPAN SOCIALIST PARTY (JSP), who was active in the anti-Security Treaty struggle of 1960 (see SECURITY TREATY REVISION CRISIS), became Mayor of Yokohama in 1963 and was JSP Chairman between 1977 and 1983.

Born in 1910, Asukata first came to prominence in the late 1950s as a left-wing Socialist parliamentarian and leader of the struggle against revision of the Security Treaty. In the early months of 1960 he was one of several Socialists who relentlessly interrogated the KISHI Government in Parliament on the definitions of 'Far East', 'prior consultation' and 'collective security'. In 1963 he moved into local politics, being elected Mayor of Yokohama, thus founding the first of what came to be called 'progressive local authorities', with a mandate to improve quality of life in Japan's crowded and polluted cities. He pioneered policies that were later taken up by MINOBE RYŌKICHI in Tokyo and others elsewhere. His left-wing and anti-Security Treaty credentials perturbed both the Japanese Government and the US military, which feared disruption of troop movements and so on. Little of this, however, eventuated.

The final phase of his career began in 1977, when he was elected Chairman of the JSP after the party had been beset by left–right conflict. He accepted the chairmanship on his own terms, which were that the Chair should be elected by the entire party membership, that it should be able to over-ride policy deadlocks, and that external advisers should be brought into the party. In office, he worked hard to expand party membership to a total of 100,000. The target was not reached, but some expansion occurred. He also tried to forge co-operation with other opposition parties, and initiated a process towards revising the party's 1960s era platform so that the party might shed its old fashioned image and take on the features of a Western European social democratic party.

Asukata's chairmanship was widely regarded as disappointing (though national and international circumstances were hardly favourable to the left at that period), and in 1983 he handed over the reins to ISHIBASHI MASASHI.

He died in October 1990 at the age of 80.

Aum shinrikyō and the politics of mass poisoning, 1995 On 20 March 1995, quantities of the poison gas 'sarin' were released on several subway trains converging on Tokyo's central administrative district. Twelve people were killed and several thousands injured, many suffering permanent physical and psychological effects. Two days later, police in large numbers raided the headquarters at Kamikuishiki village on the slopes of Mount Fuji of an extreme millenarian sect called *Aum shinrikyō* (Aum Supreme Truth Religion). The police discovered equipment for the manufacture of sarin gas, and began an investigation that uncovered a series of murders and violent acts conducted over a number of years. This was not the first occasion of mass poisoning for which the sect bore responsibility. On 27 June 1994 *Aum* members had released sarin gas in the provincial city of Matsumoto, causing seven deaths and many injuries. Despite circumstantial evidence linking this crime to the sect, the police had not felt able – or been willing – to act. Indeed, the inadequacy of police procedures became a major subsequent political issue.

Aum shinrikyō developed in the 1980s out of a yoga meditation class organised by a visually impaired mystic called Asahara Shōkō (birth name, Matsumoto Chizuo). It developed in the late 1980s and early 1990s as one of a number of so-called 'new' new religions that gained adherents principally from young people disillusioned with the materialism of Japanese society and fearful of future calamity, such as nuclear war. Among these religions the *Aum* was much the most ascetic in its practices, requiring its members to undergo extreme tests of physical endurance in pursuit of enlightenment. Asahara, who had a charismatic appeal to his followers, derived many of his ideas from Tibetan Buddhism, but also from other religious traditions, such as those of Christianity and Hinduism. Members were expected to give all their assets to the sect, and sever contact with their families and friends. In 1988 one of his followers died accidentally when an endurance test was taken too far. This proved the beginning of a cycle of violence, in which *Aum* members killed other members suspected of apostasy, disloyalty, spying or other 'crimes'. They also committed a number of murders of outsiders believed to be opposed to them. These included the murders of a lawyer retained by the estranged families of sect members, as well as of his wife and baby son, later disposing of their bodies in different parts of Japan. Despite concrete evidence linking this act to the *Aum*, the police failed to bring charges.

Reader argues convincingly that the crimes of the *Aum shinrikyō* should not be understood without consideration of the belief system developed by Asahara. He moulded certain Buddhist teachings into an extreme form of elitism, preaching that only those practising the ascetic rituals of the sect had the chance to achieve enlightenment. Thus he and his followers had no need to observe the legal or moral forms of mainstream society. Killing was justified in terms of saving those killed from the hell into which they would otherwise have fallen. But the culture of violence and deceit that he inculcated grew rapidly in the 1990s, and seems to have been fuelled by growing paranoia on the part of the leader. This followed a failed attempt to enter politics, by fielding 25 candidates in the House of Representatives elections of February 1990. Asahara himself received 0.33 per cent of the vote in the fourth district of Tokyo.

The *Aum* affair raises at least three issues of political significance. The first is the conduct of the police, and their failure over several years to pin a series of murders and other crimes onto the sect. To some extent this may be explained by limits on what the police could do, imposed by the laws on freedom of religion. The *Aum* used the courts aggressively to uphold its rights under the law, and with some success. The second issue, therefore, is that of the Religious Corporate Body Law (*Shūkyō hōjin hō*), introduced into Parliament in October 1995, designed to make it easier to deal with sects engaging in illegal activities. This was vigorously opposed by the *Sōka gakkai* and its political backers, but eventually a compromise bill was passed.

The third issue is more general. Recruits to the *Aum shinrikyō* included numbers of highly educated young people, including those trained in the natural sciences. Their services were called on for the manufacture of sarin gas, and other destructive (though abortive) enterprises. It became a matter of widespread concern why these people should have abandoned the normal expectations of family, society and career for the dubious benefits of a violent millenarian sect. Religion in general was much discredited by the affair, but the message that Japanese youth suffered from serious alienation from the materialistic norms of society became the focus of a long-running debate.

see also religion and politics

Further reading
Kisala and Mullins (2001)
Metraux (1995)
Murakami (2000)
Reader (2000)

Australasia, relations with Australia and New Zealand, being British Commonwealth countries located between the Indian and Pacific oceans, used to be regarded as outposts of European civilisation rather than as part of Asia. Over the past half-century, however, their links with Asia (including Japan in particular) have become far closer, in an economic, but also in a cultural, sense. Since the 1970s whether Australia should be regarded as 'part of Asia' has been the subject of sporadic debate, but it would be premature to say that the question has been resolved. Moreover, Asian countries tend to be sceptical about Australian claims to be part of Asia, and one does not join a club unless admitted by existing members. Much the same may be said about New Zealand, except that New Zealand also has close links with several island states of the south Pacific, and to some slight extent this tends to divert its attention from Asia. The factor of distance, however, should not be underestimated. Sydney is further from Tokyo than Tokyo is from Moscow, and Wellington is about the same distance from Tokyo as Tokyo is from Oslo.

Relations between Australia and Japan began in a small way in the late nineteenth century, and, at the time of Australian federation in 1901, approximately 3,000 Japanese were resident in Australia. But the Immigration Restriction Act passed in 1902 enshrined in law what was called the 'White Australia Policy', making it virtually impossible for people of non-European descent to obtain residence in Australia. Numbers of Japanese resident in Australia consequently declined, and in 1945 most of those who remained were returned to Japan. The Australian delegate to the Paris Peace Conference in 1919–21, William Morris Hughes (Billy Hughes), fought hard and successfully against Japanese attempts to introduce a racial non-discrimination clause into the Versailles Treaty. This caused enormous resentment in Japan, and damaged relations between Japan and Australia.

Japan, by the mid-1930s, was Australia's second largest export market after Great Britain, but in 1936 a trade diversion episode, prompted by British pressure on Australia to curb imports of Japanese textiles, brought about reduction in trade. Between December

1941 and August 1945 Japan and Australia were pitted against each other in a cruel and merciless conflict that was a defining historical experience for both.

Australia played a not insignificant role in the Allied Occupation of Japan between 1945 and 1952. At that period, however, the Australian Government was attempting to put pressure on the Americans for a more punitive approach to Japan than General MacArthur was inclined to concede. This included unsuccessful pressure to place restrictions on future rearmament by Japan. Even though conservative governments in Canberra in the 1950s accepted the need for a working relationship with Japan, trade unions and ex-service organisations were slower to adjust. As late as 1957 the Japanese Prime Minister, KISHI NOBUSUKE, made an official visit to Australia and had to face protests organised by the Returned Servicemen's League (RSL).

The year 1957, however, was significant in a much more positive sense. The Agreement on Commerce, signed in that year, provided a framework for an expansion of Australia–Japan trade that, by the early 1970s, had turned Japan into Australia's largest market by far. To agricultural exports were added the products of a rapidly expanding mining industry that was increasingly geared to provide the needs of Japanese manufacturing industry in the period of rapid economic growth.

In 1972, the last vestiges of the 'White Australia' policy disappeared and immigration was placed in a controlled regime that did not discriminate according to ethnic origin, colour or nationality. This was followed in 1976 by a Basic Treaty of Friendship and Co-operation between Japan and Australia, which put relations between them on what amounted to a most-favoured nation basis.

During the 1980s and 1990s the relationship between the two countries matured and deepened, with linkages developing on a personal and organisational level covering many walks of life. In the Japanese boom period of the late 1980s, investment by Japanese companies in tourist facilities, particularly in Queensland, caused some local disquiet, and a grandiose scheme called the 'Multi-Function Polis' eventually proved abortive. But the downturn in the Japanese economy from the early 1990s meant that withdrawal of Japanese investment, rather than excessive investment, became a matter for concern.

From the 1980s Japan and Australia were involved together in a range of regional institutions designed to facilitate economic interaction in the region. These arrangements worked reasonably well until the late 1990s, when, as Drysdale points out, a preference for bilateral economic arrangements in the region began to prevail over multilateral agreements. In Drysdale's words:

> The foundation for regional cooperation with Japan rests on the strength of our bilateral relationship. But it is a relationship that has outgrown the framework that gave birth to it. A new framework is required to encompass interests in investment, services, the information economy, education and research, as well as trade in commodities and merchandise.
>
> (p. 1)

Behind the concern expressed in Drysdale's article is the danger of Australia becoming isolated in an economic world increasingly dominated by big players and regional blocs.

Relations between New Zealand and Japan have paralleled those between Japan and Australia, though on a much smaller scale. The 1958 Commerce Treaty followed on the heels of the Australia–Japan Agreement of 1957. Like Australia, New Zealand, with its exports of agricultural products to Japan, has maintained a positive trade balance with her northern neighbour. As in Australia, knowledge and understanding of Japan has become widespread, and Japanese studies are widely taught in the education system. There have been occasional disputes, including a spat over fishing in the 1970s. Even more than Australia, New Zealand has few protections against economic isolation, and is therefore inclined to be strongly favourable to multilateral economic arrangements rather than exclusive bilateral ones.

Further reading
Drysdale (2002)

Drysdale and Kitaoji (eds) (1981)
Jain (ed.) (1998)
Kersten, in Inoguchi and Jain (eds) (2000)
Rix (1986)
—— (1999)

Rosecrance (1962)
Shimazu (1998)
Sissons, in Stockwin (ed.) (1972)
——, in Hudson (ed.) (1980)

B

'Black Mist' (kuroi kiri) scandals (1966–7) In the mid-1960s the Japanese economy was in its 'miracle' phase, and the long prime ministership of SATŌ EISAKU was in full flow. After a shaky start the LIBERAL DEMOCRATIC PARTY (LDP), founded a decade earlier, had become the most powerful political machine in the land, linked with networks of support in every region. It worked closely with the national ministries and was strongly backed by the *zaikai* (Big Business). Part of its strength was its decentralised organisational structure, and the fact that its electoral candidates were able to tap into local social and economic networks, co-opting them indirectly into the party machine. Incumbency – the fact that the LDP was in power and likely to remain in power for a considerable period – was itself an advantage because it suggested to those inclined to support the party that candidates they voted for should be able to deliver on their promises.

Problems, however, were also inherent in this structure. LDP parliamentarians came to be regarded as milch cows potentially able to deliver benefits to those prepared to pay for them. Both the factional divisions at central level and the divisions between LDP candidates in multi-member districts at local level injected a competitive element into the business of distributing benefits. This was good for the party in the sense that it helped bring out the vote, but it was also a hostage to fortune in that the more extreme examples of benefit-peddling were liable to be aired in the press and cause scandals.

In 1966 the mass media began to give publicity to what came to be called the 'black mist' scandals. This was not one scandal, but several that the press chose to group together under the same label. To an extent, the 'black mist' was the product of a media campaign, because it is not entirely clear that the level of corrupt dealing at that particular time was much greater than it usually was. Nevertheless, since publicity is the extra element needed to create a scandal, the 'black mist' took on a political life of its own.

An amusing episode was when the Minister of Transport, Arafune Seijūrō, arranged for express trains to stop at a small town in his Saitama constituency. In addition, the Defence Agency Director, Kanbayashiyama Eikichi, was accused of the misuse of official aircraft, which he had allegedly used to take him and senior defence staff to a celebratory parade in his Kagoshima constituency. The Minister of Agriculture, Matsuno Raizō, became the target of criticism for taking a party to Las Vegas and Acapulco after attending an international meeting in Canada. More importantly, the Kyōwa Sugar Refining Co. was accused of large-scale bribery of politicians with a view to obtaining a loan from a Government bank. This affair was thoroughly investigated and was found to have involved very large sums of money transferred to the pockets of politicians.

Factional rivals within the Prime Minister's own party were not slow to use these scandals against him. In December 1966 he had to contest a party presidential election, and won 289 out of 459 votes, the remaining votes divided between four other candidates. He immediately reshuffled his Cabinet to remove scandal-ridden ministers, but was forced to a general election by an Opposition boycott of Parliament. The LDP won the election, held in January 1967, with a slightly reduced majority. In years of 'miraculous' economic growth, a rash of scandals involving bribery and abuse of authority was not enough to remove either a government or a PRIME MINISTER.

Further reading
Curtis (1971)
Masumi (1995)
Mitchell (1996)

bureaucracy (kanryōsei) The role of the Government bureaucracy in Japan since 1945 is one of the most important, and at the same time one of the most controversial, topics of debate. At one end of the spectrum are those who argue that it is essentially the bureaucracy that runs Japan – that Japan is a bureaucratic polity. At the other are some who believe that Government officials ultimately do the bidding of politicians, and that the power structure is directly driven, as it should be in a democracy, by the people's representatives.

To arrive at a balanced understanding of this issue, two things need to be taken into account. One is that substantial and significant changes have taken place over time. These include not only formal administrative reorganisations, but also *de facto* shifts in the relationships between government officials and politicians. The other is that influence does not necessarily flow only in one direction. In practice the exercise of influence within the political system is extremely complex, and multi-directional.

Japan's defeat in August 1945 and the reforms instituted during the Allied Occupation might have been expected to revolutionise the relationships between politicians and Government officials. So far as the Government bureaucracy is concerned, however, most commentators have focused on the continuities between bureaucratic behaviour and influence before and after the war. It is pointed out most insistently that, unlike in the occupation of Germany, the occupying forces in Japan had no choice but to use the existing bureaucratic structures and officials in order to implement the reforms they were promoting. Partly for this reason, the purge edict was used sparingly so far as Government servants were concerned, and the degree of administrative reorganisation required was limited.

On the other hand, two ministries that had been exceedingly powerful in the pre-war and wartime period were abolished completely. These were the Ministry of War and the Ministry of the Navy. Moreover, the Home Ministry, which had been responsible for the police, control of labour and local government, among other functions, was split up, and police administration, in particular, was decentralised. A NATIONAL PERSONNEL AUTHORITY (*Jinjiin*) was set up to rationalise and co-ordinate personnel matters across the bureaucracy as a whole.

It is true that a quasi-military bureaucracy was re-established from the 1950s, with the birth of the DEFENCE AGENCY in 1954, to oversee the newly formed Self-Defence Forces (*jieitai*). Also, a partial reformation of the former Home Ministry occurred in 1960, though it failed to regain many of its pre-war functions. Police administration was recentralised in the 1950s, with careful safeguards to avoid abuse of power. The National Personnel Authority was no match for the major ministries, but it was gradually able to demonstrate the value of its services. All this suggests that, as Yamaguchi Jirō has argued, Government officials after the war not only ceased to be the servants of the Emperor (and thus proponents of an overtly chauvinistic ethic), but also lost much of their functions of maintaining social order and managing the instruments of violence.

But in place of this, they took on the primary function of engineering rapid economic growth. Here continuity with the past was crucial, in the sense that they maintained techniques and habits of interaction with politicians and the private sector that made it feasible to develop an ambitious programme of national transformation. Certain conditions, however, needed to be met for this to be possible. Most important of these was the establishment of single-party dominance under the LIBERAL DEMOCRATIC PARTY (LDP) from 1955. Another was the regime of minimal

DEFENCE spending under the US security umbrella negotiated by YOSHIDA in the early 1950s. Yet another was an ability to step back from the highly charged arena of political conflict of the 1950s and concentrate on the development of policies conducive to rapid economic growth. When KISHI stepped down as Prime Minister in 1960 in favour of IKEDA, the promotion of economic growth took centre stage, but preparations had been going on without great publicity for several years. And finally, nearly throughout the period of the economic 'miracle' (that is, until the early 1970s), the path could be kept clear for economic growth. There was no need to worry too much about spending on SOCIAL WELFARE, quality of life or environmental protection (see ENVIRONMENTAL POLITICS), because LDP dominance ensured that those things did not come to the front of the political agenda. If the LDP needed to be reminded about the priorities, the 25 per cent or so of LDP parliamentarians who had had a previous career in the Government service would remind the party about them.

Not all of the Government bureaucracy was concentrating on facilitating economic growth all of the time. But key ministries, most notably the MINISTRY OF INTERNATIONAL TRADE AND INDUSTRY (MITI, *Tsūsanshō*), were able to do so with little obstruction. The role of such ministries was that of facilitation rather than direction, and, by comparison with several European states at the same period, Government officials directly ran very little indeed of the economy. They believed that the market should take precedence in business decisions, but they made sure that so far as possible obstacles (such as excessive taxation etc.) should be removed. MITI, however, did intervene with selective allocations of foreign exchange, pressure to engage in strategic investment, and so on.

In retrospect, the 1960s were an exceptional, and from the perspective of Government officials, remarkably successful, period. With much slower growth in the (post-oil shock) 1970s, and the LDP fighting for its life against a resurgent opposition, Government ministries found themselves in a more complex and difficult environment. Slower growth and more insistent political demands meant that it was more difficult to find the funds to mobilise for strategic ends. The decade saw the rise of 'tribal parliamentarians' (*zoku giin*) (see 'TRIBES' OF PARLIAMENTARIANS), specialising in particular policy areas and demanding a say in policy-making. In one sense it is true that the interpenetration of the bureaucracy by such politicians should have led to a loss of bureaucratic power, but in fact the resultant mixture was, rather, characterised by symbiosis. Government officials and politicians with a common area of policy would find common cause, in working for budgetary allocations or other favourable treatment, against other similarly constituted nests of interests.

For the political system as a whole, the period from about 1990 posed complex challenges. Times became particularly difficult for government ministries as the movement for reform of the political system gathered force. Versions of the 'Nightwatchman State' came into vogue, fuelled by the ending of the Cold War and enhanced US dominance, a world economy whose procedures were tending towards standardisation, and a feeling that Japan as a whole was much too heavily regulated. The Government ministries fought a rearguard action to preserve as much as possible of their prerogatives, but their cause was not helped by both political instability inherent in coalition government, and the revelation of corruption scandals in which officials, not merely politicians and businessmen, were implicated.

Although deregulation did not make much progress in the early and middle 1990s, by the late 1990s plans were in place to reduce the number of ministries and agencies of Government and rationalise their activities. The ADMINISTRATIVE REORGANISATION of January 2001 was the most radical attack on long-established bureaucratic structures that had taken place since the late 1940s. Even though sceptics spoke of merely changing labels on doors, the shake up was in fact considerable in its impact. A related set of reforms being put in place after the millennium were designed to increase the effective power of the PRIME MINISTER and CABINET. Upon the success or otherwise of these reforms depended the possibility that strong central leadership might be able to assert itself against close congeries of bureaucratic, political and private-sector interests.

Meanwhile, it should not be assumed that Government officials were uniformly opposed to reform. While the instinct to preserve established areas of jurisdiction was intense, officials were sophisticated enough to understand that the politico-economic situation was changing and was sure to change further. For them to contribute effectively to the national, or even to sectional, interests, it was necessary for the bureaucracy also to change, and form new kinds of relationship with other parts of the system. In the past, the Japanese government bureaucracy had proved itself adaptable, resourceful and far-sighted. It seemed not impossible that these qualities would also be manifested over the first decade of the twenty-first century.

Further reading
Calder (1988)
—— (1993)
Hollerman (1988)
Johnson (1982)
Koh (1989)
Ramseyer and Rosenbluth (1993)
Richardson (1997)
Samuels (1987)
Tatebayashi, in Otake (ed.) (2000)
Toyonaga, in Otake (ed.) (2000)
Tsuji (1984)
Wade (1990)

business interest groups Until the amalgamation of the FEDERATION OF ECONOMIC ORGANISATIONS (*Keidanren*) and the JAPAN FEDERATION OF EMPLOYERS' ASSOCIATIONS (*Nikkeiren*) in May 2002, business was represented at national level by four separate organisations, of which all but the JAPAN CHAMBER OF COMMERCE (*Nisshō*) (having pre-war origins) were founded in the years immediately following Japan's defeat in 1945. According to a common formulation, *Keidanren* was the 'political division' of the business world, *Nikkeiren* was the 'labour affairs division', the JAPAN COMMITTEE FOR ECONOMIC DEVELOPMENT (*Keizai dōyūkai*) was the 'company research division' and *Nisshō* was the 'small and medium enterprise division'.

In the earlier post-war years, it was widely felt in business circles that these representative organisations were functionally different but worked well enough together as a whole. But with the gradual diversification of the economy, especially from the 1960s, internal co-ordination of interests and external effectiveness became gradually more problematic. In particular, structural differences between older manufacturing industries (such as steel, shipbuilding, chemicals) and newer high-technology industries (such as software manufacture) were great, and differences of view between them were wide. Thus the salience of representative groups based on individual industries (as well as regional groups) increased, and the ability of *Keidanren* and the others to make different industries pull together in their lobbying activities declined. A more sophisticated and pluralistic business world had emerged, and business groups needed to reflect the realities of that new world. In a sense the 2002 amalgamation paralleled the rationalisations that took place in January 2001 in the Government bureaucracy. In both cases the attempt was made to breathe new life into bureaucratic entities established many years before, which were suffering from a degree of sclerosis.

Further reading
Babb (2001)

C

Cabinet (Naikaku) Although a Cabinet had existed as part of the Japanese governmental structure since the Meiji period, the system of Government before 1945 could not have been termed 'Cabinet Government'. The authority of Cabinet was circumscribed by various other groups (elites around the Emperor, the military forces, etc.), and the principle of collective Cabinet responsibility was replaced by the principle of individual responsibility of ministers of state to the Emperor.

Nevertheless, however weak it may have been, Cabinet was at the centre of the governmental structure. The Occupation authorities under General MacArthur recognised the potential for stability and accountability in a system of Cabinet Government in the orthodox sense of the term. Thus the CONSTITUTION OF 1946, in its article 65, states unambiguously: 'Executive power shall be vested in the Cabinet'. Article 66 defines the Cabinet as consisting of the PRIME MINISTER, as its head, 'and other Ministers of State, as provided for by law'. In order to avoid the kind of military dominance of cabinets that occurred in the 1930s, the same article provides that: 'the Prime Minister and other Ministers of State must be civilians'. The third clause of the same article embeds the principle of collective responsibility: 'The Cabinet, in the exercise of its power, shall be collectively responsible to the Diet [Parliament]'. Article 68 gives to the Prime Minister the power to appoint and remove ministers, a majority of whom 'must be chosen from among the members of the Diet'. In practice, with few exceptions, Cabinet ministers have been parliamentarians. Article 73 provides a list of the duties of Cabinet. These include administering the law, conducting affairs of state, managing foreign affairs, concluding treaties, administering the civil service, preparing the budget, enacting Cabinet orders, deciding on amnesties, etc. According to article 75, ministers cannot be subject to legal action without the consent of the Prime Minister during their tenure of office. (Thus, using this article, YOSHIDA saved SATŌ EISAKU from arrest in 1954, but MIKI failed to protect TANAKA KAKUEI from arrest in 1976.)

Under the 1946 Constitution, the role of Cabinet nevertheless developed in a rather different direction from what was initially envisaged. In a British-type system of Cabinet Government, Cabinet will normally dominate the policy agenda so long as the party in power maintains a parliamentary majority and its own unity. The biggest threat it faces is the prospect of defeat at the next general elections. In Japan, by contrast, once the LIBERAL DEMOCRATIC PARTY had established itself as the dominant party by the 1960s, even though the threat of electoral defeat had receded, the ability of Cabinet to determine policy was much lower than in the British case.

There were several inter-related reasons for this. First of all, the pre-war traditions of bureaucratic supremacy over politicians carried through into the post-war period, in part because the Occupation chose to work through the existing bureaucracy in order to implement its programmes, and failed to reform it to any great extent. Second, although the number of ministers was similar to the number in a British Cabinet, there were (until reforms of the early 2000s) no deputy ministers or junior ministers, who lend weight to political control of the executive in the British system. There was, it is true, a Political Vice-Minister (*Seimu jikan*) shadowing each minister, but these were essentially apprenticeship positions.

Third, with the 1960s consolidation of factional rivalries in the LIBERAL DEMOCRATIC PARTY (LDP), Cabinet positions became factional quarry. Rather like the multi-party system of France in the Fourth Republic (1946–58), Cabinets had to be frequently reshuffled in order to satisfy the demands of the various factions for Cabinet office (*see* FACTIONS WITHIN POLITICAL PARTIES). An LDP President (Prime Minister so long as the party maintained a majority in Parliament) was dependent on an alliance of factions in order to stay in power. No single faction ever had enough members to dominate completely, so alliances were the order of the day. But factional alliances were alliances of convenience. If a faction saw advantage in shifting its allegiance to another presidential candidate, it was liable to do so. To forestall this, or alternatively to induce other factions to join his alliance, the Prime Minister needed to reshuffle his Cabinet rather frequently in order to satisfy insistent factional demands for Cabinet office.

For instance, the second SATŌ Cabinet was formed on 17 February 1967 soon after general elections, and it lasted until January 1970. But over that period it was reshuffled twice, in November 1967 and November 1968. The only 'holdovers' were the ministers in charge of the important Ministries of Foreign Affairs and Finance, who were retained in the first (but not the second) of the two reshuffles. The second NAKASONE Cabinet lasted from December 1983 to July 1986. During that period there were two reshuffles, in November 1984 and December 1985. Ministers in every significant ministry were reshuffled both times, except that the powerful politicians ABE SHINTARŌ (Foreign Affairs) and TAKESHITA NOBORU (Finance) remained for the whole time. Also, at the Defence Agency KATŌ KŌICHI remained Director from November 1984 until July 1986. Thus the pattern of more or less annual reshuffles of the whole Cabinet, except for ministers in a tiny number of key ministries, became the norm. In the 1960s and 1970s the alliance headed by the Prime Minister was known as the 'mainstream' (*shuryūha*) and the opposing alliance was the 'anti-mainstream' (*hanshuryūha*). Sometimes also a neutral 'non-mainstream' (*hishuryūha*) would make its appearance.

By the 1980s (and indeed earlier) a *de facto* seniority system had been established for Cabinet appointments, with calculations of seniority being made on the basis of the number of times a member had been elected to Parliament. Nearly all LDP parliamentarians had been given a Cabinet position by the time they had been elected six times to Parliament (meaning mainly the House of Representatives). But only the high flyers (or politically powerful) would achieve subsequent Cabinet positions. Interestingly, though, this outcome was achieved through an institutionalised system of bargaining between the various faction leaders and the current Prime Minister. This bore a remarkable resemblance to patterns of promotion in the public service and in large conglomerate firms.

Although the exception noted above about more lengthy tenure of key ministries is significant, the effect of this system was to make Cabinet positions more of a reward for service than appointments made on criteria of merit. This, together with the endemic shortness of tenure, made it unlikely that a minister would be able to put his (occasionally her) stamp on the way the ministry was run, or indeed on policy. So far as Cabinet policy as a whole was concerned, there were opportunities for initiative on chosen issues, but the system was far removed from a British-style Cabinet-dominance one.

The advent of coalition Cabinets from 1993 had the effect of shaking up the Cabinet appointment system out of its earlier rigidity. With different parties represented in Cabinet, more effort had to be expended on adjusting policy positions to create unified Government policy. To an extent also, the role of LDP factions declined during the 1990s, although they retain considerable power. When the

KOIZUMI Cabinet was formed in April 2001, he was able to ignore the demands of the powerful HASHIMOTO faction to be represented in Cabinet. But the decline in his popularity made a strategy of forming Cabinets without sufficient regard for factional interests less viable than it was soon after he became Prime Minister.

Fourth, as Aurelia George Mulgan has demonstrated, Cabinet government was also much diluted by the political power of LDP committees grouped in the Policy Affairs Research Council (PARC). A Prime Minister and Cabinet could not guarantee that their policy proposals would be approved by PARC committees, even though they had the numbers in Parliament. This reflected the proliferation of individual power centres within the ruling party, which could exercise effective veto power and make Cabinet Government difficult to sustain.

Reforms from the late 1990s seek to increase the effectiveness of Cabinet. In January 2001 a CABINET OFFICE (*Naikakufu*) was created, combining the PRIME MINISTER'S OFFICE (*Sōrifu*), the ECONOMIC PLANNING AGENCY (*Keizai kikakuchō*) and the OKINAWA DEVELOPMENT AGENCY (*Okinawa kaihatsuchō*) with the DEFENCE AGENCY (*Bōeichō*) and the NATIONAL PUBLIC SAFETY COMMITTEE (*Kokka kōan iinkai*) – in charge of the police – within its ambit. The creation of deputy ministers (*fukudaijin*) had much the same purpose. But it remains to be seen whether Cabinet meetings – described as normally perfunctory by some participants – will take on a more substantive decision-making character.

On the future of Cabinet as a central institution of Government rest many of the hopes of political reformers. Its strengthening seems essential if a healthy political future is to be assured.

Further reading
Curtis (1999)
George Mulgan (2002)
Nonaka, in Otake (ed.) (2000)
Stockwin, in Stockwin *et al.* (1988)
—— (1999)

Cabinet Legislation Bureau (Naikaku hōseikyoku) This bureau has enjoyed a continuous existence since 1885. Its status is now enshrined in a law of August 1952. It reports directly to CABINET, and its main tasks are to scrutinise legislative proposals coming from various ministries, to draft bills itself if required, to help in drafting the 'unified opinions' of Cabinet, and so on. Sometimes, it is criticised for being too close to the LIBERAL DEMOCRATIC PARTY, but that seems rather inevitable given its long tenure of office. It is sometimes pointed out that Cabinet is better served in terms of legislative assistance than is Parliament.

Cabinet Office (Naikakufu) The Cabinet Office was created in the ADMINISTRATIVE REORGANISATION of January 2001. The purpose of its creation was, in part at least, to strengthen the power of the PRIME MINISTER and CABINET, by bringing together into a single organ of government the PRIME MINISTER'S OFFICE (*Sōrifu*), the ECONOMIC PLANNING AGENCY (*Keizai kikakuchō*) and the OKINAWA DEVELOPMENT AGENCY (*Okinawa kaihatsuchō*). In addition, the DEFENCE AGENCY (*Bōeichō*) and the NATIONAL PUBLIC SAFETY COMMITTEE (*Kokka kōan iinkai*) were placed within the ambit of the Cabinet Office. It should be noted that some other agencies that used to answer to the Prime Minister's Office had gone elsewhere. The ENVIRONMENT AGENCY, for instance, had become a full ministry, the SCIENCE AND TECHNOLOGY AGENCY had joined the MINISTRY OF EDUCATION to become the MINISTRY OF EDUCATION, CULTURE, SPORTS, SCIENCE AND TECHNOLOGY, and so on. So the fact that the organs responsible for economic planning, Okinawa (*see* OKINAWA IN JAPANESE POLITICS), DEFENCE and the police should have made answerable to the Cabinet Office was an indication of the priority being attached to them.

This was part of the more general exercise of escaping from the situation known as 'vertical administration' (*tatewari gyōsei*), whereby individual ministries jealously guarded their respective jurisdictions without regard to overlap of function or the need for co-ordination. In the case of creating the Cabinet Office, the assault on vertical administration went along with the intention of strengthening central decision-making – by Prime Minister and Cabinet.

Cabinet Secretariat (Naikaku kanbō) The Cabinet Secretariat was established in 1947 as a body to service the needs of CABINET for research, information, liaison with various ministries and so on. In practice, however, it has concentrated on assisting the PRIME MINISTER. The Chief Cabinet Secretary (*Naikaku kanbō chōkan*) is normally one of the most senior and powerful members of Cabinet, and is a person on whom the Prime Minister relies very heavily for advice on policy, for troubleshooting in relation to the Cabinet and its members, and for representative functions.

Often, but not necessarily, the Chief Cabinet Secretary comes from the same LIBERAL DEMOCRATIC PARTY faction as the Prime Minister. For instance, throughout the period of the TAKESHITA Cabinet between November 1987 and June 1989, the Chief Cabinet Secretary was Takeshita's close factional lieutenant, OBUCHI KEIZŌ, later himself Prime Minister.

China (PRC and ROC), relations with For many years after the end of the Second World War, relations between Japan and China were greatly underdeveloped and punctuated with acrimony. This represented a massive shift in the focus of Japanese foreign and foreign economic policy by comparison with the directions it had taken up to 1945. The common wisdom in the 1930s was that Japan could not survive economically without a large-scale economic relationship with China, and that pre-eminent political influence in China was essential for Japanese national security. Between 1931 and 1945, Japan directly controlled a large area of northern China after establishing the puppet state of Manchukuo, and from 1937 Japanese armed forces wrested control of much of the rest of China. On the other hand, Japanese military operations in China between 1937 and 1945 are sometimes compared with the US experience in Vietnam three decades later. Post-war political leaders such as YOSHIDA SHIGERU regarded Japanese military experience in China as a quagmire, and his policies were not a little influenced by a determination to prevent another similar nightmare from recurring.

When Japan emerged from the Allied Occupation and regained independence in 1952, the Chinese Communist Party (CCP) was firmly in control of the Chinese mainland, having come to power by revolutionary war in October 1949. YOSHIDA, as Prime Minister in 1952, had to bow to US pressure to sign a peace treaty (separate from the San Francisco Peace Treaty), with the Chiang Kai Shek regime that had taken refuge on the island of Taiwan. There is evidence that Yoshida believed the leaders of the People's Republic of China (PRC) were likely to prove Chinese first and Communists only second. In the early period of the Cold War, however, Japan had little leverage over the United States. Since both the PRC and the Republic of China (ROC, Taiwan) both claimed to represent the whole of China, Japan's recognition of one eliminated the possibility of recognising the other.

Nevertheless, the huge scale of pre-war trade with China, particularly from the Kansai region of western Japan, meant that the Government experienced pressure from business interests to improve relations with the PRC. This was compounded by political and ideological pressure, particularly but not exclusively from the left, for a more sympathetic approach to the Beijing regime. The HATOYAMA Government that replaced that of Yoshida in December 1954 normalised diplomatic relations with the USSR, and was sympathetic to better relations with China [*see also* Soviet Union and Russia, relations with]. During the 1950s a number of small-scale unofficial (that is, lacking official sanction) trade agreements were signed between Tokyo and Beijing. But Kishi Nobusuke, Prime Minister between 1957 and 1960, had close links with Taiwan and was ideologically hostile to the PRC. A sense that the Japanese side now looked unfavourably on Beijing led to an incident in 1958 at a trade fair in Nagasaki, and to a suspension of the then current trade agreement.

The replacement of Kishi by Ikeda in July 1960 improved the atmosphere of Japan–PRC relations, and in 1962 the 'L–T' trade agreement was signed, from the initial letters of Liao and Takasaki, the chief negotiators on the Chinese and Japanese sides. Once again, the agreement did not have the formal backing of the Japanese Government, but Ikeda was sufficiently favourable that it could be called a 'semi-official' agreement. Ikeda was attempting to 'separate politics and economics' (*seikei bunri*), something necessary given that the Liberal Democratic Party (LDP) was badly divided on the China question, and that in the 1960s the United States would have strongly objected to formal Government backing for a trading relationship. He tested the waters once or twice on this. Ikeda's problem, however, was that the PRC leaders were using the carrot of trade as a means of squeezing Japan into a more and more political relationship with them, with the ultimate goal of diplomatic recognition. The half-hidden threat was that failure to conform might result in another suspension of trade. Apart from L–T trade, an extra portion of trade was dubbed 'friendly firm' trade, conducted between Chinese trading organisations and Japanese firms that the PRC considered 'friendly', often because the enterprise union was pro-PRC.

Satō Eisaku, who replaced Ikeda as Prime Minister in November 1964, was less favourably disposed towards China than his predecessor had been, though not as hostile as was his brother, Kishi. Satō was also determined to secure the return of Okinawa to Japan (see Okinawa in Japanese politics), and in pursuit of that goal he had to engage in intensive diplomacy with the United States (see United States, relations with), to convince the US authorities that Japan was serious about playing a part in the security of East Asia. Moreover, from 1966, the PRC entered into its phase of the Great Proletarian Cultural Revolution, and the United States was already engaged in the Vietnam War, so that international tensions were heightened throughout East Asia. From 1970, the PRC placed onerous extra conditions on the continuation of trade, and increased its pressure on Japan to normalise relations, relinquishing its ties with Taiwan.

Satō steadfastly resisted these pressures, and backed up the US position at the United Nations, designed to retain the China seat for Taipei and keep Beijing out of the world body. President Nixon, however, for his own reasons, deftly extracted the mat from under Satō's feet in July 1971 by announcing, with no prior consultation with the Japanese Government, that he planned to visit Beijing. This proved to be a fatal political blow to Satō, who was forced out of office a year later.

By this time, policy towards the two Chinas had become an extremely divisive issue within and between political parties. Most of the Opposition parties were in favour of recognising the PRC (though not the Japan Communist Party, since 1966 designated by Beijing as one of its 'four enemies' in Japan). The LDP, much influenced by business pressure groups having divergent interests, was divided between the majority 'Asia Group' favouring retention of ties with the ROC, and an 'Asia–Africa Group', inclined towards improving relations with the PRC. When Tanaka Kakuei became Prime Minister in succession to Satō in July 1972, he moved with lightning speed to recognise the PRC as 'China', thus breaking formal links with the ROC. This was achieved with his visit to Beijing in September of the same year. Relations with Taiwan did not, however, disappear. Economic relations continued much as usual, and a 'liaison office', or quasi-Embassy, was established in Taipei, staffed by Japanese diplomats on 'secondment'. The settlement, was, however, followed by an acrimonious airlines dispute between Tokyo and Taipei.

In contrast with this rapid action, it was not until August 1978 that a Treaty of Peace and Friendship was signed between Tokyo and Beijing. The delay was principally caused by the Chinese demand for an 'anti-hegemony' clause to be inserted in the treaty. 'Hegemony' (*baqun* in Chinese, *haken* in Japanese) was a Chinese code word for Soviet imperialism. The Japanese would not accept this, but eventually a compromise was reached whereby an anti-hegemony clause was included, but another clause stated that it was not meant to apply to any particular state. Not surprisingly, the Russians objected, even with the let-out clause added to the text of the treaty. Earlier in the same year a Japan–China long-term trade agreement was concluded, on business initiative in the Japanese case.

The year 1979 marked the beginning of the progressive opening of the Chinese economy, pioneered by Chairman Deng Xiaoping. This indicated the start of a new era in Japan–China trade and led eventually also to massive Japanese investment in China. Over the next two decades, the economic relationship developed in far greater depth than before. Various issues threatened the smooth management of the relationship from time to time. Chinese official objections to Japanese school textbook descriptions of aspects of the Asia–Pacific war caused problems in the early 1980s, as did Nakasone's official visit to the Yasukuni Shrine in 1985. Much the most difficult period was the aftermath of the Tiananmen Square episode in June 1989, following which Japan felt obliged to apply various internationally approved sanctions. The underlying Japanese policy, however, was one of engagement with China following a mild rapping of its knuckles.

Since the ending of the Cold War at the beginning of the 1990s, the Sino-Japanese relationship has entered a phase of some instability. It is described by Hughes (and others) as essentially triangular, with the other point of the triangle being the United States. Hughes considers that there is a danger of 'Japan-passing', whereby the PRC and the United States enter into deals that bypass Japan (in Hook et al., 2001, pp. 170–2). Some substance is given to this concern by the long failure of the Japanese economy to revive its former dynamism, the rapid increase in Japanese imports from an increasingly competitive Chinese economy, and a new US tendency to see China, rather than Japan, as the wave of the future.

Meanwhile, concern is evident within Japan about the long-term implications of the modernisation of Chinese armed forces. A dormant, but occasionally active, territorial issue left over from the Cold War is that of the uninhabited Senkaku islands (*Tiaoyutai* in Chinese), located between Okinawa and Taiwan, currently occupied by Japan, but claimed by China. Much more dangerous would be a confrontation over the status of Taiwan between the authorities in Beijing and Taipei. This came to the boil briefly but disturbingly in the mid-1990s, when the United States became involved. If this issue ever developed into an actual military conflict, it is difficult to see how not only the Americans, but also the Japanese, could avoid having to intervene. Should that ever happen (and we should not overstate the likelihood), it would greatly change the shape of international relations in East Asia.

Finally, relations between Japan, the PRC, the ROC, the two Koreas (*see* Korea (ROK and DPRK), relations with) and the United States lack a multilateral framework of sufficient effectiveness to maintain stability. This contrasts greatly with the situation in Europe, where powerful multilateral organisations exist at the political, economic and strategic level. Bilateral thinking is a problem more generally in Asia in the new century, as Drysdale has pointed out. But the rapidly changing economic and strategic environment affecting relations between Japan, China and the United States make thinking about a multilateral framework particularly urgent.

Further reading
Drifte (1998)
—— (2003)
Drysdale (2002)
Hook *et al.* (2001)
Rose (1998)
Vogel, Steven K. (2002)
Welfield (1988)

Clean Government Party (CGP, Kōmeitō)
This is the only significant party founded by a religious group since 1945 [*see also* religion and politics]. After the war the *Sōka gakkai*, an offshoot of *Nichiren* Buddhism, soon became the most successful post-war 'new religion', attracting several million members. Dissatisfaction with corrupt politics led to candidates standing in local elections from 1955. Three of its candidates were elected to the House of Councillors in 1956, six in 1959 and 15 in 1962. Although these candidates campaigned under 'association'-type labels, it was not until 1964 that the Clean Government Party (CGP, *Kōmeitō*) was born. The CGP astonished the political world by electing all its 25 candidates to the House of Representatives at the general elections of 1967, and 47 of its 76 candidates in 1969. After that it consolidated but did not much increase its support, and its best result was 58 seats in 1983.

In its early years the CGP was manifestly a religious party, with officials holding positions in both the parent religion and the party. In

1969–70, however, *Sōka gakkai* was accused of trying to suppress a book, by the political commentator Fujiwara Hirotatsu, which savagely criticised it. This led to formal separation of the two organisations, with officials forbidden from holding office in both. In practice, however, links between them remained close, and the great bulk of their electors were members of the religion. This is demonstrated by the fact that in the 1970s *Sōka gakkai* electors for the Upper House national constituency were instructed to vote for particular candidates according to region, so as to optimise the effect of the total vote. The policy was spectacularly successful, showing that the party knew accurately who its voters were, and that they would agree to vote for the right candidates.

For most of its existence the CGP has been a centrist party, seeking alignment with left-of-centre parties in the 1970s, but tending rather towards the right in the 1980s and 1990s. Early fears that it might turn towards the extreme right have not been fulfilled. At its foundation in 1964 the party spoke of 'humanistic Socialism', 'Buddhist democracy' and 'global nationalism', though later 'middle-of-the-road politics' became a principal slogan, and 'peace' a constant theme. The CGP leaders gradually became more independent. In 1975 they clashed with Ikeda Daisaku, leader of the *Sōka gakkai*, repudiating his attempt at reconciliation with the Japan Communist Party, and in 1984 the CGP Chairman, Takeiri Yoshikatsu, took part in an abortive plot to split the Liberal Democratic Party (LDP) and form a centrist coalition government under Nikaidō Susumu.

The 1990s provided new opportunities for the CGP. With the LDP lacking an Upper House majority, the CGP found itself in a strategic bargaining position, and courted by the LDP Secretary-General, Ozawa Ichirō, at the time of the Gulf crisis of 1990–1. The party joined the Hosokawa and Hata coalition governments of 1993–4 (without the LDP), and in December 1994 it merged into the newly formed New Frontier Party (NFP, *Shinshintō*). The arrangement, however, was peculiar, in that neither CGP local branches nor Upper House members joined the NFP, and even in the Lower House the former CGP members maintained a sense of separate identity. But they brought formidable organisational strength to the new party, and in this sense they were indispensable to it. When the NFP flew apart in December 1997, nearly all former CGP Lower House members formed the New Party Peace (*Shintō heiwa*), in January 1998. This party merged in November with the Upper House group known as *Kōmei*, to form a reconstituted CGP. The previous month the about-to-be-formed party entered a coalition Government under Obuchi Keizō, with the LDP and Liberal Party (III).

The CGP remains essentially centrist, and a moderating influence on LDP right wingers over certain issues. But over the years it has itself become more conservative, no doubt reflecting the fact that its own supporters, originally concentrated among declining industries, small firms and less educated electors, have gradually become more prosperous and better educated, developing middle-class aspirations. The religious orientation of the early years has been tempered by secular concerns, but the party's tight, disciplined organisation remains.

Further reading
Johnson (2000)
White (1970)

Congress of Industrial Unions (Zenkoku Sangyōbetsu Kumiai Kaigi, Sanbetsu Kaigi)
This labour union federation was established in June 1946 under JAPAN COMMUNIST PARTY influence, soon after the Occupation had lifted restrictions on union organisation. Like most union federations, its constituent parts were single industry unions (*tansan*), and unions in the public sector. At the outset it accounted for over one and a half million workers. In the inflationary and chaotic conditions of the early Occupation, the federation campaigned against dismissals of labour and in favour of a minimum wage. It also took the lead in organising the general strike planned for 1 February 1947, but, when this was banned by General MacArthur, the federation began to fall apart. In particular, it was accused of being manipulated by the Japan Communist Party, and the Democratisation Leagues (*Minshuka Dōmei*, or

Mindō) challenged its leadership. These Leagues gained control of many major constituent unions of *Sanbetsu Kaigi* in the years to 1950. Separately, a group under Hosoya Matsuta defected in 1949 and formed *shinsanbetsu* (New *Sanbetsu*).

Once Occupation policy became less favourable towards unions and more concerned with industrial recovery, *Sanbetsu Kaigi* rapidly lost members and influence. *Sanbetsu Kaigi* was hurt by rationalisation policies under the Dodge Line from 1949, and by the red purge from 1950. It was estimated that by 1951 its membership had dropped to 40,000, and in 1958 it was dissolved into a constituent part of the *Sōhyō* federation.

The rapid rise and fall of *Sanbetsu Kaigi* reflects a momentous struggle for control of the union movement between the Communists and other forces (mainly JSP-connected) in the years after the war, when many workers were in desperate economic straits. Had the Communists been less crude in their methods, the outcome might have been different.

Further reading
Cole et al. (1966)
Levine (1958)

consensus and conflict See Theories of Japanese politics essay, section on 'Cultural uniqueness and its critics, consensus versus conflict'.

conservative parties, 1945–55 Conservative party politics in the decade following Japan's 1945 defeat was unstable and fluid, with many splits and mergers, as well as personal rivalries for power and differences of policy prescription. It was a period of momentous change, in which conservatives had to decide how far they wanted to be part of the democratic revolution initiated by the Occupation and how far to rekindle nostalgia for the past, for nationalism and for indigenous practices. Two major figures, YOSHIDA SHIGERU and HATOYAMA ICHIRŌ, strode the political stage as rivals, while a host of lesser men jockeyed for political opportunities. Conservatives had a difficult time until the general elections of January 1949, when Yoshida's Liberals gained a clear majority in the House of Representatives. This was followed by the Yoshida ascendancy, but once the Occupation was over (in April 1952), Yoshida's power declined, and Hatoyama's star began to rise. It was to combat the threat of a newly reunited JAPAN SOCIALIST PARTY that conservatives merged into a single party in November 1955. This must be regarded as an extraordinary achievement considering the fractious nature of the movement over the previous decade.

In November 1945 two major conservative parties emerged, both with pre-war roots. One was the Japan Liberal Party (I) (JLP, *Nihon Jiyūtō*) and the other was the Japan Progressive Party (JPP, *Nihon Shinpotō*). The JLP largely consisted of former members of the Kuhara faction of the pre-war *Seiyūkai*, and its leader was Hatoyama. At its foundation it had 46 members of the House of Representatives, but this increased to 141 at the first post-war Lower House elections, in April 1946. The Americans, however, purged Hatoyama, Yoshida took over the party leadership from him and became PRIME MINISTER in a conservative coalition with the JPP. At its foundation the JPP held 273 seats in the House of Representatives, many of them originating in the pre-war *Minseitō*, and some from the Nakajima faction of the *Seiyūkai*. The purge, however, eliminated 238 of them, though the party won 94 seats in the April 1946 elections, and participated in the Yoshida Government.

Another, very moderate, conservative party formed in December 1945 was the Japan Co-operative Party (*Nihon Kyōdōtō*), dedicated to the principle of labour–management co-operation and co-operatives more generally. It became the Co-operative Democratic Party (*Kyōdō Minshutō*) in May 1946 and the National Co-operative Party (*Kokumin Kyōdōtō*), through merger with the small National Party (*Kokumintō*) in March 1947. In the same month, however, several of its members defected to the newly formed Democratic Party (I) (*Minshutō*), and its numbers were declining. Even so, the National Co-operative Party, under MIKI TAKEO, was one of three parties participating in the KATAYAMA and ASHIDA coalition Cabinets between May 1947 and October 1948.

The Japan Progressive Party between the middle of 1946 and early 1947 was torn between conservatives, led by SHIDEHARA

KIJŪRŌ, who wanted to merge with the Liberals, and younger leaders, who wanted to join with parties of the political centre. A defection from the Liberals, led by Ashida Hitoshi (Prime Minister, 1948) and one from the National Co-operative Party, mentioned above, led the JPP to change its name and form the Democratic Party in March 1947. In the first elections held under the new Constitution, in April, the Democratic Party won 126 seats in the Lower House, and it entered into the Katayama coalition Government with the Japan Socialist Party and the National Co-operative Party in May. This, however, caused strains within the party because Shidehara and others wanted to include the Japan Liberal Party in what would have been a four-party coalition, instead of the three-party coalition that emerged. The coal mine nationalisation issue brought about the defection of the Shidehara faction, which, with other defectors, joined the Japan Liberal Party in February 1948. The next month the Japan Liberal Party became the Democratic Liberal Party (*Minshu Jiyūtō*).

The Ashida Cabinet fell in October, and in December Inukai Takeru, who wanted merger with Yoshida's Democratic Liberals, succeeded Ashida as leader of the Democratic Party. The general elections for the House of Representatives held in January 1949 resulted in a sweeping victory for the Democratic Liberal Party, which won 264 seats against 69 for the Democratic Party. For several months the Democratic Party remained badly divided between the Inukai faction, angling for a general amalgamation of conservative forces, and the Ashida faction, which was determined to have nothing to do with the Yoshida Government. This led to a complete split in April 1950, with the Ashida faction merging with the National Co-operative Party and another small group to form the National Democratic Party (NDP, *Kokumin Minshutō*), and Inukai and his supporters joining the Democratic Liberals, who in March 1950 changed their name to the Liberal Party (I) (*Jiyūtō*).

The National Democratic Party did not prosper electorally, and continued to be wracked by factional bickering. The issue, as before, was whether to merge with Yoshida's Liberals – the outbreak of the Korean War in June encouraged this – but the re-emergence into active politics of formerly purged politicians added further strains. In September 1951, against the advice of progressives within the party, the NDP took into its fold members of the New Politics Club (*Shinsei Club*), a group of those freed from the purge, as well as members of another small group. This meant yet another name change, this time to the Reformist Party (*Kaishintō*). The new party accounted for 69 members of the House of Representatives and 16 members of the House of Councillors. It received a boost to its standing with the electorate after electing SHIGEMITSU MAMORU, a well-known former diplomat, as its leader, and won 85 seats in the October 1952 general elections.

Meanwhile, the Liberal Party was also seriously affected by divisive factionalism. Until the end of the Occupation in April 1952, Yoshida's position had been underpinned by the authority of the Supreme Commander, Allied Powers, and he had been used to treating his party as his fief. But with the Occupation ended, he faced opposition from within his own ranks. This was compounded by the release of former politicians from the purge, most of them long-term party politicians rather than former bureaucrats like Yoshida. His particular nemesis turned out to be Hatoyama, who re-entered active politics in August 1951. When Hatoyama was purged in April 1946, he was replaced by Yoshida, who was alleged to have promised to hand back the party leadership to him once he was released from purge. This was a promise that Yoshida failed to fulfil, and Hatoyama determined to wrest the leadership from him. He kept up a relentless campaign of criticism against Yoshida as Prime Minister. In March 1953 Hatoyama and his followers brought a motion of no-confidence in the Prime Minister, forcing a dissolution and new elections. They then broke away from the Liberal Party and formed the Separatists' Liberal Party (*Buntōha Jiyūtō*), sometimes also known as the Liberal Party, Hatoyama faction (*Jiyūtō Hatoyama ha*). In the April 1953 Lower House elections Yoshida's Liberals lost their majority, winning only 199 seats, but in November Hatoyama and 25 of his followers returned to the Liberal Party. An anti-Yoshida hard core, however, refused to rejoin, and in November formed the Japan Liberal Party (II) (*Nihon Jiyūtō*). It only consisted of eight Lower House members, but these included the powerful 'party men', MIKI BUKICHI and KŌNO ICHIRŌ, whose main purpose in life was to topple Yoshida.

A year later, in November 1954, a merger took place between the Reformist Party, with 75 Lower House seats, the eight members of the Japan Liberal Party, and Hatoyama, with 36 followers, who had once again defected from Yoshida's Liberal Party. The result of all this manœuvring was the foundation of the Japan Democratic Party (JDP, *Nihon Minshutō*). It was a historic event because the JDP promptly agreed with the Socialists to put forward a motion of no-confidence in the Yoshida Government. Yoshida lost the vote and was forced to resign, being replaced as Prime Minister by Hatoyama. The next month Ogata Taketora took over as leader of the Liberal Party.

With Yoshida removed, the task of unifying conservative politicians into a single party became rather easier. But the precipitating event was the unification of the two Socialist parties into a single JAPAN SOCIALIST PARTY in October 1955. This opened the prospect of the Socialists allying themselves with some part of the conservative camp and entering government. Leaders of the business world, determined to prevent such a prospect, put intense pressure on the conservative leaders to unite into a single party with a stable majority. They complied in November, when the Liberal Party and Japan Democratic Party combined to form the Liberal Democratic Party, which went on to form every Government for the next 38 years.

The kaleidoscopic process of party formation, division, re-amalgamation and further division that occurred among conservative politicians in the first post-war decade reflected certain underlying factors. The first was the momentous series of changes that were taking place in the Japanese polity and society during the Occupation period and after. In 1945 Japan was virtually a destroyed country, and there was a sense that everything needed to be rebuilt from scratch. In these circumstances it is hardly surprising that party politics should have been exceptionally fluid. The second factor was the purge of those deemed most responsible for wartime policies, undertaken by the Occupation authorities. In the power vacuum that this created, politicians who had been Government officials entered politics, and built up their own power base. The key figure here was Yoshida, who founded his 'Yoshida School' of protégés, and who was intolerant of opposition to him within his own party. When former party politicians were released from the purge, coming back determined to make up for lost time and ambition, they challenged Yoshida's supremacy and gradually weakened his position. The key figure here was Hatoyama. Thus rivalry between former bureaucrats and former party politicians was a crucial factor in the troubles of the period.

Third, however, factionalism in this period was not entirely about personal or professional rivalries, though that was no doubt the most important aspect of it. In addition there were genuine differences of policy position. Broadly speaking the Yoshida School was hard-line conservative, but believed it was at least expedient to accept a US regime of security protection at the price of playing down any nationalist ambitions. So Yoshida, though he hated some of the Occupation reforms and was prepared to subvert them, saw the United States as essential for Japan for the foreseeable future. By contrast, Hatoyama, and some other conservatives with a pre-war political background, wanted to assert Japanese foreign policy autonomy and roll back some of the Occupation reforms, including rewriting the CONSTITUTION OF 1946. In addition there were many nuances of policy to be found among conservatives concerning possible relations with the Socialists. The Yoshida camp was viscerally hostile to them, whereas some others saw an alliance with elements on the left as a lesser evil to alliance with Yoshida-style conservatism.

Fourth, it is difficult to escape the conclusion that FACTIONS WITHIN POLITICAL PARTIES at this period reflected social norms endemic within the society. The idea that Japan is a consensus-based society is hardly confirmed by the experiences of party politics in Japan's first post-war decade. Rather, cliques of politicians seem to have operated on the principle of the zero-sum game, constantly seeking narrow advantage against embattled rivals. Once they were united into a single party, from November 1955, their rivalries continued to be fought out as factional contests within the LDP. But the difference was that whereas after 1955 these contests were conducted within the framework of a party organisation that was effective enough, for the most part, to hold the ring, no such single organisation existed in the first post-war decade. If conservative party politics between 1945 and 1955 was that of the 'anarchical society', from 1955 on there was a form of 'world government' – not admittedly very strong – to moderate the anarchy.

Further reading
Colton (1956)
Fukui (1970)
—— (ed.) (1985)
Kataoka (ed.) (1992)
Masumi (1985)
Quigley and Turner (1956)
Stockwin (1999)

Conservative Party (Hoshutō) In April 2000, OZAWA's LIBERAL PARTY (III) (*Jiyūtō*) decided to pull out of its coalition with the LIBERAL DEMOCRATIC PARTY (LDP) and CLEAN GOVERNMENT PARTY (CGP) that formed the OBUCHI Government. About half the Liberal Party parliamentarians, however, decided to stay with the coalition, defected from the Liberal Party and reconstituted themselves as the Conservative Party. But in the June elections for the House of Representatives, their representation was reduced from 18 to seven seats. In the House of Councillors elections of July 2001, they fell from seven to five seats. Being part of the Government coalition, however, a Cabinet position was allocated to their leader, Ms Ogi Chikage, an Upper House member.

Constitution of 1946 The Constitution of Japan that existed in 2002 was promulgated in November 1946 and came into force in May 1947. Long regarded as the 'new' Constitution, it is now one of the oldest in the world. Described in the title of a recent book as 'Japan's Contested Constitution', it has never yet been revised in the smallest detail. Like all long-standing constitutions, it is the basis for much subsequent legislation and interpretation, which gives it an elasticity in practice that in part explains the extreme longevity of the original text. But, though a piece of elastic will stretch, it will not stretch to infinity. Similarly a constitution may be interpreted elastically, but there comes a point where it will not stretch any further without destroying the credibility of the constitution itself. On the other hand, the defenders of the 1946 Constitution have been many and articulate, seeing it as the 'Peace Constitution', and as a bastion against Japan's remilitarisation and incorporation into a United States-led regional military alliance. Their opponents, however, argue that these things have in any case already happened despite the apparent constitutional ban, and that the new situation ought to be recognised through a carefully considered revision of the text. Since the early 1990s there has been an important shift of public opinion in the direction of revision, but a substantial minority remains implacably opposed.

Though debate has concentrated heavily upon the 'peace clause' (article 9), the Constitution is a comprehensive document, and many other parts of it are of great significance. We summarise very briefly below the content of the chapters:

Preamble

The language is that of popular sovereignty, and the emphasis is on preserving peace.

Chapter 1. The Emperor

Here the most significant article is article 1: 'The Emperor shall be the symbol of the State and the unity of the people, deriving his position from the will of the people with whom resides sovereign power.' The remaining articles outline his functions and make clear that he has no political power whatsoever.

Chapter 2. Renunciation of War

Article 9 (the sole article in this chapter) reads:

> Aspiring sincerely to an international peace based on justice and order, the Japanese

people forever renounce war as a sovereign right of the nation and the threat or use of force as means of settling disputes.

In order to accomplish the aim of the preceding paragraph, land, sea and air forces, as well as other war potential, will never be maintained. The right of belligerency of the state will not be recognised.

Chapter 3. Rights and Duties of the People

This chapter, extending from article 10 to article 40, was for its time a most advanced statement of human rights (not excluding duties), and stands up well even today. Some of the rights are justiciable, while others are more declamatory. Article 12 applies a 'public welfare' qualification to the exercise of these rights as a whole, and articles 13 (right to life, liberty and the pursuit of happiness), and 29 (property rights), include a specific 'public welfare' qualification.

Chapter 4. The Diet (Parliament)

Article 41 reads: 'The Diet shall be the highest organ of state power, and shall be the sole lawmaking organ of the State.' Articles extend from numbers 41 to 64, and constitute a detailed statement of the procedures of this bicameral legislature.

Chapter 5. The Cabinet

This chapter (articles 65–75) established a Westminster-style system of CABINET Government, in which the PRIME MINISTER was to be 'designated from among the members of the Diet by a resolution of the Diet' (article 67). Moreover, the Prime Minister appoints ministers of state, 'a majority [of whom] must be chosen from among the members of the Diet' (article 68). These articles were intended to eliminate the possibility of 'transcendental cabinets', which under the 1889 Constitution could be appointed from outside Parliament without responsibility to it. Under the 1946 Constitution in practice, very few Cabinet ministers have not been members of Parliament.

Chapter 6. Judiciary

Under this chapter (articles 76–82), the Supreme Court is placed at the apex of the judicial system (*see* SUPREME COURT POWER OF JUDICIAL REVIEW), with Cabinet essentially in charge of appointing JUDGES. Interestingly and controversially, the Supreme Court was designated 'the court of last resort with power to determine the constitutionality of any law, order, regulation or official act'. It has used this power sparingly.

Chapter 7. Finance

Articles 83 to 91 place administration of national finances in the hands of Parliament (in practice through the annual budget) and bring Imperial Household expenditure under parliamentary control (article 88).

Chapter 8. Local self-government

This chapter (articles 92–5) most significantly establishes popular election as the only method of electing local chief executives.

Chapter 9. Amendments

The only article here is article 96, which erects a series of high hurdles facing any attempt at constitutional amendment. To succeed, an amendment must be voted for by at least two-thirds of all the members of each House, and must then receive a simple majority in a referendum of the people. For most of the time since 1947, hostility to amendment has been strong enough to ensure failure should amendment be attempted.

Chapter 10 establishes the Constitution as the supreme law of the land, and Chapter 11 provides supplementary provisions in the transition to operating the new Constitution.

One of the principal arguments of constitutional revisionists has been that the Constitution was 'imposed' by the Americans on the initiative of General MacArthur. There is substance in this argument in that in February 1946 the Supreme Commander set up a committee in his Government Section to work on a draft to be presented to the Japanese Government as the basis for a constitution, giving the committee a week to complete its work. MacArthur gave the committee three basic principles to guide their work. The first was that the Emperor's powers as head of state (later changed to 'symbol') should be exercised in accordance with the Constitution and responsive to the will of the people. The second was the renunciation of war. And the third was the abolition of feudalism and of the peerage. An addendum was that the budget should be patterned on the British system.

There seem to have been two principal reasons why MacArthur decided to be proactive on constitutional drafting, and with such haste. One was that the efforts of the Japanese Government to amend the 1889 Constitution (in the shape of the Matsumoto draft) were plainly inadequate, consisting of rather minor adjustments to the existing document. The second was that in December 1945 it was decided to set up the Far Eastern Commission in Washington, DC, and that its terms of reference appeared to give a veto to the USSR in respect of fundamental matters such as constitutional revision. MacArthur therefore judged that the SHIDEHARA Government needed to be persuaded into a more radical approach. The draft produced by the Government Section committee became known as the 'GHQ draft'. The Americans then embarked on a complicated process of negotiation with the Government, which in the end reluctantly agreed to drop the Matsumoto draft, and to use the GHQ draft as the basis of its own constitution-making efforts. In this process of persuasion, the Americans emphasised their desire to retain the Emperor, as a constitutional monarch. They insisted that this would be far easier to achieve, in the face of international threats to try the Emperor as a war criminal, with a constitution based on democratic principles than with one mired in the ambiguous principles of the 1889 Constitution. Revisionists, however, later castigated this as an example of US blackmail. Major-General Courtney Whitney, Head of the Government Section, also threatened to place the GHQ draft before the electorate in a referendum, bypassing Cabinet, if Cabinet would not accept it as the basis for its drafting.

While one of the principal charges levelled against the Constitution by revisionists has been that it was 'imposed', a distinguished list of commentators has demurred. The President of the Constitution Research Commission (*Kenpō Chōsakai*), 1957–64, Takayanagi Kenzō, maintained that it was a joint production of Americans and Japanese. More recent writers, such as Beer, Koseki, as well as Moore and Robinson, have taken the view both that there was a substantive Japanese input and that the high level of popular acceptance that it subsequently obtained legitimated the Constitution. Certainly, when the draft was put before Parliament in the summer of 1946, it received 421 votes in favour and eight against. The sharpest divergence between the early drafts and the final draft was the introduction of an elective second chamber, the HOUSE OF COUNCILLORS, to replace the non-elective House of Peers.

If the origins of the Constitution have created controversy, the most contested article has also been the most famous, article 9, the 'peace clause'. The issues relating to it are difficult to put into focus. The fact that Japan from the 1950s developed what plainly are armed forces, even though they are euphemistically defined as 'Self-Defence Forces' (*jieitai*) suggests the article is a dead letter, or at least rather toothless. In fact, however, a series of inhibitions, including a ban on arms export, limitation of defence spending to 1 per cent of GNP, a ban (absolute until the 1990s) on the dispatch of ground troops overseas, and a ban on nuclear weapons, indicates that the article has had a few teeth, at least. Moreover, whereas constitutional revision began to attract majority support in the 1990s, a majority of respondents to public opinion polls have continued for the most part to champion the retention of article 9.

A key to understanding the politics of the peace clause is two crucial insertions into the article before it reached final form, on the initiative of ASHIDA HITOSHI. 'Aspiring to an international peace based on justice and order' now headed the first paragraph, and 'In order to accomplish the aims of the preceding paragraph' began the second. These insertions opened the way to an interpretation that 'land, sea and air forces...will never be maintained...*in order to accomplish the aims of...aspiration to an international peace ...* ', but that for other purposes, for instance defence of national territory, they might be constitutional. This was a legalistic interpretation, but one consistently applied by post-Occupation governments. It turned out that the Occupation authorities were aware of the implications of

Ashida's insertions. Governments also maintained, after entry to the United Nations in 1956 (see UNITED NATIONS, RELATIONS WITH), that the UN Charter gave Japan the right to defend itself. There have been a number of high-profile attempts to challenge through the courts the legality of US and Japanese military bases on Japanese soil. But every time when a case has reached the Supreme Court, it has been rejected. The most famous of these is the Sunakawa decision of 1959, which overturned a judgment by the Tokyo District Court that the Japan–United States Administrative Agreement was illegal under article 9. The Supreme Court, in this and other cases, judged that the article could not be applied in cases where there was a 'political question' – thus in effect drastically limiting its own power of judicial review.

Another constitutional issue that has caused controversy is the status of the Emperor (*tennō*). Revisionists have maintained that his designation as 'symbol of the State and of the unity of the people' deprives him of the status that he would have as 'Head of State', and that this is a problem when he meets foreign heads of state. On the other hand, some on the left have argued that the retention of the Emperor facilitated dangerous continuities with the authoritarian culture of the past, and that the institution has been a useful prop for political conservatism. The status of the Emperor, however, represents a canny compromise devised early in the Occupation to meld change with continuity. MacArthur judged that to abolish the emperor-institution – still more, to allow him to be tried as a war criminal – would jeopardise popular support for the Occupation reforms. Therefore, it made sense to retain the institution but strip it of all vestiges of power. It is interesting in retrospect that, after the immediate post-war period, few revisionists advocated a return of power to the Emperor. Indeed, when the conservative *Yomiuri Shinbun* (newspaper) in 1994 proposed a full text of a revised constitution, the first article no longer related to the Emperor but to the principle of popular sovereignty.

The chapter on human rights has been the source of litigation over the years, although the process of redress through the courts has been cumbersome and slow. To a certain extent the reluctance of citizens to pursue constitutional guarantees through the courts has diminished. By the 1990s some cases were resulting in substantial compensation payments in cases relating to environmental pollution and similar issues. Other constitutional issues dealt with in the courts include equality of rights under the law, economic freedoms, quality of life issues, electoral rights, procedural rights, and rights and freedoms of belief and expression.

As of 2002, the 1946 Constitution has never been amended, though, as we have seen, parts of it have been elastically interpreted. But various moves to change it have been made, and constitutional amendment has always been an official aim of the LIBERAL DEMOCRATIC PARTY. The most comprehensive attempt was the Constitution Research Commission between 1957 and 1964. It was launched by the revisionist KISHI Government, but, when it finally reported, the political atmosphere had changed, and the IKEDA Government quietly buried its report, which, in any case, was not unanimous. Revision became an issue briefly in the early 1980s, and again in the 1990s, when the ending of the Cold War, and in particular criticism of Japan for failure to participate (except financially) in the United States-led expedition to liberate Kuwait, led to some rethinking about the Constitution.

The *Yomiuri Shinbun* wrote its revision proposal in 1994, and this was followed by others, from various perspectives. A particular point to note about the *Yomiuri* proposal is that the second paragraph of article 9 was to be replaced by a paragraph banning weapons of mass destruction, glossed to mean biological, chemical *and nuclear* weapons (see NUCLEAR ISSUES). This is significant in that successive prime ministers had stated that the 1946 Constitution did not rule out nuclear weapons, though the Government had no intention of obtaining them. Other elements in the *Yomiuri* proposals were a strengthening of the power of the PRIME MINISTER, and a separation of the roles of the two houses of Parliament, giving new functions to the House of Councillors. They also included an easing of the requirements for constitutional revision. These revisions represented political priorities of the 1990s that were different from those of the 1950s, when revisionist sentiment was at its height, in an atmosphere of extreme political tension. By the 1990s, the political institutions and practices embodied in the 1946 Constitution were no longer fragile, but well established and understood.

In conclusion, it may be suggested that a major reason why the 1946 Constitution has survived is that political conservatives long ago discovered that its provisions were compatible with the quasi-permanent exercise of political power, in a system that depended for its stability on networks of vested interests. The 'Westminster' form of the Constitution eliminated the danger of maverick politics embodied in presidential systems, while doing little to prevent the emergence of a 'power elite' of politicians, bureaucrats and interest groups that came to dominate the system. Even the 'peace clause', though officially disliked by conservatives, could be a useful weapon against US pressure to rearm. But in the uncertainties of the post-Cold War world, with economic growth badly stalled, pressure to reform the political system has grown, and reform of the Constitution has come on to the active agenda. Even though both houses of Parliament have established special committees to examine constitutional revision, action seems unlikely until at the least the second half of the present decade.

Further reading
Beer (1992)
Beer and Itoh (1996)
Henderson (1968)
Hook and McCormack (2001)
Itoh and Beer (1978)
Koseki (1997)
Maki (1964)
—— (1980)
Moore and Robinson (2002)
Stockwin (1999)
Ward (1965)

consumer groups It is well known that in modern Japan producer interests have been in a much superior power position to consumer interests. This was particularly the case during the period of rapid economic growth from the late 1950s to the early 1970s, when manufacturing industry was favoured with all kinds of preferential treatment by Government, but there were few controls placed on product quality, reliability or price.

In reaction against the low priority given to consumer interests, a variety of groups emerged in the early 1960s (though the movement had a history before that), setting itself a principal role of furnishing information about the reliability, safety, etc. of consumer products. In 1961 the Japanese Consumers Association (*Nihon shōhisha kyōkai*) was founded, which published a journal called *Consumers Monthly* (*Gekkan shōhisha*). The movement received a boost from a visit to Japan in 1971 by Ralph Nader, the US consumer advocate. Reflecting the enhanced environmental and conservationist concerns of the 1970s, the movement came to emphasise the need to save energy and resources. Although it became increasingly sophisticated in its capacity to evaluate products and advocate the cause of the consumer, it suffered from great fragmentation. Most of the groups were local rather than national or even prefectural, and by the late 1980s there were several thousand local groups.

One characteristic of Japanese consumer groups that has often been noted with surprise by foreign observers is their concentration on issues of safety and reliability rather than value for money. Indeed, the question of 'food safety', and to a lesser extent 'food security', has been of prime concern to them. 'Food safety' means that food should be wholesome and not cause health problems, while 'food security' means that supplies of food should be secure in case of international emergency, embargo and so on. These two concerns have combined at times to impart an anti-foreign colouring to the public attitudes of consumer groups. In 1993–4 when the HOSOKAWA Government finally accepted the necessity to import some foreign rice to enable Japan to enter the World Trade Organization, many consumer groups protested [*see also* international organisations and Japan]. The fact that this might allow consumers to buy cheaper rice was outweighed in their eyes by their perception that foreign rice might not be wholesome, and that the lifting of protection might seriously reduce the viability of domestic rice production. The 'value for money' argument lost saliency in part because rice had already fallen to a small percentage (in some accounts, around 2 per cent) of the average family's food budget. However this may be, consumer groups found themselves in the surprising position of backing farmers in their demand for continued high levels of protection, rather than urging them to become more efficient in order to lower prices to the consumer.

Consumer groups may, however, be regarded as one aspect of a gradual evolution of consumer behaviour in the direction of greater sophistication, and plurality of lifestyles. Despite economic difficulties, Japan remains in aggregate a prosperous society, and consumers have become extremely discriminating and therefore demanding of producers. Producers (particularly in the ever more dominant tertiary sector) have had to be sensitive to vagaries in consumer taste, and adapt their production accordingly. This has more to do with economic and social trends than with consumer groups as such, though the latter have performed a useful information function.

Further reading
Maclachlan (2002)

Co-operative Democratic Party (Kyōdō Minshutō) *see* conservative parties, 1945–55

court system In pre-war Japan, courts were to a large extent controlled by the Ministry of Justice, which appointed JUDGES and administered the court system. Judges could not normally be dismissed, but public prosecutors, closely linked to the Ministry, diluted the power of judges. The courts dealt with civil and criminal cases, but administrative cases were handled by separate administrative courts. A limited jury system operated between 1923 and 1943, but jury verdicts were treated as advisory, not binding. Since the war, juries have not been revived.

The CONSTITUTION OF 1946 guaranteed independence of the judiciary. Article 76 states:

> The whole judicial power is vested in a Supreme Court and in such inferior courts as are established by law. No extraordinary tribunal shall be established, nor shall any organ or agency of the Executive be given final judicial power. All judges shall be independent in the exercise of their conscience and shall be bound only by this Constitution and the laws.

Article 77 places in the hands of the Supreme Court 'the rule making power under which it determines the rules of procedure and of practice, the internal discipline of the courts and the administration of judicial affairs'. Public procurators (prosecutors) were made subject to the rule-making power of the Supreme Court. The courts were also put in charge of administrative cases, replacing the old administrative courts.

The Supreme Court (*Saikō saibansho*) is the ultimate court of appeal. Essentially, it now only handles cases where constitutional issues are involved [*see also* Supreme Court power of judicial review]. Only in a tiny fraction of several thousand cases a year do appeals to the Supreme Court succeed. The Court actively exercises its rule-making power for the courts, though it is also bound by statute law passed by Parliament. It consists of fifteen Justices (judges), who divide into three benches of five each to hear most cases. Article 79 of the Constitution provides that Cabinet shall appoint Justices of the Supreme Court. But it is the Prime Minister who, in effect, appoints the Chief Justice. (Technically, it is the Emperor on the advice of the Prime Minister.) Not all Justices of the Supreme Court are professional judges; some are the equivalent of solicitors and barristers, and there are also prosecutors, law professors and even the occasional diplomat. They must be over 40, are normally appointed over the age of 60 and have to retire at 70.

Article 79 also provides, as a democratic safeguard, for regular referenda on the suitability of Supreme Court Justices. These are held at the time of a general election for the House of Representatives. In the words of the article: 'when the majority of voters favours the dismissal of a judge, he shall be dismissed'. At the Lower House general elections held in June 2000, nine Supreme Court Justices were subject to referendum. The number of votes in favour of dismissal ranged between 5,919,825 and 4,979,746, whereas the number of votes against dismissal ranged from 52,550,174 to 51,609,972. The most 'popular' Justice received 10.55 times more favourable votes than unfavourable, and even the least 'popular' Justice received 8.72 times more favourable votes than unfavourable. No case of dismissal as a result of a referendum has yet occurred.

Below the Supreme Court are eight high courts (*kōtō saibansho*), based on the major cities, 50 district courts (*chihō saibansho*), a considerable number of family courts (*katei saibansho*) and over 400 summary courts (*kan'i saibansho*). Most important cases are taken first to a district court, whereas the summary courts deal with more minor cases. High courts hear appeals against judgments of lower courts. Family courts, which are a post-war innovation, deal with problems of juvenile delinquency as well as family problems. Probation officers and other professionals are involved in their proceedings.

The court system in Japan is criticised for the slowness of its procedures. There are various reasons for this, including a lack of judges. But in fact delays are far from uniform throughout the system, and, in the summary courts in particular, cases are often disposed of quickly. This discussion also touches on the issue of the alleged lack of litigiousness inherent in Japanese culture. Certainly, there is a preference for out-of-court settlement of disputes, and this preference has deep historical roots. Even so, more people have been prepared to take legal action in recent years than in the immediate post-war years. The cultural point is that to take somebody to court is to make that person lose face, and it is better to engage in conciliation procedures that may avoid that danger. But there is also some evidence of reluctance among the authorities to embark on reforms of court procedure that would make litigation less painful and thus encourage more of it. The question whether cultural or institutional factors are behind low levels of litigation is interesting and of great importance.

Further reading
Beer (1992)
Beer and Itoh (1996)
Oda (1999)

cow walking (gyūho) Cow walking was a filibustering technique used by some opposition parties (principally the Japan Socialist Party, JSP) to delay parliamentary business. It consisted of having affiliated parliamentarians walk through the voting lobbies extremely slowly, imitating the pace of a cow. Significant examples of cow walking were in opposition to coal industry legislation in 1962, and against ratification of a treaty between Japan and the Republic of Korea in 1965. In the second case, the JSP strongly disapproved of the treaty, because it appeared to tie Japan in with the anti-Communist side in the Cold War and excluded North Korea [*see also* Korea (ROK and DPRK), relations with]. The party demonstrated its opposition by radical delaying tactics of this kind.

Cow walking and similar techniques had some effect because of rigidities in parliamentary timetabling. A bill that was not passed by Parliament in a regular session would die and procedures would have to begin again in the next session. This was modified by the provision for extraordinary sessions, but these could not be infinitely extended. It was therefore imperative for the Liberal Democratic Party (LDP), through the Parliamentary Management Committees (*kokkai taisaku iinkai, kokutai*) of the two houses, to cultivate opposition party co-operation so far as possible. This led, from the 1960s, to the phenomenon of Management Committee politics (*kokutai seiji*), whereby the relevant party officials on both sides developed relations of understanding with each other. But when the system broke down, as it did on issues of extreme ideological sensitivity, the result could be disruptive.

But such techniques also had a demonstrative purpose. Disruptive techniques were designed to gain maximum media publicity. In this sense cow walking should be seen in conjunction with the technique of boycotting votes on contentious issues, in parliamentary committee or plenary session, so that the LDP could only pass the legislation by a 'forced vote', in other words a vote with only LDP members present. This strategy was designed to persuade the electorate that the LDP was acting arrogantly, and breaking the principle of consensus. Cow walking had a similar aim.

The efficacy of these techniques, however, was proved to have declined sharply by the 1990s. Following the Gulf crisis and war of

1990–1, the JSP in June 1992 once again had recourse to the technique of cow walking in a vain attempt to block the Peace-Keeping Operations bill. But it soon became plain that the electorate was reacting extremely negatively to such demonstrations, and the party suffered badly in subsequent elections. What had worked, to some extent, in an era of ideological polarisation, ceased to work in the post-Cold War era of the 1990s and early 2000s.

Further reading
Baerwald (1986)
Langdon (1967)

criminal justice system Judged by low crime rates, the Japanese criminal justice system might be regarded as a success. It is, however, worth examining how this has been achieved. As in some continental European legal systems, the role of the prosecutor (*kenji*) in criminal cases is crucial. Prosecutors, who have the same training as judges, investigate cases where the police suspect an individual of having committed a crime. Wherever possible, the prosecutor will seek to avoid formal prosecution, but, in those cases where prosecution takes place, subsequent acquittal is rare (less than 1 per cent of cases). Where the convicted person shows remorse and does not act in a difficult manner, penalties may even be suspended. The emphasis is placed less on the rights of the accused/convicted person, but rather on rehabilitation and return to the community. The prison population is low by comparison with most other comparable countries, but criticisms are sometimes heard about harsh treatment in prisons, and a deliberate policy of humiliating prisoners. After a limited experiment in the pre-war period, the jury system has not been revived. The concept of trial by one's peers meets some cultural resistance in Japan, though there are those who argue that trial by jury would not only be more democratic, but also raise the acquittal rate and avoid miscarriages of justice.

The system has been criticised for over-reliance on confessions. Confessions appear to be culturally sanctioned, but it is argued that too much pressure is applied by the police. Some critics also maintain that the rights of suspects, while in custody, to legal representation, access to documents, etc. is not sufficiently upheld.

Another target of criticism is the continued existence of capital punishment, now abolished throughout almost the whole of Europe, where it is seen as morally objectionable. The number of executions has greatly declined since the post-war period, and in most years they are in single figures. Executions have to be sanctioned by the Minister of Justice, and in the early 1990s the Minister of Justice in the Miyazawa Government refused to allow any executions on grounds of conscience, being a devout Buddhist. Between 1995 and 2000 executions ran evenly at about six per year. In this period the issue of capital punishment came to be widely discussed, in part because of the *Aum shinrikyō* affair and the likelihood of capital penalties being decreed for some of the accused in the sarin poisoning and other crimes of which members of the sect stood accused. In 1998 the Minister of Justice indicated that the Government would henceforth break with past precedent and announce numbers and dates of those executed. Previously, governments had insisted on avoidance of publicity. Even though opposition to capital punishment was growing, the Ministry of Justice and the Public Prosecutors Office remained firmly attached to it. On 7 November 1995, in reply to a parliamentary question, a Government minister replied that 'Taking into account public opinion and a situation in which heinous crimes recur, it would not be appropriate to abolish capital punishment completely.' The impact of the Menda case, where a man was condemned to death for murder in 1950 and finally acquitted in 1983, has by contrast reinforced the case of the abolitionists.

If there is a common theme running through different aspects of the criminal justice system, it is that more emphasis is placed on keeping the crime rate low than on the human rights of the accused. Considerable success has been achieved in the former, but often at the expense of the latter. Much reliance is placed on confessions, while apologetic, co-operative and remorseful attitudes by the accused are rewarded, except in the case of particularly heinous crimes, where punishment can be extreme. The criminal justice system is another area where excessive litigiousness is seen as an evil to be avoided, and the harmony of society as a good to be cultivated.

Further reading
Beer and Itoh (1996)
Oda (1999)
Williams, Noel (1997)

D

Daybreak Club (Reimeikai) Following the break-up of the NEW FRONTIER PARTY (NFP) at the end of December 1997, the Upper House *Kōmei* group, which had stood apart from the NFP but was allied with it, in January 1998 formed the Daybreak Club. This then formed an important element in the process of reconstruction of the CLEAN GOVERNMENT PARTY, finalised in November.

defence Since the 1960s, except for the years 1986, 1987 and 1989, Japanese defence spending has been running at less than 1 per cent of gross national product. Nakasone, as Prime Minister in the mid-1980s, deliberately broke the '1 per cent ceiling', but after three years, during which the proportion marginally exceeded 1 per cent, it sank back to its usual levels. As a proportion of annual Government expenditure, defence spending has averaged slightly more than 6 per cent since 1986. The figures, however, need careful scrutiny. Japan does not include pensions and other benefits provided to former service personnel in the defence budget, as is standard among NATO countries. If these payments were added, the proportion of GNP would rise to substantially over 1 per cent.

Because of the constitutional constraints created by article 9 of the 1946 Constitution, and because of the great sensitivity of defence as a political issue, Japan does not possess an army, navy or air force. In their stead it has Ground Self-Defence Forces, Maritime Self-Defence Forces and Air Self-Defence Forces. The titles of ranks in these three services were deliberately made different from those of the former Imperial Armed Forces. The military capacities of the Self-Defence Forces (SDF, *jieitai*) are, however, substantial. Total personnel numbers are close to a quarter of a million, and in 1997 the three services between them 'deployed over 1,000 battle tanks, 510 aircraft, and 160 surface ships and submarines' (Hook *et al.*, 2001, p. 12). It is sometimes stated that Japan ranks number three or number four in the world in defence capacity. This needs to be qualified, however. Japan has no nuclear weapons capability, virtually none of her troops have any battle experience, and the SDF have had to keep a low profile in the face of widespread pacifist sentiment, even though this may now be declining to some extent. There is no conscription for military service.

In a somewhat paradoxical fashion, public opinion polls show an overwhelming majority approving the existence of the SDF, but a majority also supporting the peace clause of the Constitution that purports to ban armed forces. Moreover, many people, when polled, appear to regard the SDF as much as a disaster relief organisation as a body whose principal task is to fight wars. On the other hand, since the passage in 1992 of the Peace-Keeping Operations (PKO) bill, contingents from the SDF have assisted with UN peace-keeping exercises, in a non-military capacity, in various trouble spots, most notably Cambodia in 1992–3. This has not met the degree of domestic opposition that was widely predicted at the time. In the aftermath of the terrorist attacks on New York and Washington on 11 September 2001, Parliament authorised the dispatch of a limited force from the SDF to help with United States-led operations centred on Afghanistan.

Japanese defence policy cannot be understood outside the framework of the security relationship with the United States [see also United States, relations with]. The Japan–US Mutual Security Treaty, created as part of the peace settlement with Japan in 1951–2, and revised amidst great controversy in 1960, led to substantial co-ordination of effort between the US forces and the SDF. The scope of co-ordination was expanded substantially by the Guidelines Agreement of 1997. It would be exaggerated to say that the SDF are an integral part of the US military machine in East Asia, but that they work closely together is uncontroversial. This, indeed, is one reason why there has been a streak of nationalism, not just on the right, but also on the left, of Japanese politics, since left-wing pacifism has gone along – particularly in the post-war years – with a marked degree of anti-Americanism.

The non-nuclear character of Japanese defence policy was established by the end of the 1960s [see also nuclear issues]. The Miki Government (1974–6), which was further to the left than most Liberal Democratic Party administrations, introduced a strengthened ban on arms exports, including technology related to military purposes. This was to cause problems of definition (is a civilian truck defence-related, given that it could be adapted as a gun-carriage?), but broadly speaking was enforced by later governments. Miki also introduced the above-mentioned defence spending limit of 1 per cent of GNP. But Miki also launched, in October 1976, the National Defence Programme Outline (NDPO), which for the first time adumbrated a defence doctrine for Japan, the essence of which was that the SDF should concentrate on preparing against 'limited and small-scale aggression', with help, if necessary, from US forces (Hook et al., 2001, pp. 132–3).

The period from the mid-1970s to the end of the 1980s was a difficult one for Japanese defence policy makers. After a period of *détente* in the 1970s, what has been called the 'Second Cold War' began from the end of that decade, with the Soviet invasion of Afghanistan. This led inevitably to greater emphasis being placed on defence, and to a substantial upgrading of defence capacities. Much careful thinking went in to the development of justifications for defence improvements, the most interesting of which was the 'comprehensive security' ideas that emerged during the Ohira administration between 1978 and 1980. 'Comprehensive security' meant, essentially, that the concept of security was broadened well beyond the sphere of military defence, to include resource and food security measures, and even overseas development aid (ODA), since this could be seen as contributing to Japanese security by aiding less fortunate countries in the region.

During the 1980s the Nakasone administration promoted measures to enhance the profile of defence. Nakasone lifted the '1 per cent of GNP ceiling', but as we have seen this did not lead to a permanent result. He also authorised the export of certain kinds of military technology to the United States, but this had less practical application than was expected. In any case, some two years after Nakasone left office, the Soviet Union was facing collapse and the ending of the Cold War was in sight.

The Gulf crisis and war of 1990–1 led, in a stumbling fashion, to the passage of the PKO bill in July 1992, and the despatch of SDF contingents to UN peace-keeping missions around the world, albeit with restrictions on what they could actually do in the field. This meant breaking an important defence taboo, and was accompanied by a definite shift of public opinion in favour of greater 'international security contribution' by Japan. A new NDPO in 1996 replaced that of 1976, and in 1997 the enhanced co-operation between the SDF and the US forces came into being through the Guidelines Agreement.

Inhibitions on a positive defence policy by Japan have stemmed from domestic public opinion, as we have seen, but also from fears about Japanese intentions expressed from time to time by politicians and others in neighbouring countries. Both these factors have to an extent declined. The Japan Socialist Party, always in the vanguard of resistance to enhanced defence efforts, has shrunk to insignificance, especially after Murayama Tomiichi, as Prime Minister in 1994, abandoned the party's traditional opposition to the SDF and the

Security Treaty. So far as the views of neighbouring countries are concerned, while they have not fundamentally changed, the rapid economic development of China creates fears in South-East Asia that have fuelled a tendency to reassess the possibilities for defence co-operation with Japan.

Even so, Japan's key security relationship remains that with the United States. Since the early 1990s the two governments have discussed plans for Theatre Missile Defence (TMD), essentially a plan to destroy enemy missiles before they arrive. This seems to be a factor that impels closer military co-operation between the United States and Japan. One reason for Japan to co-operate with TMD is that it guarantees continued US involvement in the defence of Japan. As Hook and his co-writers argue, whereas the old Socialist fear was of 'entrapment' – that is, that the Security Treaty would force Japan to participate in wars not of her own making – the fear of Japanese Government officials has rather been that of 'abandonment', namely that without sufficient *quid pro quo*, Japan risked being abandoned by the United States so far as security was concerned.

The idea, therefore, that Japan in the foreseeable future might 'go it alone' on defence, seems far-fetched. But important constraints on Japanese defence policy, within the framework of a security relationship with the United States, nevertheless remain.

Further reading
Buck (ed.) (1975)
Hook *et al.* (2001)
Inoguchi and Jain (eds.) (2000)
Keddell (1992)

Defence Agency (Bōeichō) The Defence Agency was set up in July 1954, simultaneously with the establishment of the Self-Defence Forces (*jieitai*). Its predecessor had been the Public Security Agency (*hoanchō*), in existence since 1952. Some sort of defence (or quasi-defence) preparation had been under way in Japan since General MacArthur in 1950 authorised the formation of the Police Reserve Force, after the outbreak of the Korean War. This had been upgraded to the Public Security Force (*hoantai*) in 1952 before the further renaming in 1954. The use of euphemisms did not hide the fact that Japan was once more developing what in effect was an army, navy and air force, albeit with limited capacity and restrictions on its rules of engagement. Restrictions and euphemisms were occasioned by the peace clause of the CONSTITUTION OF 1946, and the highly controversial nature of 'military' preparations and activities in the politics of the 1950s.

One indication of this was its designation as an 'Agency' of the PRIME MINISTER'S OFFICE (*Sōrifu*), rather than as a 'Ministry'. Despite agitation from right-wing politicians and others at various stages, it retained the name 'Defence *Agency*' even after the ADMINISTRATIVE REORGANISATION that took place in January 2001. Nevertheless, its responsibilities expanded. In 1958 it assumed responsibility for defence procurement, and in 1962 for liaison with US forces stationed in Japan. Even though the politician at the head of the Defence Agency was designated 'Director' (*Chōkan*), he was treated in practice as equal to other Cabinet ministers, and the post of Defence Agency Director was an important one, capable of enhancing the careers of any politician appointed to the position. For instance NAKASONE YASUHIRO substantially increased his national and international profile with his tenure of the Defence Agency Directorship in 1970–2.

Unlike the pre-war division of ministries with military responsibility into the Ministry of War (in charge of the army) and Ministry of the Navy, the Defence Agency has combined charge of all three branches of the Self-Defence Forces, Ground, Maritime and Air. Close relations are maintained between the civilian organisation of the Defence Agency and the military staff organisational structure of the Self-Defence Forces themselves. The issue of civilian control is, not surprisingly, a politically sensitive issue in Japan, and some have questioned the ability of a bureaucratic agency staffed by civilians to control a specialist military organisation. With the enhanced roles for the Self-Defence Forces authorised since the terrorist attacks in the United States on 11 September 2001, the issue of civilian control may well again become more prominent.

Democratic Liberal Party (Minshu Jiyūtō)
see conservative parties, 1945–55

Democratic Party (I) (Minshutō) see conservative parties, 1945–55

Democratic Party (II) (Minshutō) The Democratic Party was founded in September 1996, following a split in the Social Democratic Party (formerly JAPAN SOCIALIST PARTY). The two principal leaders were HATOYAMA YUKIO and KAN NAOTO, both from the NEW PARTY HARBINGER (*Sakigake*), and they became joint 'Representatives' (*daihyō*) of the Democratic Party. At the time of its foundation, 39 parliamentarians affiliated with it, but, in the elections for the House of Representatives on 20 October, the party won 52 seats. In April 1998, several weeks after the NEW FRONTIER PARTY (*Shinshintō*) collapsed in December 1997, substantial fragments of that party entered the Democratic Party, boosting its Lower House representation to over 90. This infusion of new members resulted in a relaunch of the party, which brought together members of the existing Democratic Party, the untranslatable MINSEITŌ, the NEW PARTY AMITY (*Shintō yūai*) and the DEMOCRATIC REFORM LEAGUE (*Minshu kaikaku rengō*, or *Minkairen*). The new party then received nine extra seats in elections for the House of Councillors in July. Lower House elections in June 2000 gave it a total of 127 seats (out of 480), and Upper House elections in July 2001 boosted its seats in that house to 59 (out of 247).

From the beginning, the Democratic Party was a somewhat uneasy amalgam of politicians with a left-of-centre background with some who had been further to the right. In a sense, left and right wings in Japan came with differing cultures, so that putting them together caused strains. This could be seen in the relationship between the two principal leaders of the party, Hatoyama and Kan. Initially, the two men shared the status of 'Representative'. But in September 1997 while Kan remained 'Representative', Hatoyama became Secretary-General. Then, in September 1999, Hatoyama challenged him for the top position, and narrowly won. Thus Hatoyama became 'Representative' and Kan was Chairman of the Policy Committee, later becoming Secretary-General.

The Democratic Party sought to appeal specifically to younger voters. The platform drawn up on its initial founding in 1996 began by describing the party as a 'political network centred on that generation born and educated since the war, which looks to the future'. The platform of the expanded party launched in 1998 included the phrase: 'Japan is bogged down in a structure of bureaucrat-led protectionism and uniformity, dependency and backstage deals. It is thus unable to cope with the changing times.' It also contained the following passage:

> We represent those who earn their living, who are taxpayers and consumers. We wish to transcend the conflict between those who say that the market is all and those who say that welfare is all. We aim for a society in which independent individuals live together symbiotically, and would limit the role of government to that of ensuring this.

The language of the latter passage gives a good indication of the different strands of thinking within the party and of how formulae were devised to transcend the divergences. On the one hand the party was trying to appeal to younger voters who were fed up with the existing politics of vested interests. Thus it called for small (or smaller) government. At the same time it felt the need to use language that would preserve a sense of social harmony and solidarity, rather than advocating naked market forces.

The problem was especially acute in the area of defence policy, where Hatoyama, representing a 'normal State' approach, and inclined to support Government initiatives for greater international security contribution, was criticised from those who originated on the left. After the terrorist attacks in New York and Washington on 11 September 2001, Hatoyama led the Democratic Party into supporting the KOIZUMI Government's bill to send a Self-Defence Forces contingent to assist with the United States-led operations in Afghanistan. But 21 Democratic Party members from the Lower House, and seven from the Upper House, opposed, abstained or absented themselves from the parliamentary voting. These were led by Yokomichi Takahiro, former Governor of Hokkaidō, who originated in the JAPAN SOCIALIST PARTY. The party disciplined him and his supporters, but the affair revealed a serious intra-party rift.

On 23 September 2002 Hatoyama was re-elected to the party's presidency, narrowly defeating Kan in a runoff election, after Noda Yoshihiko and Yokomichi Takahiro had been eliminated in the first round of voting. The divisions in the party were highlighted by the fact that Kan won slightly more votes among party parliamentarians, though Hatoyama was ahead among local supporters eligible to vote, and local council members affiliated with the party. His subsequent appointment of Nakano Kansei as Secretary-General caused serious dissent among younger members and seriously delayed further appointments. It marked an inauspicious start to his new regime. Following an abortive attempt by Hatoyama to merge his party with Ozawa's Liberal Party, he was forced to resign in December and was replaced by Kan Naoto.

The Democratic Party by 2002 had become the second largest party, but with no more seats in Parliament than those of the JSP before its collapse in the 1990s. It gave support to LDP-based Governments, and criticised them, on an *ad hoc* basis, avoiding entering into any coalition Government. Despite its affirmation of the need for drastic reform of the politico-economic system, its policies and performance only gave modest assurances of its capacity to engineer the reforms that were required.

Further reading
Neary (2002)

Democratic Reform League (Minshu kai-kaku rengō, Minkairen) The Democratic Reform League was a grouping based in the House of Councillors that emerged from the Japanese Trade Union Council (*Rengō*).

In June 1989 the newly formed *Rengō* established a political association called the *Rengō* Association (*Rengō no kai*), which contested the July Upper House elections. With electors disillusioned with government by the Liberal Democratic Party, not only many Socialists, but also 11 candidates of the *Rengō* Association were elected. In June 1993, the group changed its name from *Rengō* House of Councillors (*Rengō sangiin*) to Democratic Reform League. When the HOSOKAWA Government was formed in August of the same year, the Democratic Reform League was one of eight political formations participating. Its political stance was progressive and supportive of the CONSTITUTION OF 1946.

The initial electoral impact was not maintained. Only two of its candidates were elected in the 1995 Upper House elections, and in April 1998 it disbanded.

Democratic Socialist Party (DSP, Minshatō)
To understand the origins and approach of the Democratic Socialist Party, founded in 1960, it is necessary to go back to political developments in the pre-war period, as well as in the late 1940s and the mid-1950s. One of the principal tendencies of the left-wing movement from the late 1920s was the *Shamin-kei* (Social Democratic group), which was close to those embryo labour unions of the period that favoured non-confrontational unionism. A key figure in this movement was NISHIO SUEHIRO, himself a labour leader, who was the 'power behind the throne' in the KATAYAMA coalition Cabinet of 1947–8. In the late 1950s, with the JAPAN SOCIALIST PARTY (JSP) leadership driven towards the left in confrontations with the revisionist KISHI Government, Nishio saw the need for a more moderate socialism, where democratic norms and procedures would be maintained. In 1954, a group of private-sector unions had defected from the major *Sōhyō* union federation (GENERAL COUNCIL OF JAPANESE TRADE UNIONS), and formed the ALL-JAPAN TRADE UNION CONGRESS (Zenrō), which later became the JAPAN CONFEDERATION OF LABOUR (*Dōmei*) promoting non-confrontational unionism based on the principles of labour–management co-operation.

In practical terms, therefore, Nishio had a potential base of organisational support from a union grouping congenial to his politics, on which he could build a new party. An electric atmosphere had been created by the SECURITY TREATY REVISION CRISIS of 1960, and ASANUMA, the JSP Secretary-General, had spoken in Beijing of 'American imperialism [being] the common enemy of the peoples of Japan and

China'. Reacting against left-wing radicalism, Nishio decided to pull his supporters (the *Shamin-kei* and a portion of the *Nichirō-kei*) out of the JSP and form a new party of political moderates. Putting 'democracy' ahead of 'Socialism', it was called the Democratic Socialist Party. The DSP was influenced by the British Labour Party and ideas of the welfare state. In practice, however, its union base of support proved too narrow to sustain a major party, and from the 1970s LIBERAL DEMOCRATIC PARTY (LDP) governments were expanding social provision. The party performed poorly in its first general election (November 1960), but later stabilised at around 30–5 seats in the Lower House at most elections. It maintained its ideological distance from the JSP (while occasionally co-operating for electoral purposes), and came to take a much more positive attitude towards DEFENCE than the JSP. Nishio served as party Chairman until 1967. Subsequent chairmen were Nishimura Eiichi (1967–71), Kasuga Ikkō (1971–7), Sasaki Ryōsaku (1977–85), Tsukamoto Saburō (1985–9), Nagasue Eiichi (1989–90), Ouchi Keigo (1990–4) and Yonezawa Takashi (June–December 1994). During the 1970s the DSP developed reasonably close relations with the CLEAN GOVERNMENT PARTY (*Kōmeitō*), but attempts to mend fences with the JSP foundered on differences in policy on defence and nuclear power.

Nevertheless, with the amalgamation of the principal union federations into the JAPANESE TRADE UNION COUNCIL (*Rengō*) in 1989–90, and the modernisation in 1986 of the JSP platform, the possibility of closer co-operation opened up. It was promoted vigorously by the labour leader Yamagishi Akira, who saw labour unity as the first step to unity of social democratic parties. Indeed, in 1993–4 the DSP found itself co-operating within the same government as the JSP. OZAWA's attempt, however, during the HATA Government period, to create a new party which would have excluded the JSP, perversely led to a return to power by the Liberal Democrats in coalition with the Socialists. The DSP Chairman, Ouchi Keigo, who had co-operated with this endeavour, resigned to take responsibility for the fiasco in June 1994. In December, the DSP dissolved itself, and most of its members joined the newly formed NEW FRONTIER PARTY (NFP, *Shinshintō*). Following the collapse of the NFP in December 1997, the DSP was briefly reincarnated as the NEW PARTY AMITY (*Shintō Yūai*), which led a tentative existence between January and April 1998. In April this group dissolved itself into the DEMOCRATIC PARTY.

Note: Between 1960 and 1970 the party was called *Minshu Shakaitō*, but in 1970 this was abbreviated to *Minshatō*, without changing the meaning.

Further reading
Christensen (2000)
Curtis (1999)
Hrebenar (1986, 1992)
Johnson (2000)
Stockwin (1968)
—— (1999)

Doi Takako Doi Takako was the first woman to head a Japanese political party, and the first woman to be Speaker of the HOUSE OF REPRESENTATIVES [*see also*: WOMEN AND POLITICS]. She was elected Chair of the JAPAN SOCIALIST PARTY (JSP) in September 1986, and remained in that position until she resigned in June 1991. The high point of her leadership was the JSP victory in the July 1989 HOUSE OF COUNCILLORS elections, followed by a very respectable performance in the February 1990 HOUSE OF REPRESENTATIVES elections (*see* ELECTORAL HISTORY, HOUSE OF COUNCILLORS; ELECTORAL HISTORY, HOUSE OF REPRESENTATIVES). These successes reflected disarray in the LIBERAL DEMOCRATIC PARTY (LDP) following the RECRUIT SCANDAL, but her 'Madonna strategy' of encouraging numbers of women to stand as JSP parliamentary candidates contributed to the party's (briefly) strong performance. With the formation of the HOSOKAWA coalition Government in August 1993, Doi Takako became speaker of the Lower House.

She was born in 1928 in a middle-class family in Kōbe, and her early career was as a university lecturer in Constitutional Law. She was elected to Parliament for a Lower House Kōbe constituency in 1969, and pursued an unremarkable course as a parliamentarian until 1986.

When she took over the JSP Chair in that year, the party had just suffered a severe defeat in the Lower House general elections of July. The radical conservative Prime Minister, NAKASONE, was at the height of his power. Her predecessor, ISHIBASHI MASASHI, had resigned, taking responsibility for electoral defeat. But he had bequeathed to her a modernised party platform, making it easier to appeal to floating voters. She became popular through media exposure, and was helped by unpopular LDP taxation and agricultural policies, as well as by a series of corruption scandals engulfing establishment politicians. The 1989 Upper House elections were a signal victory, in which many rural seats as well as urban ones swung to the JSP. As she famously put it, quoting the poetess Yosano Akiko: 'The mountains have moved.' In the Lower House elections of February 1990, the party won about 50 extra seats, but its vote percentage had declined from the previous year. The electoral successes of her leadership in 1989–90 were, however, short-lived. Her party was unable to present a credible policy in relation to the Gulf crisis and war of 1990–1. The humiliating defeat of the JSP candidate in the April 1991 elections for Tokyo Governor forced her resignation. Two years later, however, she became Speaker of the House of Representatives following the formation of the HOSOKAWA Government.

A few days after the party split in September 1996, Doi Takako was elected Chair once again. This time, however, the party was at its lowest ebb, and about to be reduced to a mere rump of 15 seats in the House of Representatives elections held in October. At the next elections nearly four years later, she could derive modest satisfaction from an increase of seats to 19, and from the fact that the majority of these were women. Under her leadership, the party concentrated on peace issues and the rights of women.

Doi Takako had both strengths and weaknesses as a politician. For a while, through her vision and personality, she made a conspicuous impact on public opinion, transcending that of her party. But ultimately her vision, rooted as it was in a rather fundamentalist pacifism, was not broad enough to sustain the enthusiasm she originally inspired. She also confronted a sclerotic and fractious party organisation, which in the end overwhelmed her. Her modest success in leading a niche party in the period from 1996 is an interesting footnote to a career that, in its heyday (1986–90), seemed capable of moving the political mountains of corruption and special interests that continue to plague Japanese politics.

Further reading
Stockwin (1994)

E

Economic Planning Agency (EPA, Keizai kikakuchō) The origins of the Economic Planning Agency go back to the Economic Stabilisation Board (ESB, *Keizai antei honbu*), set up under the Occupation in August 1946 and abolished in July 1952. The ESB was succeeded by the Economic Deliberation Agency (*Keizai shingichō*), which changed its name to Economic Planning Agency in July 1955. It was an external agency of the PRIME MINISTER'S OFFICE, with a Minister of State as its Director.

With the establishment of the ENVIRONMENT AGENCY in 1971, the EPA lost most of its environmental policy functions, and, after the NATIONAL LAND AGENCY was set up in 1974, it lost certain functions concerning land planning and regional development. This enabled it to concentrate on its core functions of detailed investigation of economic indicators, preparing economic forecasts, publishing a variety of 'white papers' on the international economy, national economy, costs and standard of living, etc., as well as seeking to co-ordinate policy between major ministries. It developed a model of the Japanese and international economy, as a tool for economic forecasting.

The EPA has been widely regarded as an important part of the Government structure, with exceptionally high-quality personnel. Its importance may be gauged by the fact that its Director has often been a top-ranking Cabinet minister. At the same time, it would be incorrect to regard it as wholly independent of the main economic ministries. In the past, the MINISTRY OF INTERNATIONAL TRADE AND INDUSTRY (*Tsūsanshō*), and to a lesser extent the MINISTRY OF FINANCE (*Okurashō*), have played an important role in appointments at the EPA. Moreover, its role in the formation of economic policy has been controversial. The idea that EPA economic plans are meant to be implemented in detail by Government has long been discredited, and is based on a misunderstanding about the character of the Japanese economy. Rather, in the words of Chalmers Johnson, 'EPA's forecasts and indicative plans are read not so much for their accuracy or econometric sophistication as for official statements of what industries the government is prepared to finance or guarantee for the immediate future' (Johnson, 1982, p. 76). Taking this into account, it is evident that the relative lack of independence of the EPA from the major ministries may have actually enhanced its credibility.

In any case the notion of the Japanese economy as expertly *dirigiste* belongs largely to the past, and this is perhaps reflected in what happened to the EPA in the administrative reorganisation of January 2001. Together with the Prime Minister's Office and the OKINAWA DEVELOPMENT AGENCY, it was merged into the CABINET OFFICE (*Naikakufu*). This suggests that its expertise has come to be tapped by a Prime Minister and Cabinet seeking to impose their will on powerful and recalcitrant ministries intent on protecting their privileged clienteles.

Further reading

Johnson (1982)
Kosai, in Yamamura and Yasuba (eds) (1987)

Eda Saburō Born in 1907 in Okayama, Eda Saburō first came to prominence as JAPAN SOCIALIST PARTY (JSP) Secretary-General under ASANUMA as Chairman from March 1960, and then acting Chairman following Asanuma's assassination in October 1960. He was again Secretary-General under KAWAKAMI from March 1961 to November 1962. He had been a member of the SUZUKI MOSABURŌ faction, first in the Left Socialist Party and then in the united JSP from 1955, and was known as a specialist on agricultural policy.

He proved himself an accomplished orator on television in the November 1960 general election campaign, and in 1961 developed the doctrine known as 'structural reform'. This was strongly influenced by a group that had been expelled from the JAPAN COMMUNIST PARTY in 1961 for their support of the 'structural reform' theories of the Italian Communist Party leader, Palmiro Togliatti, and by some activist JSP officials. The new approach – still Marxist, but highly flexible – was an attempt to get away from stale confrontation between rigid concepts of 'monopoly capitalism' and 'Socialism'. It sought to develop new policies appropriate to an age in which Japan was no longer a backward country dominated by the United States, but rapidly approaching advanced country status. Then in July 1962, Eda announced his 'Vision', not of a Japan modelled on the USSR or PRC, but as a modern society based on 'the high standard of living of the USA, the developed welfare system of the USSR, British-style parliamentary democracy and the Japanese peace Constitution'.

'Structural reform' did not initially cause much controversy. But with the 'Eda Vision', and a growing perception that Eda wanted to dominate the party, it came under sustained attack from the leftist mainstream of the SASAKI KŌZŌ (formerly Suzuki) faction, the far-left Peace Comrades Association (*Heiwa Dōshikai*), Professor Sakisaka's Socialism Association (*Shakaishugi Kyōkai*) and, outside the party, the leaders of the General Council of Japanese Trade Unions (*Sōhyō*). These argued that Eda was ignoring the necessity of class struggle under capitalism, and was falling into DEMOCRATIC SOCIALIST PARTY (DSP)-style revisionism. Eda fought off a challenge from Sasaki in January 1962, but by November did not have enough backing within the party to win against such opposition. By the end of 1962 both 'structural reform' and the 'Eda Vision' were put to flight and he himself was out of office. This failure aborted a promising modernisation movement, condemned the JSP to long-term irrelevance and gravely weakened the potential effectiveness of a modernised social democratic politics. It was a tragedy for the JSP and arguably for Japan itself.

Eda unsuccessfully challenged his erstwhile ally, NARITA TOMOMI, for the party Chairmanship in November 1970. During the 1970s he attempted to organise a structure of co-operation between the JSP, DSP and CLEAN GOVERNMENT PARTY, based on a common moderate platform. Marxists on the JSP left wing, still dominant, kept up a barrage of attack, and in 1977 he finally left the party. This led to the formation of the SOCIAL DEMOCRATIC LEAGUE (*Shaminren*), but Eda died before the launch of the new party, which came to be led by his son, Eda Satsuki.

Further reading

Johnson (2000)
Stockwin (1968)

Eda Satsuki EDA SABURŌ defected from the JAPAN SOCIALIST PARTY (JSP) in March 1977, began preparations for a new party, but died unexpectedly in May. He had planned to run in the national constituency of the Upper House in elections scheduled for July, but his son, Eda Satsuki, ran in his stead, and was elected in second place (of 50 elected) with nearly 1,400,000 votes. In March 1978 the SOCIAL DEMOCRATIC LEAGUE (SDL, *Shaminren*) was launched, and within this mini-party Eda exercised a central role until it was dissolved in 1994.

Born in 1941, Eda was a judge before entering politics, and had taken a graduate degree in Law from Linacre College, Oxford. Following his father's mission, he worked within the SDL to inject modernising ideas into the social democratic stream of Japanese politics. In 1990–1 he maintained close links with the reformist New Wave Society within the JSP, and later formed a similar group called 'Sirius'. The SDL joined the HOSOKAWA coalition

Government (August 1993–April 1994), and Eda became Minister for Science and Technology. After that Government fell, the SDL disbanded, and Eda became an executive of the NEW FRONTIER PARTY formed in December 1994. After that party's demise in December 1997, he joined the DEMOCRATIC PARTY. He narrowly failed to be elected Governor of Okayama Prefecture in October 1996, but was later re-elected to the House of Councillors.

education and politics If education is politically controversial in most countries, it is especially so in Japan. The reasons are not far to seek. In the late nineteenth century the Meiji regime regarded education as an essential instrument of economic development, national unity and loyalty. Primary schools were built throughout the country in the 1870s, and primary education approached universality almost as early as in Britain. At secondary and tertiary level education was available to a far smaller, though expanding, part of the population, and its quality was generally high. The intention to promote dedication to the State through the education system was revealed in the Imperial Rescript on Education, an exhortatory document read aloud regularly in all schools. Later, as the Emperor cult was developed, the portrait of the Emperor kept in schools became an object of reverence. In the 1930s and early 1940s schools became increasingly militarised, with military officers stationed in schools.

A principal intention of the Allied Occupation was to eliminate militaristic indoctrination and substitute democratic education in schools. Many textbooks were withdrawn and then rewritten. The school system was reorganised and expanded for equality of educational provision on a 6-3-3-4 basis: primary (six years), junior high (three years), senior high (three years) and university (four years). Control of education was decentralised, being placed in the hands of elective prefectural boards of education.

With restrictions on unions removed, most teachers were rapidly organised into the JAPAN TEACHERS' UNION (*Nikkyōso*), formed in June 1947. Enthusiastic supporters of democratic education, many union leaders were also militant and left wing, defining teachers as 'workers'. Early co-operation between the Occupation authorities and unionised teachers quickly turned into mutual suspicion, as Occupation policy became more conservative. As independence approached and became a reality in 1952, the conservative Japanese Government took every opportunity to regain control of education. Election to local boards of education was replaced by appointment, and the MINISTRY OF EDUCATION asserted its control by refusing to deal with *Nikkyōso* at central level, on the ground that the legal decision-makers were the prefectural boards. Since these, however, were now under Ministry control, this was merely a device for excluding the union from any say in decision-making. The Ministry gradually reasserted its control over textbook accreditation, and a clash with the union and Socialist politicians on this issue in 1956 in effect confirmed Ministry textbook control. On the other hand, *Nikkyōso* was able to subvert the imposition of a teachers' efficiency rating system in 1958. There were also fierce clashes over the reintroduction of 'ethics' classes, and pupil assessment. From the 1950s until the 1980s educational politics was characterised by confrontation and non-communication between the two sides.

The philosophy of education that emerged was that of universality, equality and uniformity of provision, particularly at the lower levels. Cramming of knowledge and skills was privileged over fostering creativity. This fitted the requirements of industry and commerce in the period of rapid economic growth for a workforce that was literate, numerate, technologically adaptable and docile. At the higher levels, however, a more elitist practice came to prevail. Entry to senior high school, and, most acutely, entry to university, were subject to intense competition for the most prestigious institutions. This became known as 'examination hell'. In turn, this gave rise to an industry of cram schools (*juku*), whose main purpose was to train pupils to pass examinations.

The system gained international praise for the level of accomplishment, especially in mathematics, where Japan normally came top in tests comparing various countries. On the other hand, there was a growing list of complaints that came to a head in the 1980s with NAKASONE's Extraordinary Commission on Education (*Rinji Kyōiku Shingikai, Rinkyōshin*), set up in 1984. The complaints centred on excessive uniformity of provision, mechanical techniques of rote learning, over-regulation in schools (described as 'repression' by some), requirements that teachers 'police' pupil behaviour outside school as well as within, excessive concentration on examinations, and failure to cultivate creativity. By the 1980s and particularly the 1990s and 2000s, problems of bullying, violence against teachers (occasionally by teachers against pupils), as well as truancy, became matters for acute concern.

Nakasone had his own agenda in setting up the *Rinkyōshin*. Fundamentally, he wanted to modify State control of education by the infusion of market principles, in line with his policies on privatisation of the national railways and other Government-run enterprises. He believed that excellence of provision should take precedence over uniformity of provision. In practice, the private sector was the most dominant at higher levels, with four-fifths of universities and nearly a third of senior high schools being in the private sector. But the Ministry exercised much influence even within those parts of the system that were in private hands. The other great concern of Nakasone was to promote 'internationalisation' (*kokusaika*) – a term hard to define, but implying for Nakasone that Japanese education should stand shoulder to shoulder with the most advanced systems of education overseas, and interact with them.

Schoppa argues that the *Rinkyōshin* was essentially a failure, having being subverted by the Ministry of Education and by LIBERAL DEMOCRATIC PARTY parliamentarians concerned to retain the essence of the existing system. Even the union, *Nikkyōso*, was unenthusiastic about changing a way of doing things that guaranteed its members security and high incomes. Nakasone himself is said to regard *Rinkyōshin*, in retrospect, as a failure. Hood, and to some extent Aspinall, both writing a decade later, have challenged Schoppa's view, arguing that Nakasone triggered a movement of reform that has gradually achieved results. To take one example that would support their case, at the tertiary level, universities have been extensively reorganised to eliminate the uniform two years of 'general education', to develop postgraduate study and research, and to introduce systems of peer review based on overseas models, and even including foreign advisers. On the other hand, it is arguable that the changes that have come about do not derive solely from the Nakasone initiatives of the 1980s. They may rather result from a variety of concerns voiced over a long period, from economic transformation requiring more 'creative' educational provision, and from demographic trends that have drastically reduced the numbers of pupils in education.

The political divisions over the Nakasone reforms have not entirely superseded the left-wing–right-wing divisions of the post-war period. But the teachers' unions are much reduced in membership and influence. *Nikkyōso* split in 1989, with a left-wing group breaking away to form the ALL-JAPAN COUNCIL OF TEACHERS' AND STAFF UNIONS (*Zenkyō*), and *Nikkyōso* itself moving to more moderate positions than hitherto. But some older issues continue to provoke heat. Notable among these is that of the *hinomaru* flag and *kimigayo* anthem in schools, which the left regards as militarist by association. The extent of union activity depends on the prefecture, but it would be wrong to see teachers – unionised or not – as passive spectators of educational policy. They are highly professional transmitters of knowledge and ideas in an environment that remains closely connected with politics.

Further reading
Aspinall (2001)
Cummings (1980)
Duke (1973)
Hood (2001)
Pempel (1978)
Roesgaard (1998)
Rohlen (1983)
Schoppa (1991)
Thurston (1973)
Yoneyama (1999)

election systems Japan, like other working democratic systems, has never found an electoral system that is wholly satisfactory. Its electoral systems have tended to reflect compromises between different political interests.

This is hardly surprising, since most election systems result from political fixes, and different kinds of system create divergent outcomes. Pure proportional representation (PR) is permissive towards small parties and thus tends to promote party fragmentation. By contrast, single-member districts with first-past-the-post voting usually favour large parties able to aggregate interests, and exaggerate vote majorities into larger seat majorities.

Experience has shown, however, that it is unwise mechanically to apply rules derived from European experience to the understanding of how Japanese election systems work in practice. One reason for this is the lower salience of party and party policy as a focus of voter choice. Another reason, closely connected, is the importance of personality, personal networks and candidate support machines in voting decisions. This may explain why public opinion polls asking questions about policy register major fluctuations of opinion over time, but these are poor predictors of voting behaviour in actual elections. Japanese election systems have often been uneasy compromises between the interests of individual politicians and those of political parties.

The language used in Japan to distinguish electoral systems is instructive. Systems (apart from proportional representation) are divided into electoral systems that are small (*shōsenkyokusei*), medium-sized (*chūsenkyokusei*) and large (*daisenkyokusei*). 'Small' means single-member districts (constituencies), 'medium' means districts mostly electing three, four or five members (with no vote transferability), and 'large' means districts electing up to 12 or even 14 members (the voter sometimes having more than one vote). This is a classification based on the number of candidates elected per district. It should be noted that the 'medium-sized' system, which has been so important in Japanese electoral history, while differing from a system based on proportional representation, nevertheless has a rough proportionalising effect. For instance, in a district electing five members, a candidate may well be elected with a mere 15 per cent of the vote, and this plainly favours fringe or niche parties. At the same time a broad, loosely structured, aggregative party, the LIBERAL DEMOCRATIC PARTY (LDP), was able to use it to its advantage.

House of Representatives, election system 1947–94

Although the first post-war Lower House elections (April 1946) were held under the 'large' electoral district system, elections starting with those of April 1947 were held under the 'medium-sized' system. A very similar system had been used between 1925 and 1942, initiated in the 1920s as a means of preserving a balance of representation between the three major parties of that period. Technically, the system was one based on a single non-transferable vote in multi-member districts. At the 1947, and subsequent, elections, the breakdown of districts was as follows:

5-member	38 districts
4-member	39 districts
3-member	40 districts
Total districts	117
Total members	466

In 1953, Amami Oshima (between Kyūshū and Okinawa) was returned to Japan from US administration, and added as a unique single-member district, existing as such for nearly 40 years.

A serious defect of the post-war election law was that it did not make adequate provision for redrawing of electoral boundaries. No neutral body was set up to determine electoral boundaries without political interference. With the rapid migration of population after the war from rural to urban areas to work in factories and offices, a huge imbalance developed between the value of rural and urban (particularly big-city) votes. This was of great political significance, because the over-weighting of votes in country districts favoured the conservative side of politics, and helped maintain the LIBERAL DEMOCRATIC PARTY (LDP) (formed 1955) in power. The discrepancy became difficult to defend, however, so that in June 1964 Parliament passed a Government bill to add a total of 19 seats in the congested prefectures of Tokyo, Kanagawa, Aichi and Osaka, lifting the total number of seats to 486. But a parallel proposal to reduce the number of rural seats was rejected. Five extra seats were added with the return of Okinawa in 1972, making the total 491. Then before the general elections of December 1976, a further 20 seats were added in urban prefectures, making the total 511.

These adjustments, however, still left urban areas seriously under-represented, and the courts began to exert pressure in favour of further correction. In 1976 the Supreme Court declared unconstitutional the Lower House general elections in a Chiba electoral district, on the grounds that the district was disadvantaged by a vote–value discrepancy of 499 per cent. Plainly, further adjustments could not be made simply by adding more seats in urban areas, since this would increase the size of the House to unacceptable levels. Therefore, in 1986, eight seats were added in under-represented districts, and seven seats, where there was gross over-representation, were eliminated. This had the effect of creating one six-member seat (in Hokkaidō), and four two-member seats (in Niigata, Ishikawa, Hyōgo and Kagoshima) and increasing total seats to 512. A further adjustment was made – both adding and subtracting seats – in time for the 1993 elections, the last under the 'medium-sized' system. Total seats were reduced back to 511, and seat numbers per district were as follows:

6-member	2 districts
5-member	47 districts
4-member	33 districts
3-member	39 districts
2-member	8 districts
Total districts	129
Total seats	511

Eighteen successive elections were held under the 'medium-sized' system from 1947 to 1993. The electorate increased from 40,907,493 in 1947 to 94,477,816 in 1993. Turnout rates ranged from a high of 76.99 per cent in 1958 to a low of 67.26 per cent in 1993, but the trend was only marginally downwards (though it was to accelerate later). Despite the various seat adjustments made, vote malapportionment (the 'negative gerrymander') remained a serious problem to the end. For instance, in October 1990, it took 140,782 voters in the second district of rural Miyazaki (Kyūshū) to elect one candidate, whereas in the fourth district of Kanagawa (just south of Tokyo) the figure was 459,661, making a discrepancy of 3.35 times (335 per cent).

The decision to abolish the 'medium-sized' district system and substitute for it a quite different system was the result of various considerations. The most important was the belief that it fostered corruption, and 'money politics'. There was a particular reason for believing this in relation to LDP candidates. Being the majority party in many districts, the LDP could rationally expect to have more than one of its candidates elected. From the party's point of view, it was crucial not to run too many candidates and risk splitting an inadequate vote between them. It was also important, if possible, to run candidates of roughly equal appeal, so that no one candidate would gain too many votes at the expense of the party's other candidates. The LDP became remarkably skilled at making sure it met these conditions. Indeed, in most elections, more than 80 per cent of votes cast for LDP candidates were cast for successful candidates. The dangers of running too many candidates is illustrated by the results of the 1990 elections in the first district of Fukushima, normally a conservative bastion (Table 4).

In other words, the LDP ran three candidates, who split an evenly distributed vote between them. Had their votes been divided evenly between two candidates, each would have won around 80,000 votes, and headed the poll (though we should not assume that the votes of the candidate who dropped out would have gone to the other two). A further interesting factor here, however, was that Mashiko stood as an Independent, but joined the LDP after being elected. He was a new candidate, initially refused LDP endorsement, but with sufficient personal popularity to beat all other candidates. If we treat Mashiko as an LDP candidate, the LDP vote totalled 219,618, and the votes for all other candidates totalled 228,164. Thus, in the end, the LDP won two out of four seats with 49 per cent of the vote.

Another significant aspect of this case is that Mashiko belonged to the ABE faction, Kaneko to the TAKESHITA faction, Amano to the NAKASONE faction and Kuriyama to the MIYAZAWA faction. In other words, the election in this

Table 4 Results of the 1990 elections in the first district of Fukushima

Name	Party	Votes	
Mashiko Teruhiko	Independent	58,301	Elected
Satō Tsuneharu	JSP	58,032	Elected
Satō Tokuo	JSP	56,588	Elected
Kaneko Tokunosuke	LDP	55,535	Elected
Amano Mitsuharu	LDP	54,968	Not elected
Kuriyama Akira	LDP	50,804	Not elected

Note: There were, in addition, four other Independent candidates and a Communist.

district was a contest between four major factions of the LDP. It was also very much a personal popularity contest, based on the *kōenkai* (personal support machines) of individual candidates. Reliance on factional backing and personal support machines privileged locality over nation, faction over party and personality over policy. It was also closely bound up with money politics in that local communities, especially outside the big cities, had come to regard elections as opportunities to bid for local benefits, and candidates as worth supporting if they could deliver those benefits. That, in turn, favoured those candidates having the closest links with Government and with centres of power, meaning essentially candidates belonging to the LDP. For candidates, elections had become extremely expensive affairs, which also rendered them liable to charges of corruption if they did what they had to do to be elected.

The system also disfavoured opposition party unity. Since it was permissive to small parties, it tended to fragment the opposition. Even though the decline of the JAPAN SOCIALIST PARTY (JSP) from its high point in the late 1950s owed more to internal factors than to the election system, the election system made it easy for breakaway and new parties to probe JSP weaknesses. A further factor paradoxically made it difficult for the JSP to advance towards being a credible alternative Government party. By the 1970s the JSP ran a single candidate in the bulk of districts. These candidates could normally rely on sufficient backing from unions and other groups to be elected without the need for strong campaigning. This fostered complacency and a 'permanent opposition' mentality. By contrast, the LDP, running multiple candidates in most districts, created an atmosphere of intense competition between its own candidates campaigning in the same district. LDP candidates had to work hard to bring out the vote, whereas JSP candidates could sit back and let sympathetic unions do much of their campaigning for them.

House of Representatives election system, 1994–

Proposals to reform the 'medium-sized' electoral system were discussed from the 1950s. The Prime Ministers HATOYAMA, in the mid-1950s, and TANAKA, in the early 1970s, proposed changing essentially to a 'small' district system, on the British model. KAIFU, as Prime Minister, in 1981 put forward a mixed system of single-member districts and constituencies based on proportional representation. Miyazawa, two years later, reverted to the 'small' district system in a reform proposal that he seems to have expected to fail (as it did), but its failure precipitated a party split that cost him his prime ministership. It was left to the HOSOKAWA coalition Cabinet from August 1993 to put forward a serious reform proposal. Given the multi-party composition of the Hosokawa Government, and the fact that it was also necessary to obtain the consent of the LDP, now in opposition, the proposals went through many modifications in the course of negotiation. Finally, a package of reform measures passed a joint session of both houses of Parliament on 29 January 1994. It was not until late in 1994, two governments later, that all the arrangements for a change of system were put in place.

The new system as it finally emerged was rather similar to the Kaifu model proposed three years earlier. The 511 members were reduced to 500. Of the 500, 300 were to be elected from single-member constituencies on the British model, while 200 were to be elected by proportional representation from 11 regional constituencies, according to the d'Hondt system of calculation. The system was the product of hard-fought compromise between those who wanted a maximum number of seats to be elected from single-member districts, and those (mostly on the left and centre-left) who held out for the highest component of proportional representation seats obtainable. Those who favoured the former included both those who saw single-member districts as the best way of returning to LDP majorities, and those (like OZAWA) who saw them as the best recipe for two-party alternation in power. The smaller parties struggled to maximise the PR component as their means of survival. Although 200 seats were decided by PR in 1996, by the elections of 2000, the number had been cut to 180. The allocation of seats to the 11 regions was uneven, as shown on Table 5.

Table 5 Allocation of seats to the 11 regions

Regional bloc	Seats at 1996 elections	Seats at 2000 elections
Hokkaidō	9	8
Tōhoku	16	14
Kita Kantō	21	20
Minami Kantō	23	21
Tokyo	19	17
Hokuriku-Shin'etsu	13	11
Tōkai	23	21
Kinki	33	30
Chūgoku	13	11
Shikoku	7	6
Kyūshū	23	21
Total	200	180

The new system was a rather awkward compromise between different interests, purposes and visions. On paper it looks completely different from the system that preceded it. In practice, however, certain elements had been incorporated into the new system that were reminiscent of the old. Each voter had two votes, one for the single-member district, and one for the regional bloc. But, more surprisingly, candidates had the right to stand simultaneously in both types of district. For instance, a candidate for Tokyo No 1 (single-member) district, could also run for the Tokyo regional bloc. Essentially, this was a device to protect the vested interests of those who had a firm base of support in the old multi-member districts, but who might well be squeezed out in the fewer and larger single-member districts. They were given a second chance by being allowed also to stand for election in their regional bloc. In the 1996 elections 566 out of 1,503 candidates stood for both types of constituency.

But this was not the end of the story. Using a device of stunning originality, it was made possible for a party to make its allocation of seats in a regional bloc dependent upon performance of its candidates in single-member constituencies. A party could number its candidates in order of precedence on its list of candidates for the bloc, in which case a party obtaining, say, six quotas would have candidates numbers one to six elected. But if it wished it could number candidates equal, or some of its candidates equal. In that case, that party's quotas would be allocated according to the percentage of the votes of the winning candidates (*seikihairitsu*) in single-member constituencies won by the candidates in contention. For instance, in the 1996 elections, the Democratic Party marked all of its candidates equal in the Kita Kantō bloc. The party received four quotas, and the candidates elected were those who won, respectively, 81.47 per cent, 77.11 per cent, 75.53 per cent and 71.11 per cent of the votes of the winning candidates in the single-member constituencies in which they also stood. Although we should not exaggerate the impact of this system, since not all parties made use of it, its effect was to mitigate the stark 'win or lose' alternatives in the single-member districts by making it possible for candidates coming second in those districts to win a seat. In this sense, it revived in a weaker form something of the 'multi-member' aspect of the old system.

We need to ask whether the new mixed system has fulfilled its principal aims of shifting the focus of elections away from personality and pork-barrel politics towards politics based on party and policy. Our tentative conclusion is that, although in the long term it may make a difference, it has failed to break the crucial *kōenkai* system at district level. Indeed, since candidates in single-member districts need to appeal to a larger number of voters than they did under the 'medium-sized' district system, the effect has been to force them to strengthen and expand their *kōenkai*, rather than to rely on party organisation. Clearly also, the single-member districts, as was widely predicted, have proved advantageous for the LDP. In the 1996 elections, the LDP won 169 out of 300 single-member seats, and in the 2000 elections 177. The results were much poorer in the PR seats: 70 out of 200 in 1996, 56 out of 180 in 2000. On the other hand, the strength of personality voting and candidate-oriented machines means that even small parties may survive in single-member districts if their candidates have strong local ties. For instance the only candidates of the recently formed Conservative Party that were elected in the 2000 elections were seven in single-member districts.

Another concern about the old system was the 'negative gerrymander'. The extent of this was reduced with the introduction of the new system. But in 1994 there were 255,273 electors on the role in the third constituency of Shimane, and 538,616 in the eighth district of Hokkaidō. The discrepancy was 2.14 times, and it has increased since.

It seems reasonable to conclude that the change in the election system has been much less radical in its effects than those who devised it expected.

House of Councillors electoral system

The HOUSE OF COUNCILLORS was set up as an elective second chamber, replacing the non-elective House of Peers, under the 1946 Constitution. The hope was that it would be functionally different from the more important House of Representatives. To that end, it was given a fixed term, so that half its members would be subject to re-election every three years, and the term of a member would thus be six years. Elections normally take place in July at three-year intervals, and the most recent Upper House election was in July 2001. On two occasions – 1980 and 1986 – elections for the two houses have taken place on the same day, and the first Upper House elections – those of 1947 – preceded elections for the Lower House by five days.

The House of Councillors election system has been modified at certain stages, but has not been completely redesigned as in the case of the House of Representatives in 1994. Until recently, the number of seats has hardly fluctuated, having been 250 between 1947 and 1972, when two extra seats were added for Okinawa, and the total rose to 252. Of these, 100 were elected from a constituency consisting of the whole of Japan, and the remaining 152 (previously 150) from districts coincident with the prefectures. Only half the seats were renewed in each election, meaning 50 in the national constituency and 76 (75) in the prefectural districts. This is represented on Table 6, showing two consecutive elections:

Prefectural districts elect a varying number

Table 6 Renewed seats in two consecutive elections

	Seats in national constituency	Seats in prefectural districts	Total
Election in year X	50	76	126
Election in year X+3	50	76	126
Total	100	152	252

of members, depending on population (though the 'negative gerrymander' remains severe). Until adjustments in the early 1990s, the distribution was that given in Table 7:

By the late 1980s malapportionment in the House of Councillors had reached extreme levels. In March 1989 there were 310,108 electors for one seat in Tottori, but 1,942,319 electors for one seat in Kanagawa. This was a discrepancy of 626 per cent. An adjustment was therefore made in the early 1990s. Two seats (per election) were taken away from Hokkaidō, and one each from Hyōgo and Fukuoka. One each was added to Miyagi, Saitama, Kanagawa and Gifu. In terms of the 'negative gerrymander', these measures were a palliative, but the drastic medicine applied to Hokkaidō seems hard to justify on population grounds. But the agenda has shifted to the aim of reducing the size of both houses. In time for the 2001 elections, the total number of seats in the prefectural districts was reduced from 76 to 73, and in the proportional representation (national) district from 50 to 48. Assuming that the same happens for the 2004 elections, the total number of seats in the Upper House will have been reduced from 252 to 242.

The most far-reaching revision to the House of Councillors electoral system took place in August 1982. Before that point, the national constituency elected 100 members, 50 in each election. The whole country was treated as a single district, each elector had a single vote, and the first 50 in terms of vote score were declared elected. This might be termed 'first-50-past-the-post'. This method meant that great importance was placed on name recognition, since an elector had to select one name from a list that in the 1980 Upper House elections (for instance) included 93 names. Though most successful candidates had party affiliation, it boosted a candidate's chances to have the backing of some major organisation, for instance a sports federation or a labour union. Moreover, a sprinkling of so-called 'talent candidates', such as television stars, were usually elected. The two top-scoring candidates in the 1980 national constituency were Ichikawa Fusae, a well-known woman campaigner against political corruption, and Aoshima Yukio, a television comedian. Both stood as Independents.

In 1982 the method of election to the national constituency was changed to the d'Hondt system of PR. Most significantly, it was no longer possible to stand as an Independent, since only party lists were recognised. But unlike PR in the House of Representatives from 1994, a single national constituency (now called the 'proportional representation constituency' [*hirei daihyō ku*]) was retained.

An important consequence of this reform was that the LDP came to perform much less

Table 7 Distribution of prefectural members

Prefectures	Seats renewed each election	Total seats
Hokkaidō, Tokyo	4	8
Aichi, Osaka, Hyōgo, Fukuoka	3	6
Fukushima, Ibaragi, Tochigi, Gunma, Saitama, Chiba, Kanagawa, Niigata, Nagano, Shizuoka, Kyōto, Okayama, Hiroshima, Kumamoto, Kagoshima	2	4
Aomori, Iwate, Miyagi, Akita, Yamagata, Toyama, Ishikawa, Fukui, Yamanashi, Gifu, Mie, Shiga, Nara, Wakayama, Tottori, Shimane, Yamaguchi, Tokushima, Kagawa, Ehime, Kōchi, Saga, Nagasaki, Oita, Miyazaki, Okinawa	1	2

well in the PR constituency than in prefectural districts, where local ties and personality were important. Many electors seem to have been turned off by having to vote for Liberal Democrats in a party list, rather than for an individual candidate. In the 1983 elections, the first held under the new system, the LDP won 43.24 per cent of the vote in the prefectural districts, but only 35.33 per cent in the PR constituency.

Not surprisingly, the LDP came to dislike the PR element in Upper House elections, and in time for the July 2001 elections it was made possible for the elector to indicate a preference for an individual as well as for a party, in the PR constituency. In some cases, this led to one individual candidate attracting a very high proportion of the individual votes cast for candidates of a given party. In the case of the LDP in 2001, Masuzoe Yōichi won 25.7 per cent of the LDP personal vote, and his nearest LDP competitor a mere 7.7 per cent. The well-known woman leading the small CONSERVATIVE PARTY, Ogi Chikage, received 91.7 per cent of the personal votes cast for candidates of that party. The ratio between votes for parties and votes for individual candidates of those parties is given in the table below. It may be noted in particular that the JAPAN COMMUNIST PARTY, which places party before personality, had few individual votes. By contrast the CLEAN GOVERNMENT PARTY (Kōmeitō) had a high proportion of individual votes, and 99.4 per cent of those votes went to candidates who were elected, the distribution of votes between them being extraordinarily even. In other words, that party exercised a remarkable degree of discipline over the voting behaviour of its supporters, instructing all its known voters to vote for specific candidates.

Conclusions

The first general elections in Japan were held in 1890. Even though the pre-war political system was hardly democratic, elections were regularly held. Since the war there have been 21 national elections for the House of Representatives and 19 for the House of Councillors. This represents an accumulation of experience in running elections that matches that of European democracies. There has been a good deal of experimentation with election systems, and political interests have often affected the resultant arrangements. Perhaps the gravest flaw has been the failure adequately to correct malapportionment, and, plainly, political interests are to blame here, if only in a negative sense. The systems that have been introduced have typically been mixed systems, rather than pure British-type, or conversely PR, systems. This reflects a persistent theme of political practice in Japan, namely whether politics should be based on personality or on party. Because of the salience of this issue, and the complexity of it in the Japanese context, we should beware of making easy extrapolations from European experience to the understand-

Table 8 Votes for party and votes for candidates, House of Councillors PR constituency, July 2001 elections

Party	Votes for the party	Votes for candidates
Liberal Democratic Party	14,925,437	6,189,290
Democratic Party	6,082,694	2,907,830
Clean Government Party	1,865,797	6,322,007
Japan Communist Party	4,965,047	264,163
Liberal Party	3,642,884	584,264
Social Democratic Party	2,298,104	1,330,531
Conservative Party	609,382	665,620

Note: Parties failing to gain representation have been omitted.

ing of Japanese electoral systems and their relationship to political practice.

Further reading

Baerwald (1986)
Blaker (1976)
Christensen (2000)
Curtis (1971)
—— (1988)
—— (1999)
Ishikawa, in Jain and Inoguchi (1997)
Kohno (1997)
Mason (1969)
Quigley and Turner (1956)
Stockwin (1999)

electoral behaviour, campaigning and the control of malpractice Any system of regular democratic elections creates a set of inter-relationships between candidates and those who elect them – the electorate. The nature of these relationships will depend on many factors, cultural, institutional, historical and political. A culturally homogeneous electorate will tend to vote differently from one riven by ethnic, religious or linguistic divisions. An electorate where the electoral law keeps a tight control over campaign expenditure may vote with different considerations in mind from one where control is lax. More subtly, when the act of voting is seen as the individual's democratic right, behaviour is likely to differ from when it is seen as a duty owed to the State. Where the electorate has experience of elections going back for many decades, electors may well vote more predictably than where electoral experience is shallow. The electorate will also no doubt be influenced by the political landscape at the time of a particular election. Where there is a clear choice between, say, two cohesive parties with clearly differentiated platforms, electors will behave differently from a multi-party situation where parties frequently split and reform, and their platforms are not clearly distinguished. A political culture that favours local notabilities with loose party ties will create different voting behaviour from one that privileges centrally organised parties with clear policy platforms.

Japan has experience of elections and electoral campaigning going back to 1890. Even though Parliament in the pre-war period had limited powers, regular elections were held and some parties developed sophisticated organisation. Hara Kei was the first to diffuse local branches of his party (the *Seiyūkai*) throughout the country. These were based on local notabilities, each with his own personal vote-gathering machine. In the late nineteenth century and at the start of the twentieth, candidates had useful tricks up their sleeves to persuade the voters to vote for them. For instance, a day or two before the election, a candidate might spread a rumour that his rival had died. Without electronic means of communication, this would be difficult to refute in time.

After 1945 the electoral process was made a much more central part of politics than it had been under the *ancien régime*. The size of the electorate was greatly increased with the granting of the vote to women and the reduction of the voting age from 25 to 20. There were now many more elections, given that the upper chamber was made elective, as were local assemblies and the posts of local executive (prefectural governors, mayors of cities, towns and villages). It seems reasonable to argue that an electoral culture had taken root in Japan fairly early in the post-war period. Turnout rates were at European levels. Over the history of the 'medium-sized' electoral system in the House of Representatives, average turnout rates were as follows:

Average of elections 1946–55: 73.43 per cent
Average of elections 1958–76: 72.76 per cent
Average of elections 1979–93: 70.41 per cent

Remarkably, however, turnout rates have been substantially higher in rural areas than in urban. In the Lower House elections of 1969, for instance, where the overall turnout was 68.51 per cent, the average turnout in the 21 districts classified as 'metropolitan' was 53.11 per cent, whereas in the 33 districts classified as 'rural' the average turnout was 71.55 per cent. The gap was very marked in the post-war period, and has declined somewhat since, no doubt reflecting the gradual urbanisation of formerly rural areas. Various explanations have been advanced for this difference, which is the reverse of British experience, for example. One is that in the remoter and more conservative parts of Japan, voting is regarded more as a duty than as a right. Another is that high turnout reflects the greater sense of local solidarity in rural areas than in urban. A third is that there may even be (or have been in the post-war period) an element of coercion by highly organised political machines able to put pressure on an electorate where face-to-face relationships are pervasive. A fourth is that it reflects a greater objective need to protect local interests in rural than in urban areas.

The question of turnout is not unconnected with the nature of campaigning, where rural-urban differences may also be detected. In a classic formulation (described by Ike in his 1957 book) the three requirements for winning elections are *jiban, kanban, kaban*.

Jiban literally means 'base', or 'base of support', but more specifically it can be regarded as a set of core supporters, who have to be cultivated at all opportunities. Electoral candidates in Japan are famous for their attendance at weddings, funerals and other occasions significant for their constituents, and these activities may be seen as part of the exercise of cultivating a *jiban* of supporters personally committed to the candidate. Significantly, this typically has little to do with either party or policy. The pre-war politician Inukai Tsuyoshi had what was termed an 'iron *jiban*' in Okayama. It was so firm and loyal that he scarcely needed to campaign. Thayer makes a distinction between 'vertical' and 'horizontal' *jiban*. When it is horizontal, it extends over the whole electoral district. Where it is vertical, it is concentrated in one part of the district, typically a particular town or set of villages, where the candidate has his roots and can most easily concentrate his base of support. A *jiban* that is horizontal may be regarded as more modern than one that is vertical.

Kanban literally means 'billboard', but it connotes 'reputation'. This brings us back to the importance of local notabilities. Someone with status or prestige within a community, or with broader, even national, reputation, will have an advantage when standing as a candidate in elections. As in the case of *jiban*, a candidate may be better known in one part of an electoral district than in others, so that his *kanban* is concentrated rather than dispersed.

Kaban has the meaning of 'briefcase' or 'satchel', but it connotes financial expenditure. Money spent in electoral campaigns has been a highly controversial issue since the Occupation period. Stringent regulations concerning electoral expenditure have been widely ignored, and political finance has been a difficult area to research. Nevertheless, it is plain that far more has been spent in campaigns than permitted under the law. A tightening of the law in the 1990s has made this more difficult, but elections remain exceedingly expensive. Money is particularly important because of the expectation by the electors that their parliamentary representatives will be able to help them out in all sorts of practical situations, and will, for instance, pay for group excursions to Tokyo.

A classic study by Curtis of the campaign of a candidate in a semi-rural district of Oita Prefecture in the 1967 elections for the HOUSE OF REPRESENTATIVES demonstrated the emerging importance of the *kōenkai* (personal support groups) in elections. These are essentially extensions of *jiban*, but they manifest a degree of corporate identity lacking in most *jiban*. They are, in effect, formal associations of the supporters of a candidate. It is up to the candidate, not to the party or faction, to create and cultivate a *kōenkai*. Its effectiveness is shown by the fact that, since Curtis wrote, it has become nearly universal as an instrument of campaigning among candidates for the mainstream parties, especially the LIBERAL DEMOCRATIC PARTY (LDP). It typically consists of the candidate's family connections, school and university friends, business associates and representatives of local interest groups. As an institution, it has survived the abolition of multi-member districts that occurred in 1994. Since there are more electors to cultivate in single-member districts, *kōenkai* have become bigger rather than giving way to campaigning based on party.

Once a *kōenkai* has been created, the candidate must continue to cultivate it, even after he or she has been elected to Parliament. Many *kōenkai*, however, enjoy a long life. This means that the easiest way to have an effective *kōenkai* is to inherit one. The extent of this practice is extraordinary. Of LDP candidates elected at the Lower House elections of October 1996, 37 per cent had taken over their *kōenkai* from a relative (typically father). In addition, a substantial number of secretaries of former parliamentarians had 'inherited' their *kōenkai* from their former employer. Indeed, the organisational structure centred on a parliamentarian is similar to that of a family firm – a pattern that may be observed elsewhere in Japanese society, for instance among Shinto priests, traditional craftsmen, or dentists. There is some evidence that sons of parliamentarians feel constrained to 'take over the family firm'. 'Inheritance', however, is much less widespread in other parties and almost absent in the parties of the left.

It should not be assumed from the above that in Japanese elections votes are cast entirely on the basis of local loyalties and personality. As Flanagan and his co-authors argue in their study of the 1976 Lower House elections, party identification and image also play an important part. Indeed, they argue that since most electors have more ready access through the media to information about PARTIES and party leadership than to the activities of their local candidates, they may well have a clearer impression of party than of candidate. So many variables are involved, however, that it is difficult to be sure how far electors vote on the basis of party and how far on the basis of candidate image and identification. Increased volatility of electoral behaviour since the 1980s might suggest that the trend is towards greater emphasis on party, but, since the near-collapse of the Socialists in the 1990s, surviving parties have become hard to distinguish from each other. This has gone along with declining voting turnout rates, suggesting, perhaps, that electors, lacking a real policy choice, have switched their attention away from parties.

Controlling electoral practice has been the main purpose of the electoral laws. From a European perspective the Public Offices Election Law (*Kōshoku senkyo hō*) appears unduly to restrict contact between the candidate and the elector. For instance, door-to-door canvassing is strictly prohibited during the election campaign, though in practice there are ways of getting round this ban. (The HOSOKAWA Government tried, but failed, to remove the ban.) The campaign period has been repeatedly shortened, and is now a few days over a week. Strict limits are imposed on the quantity of promotional literature that a candidate may distribute, and on the amount of entertainment (meals etc.) that may be provided within the electorate. The use of television in election campaigns has increased, but is subject to clear legal limits. An interesting recent development is the use of e-mail and the Internet in campaigning. Campaign expenditure has to be reported, with a low upper limit that led to massive under-reporting.

In 1994, coincident with the change in the Lower House electoral system, changes in the law on election campaigning were introduced. There were three main changes: the introduction of public financing of political parties, tightened restrictions on political donations, and the principle of complicity (*renzasei*), whereby a candidate could be prosecuted as the result of a misdemeanour committed by a member of his staff or his family.

After much debate, public financing was introduced at the level of ¥150 per head of population, with the provision that it should not account for more than two-thirds of a party's total income. For a party to be eligible for such funding, it had to have at least five members of Parliament or to have received at least 2 per cent of the total valid vote. Politicians had been able to maintain several different funding organisations and thus evade the legal limits on contributions. This loophole was closed by a provision that donor organisations could only contribute funds (up to a stated limit) to one financial control body representing a party, political funding body or politician. Finally, the complicity provision included the penalty of suspension of civil rights for both donor and, crucially, receiver. To deprive a candidate of the right to stand for election over a period of years was deemed a better deterrent than a fine that could be treated as 'campaign expenses'.

Although substantial numbers of cases involving alleged violations of the electoral law were brought following most elections, the tightening of the law in 1994 has clearly made it more difficult to evade the law – particularly concerning campaign contributions. Nevertheless, there is anecdotal evidence that much more money is still spent on campaigning than is allowed under the law.

There is much argument about how far cultural factors affect electoral behaviour and the nature of campaigning. In practice, it is difficult to distinguish clearly between the cultural and the institutional, while the balance between them has been gradually changing. We shall probably never reach a satisfactory answer to the question how far cultural values of deference to authority and to the group affect voting behaviour, and how far the same outcomes can be explained in terms of rational considerations of interest by the voter (or non-voter). Cultural norms are undoubtedly involved, but so are institutional arrangements, historical memory and the vagaries of contemporary politics.

Further reading
Bestor (1989)
Curtis (1971)
Flanagan *et al*. (1991)
Ike (1957)
Reed (forthcoming, 2003)
Stockwin (1999)
Thayer (1969)

electoral history, House of Councillors
Whereas the HOUSE OF REPRESENTATIVES has a history going back to 1890, the HOUSE OF COUNCILLORS was set up as an elective second chamber under the terms of the 1946 Constitution. It replaced the House of Peers, which had been a non-elective chamber. It was hoped that the House of Councillors would be less dominated by party than the House of Representatives, and that it would take a more measured and reflective view of political issues. To this end elected members were given a fixed term of three years, with half the seats being renewed every three years. The system of election was also quite different from that of the Lower House. Out of 250 seats (252 after the reversion of Okinawa in 1972), 150 (152 from 1972) were elected from constituencies coincident with the prefectures, and the remaining 100 from a national constituency. Until 1982 the national constituency members were elected according to the principle of 'first-50-past-the-post', but after 1982 according to the d'Hondt system of proportional representation.

The first elections for the House of Councillors were held on 20 April 1947. All 250 seats were subject to election. No less than 44 per cent of those elected were standing as Independents.

In the 1947 elections, half of those elected were given a full six-year term, and the remaining 125 were elected for three years. It was seats in this latter category that had to be renewed in 1950. In these elections, the number of Independents elected was drastically reduced. Moreover, only three of those elected as Independents in 1947 for a six-year term were still categorised as Independents in 1950. The rest were now affiliated with parties. On

Table 9 House of Councillors elections, 20 April 1947

Party	Prefectural districts	National constituency	Total
Japan Socialist Party (*Nihon Shakaitō*)	30	17	47
Liberal Party (*Jiyūtō*)	30	8	38
Democratic Party (*Minshutō*)	24	6	30
National Co-operative Party (*Kokumin Kyōdōtō*)	6	3	9
Japan Communist Party (*Nihon Kyōsantō*)	1	3	4
Independents	53	58	111
Others	6	5	11
Total	150	100	250

the other hand the Green Breeze Society, which became prominent in the 1950s, was a loose grouping of Upper House conservatives rather than a party in the true sense. (See Table 10.)

The six-year term of those elected in the first elections for the House of Councillors in April 1947 was completed in 1953, and elections held on 24 April. YOSHIDA's Liberal Party was still the strongest party, but with some loss of seats. The Socialists were at this stage divided into two parties, one of the left and one of the right. The numbers of Independents had once again increased, and the Green Breeze Society had consolidated its position. Independent-minded parliamentarians were thus numerically significant in the Upper House at this period. The Communists and Labour Farmer Party (extreme left) ran candidates but won no seats. (See Table 11.)

In October–November 1955, first the left wing, then the right wing, consolidated their forces into the JAPAN SOCIALIST PARTY (JSP) and LIBERAL DEMOCRATIC PARTY (LDP), respectively. For a while, Japan appeared to have a two-party system, and this was reflected in the results of the House of Councillors elections as well as in the Lower House. Correspondingly, Independents and Green Breeze Society members were reduced. The Communists once more gained some representation. The LDP came close to obtaining an absolute majority of Upper House seats. The date of the

Table 10 House of Councillors elections, 4 June 1950

Party	Prefectural districts	National constituency	Total
Liberal Party	34	18	52
Japan Socialist Party	21	15	36
Democratic Party	8	1	9
Green Breeze Party (Ryokufūkai)	3	6	9
Agricultural Co-operatives (Nōkyō)	2	1	3
Japan Communist Party	0	2	2
Labour Farmer Party (Rōnōtō)	1	1	2
Independents	7	12	19
Total*	76	56	132

Note: *Totals include the filling of seven vacancies among seats allocated for a six-year term.

Table 11 House of Councillors elections, 24 April 1953

Party	Prefectural districts	National constituency	Total
Liberal Party	30	16	46
Left Socialist Party (Saha Nihon Shakaitō)	10	8	18
Green Breeze Society	8	8	16
Right Socialist Party (Uha Nihon Shakaitō)	7	3	10
Reformist Party (Kaishintō)	5	3	8
Independents	15	15	30
Total	75	53*	128*

Note: *Includes filling of three vacancies.

election moved to June–July, where it was to stay in future years. (See Table 12.)

The 1959 House of Councillors elections consolidated the LDP lead over the JSP, but also demonstrated two-party dominance over all other candidates. (See Table 13.)

Despite the upheaval of the Security Treaty revision crisis in 1960, the results of the House of Councillors elections in 1962 showed very little change from those of 1959, the main differences being the appearance of the DEMOCRATIC SOCIALIST PARTY (DSP) and a slight increase in Communist seats. (See Table 14.)

The principal development in the 1965 House of Councillors elections was the emergence of the CLEAN GOVERNMENT PARTY (CGP, Kōmeitō), formed the previous year. In fact, the Sōka Gakkai, parent body of the CGP, had run a few candidates in Upper House elections since 1956, under the euphemism of 'Independent'. Now, however, they emerged under their own label, and were clearly a force to be reckoned with. As before, they had a clear majority, and nearly twice as many seats as the JSP, their closest rivals. The Green Breeze Society had now disappeared. (See Table 15.)

The 1968 elections did not mark significant change, except that the Socialists lost a number of seats and the CGP and DSP made some progress. This was the high economic growth and Vietnam War period, when the Socialists had moved sharply to the left, against the electoral trend. (See Table 16.)

Table 12 House of Councillors elections, 8 July 1956

Party	Prefectural districts	National constituency	Total (grand tot.)
Liberal Democratic Party (*Jimintō*)	42	19	61 (122)
Japan Socialist Party	28	21	49 (80)
Green Breeze Society	0	5	5 (31)
Japan Communist Party	1	1	2 (2)
Others	0	1	1 (1)
Independents	4	5	9 (14)
Total	75	52*	127* (250)

Note: *Includes filling of two vacancies.

Table 13 House of Councillors elections, 2 June 1959

Party	Prefectural districts	National constituency	Total (grand tot.)
Liberal Democratic Party	49	22	71 (132)
Japan Socialist Party	21	17	38 (87)
Green Breeze Society	2	4	6 (11)
Japan Communist Party	0	1	1 (3)
Independents	3	7	10 (16)
Others	0	1	1 (1)
Total	75	52*	127* (250)

Note: *Includes filling of two vacancies.

Table 14 House of Councillors elections, 1 July 1962

Party	Prefectural districts	National constituency	Total (grand tot.)
Liberal Democratic Party	48	21	69 (140)
Japan Socialist Party	22	15	37 (75)
Democratic Socialist Party (Minshatō)	1	3	4 (4)
Japan Communist Party	1	2	3 (4)
Association of Friends (Dōshikai) = Green Breeze Society		2	2 (8)
Independents	4	8	12 (21)
Total	76*	51*	127* (250)

Note: *Includes filling of two vacancies.

Table 15 House of Councillors elections, 15 July 1965

Party	Prefectural districts	National constituency	Total (grand tot.)
Liberal Democratic Party	46	25	71 (140)
Japan Socialist Party	24	12	36 (73)
Clean Government Party	2	9	11 (20)
Democratic Socialist Party	1	2	3 (7)
Japan Communist Party	1	2	3 (4)
Independents	1	2	3 (5)
Total	75	52*	127* (250)

Note: *Includes filling of two vacancies.

Table 16 House of Councillors elections, 13 June 1968

Party	Prefectural districts	National constituency	Total (grand tot.)
Liberal Democratic Party	48	21	69 (140)
Japan Socialist Party	16	12	28 (64)
Clean Government Party	4	9	13 (24)
Democratic Socialist Party	3	4	7 (10)
Japan Communist Party	1	3	4 (7)
Independents	3	2	5 (8)
Total	75	51*	126* (250)

Note: *Includes filling of one vacancy.

The 1971 House of Councillors elections reflected changed priorities within the electorate. The negative, rather than positive, aspects of the economic 'miracle' were becoming apparent in the shape of environmental degradation, poor quality of life and inadequate welfare provision. This was the period of 'progressive local authorities' (*kakushin jichitai*) of left-wing orientation. The Liberal Democrats lost seats and the Socialists (also the Communists) improved their position. (See Table 17.)

The return of Okinawa from US administration in 1972 added two extra seats to the Upper House prefectural districts (*see* OKINAWA IN JAPANESE POLITICS), as well as adding the Okinawan electorate to the voting roll for the national constituency. The 1974 elections were held a few months after the effects of the first oil crisis had been felt in the shape of inflationary pressure and the hoarding of goods by companies. Rumours of political corruption were also rife. In these circumstances, the LDP lost seats, holding a bare majority in the house. The JSP, however, also did badly, and the advantage was taken by the CGP and the JCP, which increased their representation. (See Table 18.)

The 1977 elections did not create any great change in vote distribution, although the NEW LIBERAL CLUB, a small splinter from the LDP, formed in 1976 in protest against the LOCKHEED SCANDAL, won three seats. The Communist resurgence of 1974 was not sustained. (See Table 19.)

The 1980 House of Councillors elections took place, for the first time in Japan's electoral history, on the same day as elections for the House of Representatives. The electorate

Table 17 House of Councillors elections, 27 June 1971

Party	Prefectural districts	National constituency	Total (grand tot.)
Liberal Democratic Party	42	21	63 (132)
Japan Socialist Party	28	11	39 (67)
Clean Government Party	2	8	10 (23)
Democratic Socialist Party	2	4	6 (13)
Japan Communist Party	1	5	6 (10)
Independents	1	1	2 (7)
Total	76*	50	126* (250)

Note: *Includes filling one vacancy.

Table 18 House of Councillors elections, 7 July 1974

Party	Prefectural districts	National constituency	Total (grand tot.)
Liberal Democratic Party	46	16	62 (125)
Japan Socialist Party	18	11	29 (68)
Clean Government Party	5	9	14 (24)
Japan Communist Party	5	6	11 (17)
Democratic Socialist Party	1	4	5 (11)
Independents	1	3	4 (6)
Total	76	49	125 (252)

was shocked by the death of the Prime Minister, OHIRA MASAYOSHI, during the electoral campaign, after he had been defeated in a no-confidence motion because of LDP factional abstentions. These two factors led to a higher than usual turnout, and a sympathy vote for the LDP. The JSP vote was adversely affected by the defection of a small splinter group in 1977, which had led to the formation of the SOCIAL DEMOCRATIC LEAGUE. (See Table 20.)

In 1982 the national constituency became a constituency elected, no longer by 'first-50-past-the-post', but by the d'Hondt method of proportional representation (PR). It came to be known as the 'proportional representation constituency', but this did not indicate a boundary change, since the boundaries remained those of the State. It soon became evident that the change did not favour the LDP, since electors were more reluctant to vote

Table 19 House of Councillors elections, 10 July 1977

Party	Prefectural districts	National constituency	Total (grand tot.)
Liberal Democratic Party	45	18	63 (125)
Japan Socialist Party	17	10	27 (56)
Clean Government Party	5	9	14 (28)
Japan Communist Party	2	3	5 (16)
Democratic Socialist Party	2	4	6 (11)
New Liberal Club	2	1	3 (3)
Others (*Shashiren, Kakujiren*)	1	2	3 (3)
Independents	2	3	5 (9)
Total	76	50	126 (251)*

Note: *One vacancy.

Table 20 House of Councillors elections, 22 June 1980

Party	Prefectural districts	National constituency	Total (grand tot.)
Liberal Democratic Party	48	21	69 (132)
Japan Socialist Party	13	9	22 (49)
Clean Government Party	3	9	12 (26)
Japan Communist Party	4	3	7 (12)
Democratic Socialist Party	2	3	5 (11)
New Liberal Club	0	0	0 (3)
Social Democratic League (*Shaminren*)	0	1	1 (3)
Others	1	1	2 (2)
Independents	5	3	8 (13)
Total	76	50	126 (251)*

Note: *One vacancy.

for a party list than for individual candidates. This begins to become evident in the 1983 elections, where the LDP vote was only 35.33 per cent in the PR constituency. Another result of the change was the ability of some mini-parties to win seats. (See Table 21.)

The general elections held on 6 July 1986 were, like those of 1980, simultaneous elections for both houses, held on the same day. This was the zenith of NAKASONE's tenure as Prime Minister; the LDP did well, and the JSP performed badly. The proliferation of mini-parties precipitated by the introduction of PR continued. (See Table 22.)

Table 21 House of Councillors elections, 26 June 1983

Party	Prefectural districts	PR constituency	Total (grand tot.)
Liberal Democratic Party	51	19	70 (139)
Japan Socialist Party	13	9	22 (44)
Clean Government Party	5	8	13 (25)
Japan Communist Party	2	5	7 (14)
Democratic Socialist Party	1	4	5 (10)
Salary Man New Party (*Sarariman Shintō*)		2	2 (2)
Welfare Party (*Fukushi tō*)		1	1 (1)
New Liberal Club Democratic League (*Shin Jiyū Club Minshu Rengō*)	1	1	2 (3)
Second Chamber Club (*Niin Club*)		1	1 (1)
Others	2		2 (4)
Independents	1		1 (9)
Total	76	50	126 (252)

Table 22 House of Councillors elections, 6 July 1986

Party	Prefectural districts	PR constituency	Total (grand tot.)
Liberal Democratic Party	50	22	72 (142)
Japan Socialist Party	11	9	20 (42)
Clean Government Party	3	7	10 (23)
Japan Communist Party	4	5	9 (16)
Democratic Socialist Party	2	3	5 (10)
New Liberal Club	–	1	1 (3)
Social Democratic League	–	–	– (1)
Second Chamber Club	–	1	1 (2)
Salary Man New Party	–	1	1 (3)
Taxpayers' Party (*Zeikintō*)	–	1	1 (1)
Independents	6	–	6 (7)
Total	76	50	126 (252)

Considering the overwhelming superiority of the LDP over a fragmented opposition in the 1986 Upper House elections, the severe LDP reverse in the elections of 1989 was a great surprise. A series of events in 1988–9, most notably the RECRUIT SCANDAL, the imposition of consumption tax and the lifting of tariff protection on beef and citrus products, combined with the popularity of the JSP Chair, DOI TAKAKO (the first woman to head a Japanese political party), created a massive shift of votes from the LDP to the JSP. In the 26 prefectural districts that in each election only returned one member, an LDP majority of 24 seats out of the 26 was converted into a JSP/*Rengō* majority of 23 out of the 26. Since these seats were largely away from the big cities, it indicated a massive, if temporary, rural disillusionment with the LDP. Most significantly, even though the Socialist success proved short-lived, the LDP lost its Upper House majority for the long term. (See Table 23.)

The 1992 elections were held in the aftermath of the Gulf War, and not long before the events that preceded the fall from office of the LDP in August 1993. The first sign of this had already appeared, in the shape of the JAPAN NEW PARTY (*Nihon Shintō*), founded by HOSOKAWA MORIHIRO, the future Prime Minister, which contested the 1992 Upper House elections. JSP successes three years earlier were not sustained, and nor were those of the Japanese Trade Union Council (*Rengō*). By contrast, the LDP had recovered to about its normal strength, but, since only half the seats are re-elected in each election, it remained substantially below a majority in the House of Councillors. (See Table 24.)

The interval between the 1992 and 1995 Upper House elections brought dramatic events in Japanese politics. First, the LDP split, allowing a coalition Government, excluding the LDP, to take over in August 1993, but in June 1994 the LDP was back in power, in coalition with the JSP and the recently formed NEW PARTY HARBINGER (NPH, *Sakigake*), under a Socialist Prime Minister. New parties came and went, but the most significant piece of party formation was that of the NEW FRONTIER PARTY (NFP, *Shinshintō*) in December 1994, absorbing the parties of the Hosokawa coalition except for the Socialists and the

Table 23 House of Councillors elections, 23 July 1989

Party	Prefectural districts	PR constituency	Total (grand tot.)
Liberal Democratic Party	21	15	36 (109)
Japan Socialist Party	26	20	46 (66)
Clean Government Party	4	6	10 (20)
Japan Communist Party	1	4	5 (14)
Japanese Trade Union Council (*Rengō*)	11	–	11 (12)
Democratic Socialist Party	1	2	3 (8)
Taxation Party	1	1	2 (3)
Second Chamber Club	–	1	1 (2)
Salary Man New Party	0	0	0 (1)
Sports Peace Party (*Supōtsu Heiwatō*)	0	1	1 (1)
Others	1	0	1 (1)
Independents	10	0	10 (15)
Total	76	50	126 (252)

NPH. As the results of the 1995 elections showed, the LDP was much weakened by splits and defections, even though it remained the single largest party. Between the 1992 and 1995 elections there was an adjustment of seats in the prefectural districts [see also election systems]. (See Table 25.)

By 1998 the New Frontier Party had broken up, and various new parties had been formed, most notably the Democratic Party (now the second largest party after the LDP), and the Liberal Party (the hard core supporters of Ozawa Ichirō). The LDP was still far short of a majority, and the JSP (now called the Social Democratic Party, or SDP) was reduced to minor party status. The Clean Government Party, having extracted itself from the defunct NFP, had been revived. New minor parties had come and gone, like bamboo shoots after rain. The country was in the grip of a recession associated with the 'Asian economic crisis'. (See Table 26.)

The July 2001 elections were held soon after the election of Koizumi Junichirō as LDP President and Prime Minister. The great popularity that he enjoyed after his election helped the LDP to increase the number of its seats, though they remained well short of a majority. Another factor that may have helped the performance of the LDP was a change in the election law enabling voters to express preference for particular candidates in the PR constituency, not just their preference for a party. Since the 1998 elections, the number of seats in the House of Councillors had been reduced by five. Among the prefectural districts, Okayama, Kumamoto and Kagoshima had lost one seat each, meaning that in each three-yearly election they returned one member, not two, and two seats had been shaved from the PR constituency for each election [see also election systems]. (See Table 27.)

When we survey the House of Councillors elections between 1947 and 2001, we find four points of particular significance. First, the dominance of the LDP, unchallenged until the late 1980s, has fallen short of an absolute majority since its defeat in 1989. This has had profound effects on the development of Japanese politics, because of the veto powers of the Upper House. Second, non-LDP parties have proliferated since the 1950s, with an acceleration of that process since the early 1990s. This has greatly weakened the opposition to the LDP in the Upper House, despite its loss of an absolute majority. And, third, the PR constituency is less LDP-friendly than the prefectural districts, confirming once again

Table 24 House of Councillors elections, 26 July 1992

Party	Prefectural districts	PR constituency	Total (grand tot.)
Liberal Democratic Party	50	19	69 (108)
Japan Socialist Party	12	10	22 (71)
Clean Government Party	6	8	14 (24)
Japanese Trade Union Council	0	–	0 (12)
Japan Communist Party	2	4	6 (11)
Democratic Socialist Party	1	3	4 (7)
Japan New Party	–	4	4 (4)
Sports Peace Party	–	1	1 (2)
Second Chamber Club	–	1	1 (2)
Social Democratic League	–	0	0 (1)
Others	2	0	2 (3)
Independents	4	–	4 (7)
Total	77	50	127 (252)

Table 25 House of Councillors elections, 23 July 1995

Party	Prefectural districts	PR constituency	Total (grand tot.)
Liberal Democratic Party	31	15	46 (107)
New Frontier Party (Shinshintō)	22	18	40 (56)
Japan Socialist Party	7	9	16 (38)
Japan Communist Party	3	5	8 (14)
Clean Government Party*	–	–	– (12)
New Party Harbinger	1	2	3 (3)
Second Chamber Club	0	1	1 (2)
Peace Citizens' Party (Heiwa Shimintō)	1	0	1 (2)
Democratic Reform League (Minkairen) (formerly Japanese Trade Union Council – Rengō)	2	–	2 (2)
Sports Peace Party	–	0	0 (1)
Others	0	0	0 (1)
Independents	9	–	9 (15)
Total	76	50	126 (252)

Note: *Although the CGP had formally merged into the NFP, part of its Upper House contingent maintained a semi-separate existence under the name Kōmei.

Table 26 House of Councillors elections, 12 July 1998

Party	Prefectural districts	PR constituency	Total (grand tot.)
Liberal Democratic Party	30	14	44 (102)
Democratic Party	15	12	27 (47)
Japan Communist Party	7	8	15 (23)
Clean Government Party	2	7	9 (22)
Social Democratic Party (Shakai Minshutō, Shamintō), formerly Japan Socialist Party	1	4	5 (13)
Liberal Party (Jiyūtō)	1	5	6 (12)
Reform Club (Kaikaku Club)	–	0	0 (3)
New Party Harbinger	–	0	0 (3)
Second Chamber Club	–	0	0 (1)
Independents	20	–	20 (26)
Total	76	50	126 (252)

Table 27 House of Councillors elections, 29 July 2001

Party	Prefectural districts	PR constituency	Total (grand tot.)
Liberal Democratic Party	45	20	65 (111)
Democratic Party	18	8	26 (59)
Clean Government Party	5	8	13 (23)
Japan Communist Party	1	4	5 (20)
Liberal Party	2	4	6 (8)
Social Democratic Party	0	3	3 (8)
Independent Association (*Mushozoku no kai*)	–	0	0 (4)
Conservative Party	0	1	1 (5)
New Party Harbinger	–	–	– (1)
Second Chamber Club	–	0	0 (1)
Independents	2	–	3 (7)
Total	73	48	121 (247)

that conservative politics flourishes better on personality politics than on appeals based simply on party. Fourth, despite palliative remedies, the prefectural districts remain heavily weighted towards the rural vote and against the less conservative big-city vote.

Note: The statistics have been compiled using the following sources:

Asahi Nenkan (Asahi Yearbook), various years.
Asahi Shinbun (Asahi Newspaper), various dates.
Yomiuri Nenkan (Yomiuri Yearbook), 2002.

Because of changes of affiliation etc., between elections, some figures may be subject to interpretation and there are minor discrepancies between individual figures and totals.

electoral history, House of Representatives
The purpose of this entry is to give an annotated set of data concerning Lower House elections since 1946. We shall divide the 21 elections that have taken place between 1946 and 2000 into four periods, viz.:

Period 1	1946–55 (6 elections)
Period 2	1958–76 (7 elections)
Period 3	1979–93 (6 elections)
Period 4	1996–2000 (2 elections)

The divisions are not entirely arbitrary. Period 1 covers the democratic reforms that followed the defeat, and the unstable multi-party politics that preceded the reunification of the Socialists into the JAPAN SOCIALIST PARTY (JSP) in October 1955 and the formation of the LIBERAL DEMOCRATIC PARTY (LDP) the following month. Period 2 is essentially the period of the economic 'miracle', when the Liberal Democrats were consolidating their power and attempting to respond to new interests in the electorate, but nevertheless gradually losing votes. Period 3 saw greater electoral volatility, with the LDP doing extremely well in some elections and poorly in others. It ends with power temporarily shifting out of the LDP's hands. Period 4 consists of two elections conducted under the new electoral system, and is a time when LDP monopoly of power has given way to dominance within shifting coalition governments.

Period 1 (1946–55)

The political conditions in this period were full of change and turbulence. It is hardly surprising that party politics was fluid and unstable. But by 1955 the parameters of a more stable system were beginning to be evident.

The April 1946 elections were conducted under the 'large' electoral system (*daisenkyo-*

kusei), with districts electing between four and 14 members. This was the first election in which women had been granted the vote, the age of suffrage had been reduced from 25 to 20, and the age of candidacy from 30 to 25. A total of 2,770 candidates stood for election, nearly twice as many as in any subsequent election, and 39 women were elected, a figure that was to fall below ten in most later elections. Literally hundreds of parties, some of them local, ran candidates. Many Independents and minor party candidates were elected. The elections a year later were held under the 'medium-sized' district system, as were all elections up to and including that of 1993. Three parties, Socialists, Liberals and Democrats (in that order), dominated the results, leading to the KATAYAMA coalition Government in which the Socialists were the largest party. The relative failure of this and its successor ASHIDA coalition Cabinet led to a victory by YOSHIDA's Democratic Liberals in the elections of January 1949, and a severe defeat for the Socialists. The elections of 1952, 1953 and 1955 saw complex manœuvrings by different conservative leaders (principally Yoshida and HATOYAMA) and frequent changes of party name and composition. Meanwhile the Socialists – who split into a right-wing party and a left-wing party over the peace settlement in 1952 – were gradually gaining electoral ground, and had 156 Lower House members when they reunited in October 1955. It was the Socialist strength in numbers that persuaded conservative forces to form the Liberal Democratic Party in November [*see also* conservative parties, 1945–55]. (See Table 28.)

Period 2 (1958–76)

Party politics became much simpler at the outset of this period, because of the creation in 1955 of two major parties, the LDP and the JSP. In the 1958 elections, only 14 seats were not won by these two parties, and 12 of those were won by Independents (some of whom subsequently joined the major parties). From the beginning of the 1960s, however, the Socialists decline in strength. This is partly because of the split in that party and formation of the Democratic Socialist Party (DSP) in 1960, and partly because of the formation of the Clean Government Party (CGP) in 1964. An additional factor was the resurgence of the Japan Communist Party (JCP) from the late 1960s. All these parties eroded the big-city heartland of the JSP. But the LDP was also losing ground throughout the 1960s and into the 1970s, as new issues (welfare, environmental protection, quality of life) entered onto the political agenda and weakened the appeal of economic growth for its own sake. The 1976 elections were the low point of LDP performance since their formation in 1955, though this was partly because of a minor defection leading to the foundation of the New Liberal Club (NLC) in 1976. (See Table 29.)

Period 3 (1979–93)

This period was characterised by greater fluctuations in electoral outcomes than Period 2, but the most salient underlying trend was LDP recovery from its low point of the mid-1970s. Even though the 1979 and 1983 elections were disappointing for the LDP, the elections of 1980 and 1986 were spectacularly successful. Both of these were double elections, for both houses simultaneously, and it seems that the extra dynamism created by this innovation helped the chances of the LDP. The late 1980s, however, were a period of political turbulence, associated with political scandals, some unpopular policies and what came to be known as the 'bubble economy'. The JSP enjoyed a brief period of resurgence under its popular leader, Doi Takako, the first woman ever to lead a political party in Japan. In the 1990 elections the JSP did well, but the LDP also performed creditably. The elections of 1993 were preceded by the defection of groups led, respectively, by Ozawa Ichirō and Takemura Masayoshi, so that the LDP lost that election and had to cede power to the short-lived Hosokawa coalition. Socialist electoral successes proved ephemeral and the party lost many seats, many of them to new parties that had emerged. (See Table 30.)

Period 4 (1996–2000)

The formation of the Hosokawa multi-party coalition Government in August 1993 entailed

Table 28 Elections for the House of Representatives, 1946–55

	Seats (% of total seats) Votes [thousands] (% of total vote)					
	10/4/46	25/4/47	23/1/49	1/10/52	19/4/53	27/2/55
Progressive Party (Shinpotō)	94 (20.3) 10,351 (18.7)					
Democratic Party (Minshutō)		121 (26.0) 6,840 (25.0)	69 (14.8) 4,798 (15.7)			185 (39.6) 13,536 (36.6)
Reformist Party (Kaishintō)				85 (18.2) 6,429 (18.2)	76 (16.3) 6,186 (17.9)	
Liberal Party (Jiyūtō)	140 (30.2) 13,506 (24.4)	131 (28.1) 7,356 (26.9)		240 (51.5) 16,939 (47.9)		112 (24.0) 9,849 (26.6)
Democratic Liberal Party (Minshujiyūtō)			264 (56.7) 13,420 (43.9)			
Hatoyama Liberal Party (Jiyūtō Hatoyama-ha)					35 (7.5) 3,055 (8.8)	
Yoshida Liberal Party (Jiyūtō Yoshida-ha)					199 (42.7) 13,476 (39.0)	
Co-operative Party (Kyōdōtō)	14 (3.0) 1,800 (3.2)					
National Co-operative Party (Kokumin Kyōdōtō)		29 (6.2) 1,916 (7.0)	14 (3.0) 1,042 (3.4)			
Japan Socialist Party (Nihon Shakaitō)	92 (19.8) 9,858 (17.8)	143 (30.7) 7,176 (26.2)	48 (10.3) 4,130 (13.5)			

Table 28 continued

	Seats (% of total seats) Votes [thousands] (% of total vote)					
	10/4/46	25/4/47	23/1/49	1/10/52	19/4/53	27/2/55
Left Socialist Party (*Saha Nihon Shakaitō*)				54 (11.6) 3,399 (9.6)	72 (15.4) 4,517 (13.1)	89 (19.1) 5,683 (15.3)
Right Socialist Party (*Uha Nihon Shakaitō*)				57 (12.2) 4,108 (11.6)	66 (14.2) 4,678 (11.6)	67 (14.3) 5,130 (13.9)
Labour Farmer Party (*Rōnōtō*)			7 (1.5) 607 (2.0)	4 (0.9) 261 (0.7)	5 (1.1) 359 (3.0)	4 (0.9) 358 (1.0)
Japan Communist Party (*Nihon Kyōsantō*)	5 (1.1) 2,136 (3.8)	4 (0.8) 1,003 (3.7)	35 (7.5) 2,985 (9.7)	0 (0) 897 (2.6)	1 (0.2) 656 (1.9)	2 (0.4) 733 (2.0)
Independent	81 (17.4) 11,325 (20.4)	13 (2.8) 1,581 (5.8)	12 (2.6) 2.008 (6.6)	19 (4.1) 2,355 (6.7)	11 (2.4) 1,524 (4.4)	6 (1.3) 1,229 (3.3)
Others	38 (8.2) 6,473 (11.7)	25 (5.4) 1.490 (5.4)	17 (3.6) 1.602 (5.2)	7 (1.5) 949 (2.7)	1 (0.2) 152 (0.4)	2 (0.4) 497 (1.3)
Total	464 26,582	466 27,798	466 31,176	466 35,750	466 34,948	467 37,338
Turnout (%)	72.08	67.95	74.04	76.43	74.22	75.84

the exclusion of the LDP from power until late June 1994, when the LDP returned to office in a coalition with the JSP and the New Party Harbinger (NPH, *Sakigake*), under a Socialist Prime Minister, Murayama Tomiichi. During the 1993–4 period, a new Lower House electoral system was put in place, with 300 seats elected from single-member constituencies on the principle of first-past-the-post, and 200 seats elected from 11 regional blocs by the d'Hondt system of proportional representation.

The mid-1990s saw extraordinarily fluid party politics, but a major development was the formation of the New Frontier Party (NFP) in December 1994, as a putative alternative party of government. The high point for this party was the House of Councillors elections of July 1995, where the NFP did well, but thereafter it suffered a series of internal disputes and defections of parliamentarians.

The second event of particular electoral significance was the split in the JSP (now

Table 29 Elections for the House of Representatives, 1958–76

	Seats (% of total seats) Votes [thousands] (% of total vote)						
	22/5/58	20/11/60	21/11/63	29/1/67	27/12/69	10/12/72	5/12/76
Liberal Democratic Party (*Jimintō*)	287 (61.5) 22,977 (57.8)	296 (63.4) 22,740 (57.6)	283 (60.7) 22,424 (54.7)	277 (57.0) 22,448 (48.8)	288 (59.2) 22,382 (47.6)	271 (55.2) 24,563 (46.8)	249 (48.7) 23,654 (41.8)
New Liberal Club (*Shin Jiyū Club*)							17 (3.3) 2,364 (4.2)
Japan Socialist Party (*Nihon Shakaitō*)	166 (35.5) 13,094 (32.9)	145 (31.0) 10,887 (27.6)	144 (30.8) 11,907 (29.0)	140 (28.8) 12,826 (27.9)	90 (18.5) 10,074 (21.4)	118 (24.0) 11,479 (21.9)	123 (24.1) 11,713 (20.7)
Democratic Socialist Party (*Minshatō*)		17 (3.7) 3.464 (8.8)	23 (4.9) 3,023 (7.4)	30 (6.2) 3,404 (7.4)	31 (6.4) 3,637 (7.7)	19 (3.9) 3.661 (7.0)	29 (5.7) 3,554 (6.3)
Clean Government Party (*Kōmeitō*)				25 (5.1) 2,472 (5.4)	47 (9.7) 5,125 (10.9)	29 (5.9) 4,437 (8.5)	55 (10.8) 6,177 (10.9)
Japan Communist Party (*Nihon Kyōsantō*)	1 (0.2) 1,012 (2.6)	3 (0.6) 1,157 (2.9)	5 (1.1) 1,646 (4.0)	5 (1.0) 2,191 (4.8)	14 (2.9) 3.199 (6.8)	38 (7.7) 5,497 (10.5)	17 (3.3) 5,878 (10.4)
Independent	12 (2.6) 2,381 (6.0)	5 (1.1) 1,119 (2.8)	12 (2.6) 1,956 (4.8)	9 (1.9) 2,554 (5.5)	16 (3.3) 2,493 (5.3)	14 (2.9) 2,646 (5.0)	21 (4.1) 3.227 (5.7)
Others	1 (0.2) 288 (0.7)	1 (0.2) 142 (0.3)	0 (0) 60 (0.1)	0 (0) 101 (0.2)	0 (0) 81 (0.2)	2 (0.4) 143 (0.3)	0 (0) 45 (0.1)
Total	467	467	467	486	486	491	511
Turnout (%)	76.99	73.51	71.14	73.99	68.51	71.76	73.45

calling itself 'Social Democratic Party' [*Shakaiminshutō*]) and formation of the Democratic Party (*Minshutō*) in September 1996, a month before the October 1996 elections for the House of Representatives. The elections saw an improvement (short of a majority) in

Table 30 Elections for the House of Representatives, 1979–93

	Seats (% of total seats) Votes [thousands] (% of total vote)					
	7/10/79	22/6/80	18/12/83	6/7/86	18/2/90	18/7/93
Liberal Democratic Party	248 (48.6) 24,084 (44.6)	284 (55.6) 28,262 (47.9)	250 (48.9) 29,875 (45.8)	300 (58.6) 29,875 (49.4)	275 (53.7) 30,315 (46.1)	223 (43.6) 23,000 36.6
New Liberal Club	4 (0.7) 1,632 (3.0)	12 (2.3) 1,766 (3.0)	8 (1.6) 1,341 (2.4)	6 (1.2) 1,115 (1.8)		
Japan Socialist Party	107 (20.9) 10,643 (19.7)	107 (20.9) 11,401 (19.3)	112 (21.9) 11,065 (19.5)	85 (16.6) 10,412 (17.2)	136 (26.6) 16,025 (24.4)	70 (13.7) 9,687 (15.4)
Democratic Socialist Party	35 (6.3) 3,664 (6.8)	32 (6.3) 3,897 (6.6)	38 (7.4) 4,130 (7.3)	26 (5.1) 3,896 (6.4)	14 (2.7) 3,179 (4.8)	15 (2.9) 2,206 (3.5)
Clean Government Party	57 (11.2) 5,283 (9.8)	33 (6.5) 5,330 (9.0)	58 (11.3) 5,746 (10.1)	56 (10.9) 5,701 (9.4)	45 (8.8) 5,243 (8.0)	51 (10.0) 5,114 (8.1)
Japan Communist Party	39 (7.6) 5,626 (10.4)	29 (5.7) 5,804 (9.8)	26 (5.1) 5,302 (9.3)	16 (3.1) 5,313 (8.8)	16 (3.1) 5,227 (8.0)	15 (2.9) 4,835 (7.7)
Social Democratic League (Shaminren)		3 (0.5) 402 (0.7)	3 (0.6) 381 (0.7)	4 (0.8) 500 (0.8)	4 (0.8) 567 (0.9)	4 (0.8) 461 (0.7)
Japan Renewal Party (Shinseitō)						55 (10.8) 6,341 (10.1)
New Party Harbinger (Shintō Sakigake)						13 (2.5) 1,658 (2.6)
Japan New Party (Nihon Shintō)						35 (6.8) 5,054 (8.0)

Table 30 continued

	Seats (% of total seats) Votes [thousands] (% of total vote)					
	7/10/79	22/6/80	18/12/83	6/7/86	18/2/90	18/7/93
Japan New Party (*Nihon Shintō*)						35 (6.8) 5,054 (8.0)
Independent	19 (3.7) 2,641 (4.9)	11 (2.1) 2,057 (3.5)	16 (3.1) 2,769 (4.9)	9 (1.7) 3,515 (5.8)	21 (4.1) 4,807 (7.3)	30 (5.8) 2,711 (4.3)
Other	0 (0) 69 (0.1)	0 (0) 109 (0.2)	0 (0) 62 (0.1)	0 (0) 58 (0.1)	0 (0) 58 (0.1)	0 (0) no data
Total	511	511	511	512	512	511
Turnout	68.01	74.57	67.94	71.40	73.31	67.26

the position of the LDP, the reduction of the Socialists to minor party status, the near-elimination of the NPH, a rather disappointing result for the NFP (which nevertheless was established as the runner-up to the LDP), and a respectable result for the newly-formed Democratic Party, an amalgam of former Socialists and centrists with varying pedigrees.

In December 1997, the NFP disintegrated, and the fragments from that doomed experiment essentially moved in three directions. Some joined the Democratic Party, turning it into a much more substantial party than it had initially been. The former CGP (*Kōmeitō*), which had been a semi-detached part of the NFP, came back into more or less its old form, and with its old name. And the true followers of Ozawa Ichirō and of his market liberal reformism created a small and close-knit party called the Liberal Party (III) (*Jiyūtō*). This party, however, split in two roughly equal halves when Ozawa pulled it out of coalition with the LDP in April 2000.

Those wishing to remain with the coalition formed the Conservative Party (*Hoshutō*), which lost 11 of its 18 Lower House seats in the subsequent elections. The LDP regained some of its support, but could only govern effectively in coalition with various small parties. In the mid-1990s its coalition parties were from the centre-left, but from 1998 they were from the centre-right. Finally, the Japan Communist Party continued more or less as it had been, largely aloof from the manœuvrings of all the other parties.

In the general elections to the House of Representatives held in June 2000, the LDP lost ground, falling several seats short of an absolute majority, but the three-party coalition retained its majority. The most successful party in the elections was the Democratic Party, already boosted by the collapse of the NFP and now occupying more than a quarter of the total Lower House seats. The performance of the smaller parties was not much changed by comparison with the elections of 1996. (See Table 31.)

Table 31 Elections for the House of Representatives, 1996 and 2000

	Seats (% of total seats), seats in single-member districts (smd), seats in PR regional blocs (pr)	
	20/10/96	25/6/00
Liberal Democratic Party (Jiyūminshutō, Jimintō)	239 (47.8) smd 169 pr 70	233 (48.5) smd 177 pr 56
New Frontier Party (Shinshintō)	156 (31.2) smd 96 pr 60	
Democratic Party (Minshutō)	52 (10.4) smd 17 pr 35	127 (26.4) smd 80 pr 47
Clean Government Party (Kōmeitō)		31 smd 7 pr 24
Liberal Party (Jiyūtō)		22 smd 4 pr 18
Japan Communist Party (Nihon Kyōsantō)	26 (5.2) smd 2 pr 24	20 smd 0 pr 20
Social Democratic Party (Shakaiminshutō) – formerly Japan Socialist Party (Nihon Shakaitō)	15 smd 4 pr 11	19 smd 4 pr 15
Conservative Party (Hoshutō)		7 smd 7 pr 0
New Party Harbinger (Shintō Sakigake)	2 smd 2 pr 0	
Independent Association (Mushozoku no kai)		5 smd 5 pr 0
Liberal League (Jiyū Rengō)	0 smd 0 pr 0	1 smd 1 pr 0

Table 31 continued

	Seats (% of total seats), seats in single-member districts (smd), seats in PR regional blocs (pr)	
	20/10/96	25/6/00
Democratic Reform League (*Minkairen*)	1 smd 1 pr 0	
Independent	9 smd 9 pr 0	15 smd 15 pr –
Others	0	0
Total	500	480
Turnout	smd 59.65 pr 59.62	smd [no data] pr [no data]

Source: Statistics are from the following sources: *Asahi Nenkan* (Asahi Yearbook), various years; *Asahi Shinbun* (Asahi Newspaper), various issues; *Yomiuri Nenkan* (Yomiuri Yearbook), various years.

Emperor (Tennō) and politics The position of the Emperor (*Tennō*)* has been one of the most sensitive political topics in Japan since 1945, and while the Shōwa Emperor was still alive (up to 1989) the mass media tended to be circumspect in discussing it. To an extent, it was a taboo subject. Moreover, the institution itself for the most part kept a remarkably low profile.

The key event in Japan's modern history, known in English as the Meiji Restoration (in Japanese *Meiji ishin*), used as its legitimising symbol the *Tennō*, translated rather freely into English as 'Emperor'. The *Tennō* was the latest in a dynasty confined to the ancient capital of Kyōto, performing certain religious functions but not having exercised political power for several centuries. Following the Meiji Restoration the role of the *Tennō* was transformed into that of supreme legitimiser of the new regime. Gradually an imperial cult was built up, underscored by such rituals as the regular reading in schools of the Imperial Rescript on Education. The *Tennō* was portrayed as the father of his people, in a symbolic extension of the structure of the traditional Japanese family (see FAMILY AND POLITICS), and the demands for loyalty to him became intense.

For the most part, he did not take part in political decision-making (though there is controversy about his role in the Asia–Pacific War), but decisions were made in his name. During the first three decades of the twentieth century, constitutional specialists argued whether he was an 'organ' of the polity, or above it, a supreme ruler. The implication of the 'organ theory' was that he was dependent on other 'organs' (like different organs of the human body are dependent on each other), whereas the 'suprematist' theory would have removed limits to his power. Even the 'suprematists', however, would not have placed actual day-to-day decision-making power into the *Tennō*'s hands. Ironically, even if one accepts the arguments of those who think the *Tennō* played a certain part in decision-making at various periods, it is clear that he did not control the political agenda, in the manner, say, of the late Shah Reza Pahlavi of Iran.

It is now clear that the Japanese surrender in 1945 was delayed, with tragic results, in part because of Government concerns about the survival of the *Tennō* system. When the Allied Occupation was set up, following the defeat, General MacArthur, as Supreme Commander, Allied Powers, had to decide whether to retain the *Tennō* or introduce a republican form of Government. The fact that the former choice was made reflected MacArthur's view that retention of the *Tennō* was necessary in order to obtain the population's acquiescence in reform. In particular, he was strongly convinced that to try him as a war criminal, as some were urging, would seriously jeopardise the whole Occupation effort.

The solution adopted, and written into the CONSTITUTION OF 1946, was to retain the *Tennō*, but to strip him of all possibility of exercising political power. The position and roles of the *Tennō* are described in the Constitution's chapter 1 – a primary position that some 1990s revisionists have regarded as anachronistic. Chapter 1, article 1, reads: 'The Emperor shall be the symbol of the State and the unity of the people, deriving his position from the will of the people with whom resides sovereign power.' A list of his functions follows, in which it is stipulated that his formal decisions require a counter-signature of a Minister of State. He could not, as is theoretically possible for the British monarch, choose between different candidates for Prime Minister, since the designation of PRIME MINISTER is determined by a vote in Parliament. Other important changes were the abolition of the aristocracy, except for immediate relatives of the *Tennō*, and a severe reduction in the extent of imperial property holdings. The former Imperial Household Ministry, which used to exercise extensive power, was abolished, and replaced by an IMPERIAL HOUSEHOLD AGENCY (*Kunaichō*), made directly responsible to the Prime Minister.

Several controversial aspects of the *Tennō* institution have remained following the end of the Occupation in 1952. Early constitutional revisionists – many of whom were highly conservative – objected to the term 'symbol' as the official designation of the *Tennō*, on the ground that it gave him a lower status than other national leaders, who were normally termed 'Head of State'. The Japanese word *shōchō* ('symbol') was itself a constitutional neologism. But the heat gradually went out of this controversy and *shōchō* became assimilated into normal constitutional discourse.

Another area of friction concerned the person of the *Shōwa Tennō* and the question of his war responsibility. Until he died in 1989 it was difficult to raise this question openly in Japan, not least because of threats of violence from mini-groups of ultra-right-wing nationalists. The issue, in any case, raised difficult historical and interpretative questions. Adequate archival material did not exist, evidence that might have been incriminating had quite possibly been destroyed at the end of the war, and there were questions about the reliability of accounts that were extant. The *Shōwa Tennō* was understandably reticent on the subject.

Foreign writers were in a position to be less inhibited in exploring this sensitive issue. At one end of the spectrum were those who saw the role of the *Shōwa Tennō* as similar to that of King George VI of Great Britain during the Second World War, of presiding and endorsing, but not deciding. Stephen Large's 1992 biography of the *Shōwa Tennō* came rather close to this position, though he admitted a certain activism by the *Tennō* during the war. An important point made by Large was that by the late 1930s the *Tennō* and his advisers were seriously concerned by potential threats to his person by elements of the extreme right. He argued that this created intense pressure on both the man and the institution to become more accommodating to advocates of war with the United States.

At the other end of the spectrum was a book by a US journalist, David Bergamini (published in 1971), who outlined an 'imperial conspiracy', going back several decades. According to this the *Tennō* was at the nerve centre of a plot to have Japan militarily conquer and dominate the Asian region. Large parts of the argument rest on the flimsiest of evidence, and there is much apparent misinterpretation of archival material. Nevertheless, the book had a certain vogue after its publication. A more recent and far more scholarly book on the subject is by Herbert Bix, who concludes that the *Shōwa Tennō* played a rather more active role in policy-making during the war than is often realised. It seems likely that even Bix's book will not be the last word on this difficult subject.

The illness of the *Shōwa Tennō* from the autumn of 1988 and his death on 7 January 1989 happened to come at a particularly complex point in Japan's political evolution. It was marked by an outpouring of concern that greatly surprised both foreign, and even many Japanese, observers. Immediately after his death condolence books were opened all over the country, and various forms of sport and entertainment were suspended for a period. Plainly, as Watanabe Osamu has argued, there was a degree of official orchestration in relation to these manifestations of grief, and the private sector (especially large firms) went along with this to a surprising extent. During his illness the media reported his vital signs in clinical detail every day. When he died they used formal language hardly seen for decades to refer to the death of the *Tennō* and related matters. Various interpretations were put forward to explain all this, ranging from 'revival of the emperor-cult' theories to assumptions that it was all simply a spontaneous outpouring of grief. Undoubtedly official attempts to re-emphasise the importance of the *Tennō* institution were far from absent. But also a major factor seems to have been that the population at large, few of whom remembered the death of the previous *Tennō* in 1926, sensed that a turbulent era in the nation's history had come to an end, and that in more than a formal sense a new era was about to begin.

The new *Tennō*, whose era name was to be *Heisei*, succeeded his father and his accession was symbolised by ceremonies revived and refurbished from a distant past. One problem that arose with these ceremonies was the constitutional separation of religion from the State. This meant that the religious and political elements in the ceremonies had somehow to be separated, and this required ingenious – and not particularly transparent – solutions.

Perhaps the clearest indication that a new era might truly be beginning was to be found in the language used by the new *Tennō* in his early speeches following his succession. Eschewing the formal court language of his father, he addressed audiences as *minasan* (literally 'everybody', perhaps better translated as 'Ladies and Gentlemen'). He also referred to the 1946 Constitution as the only constitution he had ever known, which was clearly calculated as a riposte to right-wing constitutional revisionists.

One issue that has come to cause concern is the absence of a male heir to follow the current Crown Prince. Indeed, no male child has been born to the Imperial Family for several decades. This has given rise to active discussion of whether the succession law should be altered to permit female succession. There are some precedents for this in the family's history, but not in modern times.

*Although each *Tennō* bears a personal name, this is rarely used in Japan outside his family. The normal method of referring to, or addressing, a *Tennō* is '*Tennō heika*' (roughly 'His (Your) Majesty'). The era name of a *Tennō* becomes his official title after death. Thus 'Emperor Hirohito', as he was often referred to outside Japan, became *Shōwa Tennō*, or 'The Emperor Showa', after his death. The personal name of the present *Tennō* is Akihito (though hardly used in Japan), but after his death he will be referred to as the *Heisei Tennō* (Heisei Emperor).

Further reading

Bergamini (1971)
Crump (1989)
Large (1992)
Watanabe (1989)
Williams (1990)

Environment Agency (Kankyōchō) The Environment Agency was established in July 1971 following several appalling environmental disasters resulting from lax controls during the rapid economic growth of the late 1950s and 1960s. It was an external agency of the PRIME MINISTER'S OFFICE (*Sōrifu*), with a Minister of State as its Director. Environmental degradation had become a major political issue by the late 1960s, but it took four years from the passage of a Basic Law on Pollution Policy in 1967 before a single Government body with responsibility for environmental policy could be created. The 1967 law was in any case deeply flawed from an environmental point of view, being based on a clause decreeing that environmental protection should advance 'in harmony' with economic development.

The new agency was divided into a Director's Secretariat, and four bureaux, namely Planning and Adjustment, Protection of Nature, Conservation of the Atmosphere, and Preservation of Water Quality. Bodies attached to the agency included the National Pollution Research Institute, National Minamata Disease Research Centre, and the Pollution Training Institute.

In its earlier years the Environment Agency suffered from its youth, small size and low prestige by comparison with the major established ministries, such as the MINISTRY OF INTERNATIONAL TRADE AND INDUSTRY or the MINISTRY OF AGRICULTURE, FORESTRY AND FISHERIES. It nevertheless had successes in tackling at least the more severe areas of environmental damage, and was most successful where it received political backing resulting from perceptions within the LIBERAL DEMOCRATIC PARTY (LDP) that environmental disasters meant fewer votes. Laws were brought in that had the effect of forcing polluting industries out of cities, and ultimately out of Japan altogether. This led to accusations that Japan was 'exporting pollution', particularly to South-East Asian countries. Car exhaust standards were also drastically tightened. Increasing international pressure on Japan to conform to new environmental standards also gradually effected some strengthening of the agency's position.

In the administrative reorganisation of January 2001, the Environment Agency was upgraded to the MINISTRY OF THE ENVIRONMENT, also acquiring some extra functions from the MINISTRY OF HEALTH AND WELFARE, and from MITI.

Further reading

Schreurs, in Schreurs and Economy (eds) (1997)

environmental politics Japan is often seen as inclined to drag its feet on environmental issues, but the environment has had a profound impact on the politics of Japan at various times since the 1960s.

Japan is particularly vulnerable to environmental degradation for reasons of geography and population. Her population is currently approximately 126 million, in a land area that is 151 per cent of the land area of the United Kingdom and 68 per cent of the land area of France. Both those countries have a population of nearly 60 million, less than half that of Japan. Moreover much of Japan is mountainous, forcing the bulk of the population to concentrate on coastal plains. As many as 50 million people live along the Pacific coast from the Tokyo conurbation to northern Kyūshū, and industrial production has been similarly concentrated in that narrow strip of land.

Environmental issues did not begin to make a political impact until the mid-1960s. Government policies devised in the 1950s gave absolute priority to economic growth, with hardly any attempt being made to impose controls on pollution. Air and water pollution in congested urban areas rapidly reached levels that were difficult to tolerate. Three cases in particular drew widespread attention and by the late 1960s were having major political effects. The first, and most serious, was mercury poisoning resulting from industrial effluent discharged by the Chisso Corporation into Minamata Bay in Kyūshū (there was also a similar case in Niigata). The second was widespread asthma brought about by emissions from a petrochemical plant at Yokkaichi, near Nagoya. And the third was the case of poisoning from rice polluted with cadmium, in Tōyama Prefecture. But there were many other less publicised cases having grave results for those involved as victims.

These three cases, like others, were caused by poisonous emissions or effluent discharge from industrial plants. The Minamata case was the earliest, first becoming apparent as early as 1953, and is in many ways the most shocking. The Chisso Corporation was a long-established chemical fertiliser company that economically dominated the local town, creating much of its employment. As subsequently became clear, mercury effluent discharged into the bay by Chisso had entered the food chain, and was polluting fish, which were eaten by animals that then developed neurological disorders. By the later 1950s substantial numbers of people, mainly from fishing families, came down with similar symptoms, including deformities and mental impairment, and a high proportion of them died. The company did everything in its power to suppress research demonstrating that it was responsible, and it was backed by the company union, fearful for jobs. The victims were locked into a culture of submission to authority, and were in any case mostly of low socio-economic status. The company came to an agreement with the victims in 1959, but avoiding any admission of responsibility. Even though the MINISTRY OF HEALTH AND WELFARE had pinpointed the cause with near certainty as early as 1958, other Government agencies (notably the MINISTRY OF INTERNATIONAL TRADE AND INDUSTRY and the MINISTRY OF JUSTICE) were able to delay any real investigation of Chisso for another decade.

Between 1967 and 1969 a chain of events led to victims of the four most appalling pollution cases filing suits against the companies concerned. The Big Four cases, as they were called, attracted huge publicity, and were a principal cause of citizens' movements (*shimin undō*) developing in many parts of the country to fight local issues involving pollution and quality of life issues. Eventually the courts handed down verdicts favourable in many cases to the victims, though it took many years before the legal process was exhausted.

By the early 1970s, pollution problems had become so serious that the Government was coming to realise it could not carry on promoting economic growth with no concern for the environment, without risking a major alienation of its support base. Indeed, Government action began even before this. It passed a Basic Law for the Environment in 1967, but this law contained a clause stating that concern for the environment should be balanced by a healthy concern for the development of the economy. This, in effect, neutralised the impact of the law, since the clause could always be cited as a means of avoiding environmental controls. It was not until the 'Pollution Parliament' of December 1970 that real teeth were attached to the laws on environmental protection, and a new era began. An ENVIRONMENT AGENCY, attached to the PRIME MINISTER'S OFFICE, was established in July 1971. Nearly 30 years later, in January 2001, it was upgraded to a full ministry.

From this point on, LIBERAL DEMOCRATIC PARTY (LDP) governments, undoubtedly motivated by the threat to their survival caused by citizens' movements riding high with indignation on a variety of pollution and other issues, set about improving environmental quality. Severe sanctions were placed on companies found guilty of transgressing rigorous air and water pollution standards, while car manufacturers were faced with severely tightened requirements concerning exhaust emissions. This led to the 'export of pollution' by Japanese companies relocating to other countries in the Asian region, but air and water quality greatly improved within Japan itself.

Both Pempel, and much later Schreurs, argue that by acting so vigorously to clean up the environment during the 1970s, the LDP took the steam out of environmentally oriented citizens' movements, and, in the process, earned itself several more years in government. What happened is actually rather more complicated than that, but the political momentum generated by citizens' movements, and opposition parties backing them, was certainly perceived as a threat by LDP governments for much of the 1970s. This may well explain the vigour of the official response. Once the threat had receded, however, the momentum of environmental regulation also diminished.

In more recent years, as global issues such as the depletion of the ozone layer and global warming have become major concerns internationally, Japan has gradually been drawn into international regimes attempting to do something positive about these problems. Successive governments manage to create the impression that they are belatedly reacting to international pressures, rather than taking any kind of initiative, but gradually Japan has become more active in terms of the international environmental agenda. Such issues as whaling, and logging by Japanese companies in the forests of South-East Asia, have continued to give Japan an unfortunate reputation on environmental issues. But latterly the well-publicised US refusal to co-operate with a multi-lateral environmental regime concluded on Japanese soil, at Kyōto, leaves Japan looking respectable, by comparison with an economy that now causes far more pollution than Japan.

Further reading
McCormack (1996)
McKean (1981)
Miyaoka (forthcoming)
Pempel (1982)
Schreurs, in Schreurs and Economy (1997)
Steiner *et al.* (1980)
Upham (1987)
Upham, in Gordon (ed.) (1993)

Europe, relations with Relations between Japan, the United States and Europe have sometimes been portrayed as a triangle, of which two sides are drawn in bold, and the third side drawn as a faint, dotted line. The lines drawn in bold are those between Japan and the United States, and between Europe and the United States. The faint, dotted line is that between Japan and Europe.

This image comes out of the geo-strategic situation prevailing in the Cold War, in the sense that Japan and (Western) Europe were allies of the United States, confronting the Communist bloc. It was the United States that was the undisputed leader of these alliances, so that Japan and Europe each looked primarily to the United States for guidance rather than to each other.

To some extent, this model has entered a phase of evolution since the ending of the Cold War and the collapse of the Soviet Union. The first thing to examine is the concept of 'Europe'. Up till the early 1990s 'Europe' for Japan principally meant the major states of Western Europe, namely Britain, France and (West) Germany. Japanese governments were most comfortable pursuing bilateral relations with them, rather than with the institutions of the European Union (in those days European Economic Community, then European Community).

From 1989, however, Europe entered a phase of dramatic development. The breaching of the Berlin Wall in that year was followed by the unification of Germany, the collapse of Communist governments throughout Eastern Europe, the break-up of Czechoslovakia into two states, and civil war in Yugoslavia, leading to the fragmentation of that country. In 1992, the Maastricht Treaty was signed, propelling the union – though the ride was to prove bumpy – towards further integration, including adoption of the Euro as a common currency. The process of expansion was also put in train, so that, while the twenty-first century was still young, it could reasonably be expected that almost the whole of historical Europe would be united in the European Union.

The momentous significance of these trends was gradually comprehended in Japan. In July 1991 Japan and the EC (as it then was) signed the Hague Declaration. This established a list of common aims and provided a sophisticated framework for regular consultations between Japan and senior European officials. In addition to this, contacts and regular consultations have become institutionalised between a wide variety of bodies in Japan and Europe.

An important aspect of Japanese relations with Europe is that of foreign investment. Of the European nations, the United Kingdom has been the most favoured by Japanese companies wishing to invest in Europe. This may be attributed in part to the English language, but also to what Japanese businessmen have regarded as relatively favourable conditions for their investment in the United Kingdom, by comparison with some, at least, of the other European States. But since the introduction of the Euro in the EU in 1999, British reluctance to enter the common currency has been regarded with disquiet by a considerable portion of the Japanese business community in Britain.

A particularly interesting forum for communication between Japan and Europe is the Asia–Europe Meeting (ASEM), established in 1996. On the Asian side 10 states from East and South-East Asia belong (including Japan), and, on the European side, all the EU members are represented, as well as the President of the European Commission. Julie Gilson argues (in Hook *et al.*, 2001, pp. 251–2) that, from the Japanese point of view, ASEM fulfils five useful functions. First, it enables Japan 'to play a greater international political role without military implications'. Second, it provides a forum for proxy diplomacy, 'by getting the EU to voice some of [Japan's] regional proposals without raising East Asian fears regarding

Japanese motives'. Third, it helps Japan strengthen its relations with the rest of East Asia. Fourth, since ASEM does not include the United States, it can therefore 'establish an agenda which does not prioritize US concerns'. Fifth, ASEM seeks to deepen 'relations between the two weakest sides of the Japan–US–Europe triangle', by expanding 'the "Japan" pole to include other major East Asian players'.

As late as the 1980s Europe was regarded in some Japanese circles as a region in relative, if not absolute, decline, a nice place to visit for cultural or gastronomic tourism, but hardly serious in terms of technological innovation or economic development. Early in the 1980s the present writer even heard Spengler's *Decline of the West* put forward in Japan as a serious guide to the understanding of Europe. Such views are far more rarely heard today. In their place, increasing numbers of Japanese are coming to appreciate the boldness and dynamism with which the European vision is being pursued, and to understand that Europe is emerging as a global power centre in its own right.

The third side of the triangle is not yet drawn in bold, but the spaces between the dots are being filled in.

Further reading

Bridges (1999)
Drifte, in Inoguchi and Jain (eds) (2000)
Gilson (2000)
Hook *et al.* (2001)
Rothacher (1983)

extremist movements (left) Left-wing groups with extremist revolutionary views and favouring the use of violence were an offshoot of STUDENT POLITICAL MOVEMENTS in the 1960s. Student radical activity in the 1950s and early 1960s (particularly that associated with the SECURITY TREATY REVISION CRISIS) was on a mass scale, and involved set-piece confrontations with police, but for the most part violence on both sides was kept within bounds, and deaths were rare. Guns were difficult to obtain, and not used on either side. Both police and students were well protected with helmets and padded clothing, their weapons being long sticks rather than anything more lethal.

From the late 1960s altogether more sinister behaviour began to be seen among small groups of student (and ex-student) radicals. Much of this paralleled what was happening in Europe and elsewhere, where terrorist groupings had spun off from extreme left-wing radical movements. In the Japanese case two principal types of group emerged. One consisted of groups that used some variant of the name 'Red Army', while the other were two Marxist groups that spent much of their time fighting each other on university campuses: the Middle Core Faction (*Chūkakuha*) and the Marxist Revolutionary Faction (*Kakumaruha*). We shall discuss each type in turn.

Red Army groups

In 1969 a group calling itself the Red Army Faction (*Sekigunha*) began violent activities, including throwing molotov cocktails at police boxes. In November 53 members of the group were arrested by police at a mountain training camp, where they had apparently been planning an attack on the residence of the PRIME MINISTER. In March 1970 nine members of the same group hijacked a Japan Airlines aircraft on a domestic flight and forced the pilot to fly to North Korea. The flight landed once at an airport within Japan to refuel, where some women and children were allowed to disembark. Most of the passengers, however, as well as the crew, remained as hostages. The hijackers successfully bargained to have the remaining passengers exchanged for a junior minister and a Socialist member of the House of Councillors. From Japan, the plane flew to Korea and landed first in Seoul, where an attempt was made to make the hijackers think they were in Pyongyang. They were not, however, fooled by this ruse. The plane then flew from Seoul to Pyongyang, where the hijackers apparently remained (for more than 30 years), whereas the two politicians, the crew and the plane were returned to Japan.

Also in 1969 a group calling itself the Tokyo–Yokohama Security Treaty Joint Struggle (*Keihin ampo kyōtō*) began activities that included stealing guns and explosives, and throwing molotov cocktails at police boxes, foreign embassies and US military installations.

In February 1972 the *Keihin ampo kyōtō* and the *Sekigunha* formed an alliance that became the United Red Army (*Rengō sekigun*). They carried out several bank robberies and bombings, and established a number of mountain bases. In the same month two members of the group (one of whom was a woman) carried out a purge, torturing and killing some 14 members. When police raided the house in which this was taking place, five terrorists escaped and held a woman hostage in the mountain resort of Karuizawa. Three people were killed in the subsequent police rescue, but the terrorists were all captured alive. This final drama was relayed on television, to a huge viewing audience.

At this period the United Red Army was developing links with terrorist groups in the Middle East. In June 1972 three of its members, who had undergone training with the Popular Front for the Liberation of Palestine, flew by Air France from Paris to Lod Airport in Tel Aviv. In those days before strict airport security, they were able to collect their luggage containing an arsenal of weapons, and opened fire at random on the crowd in the terminal building with automatic rifles, also throwing hand grenades. They killed 26 people, of whom 17 were Christian pilgrims from Puerto Rico, and injured a further 80. Two of the terrorists were themselves killed, but one of them, the youngest, Okamoto Kōzō, then aged 24, survived.

Patricia Steinhoff was able to interview Okamoto in prison in Israel, and reported her findings in an article in *Asian Survey* in 1976. He regarded himself as a foot-soldier, not a leader, of the movement, in which he had not been heavily involved before receiving orders to proceed to the Middle East. He was the youngest of six children of a social worker father and schoolteacher mother, and an elder brother was one of those who had hijacked the JAL plane to North Korea in 1970. Like most students at that period, he was involved in left-wing student activity, but, unlike many of the movement's leaders, he did not have a clearly formed or sophisticated ideology. He was not, like so many of them, a doctrinal Marxist hairsplitter. But as an Agriculture student at the provincial Kagoshima University, he became concerned with issues of environmental degradation. His occasional involvement in demonstrations against US bases did not satisfy him, and he was looking for a goal of world revolution. The revolutionary forces by their violent actions would profoundly shock the bourgeoisie into a realisation of their vulnerability, bring those bourgeois suffering from pollution over to the side of revolution, massacre others in a revolutionary war, and in the end create revolution throughout the world. In his trial in Israel he painted a picture of those who died in revolutionary actions – both terrorists and victims – becoming stars in the constellation of Orion.

As Steinhoff persuasively argues, there was more of classic anarchism than Marxism in Okamoto's formulations. Like his dead companions, he willed his own death, and, according to his Israeli defence lawyer, he was 'working for the prosecution' at his trial, actively seeking the death penalty. His actions need to be seen in a Japanese cultural context, for he admired the suicide of MISHIMA YUKIO and the wartime *kamikaze* pilots, while disagreeing with the cause they fought for. Action for action's sake, death as martyrdom, the idea that taking one's own life redeems shame or demonstrates commitment to a cause, however hopeless, are ideas rooted in Japanese literature and culture. It may not be entirely fanciful to see a link with the motivations for terrorist acts on the part of the *Aum Shinrikyō* religious sect in the 1990s (*see* AUM SHINRIKYŌ AND THE POLITICS OF MASS POISONING).

During the mid-1970s the United Red Army was implicated in a number of hijackings and other terrorist acts, in Europe, Singapore, Malaysia, Kuwait, Israel and in Japan itself. There was a strong link with the Popular Front for the Liberation of Palestine in many of these episodes. Indeed, to a large extent the United Red Army could be said to have moved its centre of operations to the Middle East.

The fact that a principal leader of the movement was a woman, Shigenobu Fusako, attracted much international media attention. It appears that she had been briefly married to one of the two perpetrators of the Lod Airport massacre who died in the attempt. In September–October 1977, four United Red Army hijackers, under the command of Shigenobu, hijacked a JAL flight from Bombay to Bangkok to demand the release of nine of the group's members in prison in Japan. The plane landed at Dhaka in Bangladesh, where the 151 passengers were held for six days. This episode became highly controversial, as the Japanese Government caved in to the hijackers' demands, paying a $US6 million ransom and releasing six prisoners held in Japan. Following the release of the passengers, the plane took the hijackers to Algeria, though it appears that Algeria expelled them after a week. Some ministers resigned as a consequence of the concessions they had had to make.

After this complex and confused episode, the United Red Army issued a statement that it would henceforth concentrate on the struggle within Japan, in the determination to 'crush the emperor system and Japanese imperialism, drive US forces out of Japan, and establish a People's Republic of Japan'. By this time, however, police vigilance in Japan had become sufficiently effective that the movement seems to have retreated to its hideouts in the Middle East.

Middle Core Faction (Chūkakuha) and Marxist Revolutionary Faction (Kakumaruha)

These two Marxist groups emerged from the student movement of the 1960s, and recruited substantial numbers of adherents on the campuses of many universities in the late 1960s and early 1970s. Like extremist groups generally in Japan, their organisation was hierarchical and authoritarian, while both were inclined towards violence. Much of their energies was in fact devoted to fighting each other for control of student movements on particular campuses, and a considerable number of deaths occurred in these struggles.

The *Chūkakuha* in the early 1970s found a cause dear to its heart, in the form of opposition to the construction of the New Tokyo International Airport at Narita, north-east of Tokyo. The issue is analysed by Apter and Sawa, in their book *Protest in Tokyo*. The students managed to delay substantially the opening of the airport, by occupying land, in conjunction with farmers who were to be displaced by the new construction. They also managed to penetrate the control tower, soon before the airport was due to open, and destroyed much computer equipment. The cooperation between local farmers and a Marxist-oriented student organisation attracted national and even international attention. It was a marriage of convenience, in that the farmers were protesting at the loss of their land, whereas the students were concerned to prevent what they suspected would be military uses for the airport. The students also had broader, revolutionary aims. But what is amazing is that the protest continued for more than two decades, with substantial continuity of organisation and personnel. It is also interesting that, despite repeated violent set-piece clashes between the protesters and police, the authorities stopped short of methods that would have removed the protesters entirely from the airport area.

Note: I gratefully acknowledge research assistance by Ms Carrie Steffen, in Canberra, in preparation of this entry.

Further reading
Apter and Sawa (1984)
Krauss (1974)
Steinhoff (1976)

extremist movements (right) Right-wing movements of an extreme nationalist variety have been a constant factor in Japanese politics since the 1950s, and they of course have their roots in the much more influential ultra-nationalist movements of the pre-war period.

Such groups typically have a small handful of members, owing close loyalty to a leader. The number of groups has been very large indeed, and the inter-relationships between them extremely complex. Despite the proliferation of minuscule groups, they mostly share a broad common ideology, based on reverence for the Emperor (*Tennō*) (*see* EMPEROR AND POLITICS), hostility to the peace CONSTITUTION OF 1946, belief in hierarchy and discipline, hostility to political corruption, and an intense dislike of left-wing parties, LABOUR UNIONS, intellectuals and left-leaning sections of the mass media.

When candidates of the far right have stood for election, they have only received a derisory number of votes. The durable rightist Akao Bin, whose loudspeaker trucks were well known on the streets of Tokyo, as he flamboyantly denounced Communism and other assorted left-wing enemies, was regularly on the list of candidates in elections for Tokyo Governor. But he normally received a few thousand votes out of an electorate of several millions.

The far right, however, has other weapons in its armoury besides election candidacy. Particularly at times of political tension, it has resorted to physical violence. This has typically meant small-scale acts of violence targeted on individuals, rather than the more indiscriminate bombings and hijackings favoured by extremist movements of the left in the 1970s (see EXTREMIST MOVEMENTS (LEFT)), or the type of chemical warfare attempted by the Aum Shinrikyō in the 1990s (see AUM SHINRIKYŌ AND THE POLITICS OF MASS POISONING).

For instance, in the period of the SECURITY TREATY REVISION CRISIS in 1959–60, and its aftermath, the ultra-right committed a number of violent acts, including murder. Confronting the massed ranks of protesters against the Treaty, rightists on one occasion drove a truck into the crowd. Shortly after the Treaty had been ratified, they wounded by stabbing the JAPAN SOCIALIST PARTY (JSP) leader, KAWAKAMI JŌTARŌ, and, less explicably, the recently resigned PRIME MINISTER, KISHI NOBUSUKE. Dramatically, in November 1960, the ultra-right gave world television viewing audiences their first experience of a televised assassination. The Chairman of the JSP, ASANUMA INEJIRŌ, who the previous year had roused the ire of rightists by stating in Beijing that US imperialism was 'the common enemy of the peoples of Japan and China', was making a speech in a televised election debate. A 17 year-old former member of an ultra-rightist mini-party and son of a Self-Defence Forces officer, jumped up onto the stage and killed Asanuma with a knife. In 1961 a plot was discovered, and foiled, to assassinate the members of the IKEDA Cabinet. The following year the monthly intellectual journal, Chūō Kōron, published a short story describing a fictional coup against the Imperial Family. After its publication, a member of a rightist organisation broke into the house of the journal's publisher, and killed a female servant of the publisher's family.

During the late 1960s the far right received widespread publicity with the activities of the well-known novelist, MISHIMA YUKIO. Mishima, a flamboyant and complex figure greatly influenced by European literature and tastes, nevertheless developed the view that self-sacrifice in the cause of Japan was a noble tradition in danger of being submerged under the wave of modernisation and materialistic tastes. He formed the paramilitary Shield Society (Tate no kai), which, surprisingly, was allowed to drill using facilities of the Self-Defence Forces. In November 1970 he committed ritual suicide after haranguing the troops at the Ichigaya (Tokyo) headquarters of the Self-Defence Forces, calling upon them to rise up against a corrupt political system. Mishima's dramatic gesture greatly boosted the sales of his novels, but otherwise made little direct impact on politics, or indeed on the Self-Defence Forces. The Shield Society disbanded after his death, but a former member of it was involved in a raid in March 1977 on the building of the FEDERATION OF ECONOMIC ORGANISATIONS (Keidanren), along with members of other rightist groups.

Another high-profile figure, very different from Mishima, who maintained a paramilitary group at around the same period, was an ultra-right-wing associate of KISHI NOBUSUKE, named Kodama Yoshio. Kodama was a political fixer, who had been involved in economic deals in China during the war. He became notorious after 1976 as one of the main channels to the Prime Minister (TANAKA KAKUEI) used by the Lockheed Corporation to bring about the purchase of its aircraft by All Nippon Airlines. The Kodama case suggests the curious paradox that while anti-corruption has been one of the main campaign themes of the ultra-right, some supporters of the movement and their mainstream political associates have been heavily involved in backstage financial manœuvring.

Demonstrations by ultra-rightist groups have often had a ritualistic character. For many years, certain left-wing organisations, most notably the JAPAN TEACHERS' UNION (Nikkyōso), held their annual congresses to the cacophonous accompaniment of rightist loudspeaker trucks, parked outside the hall. There also seems to be a ritualistic element in the appeals of such loudspeaker trucks that harangue the crowds at major centres in Tokyo and other cities. Hardly anybody stops to listen to what they are saying, but the noise and martial music are a regular feature of life at these centres. They are, incidentally, tolerated by the police.

Another form of rightist activity has been pressure brought on authors and publishers not to publish material objectionable to the far right. One writer who published a book about the Emperor (*Tennō*) in the 1990s was receiving threatening telephone calls for about a year after its publication. This activity has had some effect since publishers have a tendency to take the line of least resistance in the face of threats. Such threats, in any case, are known not to be empty, since journalists and others have been physically attacked. In an analogous incident, the mayor of Nagasaki was stabbed, though not fatally, for suggesting that the *Shōwa Tennō* should accept some responsibility for the war.

Despite their extremely low level of popular support, they are able to exercise a degree of indirect influence because of clandestine linkages with some 'respectable' politicians in the LIBERAL DEMOCRATIC PARTY (LDP). The Young Storm Association (*Seirankai*), founded in the early 1970s by a group of young LDP politicians, took on board some extreme right-wing themes. They included some who came to political prominence in the 1980s and 1990s, such as WATANABE MICHIO, YAMASAKI TAKU and MORI YOSHIRŌ (the last of these becoming Prime Minister in April 2000). These politicians find that some nationalist themes expressed vociferously by the far right can be useful to them in their own political campaigns. There is also some degree of overlap between extremist right-wing movements and *bōryokudan* (organised groups of gangsters), some of which are also known to have had links with some LDP politicians. For instance KANEMARU SHIN was discovered to have personally visited, in 1987, the leader of a *bōryokudan* group to thank him for ceasing the group's campaign of harassment of Kanemaru's close associate, TAKESHITA NOBORU. This became a *cause célèbre*, and was one of the issues that eventually forced Kanemaru out of politics.

The ultra-right in Japan thrives on political crisis. Although the ending of the Cold War has removed some of its former enemies (most notably the Soviet Union), political instability combined with economic stagnation provide themes that it is capable of exploiting. Moreover, the decline of the left has weakened an important factor that used to balance its influence. On the other hand, liberalising changes, in train in the new millennium, may serve to reduce the appeal of anachronistic right-wing extremism.

Note: I gratefully acknowledge research assistance from Ms Carrie Steffen, in Canberra, in preparation of this entry.

Further reading
Dixon (1975)
Morris (1960)
Stockwin (1972)

F

factions within political parties What are normally translated into English as 'factions' are endemic to most Japanese political parties of any size, and indeed exist in other kinds of organisation as well. The Japanese term is *habatsu*, which may be abbreviated to *ha* when referring to a particular faction, as in *Tanaka ha* (Tanaka faction). The second part of the word, *batsu*, when used on its own is often translated 'clique'. Other prefixes may be attached to it, making *gakubatsu* (academic clique, 'professoriate'), *zaibatsu* (financial clique, conglomerate firm) or *hanbatsu* (clan clique, in other words Meiji period leaders representing various *han*, or clans).

Even though 'factions' may readily be identified in political parties elsewhere, *habatsu* implies cultural characteristics that, while not necessarily absent outside Japan, are particularly marked within Japan itself. Central to the concept of *habatsu* is the idea of a leader–follower relationship of a paternalistic kind, whereby followers attach themselves to the leader, who is expected both to give direction to their activities and to provide benefits for them. Discussions of *habatsu* sometimes link them with OYABUN-KOBUN RELATIONSHIPS, which may roughly be translated as relations between boss and henchman. Today, however, such a comparison is regarded as derogatory. The point is though that the *oyabun* is a 'quasi-parent' to his *kobun* who are his 'quasi-children'. In other words, the language that is being used is the language of family relationships.

Some analysts maintain that the language of Japanese cultural specificity ought to be avoided in discussions of socio-political phenomena such as *habatsu*. The point is well taken, because Japanese political factions may be regarded as integral parts of a modern political system that merits comparison with other political systems in many parts of the world. Nevertheless, those who would banish cultural considerations from the understanding of *habatsu* are faced uncomfortably with the sheer pervasiveness of this phenomenon in political organisations such as parties. The quite reasonable argument that *habatsu* behave rationally in terms of their perceived interests does not quite meet the objection that they behave in significantly different ways from possibly parallel types of group in other parts of the world. In particular, many Japanese *habatsu* have long pedigrees, extending over decades. Indeed, sometimes, their histories last longer than those of the parties (or other organisations) of which they are a part. Also, though policy prescription is likely to be an aspect of their purpose, it may well be easily subordinated to the maintenance of the *habatsu* and of the integrity of its internal relationships.

The best solution to this problem may well be to regard *habatsu* as culturally conditioned, but politically adaptive. We may illustrate this by consideration of three examples of *habatsu*, and *habatsu*-systems, in operation.

Factions in the Liberal Democratic Party

The LIBERAL DEMOCRATIC PARTY (LDP) has an entrenched *habatsu*-system, which has passed through various phases of adaptation. Soon after the party's foundation in 1955, a number of well-organised internal bodies emerged, playing a particularly crucial role in votes for the party presidency and in the allocation of posts within CABINET and the LDP itself. Some of them were led by men who had been prominent in the various conservative parties that preceded the LDP. Some were known in the media as 'bureaucratic' *habatsu*, in the sense that a large percentage of their members (and of course their leader) had entered politics via a career in a Government ministry. Others were labelled 'party men' *habatsu*, since their leader and a good proportion of their members came from a career in local and national politics. This division, in turn, represented a clash between the YOSHIDA school of ex-bureaucrat politician, which had come to the fore during the Occupation period, and those pre-war politicians released from the purge in 1951–2.

The bureaucrat-party man distinction gradually lost salience, but a system developed whereby the *habatsu* became an integral part of candidate selection, fund distribution, electoral campaigning and post allocation. Each *habatsu* supported candidates in as many electoral districts as practicable, competing with the candidates of other LDP *habatsu* in multi-member constituencies. *Habatsu* collected funds to distribute to their candidates in their electoral campaigns. The leaders would campaign on behalf of their own members in the run-up to elections. They would also bargain with the LDP President (concurrently PRIME MINISTER) over the distribution of posts in Cabinet and Party. This final function led to a quite rigid system of seniority appointment to posts, where a *habatsu* leader would present to the Prime Minister a seniority-ranked list of his members, and the Prime Minister would allocate posts with primary concern for factional interests and demands. To some extent this system became modified with the more fluid politics from the early 1990s, but the essential *habatsu* logic remained.

Another characteristic of factionalism in the LDP was that of *habatsu* alliances. For many years, governments emerged out of power plays between 'mainstream' and 'anti-mainstream' alliances of rival *habatsu*. This could prove extremely disruptive (late 1970s). At other times (late 1960s, early 1980s) one *habatsu* was so dominant that it was able to dictate who formed governments. In 1992–3 the dominant *habatsu* split, leading to the downfall of the party.

Thus LDP factionalism was not primarily factionalism about policy. *Habatsu* with strong policy agendas tended to be on the fringes of the party (e.g. *Nakagawa-ha* on the right, *Miki-ha* on the left), whereas the principal factions tended to avoid conspicuous policy colouring. In the most recent period, *habatsu* have become less hierarchical, in part as a consequence of tightened rules on fund-raising. Interestingly enough, the new electoral system (see ELECTION SYSTEMS) for the HOUSE OF REPRESENTATIVES, introduced in 1994, though it abolished the multi-member districts that were widely believed to foster intra-LDP factionalism, did not in fact result in the demise of *habatsu*, though it may be helping them to evolve and further adapt.

Factions in the Japan Socialist Party

The JAPAN SOCIALIST PARTY (JSP) was formed after the war on the basis of a number of small Socialist groups operating from the late 1920s. It quickly developed factionalism that followed rather closely the lines of pre-war cleavages. Differences of ideological position (principally between various kinds of Marxist, and social democrats) were the most important markers of factional division. Thus it was normally possible to rank the different Socialist *habatsu* on a spectrum from left to right. We may regard this as an example of adapting the culturally specific *habatsu* phenomenon to the purpose of ideological assertion and disputation. But on occasion more traditional motivations broke through. Obligations between individuals and between groups would create alliances or divisions hard to explain in terms of ideological motivations or consistency.

Factions in the Japan Communist Party and the Clean Government Party

The organisational structure of both the JAPAN COMMUNIST PARTY (JCP) and the CLEAN GOVERNMENT PARTY (CGP) has been based on an anti-factional principle. In the JCP case the Leninist doctrine of democratic centralism means that factionalism is not supposed to happen. But in the 1950s and 1960s the party was beset by the most extreme factional divisions, which could be traced both to ideological and to personal differences going back many years. But in 1958, 1963 and 1966, supporters, respectively of the 'Italian', 'Soviet' and 'Chinese' lines, were summarily expelled from the party. Democratic centralism was ruthlessly upheld, so long as the leadership was strong enough to impose its will.

The CGP also maintains a policy of suppressing internal factionalism, though this was sorely tested in the 1990s with the doomed experiment of merging into the NEW FRONTIER PARTY. In both the Communist and CGP cases, party organisation is highly centralised. These two parties may be seen as the exceptions that prove the rule of Japanese political parties, that *habatsu* or *habatsu*-like activity is an endemic and entrenched part of their method of functioning.

Further reading
Baerwald (1986)
Curtis (1988)
—— (1999)
Kato, in Schmiegelow (1997)
Leiserson (1968)
Morris (1989)
Scalapino and Masumi (1962)
Stockwin (1968a)
—— (1989)
—— (1999)
Totten and Kawakami (1965)

Fair Trade Commission (Kōsei torihiki iinkai) and anti-monopoly policies Anti-monopoly policy (anti-trust policy, in US usage) is an area where the aims and ideals of the Allied Occupation have clashed sharply with standard Japanese practice. Interestingly, however, while the measures to curb monopolistic practice have been weakly enforced in Japan, the promotion of competition has remained a live issue, and the apparatus of enforcement has survived against the odds.

The Occupation authorities after the war were concerned with what they saw as excessive concentrations of economic power in industry and commerce. They set out to break up the conglomerate firms known as *zaibatsu* (financial cliques), though that policy was not pushed through to completion. The other approach that they adopted was to put in place legislation against cartels and other forms of trade restriction. In March 1947 the Anti-Monopoly Law (*Dokusen kinshi hō*)* was passed through Parliament. It contained bans on certain *zaibatsu* practices such as the maintenance of holding companies, and it also banned private monopolies, cartels (between companies of any size) and various forms of unequal or unfair practice.

The Fair Trade Commission (FTC) was set up at the same time that the Anti-Monopoly Law came into force. It was given formal freedom from political control, and accorded quasi-legislative and quasi-judicial powers.

Anti-monopoly policy is relatively easy to enforce where the prevailing ethos is founded in the primacy of free competition so as to foster efficiency and economic dynamism. But that was not the ethos that prevailed in postwar Japan. Rather, priority was given to 'force fed' economic growth, with the closest of linkages between Government ministries and oligopolistic firms. Anxiety about 'practices in restraint of trade' was not allowed to stand in the way of policies and practices designed to promote growth. The model was highly successful, in that economic growth over the 15-year period from 1958 to 1973 averaged around 10 per cent per annum. In these years Government agencies, particularly the MINISTRY OF INTERNATIONAL TRADE AND INDUSTRY (MITI), and business interest groups, especially the FEDERATION OF ECONOMIC ORGANISATIONS (*Keidanren*), were repeatedly able to demonstrate their dominance over the Fair Trade Commission. Indeed, there were occasions where the FTC threatened legal action, and in turn was threatened with abolition.

Following the economic disruption caused by the first oil crisis in 1973–4, the Anti-Monopoly Law was strengthened, though it took four years for this process to be completed. MIKI TAKEO (Prime Minister, 1974–6) was sympathetic to revision of the Law, but in his time two attempts to revise it were unsuccessful. Under FUKUDA TAKEO (Prime Minister, 1976–8), the Government found itself with a paper-thin parliamentary majority, and lacking control of key parliamentary committees. The views of opposition parties had to be taken into account, and, in these more propitious circumstances, revision of the Anti-Monopoly Law was finally accomplished in May 1977.

During the 1980s, the LDP was able to consolidate its grip on power through more generous parliamentary majorities, and the effectiveness of the FTC tended to recede. In the 1990s, on the other hand, a combination of unstable party politics and external pressure from the United States conspired to give rather more effectiveness to the FTC. The Commission had now become sophisticated in the arts of persuasion and pressure geared to a correct understanding of political balances. In Beeman's words: 'the equilibrium shifted according to political balances of power, economic conditions, and the concentration of interests that were threatened by stronger antimonopoly policy....the multiplicity of competing interests and ideas often required the deep involvement of politicians to broker final agreements' (p. 175).

Scholarly opinion is divided on the degree to which the FTC has been able to enforce anti-monopoly policy. Tilton, and to a lesser extent Schaede, emphasise the weakness of its enforcement. Beeman, Uriu and Haley make rather more positive assessments. The ban on holding companies, long maintained in the Anti-Monopoly Law, was lifted in 1997, suggesting a weakening of anti-monopoly policy. But moves to reshape the economy in the new century may perhaps see a period of more vigorous enforcement.

*The full title of the law is: Law concerning the Prohibition of Private Monopolisation and the Methods of Preserving Free Trade (*Shiteki dokusen no kinshi oyobi kōsei torihiki no kakuho ni kansuru hōritsu*).

Further reading

Beeman (2002)
Haley, in Yamamura (ed.) (1990)
Schaede (2000)
Tilton (1996)
Uriu (1996)

family and politics In both pre-war and post-war political ideology, enormous emphasis has been placed on the Japanese family as the bedrock of society. The family has been seen as a kind of built-in SOCIAL WELFARE system, responsible for the care of elderly or disadvantaged relatives, as part of a policing system to maintain social order and as an integral part of the education system through close liaison between families and schools (*see* EDUCATION AND POLITICS).

In the pre-war system the ideological content of the family system was overt and fundamental to the ideology of the regime. Hierarchy was stressed, and with it the leadership role of the family head, nearly always the most senior male. The role of women was subordinate to that of men, and this was enshrined in the legal system. The 'corporate' character of the family was perpetuated by a system of family registers (*koseki*), which still exist, and until recent decades were open to public inspection. A bride, on her marriage, would be removed from the register of her parental family and be entered onto the register of the family of her husband. Many works of literature and reportage were devoted to the travails of the new bride, who, as the most junior member of her husband's family, was expected to obey the orders of her mother-in-law, and occupy a position akin to that of an (unpaid) servant.

The myth was maintained of a 'Family State', with the Emperor (*Tennō*) at its head (*see* EMPEROR AND POLITICS), and a metaphor of national paternalism was insistently used. Industrial companies, and other sorts of organisation, were expected to be corporate bodies with a paternalistic and quasi-familistic ethic. Unlike in China, the larger firms were in many cases not literally family firms, but they adopted family-like organisational structures, based on a paternalistic ethic. One thing that is often misunderstood about the pre-war system is that it was to a considerable extent constructed on the basis of a *samurai* ethic that before 1868 had been the ethic of perhaps 10 per cent of the population. This had been extended to the rest of the population as the result of political engineering, but not surprisingly it was observed with greater or lesser commitment depending on the social origin of the sections of the community concerned.

The family was an integral part of a system of social control at local level. The Neighbourhood Association (*tonarigumi*) was an association of a small number of families living typically in a local bloc of houses. The families co-operated, through the Association, with such tasks as street cleaning, but increasingly towards the period of the Asia–Pacific War it was used by Government as a uniform system whereby tasks relating to the war effort could be enforced, and loyalty could be ensured.

The post-war Constitution and civil code gave to women a degree of legal equality they had not enjoyed before, as well as extending the vote to them. In a quip current in the Occupation period, after the war 'women and stockings became stronger'. In practice, of course, social change occurs far more slowly than changes to the legal system. Families still interacted in much the way as they had before, and indeed neighbourhood associations, under a new name in Japanese (*chōnaikai*), continued to flourish, as they still do, though today they are widely regarded as a conservative institution.

Two social developments of the early postwar decades wrought changes in the family system that ultimately worked along with the paper democratisation brought in during the Occupation. One of these was a drastic reduction in the birth rate, following the easing of the abortion laws in 1948. The average number of children per family rapidly reduced until by the late 1990s it was below 1.5. This meant that the number of years in which a woman was primarily engaged in child-rearing was greatly reduced, and it gave her much more freedom to go out to work once her children were no longer in need of full-time care. The average age of marriage for both women and men gradually increased, as more and more highly educated young women were giving priority to career rather than family.

The second, closely related, social development was the extraordinary wave of population shift to the big cities that occurred from the 1950s onwards. This had the effect of rapidly modernising attitudes towards family relationships and to the balancing of family and career. But it also imposed a series of changes on pre-existing family attitudes because of the restricted living space available to most families in a big-city environment. Whereas in the countryside or small towns houses had enough space to accommodate grandparents in reasonable comfort, this was often no longer possible in the cities. By the 1970s this was creating a boom in demand for old people's nursing homes, where few had existed before. Even though in the 1990s some construction companies were specialising in building houses with 'granny flats' incorporated within them, and were even using the term 'traditional family' in some of their advertising, this hardly stemmed the trend towards the nuclear family, consisting only of parents and one or two children. Respect for earlier generations, whether living or dead, had atrophied to a remarkable extent, particularly when compared with another country influenced by Confucian values, South Korea.

A further trend that stemmed from the two mentioned above was the problem of the 'absent father'. Commuting times of up to two hours each way in metropolitan environments meant that many fathers only had significant interaction with their children on Sundays. This greatly shifted the balance of family responsibilities onto the mother, and it was the women in a suburban community who typically came to participate most consistently in local community life. Parent–teacher associations attached to schools, as well as local hobby, sport and interest groups of various kinds, came to be predominantly staffed by women (though often men still occupied the top positions). The inability of fathers to interact sufficiently with their children also led to much soul-searching about family discipline, worries about juvenile delinquency and school violence. Articles came to be written in newspapers suggesting that the current generation of children were growing up soft, and various remedies were advocated, including a return to traditional themes of hierarchy, respect for elders and family discipline.

This kind of theme was hammered home with particular insistence by some religious-political groups of a conservative character, such as *Seichō no ie* (House of Growth) [*see also* RELIGION AND POLITICS]. These had a limited political impact. But concern that family life was breaking down and that this was having potentially adverse effects on social discipline and social order was a theme that resonated with many members of the older generation, and with those of conservative views more generally, particularly outside the major metropolitan areas. As such it was something that politicians needed to take into account in electoral campaigns, even though international comparisons suggested that in these areas Japan's problems were comparatively mild. The prospects that by the second or third decade of the twenty-first century the population of Japan would include unprecedented numbers of elderly people made it tempting for politicians and bureaucrats to implement extremely conservative policies towards the family. But the changes that have taken place in the structure and behaviour of Japanese families over the past half-century make it extremely difficult to treat the family as though it were the kind of entity that existed in 1940 or 1950. Such attempts may well be doomed to failure.

Further reading
Dore (1958)
Hendry (1981)
—— (1995)
Waswo (2002)

Federation of Economic Organisations (Keizai dantai rengōkai, Keidanren) Many commentaries on Japanese government and politics have emphasised the influential position of 'Big Business' – often collectively referred to as *zaikai* (literally 'the financial world') – especially in relation to economic policy. The notion that *zaikai* influence is salient is a central element in the journalistic cliché 'Japan Incorporated', and also to corporatist interpretations of the Japanese politico-economic system (*see* Theories of Japanese politics essay).

Keidanren (as it is universally known) is the most important of the four 'peak associations' of corporate Japan. It was founded in 1946 on the basis of several previously existing bodies. During the Allied Occupation it was a body seeking to represent business interests in general, but in 1952 the JAPAN CHAMBER OF COMMERCE (*Nisshō*) and the Federation of Small and Medium Industries (*Chūshō kigyō renmei*) moved from under the *Keidanren* umbrella and set up independently. This left *Keidanren* essentially representing large corporate interests.

Keidanren is based largely on corporate membership, though a few prominent persons have been individual members. It functions as a liaison organisation for its membership, and, because of its excellent access to the top levels of politics and Government, its voice is clearly heard and its policy perspectives are often reflected in Government action. Its expertise on matters of macro-economic policy is widely respected, even though its viewpoint may be regarded as sectional. But its proposals have ranged over areas not confined to the economic. For instance, at various times it has made interventions into debate about education, advocating structural and syllabus changes to make what is taught in schools as relevant as possible to the needs of industry. At times also, it has intervened in defence debates, in the interests of domestic armaments production – a highly sensitive subject in the Japanese political context.

There is no doubt that *Keidanren* has favoured the LIBERAL DEMOCRATIC PARTY (LDP) since its foundation in 1955. Indeed, it was corporate fear of the prospect of a Socialist Government that led to business pressure on the fractious conservative politicians of the 1950s to merge into a single conservative party in order to head off the Socialist 'threat'. But for the most part until the 1990s *Keidanren* was sufficiently satisfied with the political status quo that it did not need to intervene too directly or insistently in the political process. Political instability from the early 1990s, however, required a change of approach. When the LDP temporarily went into opposition in 1993, *Keidanren* announced that it would no longer channel funds to political parties. Previously it had acted as a clearing house for political funding from corporate firms. The tightening of the laws on political contributions in 1994, and the introduction of public funding of political parties, also required rethinking of its political funding role, although *Keidanren* in the end did not abandon this function altogether. Unsurprisingly, it has been greatly exercised by the difficult business conditions facing the corporate sector in the late 1990s and early 2000s. Moreover, with the increasing diversification of the domestic economy, it finds its membership less united than before on key policy issues, and in broad terms its influence has been declining.

The influence of *Keidanren* in international economic policy is indicated by the fact that it is able to post its representatives in Japanese embassies in major countries. Its involvement in global economic issues has expanded with the transformation of some corporate firms effectively into multinational corporations.

In May 2002, *Keidanren* merged with the JAPAN FEDERATION OF EMPLOYERS' ASSOCIATIONS (*Nikkeiren*) to form the JAPAN FEDERATION OF ECONOMIC ORGANISATIONS (*Nihon keizai dantai rengōkai*).

Further reading
Babb (2001)
Curtis (1988)
Pempel (1998)
Richardson (1997)

forced passage (kyōkō saiketsu, kyōkō kaketsu) of parliamentary legislation In parliaments of most Western nations it is rare for a party or parties to boycott a session in protest against legislation of which it disapproves. Indeed, the principle of decision by majority vote so entrenched in Western democracies would make it a meaningless gesture. In the Japanese Parliament, however, there have been many instances in the past where opposition parties have absented themselves from the vote, either in committee or in plenary session of either house.

This is one of a number of techniques (another being 'COW WALKING') whereby the opposition seeks to show up the Government as arrogant and inclined to ride roughshod over the interests of the minority. In turn it indicates an attitude towards decision-making in which the majority-take-all principle is tempered by the principle of consensus-making. A Government party that passes a bill through Parliament in the absence of opposition parties is accused of committing 'forced passage' of that bill. The implication is that the Government should have listened to the views of the opposition and taken their views into account in the framing of the legislation. That, in the nature of things, is possible where the legislation relates to issues of 'more or less', for instance a bill to compensate workers made redundant, where compromise can be reached about the level of compensation. But it is much more difficult in 'papal infallibility'-type issues, where there is no middle ground between one position and its opposite (a Pope is infallible or he is not).

It is primarily in this latter type of issue that forced passage has occurred. Perhaps the most famous example of it was Prime Minister Kishi's snap vote on the revised Japan–US Mutual Security Treaty in May 1960, in the absence of opposition parliamentarians (who had been evicted from the Chamber by the police) (*see* SECURITY TREATY REVISION CRISIS). Any possibility of compromise had been practically made impossible by the intransigence of both sides. Forced passage was a rather common phenomenon of the 1960s, but much less so from the early 1970s because the LIBERAL DEMOCRATIC PARTY (LDP) majority over the opposition parties was greatly reduced. Even in the 1960s the LDP used it sparingly, because, in Baerwald's words, frequent boycotts by the opposition 'could raise doubts in the minds of the Japanese public concerning the viability of [Parliament] as a viable institution' (Baerwald, 1986, p. 90).

From an LDP perspective, in circumstances of ideological polarisation between the two sides of party politics, the alternative to forced passage – consultation with the opposition – looked unattractive. Baerwald quotes a Cabinet Minister he interviewed in 1985 as deriding the inefficiency of Parliament: 'The Opposition knows that we [LDP] will not use *kyōkō saiketsu*, and that everything will be handled by means of mutual consultations. In effect, it is the opposition parties that have controlled [Parliament's] agenda' (ibid., p. 152). Since the 1970s forced passage has more or less faded from the scene. Relations between Government and opposition parties have become less ideologically polarised, and, with coalition Government becoming the norm from the early 1990s, opposition parties are more likely to place themselves in a position where they might join the Government than to shame it into a forced passage. In the mid-1990s, however, it returned in a new form, when the New Frontier Party (NFP, *Shinshintō*) members absented themselves from the vote on 9 June 1995 to endorse a resolution of the Murayama coalition Government expressing regret for Japan's military actions in Asia between 1937 and 1945. The NFP also picketed Parliament in March 1996 in a disagreement about the budget.

Forced passage constitutes an interesting case study of how far socio-cultural factors (preference for consultation and consensus-formation over majoritarianism), and how far pragmatic calculations of political advantage, shape political behaviour in the Japanese context. Plainly both are significant, and one might generalise, following Bailey, that politicians operating under 'normative rules' formed by the socio-cultural context seek to maximise advantage by applying 'pragmatic rules', rather as footballers follow rules of play in the general context of the rules of the game.

Further reading
Baerwald (1974)
—— (1986)
Bailey (1969)

foreign aid During the post-war decades, Japanese foreign aid was often criticised for its commercial bias, being allegedly geared to promoting the interests of Japanese firms seeking to penetrate new areas to their advantage. Thus agreements tying aid to the provision of goods and services by Japanese contractors were a feature of aid agreements entered into by Japan, especially in South-East Asia, in the 1950s and 1960s. From the 1980s, however, overseas development aid (ODA) became a matter of much higher priority for the Japanese Government. The doctrine of 'comprehensive security' that emerged from the Ohira Government of the late 1970s envisaged ODA as part of a national security policy in the sense that providing aid was a way of ensuring at least relative levels of friendship.

In the 1970s and early 1980s, Japanese aid was poorly co-ordinated between a remarkable number of different ministries and agencies of Government. Later, however, it was subjected to careful thought and planning with a view to making it more effective in terms of the aims it was supposed to fulfil. In part, this was in reaction to criticism of much previous poor planning and waste in the administration of ODA.

By the late 1980s, Japanese ODA was of a similar amount, on an annual basis, to that of the United States, or had actually surpassed it. The provision of ODA in a carefully targeted fashion was becoming an important instrument for the projection of low-key influence by Japan in sensitive regions of the world. Partly to avoid the kinds of criticism that had plagued its aid provision in its earlier years, Japan has recently tended to prefer channelling its aid through multilateral channels, such as the Asian Development Bank, in which it has a large stake.

Further reading
Arase (1995)
Rix (1993)

foreign policy A British Foreign Minister claimed in the early 1990s that the United Kingdom 'punched above its weight' in international affairs. In the eyes of many observers, Japan has, rather, 'punched below its weight' since the war, in the international arena. Those who believe that this is the case point to a number of factors that might explain it. Foremost among them is the close security and economic linkages with the United States (*see* UNITED STATES, RELATIONS WITH), which some maintain have made Japan too United States-dependent. Another factor is the pacifist legacy from the post-war years, stemming from appalling wartime destruction (including atomic holocaust in two major cities and air raids creating fire storms in many others), and the peace clause of the CONSTITUTION OF 1946. A third factor frequently cited is an alleged lack of leadership embedded, according to some analysts, in the very structure of the political system.

On closer inspection, however, these factors are more problematic than they appear. Moreover, it is important not to assume that what was true for one period is equally true for other periods. Very roughly speaking, we may divide the years from 1945 to 2002 into four discrete periods, though with the understanding that there is continuity and overlap between them.

The first period is that of post-war recovery and reorganisation, 1945 to 1956. It begins with the defeat and ends with Japan's admission to the United Nations (*see* UNITED NATIONS, RELATIONS WITH). Japan experiences nearly seven years of tutelage under the Allied Occupation (1945–52). Japanese authorities were subject to the authority of the Supreme Commander, Allied Powers, and the State was not able to have an independent foreign policy in a full sense. The course of the Occupation was changed by the development of the Cold War from the late 1940s, followed by a fighting war in Korea from June 1950. The San Francisco peace settlement that came into force in April 1952 had the effect of linking Japan closely with US interests in Asia. Thus, even after recovery of independence, it was easy to argue that Japan was a 'semi-sovereign power', so far as her foreign policy was concerned. Japan recognised the Taipei Government as the Government of China, largely because of US pressure. Nevertheless, the MINISTRY OF FOREIGN AFFAIRS revived, and was able to re-establish embassies and consulates in many countries. A *de facto* military force, known euphemistically as the Self-Defence Forces (*jieitai*) was established in 1954, becoming an integral part of a Japan–United States security relationship founded on the Security Treaty of 1952 (which would be revised, creating a political crisis, in 1960). In this period emerged what later came to be called the 'YOSHIDA doctrine', whereby Japan maintained limited military capacity, but accepted a close security relationship with the United States and concentrated on building up its economy. In 1956 Japan was admitted to the United Nations, and also normalised diplomatic relations with the Soviet Union, though the negotiations left unresolved the status of some minor island territories to the north-east of Hokkaidō.

The second period lasted from 1957 to 1973, and more or less coincided with the economic 'miracle', which transformed both Japanese society and the nation's international economic importance. By 1968 the GNP of Japan surpassed that of West Germany, and so became larger than any in Europe. Japan was coming to be noticed as an international economic power, and as a potential model for rapid economic development elsewhere. Early signs of trade friction were beginning to emerge between the United States and Japan, manifested in a textile trade dispute and President Nixon's *démarche* of August 1971 designed to force revaluation of the Japanese currency.

Standard English-language textbooks of international relations published in the 1960s scarcely mentioned Japan as an actor in international affairs. In fact, a great deal was going on domestically in terms of debate about foreign relations. Political opinion was severely polarised between right and left over the China recognition question, the Vietnam War, the security relationship with the United States, and Japan's claim for the return of Okinawa to Japanese sovereignty (*see* OKINAWA IN JAPANESE POLITICS). The last three of these (and the first to a lesser extent) were inter-related in the sense that Okinawa functioned as a key US military base in pursuit of the Vietnam War, and US bases both in Okinawa and Japan proper were there under the terms of the Security Treaty. SATŌ EISAKU, the Prime Minister in the late 1960s and early 1970s, was placed under intense pressure by the US Government to increase the Japanese contribution to the defence of the East Asian region, particularly in respect of Korea and Taiwan. But these principal issues of the 1960s were mostly brought to a satisfactory solution. Satō negotiated an agreement for the return of Okinawa, which duly reverted to Japanese sovereignty in 1972 (though US bases remained, albeit with their nuclear weapons removed). Anxieties about renewal of the Security Treaty in 1970 failed to materialise, and the Treaty was automatically extended. Nixon, in July 1971, announced that he would visit Beijing, and Satō's successor, Tanaka Kakuei, quickly negotiated normalisation of diplomatic relations with the People's Republic of China in 1972 [*see also* CHINA (PRC AND ROC), RELATIONS WITH]. This, of course, meant de-recognition of the Republic of China on Taiwan, but a *de facto* economic relationship was preserved. Seven years earlier, in 1965, Japan and the Republic of Korea (South Korea) had brought long negotiations to a conclusion and normalised their relationship [see also KOREA (ROK AND DPRK), RELATIONS WITH].

By the early 1970s, therefore, the main contentious issues that had faced Japanese foreign policy-makers in the 1960s were largely resolved, and Japan had been spectacularly transformed into a major economic power. This takes us to the third of our periods, lasting from 1974 to 1991. This third period began with a sharp break from the previous one, since the quadrupling of the price of oil in the OPEC oil crisis of 1973–4 brought economic growth to a sudden halt and created severe inflation, though for a short period only. A combination of the two 'NIXON SHOCKS' of July and August 1971, and the 'oil shock' of 1973–4, led to some reappraisal of foreign policy priorities. For a while the idea gained some currency that Japan should assert greater independence from the United States. This led to some rather minor moves, such as the diplomatic recognition by Japan of the Mongolian People's Republic.

Residual issues with the PRC were sorted out during the 1970s, and in 1978 a Japan–China trade treaty was followed by a peace and friendship treaty. In parallel, however, Japanese relations with the USSR worsened, and Japan was one of a number of nations that boycotted the Moscow Olympics in 1980, following the Soviet intervention in Afghanistan [see also SOVIET UNION AND RUSSIA, RELATIONS WITH]. The period when OHIRA MASAYOSHI was Prime Minister (1978–80) was a formative period in Japanese foreign and defence policy thinking, because Ohira set up a number of *ad hoc* commissions to examine relevant questions. Out of this exercise came the doctrine of 'comprehensive security', whereby the security of Japan was to be regarded not just in terms of military security, but also bearing in mind security of food and energy supplies. A closely related idea, pushed hard through the 1980s, was that Japanese contributions to international security should emphasise assistance to less developed countries, based on rapid increases in overseas development aid.

The NAKASONE administrations of the mid-1980s emphasised the building up of DEFENCE capacity, and indeed throughout the 1980s the defence budget grew at a rate of approximately 6.5 per cent per annum. Nakasone considered himself a revisionist in several areas of national policy, and in foreign affairs was concerned that Japan should be seen to be pulling her weight in the interests of international stability. The Japanese economy was in another phase of rapid growth, but this time Japan accounted for such a high proportion of world output, trade and foreign investment that frictions inevitably resulted. Accusations of mercantilist trading practices, with an essentially closed domestic economy contrasting with expansionist, and even predatory, policies overseas, flew about. It was a time, therefore, of increasingly severe strain on economic issues between the United States and Japan, so that relations between those two countries were punctuated by frequent acrimonious negotiations on a variety of trade-related issues. Nevertheless, at least until 1991, when the third period ends, Japan appeared to be securely locked in to a stable security relationship with the United States, directed largely against the Soviet Union and its Communist allies. US complaints about Japan 'taking a free ride on the Security Treaty' were still heard. But since Japan now paid most of the costs for US military bases on Japanese soil, it was widely accepted that the United States was obtaining a favourable deal from its defence pact with Japan. This was, after all, a state that constituted a '2,500 kilometer-long aircraft carrier moored off the coast of East Asia', to adapt a phrase once used by Nakasone.

Between 1989, with the fall of the Berlin Wall, and December 1991, when the Union of Soviet Socialist Republics fragmented into its constituent republics, the world changed dramatically, and Japan also entered a period of far-reaching change. The year 1991 marks the transition from our third to our fourth periods.

The removal of the Soviet Union as the primary threat for both the United States and Japan was thought likely by some to bring to an end the Japan–United States security relationship, or at least to result in its radical downgrading. The fact that, if anything, the reverse of this has occurred – that there has been a notable strengthening of the relationship – is one of the more surprising developments of the fourth period. Several reasons may be adduced to explain it. First of all, despite the brief popularity in the early 1990s of dubious 'End of History' arguments, the removal of one major 'enemy' did not automatically guarantee a peaceful world, or a peaceful East Asia. Moreover, although the Cold War had ended in Europe, it was not immediately so clear that it had ended in East Asia. The Korean peninsula remained divided between a Stalinist North and a capitalist South, each facing the other across a fortified frontier with huge armies on either side, and far less communication between them than there had been between the two Germanys. The PRC had opened its economy, but the Chinese Communist Party continued to monopolise political power. Despite the development of some economic interaction, relations between the PRC and Taiwan remained tense, and were to become worse later in the 1990s. Rightly or wrongly, the long-term ambitions of the PRC were a continuing focus of concern for Japanese policy makers, as for their US counterparts, even though US administrations were to reveal some ambivalence of attitude between China and Japan.

A formative moment in the development of Japanese foreign policy thinking in our fourth period was provided by the Gulf crisis and war of 1990–1. After some delay and indecision, the Government of KAIFU TOSHIKI provided $13 billion towards the costs of the United States-led expeditionary force that eventually liberated Kuwait. But Kaifu was unsuccessful in gaining parliamentary approval for a bill to permit the use of Self-Defence Forces in such expeditions overseas, and it was left to his successor, MIYAZAWA KIICHI, to achieve this in July 1992. The considerable international criticism to which this apparent indecisiveness gave rise led over the course of the 1990s to a shift in the balance of public opinion in favour of more proactive and co-operative policies in defence of international stability. In 1997 Japan and the United States signed a Guidelines Agreement, increasing Japanese obligations to assist with various aspects of any US military (especially naval) actions outside the territory of Japan. Following the terrorist attacks on New York and Washington in September 2001, the Koizumi Government brought in legislation enabling Self-Defence Force contingents to join the international effort in Afghanistan. The net result has been a considerable strengthening of co-operation in security matters between Japan and the United States, even though the 'principal enemy' (the USSR) has disappeared.

The fourth period, on the other hand, has been a time of major economic difficulty and stagnation for Japan, and in this respect it contrasts markedly with the previous periods. To some extent this has taken the pressure off Japan in respect of its foreign and defence policies. Trade frictions between Japan and other countries (most notably, the United States) have much diminished by contrast with the 1980s. The United States is the sole remaining superpower, and Japan a major middle power, rather than (as it appeared to be) an aspiring superpower. In this respect, Japan has become somewhat less exposed, so that modest increases in contributions to international security are easier to manage domestically than they might have been in previous decades. Since 11 September 2001, Japan's situation *vis-à-vis* the United States has been compared with that of Britain. But the endemically cautious leadership of Japan is less inclined to take a high profile in support of US exercises against terrorism than is the Government of the British Prime Minister, Tony Blair.

In conclusion, let us return to the points made in our opening paragraph. We suggested that Japan's tendency to 'punch below its weight' in international affairs might be induced by some combination of a dependency syndrome in relation to the United States, a pacifist legacy stemming from the atomic holocaust and the peace Constitution, and by structural weaknesses in political leadership. But though each of these factors holds some explanatory value, it seems explicable also in terms of national interest. Again, we need to be careful about periodisation. In the earlier post-war decades Japan had little choice but to follow the United States. It was only when the economic 'miracle' had sufficiently enhanced Japan's international status that any loosening of the bonds with the United States might rationally be contemplated. In the early 1950s Yoshida Shigeru, as Prime Minister, resisted pressure from John Foster Dulles for massive and immediate rearmament by Japan, arguing that this would be unacceptable to neighbouring countries, politically destabilising and economically damaging. A compromise was reached leading to the construction of modest Self-Defence Forces with highly restrictive rules of engagement. We may well ask what the effect would have been on Sino-Soviet relations in the 1950s and 1960s had the two Communist powers suddenly been faced by a militarily resurgent Japan. The Sino-Soviet rift, which turned out to be massively beneficial to the Western side in the Cold War, might well not have occurred – or not have been so divisive – had that been the case.

Later, particularly in the 1980s, the really quite severe economic conflicts between Japan and the United States might have taken a different turn had Japan been militarised in such a way as to give power to extreme nationalist elements. As the left pointed out on many occasions, this was a real danger given the historical and cultural background. As it was, the disputes were noisy, but reasonably manageable.

Finally, during our fourth period, both the domestic and international political environments of Japan have been much more unstable and unpredictable than before. The pacifist inhibitions against more proactive foreign policies have been somewhat reduced, though the residue of pacifist sentiment runs very deep, and is not about to disappear. Relations with the United States remain complex and multifaceted, but have been strengthened rather than weakened over the past decade. Structural weaknesses in political leadership remain an inhibiting factor, but this is seen as a problem and remedies are being attempted. What has changed over the long term is a gradual increase in the sophistication and complexity of foreign policy-making in Japan. Japanese foreign policy makers today have a depth and breadth of experience of contemporary international relations that they lacked three or four decades ago. Even though the low profile remains, Japan is in fact a major international player in many fields centrally important to the stability of global systems of interaction. Since the early 1990s Japan has been bidding for permanent membership of the UN Security Council. In terms of the potential contribution Japan could make to the world body if admitted to permanent membership, Japan would seem to have impressive credentials with its international sophistication and experience.

Further reading
Chapman *et al.* (1983)
Curtis (ed.) (1993)
Dore (1997)
Drifte (1998)
—— (2000)
Hellmann (1972)
Hook *et al.* (2001)
Inoguchi (1991)
—— (1993)
Langdon (1973)
Mochizuki (1997)
Newland (ed.) (1990)
Ozaki and Arnold (eds) (1985)
Scalapino (ed.) (1977)
Schoppa (1997)
Vogel, Stephen K. (2002)
Welfield (1988)

foreign pressure (gaiatsu) In the often acrimonious negotiations that took place over trade and investment issues between Japan and the United States during the 1980s, it was noticed that foreign pressure could sometimes be effective in shifting Japanese policy where domestic political actors could do little.

This appeared to be a consequence of the immobilist character of the Japanese political process, whereby the total effect of checks and balances was such that real shifts of policy were difficult to bring about. In these circumstances, foreign political actors became *de facto* participants in the domestic Japanese political process. In some instances, a political or bureaucratic group within Japan would enlist the help of foreign negotiators in order to overcome resistance from other domestic groups to policy change. It is important not to exaggerate the extent of this phenomenon, but its existence even to a limited extent is some indication of the difficulties experienced with the implementation of necessary change.

Needless to say, much of the foreign pressure came from US sources, so that *gaiatsu* was often referred to as *beiatsu* (US pressure).

Further reading
Inoguchi and Jain (2000)
Schoppa (1997)

From Five In June 1997 HOSOKAWA MORIHIRO and four of his associates defected from the NEW FRONTIER PARTY (NFP) and formed what is probably the only party in Japanese history to give its name only in English, signifying, presumably, that it was destined to grow beyond its original five members. Like HATA, whose group defected a few months earlier and formed the SUN PARTY, Hosokawa found OZAWA's leadership style difficult to accept. After the collapse of the NFP, From Five joined with three other groups to form the MINSEITŌ in January 1998, and ended up as part of the DEMOCRATIC PARTY in April of the same year.

Fujiyama Aiichirō Fujiyama Aiichirō was a prominent example of a successful businessman turned politician, and a central figure in the KISHI Government's negotiation of a revised security treaty with the United States between 1958 and 1960 [*see also* SECURITY TREATY REVISION CRISIS]. Unlike Kishi, however, he was an enthusiast for normalising relations with the PRC [*see also* CHINA (PRC AND ROC), RELATIONS WITH].

Born in 1897, as a young man he entered (and soon inherited) his father's business empire, based on sugar refining, and in 1941 became President of the Japan Chamber of Commerce and Industry. He was involved in efforts to remove Tōjō from office during the war, but even so was purged from public life during the Allied Occupation, returning to his business career in 1951. When the Kishi administration was formed in 1957, Fujiyama, a confidant of Kishi, was brought in as Foreign Minister. His contribution to the shape of the revised Treaty was significant, and the exercise was ultimately successful, but he was inevitably damaged by the severe crisis that it provoked in 1960.

In 1960, 1964 and 1966 he stood unsuccessfully for the LIBERAL DEMOCRATIC PARTY presidency, which would have carried with it the prime ministership, spending much of his personal fortune on the attempt, in the course of which he had formed his own intra-party faction. During the later 1960s he was disappointed in the negative attitudes of the party leadership towards the PRC, being convinced that there was a 'natural linkage' between two Confucian civilisations.

He died, aged 87, in February 1985.

Fukuda Takeo Fukuda's was the type case of an elite political career path. He came from an old established family of local notabilities, attended top schools and Tokyo Imperial University, had a brilliant career in the MINISTRY OF FINANCE, then rose to the very top in politics. Born in 1905, he had attained senior positions in the Finance Ministry by the late 1940s. He then faced a setback, being implicated in the SHŌWA DENKŌ SCANDAL of 1948, which forced his resignation from the ministry before he could become Vice-Minister. He was first elected to the HOUSE OF REPRESENTATIVES in 1952 for his home district in Gunma, which went on to return him a total of 14 times. It was not until 1958 that he was found not guilty of financial malpractice. Although briefly a member of the Liberal Party, he was far from happy with YOSHIDA, and joined the Japan Democratic Party when it was formed in November 1954, and the LIBERAL DEMOCRATIC PARTY (LDP) on its formation a year later. In the KISHI administration (1957–60) he was Chairman of the Policy Affairs Research Council, and later Secretary-General, of the LDP, before becoming Agriculture Minister in 1959. Kishi he found congenial, but the story was different with IKEDA, of whose 'income doubling' policies he disapproved. Once SATŌ was PRIME MINISTER (1964–72) he was in his element again and his career blossomed. He became successively Finance Minister, Foreign Minister and LDP Secretary-General.

Although Fukuda was regarded as the natural successor to Satō as LDP President and Prime Minister, by 1972 Satō was discredited and the party preferred the earthy dynamism of TANAKA to the patrician polish of Fukuda. Thus began a decade of rivalry between Tanaka and Fukuda, causing severe intra-party strain. Nevertheless, Fukuda served in the Tanaka Government, first as Administrative Board Director and then, once again, as Finance Minister.

Tanaka, however, he thought too inclined to fuel inflation, and in July 1974 both he and MIKI TAKEO resigned their ministerial posts. Tanaka was forced out of office later in the year, and Miki succeeded him as Prime Minister. Under Miki, Fukuda became Deputy Prime Minister and Economic Planning Board Chairman, but he was critical of Miki and resigned his positions in November 1976. Next month, following poor election results, Miki resigned and Fukuda was elected party President – and thus Prime Minister – in his stead.

As Prime Minister, Fukuda pursued cautious financial policies, and took important initiatives in policy towards South-East Asian economic development. In 1978 the LDP for the first time ran primary elections among local party members for the presidency. The combined organisational efforts of the Tanaka and OHIRA factions secured Ohira's victory over Fukuda, who was denied a second prime ministerial term. The defeat rankled, and, after the general elections of October 1979, Fukuda challenged Ohira for the leadership, precipitating a 40-day crisis that was only resolved by a close vote in Parliament in favour of Ohira. The following summer Fukuda's faction was one of three to abstain in a vote of no-confidence against the Ohira Government, thus precipitating the Government's resignation and new general elections. Fukuda died in 1995, aged 90.

Further reading
Curtis (1999)
Stockwin (1999)

Fuwa Tetsuzō Known earlier as the 'Crown Prince' of the JAPAN COMMUNIST PARTY (JCP), Fuwa Tetsuzō (original name Ueda Kenjirō) has been at the centre of JCP decision-making since 1970.

Born in 1930 in Tokyo, he graduated from Tokyo University, bringing elite educational credentials to the JCP leadership. Elected to the HOUSE OF REPRESENTATIVES for a Tokyo constituency in 1969, he became Secretary-General in 1970, launching a stable MIYAMOTO–Fuwa regime in the party, even though NOSAKA remained Chairman of the Central Committee. When Nosaka retired in 1982, and Miyamoto stepped into his position, Fuwa became Chairman of the Secretariat of the Central Committee. It was not until Miyamoto retired, aged 89, in 1997, that Fuwa – no longer young – graduated to the Central Committee chairmanship.

Even though the JCP never repeated its electoral successes of the 1970s, it is significantly owing to Fuwa that the party survived the ending of the Cold War. It attracted significant numbers of electors because of its criticism of Government and refusal to make deals with other parties, especially the LIBERAL DEMOCRATIC PARTY.

G

General Council of Japanese Trade Unions (Nihon Rōdō Kumiai Sōhyōgikai, Sōhyō)
Sōhyō was much the largest of Japan's labour union federations throughout the period of its existence (1950–89). At the height of its influence it accounted for some 4,800,000 unionists in their constituent industrial unions (*tansan*). These included *Kokurō* (the national railwaymen's union), *Nikkyōso* (the JAPAN TEACHERS' UNION), *Zendentsū* (the electricians' union), *Zentei* (the communications workers' union), *Shitetsu sōren* (General Federation of Private Railway Workers' Unions of Japan), *Jichirō* (All-Japan Prefectural and Municipal Workers' Union) and *Tekkō Rōren* (Japan Federation of Steel Workers' Unions).

On its foundation in July 1950 it was regarded as a bulwark against far-left influences that had dominated, in particular, the CONGRESS OF INDUSTRIAL UNIONS (*Sanbetsu kaigi*). There is evidence of Occupation involvement in the process leading to its birth. Different constituent unions, however, had contrasting political views, and, in the turbulent ideological climate after the outbreak of the Korean War and the approaching Japanese peace settlement, *Sōhyō* soon moved towards the left. This was already evident in its second Congress in March 1951, which backed positions on a peace settlement and possible rearmament close to those of the left-wing Suzuki faction of the JAPAN SOCIALIST PARTY (JSP). After the JSP split into Left Socialist and Right Socialist Parties in October 1951, *Sōhyō* became the principal organisational support for the Left Socialist Party, strongly opposing US pressure on Japan to become part of an anti-Communist alliance. In July 1953, the *Sōhyō* Secretary-General, Takano Minoru, took the federation even further to the left. Reflecting on the international situation following the death of Stalin, Takano supported the 'peace forces', including the USSR and China, but excluding the United States. Takano once famously remarked that, being responsible for *Sōhyō*'s birth, 'the Occupation hatched a chicken that turned into a duck'.

In April 1954, a substantial group of unions that opposed the turn to the left orchestrated by Takano defected from *Sōhyō*, and formed the ALL-JAPAN TRADE UNION CONGRESS (*Zenrō Kaigi*) (later the JAPAN CONFEDERATION OF LABOUR, or *Dōmei*), which became the principal federation of private-sector unions. Takano's far-left position, however, was under attack from those close to the left-wing factions of the JSP, so that he was eased out of the leadership and replaced by that of Ota Kaoru (Chairman from 1958) and Iwai Akira (Secretary-General from 1955). Ota and Iwai were Marxist-influenced and confrontational towards the revisionist KISHI Government of the late 1950s (and later governments), but hostile to the JAPAN COMMUNIST PARTY.

Their best-known achievement was the establishment of the annual 'spring struggle' from 1955. (This was initiated by Ota as Chairman of the Synthetic Chemical Workers Union.) They recognised that the great weakness of the Japanese enterprise union system was lack of co-ordination between the wage claims of thousands of individual unions.

Therefore they instituted a wage negotiation process, announced in advance and conducted in April of each year, so as to unify union struggles for improved wages and conditions, and thus increase the bargaining power of unions as a whole. This proved a remarkably efficient instrument for achieving reasonably equitable distribution of the improvements in the standard of living taking place during a period of rapid economic growth. By the 1980s, however, declining union membership and bargaining power had reduced its effectiveness.

An important feature of *Sōhyō* was that around two-thirds of its membership was provided by unions in the public sector. These included unions of national railwaymen, teachers and local public servants. But these assembled workers whose rights of industrial bargaining and strike were severely curtailed by legislation introduced in the late 1940s. Thus the concern to have this legislation modified or repealed became a major *Sōhyō* concern, so that in the 1970s 'strikes for the right to strike' became part of its repertoire. To an extent this helped create an image of the federation as more concerned with political and ideological issues than with grass roots concerns about wages and conditions of workers. The 'political' stance of *Sōhyō*, contrasting with the 'economic' approach of *Dōmei* and other union groups, made sense in the 1950s and 1960s, when the direction for Japan to take was unclear and in dispute. It made less sense from the 1970s, when political institutions had stabilised and a prosperous working population was more concerned with its own narrow interests than with overarching ideology.

This in turn greatly affected the JSP. From the 1950s *Sōhyō* unions became the principal organising base for the JSP, and indeed provided many of its parliamentary candidates. But for the party this was a reliable, but far too narrow, set of interests on which to found its basic structure. Indeed, the very reliability of *Sōhyō* support led the party to be too satisfied with permanent opposition status, and, with *Sōhyō* removed in the 1990s, it faced division and near-collapse.

With the rise of 'post-industrial society' and weakening of union bargaining power in the 1980s, *Sōhyō* fell on hard times. Privatisation by the NAKASONE Government of the National Railways devastated *Kokurō* (the national railwaymen's union), as other privatisations harmed their respective unions. Being principally a federation of public-sector unions, *Sōhyō* was hit badly. Negotiations took place between the various federations from 1987 to form a single national federation. This was achieved with the formation of the JAPANESE TRADE UNION COUNCIL (*Rengō*), and in 1989 *Sōhyō* dissolved.

Further reading
Cole *et al.* (1966)
Levine (1958)
Masumi (1995)
Stockwin (1968)

giri-ninjō The idea that mutual obligations are a key feature of Japanese society has a long pedigree in literature on Japan, particularly in the discipline of social anthropology. Ruth Benedict, in her classic 1946 book, *The Chrysanthemum and the Sword*, portrayed Japanese people as 'debtors to the ages and the world', that is, locked into a network of social relationships based on acquired obligations that they could never expect completely to repay. These included obligations both to living people (family members, work superiors, business associates, the Emperor, etc.) and to ancestors, for Japanese were especially meticulous in showing reverence to the memory (or souls) of family members that had gone before. An implication of Benedict's work was that this network of obligations constituted an incentive system of great effectiveness, since the repayment of obligations that could never be completely paid off required self-sacrifice and ascetic behaviour. This theory appeared to go some way to explaining the willingness of ordinary Japanese to die for the Emperor during the war with what was often regarded by their foreign adversaries as fanatical determination.

A term used to express this kind of obligation was *giri-ninjō*. The basic meaning of *giri* is obligation, or duty, so that *giri shirazu* (literally 'not knowing *giri*') means 'lacking a sense of duty'. *Ninjō*, on the other hand, may be translated 'human feeling', so that *giri* and *ninjō* may well come into conflict with each other, as they often do in modern Japanese literature. What is interesting, however, is the common juxtaposition of the two words, implying that relations of obligation are not merely cold and impersonal but warm and 'affective'. Even though this may refer more to the ideal than to the reality, the relationship between the ideal and the reality is complex, with beliefs about how relationships ought to work influencing to a marked extent the ways in which they work in practice.

Under the system in operation before 1945, a pervasive official ideology was propagated, lauding *giri-ninjō*-type relationships. It is therefore difficult to unravel how far these relationships were a product of the ideology and how far they stemmed from genuine social roots. When the official ideology was replaced by democratic prescriptions about behaviour after the war, the influence of *giri-ninjō* nevertheless survived and was particularly evident in politics.

Two examples stand out. First, factionalism remained pervasive in party politics, especially, but by no means exclusively, within conservative parties (*see* FACTIONS WITHIN POLITICAL PARTIES). Although rational choice-type explanations of intra-party factional behaviour carry the argument a considerable distance, they fail to explain the intensity and longevity of relationships between faction leaders and followers, at least in the post-war period. Relations between a politician and his followers were often based in close personal interaction over a long period, resulting in a build-up of mutual obligations linked with human feeling: in other words *giri-ninjō*. The classic faction boss – of whom TANAKA KAKUEI was an excellent example – was adept at providing his followers with material benefits, as well as creating a close and warm community atmosphere. The material benefits were real and substantial, comprising most obviously political funds, but also easy access to contacts and expertise, so that some factions became political information centres apart from anything else. But the *giri-ninjō* element was perhaps equally crucial. Abe Shintarō, a leading member of FUKUDA TAKEO's faction, stated that when he found his faction leader was going to abstain in a vote of no-confidence against the Ohira Government in 1980, he felt he could not go against the decision of a leader to whom he was so close and so obliged, even though it jarred with his better instincts.

A second example of *giri-ninjō* in politics is the pervasive institution of the *kōenkai* (personal support group) set up by parliamentary candidates at constituency level. Here again, there is a complex mixture of instrumental and social motivations operating. The principal purpose of a *kōenkai* is to gather local support for the candidate by bringing together influential people who can influence others to vote for him or her. One particular method used in constructing a *kōenkai* is for the candidate to call on university contemporaries to join the campaign or otherwise give support. This is likely to be on personal friendship/personal obligation grounds, rather than ideological similarity, and such a request is difficult to turn down. Here again, *giri-ninjō* is at work.

There is evidence that instrumental motivations have been gaining ground to some extent in recent years over motivations based on *giri-ninjō*, but the latter are by no means dead, and continue to influence politics, as they do other spheres of life.

Further reading
Benedict (1946, 1954)
Hendry (1995)
Ike (1957)
Krauss *et al.* (1984)

Great Hanshin–Awaji Earthquake (Dai Hanshin Awaji shinsai) of January 1995 and politics On 17 January 1995, a heavily populated area of Japan not normally associated with seismic activity was hit by a severe earthquake. The worst affected area was the city of Kōbe, but parts of Osaka and the Inland Sea island of Awaji were also badly hit. In Kōbe the parts of the city adjacent to the sea front, where there were many old wooden houses with heavy tiled roofs, caught the full brunt of the quake. Fires took hold over a large area. Long sections of overhead road collapsed sideways and rail links between the east and west of Japan were cut, taking some months to re-establish. The port of Kōbe – one of the busiest in Japan – was closed for many months. Reclaimed land, including two artificial offshore islands, were subject to 'liquefaction' of their ground base. The death toll exceeded 6,000, and there was enormous property damage, though newer buildings, built to exacting safety standards, survived much better than old ones. Though usually known outside Japan as the Kōbe Earthquake, the title that came to be applied in Japan reflected its geographic spread, 'Hanshin' meaning 'Osaka–Kōbe'.

The earthquake revealed severe deficiencies in the organisation of rapid reaction for disaster relief. Different agencies failed to co-ordinate their activities. The Self-Defence Forces (*Jieitai*) – the entity best prepared to deal with disasters – were not immediately called. Many lives that could have been saved were needlessly lost in the first few hours because of the failure of relief services to arrive. Admittedly, firefighting and ambulance services were greatly hampered by blocked roads, severed water mains and the fact that in some cases their own facilities had been wrecked. The Kōbe area had not suffered an earthquake on this scale for some 400 years, so that the kinds of preparation in place in Tokyo hardly existed. But over the weeks and months following, public criticism of bumbling officialdom became intense. Officials, for instance, proved inept in handling international offers of technical aid in the relief effort. The principle of NAWABARI (roping off different spheres of jurisdiction) was pilloried, and the press noted that the PRIME MINISTER had first heard of the disaster on the TV news.

The earthquake had several effects of political significance. First, it gave a boost to moves for reform of the Government's administrative structure, with a view to creating better co-ordination between agencies. Coupled with the *sarin* gas attack on the Tokyo subway a few weeks later [*see also* AUM SHINRIKYŌ AND THE POLITICS OF MASS POISONING], the earthquake focused intense national attention on the preparations for disaster relief. Second, it raised complex and long-running issues of compensation, in which Government had to become involved. The affected areas were rebuilt with remarkable speed, but property claims dragged on for much longer. Third, the slow reaction of official relief services led to spontaneous relief efforts by local groups. This in turn gave rise to heightened interest in civic society, and a realisation of its potential to act with better understanding of local needs and conditions than sclerotic official agencies.

There were also more immediate political effects. The earthquake occurred just six months into the Murayama coalition Government, of Socialists, Liberal Democrats and *Sakigake* members. On the very day the disaster occurred a new party was due to be formed by dissident Socialists, threatening the power base of the Prime Minister. But the earthquake resulted in an immediate suspension of competitive party politics, and the new party was placed on hold (the JAPAN SOCIALIST PARTY split over 18 months later, in September 1996).

Undoubtedly the most important legacy of the Great Hanshin–Awaji Earthquake was the debate it precipitated about the inadequacies of administrative structures and practice, together with its boost to civic society. McCormack gives a particularly provocative account of the administrative inadequacies exposed by the disaster, inherent in what he calls the 'Construction State'.

Further reading
McCormack (1996)

H

Hashimoto Ryūtarō When Hashimoto Ryūtarō became PRIME MINISTER in January 1996, it signalled that power had moved definitively back to the LIBERAL DEMOCRATIC PARTY (LDP) after two and a half years painfully trudging back from the political wilderness. When he resigned in July 1998, it indicated that, to survive, a Prime Minister now had to please a fickle electorate, not just the party.

Born in 1937, he graduated from Keiō University and first entered the House of Representatives for an Okayama constituency in 1963 at the age of 26, thereafter ensuring it was a safe seat. He joined the TANAKA faction, which he eventually came to lead. He was Health and Welfare Minister under OHIRA (1978–9), Transport Minister under NAKASONE (1986–7), Finance Minister under KAIFU (1989–90), MITI Minister under MURAYAMA (1994–6), and at one stage was LDP Secretary-General.

As Prime Minister from January 1996, he promoted reform of the financial system, with deregulation proceeding over a four-year period from 1997, and planned to reduce the number of government ministries over a similar period. Nevertheless, there was little in Hashimoto's record to suggest passionate commitment to reforming the system of government, and he proceeded cautiously. A huge issue for him was consumption tax. After much debate and uncertainty, he raised the rate from 3 to 5 per cent in 1998, following an intense campaign by the MINISTRY OF FINANCE. The timing was unfortunate, however, since it deepened the recession associated with the Asian economic crisis. The electorate reacted savagely, and in the Upper House elections of July 1998 the LDP lost many seats. Hashimoto consequently resigned at the end of July, to be replaced by OBUCHI KEIZŌ of the same faction.

Obuchi was incapacitated by a stroke on April 2000 and was replaced by MORI YOSHIRŌ, who quickly lost popularity. When Mori resigned in April 2001, the former Tanaka faction chose Hashimoto, now its leader, as its candidate for the succession. In primary elections conducted by party branches, Hashimoto and two other candidates were overwhelmed by the whirlwind candidacy of KOIZUMI JUNICHIRŌ. It undoubtedly hurt Hashimoto's chances of making a comeback that he was now seen as an election loser. Koizumi, in constructing his Cabinet, pointedly ignored the claims of the Hashimoto faction, thus risking its revenge once his own popularity began to decline, as it did from early in 2002.

Further reading
Curtis (1999)
Stockwin (1999)

Hata Tsutomu Born in 1935 in Nagano, Hata Tsutomu was briefly Prime Minister of a minority Government in the summer of 1994.

He was first elected from Nagano to the HOUSE OF REPRESENTATIVES for the LIBERAL DEMOCRATIC PARTY (LDP) in its 1969 landslide, and became a rising star of the TANAKA (later TAKESHITA) faction that dominated the LDP by the 1980s. He was Agriculture Minister for brief periods under NAKASONE in 1985–6, and again under Takeshita in 1988–9. Later he was Minister of Finance under MIYAZAWA between November 1991 and December 1992.

The split that occurred in the LDP in 1992–3 was initially a split in the Takeshita faction, following the disgrace of KANEMARU SHIN, its *de facto* leader, in the middle of 1992. In December 1992 Hata and OZAWA ICHIRŌ set up a group called 'Reform Forum 21'. Subsequently, in June 1993, following the withdrawal of Prime Minister Miyazawa's electoral system reform proposals, members of this group voted in favour of a motion of no-confidence in the Government introduced by most opposition parties. On 23 June Hata and Ozawa set up the JAPAN RENEWAL PARTY (*Shinseitō*), with 44 former LDP parliamentarians from both houses. In Lower House general elections in July, the new party won 55 seats, and became the core element in the Hosokawa coalition Government formed on 9 August.

Even though Ozawa was the brains behind the establishment of the Hosokawa Government, Hata was made President of the Japan Renewal Party (JRP), and became both Deputy Prime Minister and Foreign Minister. Ozawa seems to have initially considered Hata for Prime Minister, but, seeking to broaden the new Government's appeal, passed him over in favour of Hosokawa. Hata did become Prime Minister, however, once the Hosokawa Government collapsed in April 1994. Initially, the parties composing the Hata coalition were the same as those in its predecessor, but once the Socialists realised Ozawa was planning to exclude them from a new consolidated anti-LDP party, they pulled out, leaving the Hata Government in a minority position. The Government passed a much-delayed budget, before resigning in June.

In December 1994 Ozawa's dream of a consolidated party of opposition was finally realised, and the NEW FRONTIER PARTY (NFP, *Shinshintō*) was born. Its founding President was KAIFU TOSHIKI, but in December 1995 elections were held for the presidency between the two former allies, Ozawa and Hata. In the event, Ozawa won easily, in a contest based on a wide popular electorate. Relations between them subsequently deteriorated, and, a year later, Hata left the NFP, forming a small party called the SUN PARTY (*Taiyōtō*). Following the break-up of the NFP at the end of 1997, Hata and his followers eventually (April 1998) found their way into the expanded DEMOCRATIC PARTY (*Minshutō*).

Further reading
Curtis (1999)
Stockwin (1999)

Hatoyama Ichirō Hatoyama Ichirō represented the second of four generations of a famous political family. His father, Kazuo, entered the House of Representatives in 1892, his younger brother, Hideo, was a parliamentarian in the 1930s, his son, Iichirō, was Foreign Minister in the 1970s, and, among his grandsons, in 2002 Kunio was a LIBERAL DEMOCRATIC PARTY (LDP) parliamentarian and Yukio leader of the DEMOCRATIC PARTY.

Born in 1883, he was elected to Parliament in 1915 for the *Seiyūkai*, and occupied senior party and Cabinet posts from the late 1920s. As Minister of Education in 1933 he acted repressively against Takikawa Yukitoki, a Kyōto University law professor of moderate liberal views, who was dismissed from his position. During the war he criticised the Konoe regime, and was elected to Parliament in 1942 as a 'non-recommended' candidate.

Immediately after the war he founded the JAPAN LIBERAL PARTY (I) and became its President. The general elections of April 1946 produced a plurality for his party, and he began to construct a Cabinet, but was promptly purged by the Occupation and had to concede the party leadership to YOSHIDA SHIGERU. It was widely believed (though later denied by Yoshida) that they had agreed Yoshida would hand back the leadership to Hatoyama once the latter was depurged. In 1951 Hatoyama was free to return to politics, rejoined the Liberal Party, but engaged in a fierce faction fight with Yoshida. Early in 1953 he formed the SEPARATISTS' LIBERAL PARTY (*Buntōha Jiyūtō*) – also known as the Liberal Party Hatoyama faction – which won 35 seats in the April elections. Hatoyama and most of its parliamentarians returned to the Liberal Party in November, but relations with Yoshida remained tense. In November 1954, Hatoyama formed the Japan Democratic Party, consisting of the Reformist Party (*Kaishintō*) and his own dissidents from the Liberal Party. This move ensured that he became PRIME MINISTER in December 1954 [*see also* CONSERVATIVE PARTIES, 1945-55].

As Prime Minister, he put forward a radical programme having a less pro-United States and distinctly more nationalist flavour than that of Yoshida. Prominent among his aspirations was to revise the CONSTITUTION OF 1946, and he also promoted – but failed to deliver – a reform of the Lower House electoral system (*see* ELECTION SYSTEMS). As a 'party-man' politician, he sought to ban mah jongg playing by Government officials, often associated with corruption. Undoubtedly the most important political achievement of his period in office was the amalgamation of all significant conservative groups into the LDP in November 1955. In addition, he negotiated the restoration of diplomatic relations between Japan and the USSR in October 1956. Failure to agree on the territorial issue, however, stymied moves towards a peace treaty, and this remained unfinished business nearly fifty years later [*see also* SOVIET UNION AND RUSSIA, RELATIONS WITH].

Hatoyama, in ill health as Prime Minister, stepped down in December 1956, and was succeeded by ISHIBASHI TANZAN. He died in 1959.

Further reading
Kohno (1997)
Quigley and Turner (1956)

Hatoyama Yukio Grandson of HATOYAMA ICHIRŌ (Prime Minister, 1954-56), Hatoyama Yukio became leader of the DEMOCRATIC PARTY in 1999.

Born in 1947 in Tokyo, he graduated from Tokyo University in Engineering and took a doctorate at Stanford University in Operations Research. He was an associate professor at Senshū University in Tokyo, before being elected for the fourth constituency of Hokkaidō in 1986 on the LIBERAL DEMOCRATIC PARTY (LDP) ticket. He was re-elected in 1990 for the LDP, where he was an active committee member. But in 1993 he was one of those who defected to the NEW PARTY HARBINGER (*Shintō Sakigake*), and in the new party boom manifest in those elections, he polled over 30,000 votes more than his nearest rival.

During the coalition governments of the mid-1990s, he occupied junior Cabinet positions. He joined the Democratic Party (*Minshutō*) on its formation in September 1996, becoming one of its two 'representatives' (*daihyō*), the other being KAN NAOTO. This two-headed leadership did not work well, and in September 1997 was replaced by an arrangement whereby, more conventionally, Kan would be 'representative' and Hatoyama 'secretary-general'. In September 1999, however, Hatoyama narrowly beat Kan for the top position in the party, and retained it until 2002. Under his leadership the Democratic Party consolidated its position, and did reasonably well in elections, but, although from 1997 it became the largest party of opposition, it never came close to replacing the LDP in office.

In September 2002, Hatoyama was re-elected to the leadership of the Democratic Party, narrowly defeating his challenger, Kan, and two other candidates. The divisions within his party were reflected in the difficulties he subsequently faced in selecting party executives. In December 2002, after an abortive attempt to merge the Party with Ozawa's Liberal Party, he was forced to resign and was replaced by Kan Naoto.

Further reading
Neary (2002)

HIV-tainted blood scandal (1980s–90s) In the mid-1980s many patients (mainly haemophiliacs) were treated with blood products that turned out to have been infected with the HIV virus, and several hundred of them died. It was alleged that officials of the Ministry of Health and Welfare (*Kōseishō*), knowing of the risk, had failed to insist that the products were heat-treated in order to eliminate the virus. It was further alleged that this failure had been motivated by a desire to protect the profits of pharmaceutical companies. The affair bears some resemblance to a HIV-tainted blood scandal in France at about the same period.

Court cases brought by patients and their relatives against pharmaceutical companies began in the late 1980s. On 9 February 1996 KAN NAOTO, the newly appointed Minister of Health and Welfare in the first HASHIMOTO Government, held a press conference in which he revealed the existence of files in the ministry. These demonstrated that already in 1983 the ministry had known about the dangers of treating patients with unheated blood products. Previously, the ministry had denied the existence of such documents. On 16 February Kan met with a group of about 200 haemophiliacs who had been treated with HIV-tainted blood. He apologised to them, bowing deeply, for the previous failure of the ministry to accept responsibility, and for having infected them with the AIDS virus. This caused a political sensation, not only because of the gravity of the affair, but because the Minister had broken a long-standing taboo against Government officials apologising for faults committed by their ministries.

This affair was different from previous political scandals in that it involved bureaucrats rather than politicians. Indeed, it seems to have been part of a trend in the 1990s whereby accusations of corrupt and/or incompetent behaviour were targeted increasingly at officials of Government ministries. It also affected people's lives more directly than political scandals, where large sums of money had changed hands but for the most part this took place at a level removed from the concerns of ordinary people. The image of Government service was severely tarnished by this scandal, and this no doubt facilitated later reforms of the bureaucratic structure.

Kan's revelations about ministry documents, and his apology to the AIDS sufferers, greatly enhanced his reputation, and he became one of the two key leaders of the DEMOCRATIC PARTY after its foundation in September 1996.

homogeneity and politics Statements may be found in profusion from Japanese sources that the Japanese are a homogeneous people. This is plainly true if the standard of comparison is India, Congo-Kinshasa or even Belgium. It may be true by comparison with major European countries in so far as Japanese governments have permitted far less immigration from abroad than have European governments. But if we except recent immigration, it is not entirely clear that the degree of difference that can be found in different parts of Japan is of a different order from that found in, say, the United Kingdom or France. The following example may seem a trifle facetious, but seems worth making. The present writer once interviewed local officials in Akita and Aomori prefectures of the Tōhoku region in northern Japan. They spoke with accents as thick and difficult to understand* from the perspective of standard (i.e. Tokyo) Japanese as the inhabitants of Kirkcaldy, in Fife, Scotland, sound to anyone whose 'standard English' is based on the south-east of England. Moreover, the officials in Akita and Aomori exhibited attitudes towards central government in Tokyo that probably had much in common with those that would be found among local officials in Kirkcaldy.

Rivalries between different regions of Japan are notorious: Kantō (Tokyo region) versus Kansai (Osaka region), even Kōbe versus Osaka within the Kansai. Social class is said to have been largely eliminated in Japan, since huge majorities answer 'middle class' when asked what social class (or stratum) they belong to. Much of this, however, is a question of perception, since objectively such differences do exist, even if not to an extreme extent. There are also significant differences of religious affiliation, including a plethora of new (and 'new new') religions that have sprung up since the war. The largest of the new religions, *Sōka Gakkai*, claims well over ten million adherents, and, even today (though significantly less than in the past), they are regarded in mainstream society with varying degrees of suspicion [*see also* RELIGION AND POLITICS].

A crucial element in relation to homogeneity is Government policy and ideology. From the late nineteenth century, when governments were striving to construct a modern nation out of scattered fiefdoms, through the intense Emperor-centred indoctrination that reached its apogee in the early 1940s, governments were seeking to *create* a homogeneous people and to iron out diversity, especially diversity with a political agenda. With new and democratic institutions from the Occupation period onwards, governments could no longer be so direct in their approach. But one method was to put in place social and economic measures to even out differences and standardise institutions (the education system (*see* EDUCATION AND POLITICS) is a good example of this, but so are efforts to improve the lifestyle of minorities, especially the *Burakumin*) [*see also* MINORITIES AND POLITICS]. A second method, which has developed considerable sophistication since the 1980s, has been to use what may be called the 'ripples in the pond' approach, whereby the Government incorporates into its patronage structure wider and wider sections of the population. A fourth has been a highly restrictive policy on immigration. And finally, Government has, in a variety of subtle ways, inculcated the notion that the Japanese are a homogeneous – and indeed uniquely homogeneous – people. Statements by NAKASONE YASUHIRO, as Prime Minister in the 1980s, that Japan lacked minorities – implying that so-called minorities were really part of the Japanese family – are a case in point.

*The mayor of one small town spoke adenoidally of *utsu no matsu no fukusu chiikaku* ('our town's welfare plan'), where in standard Japanese it would be *uchi no machi no fukushi keikaku*.

Further reading
Dale (1986)
Kelly, in Gordon (ed.) (1993)
Kinmonth (1985)
Neary (2002)

Hosokawa Morihiro Scion of an ancient aristocratic family from which sprang the lords (*daimyō*) of the Higo Domain (*han*) in the Tokugawa period, Hosokawa led the first non-LIBERAL DEMOCRATIC PARTY (LDP) Government for 38 years in 1993–4.

Born in 1938 in Kumamoto (formerly Higo), Hosokawa was briefly a journalist before being elected to the HOUSE OF COUNCILLORS for the LDP in 1971 from Kumamoto. Between 1983 and 1991 he was Governor of Kumamoto Prefecture, during which time he claimed that he needed 'permission from Tokyo even to move a bus stop'. Disillusioned with LDP-centred politics, in 1992 he founded the JAPAN NEW PARTY (*Nihon Shintō*), and in July of that year was elected under that label from the proportional representation constituency of the House of Councillors. In July 1993, when splits had already occurred in the LDP, he stood for the HOUSE OF REPRESENTATIVES in Kumamoto, and saw his party win 35 seats in the general elections.

With the departure of the LDP from power on 9 August, Hosokawa found himself PRIME MINISTER of an administration consisting of seven parties and one Upper House grouping. He also at first enjoyed popular approval ratings at the unprecedented level of over 70 per cent. His Government set out a programme of structural and policy reform, including deregulation of the economy, decentralisation of Government, reform of the electoral system, tightened anti-corruption measures and public funding of political parties, and economic reforms including reforming the taxation system. This in effect set out the agenda of political reform for the next several years, but Hosokawa achieved little in terms of deregulation and decentralisation. Indeed Government officials soon discovered that they could more easily manipulate inexperienced ministers and so maintain their regulatory grip on power than battle-hardened ministers of the LDP. Hosokawa with difficulty achieved a radical reform of the Lower House electoral system, an anti-corruption law and public funding law, though these measures were not finalised until after his Government ended. He also negotiated a conclusion to the Uruguay round of trade negotiations, which involved importation of foreign rice and was bitterly opposed by the farming lobby. This he regarded as his most important achievement as Prime Minister. Unlike his predecessors, he made a forthright apology to other Asian nations for Japan's actions during the war. On taxation policy, however, he was persuaded by OZAWA and the MINISTRY OF FINANCE to promote a rise in consumption tax (packaged as a 'welfare tax') from 3 to 7 per cent. This placed him in conflict with his Chief Cabinet Secretary, Takemura Masayoshi, whom he tried, unsuccessfully, to expel from Cabinet.

In April 1994, he abruptly resigned as Prime Minister, for reasons that were not fully elucidated. He was later involved in forming the NEW FRONTIER PARTY (*Shinshintō*), and served as its deputy leader. In June 1997, however, he left and formed a group called 'FROM FIVE' that joined up with the DEMOCRATIC PARTY (*Minshutō*) in April 1998. Shortly thereafter he left politics altogether and devoted himself to making pottery.

Further reading
Curtis (1999)
Stockwin (1999)

House of Councillors (Sangiin) The GHQ draft of a new Constitution in February 1946 envisaged a unicameral legislature. The introduction of a second chamber was perhaps the most significant example of a Japanese contribution to the Constitution-drafting process.

The House of Councillors succeeded to the House of Peers, whose membership was filled entirely by appointment or by birth. While the British House of Lords had served as a model for the House of Peers, the decision to create a wholly elective second chamber in Japan preceded by many decades any such reform of the House of Lords. Article 43 of the 1946 Constitution states that *both* houses 'shall consist of elective members, representative of all the people'. Various ideas were put forward in the formative period to make the House of Councillors different in character and function from the HOUSE OF REPRESENTATIVES. It was hoped that it would prove less partisan, more restrained and reflective, including as members 'persons of learning and experience', and perhaps acting as a check on the excesses of the Lower House. To this end it was given a fixed term, which could not be varied by the whim or strategy of the Government. Article 46 of the Constitution states: 'The term of office of members of the House of Councillors shall be six years, and election for half the members shall take place every three years.' The effect of holding a half-election every three years for members who sit for a six-year term is to delay and blunt the impact of opinion shifts, so that, potentially at least, the Upper House may indeed become a check on a Lower House seeking to ride a surge of fashionable doctrine.

The aspiration towards a house that would contain many 'persons of learning and experience' was quickly dashed. Already by the 1950s, party and factional machines had for the most part taken over the organisation of most Upper House candidates' electoral campaigns. Although there were a few exceptions, for the most part those elected on the basis of their personal image had stood for the national constituency (50 seats in each election) and were nationally known television personalities, sporting heroes and the like. Even this phenomenon declined after the method of election to the national constituency changed to proportional representation in 1982.

The House of Councillors has certain special functions and powers. Under the terms of Constitution, article 54, 'the Cabinet may in times of emergency convoke the House of Councillors in emergency session' when the House of Representatives is dissolved. Much more important is the provision in article 59 that, if the Upper House rejects a bill coming to it from the Lower House, the latter can over-rule such a veto 'with a majority of two-thirds or more of the members present'. In fact, this gives to the House of Councillors effective blocking power, should it care to use it, because the Government of the day rarely commands a two-thirds majority in the House of Representatives. It may, on the other hand, convoke a meeting of a committee of both houses, but there is no guarantee that this will resolve the issue in dispute. A Government facing a recalcitrant Upper House is also not likely to be much helped by the additional provision of article 59, that the Lower House can take a failure to act on a bill by the Upper House to constitute a rejection of that bill, after 60 days have passed. In two key areas the House of Councillors merely has the power to delay a bill for 30 days. These are the budget and treaties (articles 60 and 61). In addition, it is open to the House of Councillors to vote for a different candidate for PRIME MINISTER from the candidate supported by the House of Representatives. According to Constitution, article 67, where the two houses disagree, 'and no agreement can be reached even through a joint committee of both Houses, provided for by law, or the House of Councillors fails to make designation within ten (10) days, the decision of the House of Representatives shall be the decision of the Diet'.

The powers of delay and rejection in the hands of the House of Councillors were of little consequence so long as the LIBERAL DEMOCRATIC PARTY (LDP) maintained a majority of seats in both houses. In the Upper House elections of 1989, however, that party lost its majority in the House of Councillors, and has never subsequently regained it (though it may have a majority together with other parties with which it is in coalition). This made a major – and often underestimated – difference to the way in which party and parliamentary politics is conducted. It has been the principal reason why, despite possessing a Lower House majority in its own right since September 1997, the LDP continues to allow other parties to serve in a coalition Government of which it is the dominant partner.

From the 1990s various proposals were made to distinguish the functions of the House of Councillors more clearly from those of the House of Representatives. For instance the proposal for constitutional revision published by the *Yomiuri Shinbun* in 1994 included the suggestions that treaties should first be presented to the Upper House, which should also have sole power of appointing judges of a proposed Constitutional Court, and the right to impeach judges.

The profile of the House of Councillors has become higher since the LDP defeat in the 1989 Upper House elections, and it has the potential to exercise an enhanced democratic role within the political system as a whole. But it remains the weaker of the two houses [*see also* CONSTITUTION OF 1946; ELECTION SYSTEMS; ELECTORAL HISTORY, HOUSE OF REPRESENTATIVES].

Further reading
Baerwald (1974)
—— (1986)
Curtis (1999)
Langdon (1967)
Quigley and Turner (1956)
Richardson (1997)
Stockwin (1999)

House of Representatives (Shūgiin) The history of the House of Representatives goes back to 1890, when the Imperial Diet (Parliament) was first established under the 1889 Constitution. It was the only elective house, but had limited powers and was not superior to the appointive House of Peers. Its members were elected at general elections held regularly, but it only ever produced three prime ministers.

Under the CONSTITUTION OF 1946 the powers of the House of Representatives were immeasurably strengthened, even though it is known as the 'Lower House' (*ka-in*). Article 46 of the Constitution states: 'The Diet [Parliament] shall be the highest organ of state power, and shall be the sole law-making organ of the State.' Both houses of Parliament were made elective, and in many respects their powers were similar. In practice, however, the House of Representatives has been the superior house, in that the great bulk of Cabinet ministers belong to it, and it is more important for a Government to have a majority in the Lower House than in the Upper. A Government also has more potential control over the composition of the Lower House, which, as a matter of practical politics, it is able to dissolve more or less when it wishes, and hold new elections. (It has no such powers over the Upper House, which operates according to fixed terms.)

Article 59 of the Constitution provides that if the Upper House (HOUSE OF COUNCILLORS) rejects a bill sent to it from the Lower House, the latter may over-ride the rejection if it can muster a two-thirds majority. Few governments, however, have had majorities as large as that, so that this is a real constraint on a Government not enjoying an Upper House majority (the case of the LIBERAL DEMOCRATIC PARTY (LDP) after 1989). The constraint is slightly mitigated by the provision, in the same article, for a meeting of a joint committee of both houses, to seek to resolve the issue.

On the other hand, the House of Representatives has clear constitutional precedence in respect of the budget (article 60) and treaties (article 61). The budget (but not necessarily a treaty) must first be submitted to the House of Representatives. If there is a dispute between the two houses over either the budget or a treaty, the decision of the Lower House becomes final after a lapse of 30 days. On 19 May 1960 the Prime Minister, KISHI NOBUSUKE, knew that the revised Security Treaty would automatically come into effect on 19 June, when President Eisenhower was due to arrive in Japan. This was what prompted him to bring police into the Lower House to expel the Socialists who were obstructing passage of the Treaty [*see also* SECURITY TREATY REVISION CRISIS].

Designation of the Prime Minister (which takes precedence over all other business) is the third matter where the Lower House has the advantage over the upper. Article 67 of the Constitution provides that the candidate of the House of Representatives prevails over that of the House of Councillors where a joint committee has failed to resolve the issue and the Upper House has failed to make a designation within ten days. This happened in 1948 (ASHIDA prevailed over YOSHIDA) and in 1989 (KAIFU prevailed over DOI).

An important innovation of parliamentary procedure under the 1946 Constitution was the establishment of a committee system in both houses of Parliament. Nearly all substantive deliberation takes place in committees, not in plenary session. This came about on the basis of the exiguous article 62: 'Each House may conduct investigations in relation to government, and may demand the presence and testimony of witnesses, and the production of records.' The committee system may be considered as an 'American' element in a political system basically modelled on the British system, as it mirrors the system of the US Congress. In the House of Representatives, powerful committees such as the Budget Committee and the Foreign Affairs Committee operate with a very broadly defined brief. All bills are first referred to a committee, but, unlike US congressional committees, it is difficult to 'bury' a bill in a committee. A bill must be taken out of the committee and submitted to the plenary session if 20 or more members of the house demand it.

There have normally been 20 standing committees of the House of Representatives and a varying number of special committees. All members of the House except for the Speaker and Cabinet ministers have to belong to at least one committee. The Management Committee allocates members to committees, in proportion to party strengths, while the speaker uses the same principle to choose committee chairmen. In periods of near-parity between the LDP and Opposition parties (such as in the 1970s), the latter controlled some key committees because of vagaries in the way this proportional system actually operated. To be sure of controlling all the committees, the LDP needed to obtain a 'majority plus' at a general election. This came to be known as a 'stable majority'. During the coalition governments from the early 1990s, committees became a forum for policy adjustment between different coalition members, as well as between Government and opposition parties.

Committees may summon witnesses, and, unlike the rules of the US Congress, Cabinet ministers have a right to speak in committee, as well as in plenary session. This reflects the 'British', rather than 'American' character of the system as a whole. Until the reforms of the late 1990s, unelected Government officials were permitted to speak also, assisting the minister. The reformist politician, OZAWA ICHIRŌ, was particularly scathing about this practice, and it was eventually abolished, leaving ministers more exposed to direct questioning.

The reputation of the House of Representatives has not always been high. It has been seen as a part of the political process that had been reduced to relative impotence by single-party dominance and the semi-independent decision-making power of Government ministries. It has also variously been regarded as a hotbed of scandal and (mainly in the earlier post-war decades) as an arena where physical confrontations regularly occurred between Government and opposition parties. But there is some evidence of change. Reform of parliamentary procedures is a live issue in the 2000s, and is part of an attempt to strengthen both the power and accountability of politicians in relation to that of unelected Government officials. The issue became particularly salient after KOIZUMI became Prime Minister in April 2001, but it also preceded that event. A small, but not insignificant, part of the reform movement has been the introduction of 'Prime Minister's question time', on the British model. In part because of coalition Government, in part because of reforms designed to strengthen political leadership, in part possibly because of changes in the electoral system, the House of Representatives has been experiencing something of a revival that may enable it to fulfil its role as envisaged in the democratic Constitution of 1946 [*see also* CONSTITUTION OF 1946; ELECTION SYSTEMS; ELECTORAL HISTORY, HOUSE OF COUNCILLORS].

Further reading
Baerwald (1974)
—— (1986)
Curtis (1999)
Langdon (1967)
Quigley and Turner (1956)
Richardson (1997)
Stockwin (1999)

I

Ikeda Hayato Ikeda, PRIME MINISTER 1960–4, altered the course of Japanese history from political confrontation towards consensus in pursuit of economic prosperity. He with SATŌ EISAKU, who succeeded him as Prime Minister, were the core of the 'YOSHIDA School' of elite ex-bureaucrat politicians.

Born in 1899 in Hiroshima, Ikeda pursued an elite path through Tokyo Imperial University into the MINISTRY OF FINANCE, whose Vice-Minister he became after the war. Entering Parliament in the 1949 general elections, representing Yoshida's Democratic Liberals, he was made Finance Minister – a rapid promotion that would have been impossible in later years. His tenure coincided with the Occupation-sponsored 'Dodge Line' of economic policies designed to squeeze inflation out of the system, and he applied these tough policies with zeal. In the early 1950s he played a major role in Japan–United States relations, most significantly in the Ikeda–Robertson talks in 1953 concerning the establishment of Japanese DEFENCE capacity [*see also* UNITED STATES, RELATIONS WITH]. During the 1950s he was Minister of International Trade and Industry (*see* MINISTRY OF INTERNATIONAL TRADE AND INDUSTRY) and Director of the ECONOMIC PLANNING AGENCY under Yoshida, Finance Minister under ISHIBASHI, Finance Minister again under KISHI, as well as occupying various party positions. He had two setbacks: in 1952 he had to resign the MITI portfolio after making a speech in which he suggested that 'poor people should eat barley', and from 1954 when he and Satō were under investigation concerning a shipbuilding scandal but exonerated on the orders of the Justice Minister.

Following Kishi's resignation as Prime Minister in July 1960, Ikeda, now leader of a major LIBERAL DEMOCRATIC PARTY (LDP) faction, succeeded him. During his four and a half years in the post, he developed policies markedly at variance with those of Kishi. Perceiving that the political temperature had risen too high, he de-emphasised confrontational issues and established a *modus vivendi* with the JAPAN SOCIALIST PARTY (JSP) under its moderate Chairman, KAWAKAMI JŌTARŌ. When the controversial Constitutional Research Commission reported in 1964, he in effect buried the report. On the positive side, he did all he could to promote economic growth and to have Japan accepted as an equal in international organisations (Japan joined the OECD in 1964 and attained IMF article 8 status) (*see* INTERNATIONAL ORGANISATIONS AND JAPAN). His 'Income Doubling Plan' came under criticism, on inflationary and environmental grounds, but it essentially extrapolated the high growth rates of the economy from the late 1950s. In foreign policy, he strove to improve relations with China, but had to tread carefully given US official attitudes and pro-Taiwan opinion within the LDP [*see also* CHINA (PRC AND ROC), RELATIONS WITH]. He also attempted to mediate in the *konfrontasi* dispute between Indonesia and Malaysia, this being a rare example of such a positive FOREIGN POLICY initiative. He piloted the LDP to comfortable victory in the general elections of 1960 and

1964, and was Prime Minister at the time of the 1964 Tokyo Olympics.

In July 1964 he beat off a challenge to his party presidency from Satō, but contracted throat cancer and resigned in November, dying the following year.

Further reading
Masumi (1995)

Imperial Household Agency (Kunaichō) The Imperial Household Ministry (*Kunaishō*) had been one of the most powerful ministries under the pre-1945 system. The Occupation authorities, even though retaining the Emperor (*Tennō*) (*see* EMPEROR AND POLITICS), were determined to avoid at all costs the kind of power concentration around the Emperor that had previously occurred. Therefore, in May 1947, it was downgraded to an Imperial Household Office (*Kunaifu*), answering directly to the PRIME MINISTER. With the establishment of the PRIME MINISTER'S OFFICE (*Sōrifu*) in June 1949, it was renamed as the Imperial Household Agency with the status of 'external' bureau of the Prime Minister's Office. It was placed under the direct jurisdiction of the Prime Minister, so that it does not figure in lists of Cabinet members and their portfolios. The Prime Minister appoints the Agency Chairman (*Kunaichō chōkan*). As a result of the administrative reorganisation of January 2001, it became an 'external' bureau of the CABINET OFFICE (*Naikakufu*).

The agency administers the affairs of the Imperial Palace, as well as other Imperial properties, although these are sparse by comparison with the pre-war period. It even runs its own hospital. Perhaps as a result of the extreme sensitivity of the Imperial institution in the post-war period, the agency has a reputation for lack of transparency, and it is also sometimes accused of breaking the constitutional separation of religion and the State with its promotion of Imperial rituals of various kinds. Its biggest test came in 1988–89, with the illness and death of the Shōwa Emperor, and the transition to the current Emperor.

International Metal Workers' Federation – Japan Chapter (IMF-JC) In May 1965 a number of powerful unions in the metal-working field founded the IMF-JC, in close conjunction with the recently established JAPAN CONFEDERATION OF LABOUR *Dōmei*). The philosophy behind this organisation was co-operation between management and labour, as well as opposition to left-wing unionism as represented by some unions affiliated with the GENERAL COUNCIL OF JAPANESE TRADE UNIONS (*Sōhyō*). It was seen as especially significant at the time that the IMF-JC included unions affiliated with all the four union federations: *Sōhyō*, *Dōmei*, the NATIONAL LIAISON COUNCIL OF INDEPENDENT UNIONS (*Chūritsu Rōren*) and SHINSANBETSU. It did not aspire to be a national centre, but to represent the interests exclusively of metal workers.

The founding of the IMF-JC was an important indication of the transformation of private-sector unionism taking place in the 1960s from confrontational to co-operative strategies in relation to management.

Further reading
Masumi (1995)

international organisations and Japan Japan has often been regarded as 'punching below its weight' in international organisations, but Japanese membership of many such institutions goes back a long way, and in some of them she has been taking an increasingly active role. Whereas, in the earlier post-war years, Japan's international policy was overwhelmingly focused on the bilateral security and economic relationship with the United States, in more recent decades, the trend has been towards diplomacy to cement relations with East and South-East Asia [*see also* CHINA (PRC AND ROC), RELATIONS WITH; KOREA (ROK AND DPRK), RELATIONS WITH; SOUTH-EAST ASIA, RELATIONS WITH]. Even today, however, the United States–Japan relationship places limits on possible Japanese initiatives towards the region utilising international or regional organisations. On the other hand, the size of the economy, and consequent capacity to contribute financially to international institutions, gives greater flexibility than would otherwise be the case.

Japan's relations with the United Nations (UN) have been treated in another entry (*see* UNITED NATIONS, RELATIONS WITH). While the

UN has been central to Japanese diplomatic language and even practice, she has also taken other international organisations, mostly economic in nature, extremely seriously. Japan was admitted to the World Bank in 1952, shortly after the ending of the Allied Occupation, and has become an influential force in that organisation. In the same year she joined the International Monetary Fund (IMF). In 1955 (a year before admission to the UN), Japan was admitted to membership of the General Agreement on Tariffs and Trade (GATT). Several European states, however (including the United Kingdom), continued until 1964 to apply the exemption, permitted under the GATT article 35, from granting Most Favoured Nation (MFN) treatment to Japan. Also, 1964 was the year in which Japan was admitted to the Organization for Economic Co-operation and Development (OECD).

Thus from the mid-1960s Japan had come of age, as it were, and was accepted (more or less) as a member of the 'club' of advanced industrial states. Moreover, in 1966, a regional body was created in which Japan was to have a leading role to play. This was the Asian Development Bank (ADB), whose Chairman has always been Japanese (nearly always an ex-official of the MINISTRY OF FINANCE). Japan has also contributed a substantial proportion of the Bank's capital, and has a degree of influence in the choice and design of its projects that parallels or exceeds that of the United States.

Japan was a signatory to the World Trade Organization (WTO), established in 1995 as the successor to the GATT following the conclusion of the Uruguay round of trade negotiations. Japanese influence has gradually increased in the IMF, which, since the 1980s, has been heavily impregnated with US-style philosophies mandating *laissez faire* and free market economics. Japan, although very much in a minority position within it, has struggled hard to embed its own alternative economic philosophy of State-led, market-conforming, development. This also tends to assume a regional flavour, with Japan taking on the mantle of regional leader within the WTO. That there are limits to this approach was demonstrated in the successful US veto of the Japanese proposal for an Asian Monetary Fund (AMF), to help alleviate the Asian economic crisis, in 1997. Specifically regional organisations in which Japan is involved are discussed in the entry SOUTH-EAST ASIA, RELATIONS WITH.

Finally, Japan has been a member since its establishment in 1976 of the regular G7 (later G8) summit meetings of the leaders of major states. It would be overstating the matter to argue that Japan had been a major force within these summit meetings, but her low-key diplomacy within them has on occasion swung the argument on a particular issue.

Many of those who have observed Japan's performance in international organisations (e.g. Hook *et al.*, 2001) have concluded that she behaves more as an outsider than as a committed member of the international 'club' of the most advanced states. The number of Japanese nationals employed in most international organisations is well below what might be expected, although almost imperceptibly Japanese commitment and influence have been increasing. The single most significant element in Japanese foreign policy, namely the strength of her bilateral relationship with the United States, has inhibited the rapid emergence of an independent philosophy, forcefully projected in international organisations. But broadly speaking, Japan is playing a more confident and quietly sophisticated role in such institutions than was the case up to the 1980s.

Further reading
Drifte (1998)
Hook *et al.* (2001)
Inoguchi and Jain (eds) (2000)
Wihtol (1988)

Ishibashi Masashi Born in 1924, Ishibashi was first elected to the Lower House for his home area of Nagasaki in February 1955, representing the Left Socialist Party. After the two Socialist Parties united later in that year, he occupied various party offices, and eventually reached the position of Secretary-General, replacing the controversial EDA SABURŌ, in November 1970.

As deputy to the Chairman, NARITA TOMOMI, between 1970 and 1977, he was closely involved in the controversies of that period between the Eda-style 'modernisers' and the Marxist 'Socialism Association' (*Shakaishugi Kyōkai*). He acted in parallel with the Eda group to forge solid co-operation with moderate centrist parties, but he also had some sympathy for the Socialism Association, and for its pro-Soviet stance. At the same time he had to respond to the electoral threat from a resurgent JAPAN COMMUNIST PARTY, sometimes promoting co-operation with it in local level elections, and at times attacking it.

The Eda group's defection in 1977 coincided with the resignation of Narita and Ishibashi, a crackdown on the Socialism Association and the emergence of ASUKATA as party Chairman. When Asukata resigned in 1983, Ishibashi was the obvious candidate to succeed him. The national and international situation in the early 1980s was less favourable to the JAPAN SOCIALIST PARTY (JSP) than the 1970s were, and Ishibashi as Chairman worked to revise the party's policies to reflect new circumstances. At the February 1984 Congress, he successfully promoted a revised formula concerning the Self-Defence Forces (SDF), that they were 'unconstitutional' but, since their existence was based on parliamentary approval, they were 'legal'. This awkward compromise at least marked a departure from previous blanket hostility to the SDF. But most importantly, he rewrote the 1964 Platform, 'The Road to Socialism in Japan', to exclude its Marxist rhetoric and create the basis for a modernised party. This was approved at the party Congress of January 1986.

At the double elections of July 1986 the JSP was badly defeated, and Ishibashi resigned as Chairman, to be replaced by DOI TAKAKO, the first woman to head a Japanese party. His modernising efforts paved the way, in an important sense, for electoral successes of the party under Ms Doi in the late 1980s and early 1990s.

Further reading
Hrebenar (2000)
Johnson (2000)

Ishibashi Tanzan In the pre-war period Ishibashi was a liberal journalist, who in 1939 became Chairman of the Oriental Economist Co. Ltd (*Tōyō Keizai Shinpōsha*). Born in 1884, son of the abbot of a Buddhist temple, he graduated from Waseda University, and in his journalism during the 1930s he strongly opposed the militarists and championed ideas of liberal democracy and internationalism. His political ideas were influenced by J.S. Mill, while his economics derived substantially from J.M. Keynes.

After the war he entered politics, joining the Liberal Party, and became Finance Minister in the YOSHIDA Cabinet of 1946–7. Some regarded his financial policies as inflationary, and he was not afraid to challenge Occupation policy on some issues. In any case, he was purged from public life by the Occupation between 1947 and 1951. On his return to politics, he was on bad terms with Yoshida and came to support HATOYAMA in his bid to replace him. Early in 1953 he joined Hatoyama, KŌNO ICHIRŌ and others in founding the Liberal Party Dissident faction (*Buntō ha Jiyūtō*), which returned to the Liberal Party in November. Then in 1954 he co-operated with Hatoyama, KISHI, MIKI BUKICHI and Kōno in founding the Japan Democratic Party (*Nihon Minshutō*). When the Hatoyama Cabinet was formed in December 1954, Ishibashi was appointed Minister of International Trade and Industry, a post that he held for two years [*see also* CONSERVATIVE PARTIES, 1945–55]. When Hatoyama retired as President of the unified Liberal Democratic Party in December 1956, and its first presidential election was held, Ishibashi defeated Kishi by seven votes in an electorate consisting largely of LIBERAL DEMOCRATIC PARTY (LDP) parliamentarians, becoming party President and Prime Minister. He fell ill, however, and surrendered his post to Kishi in February 1957.

He devoted the rest of his life to improving relations between Japan and China [*see also* CHINA (PRC AND ROC), RELATIONS WITH], as well as to writing on peace and economic issues, while remaining active in the LDP. He died in 1973.

Further reading
Masumi (1995)

Ishida Kōshirō Born in 1930 in Hokkaidō, and a graduate of Meiji University, Ishida

Kōshirō was first elected to the House of Representatives for an Aichi constituency in 1967 – the first election contested by the CLEAN GOVERNMENT PARTY (CGP, *Kōmeitō*) after its formation in 1964.

In 1989 he became party Chairman in succession to YANO JUNYA. During the HOSOKAWA and HATA coalition governments (1993–4), which included the CGP, he was Minister of State in charge of the MANAGEMENT AND CO-ORDINATION AGENCY (*Sōmuchō*). As leader of one of the larger parties participating in the non-LDP coalition, he was a key player during that period. He took the CGP into the NEW FRONTIER PARTY (NFP, *Shinshintō*) in December 1994 and became one of its three vice-chairmen. He later became Chairman of the Permanent Council of Advisers (*Jōnin komon kaigi zachō*) of the NFP. When the party set up its 'tomorrow's Cabinet' (*Asu no naikaku*) in 1996, Ishida shadowed the Deputy Prime Minister, in charge of administrative reform. With the new electoral system in place in 1996, he was elected for the NFP from the Tōkai bloc – his tenth successful election.

Ishihara Shintarō A famous novelist before he became a politician, Ishihara Shintarō appealed to the electorate on a strongly nationalist platform. Born in 1932 in Hyōgo, he attended Hitotsubashi University. He was first elected to the House of Councillors in July 1968, representing the LIBERAL DEMOCRATIC PARTY (LDP), polling over three million votes in the national constituency. In December 1972 he moved to the House of Representatives, being elected at the top of the poll, in the five-member second constituency of Tokyo. He went on to win the next seven elections, in all but one receiving more votes than any other candidate. In 1975 he stood for governor of Tokyo Prefecture, but was beaten into second place by the incumbent, Minobe Ryōkichi. Ishihara nevertheless polled 43.88 per cent of the total valid vote.

He did not contest the first Lower House elections under the new electoral system in 1996. In 1999, however, he was successful in his second attempt to be elected Governor of Tokyo. This time, he confronted a badly divided field, and, standing as an Independent, he won nearly twice as many votes as his nearest rival. Part of Ishihara's popularity was attributed to the memory of his brother, a famous actor, who had died prematurely, and indeed he recalled his brother's name in many of his election appeals. The LDP candidate, Akashi Yasushi, was forced into fourth place. On the other hand Ishihara's percentage of the total valid vote was only 30.56 per cent.

As Tokyo Governor, he developed a number of initiatives, including an attempt to tax those banks with headquarters in Tokyo, so as to close the city's chronic budgetary deficit. He also called for the return of the US military base at Yokota, in Tokyo, to Japanese control.

In 1989 Ishihara published a book, together with Morita Akio, entitled *The Japan that Can Say No*, arguing that Japan should stand up to US pressure far more firmly than she was doing. It was published only in Japanese, but an unauthorised translation soon appeared in the United States, causing sharp reactions. Morita later publicly regretted his joint authorship. Ishihara's election as Governor of Tokyo a decade later caused a hostile reaction in China, because of his consistent stand that the Nanjing massacre was a fabrication.

Further reading
Ishihara and Morita (1989)

Itō Masayoshi Born in Fukushima in 1913, Itō Masayoshi was a LIBERAL DEMOCRATIC PARTY (LDP) politician of a liberal and reformist bent. He was first elected to the House of Representatives for a Fukushima constituency in 1963, was defeated in 1967, but was then returned comfortably in every election up to and including that of 1990.

Itō is famous in particular for two episodes in his career. The first was in May 1981, when he resigned as Foreign Minister after the PRIME MINISTER, SUZUKI ZENKŌ, having returned from an official visit to the United States, publicly criticised the idea of an 'alliance relationship' between the two states – a phrase included in the joint communiqué he had himself signed.

The second episode came in advance of the anticipated resignation of TAKESHITA NOBORU as Prime Minister in June 1989. Itō's name was the first to be seriously considered within the LDP as a possible successor. This was the time of the RECRUIT SCANDAL, when many politicians, including most faction leaders, were facing criticism for accepting unlisted shares from the Recruit company. Itō was vigorously attacking political corruption, and insisted that he would only accept the leadership if the following conditions were fulfilled: (1) rejuvenation of the party executive with the insertion of young members; (2) abolition of factions; (3) resignation from Parliament of the Prime Minister, Takeshita Noboru, the LDP Secretary-General, ABE SHINTARŌ, the former Prime Minister, NAKASONE YASUHIRO, the Finance Minister, MIYAZAWA KIICHI, and the Chairman of the LDP Policy Affairs Research Council, WATANABE MICHIO. He insisted that superficial change was not sufficient, since genuine sweeping reform was necessary. To his great annoyance, the composition of his prospective Cabinet had become a matter for open bargaining between LDP factions, and, when it became clear to him that his conditions would not be met, he withdrew his candidacy.

J

Japan Chamber of Commerce (Nihon shōkō kaigisho, Nisshō) The Japan Chamber of Commerce is the only one of the four 'peak associations' of Japanese business to have a pre-war history. It was originally founded in 1892 as the Liaison Council of Chambers of Commerce (*Shōkō kaigisho rengōkai*), and was consolidated under its present name in 1927, following a change in the law. Between 1943 and 1952 it experienced various changes of name and status, being for a while up to 1952 under the umbrella of the Federation of Economic Organisations (*Keidanren*). From 1952, however, it has been organisationally rather stable.

Its function is to represent Chambers of Commerce throughout the country, and conduct research and liaison activities of benefit to them. Of the four peak associations it is the closest to the small- and medium-firm sector, and as such contrasts most sharply with *Keidanren*.

Japan Committee for Economic Development (Keizai dōyūkai) This organisation of businessmen was founded in April 1946. Its name in English is not a translation of its name in Japanese, which literally means 'Association of Economic Friends'. It differed from the Federation of Economic Organisations (*Keidanren*) in being based on individual, rather than corporate, membership. Its members were middle-ranking rather than at the top of their companies, and, at least in its early years, it maintained a relatively progressive vision promoting economic democratisation and the creation of a State committed to peace. It was prepared to confront the more atavistic businessmen from the pre-war period, and favoured communication with labour unions in preference to confrontation. Its ideas about management were progressive and in the immediate post-war years it advocated something close to what today would be called 'stakeholder democracy'.

Gradually, however, *Keizai Dōyūkai* became more conservative, so that by the 1960s and 1970s it had become difficult to distinguish its views from those of the other business federations. Although it continued to pronounce on certain issues, generally speaking its pronouncements had become bland and in conformity with mainstream business thinking, rather than radical and thought-provoking as they had been in the immediate post-war years.

Japan Communist Party (JCP, Nihon Kyōsantō) On some definitions, the Japan Communist Party is the oldest political party in the country. An illegal party was founded in 1922, and existed in a spasmodic fashion, persecuted by the authorities, until at least the mid-1930s. From the early 1930s it also suffered from recantations by leading members (the so-called *tenkō* phenomenon). Most of its leaders who had not recanted were in gaol. Such political activity as they could still conduct was influenced by a series of 'theses' from the Comintern – an organisation that had scant appreciation of the conditions under which the movement was operating. This was, however, the only party in Japan that called for the abolition of the Emperor system (*see* EMPEROR

AND POLITICS) and railed against aggressive military policies by the Government.

The Allied Occupation released Communist leaders from prison in October 1945, including TOKUDA KYŪICHI and SHIGA YOSHIO. The party was re-founded at its 'fourth' congress in December, and was for the first time able to conduct its affairs legally, free of police persecution, and enjoying guarantees of freedom of speech. It could even criticise the Emperor system without fear of arrest. Being virtually the only political group that had not compromised its principles up to 1945 (though many members had recanted and left), it enjoyed some popularity in the dark days after the defeat. The Congress of Industrial Unions (*Sanbetsu kaigi*) was quickly set up under its control. On the other hand its association with the USSR, which had entered the war a week before Japan's surrender, as well as its harsh criticism of other groups, created widespread concern.

NOSAKA SANZŌ, the Communist leader who had been in exile in Moscow since 1928 and then in the caves of Yenan with Mao, appeared dramatically at the party's fifth congress in February 1946, and from then on Tokuda and Nosaka occupied the two top party posts. Nosaka's return led to a softer approach, and to the era of the 'lovable Communist Party'. Rather than attacking the Emperor institution, the party now talked of peaceful revolution and a united front. This was consistent with the 'two-stage revolution' argument of the 1932 Comintern thesis. In 1947, however, attempts by the JCP to persuade the JAPAN SOCIALIST PARTY (JSP) to form a united front with it irretrievably broke down. The parties fought over control of the union movement, and Communist electoral performance was too weak to make them attractive partners for the Socialists. Moreover, the gathering clouds of the Cold War were creating a conservative shift in Occupation policies, and a corresponding hardening of the JCP line.

In the general elections of January 1949, following the collapse of the KATAYAMA and ASHIDA coalition Cabinets, the JCP won a remarkable 35 seats in the House of Representatives, with 9.7 per cent of the total vote. A year later, however, it was publicly criticised for 'softness' by Moscow, and began factional conflict between a moderate 'Mainstream' faction (Nosaka, Tokuda) and a militant 'Internationalist' faction (Shiga, MIYAMOTO). The party embarked on a path of amateurish militancy. The Americans took the opportunity to subject it to the purge, and it was virtually forced underground. Electoral support evaporated, and did not begin to recover for a decade.

The Sixth National Congress of the JCP in July 1955 marked the beginning of recovery from these disasters. But there was a long way to go. Between 1958 and 1961, the party was divided between those who still saw 'American imperialism' as the main enemy, and a group influenced by the Italian Communists, arguing that indigenous 'monopoly capitalism' should be principally targeted. This latter group, led by Kasuga Shōjirō, was expelled from the JCP in 1961, and some of them established links with the 'structural reform' group in the JSP.

Thus what had become the mainstream of the party, led by Miyamoto Kenji, could consolidate its control. But first, the party had to decide policy towards the Sino-Soviet dispute. In 1964 the Miyamoto leadership distanced itself from the Soviet Union by opposing the nuclear test ban treaty, which the Soviets had signed. The pro-Soviet Shiga therefore departed, and formed the 'Voice of Japan' Communist Party, which was an electoral flop. For a while the JCP clove to the Chinese line, but in 1966 relations between the Japanese and Chinese Communist Parties broke down completely, and they remained estranged for a generation. The result was that the JCP was independent as never before. Under Miyamoto, the party began to cultivate broad electoral support, softening much of its platform. Party membership and sales of *Akahata* (Red Flag) newspaper rose rapidly, and elections went well. In the 1972 and 1979 Lower House elections the JCP won 38 and 39 seats respectively. Early in the 1970s, some within the LIBERAL DEMOCRATIC PARTY began to regard the JCP as a potentially more dangerous rival than the JSP. Thus the party found pre-war skeletons dragged out of the cupboard, and Miyamoto was publicly reminded that he had been involved in the lynching of a police spy in 1933.

After the 1970s, the JCP settled down as a minor but stable force in Japanese politics, normally polling slightly under 10 per cent of the vote, and 5 or 6 per cent of Lower House seats. Miyamoto was Chairman of the Central Committee between 1982 and 1997, but increasingly power was wielded by FUWA TETSUZŌ, who formally succeeded him on his retirement in 1997. From the early 1990s Fuwa worked hard to ensure the JCP's survival in the post-Cold War world. His number two was the youthful and dynamic SHII KAZUO, who helped him form the party in a more attractive mould.

The JCP is largely an urban party. It can attract votes of the disaffected, but any sense (as hinted at by Shii) that it might follow the example of the French and Italian Communist Parties and join coalition governments tends to alienate the support of those who support it because it opposes.

Further reading
Beckmann and Okubo (1969)
Central Committee, Japanese Communist Party (1984)
Hrebenar (2000)
Scalapino (1967)
Stockwin (1965)
Swearingen and Langer (1952, 1968)

Japan Confederation of Labour (Zen Nihon Rōdō Sōdōmei, Dōmei) This national union centre was formed in November 1964, as successor to the ALL-JAPAN TRADE UNION CONGRESS (*Zenrō Kaigi*) (1954–62) and *Dōmei Kaigi* (1962–4), as well as the ALL-JAPAN GENERAL FEDERATION OF LABOUR UNIONS (*Sōdōmei*) (1946–62). Most of its affiliated unions were in the private sector, and it pursued a relatively pragmatic economic unionism, eschewing where possible the kinds of ideological campaigns favoured by some elements within the General Council of Japanese Trade Unions (*Sōhyō*). It inherited a tradition, going back to the pre-war *Sōdōmei*, of labour–management co-operation that sprang logically from private-sector enterprise unionism. Following from this it was happy to participate in productivity improvement drives.

Dōmei consistently supported the DEMOCRATIC SOCIALIST PARTY, and provided much of its organisational backing. With this went positive efforts in the area of welfare policy, a professed concern with democratic practice and rather pro-US attitudes towards foreign policy. Concern with defence policies no doubt sprang from the fact that its constituent unions included some in firms manufacturing armaments.

With the amalgamation of the bulk of the union movement into a single Japanese Trade Union Council (*Rengō*) in 1987–9, the organisation dissolved itself in November 1987. For a while it continued to exist under the name of *Yūai Kaigi*. At the time of its dissolution 29 industrial unions involving some 2,200,000 unionists belonged to it.

Further reading
Johnson (2000)
Kume (1998)

Japan Co-operative Party (Nihon Kyōdōtō) *see* conservative parties, 1945–55

Japan Democratic Party (JDP, Nihon Minshutō) *see* conservative parties, 1945–55

Japan Federation of Economic Organisations (Nihon keizai dantai rengōkai) This federation was formed in May 2002 from the merging of the FEDERATION OF ECONOMIC ORGANISATIONS (*Keizai dantai rengōkai, Keidanren*), and the JAPAN FEDERATION OF EMPLOYERS' ASSOCIATIONS (*Nihon keieisha dantai renmei*). Its founding was a rather natural coming together of two long-standing organisations of similar composition and interests, but different functions – general economic policy in the case of the former and labour relations in the case of the latter. It also represented a sense of economic crisis and the need for strengthened organisational effort to solve structural economic problems, some having a political character. Both component federations had declined somewhat in influence in recent years with the diversification of the economy.

Its foundation President, Okuda Hiroshi, Chairman of Toyota, spoke of the need for radical medicine if economic health were to be restored.

Japan Federation of Employers' Associations (Nihon keieisha dantai renmei, Nikkeiren) This Federation, commonly known as

Nikkeiren, was founded in April 1948, at a time of widespread labour unrest, in order to mobilise the strength of employers in the face of militant labour demands. Its membership has been based on local employers' federations and groups representing particular industries.

During the 1950s and into the 1960s *Nikkeiren* maintained a tough stand against labour unions in its policies towards bargaining over wages and conditions. The institution of the spring struggle (*shuntō*) from the mid-1950s had the gradual effect of routinising and bureaucratising such negotiations, making them more predictable. Rapid economic growth also eventually transformed average standards of living, so that relations between labour and management became less confrontational than they had been in the late 1940s and 1950s. Even so, *Nikkeiren* continued to perform an information function for employers and help them to co-ordinate their activities in matters relating to labour relations. It maintained close links with the LIBERAL DEMOCRATIC PARTY.

In May 2002 *Nikkeiren* merged with the FEDERATION OF ECONOMIC ORGANISATIONS (*Keidanren*) to form the JAPAN FEDERATION OF ECONOMIC ORGANISATIONS (*Nihon keizai dantai rengōkai*).

Japan Liberal Party (I) (JLP, Nihon Jiyūtō)
see conservative parties, 1945–55

Japan Liberal Party (II) (Nihon Jiyūtō) see conservative parties, 1945–55

Japan Medical Association (JMA, Ishikai)
The Japan Medical Association, like its counterparts in other comparable countries, has exercised impressive political influence.

Although over-generalisation should be avoided in so complex an area as health care and the provision of medical services, it is broadly true that the JMA has fought tenaciously for the rights, and particularly for the right to independent practice, of its members. It gained a reputation for determined lobbying under Takemi Tarō, its Chairman between 1957 and 1972. This often placed it at loggerheads with the former MINISTRY OF HEALTH AND WELFARE (MHW, *Kōseishō*), which was in charge of administering the health insurance system. In Campbell's graphic description, struggles between the MHW and the JMA reflected 'a prolonged struggle for control of health care, between what Takemi Tarō liked to call totalitarian administration, and those seen by Welfare Ministry Officials as greedy medical entrepreneurs' (Campbell, 1992, p. 287). In 1971 it confronted the ministry with a tough approach and won. The JMA is careful to make regular financial contributions to the LIBERAL DEMOCRATIC PARTY, and normally elects several of its members to Parliament, especially for the HOUSE OF COUNCILLORS. For many conservative politicians, the support of doctors – through local JMA branches – is a valuable prize because of the social influence of the medical profession in local communities.

As with health insurance systems in other countries, confrontations take place over levels of remuneration to doctors for a range of services. To this are added struggles over pharmaceutical remuneration, given that in Japan medical doctors make money by selling medicines to their patients, a system that leads to problems of over-prescribing. Campbell speaks of a 'standoff', or 'equilibrium', between the JMA and the ministry.

The JMA has been involved in other sorts of controversy. It has vigorously supported the retention of the relaxed abortion laws that have existed since 1948, but for years opposed the introduction of the birth control pill. Critics have argued, not entirely without evidence, that its motives on these two related issues were mercenary rather than principled.

The political influence of the JMA has declined since the days of the redoubtable Takemi. Its membership has slipped and salaried medical practitioners now make up a substantial proportion of the whole. Given Japan's ageing society, financing health service provision has become problematic. Whatever the defects of the service, however, the standard of health care throughout the country is extraordinarily high, reflected in the fact that Japanese since the 1970s have enjoyed the highest life expectancy of any people in the world.

Further reading
Calder (1988)
Campbell (1992)
Curtis (1999)

Norgren (1998)
Steslicke (1973)

Japan New Party (JNP, Nihon Shintō) The Japan New Party only lasted for about two years, but it represents one of the few recent attempts to open up a radically different kind of party politics. It is closely bound up with the career of HOSOKAWA MORIHIRO, who founded it in the middle of 1992. After modest success in the Upper House elections of July of that year, it won a spectacular total of 35 seats in the Lower House elections of July 1993, which were followed shortly thereafter by the election of Hosokawa as PRIME MINISTER in the first non-LIBERAL DEMOCRATIC PARTY (LDP) administration for 37 years. The average age of those elected was only 42, several of them being graduates of the MATSUSHITA INSTITUTE OF POLITICS AND MANAGEMENT.

In the early months of the Hosokawa Government, many expected that the JNP and the NEW PARTY HARBINGER (NPH, *Sakigake*) would merge, as their programmes were very similar. Early in 1994, however, a clash between Hosokawa and Takemura of the NPH over taxation policy drove the two parties apart. As Prime Minister, Hosokawa showed little interest in the welfare of his party, and in December, after the fall of his Government in April, it merged into the NEW FRONTIER PARTY.

Japan Political League of Small and Medium Enterprises (Nihon chūshō kigyō seiji renmei) While disproportionate power has been in the hands of the corporate sector and its representatives, the Japanese economy has benefited from an unusually extensive small and medium enterprise sector, which has contributed to diversity of manufacture. To a marked extent the relationship between large corporate firms and the small and medium firm sector has been hierarchical, with many large firms sub-contracting work to smaller firms, which became highly dependent upon them. Particularly in the earlier post-war years, the Japanese economy manifested extreme duality between a few very large, wealthy and powerful firms, and a huge number of small and medium-sized firms, which in economic terms were far weaker and experienced a high rate of bankruptcy. In later years the situation became rather more balanced, with some medium-sized and small firms attaining high levels of efficiency and profitability.

On the other hand, in one respect at least, small and medium industry in Japan enjoys one significant advantage giving it the potential for political influence. It employs very large numbers of people. In many parts of the country parliamentary candidates find it difficult to ignore the votes of its employees.

With this factor in mind, the Japan Political League of Small and Medium Enterprises was founded as an interest group in 1956 under the dynamic leadership of Ayukawa Yoshisuke, a wealthy businessman. Ayukawa was able to fund the group rather lavishly and recruited large numbers of members. He focused the group's lobbying activities on various pieces of legislation going through Parliament in the late 1950s affecting the interests of small and medium industry. Principal among these was the Small and Medium Industries Organisation Law (*Chūshō kigyō dantai soshikihō*), where Ayukawa, using the metaphor of boosting the pressure within a steam boiler, applied intense pressure on Parliament and parliamentarians. He took labour union organisation as his model, while realising that small and medium-sized enterprises were much harder to meld into a political force than labour unions.

The League only had a short life, and some time after the 1959 HOUSE OF COUNCILLORS elections it disbanded. It had faced contradictory demands from its members, its style of organisation was rather chaotic, and many of its constituent groups had links with the LIBERAL DEMOCRATIC PARTY (LDP). Ayukawa himself was a dominant leader but his organisation was unduly fragmented. One of his close relatives was accused of violating the electoral law during the 1959 House of Councillors campaign.

After the demise of the League, small and medium industry remained a capacious pool of political support that few politicians could afford to ignore. But the fragmentation problem remained, and much political activity was conducted through political parties: most notably the LDP, but also some opposition parties, particularly the DEMOCRATIC SOCIALIST PARTY and the CLEAN GOVERNMENT PARTY (*Kōmeitō*).

Special financial facilities for small and medium enterprises, as well as such protectionist legislation as the Large Stores Law, reflected the extensive political clout of this sector.

Further reading
Kobayashi, in Itoh (1973)

Japan Progressive Party (JPP, Nihon Shinpotō) *see* conservative parties, 1945–55

Japan Renewal Party (JRP, Shinseitō) The origins of the Japan Renewal Party are in a group called 'Reform Forum 21', created by HATA TSUTOMU and OZAWA ICHIRŌ in December 1992 following the split in the TAKESHITA faction. About half the Takeshita faction members formed this group. Following the passage of a no-confidence motion against the MIYAZAWA Government in June 1993, the Hata–Ozawa group defected from the LIBERAL DEMOCRATIC PARTY (LDP) and formed the JRP. It initially consisted of 44 members, but at the Lower House elections in July this figure increased to 55.

With the formation of the HOSOKAWA coalition Cabinet in August, it was widely remarked that the JRP (though not the largest party) took the bulk of the key Cabinet positions. This confirmed observers in the view that Ozawa was both the brains behind this unorthodox Cabinet, and the power behind the throne. After the resignation of Hosokawa in April 1994, the JRP participated in the brief minority Hata Cabinet, but with the return to office of the LDP in a three-way coalition in June, Ozawa worked hard to unite the Hosokawa coalition parties (minus the JSP and NPH) into a single party. This he achieved in December 1994, forming the 'New New Party' later renamed the NEW FRONTIER PARTY.

Japan Socialist Party/Social Democratic Party (JSP, SDP, Nihon Shakaitō, Shakai Minshutō)* The Japan Socialist Party was the largest party of opposition to the LIBERAL DEMOCRATIC PARTY (LDP) over the period that corresponds with the Cold War – the late 1940s to the early 1990s. Broadly speaking it could be described as ideologically left wing, though sharply differing doctrines contended within it. It bore some resemblance to social democratic and labour parties in Europe and Australasia, in that it was backed by a combination of labour unions, citizens' groups and intellectuals, with labour unions being its main organisational base. But there were two principal differences. First, Marxist influence within it ran deep, even though it was declining by the 1980s. Second, it was fundamentally a pacifist party, for which defence of the peace clause of the CONSTITUTION OF 1946 was a primary article of faith. Even though it was never able to attain power in its own right, it exercised sufficient veto power over a long period to prevent constitutional revision and inhibit right-wing aspirations towards a 'normal state' in defence. Its relations with the LDP during the 1950s and to a lesser extent in the 1960s were extremely confrontational, but at least from the 1960s back-stage negotiation between the LDP and JSP became the norm in Parliament concerning the more routine areas of legislation. The party provided two prime ministers, one in the late 1940s and the other in the mid-1990s, but both presided over fragile coalition governments in turbulent times, and in both cases the electoral consequences were disastrous.

In November 1945, several Socialist and social-democratic factions from the pre-war period came together and founded the JSP. It consisted broadly of three factional-ideological tendencies: the *Rōnō-kei* (Labour-Farmer group) on the left, the *Nichirō-kei* (Japan Labour group) in the centre and the *Shamin-kei* (Social Democratic group) on the right. Initially the balance was towards the right, so that, when the party emerged from the April 1947 Lower House elections with a plurality of seats, it formed a coalition Government with two other parties under a Prime Minister, KATAYAMA TETSU, from the *Shamin-kei*. The collapse of this Government, and of its successor (in which the JSP also participated), led to a catastrophic result in the January 1949 elections. After this, the left of the party began to gain ground over the right. The party split in October 1951 into the Left Socialist Party (principally *Rōnō-kei* and the 'bureaucrat' WADA faction), and the right Socialist Party (mainly *Shamin-kei* and *Nichirō-kei*). Over the next four years both parties made electoral progress, but the Left Socialists were particularly successful, having consolidated their organisational links with the *Sōhyō* union federation.

In October 1955, the two wings of the Socialist movement reunited into a single party, which in the late 1950s was the only significant opposition party. At the general elections of May 1955 it polled 32.9 per cent of the vote and 35.5 per cent of the seats in the Lower House. But the late 1950s were a turbulent period with the Socialists confronting the revisionist policies of Prime Minister KISHI. The JSP leadership moved significantly towards the left, precipitating the defection in 1959–60 of the *Shamin-kei* and a good part of the *Nichirō-kei*, which formed the DEMOCRATIC SOCIALIST PARTY. The SECURITY TREATY REVISION CRISIS in the summer of 1960, and the assassination of the JSP Chairman, ASANUMA INEJIRŌ, in November 1960, ushered in a period of reflection.

For the JSP, however, the 1960s were a period of political decline, with other opposition parties eating into its support, especially in big cities. The failure of EDA SABURŌ's 'structural reform' in 1962 and the influence of the Vietnam War in the late 1960s, reinforced the left and inhibited party modernisation. Support returned to a minor extent in the 1970s, when 'progressive local authorities' were in vogue in urban areas. The year 1986 was significant, with a modernised party platform, followed by defeat in double elections, and the succession to the party chairmanship of the first woman to head a Japanese political party, DOI TAKAKO. Ms Doi turned out to have charismatic appeal, and, in the confused politics of the late 1980s, gave the party a fresh image. In the Upper House elections of July 1989 (following the RECRUIT SCANDAL) the JSP actually forced the LDP into a minority position. It also much improved its position in the Lower House elections of February 1990. Doi Takako resigned her Chair in 1991, and in the Lower House elections of July 1993 the party lost many seats.

Ironically, despite this defeat, the JSP found itself the largest party in the eight-party HOSOKAWA coalition Government that excluded the LDP. When Hosokawa resigned in April 1994, the JSP strongly objected to OZAWA's plan of forming a new party from which it would be excluded. It therefore negotiated with its old enemy, the LDP, which offered the prime ministership to the JSP Chairman, MURAYAMA TOMIICHI, as its price for returning to power, albeit as part of a coalition. Murayama was able to further certain causes dear to the JSP, but he surrendered traditional party positions on the Self-Defence Forces, the Security Treaty and other issues, thus disillusioning many loyal supporters of his party.

In September 1996 the party split once again, and most of its right wing (and some centrists) joined with others to form the DEMOCRATIC PARTY. In elections the following month, the left and centrist remainder was reduced to a rump of 15 Lower House members. Doi Takako returned as Chair, and in the 2000 elections 19 members were elected, the majority of them women. The party now occupied a niche position, emphasising issues of peace and women's rights.

*For most of its existence, the official name was *Nihon Shakaitō* (Japan Socialist Party). But in the early post-war period, and from 1996, it has been *Shakai Minshutō* (Social Democratic Party). Between 1991 and 1996, the name was, in Japanese, *Nihon Shakaitō*, but in English 'Social Democratic Party'. Here, for simplicity, we use 'Japan Socialist Party'.

Further reading
Cole *et al.* (1966)
Curtis (1999)
Hrebenar (2000)
Johnson (2000)
Stockwin (1968)
—— (1999)

Japan Teachers' Union (JTU, Nihon Kyōshoku in Kumiai, Nikkyōso) *Nikkyōso* was founded in June 1947 as a single union for teachers, succeeding several early Occupation period unions. The zeal of the Occupation to democratise education and remove militaristic influences helped create a union of teachers determined to combat militarism and promote democratic reform. But the Americans were surprised to find that *Nikkyōso* leaders were influenced by Marxism, as well as by the ideals of liberal democracy. This meant that relations between *Nikkyōso* and the Occupation authorities rapidly soured, facilitating 'reverse course' policies on education by successive Japanese governments from the late 1940s onwards.

Unlike unions mainly concerned with improving the wages and conditions of their members, *Nikkyōso* also campaigned against militarism, and in particular against the militaristic education of the pre-war and wartime periods. Over 20 per cent of teachers had been purged by the Occupation as being militarist, and *Nikkyōso* was quickly able to secure the membership and loyalty of most remaining teachers. The union was enthusiastic about the rewriting of textbooks to emphasise peace and democracy, promoted by the Occupation. It gained the widespread allegiance of teachers with its slogan 'Never send our children to war again'. But the Marxist element in its thinking led to a definition of teachers as workers, who were expected to strike and demonstrate, in solidarity with other members of the working class. The banning by General MacArthur of the general strike planned for 1 February 1947, and restrictions on the right of public servants to strike and organise, quickly created confrontation with *Nikkyōso*. In 1949 disagreements developed between Communist and Socialist-backed *Nikkyōso* unionists, and the balance of power shifted towards the Socialists. The union was a key player in the creation of the General Council of Japanese Trade Unions (*Sōhyō*) in 1950, which also had the support of Occupation authorities, who prematurely regarded the new federation as anti-Communist.

Once the Occupation was over, *Nikkyōso* found itself in frequent dispute with the MINISTRY OF EDUCATION, over attempts by the ministry to control the content of textbooks, to reintroduce 'ethics' courses into schools (previously an instrument of nationalist indoctrination) and introduce a 'teachers' efficiency rating' system. They were also often at loggerheads over the wages and conditions of teachers, the legislation banning strike action and political campaigns by *Nikkyōso* on peace issues. The ministry held one trump card over the union, and this it exploited to the full. Occupation attempts to decentralise educational administration were emasculated by the Government in the early 1950s, but one aspect of it was retained. Teachers were legally permitted to bargain with their employer (the State) at prefectural, but not at national, level. This meant that the central organisation of *Nikkyōso* was almost entirely excluded from negotiations with the ministry, and, since prefectural educational authorities had little effective power, the negotiating process was heavily skewed in favour of the ministry.

The 1950s were extremely turbulent in education policy, with a militant union facing a Ministry of Education (backed by right-wing elements in Government) determined to impose its own control over education and roll back progressive Occupation reforms. Confrontation over textbook control in 1956 and over teachers' efficiency rating in 1958 created great tension, with the ministry essentially winning the first struggle but the union managing to subvert its intention over the second. *Nikkyōso* gradually came to realise that absolute opposition worked less well than more subtle ways of doing battle with the ministry. This gave the union some degree of success in its campaign against a system of pupil assessment in the early 1960s.

The membership of *Nikkyōso* stood at over 85 per cent of all teachers in the late 1950s but was down to below 50 per cent by 1987 (Aspinall, 2001, p. 48). Reasons for this included high union dues, growing political apathy in a society that had become stable and prosperous, widespread criticisms of *Nikkyōso* militancy, and splits within the union, principally between JAPAN COMMUNIST PARTY (JCP) and JAPAN SOCIALIST PARTY (JSP)-oriented factions. These divisions had been containable while *Nikkyōso* remained within the *Sōhyō* federation, which was largely composed of public-sector unions and favoured political unionism. But moves in the 1980s towards a single national union centre upset this balance. Fearing that entry into *Rengō* would force *Nikkyōso* into 'co-operative' unionism, the more traditionally left-wing (and especially Communist-linked) elements in it refused to follow the line of the central leadership. Instead, they broke away from *Nikkyōso*, forming the ALL-JAPAN COUNCIL OF TEACHERS' AND STAFF UNIONS (*Zenkyō*) in November 1989. Even though the JTU was weakened by the departure of *Zenkyō*, it remained much the bigger of the two main teachers' unions, and relations between it and the ministry became more co-operative than hitherto. Since the early 1990s *Nikkyōso* has been active in moves to modernise the education system and make it more relevant to the sophisticated society that Japan has now become.

Further reading
Aspinall (2001)
Cummings (1980)
Duke (1973)
Hood (2001)
Pempel (1978)
Schoppa (1991)
Thurston (1973)

Japanese Trade Union Council (Zen Nihon Rōdō Kumiai Rengōkai, Rengō) The formation of *Rengō* represented the fulfilment of a longstanding ambition to unify the labour movement into a single federation. Divisions formed within the union movement in the late 1940s and the 1950s ran deep, but by the 1980s it was widely felt that the causes of these divisions were far less salient than they had been three decades before. The process was also facilitated by the fact that the more militant public-sector unions within the GENERAL COUNCIL OF JAPANESE TRADE UNIONS (*Sōhyō*) had been seriously weakened by the privatisations of the NAKASONE period in the mid-1980s. Nevertheless, the process of amalgamation took two years. In November 1987, a consultative group called the ALL-JAPAN COUNCIL OF PRIVATE SECTOR TRADE UNIONS (*Zenmin Rōkyō*), formed in 1982, turned itself into a full-blown union federation, and around the same time the JAPAN CONFEDERATION OF LABOUR (*Dōmei*), SHINSANBETSU and the National Liaison Council of Independent Trade Unions (*Chūritsu Rōren*) – all of long standing – joined *Rengō* and dissolved their own organisations. It took a further two years before, in November 1989, the *Sōhyō* unions came on board and *Rengō* was born in its final form. Even then, the amalgamation did not embrace all unions. A group of unions close to the JAPAN COMMUNIST PARTY formed their own federation, the National Labour Union Alliance (*Zenrōren*), in disagreement with the 'accommodationist' policies of *Rengō*. A little later a separate group called the NATIONAL LIAISON COUNCIL OF LABOUR UNIONS (*Zenrōkyō*) was formed outside the *Rengō* umbrella by unions associated with the left wing of *Sōhyō*.

It is estimated that at its foundation *Rengō* accounted for 66 per cent of unionised workers, or a total of 8,100,000, making it one of the three or four largest union federations in the world. Nevertheless, it was evident to all concerned that union membership was gradually reducing, as manufacturing industry declined in favour of employment in the tertiary sector, where unions were harder to organise. By the mid-1990s not much over 20 per cent of the workforce was unionised, down from over 55 per cent in the peak year of 1949.

The early years of *Rengō* coincided with a bold plan to unify left-of-centre parties developed by the leading unionist, Yamagishi Akira. Given the fact that the split in *Sōhyō* in 1954 had led a few years later to a split in the JAPAN SOCIALIST PARTY (JSP) and the formation of the right-of-centre DEMOCRATIC SOCIALIST PARTY (DSP), Yamagishi wished to reverse the process and unify the left. This led to an unprecedented electoral campaign in the July 1989 House of Councillors elections, in which 12 *Rengō* candidates were put forward, of whom 11 won, all in what in effect were single-member districts in non-city areas. Even though this spectacular success was not subsequently repeated, it showed that the federation could be a political force.

With the formation of the Hosokawa coalition Government in August 1993, Yamagishi's ambition of using labour unification as a first step to unifying left-of-centre parties seemed on the way to fulfilment. The JSP and the DSP were together in the same Government (as was the *Rengō* group in the Upper House, under the name of *Minkairen*). His ambition was, however, to be disappointed by the formation of the LIBERAL DEMOCRATIC PARTY (LDP)–JSP–*Sakigake* coalition Government in June 1994, and Yamagishi resigned his positions.

Undoubtedly the formation of *Rengō* – incomplete though it might be – strengthened the political muscle of labour unions as a whole. Being co-operative with management rather than confrontational, organised labour found itself being regularly consulted by Government and its representatives invited onto Government commissions of various kinds. Nevertheless, the general trend was of decline in union membership and a gradual slippage of influence.

Further reading
Curtis (1999)
Kume (1998)
Tsujinaka, in Allinson and Sone (1993)

judges It is notoriously difficult to become a judge in Japan. There are less than 3,000 judges for a total population of about 126 million people. The number of cases handled throughout the court system has been steadily increasing, but the number of judges increases only very slowly. Almost all judges receive training in the Supreme Court's Legal Training and Research Institute, but its intake is low (about 700 per year) and depends on passing the National Law Examination. According to Beer and Itoh, each year about 50 of these become judges. Formally speaking, Cabinet appoints judges, but only rarely does Cabinet interfere with choices made within the judiciary.

Justices (judges) on the Supreme Court include some that have not risen by this route, including former academics teaching law. They include several who have been influential in the area of human rights. There is also a category of 'persons of learning and experience', and these have included, for instance, former diplomats.

Many believe that judges are not produced in sufficient numbers to staff the system adequately, and that this is one of the main reasons for excessive delay in the processing of cases. Others argue that there are enough judges to fulfil demand because of powerful cultural restraints on willingness to engage in litigation. Conversely, some observers maintain that the principal reason why people are wary about engaging in litigation is the inordinate delays to which cases are subject, in part because of this very same lack of judges. The mind-set of the politico-bureaucratic elite is generally hostile to open conflict and dispute, and favourable to harmony and conciliation. It may thus even be possible to make a causal connection between low litigation levels, the shortage of judges and official policy on the training and appointment of judges. This is, however, highly controversial territory.

Another controversial topic is the widespread view that judges (particularly at the upper levels of the system) are unduly conservative, and willing to make decisions that broadly follow the preferences of officialdom. The extremely sparing use by the Supreme Court of its powers of JUDICIAL REVIEW might seem to justify this concern, though the Court explains it in separation-of-powers terms. Other comparable countries (such as the United Kingdom) are no strangers to controversy over judges whose mind-set is more conservative than that of society at large. Whether Japan presents us with a particularly marked example of this phenomenon is more difficult to answer. In the 1970s some judges found their promotion prospects blocked by their membership of the left-leaning Young Lawyers Association. Today, it may well be the case that judges, in general, reflect the conservative preferences of the bulk of the population as well as of the Government, rather than that they are exceptionally conservative in terms of the prevailing ethos.

Further reading
Beer (1992)
Beer and Itoh (1996)
Oda (1999)

K

Kaifu Toshiki Kaifu Toshiki became PRIME MINISTER unexpectedly in August 1989 and remained in the post until November 1991, his main qualification being his uncorrupt reputation.

He was born in Aichi in 1931, shone in the Waseda University debating society and was known as an eloquent speaker. He was elected from a Lower House district of Aichi Prefecture at every election between 1960 and 2000. A member of the small MIKI–KŌMOTO faction of the LIBERAL DEMOCRATIC PARTY (LDP), as Prime Minister he had neither strong factional backing nor extensive ministerial experience. He was regarded as an educational specialist, having spent two terms as Education Minister.

He became Prime Minister at a low point in LDP fortunes. The party had just lost the Upper House elections of July 1989, following the RECRUIT SCANDAL and unpopular policies such as the imposition of consumption tax. The brief reign of UNO SŌSUKE had come to an ignominious end and the party was looking for an acceptable replacement. Kaifu presented a clean and attractive image. For the first time in 41 years, a joint session of both Houses had to be held to determine who should become Prime Minister, since DOI TAKAKO of the JAPAN SOCIALIST PARTY (JSP) was the choice of the Upper House. Duly elected at that session, Kaifu appointed two women to his first Cabinet (a record number), in a bid to counter Doi's appeal to women. (They did not survive into his second Cabinet, however.)

Kaifu began well, leading his party to a comfortable win in the Lower House elections of February 1990 (though the Socialists won an extra 50 seats, mainly at the expense of minor parties). His weak factional position, however, and the absence of an LDP majority in the Upper House, caused him severe problems. Pressured by the Americans to contribute men and materiél to the force seeking to dislodge Saddam Hussein from Kuwait, Kaifu tried but failed, in October–November 1990, to pass a bill through Parliament authorising despatch of military personnel to the Gulf. When, in 1991, his attempt to reform the Lower House electoral system was vetoed by party elders, he left office.

This was not the end of his career. When an LDP–JSP–NEW PARTY HARBINGER coalition was proposed to replace the Hata minority Government in June 1994, he ran against the Socialist Murayama for the prime ministership with backing from most of the Hata coalition and some dissidents from the LDP and JSP. He was narrowly defeated. When the NEW FRONTIER PARTY (NFP) was constructed by OZAWA ICHIRŌ in December 1994, he was elected leader of it, but replaced a year later by Ozawa in a general vote. When the NFP broke up in December 1997, he joined Ozawa's LIBERAL PARTY (III).

Kaifu had ambitions to reform the political system, but even as Prime Minister was too politically weak to do much about it.

Further reading
Curtis (1999)

Kajiyama Seiroku First elected to the HOUSE OF REPRESENTATIVES in 1969, Kajiyama Seiroku was a LIBERAL DEMOCRATIC PARTY (LDP) politician who honed the arts of factional manipulation.

Born in 1926 in Ibaragi, he attended an army air school towards the end of the war (mentioned in his election literature, as was sponsorship by ex-service organisations), and after the war graduated from Nihon University. His career as a prefectural councillor culminated in the presidency of the Ibaragi prefectural council. Representing the LDP in Parliament from 1969, he served as Secretary-General and Chairman of its Parliamentary Policy Committee, as well as being successively Minister of Justice, of International Trade and Industry, of Home Affairs and from 1996 being Chief Cabinet Secretary to the Prime Minister, HASHIMOTO.

His machinations in 1992–3 in relation to electoral system reform were designed to combat OZAWA's ambitions, but in practice contributed to the fall of the MIYAZAWA Government and to the LDP's temporary exit from office. Curiously enough, in the late 1990s, he worked for a 'conservative–conservative' alliance, to replace the earlier coalitions of centre-left parties with the LDP. This involved accommodation with Ozawa, whom he had previously done so much to frustrate.

In July 1998, Hashimoto resigned after poor results in the Upper House elections, and Kajiyama was one of three contenders for his succession. He was badly beaten, however, by the factional strength of OBUCHI KEIZŌ, the results being: Obuchi 225 votes, Kajiyama 102 and KOIZUMI 84. In his campaign, Kajiyama placed overwhelming emphasis on the need to solve the bad loan crisis affecting the banking system, including forcing banks into liquidation if necessary. Some observers thought he might have had the clout and toughness to make progress on this vital issue.

Further reading
Curtis (1999)

Kan Naoto Influenced by the veteran female anti-corruption politician Ichikawa Fusae, Kan Naoto came to exemplify the possibilities of citizen organisations as a basis for political campaigning, at least in cities.

Born in 1946 in Yamaguchi, Kan attended the Tokyo Institute of Technology, and worked as a lawyer. In the 1970s he was active in housing pressure groups in Tokyo and in 1976 organised Ichikawa Fusae's highly successful campaign for the Upper House. He failed in several attempts to enter national politics, but was elected spectacularly from an outer Tokyo constituency in the Lower House elections of 1980. During the 1980s, as a member of the mini-party, SOCIAL DEMOCRATIC LEAGUE (SDL, *Shaminren*), Kan made a name for himself as expert on urban issues, notably housing, and as an activist in citizen movements. In 1992, with EDA SATSUKI of the SDL, he formed a centre-left discussion group called 'Sirius', and the next year was closely involved in formulating policy initiatives of the HOSOKAWA coalition Government. With the formation of the Hosokawa Government in 1993, Kan began to disengage from the SDL (which broke up in 1994) and joined the NEW PARTY HARBINGER (*Shintō Sakigake*).

Appointed Minister of Health and Welfare in the first Hashimoto coalition Government in January 1996, Kan reversed years of bureaucratic denial of responsibility by publicly apologising to a large group of relatives of victims of an HIV-TAINTED BLOOD SCANDAL, dating back to the 1980s, and insisting on a full investigation.

Kan joined the DEMOCRATIC PARTY (*Minshutō*) on its formation in September 1996, becoming one of its two 'representatives' (*daihyō*), the other being HATOYAMA YUKIO. This two-headed leadership did not work well, and in September 1997 was replaced by an arrangement whereby, more conventionally, Kan would be 'Representative' and Hatoyama 'Secretary-General'. He remained in this top position until September 1999, when he was narrowly defeated by Hatoyama, and became Chairman of the party's Policy Committee. He was again defeated narrowly by Hatoyama in September 2002, but in December, after the latter was forced to resign following an abortive attempt to merge the Party with Ozawa's Liberal Party, Kan replaced him.

The popularity of Kan among the urban middle class, particularly in Tokyo, remained high, but by 2002 he had hardly 'broken the mould' of politics as some had predicted early in his career.

Kanemaru Shin Born in 1914 in the largely rural prefecture of Yamanashi, Kanemaru Shin graduated from Tokyo Agricultural University, and was first elected to the HOUSE OF REPRESENTATIVES in the general elections of 1958 on the LIBERAL DEMOCRATIC PARTY (LDP) ticket.

From the early 1970s he became an important member of the TANAKA faction, and received his first full Cabinet position – that of Minister of Construction – in the second Tanaka Cabinet between December 1972 and November 1973. He was then Director of the NATIONAL LAND AGENCY in the MIKI Cabinet between December 1974 and September 1976, and Director of the DEFENCE AGENCY in the FUKUDA Cabinet between November 1977 and December 1978. He was Deputy Prime Minister in the third NAKASONE Cabinet between July 1986 and November 1987. In addition he also held at various times the party positions of Secretary-General, Chairman of the Executive Board and party Vice-President.

When TAKESHITA took over control of most of the Tanaka faction in 1985, after Tanaka's stroke, Kanemaru, whose son was married to Takeshita's daughter, became extremely influential within it. After Takeshita was forced to step down as Prime Minister in June 1989, following the Recruit stocks for favours scandal (see RECRUIT SCANDAL), Kanemaru gradually evolved into the effective leader of the faction. His political style was that of a traditional faction boss, and that meant amassing funds in order to fund faction activities. Like other such politicians, he had extensive connections with the construction industry, but his downfall was caused by links with a road delivery company called SAGAWA KYŪBIN (see SAGAWA KYŪBIN SCANDAL).

In the party presidential elections of 1987, Takeshita had been embarrassed by a gangster organisation giving him public support in an attempt to discredit him. Kanemaru asked the head of *Sagawa Kyūbin* to intervene, and, after the gangsters were persuaded to desist from such activities, Kanemaru controversially went to thank them. He was also forced to admit he had received an unreported ¥500,000 from *Sagawa Kyūbin*. In September 1992 police investigating the *Sagawa Kyūbin* scandal raided his house and discovered a huge cache of money, including gold bars. The total amount was estimated at more than ¥4.5 billion. He was fined ¥200,000 for contravention of the Political Contributions Control Law. The derisory nature of the fine created a public outcry, and Kanemaru resigned all his political positions as a result. He resigned from Parliament in October. In March 1993 he was arrested and subjected to various charges. Pressure for reform of the anti-corruption laws became intense as a result.

Kanemaru's resignation was a key event precipitating the split in the Takeshita faction, and ultimately the split in the LDP itself, which led to the formation of a non-LDP government in August 1993, and a decade of political confusion that followed.

Further reading
Curtis (1999)

Kanzaki Takenori Born in 1943 in Fukuoka, Kanzaki Takenori was first elected to the House of Representatives for a Fukuoka constituency, as a CLEAN GOVERNMENT PARTY (CGP, *Kōmeitō*) candidate in 1983. When the CGP entered the HOSOKAWA coalition Government in August 1993, he became Minister for Posts and Telecommunications.

With the collapse of the NEW FRONTIER PARTY (*Shinshintō*) in December 1997, the CGP element within that party, which had merged with it three years earlier, began to reform. Kanzaki became the Representative (*Daihyō*) of the NEW PARTY PEACE (*Shintō Heiwa*), created by Lower House members in January 1998, and then of the reconstituted CGP (absorbing the *Kōmei* members of the Upper House) in November.

In October 1999, with OBUCHI KEIZŌ as Prime Minister, Kanzaki took the CGP into a three-way coalition with the LDP and Ozawa's Liberal Party. A condition of joining was that the proportional representation seats in the Lower House be reduced by no more than 20. The adherence of the CGP created a Government with a commanding majority in both houses, unlike the weak administrations that had preceded it. Whereas the Liberals later pulled out of the coalition, the CGP led by Kanzaki remained with it through the administrations of Obuchi, MORI and KOIZUMI.

Katayama Tetsu Katayama Tetsu was Japan's first Socialist PRIME MINISTER, for nine months in 1947–8, the first Prime Minister under the new Constitution (*see* CONSTITUTION OF 1946), and was a Christian.

Born in Wakayama in 1887, he graduated in Law from Tokyo Imperial University and practised law in Tokyo, seeking to simplify legal explanation. He was Secretary-General of the moderate Socialist People's Party (*Shakai Minshūtō*) at its foundation in 1926, and was first elected to Parliament in 1930. After the war he was the first Secretary-General of the JAPAN SOCIALIST PARTY (JSP), created in November 1945. After the Socialists received a seat plurality in the general elections of April 1947, Katayama became Prime Minister in May of a Cabinet consisting of the JSP, the Democratic Party and the National Co-operative Party [*see also* CONSERVATIVE PARTIES, 1945–55].

The coalition Cabinet was a precarious left–right balance, and was especially shaken by dissent *within* the JSP. Initially, it was to have included YOSHIDA's Liberal Party, which demanded exclusion of the JSP left wing, the latter arguing against forming a coalition with conservative parties. The Cabinet took office amidst a desperate economic situation, which occupied much of its energies. It needed to curb galloping inflation and attempted this by economic controls. Its attempts to nationalise coal mining foundered on conservative objections, though a weak bill was brought in. But some of the most progressive legislation of the Occupation period was introduced under Katayama. The military ministries were abolished and a Ministry of Labour established, extensive revisions were made to the criminal and civil codes, land reform progressed, and other reforms came in, including an anti-monopoly law.

Katayama's first serious political crisis occurred when he had to dismiss his maverick Agriculture Minister, Hirano Rikizō. The appointment of his successor caused problems with the JSP left wing, and the Government faced severe labour problems, despite its labour reforms, in an economic situation catastrophic for workers. In February 1948 the Lower House budget committee, chaired by the left-wing Socialist, SUZUKI MOSABURŌ, rejected the Government's counter-inflationary budget. In the aftermath, the Katayama Government was forced to resign.

Katayama lost his seat in the 1949 general elections, and in 1950 resigned as party Chairman. Although he remained active in the Right Socialist Party (1951–5) and the reunited JSP from 1955, he devoted himself to defence of the CONSTITUTION OF 1946, combating corruption, improving relations with China and other issues in which he had a personal interest. In 1959–60 he defected to the DEMOCRATIC SOCIALIST PARTY led by his closest associate when Prime Minister, NISHIO SUEHIRO. But in 1963 he resigned from that party too, disagreeing with aspects of its platform. He died, aged 90, in 1978.

Further reading
Cole *et al.* (1966)

Katō Kōichi Born in 1939 in Yamagata, Katō Kōichi belonged to the YKK group of promising younger leaders much remarked on in the 1990s (the others being YAMASAKI TAKU and KOIZUMI JUNICHIRŌ). A graduate of Tokyo University, he began a career as a diplomat (specialising in China) before being first elected to the HOUSE OF REPRESENTATIVES for a Yamagata constituency at the general elections of 1972. He continued to be re-elected at every subsequent election, including that of 2000.

A member of the OHIRA – later MIYAZAWA – faction, his political preferences were, in LIBERAL DEMOCRATIC PARTY (LDP) terms, centrist or slightly to the left of centre (distinguishing him from the other two YKK members). He succeeded Miyazawa as leader of the faction in the late 1990s, and in 1999 it was the second largest of the seven factional groupings in the party. He served in senior party posts, notably those of Deputy Chairman of the Policy Affairs Research Council and LDP Secretary-General. He was also, at various times, Director of the DEFENCE AGENCY (under NAKASONE, 1984–5) and Chief Cabinet Secretary (under Miyazawa, 1991–2).

In November 2000, with the MORI Cabinet suffering from low popularity, opposition parties presented to Parliament a motion of no-confidence in the Cabinet. Katō (as did Yamasaki), announced that he and his supporters would vote in favour of the motion. Mori responded by threatening to expel them from the party. Consequently, the revolt collapsed as Katō found he could not persuade enough of his followers to support the motion (thus jeopardising their LDP endorsement) to guarantee its passage. In particular, his factional patron, Miyazawa Kiichi, refused to support him. Katō was humiliated by this retreat from the brink, and it had a catastrophic effect on his political prospects.

In March 2002, he was forced to resign from the LDP, and as head of his faction, because of a tax-evasion scandal involving one of his aides. This in turn was a blow for the Koizumi administration, which Katō and his faction had strongly backed.

Katsumata Seiichi Briefly Chairman of the JAPAN SOCIALIST PARTY (JSP) in 1967–8, Katsumata was unusual in entering that party from the Government bureaucracy. Born in 1908, he was, along with WADA HIROO and Sata Tadataka, a left-wing member of the governmental Planning Board, and with them was imprisoned following the exposure of the Sorge spy ring in 1941. After the war he and the others worked for the Economic Stabilisation Board (*Keizai Antei Hombu*) and later joined the Socialist movement. He was a leading member of the Wada faction of the Left Socialist Party in the first half of the 1950s, and of the united JSP later in that decade and into the 1960s. In 1956 he successfully led JSP resistance to a LIBERAL DEMOCRATIC PARTY (LDP) attempt to create a new electoral system highly unfavourable to JSP chances.

Katsumata became leader of the Wada faction after the latter's death in 1967. During the mid-1960s Eda–Sasaki struggles within the JSP, Katsumata first stood as the running mate of EDA SABURŌ for the top two party positions in January 1966, but SASAKI and NARITA defeated them. After convoluted factional manœuvres, Sasaki and Narita both resigned in August 1967, and Katsumata, having shifted his faction's support from Eda to Sasaki, was elected Chairman. He only lasted a year, however, and was displaced in September 1968. He later served as Deputy Speaker of the House of Representatives. He died in December 1989.

Further reading
Hrebenar (2000)

Kawakami Jōtarō Kawakami was a Kōbe lawyer and academic who became Chairman of the Right Socialist Party from August 1952 until Socialist reunification in October 1955, then Chairman of the JAPAN SOCIALIST PARTY (JSP) from March 1961 until his resignation through illness in March 1965. He is significant in the politics of the early 1960s in that he provided moderate non-confrontational leadership following the extreme tensions of the SECURITY TREATY REVISION CRISIS of 1960. In this sense he was tacitly co-operating with the Prime Minister, IKEDA HAYATO, in seeking to lower the political temperature.

Born in 1889, he initially became interested in Socialism at the time of the Russo-Japanese war of 1904–5. He later became involved in the labour movement, and was first elected to Parliament for the Japan Labour-Farmer Party in 1928. He failed to be elected in the elections of 1930 and 1932, but succeeded in the elections of 1936, 1937 and 1942. During the 1930s he belonged to the 'Japan Labour' faction that dominated the Socialist Masses Party, and in 1940, along with ASANUMA and others, became an official of the State-sponsored Imperial Rule Assistance Association. As a result of his wartime activities, he was 'purged' by the Allied Occupation, but resumed active politics once the purge was lifted.

As Chairman of the Right Socialist Party, he led its centrist faction (still known as the 'Japan Labour group'), and, when the reunited JSP split once more in 1959–60, he stayed with the JSP (unlike some in his faction who joined the newly formed DEMOCRATIC SOCIALIST PARTY). Following his narrow defeat by Asanuma in the contest for party chairman in March 1960, Asanuma's assassination in October, and the acting chairmanship of Eda Saburō, he became Chairman in March 1961 and provided needed stability for the party in the early 1960s. He died in 1965.

Further reading
Cole *et al.* (1966)
Stockwin (1968a)
Totten (1966)

Kishi Nobusuke Kishi Nobusuke was perhaps the most controversial political leader of postwar Japan, and was PRIME MINISTER during the tensions of the late 1950s. He is remembered for the political crisis over revision of the Japan–US Security Treaty, which buffeted the system in 1960 (see SECURITY TREATY REVISION CRISIS).

He was born in November 1896, in what had been the Chōshū domain of western Honshū, an area that produced many political and military leaders. He was Prime Minister between 1957 and 1960, and the elder brother of a later Prime Minister, SATŌ EISAKU (their surnames differing because of an adoption procedure). In the 1930s he worked in the Ministry of Agriculture and Commerce, and later in the Ministry of Trade and Industry. He spent a period from 1936 in the Government of Japan's puppet state of Manchukuo, planning the economic development of that territory. In 1939 he became Vice-Minister of the Ministry of Trade and Industry in Tokyo, but resigned over a disagreement with his Minister in 1941. He then, aged 44, became Minister for Trade in the first Tōjō Cabinet, formed in October 1941. Later, he was put in charge of munitions, but clashed with those in the Government who, in his view, ignored technical and economic advice. At this stage and later, he exhibited outstanding organisational ability.

Having worked for Tōjō, he was under suspicion in the post-war period. The Allied Occupation authorities arrested him and held him in prison as a suspected class A war criminal, but he was never brought to trial and was eventually released. He returned to active politics in 1952, joined YOSHIDA's Liberal Party, but after clashes with Yoshida he became Secretary-General of HATOYAMA's Democratic Party, and continued as Secretary-General of the merged LIBERAL DEMOCRATIC PARTY (LDP) after its formation in November 1955. In December 1956, on the formation of the ISHIBASHI Cabinet, Kishi became its Foreign Minister, and then acting Prime Minister when Ishibashi fell ill. On the latter's resignation in February 1957, he became Prime Minister at the age of 60.

In foreign policy, the Kishi administration pursued a staunchly pro-American and anti-Communist line, rather in contrast to that of its immediate predecessors. Kishi was determined to revise the Security Treaty to make it more equal for Japan, and soon began to negotiate with the Americans to this end. He also helped restore economic relations with much of South-East Asia, and strongly supported Taiwan against the PRC [see also SOUTH-EAST ASIA, RELATIONS WITH; CHINA (PRC AND ROC), RELATIONS WITH]. In domestic policy he confronted the militant JAPAN TEACHERS' UNION with a teachers assessment system and the reintroduction of ethics courses into schools, attacked unions generally and sought unsuccessfully to revise the CONSTITUTION OF 1946. He failed in his attempt to strengthen police powers in 1958 – an issue which provoked a major political crisis. On the other hand, he succeeded in restoring much of the powers of the former Ministry of Home Affairs over local government.

Kishi's intention in revising the Security Treaty was to place Japan–US security relations on a more equal footing by the removal of discriminatory clauses and clarifying responsibilities. But he failed to reckon with growing pacifist sentiments among the electorate, and the concerted hostility to the Treaty of the JAPAN SOCIALIST PARTY, many labour unions, students and urban intellectuals, who organised a series of anti-Treaty, anti-Kishi demonstrations. The revised Treaty was signed in January 1960, but ratification required the consent of both houses of Parliament. Assuming ratification by both houses by 19 June 1960, he invited President Eisenhower to visit Japan on that date. This meant it had to pass the Lower House by midnight on 19 May. With Socialist parliamentarians physically obstructing the taking of votes for extension of the session and ratification of the Treaty, Kishi ordered 500 police into the building to remove the obstructing Socialists.

That act turned the crisis from one involving security policy to one where the foundations of the still fragile post-war democracy appeared at risk. When the U2 incident forced Eisenhower to cancel his visit to Moscow, and confined his journey to the non-Communist states of Asia, fear of world war was added to fears about democracy. Massive demonstrations on 15 June caused the death of a girl student and forced Kishi to call off Eisenhower's state visit. The Japan–US Mutual Security Treaty was duly ratified by the House of Councillors on 19 June, but Kishi resigned four days later, having made himself vulnerable to intra-LDP factional manœuvring against him [*see also* SECURITY TREATY REVISION CRISIS]. Next month he was stabbed by an ultra-rightist, but not seriously [*see also* EXTREMIST MOVEMENTS (RIGHT)].

After his resignation, Kishi never again held Cabinet office, but remained in Parliament until 1979, exercising considerable influence, particularly during his brother's prime ministership between 1964 and 1972. He maintained close links with Taiwan and remained implacably hostile to the PRC. He died in 1987.

Kishi was a bureaucrat turned politician, but unusually for such people the reverse of a consensus-taker. He was determined to place his stamp on policy and events, even at the cost of provoking serious crises. Ironically, his most lasting legacy was negative. The scale and violence of the 1960s crisis shook the political establishment to its core. That many of his successors have been so cautious may owe something to the negative example of Kishi's decisiveness.

Further reading
Packard (1966)

Koizumi Junichirō PRIME MINISTER from April 2001 on a reformist platform, Koizumi Junichirō was for some months more popular with the general public than any of his many predecessors.

Well known from the mid-1990s as one of the most promising of younger LIBERAL DEMOCRATIC PARTY (LDP) leaders, Koizumi was one of the trio known as 'YKK', the others being YAMASAKI TAKU and KATŌ KŌICHI. He was in fact the youngest of the three, being born in 1942 in Kanagawa, just south of Tokyo, so that when he became Prime Minister he was 59. He was first elected to the House of Representatives at the general elections of 1972 for a Kanagawa constituency, which then continued regularly to elect him.

He held a number of senior positions in the LDP, but his first ministerial portfolio was as Minister of Health and Welfare in 1988–9. His original factional affiliation was with the FUKUDA faction, where he remained through various changes of leader, his most recent faction leader being MORI YOSHIRŌ. This inevitably labelled him as a distinctly right-of-centre LDP politician, but in the 1990s he was developing certain policy positions that made him distinctive. In a series of carefully argued speeches and articles, he called for the privatisation of the Post Office, and in particular its savings bank, where the highest proportion of the people's savings was deposited. Given the fact that post office savings accounts formed a huge pool of funding available for political purposes, his privatisation proposal threatened many LDP-based vested interests, not to speak of rousing the ire of the public-sector unions.

Koizumi's first bid for the LDP presidency (and thus prime ministership) was made in July 1998, after HASHIMOTO resigned. He came a poor third with 84 votes, against 225 for OBUCHI KEIZŌ and 102 for KAJIYAMA SEIROKU. In April 2001, the unpopular Prime Minister, Mori Yoshirō, who had succeeded Obuchi, was persuaded to step down, with HOUSE OF COUNCILLORS elections scheduled for July. Few expected that the LDP had any chance of success in the elections if Mori remained the party leader. Four politicians challenged for the succession, of whom the two strongest were the former Prime Minister, Hashimoto Ryūtarō, and Koizumi. When primary elections were held in prefectural party branches, Koizumi unexpectedly swept the board, and Hashimoto did not win a single prefecture east and north of Kyōto. The most probable explanation for the result was that local LDP branches were desperate to avoid disaster in the forthcoming Upper House elections, due in July. By 'borrowing' the popular media image of Koizumi, they hoped to repair their electoral fortunes, sunk to low levels during Mori's party presidency. The election results were to prove them right.

Image became a crucial factor in Koizumi's tenure of the prime ministerial position. To an extent his image was a media concoction, though the LDP exploited it, marketing Koizumi blow-up dolls, Koizumi T-shirts and the like. Polls showed that he was popular with over 80 per cent of the electorate – a higher rating even than Hosokawa early in his term in 1993. But the wavy hairstyle and rock-band image was underpinned by a rhetoric of radical reform promises. He promised to reform the system in such a way as to promote efficiency and attack the stranglehold over policy maintained by vested interests.

This worked well for several months. But by the end of 2001 questions were being asked about how far he was able to deliver on his promises. The economy remained stagnant, the bank indebtedness crisis was hardly improving, and vested interests still exercised great influence over policy. When, in January 2002 he was constrained to dismiss his maverick but popular Foreign Minister, Ms TANAKA MAKIKO, he saw his popularity fall from 80 per cent to around 50 per cent. In the early months of 2002, he had come to look more like a standard LDP prime minister than the new broom he had appeared to be at the beginning of his term.

During the summer of 2002, his position stabilised to some extent, and there were some signs of economic recovery, though any such recovery remained fragile. On 17 September 2002, he travelled to North Korea for talks with the North Korean leader, Kim Jong Il. They both signed a Declaration aimed at normalising relations between the two states, engaging in economic and security co-operation and reducing tensions. But this came to be overshadowed by the issue of Japanese nationals abducted from Japan to North Korea since the 1970s. For the first time Kim Jong Il admitted to the kidnappings, but informed Japanese officials that the majority of those kidnapped had subsequently died. This news caused grief and outrage in Japan, though there was strong support for the Koizumi initiative [see also KOREA (ROK AND DPRK), RELATIONS WITH].

In early October 2002, Koizumi reshuffled his Cabinet, replacing Yanagisawa Hakuo with Takenaka Heizō as Director of the Financial Services Agency. This was taken as indicating a new determination to tackle the problem of bank debt with greater vigour than hitherto.

Further reading
Neary (2002)

Kōmei *see* Clean Government Party, New Party Peace

Kōmoto Toshio Born in 1911 in the Kōbe area, Kōmoto was unusual among LIBERAL DEMOCRATIC PARTY (LDP) politicians in rising to the high echelons of party and Government from a background in business, specifically, in shipping. In this, however, he may be compared with FUJIYAMA AIICHIRŌ, who similarly aspired to be PRIME MINISTER but never quite succeeded.

First elected to the HOUSE OF REPRESENTATIVES in 1949, he was returned from his home district for no less than 17 consecutive elections, up to and including the elections of 1993. At various times he was Minister of International Trade and Industry, of Posts and Telecommunications, Director of the ECONOMIC PLANNING AGENCY and of the LDP Policy Affairs Research Council. Relatively liberal in his approach to economic problems, he occupied a broadly centre-left political position. For many years he was a leading member of the small MIKI faction on the left wing of the LDP, and took over its leadership in 1980. He first contested primary elections for the party presidency in November 1978, when he was Minister for International Trade and Industry, but came a poor fourth behind OHIRA, FUKUDA and NAKASONE. At his second attempt in October 1982, as Director of the Economic Planning Agency, he came second, behind Nakasone, but ahead of ABE SHINTARŌ and NAKAGAWA ICHIRŌ. Although he had been expected to give Nakasone a run for his money, he only gained 27.29 per cent of the vote against 57.62 per cent for Nakasone. Undoubtedly this poor performance reflected his limited support as head of the smallest faction in the party. But he also lacked the strategic sense of Miki, who had parleyed an implicit threat to defect against a spell as Prime Minister. His final effort came in August 1989, following the LDP defeat in the Upper House elections and the resignation of UNO SŌSUKE.

Kōmoto was attempting to forge an alliance of support for his candidacy, but was persuaded to withdraw in favour of a younger and more appealing member of his own faction, KAIFU TOSHIKI.

Further reading
Morris, David (1989)

Kon-Chiku-Shō A mildly derogatory term much used in the 1980s and early 1990s to designate three leading politicians of the LIBERAL DEMOCRATIC PARTY's Takeshita faction: KANEMARU SHIN, TAKESHITA NOBORU and OZAWA ICHIRŌ. It makes use of variant readings (pronunciations) of the same *kanji*. The *kane* (金) of Kanemaru can also be read *kon*; the *také* (竹) of Takeshita can be read *chiku*; and the *o* (小) of Ozawa can be read *shō*. *Kon-chiku-shō* sounds like a mild swearword.

Kōno Ichirō Kōno Ichirō was a powerful faction leader in the LIBERAL DEMOCRATIC PARTY (LDP) of the late 1950s and early 1960s. He maintained close links with agriculture and construction, and was generally hostile to those factions in which YOSHIDA school ex-bureaucrats predominated.

Born in 1898 in Kanagawa, he became a journalist after graduating from Waseda University, and was first elected to the House of Representatives in 1932 representing the *Seiyūkai* party. After the war he was a founder member of the JAPAN LIBERAL PARTY (I), becoming its Secretary-General. But as well as his mentor, HATOYAMA ICHIRŌ, he was purged from public life in 1946, and was out of politics until 1951. With Hatoyama as PRIME MINISTER from 1954, Kōno became Minister of Agriculture, and was a key figure in moves to form the LDP in 1955. In 1956 he was principal Japanese negotiator with the USSR for a fisheries treaty and played a major part in negotiations that restored Japan–Soviet diplomatic relations, but failed to produce a peace treaty [*see also* SOVIET UNION AND RUSSIA, RELATIONS WITH]. In the KISHI Cabinet he was Director of the ECONOMIC PLANNING AGENCY, and in IKEDA's Cabinets he was successively Minister of Agriculture and of Construction. He was also in charge of organising the 1964 Olympics and was centrally involved in the choice of a site for the New Tokyo International Airport.

At the climax of the 1960 SECURITY TREATY REVISION CRISIS, he was a crucial influence forcing Kishi to resign as Prime Minister, and for about two weeks he actively discussed pulling his faction out of the LDP and forming a new party. Ironically his son, KŌNO YŌHEI, did just that in 1976, forming the NEW LIBERAL CLUB in protest against LDP corruption as symbolised by the LOCKHEED SCANDAL.

When IKEDA resigned the leadership in November 1964, Kōno threw his hat into the ring, but was defeated by SATŌ EISAKU. He died unexpectedly in July 1965.

Kōno Yōhei Son of KŌNO ICHIRŌ, the LIBERAL DEMOCRATIC PARTY (LDP) faction leader, Kōno Yōhei succeeded to his father's Lower House seat following his death. He is known as founder of the NEW LIBERAL CLUB, as the only non-prime ministerial LDP President, and as a long-serving Foreign Minister.

Born in 1937, graduated from Waseda University like his father, he was elected first in 1967 from a Kanagawa constituency. In 1976, following exposure of the LOCKHEED SCANDAL, he founded the New Liberal Club, thus splitting the LDP for the first time. The New Liberal Club went into coalition with the LDP after the 1983 general election, and nearly all its members returned to the LDP in 1986.

With the collapse of LDP rule in August 1993, Kōno succeeded MIYAZAWA as LDP President, but, with his party out of power, did not become Prime Minister. As leader of the largest opposition party, he negotiated with the HOSOKAWA Government in late 1993 and early 1994 over reform of the Lower House electoral system (*see* ELECTION SYSTEMS). When, in June 1994, the LDP returned to power in coalition with the JAPAN SOCIALIST PARTY and NEW PARTY HARBINGER, the Socialist Chairman, MURAYAMA, became Prime Minister. Kōno was both his deputy and Foreign Minister. In 1995, however, he was challenged for the LDP presidency by Hashimoto Ryūtarō, who commanded superior factional support. Kōno declined to stand, and Hashimoto succeeded him as party President in September 1995, becoming Prime Minister in January 1996. Kōno began a second term as Foreign

Minister in October 1999, in the second OBUCHI Cabinet.

Kōno's views were broadly moderate and liberal, his ten-year defection had some reforming effect, but his weak power position in the LDP put him at a disadvantage against the party's factional heavyweights.

Korea (ROK and DPRK), relations with
Crucial to an understanding of Japanese foreign policy is the fact that one of the last remaining theatres of the Cold War divides in two the country that is physically closest to Japan and was a Japanese colony between 1910 and 1945. The Japanese city of Kitakyūshū is slightly more than 200 km, as the crow flies across the Tsushima Strait, from the Korean city of Pusan, while the nearest point on the demilitarised zone (DMZ) between the two Koreas to the nearest point on the Japanese coast is about 500 km. The DMZ is the most heavily fortified frontier in the world, where nearly two million troops confront each other across a strip of land over a kilometre wide. The city of Seoul, capital of South Korea, home to around a quarter of the South Korean population, is some 45 km, or two minutes' flying time, from the DMZ. President Clinton once described the border village of Panmunjom as 'the most frightening place on earth'. And yet, despite extreme tension punctuated by many minor incidents, on land and at sea, the border has held, without serious warfare, for nearly fifty years.

Those who expected the North Korean regime to collapse after the ending of the Cold War in Europe were disappointed, while famine conditions in the North in the late 1990s may have killed hundreds of thousands (possibly millions) of people, yet the regime survived. The cost of unifying the two Germanys frightened the Government in Seoul out of its earlier aspirations to unify the country and into a preference for a two-Korea system with reform in the North.

The degree of separation between the populations of the Republic of Korea (ROK, South Korea) and the Democratic People's Republic of Korea (DPRK, North Korea) far exceeds that between East and West Germany during the Cold War in Europe. Telephone, postal and other electronic communication between the two Koreas does not exist for ordinary people, while the two populations cannot receive each other's television programmes. Sometimes compared with Albania under the late Communist dictator, Enver Hoxha, the DPRK under Kim Il Sung, and since his death in 1994, under his son, Kim Jong Il, is a shuttered, militarised and totalitarian state with a collapsed economy. By contrast, the ROK, though its economy retains some autarchic characteristics, is increasingly integrated into the global capitalist economy. Whereas as late as 1960, the output of the two economies was probably of the same order of magnitude, by the early 2000s the economy of the South had grown to be many times larger than that of the North. Until the late 1980s, the system of government was authoritarian, but with the 1990s came a form of democratic rule, based on a president and a national assembly, which, though often turbulent, was becoming well institutionalised.

Japan's relationship with Korea has been severely affected by a bitter colonial legacy. Japanese colonial rule over Korea was harsh, and punctuated by attempts at revolt that were punitively repressed. The defeat of Japan led to the division of Korea, and to the outbreak of the Korean War in June 1950. Sometimes now referred to as the 'forgotten war', the conflict in Korea was the nearest that the Cold War came to being an all-out military conflict between the Communist and anti-Communist camps. It wrought untold destruction practically throughout the Korean peninsula, and the capital city, Seoul, changed hands four times before the armistice agreement in 1953. This left the line of demarcation between the two Koreas only a few kilometres distant from where it had been in June 1950.

The Korean War spanned Japan's transition from occupation to independence. Japan played essentially no part in the war, but it proved to be a bonanza for the Japanese economy, since the Americans placed orders with Japanese firms for goods they needed in Korea. It also set Japan on the path towards limited rearmament, since General MacArthur authorised the formation of a Police Reserve Force (*Keisatsu yobitai*), in part to replace US troops moved from Japan to Korea. Starting in 1952, Japan and South Korea found themselves under US pressure to embark on normalisation talks. The leaders of both sides, however, were so prejudiced against each other that no progress was possible. They were divided on a range of issues related to compensation claims, Korean demands for apology from Japan, territorial disputes and fishing rights. But sheer mutual dislike and distrust was the principal factor frustrating US aspirations for their two East Asian protégés to co-operate. Welfield comments ironically: 'Opponents of Japanese participation in American global strategy could at least console themselves with the thought that prejudice, ignorance and folly occasionally conspire to promote the common good' (p. 93).

By the mid-1960s the leadership on both sides had changed, both economies had entered a phase of rapid growth, and there was now sufficient temporal and psychological distance from war and colonialism. Thus, in June 1965, Japan and the ROK signed their Treaty on Basic Relations, which led to long-term and large-scale economic co-operation between them. The Treaty did not solve all the issues that divided them. The Koreans continued to demand apologies from the Japanese, fishing zones remained a problem, and a dispute continued to fester over possession of some waterless rocks that the Japanese called 'Bamboo Island' (Takeshima) and the Koreans 'Lonely Island' (Dokdo).

Compared with some other ROK Presidents before or since, Park Chung Hee, whose presidency began with his coup against an elected president in 1961 and ended with his assassination in 1979, was relatively pro-Japanese. A military man, he had been trained in the Imperial Japanese Army before the war. But in the 1970s he became increasingly authoritarian. In August 1973 agents of the Korean Central Intelligence Agency kidnapped the South Korean opposition leader, Kim Dae Jung, from a Tokyo hotel and abducted him to Korea. This caused a major political storm in Tokyo, and severe strains in relations between the two countries. The reputation in Japan of the Park regime had fallen to low levels by the late 1970s.

Over the same period relations between Japan and the DPRK were rather insubstantial, but the large pro-DPRK Korean population in Japan meant that the Japanese authorities could not ignore the Pyongyang regime. Trade talks in the early 1970s between Pyongyang and Tokyo led to a slight increase in trade (from very low levels), but after the first oil crisis this was not sustained. A series of political issues bedevilled Japanese–North Korean relations in the 1980s, including various terrorist acts and kidnappings attributed to agents of the DPRK regime.

The 1980s saw a fluctuating relationship between Japan and the ROK. Korean objections to statements in Japanese school textbooks caused a crisis in 1982, as did Korean demands for large-scale economic aid. When NAKASONE became PRIME MINISTER, however, in 1983, he made a point of visiting Seoul before any other capital. The ideological preferences of Nakasone were rather more in tune with those of the Korean leaders than had been the case with some previous Japanese prime ministers, so that relations improved, for a while at least.

The ending of the Cold War in Europe in the early 1990s led to a new and complicated phase in Japanese relations with the two Koreas. Quite apart from the reduction of international tension that the ending of the Cold War implied, politics in the ROK were moving towards a more democratic order, while politics in Japan was entering a period of instability, accompanied by economic stagnation. The issue of 'comfort women' (*ianfu*), who were women forced into prostitution by the Imperial Japanese Army during the war (and including many Koreans), proved difficult to handle, but eventually an agreement – hardly satisfactory, but better than no agreement – was reached [see also WOMEN AND POLITICS].

The DPRK, meanwhile, was experiencing the consequences for it of the demise of the Soviet Union, one of its two main backers along with the People's Republic of China. Also the PRC had normalised diplomatic relations with the ROK, with which it could do far more business than with the impoverished economy of the North. In 1994 Kim Il Sung died, provoking a crisis of leadership transition in the DPRK. But the biggest issue of the 1990s concerned the alleged development of nuclear weapons and other weapons of mass destruction by North Korea. In 1994 a dangerous crisis developed over nuclear inspections. This was eventually defused by an agreement to supply the DPRK with two light water nuclear reactors to replace existing reactors that could have produced material for nuclear weapons. Japan has participated in the Korean Peninsula Energy Development Organisation (KEDO), providing finance for light water reactors. This programme has experienced many vicissitudes, and anxieties about North Korean nuclear weapons persist.

Since 1998, with the election of Kim Dae Jung as President of the Republic of Korea, relations between the ROK and Japan have improved. Even though not all outstanding issues have been solved, the atmosphere of the relationship has been much better. The President's 'sunshine policy' towards North Korea (symbolised by his own historic visit to Pyongyang) was seriously undermined by the Bush administration after its coming to power in 2001 (and by Bush's later inclusion of the DPRK as a member of the 'Axis of Evil'). Nevertheless, it has had significant, if unspectacular, results in demonstrating at least to younger North Korean officials that there is a modern world out there that might be worth joining. Whether and to what time scale such demonstrations will continue to ferment within the rigid Stalinist structure of the regime remains to be seen. But it is worth noting that North Korea has radically de-industrialised since the early 1990s, and food production remains in crisis. Outside the capital, conditions of life lack most basic necessities.

Various groups in Japan, including political parties, have made efforts to reach out to North Korea. Most famously, in September 1990 a delegation led by Kanemaru Shin of the LIBERAL DEMOCRATIC PARTY (LDP) and Tanabe Makoto of the JAPAN SOCIALIST PARTY (JSP) visited Pyongyang and secured the release of a fishing boat crew. But events have repeatedly derailed moves towards improving relations. Of these the most disturbing, from Japan's point of view, was the launch of a *Taepodong* rocket from North Korea over Japan into the Pacific, in August 1998. Japanese concerns about alleged hijacking of several Japanese citizens from Japan towards North Korea have never been positively acknowledged by the DPRK. During 2002 numbers of North Korean refugees, fleeing appalling conditions in their own country and seeking refuge with foreign embassies (including the Japanese) in China, have faced violent preventative action by the PRC police.

Since the 1950s, Japan and the Republic of Korea have gradually succeeded in developing relations of depth and sophistication, despite many disputes and difficulties along the way. Younger politicians, officials, businessmen and so on, from South Korea, largely lack the anti-Japanese prejudices of their elders. Younger generations in Japan similarly have a much more favourable impression of the ROK than older people. An increasing rapport between the peoples of the two countries was seen throughout their joint hosting of the World Cup in May–June 2002, though it would be premature to suggest that prejudices have entirely disappeared.

Between Japan and the DPRK, however, relations remain difficult. The Japanese authorities find it perplexing to have to cope with what Foster-Carter colourfully describes as the 'militant mendicancy' of the North. In the words of Hughes: 'although the Japanese government has professed a desire for greater dialogue with North Korea...it has in fact switched its policy more to one of deterrence in the dimension of security' (in Hook *et al.*, 2001, p. 182).

On 17 September 2002, the Japanese Prime Minister, KOIZUMI JUNICHIRŌ, flew to Pyongyang for talks with the North Korean leader, Kim Jong Il. The two leaders signed a joint declaration, containing the following items:

1 The two sides would aim quickly to normalise relations between them.
2 Japan apologised to the Koreans for suffering caused while Korea was a Japanese colony, and both sides agreed on economic co-operation, mutual waiving of pre-1945 property claims, discussion of the status of Korean residents in Japan and the issue of cultural property.
3 Both sides agreed to refrain from threatening acts and the Korean side confirmed that past 'regrettable incidents' would not recur.

4 The two sides agreed to co-operate in pursuit of peace and in confidence-building measures in North-East Asia (especially concerning nuclear and missile issues), and the Koreans agreed to maintain their missile-launching moratorium in and after 2003.

For the first time Kim Jong Il admitted the truth of Japanese allegations that his operatives had kidnapped a number of Japanese from Japan and taken them to North Korea, over a 25-year period. But Japanese officials were informed that, of some 13 people concerned, eight had died. This news overshadowed the talks, and was greeted with grief and outrage in Japan, though the public broadly supported the Koizumi initiative. Subsequent events towards the end of 2002, especially the North Korean use of nuclear weapons development as a bargaining counter against US pressure, made further progress towards normalisation of DPRK-Japanese relations difficult. By December, tension on the peninsula had much increased, though the election of Roh Moo-Hyun as President of South Korea in succession to Kim Dae-Jung meant that the South would still try to engage with the North, rather than simply confronting it.

Further reading
Bridges (1993)
Drifte (1998)
Foster-Carter (2002)
Hook *et al.* (2001)
Welfield (1988)

labour unions (Rōdō kumiai) Japan's first attempt to form a national-level labour organisation was the *Yūaikai* (Friendship Society) formed in 1912. By 1920 it had 30,000 members in 120 affiliated unions under its wing. Its philosophy was influenced by Christian unitarianism, and it was moderate and co-operative in its attitudes to management. In 1921 it became the Japan Federation of Labour (*Nihon rōdō sōdōmei, Sōdōmei*), which became the vehicle of one important strand of unionism, that based on the principle of labour–management co-operation. The 1920s saw a great expansion of unionism, and in 1931 there were 370,000 members of 818 unions, though this represented only 8 per cent of the total workforce.

The decade, however, was turbulent and saw the influence, first of syndicalism, then more lastingly of Marxism, penetrate the union movement. Between 1925 and 1927 *Sōdōmei* split three ways, the most left-wing fragment, the Japanese Council of Labour Unions (*Nihon rōdō kumiai hyōgikai, Hyōgikai*) being Marxist-influenced. From this period close links developed between union groups and political parties of Socialist or social democratic persuasion. Just as the party divisions formed in the 1920s carried over into the post-war period, so did parallel divisions between union groups and their ideologies. During the 1930s the union movement came under increasing pressure from a repressive militaristic State, the Marxist left was driven underground, and the moderates were forced to move further and further to the right. The scope for union activity was rapidly reduced, and in 1940 the Government banned independent unions and formed the Patriotic Industrial Association (*Sangyō hōkokukai, Sanpō*) as a State-run labour front.

The end of the war in 1945 and the advent of the Allied Occupation created unprecedented opportunities for union organisation. The Labour Union Law (*Rōdō kumiai hō*) went into effect in April 1946, ensuring for workers the rights of organisation, collective bargaining and of strike. Further legislation was passed, over the next year, to create a framework for the settlement of labour disputes, and to guarantee minimum conditions of work for workers as a whole. The MINISTRY OF LABOUR was set up in August 1947. Growth of union membership was spectacular. By 1949 around seven million workers (50 per cent of the workforce outside agriculture) had joined some 35,000 unions grouped into various federations.

The rapid growth of unionism soon began to cause problems to which the Occupation authorities reacted. Their own experience back home made it difficult for Americans to understand the profoundly political nature of Japanese labour unionism. But that was logical enough in Japanese terms, given the endemically oppressive nature of the pre-war Japanese State. Left–right ideological differences carried over from the pre-war period were intensified in the heady atmosphere of democratic opening that followed the war. At national level the movement was divided between the right-of-centre *Sōdōmei* federation and the left-wing,

Communist-dominated, CONGRESS OF INDUSTRIAL UNIONS (*Sanbetsu kaigi*). Militant demands, some of a highly political nature, led General MacArthur to ban a planned general strike scheduled for 1 February 1947. In July 1948, following pressure from the Occupation authorities, legislation was passed by Parliament severely restricting the union rights of workers in the public sector. The 'Dodge Line' economic retrenchment measures put in place from 1949 were accompanied by mass dismissals of workers, including many union militants. These were followed by the 'Red Purge' of presumed Communists, which further weakened the militant left. *Sanbetsu kaigi* had clearly lost in its attempt to dominate unionism as a whole, and soon collapsed. In 1950, with some connivance by Occupation officials, the General Council of Japanese Trade Unions (*Sōhyō*) was formed. This signalled an end to serious Communist influence in the union movement, though *Sōhyō* was to lurch to the left a few years later. (In the words of its Chairman, Takano Minoru: 'the Occupation hatched a chicken that turned into a duck'.)

To understand the course of labour unionism in Japan since 1945, it is crucial to grasp the nature of employment patterns and labour–management relations in industry. Speaking very broadly, the following patterns predominated from at least the 1950s. A large proportion of the (male) workforce was given essentially lifetime contracts of employment (*shūshin koyō seido*), so that their commitment to their company was not tempered by the likelihood that they might seek employment elsewhere. Managers were greatly inhibited in any intention they might have to dismiss workers on lifetime contracts, but such workers were also unlikely to leave because they would have great difficulty finding work elsewhere at a comparable level of remuneration or status. Wages and salaries for those on lifetime contracts progressed by seniority increments (*nenkō joretsu seido*), dependent on length of time served, not merit. Lifetime employment in large firms was often accompanied by generous fringe benefits, such as company housing, medical facilities, holiday schemes, private insurance schemes and so on. These in turn were partly designed to foster company workforce solidarity and enthusiasm, since incentives were needed in the relative absence of reward based on exceptional merit.

On the other hand, small and medium-sized firms were for the most part too vulnerable to fluctuations in market forces to be able to propose to their workforce comparable conditions. Bankruptcy rates were much higher, and they were often dependent for survival on sub-contracting arrangements from the large firms. The large firms too employed considerable numbers of workers (particularly female) on short-term or casual contracts of labour. Even though some nominally short-term contracts were renewable and even approximated to lifetime contracts, this section of the workforce provided an economic cushion, from the perspective of the large firm, as indeed did the small and medium firm sector to which large firms sub-contracted work, often in exclusive arrangements. Another cushion was the twice-yearly bonus, which could be adjusted downwards as well as upwards, depending on economic conditions.

This structure had profound implications for unionism. With few exceptions since the war (the Seamen's Union being one), unions were organised on the basis of the company, and became known as 'enterprise unions' (*kigyō-betsu kumiai*). This explains the huge number of individual unions in the figures cited above. Now the logic of bargaining over wages and conditions where the predominant form is the enterprise union differs greatly from bargaining logic where the key unit is the craft or industrial union. Particularly in a system dominated by lifetime contracts, an enterprise union is unlikely to put in jeopardy the company's health by pressing excessive demands. This tends to bring management and union rather close together, because they have a common interest in maintaining or expanding a common 'pie'. Indeed, in many firms it has been found that the management of the union overlaps with junior management of the firm itself. That is hardly a recipe for confrontational labour–management relations.

There is, on the other hand, a problem of fragmentation in so far as bargaining is conducted separately in each of a myriad of companies. To combat this, and to introduce strength born of union solidarity across firms, the annual 'spring struggle' (*shuntō*) was instituted in 1955, initially by the leaders of the *Sōhyō* federation. Wage settlements negotiated through the spring struggle have been used as benchmarks for negotiations between enterprise unions and their employers.

Between the mid-1950s and the late 1980s, the Japanese union movement at national level was divided between two principal federations with contrasting ideologies and interests. The larger of the two federations, *Sōhyō* (General Council of Japanese Trade Unions), was the more left wing and confrontational of the two, and took some two-thirds of its members from affiliated unions in the public sector. These two factors were connected, because public-sector workers suffered from restrictions to their rights to bargain, organise and strike that did not apply to workers in private industry. Their grievances tended to be expressed in terms of radical ideology. The smaller federation, *Dōmei* (JAPAN CONFEDERATION OF LABOUR), consisted almost entirely of affiliated unions in the private sector, and its approach inherited the tradition of co-operative relations between labour and management. Partly because of privatisations in the 1980s, the two federations were dissolved at the end of the 1980s and gave way to a new federation, *Rengō* (JAPANESE TRADE UNION COUNCIL), to which the great bulk of unions affiliated themselves. There was a party political dimension to these developments, because while *Sōhyō* had consistently supported the JAPAN SOCIALIST PARTY (*Nihon Shakaitō*), *Dōmei* had backed the DEMOCRATIC SOCIALIST PARTY (*Minshatō*). Yamagishi Akira, the midwife of *Rengō*, saw its formation as a means of uniting those two parties and strengthening the political left. It seemed possible that this might be achievable at the time of the HOSOKAWA Cabinet in 1993–4, but events conspired to frustrate it.

The profound changes in the economy that occurred between the late 1940s and the early 2000s were accompanied by a gradual decline in the rate of workforce unionisation from around 50 per cent to below 25 per cent. This paralleled trends in other comparable economies, where the decline of secondary industry relative to tertiary industry (where unionisation was more difficult) has led to a fall in numbers of workers belonging to unions. There is a further factor in the Japanese case, namely that unionisation rates are far higher among workers on lifetime (or long-term) contracts of employment than among those on short-term contracts or in casual employment.

Some analysts have seen the practice of bargaining at enterprise level, and the practice of union federations supporting political parties out of power, as gravely weakening the impact of labour unions in Japan. Others have regarded the fact that unionised workers are largely permanently employed and employed by large firms as evidence for the limited impact of unions. Steven, for instance, writing from a Marxist standpoint in the 1970s, argued that the divide between workers on lifetime contracts, who might be regarded as the shock troops of corporate Japan, and those more casually employed (including workers in much of the small- and medium-firm sector and the bulk of women workers) constituted a class division of central importance.

Kume, by contrast, maintains that this last argument is difficult to sustain since wage differentials across these sectors have converged, rather than diverged, in recent years. He also argues that the incorporation of unions into regular negotiations with management through the enterprise union system has given organised labour an influence within companies that they generally lack in systems where the predominant mode of union action is confrontational. It may in addition be noted that, at least since the formation of *Rengō*, the labour movement has been given greater access to Government councils than was the case up to the 1980s. Kume's account may possibly go too far in arguing that, by contrast with Sweden, 'Japanese labour politics tends to be more resilient...because it is more deeply rooted in micro-level labour accommodation than in centralised political bargaining' (p. 232). But his argument provides a useful counterweight to the assumption of numerous writers that the Japanese labour union movement has fundamentally weak industrial and political significance.

Note: The term 'labour union' has here been

preferred to 'trade union', since most Japanese unions are based on enterprises, not trades.

Further reading
Gordon, in Gordon (ed.) (1993)
Koike (1991)
Kume (1998)
Levine (1958)
Steven (1983)

Liberal Democratic Party (LDP, Jiyūminshutō, Jimintō) Founded in November 1955, the LDP has been in government for all the years to 2002, except for the period August 1993 to June 1994. Until its temporary fall from office in 1993, the party was in power on its own, with the minor exception of 1983-6, when it was in coalition with the tiny NEW LIBERAL CLUB – itself an LDP-splinter. Between 1994 and 2002, it was the largest partner in a shifting series of coalition governments. Between its foundation and 1993, it had gained a majority over all other parties in every general election for the HOUSE OF REPRESENTATIVES, although in the elections of 1976, 1979 and 1983 its majority was only secured with the subsequent entry into the LDP of a small number of Independents. It lost the elections of July 1993, and did not recover a Lower House majority until September 1997. It fell a few seats below a majority in the elections of June 2000.

Similarly the LDP won every general election to the HOUSE OF COUNCILLORS up to and including that of July 1986, but was unexpectedly beaten by the Socialists in the elections of July 1989. Since then, the LDP has never recovered its Upper House majority, although it improved its position in the elections of July 2001. Given the potential of the House of Councillors for blocking legislation coming to it from the House of Representatives, the lack of an Upper House majority now makes it inevitable that the LDP should govern in coalition with other parties.

Even though since the early 1990s LDP power has been weakened, it has been, virtually throughout its history, in a different category from any other political party. In Fukui's terminology it is the 'party in power', or in Pempel's usage Japan is an 'uncommon democracy' in the sense of having a 'one-party dominant regime'. As in other such 'uncommon democracies', for instance Italy up to the 1990s, or Sweden, the effect of having a single dominant party is to enmesh it into the bureaucratic structures of the State. With little or no expectation of a change of party in power in the foreseeable future, policies can be devised, and careers mapped out, in the expectation of long-term stability of structures. One aspect of this that is particularly marked in the case of Japan is the symbiotic relationship that developed from the 1950s between conservative politicians, Government officials and representatives of major interest groups.

A study of the LDP in the late 1960s (by Fukui) found that around a quarter of LDP members of the House of Representatives (and an even higher proportion of members of the House of Councillors) had had previous careers as Government officials [*see also* BUREAUCRACY]. Moreover, at that time the proportion of Cabinet ministers (all being LDP members) with bureaucratic background approached 50 per cent. PRIME MINISTERS falling into this category include YOSHIDA (1946–7 and 1948–54), who preceded the LDP, but in many ways set the trend, KISHI (1957–60), IKEDA (1960–4), SATŌ (1964–72), FUKUDA (1976–8), OHIRA (1978–80), NAKASONE (1982–7) and MIYAZAWA (1991–3). It seems worth noting that ex-bureaucrat prime ministers dominated the high economic growth period from the late 1950s to the early 1970s, whereas they have been absent during the recent years of economic slowdown and crisis.

If the influence of LDP parliamentarians with experience as Government officials has been declining, that of the 'professional politician' – often with a background in local politics – has been increasing. The occupation background of such people is diverse, but today a substantial block of LDP parliamentarians have spent most of their careers as professional politicians. One reason for this is the salience of the 'inherited seat'. Elections in Japan have been locally focused and personalised, while the *kōenkai* (personal support machine at constituency level) has become ubiquitous. Today the easiest way to ensure election is to 'inherit' a *kōenkai* from a relative or patron, because its inheritor is guaranteed a base of personal support in the constituency. Of LDP parliamentarians elected in the 1996 Lower House general elections, some 37 per cent were the sons, sons-in-law, nephews, etc. of former parliamentarians, while a substantial number of candidates had been secretaries of former members, and had, in a sense, 'inherited' their personal machines.

This phenomenon is an important aspect of the professionalisation of ruling-party politics in Japan. Another aspect is the long-established system of linkages between LDP parliamentarians and powerful interest groups. Perhaps the most striking set of linkages is with agricultural interest groups, as shown in detail by Aurelia George Mulgan. These linkages have arguably distorted national economic priorities in favour of inefficient agricultural production. But this is symbolic of a far wider phenomenon, whereby the LDP is at the centre of a vast web of special interests, tending to distort economic rationality. Since the 1980s, a particular mechanism for the perpetuation of special influences has been termed that of 'tribal parliamentarians' (*zoku giin*) (see TRIBES' OF PARLIAMENTARIANS). These are groups of LDP members of Parliament who specialise in a particular policy area (transport, education, defence, or particular industries, etc.), and, co-operating with relevant Government officials and interest group representatives, in effect 'sew up' policy in these areas of concern. The 'tribe' phenomenon has been compared with 'iron triangles' in the United States.

Better known, perhaps, than 'tribes' are factions (*habatsu*) (see FACTIONS WITHIN POLITICAL PARTIES). Factions (in the Japanese sense) exist in many types of organisation in Japan, including political parties in general. But in the LDP they have taken on a very particular form. It seems likely that they are different because of the sheer magnitude of power and patronage disposed of by the LDP. Except for the occasional ideologically committed faction on the right or left fringes of the party, LDP factions are political machines whose principal members are parliamentarians, devoted to the furtherance of the interests of those parliamentarians. Principal among the interests they serve are to maximise the number and quality of Cabinet and party posts available to faction members, and to channel funding, for electoral and other purposes, to members of the faction.

Factional pressure on the Prime Minister to favour each faction with the maximum number of posts led to frequent Cabinet reshuffles, so that the average tenure of office by a Cabinet minister was a year or less. This in turn led to the introduction of a *de facto* seniority system, whereby a parliamentarian could expect to receive his or her first full Cabinet post after five terms in Parliament. Essentially this was a mechanism to dampen down disruptive factional rivalry and provide a predictable path of career advancement. But only a minority of LDP parliamentarians progressed beyond their first Cabinet post. As in the Government bureaucracy or sections of industry, seniority progression worked up to a certain level and then was replaced by merit (or pull). The advent of coalition governments in the 1990s disrupted the simplicity of this seniority promotion system, because coalition partners had to be taken into consideration also in the distribution of posts. But there is a certain sense in which coalition partners came to be treated as 'external factions' of the LDP.

Patterns of fund distribution also changed after the 1980s. Whereas in the heyday of single-party dominance funds where typically raised from companies by faction bosses and distributed to their members, tightened anti-corruption laws in the 1990s made this more difficult. Thus individual faction members became more individually responsible for raising their own funding. An attempt was made to combat corruption by providing public funding for political PARTIES, but the amount spent on elections has continued to rise.

Another aspect of LDP factionalism is organised competition for the party presidency, which in normal circumstances has carried with it the post of Prime Minister. During some periods the dominance of one faction has ensured that its wishes will be followed in the choice of party president. This was so in the second half of the 1960s with the dominance of the Satō faction, and again in the 1980s with the dominance of the TANAKA (later TAKESHITA) faction. But the periods 1955–64, 1972–80 and post-1989 have provided more disruptive scenarios, with rival groups of factions pitted against each other. One of the most difficult periods was 1979–80, when a 40-day crisis ensued from the fact that the LDP could not decide between Ohira and Fukuda as leader, and, later, when the Ohira Government fell as the result of three factions abstaining in a no-confidence motion. Even more disruptive was the split in the Takeshita faction in 1992–3, leading to a serious split in the party and its temporary fall from power.

From time to time attempts have been made to abolish LDP factions, but, though they may be suppressed, they soon reappear. With the abolition of the multi-member constituency electoral system for the House of Representatives in 1994, it was expected that factions would atrophy, since different LDP candidates for the same (multi-member) constituency had been rivals and typically members of competing factions. But after a lull in factional activity, they were fully back in business by the end of the decade. Some have considered factions to be 'parties within a party', and in certain respects this may be a reasonable view. But they are not primarily policy-oriented bodies (though there may be differences of shading), and they never run electoral candidates under factional labels.

Various attempts were made over the years to mitigate conflict associated with party presidential elections. Until the 1970s the normal method of choosing a party president was by a vote of all LDP parliamentarians from both houses, plus one representative from each of the prefectures. Sometimes (as following the resignation of Tanaka in November 1974), the succession was determined by behind-the-scenes negotiations by party elders. But in the mid-1970s a system of primary elections was introduced, whereby party members and 'friends' at local level were given a vote in an opinion-testing exercise, before a run-off vote of LDP parliamentarians. This was supposed to eliminate the evils of factionalism and vote-buying, but in 1978, when the system was first employed, competitive recruitment of 'members' by the relevant factions led to a tripling of party 'membership' and the defeat of the incumbent Prime Minister, Fukuda, by his rival, Ohira, who enjoyed the efficacious backing of the Tanaka faction. Later, the conditions that could trigger a primary election were made stricter, namely that there should be at least four candidates, and that each should be endorsed by at least 50 LDP parliamentarians. In 1982 a fourth candidate, NAKAGAWA ICHIRŌ, actually had to be 'lent' sponsors by the Fukuda faction, since his own faction contained only a handful of members. The election was held, but Nakasone won easily. A slightly different primary election system was used in April 2001, in which each prefectural branch tested local party opinion. As a result, KOIZUMI JUNICHIRŌ was elected by a comfortable margin, whereas the parliamentary party support would probably have gone to HASHIMOTO RYŪTARŌ, who had heavy factional backing.

Given factional rivalries, the LDP has experienced frequent changes of leadership. Nevertheless, the party organisation, though formally democratic and based on an annual congress, has been top-down in character. The party president (*sōsai*), secretary-general (*kanjichō*), chairman of the executive council (*sōmukaichō*), and chairman of the policy affairs research council (*seisaku chōsakaichō*) constitute the party's core executive, and work closely with key ministers, particularly the chief Cabinet secretary (*kanbōchōkan*). The policy affairs research council consists of many functional sub-committees, and these in turn liaise with relevant parliamentary committees, Government ministries and interest groups. Since the advent of coalition Government, cross-party committees have been instituted between the coalition partners, for basic decision-making.

There is no doubt that the LDP is by far the most successful political party in modern Japanese history. With a brief gap in the early 1990s it has dominated the power structure since its foundation. An important reason for this is that in policy and patronage terms it has exercised remarkable flexibility. It is formed on the model of a 'catch-all' party, and, as in the 1970s when its popularity was declining, it has been able to change policy and shift its appeal to take in sections of the population that had previously supported other parties. On the sensitive issue of constitutional revision, the LDP keeps revision as an aim in its platform, but for the most part refrains from taking serious action about it. There is also a negative reason for its success, in that its principal rivals have never managed to constitute a sufficiently cohesive or attractive political force to challenge it effectively. The JAPAN SOCIALIST PARTY (JSP) was its main rival for many years, but that party lost its way in the 1960s, and, except for a brief flowering at the end of the 1980s and beginning of the 1990s, it was an effective veto force but not an alternative party of Government. The NEW FRONTIER PARTY between 1994 and 1997 came closest to dislodging the LDP, but it fell apart through its manifest and manifold internal contradictions. The DEMOCRATIC PARTY from 1996 has established itself as the principal contemporary party of opposition, but so far is hardly a serious threat.

Nevertheless, even though the LDP has succeeded in hanging on to power, it has been far less successful in handling policy dilemmas since the early 1990s. The key reason is that it remains primarily a party of patronage. It is significant that while it was out of power in 1993–4, it was rapidly losing parliamentary members. Had it not negotiated a return to power by an unlikely but opportunistic alliance with the JSP, it is probable that it would have faded away much like the Christian Democrats in Italy, because it would have suffocated without the oxygen of access to power. The difficulty is, however, that once back in power the very logic of its electoral success makes it hard for it to modernise Japan's power structures, even though they are in desperate need of restructuring. The latest experiment with 'image' politics under Koizumi tends to confirm the view that the LDP now constitutes an obstacle to structural reform rather than a channel for it.

Further reading

Curtis (1988)
—— (1999)
Fukui (1970)
—— (ed.) (1985)
George Mulgan (2000)
Hrebenar (2000)
Pempel (1982)
—— (1990)
—— (1998)

Stockwin (1999)
Thayer (1969)

Liberal League (Jiyū rengō) The Liberal League was formed in December 1994 by Kakizawa Kōji, who had been Foreign Minister in the short-lived Hata Cabinet, and Ouchi Keigo, who had been Chairman of the defunct DEMOCRATIC SOCIALIST PARTY. Neither of them wished to join the NEW FRONTIER PARTY, formed earlier the same month. Ouchi was Chairman of the Liberal League, which consisted of eight members. In December 1995 a new party with exactly the same name was formed, consisting of six of the original eight members. Kakizawa fought the 1996 general elections successfully as a Liberal Democrat, with an appeal for radical reform of the LIBERAL DEMOCRATIC PARTY (LDP). In the June 2000 Lower House elections a Liberal League candidate won Kagoshima No. 2 (single member) district, presumably on a personal vote.

Liberal Party (I) (Jiyūtō) *see* conservative parties, 1945–55

Liberal Party (Jiyūtō) (II) In April 1994 five younger members of the LIBERAL DEMOCRATIC PARTY (LDP), led by Ota Seiichi, defected to form the Liberal Party. They persuaded Kakizawa Kōji, Foreign Minister in the HATA minority Government, to head it. A week later it was one of the parties participating in Ozawa's abortive scheme to form a new party to be called *kaishin*. Some of the members, by way of a group called the Liberal Reform League (*Jiyū kaikaku rengō*) joined the NEW FRONTIER PARTY (*Shinshintō*) in December. Ota, however, later returned to the LDP, and Kakizawa joined up with Ouchi Keigo, formerly Chairman of the DEMOCRATIC SOCIALIST PARTY (*Minshatō*) to form the minuscule LIBERAL LEAGUE (*Jiyū Rengō*), also in December.

Liberal Party (Jiyūtō) (III) The Liberal Party was founded by OZAWA ICHIRŌ in January 1998, following the collapse of the NEW FRONTIER PARTY (*Shinshintō*) into six separate fragments, of which the Liberal Party was one. At the time of its formation, 43 members of the House of Representatives and 11 members of the House of Councillors belonged to it. The

Upper House contingent increased to 12 in the subsequent July elections.

The party platform reflected a clear ideological vision, defining 'creative liberalism' as a situation in which 'autonomous individuals are able to pursue their own ways of life creatively and in freedom, having a variety of choices and under fair rules'. The platform went on to call for an international outlook, going beyond the confines of Japan. It attacked 'easy dependence on the State and on Society', emphasising the bonds of family and a patriotic people setting its own goals. It called for administrative decentralisation and thriving local politics, small government, and a free, fair and transparent society, where the rights of consumers should prevail. It defended equality of opportunity, 'irrespective of sex, age, handicap or means' over equality of outcomes. It emphasised the need for an efficient crisis-reaction regime (including national defence under this heading), effective social security to create a 'secure and safe society', and environmental protection for a 'society at one with nature'. It favoured the interests of the people as a whole, and attacked the politics of special interests. Its final paragraph read: 'We reject pacifism in one country, prosperity for one country, and one country self-righteousness. Believing in the principle of living together in international society, we shall participate actively in efforts for global peace and prosperity.'

The platform embodied Ozawa's ideas of individual autonomy, market economy, small government, transparent administration, stable society and international responsibility. In a real sense, the Liberal Party was the instrument for his ideas.

The Liberal Party suffered a blow in October 1998, when five of its parliamentarians defected to the re-formed CLEAN GOVERNMENT PARTY (CGP, *Kōmeitō*), which had been their original home. But in November three Independents joined the party. From November also, Ozawa entered discussions with OBUCHI KEIZŌ, the LIBERAL DEMOCRATIC PARTY (LDP) President and Prime Minister, over plans to enter a coalition Government. This came to fruition in January 1999, after Obuchi had accepted Ozawa's demands that politico-administrative reform, national security and taxation should be areas for active policy intervention.

During the period of coalition Government, the Liberal Party pressed for a reduction of seats from 200 to 150 in the proportional representation blocs of the HOUSE OF COUNCILLORS. But, after the CGP joined the coalition in October, that party vigorously opposed this proposal. A compromise was eventually reached, cutting back the seats from 200 to 180. But the Liberal Party was pressing for closer alignment with the LDP on policy and for local electoral pacts, while at the same time criticising Government policy on nursing insurance. Resentment in the LDP and CGP against the Liberal Party quickly built up, and in April the Liberal Party had to leave the coalition. This, however, was not to the liking of all in the Liberal Party, and 26 of its Lower House members broke away, forming the CONSERVATIVE PARTY, which remained with the coalition. Following this break, the Liberal Party became more critical of the Government, and, although weakened by the split, increased its representation by four seats to 22 seats in the House of Representatives elections in June.

The party also did well in the elections to the House of Councillors of July 2001, and developed closer co-operation with other parties of opposition. It presented its own bills to Parliament on deregulation, electoral system reform (*see* ELECTION SYSTEMS) and other issues. After the terrorist attacks in the United States in September, the party put forward its own 'International peace co-operation bill'.

Liberal Party, Hatoyama faction (Jiyūtō Hatoyama ha) *see* conservative parties, 1945–55

Liberal Reform League (Jiyū kaikaku rengō) *see* Liberal Party (II)

local government and politics The thrust of Government policy towards the localities was profoundly centralising from the Meiji period until 1945. Top priority was given to the tasks of modernisation, so that institutions permitting local initiative, or the reflection of local opinion in administrative decisions, were weak or absent. Power was concentrated in the Home Ministry, which essentially administered regional and local affairs from Tokyo. The ministry's most important instrument was the prefectural governor, who was appointed, not elected. Prefectural governors were powerful individuals in their own right, but they answered to the central government, not to the prefectures that it was their duty to govern.

By the reforms of the Allied Occupation, democratic principles were introduced into local government, along with the principle of decentralising power. The Home Ministry was broken up and its powers dispersed among various agencies, of which the most relevant for local administration was the Local Autonomy Agency (*Jichichō*). Prefectural governors were retained as chief executives, but their positions were made elective, as were those of mayors of cities, towns and villages. Local assemblies were created in every prefecture, city, town and village, and indeed the number and scope of elections that were created at local level even led the US scholar, Herbert Passin, in the 1960s, to speak of an 'overloading of the political communication circuits'.

The reality, however, as it emerged in the years following the ending of the Occupation, was rather different from the democratising and decentralising ideal of the occupying authorities. Local control of police forces, introduced in the late 1940s, was soon turned back to central control in the 1950s, and locally elected boards of education did not long survive the return of national independence in 1952. The tax base of local authorities was also insufficient to sustain decentralised administration, since they were dependent for the bulk of their revenue on the centre. Moreover, the introduction (more accurately, reintroduction) of agency-delegated functions meant that elected local officials had the obligation to undertake certain functions delegated to them by central agencies of Government. Some 70 to 80 per cent of administrative tasks performed by local authorities in the 1970s were of this nature. By the 1960s, also, the former Home Ministry had been partially reconstituted, though it never attained the degree of power it had enjoyed in the pre-war period. In 1960 the Local Autonomy Agency (*Jichichō*) was elevated in status to the Ministry of Local Autonomy (*Jichishō*), which some time later took to calling itself 'MINISTRY OF HOME AFFAIRS' in English. Many – though by no means all – of the prefectural governors were former ministry officials, thus repeating at local level the national phenomenon of ex-bureaucrats going into politics.

The period from the late 1960s to the end of the 1970s is particularly interesting in local politics. At local, as at national, level, the extremely high economic growth rates of the 15 years between 1958 and 1973 led to widespread demands for better services, more generous welfare provision and improved environmental protection. This was reflected both in a declining percentage of the vote for LIBERAL DEMOCRATIC PARTY (LDP) candidates in national elections, and also in the defeat of many conservative and LDP-backed candidates for prefectural governor and city mayor at local level. According to Muramatsu, whereas in 1964 there were only 10 members of the League of Progressive Mayors, by 1974 there were about 140 out of a possible total of 600. Even though this sounds like a smallish minority, in population terms it was impressive, since progressive local executives were mostly to be found in urban and metropolitan prefectures and cities with huge concentrations of people. In the mid-1970s the prefectures of Tokyo, Osaka, Kyōto and Saitama, and the metropolitan cities of Osaka, Kyōto, Yokohama, Nagoya, Kawasaki and Kōbe, all had progressive local executives (governors or mayors). Across the board, around 40 per cent of the total population of Japan lived in local authority areas headed by progressive executives at that time. 'Progressive' here means largely supported by left-wing parties, principally the JAPAN SOCIALIST PARTY and JAPAN COMMUNIST PARTY.

This did not necessarily mean that progressive local executives had it all their own way, since in many cases they faced a local assembly that had a conservative majority. But, in September 2002, Tanaka Yasuo, anti-establishment governor of Nagano Prefecture, who had been deposed by a vote of no-confidence passed in the prefectural assembly, was re-elected governor by a two-to-one majority over his nearest rival.

The phenomenon of agency-delegated functions meant that local executives were subject to various kinds of pressure from ministries of the central government in Tokyo. On the other hand, the kinds of environmental, welfare and quality of life issues that had brought progressive executives to power in the first place also greatly exercised the minds of both the central ministries and the LDP. The latter, indeed, mindful of its declining popularity, was anxious to satisfy the new kinds of demand that had emerged as a result of the economic 'miracle', and so gain new supporters in order to avoid electoral defeat.

To a considerable extent, the LDP was successful in this endeavour. Its electoral fortunes nationally revived in the 1980s, but even more spectacularly, at local level, nearly all the progressive local executives had been defeated by the start of the 1980s. In their place, in many areas of Japan, local executives were elected with the support of a combination of political parties of both right and left, as well as of a variety of interest groups. Various explanations may be advanced for this remarkable phenomenon of the 1980s, but perhaps the most persuasive is the revival of the old idea that it made most sense to vote for a candidate that had a 'direct channel to the centre'. Some of the progressive local authorities had become well known for less than optimally efficient administration, though a number of them had pioneered structures of local consultation and people-centred government that came to be copied in local authorities whose general political colouring was conservative. An ability to 'steal the clothes of the opposition' was combined with a widespread assumption that power flowed from the centre, so that the worst thing was to be ostracised by the central authorities. Progressive parties in the early 1980s had not yet put themselves into a position where they could project themselves as alternative sources of central power.

During the NAKASONE administration of the mid-1980s, the idea that centralised and uniform government throughout the country was not necessarily a good thing in a modern state had entered the thinking of politicians and Governmental officials alike. This was reflected in the recommendations of the Second Extraordinary Administrative Reform Commission (*Rinchō*). In 1993 decentralisation became one of the principal slogans of the non-LDP HOSOKAWA Government – though little was done about it in the short space of time accorded to that Government.

Japanese specialists in the local politics and Government of Japan have, broadly speaking, divided into those who favour a continuity emphasis, and those who prefer a discontinuity emphasis. The former, who were struck with the ways in which practices prevalent in the pre-war period were brought back into the system in the 1950s and 1960s, include the post-war scholar, Tsuji Kiyoaki, and his school. Those who believe that the discontinuities should be treated more seriously include in particular Muramatsu Michio, who tends to emphasise that the introduction of elections and party politics into local government and politics means that local opinion has to be taken more seriously, thus politicising the local decision-making process. Even though central government bureaucrats have traditionally sought to keep politics out of local government as much as possible, they now have to anticipate trends in public opinion in order to stay in control. Tsuji, writing much closer in time to the *ancien régime* than Muramatsu, was seriously worried about the possibility that conservative central governments would be able to re-establish authoritarian control of local authorities. By contrast Muramatsu, while agreeing that a high degree of central control has been maintained, is inclined to believe that such centralisation is consistent with the needs of a modern state. He sees the influence of public opinion (expressed through elections and in other ways), the development of citizens' and residents' movements, and the consolidation of the capacities of local authorities as important checks on central administrative control.

Further reading
Jain (1989)
Muramatsu (1988, 1997)
Muramatsu *et al.* (2001)
Passin (1968)
Samuels (1983)
Tsuji (1984)

Lockheed scandal (1970s) Testimony to a US congressional committee in February 1976 revealed that the Lockheed Aircraft Corporation had given huge sums of money to various individuals in Japan in an effort to secure adoption by All Nippon Airways (ANA) of its Tristar passenger jets. A Lockheed Vice-President, Carl Kotchian, testified that he (or the company) had paid a little over one billion yen to a notorious right-wing political fixer named Kodama Yoshio, some of which had been passed on to Osano Kenji, Chairman of a company called International Industrial Enterprises (*Kokusai kōgyōsha*). Money was also channelled via the Marubeni Corporation, with which Lockheed had close links in Tokyo, and whose Chairman, Hiyama Hiroshi, was also advising Lockheed about establishing the most effective political links.

The events referred to had allegedly taken place during the time in the early 1970s when TANAKA KAKUEI WAS PRIME MINISTER. Tanaka had left office in November 1974 following revelations in the press about the nature of his financial dealings. Nothing, however, was publicly known about his involvement with Lockheed until the congressional hearings of February 1976. Statements in the world press over subsequent years that Tanaka left office because of the Lockheed scandal are wholly incorrect. This is indeed an excellent example of misinformation turned into 'truth' by repetition.

The Lockheed scandal dominated Japanese politics for the rest of 1976 and for some time thereafter. The Prime Minister at the time was MIKI TAKEO, who had been chosen to replace Tanaka for the purpose of creating an image of probity for the ruling party. Miki had a weak power base within the LIBERAL DEMOCRATIC PARTY (LDP), but he combined a concern for principle with considerable political cunning and stubbornness. Two decades earlier, in 1954, YOSHIDA SHIGERU had protected his acolyte, SATŌ EISAKU, from arrest in connection with the shipbuilding scandal. On this occasion, however, Miki took no action to prevent Tanaka's arrest in July 1976 on suspicion of having received a bribe of ¥500,000,000.

Four separate trials were generated by the Lockheed affair. Various businessmen who had acted as go-betweens with Lockheed were convicted and punished, as well as several others who had been involved in the corrupt transactions. Two reasonably prominent politicians, Hashimoto Tomosaburō and Satō Kōkō (Takayuki) were treated similarly. Tanaka's trial, like the others, dragged on for several years, but in October 1983 he was found guilty of bribery, given a four-year suspended prison sentence and a large fine. He appealed, but died (in 1993) before the appeal procedures were exhausted.

After Miki's refusal to block Tanaka's arrest (as he had the power to do), mainstream leaders of the LDP determined to get rid of him. They achieved this following poor results for the party in the Lower House general elections of December 1976, forcing him to take responsibility for the election results by resigning. He had, however, succeeded in revising laws on electoral campaigning and political contributions, with a view to stamping out corrupt practices [*see also* ELECTORAL BEHAVIOUR, CAMPAIGNING AND THE CONTROL OF MALPRACTICE]. The Lockheed scandal had created a public mood in favour of electoral reform, and without it there was little likelihood that the laws would have been revised. Whether the revisions had the effects desired is a more difficult question. Curtis (p. 164) argues that they may actually have made things worse, by driving a wedge between legal forms and actual practice.

As a result of the Lockheed affair, Tanaka relinquished his membership of the LDP, standing in subsequent elections as an Independent. This made no difference to his popularity in his Niigata constituency, where he continued to be returned with big majorities. Moreover, he not only continued to lead his own LDP faction (despite being out of the party), but also ensured that it attracted increasing numbers of LDP parliamentarians as members. By the 1980s it had become much the biggest faction in that party, able to determine on several occasions who the next party President (and thus Prime Minister) should be. Critics alleged that Tanaka had expanded his own faction for protection against the courts, but for its members the Tanaka faction was forged into an extraordinarily effective instrument for the pursuit of political power, and of political aims in general.

The Lockheed scandal profoundly marked the politics of the late 1970s and early 1980s. Tanaka could and did argue that his political *modus operandi* was consistent with Japanese traditions of political action, though the sheer size of the money transfers involved made such assertions problematic. The affair pitted reformers against traditionalists within the ruling party, but, though it led to some legal reform, 'money politics' proved too deeply embedded to be eliminated. It was left to a later rash of money scandals, in the late 1980s and the 1990s, before limited success could be achieved in tackling the structural problems underlying political corruption.

Further reading

Curtis (1988)
Mitchell (1996)

Maekawa Report During the NAKASONE Government period of the mid-1980s Japan ran a substantial balance of payments surplus with the outside world. What had come to be regarded overseas as the 'unbalanced' character of Japanese trade ushered in a period of trade disputes between Japan and the United States (*see* UNITED STATES, RELATIONS WITH).

Amidst growing disquiet about the health of the Japan–US economic relationship, Nakasone set up the Advisory Group on Economic Structural Adjustment for International Harmony (*Kokusai kyōchō no tame no keizai kōzō chōsei kenkyūkai*). It began its work in October 1985 under the chairmanship of Maekawa Haruo, a former Governor of the Bank of Japan, and issued its report (known as the Maekawa Report) in April 1986.

The Report described as a 'crisis situation' the fact that over a considerable period Japan had been running a balance of payments surplus averaging 3.6 per cent of GNP. To remedy this, it recommended a shift to domestic demand and away from exports as the principal engine of economic growth. This could be achieved, first, by accelerating house building and moving as quickly as possible to a five-day working week, so as to increase domestic demand. Second, a contribution could also be made by phasing down coal mining and rationalising agriculture to make it more efficient. The Report recommended increasing imports of agricultural products, apart from staple foods, and also of manufactured goods. Another recommendation was for fundamental reform of the taxation system, including abolition of the *maruyū* system of untaxed savings much favoured by small businesses as a means of reducing their tax bills.

The Report also recommended increased foreign investment (both into and out of Japan), promotion of exchange rate stability at rates reflecting real values, liberalisation of financial and capital markets, and more favourable treatment of developing countries, particularly in respect of access for their exports to the Japanese market.

An immediate result of the Maekawa Report was that Government set up mechanisms having the aim of gradually reducing the balance of payments surplus. A propaganda campaign was launched urging people to buy imported goods, and Japanese companies were encouraged to invest overseas. This latter aim was facilitated by the strengthening of the yen following the Plaza Accords of September 1985, but a rapid rise in Japanese overseas investment created its own problems, with US resentment over Japanese purchases of some high-profile US companies.

Generally speaking, the recommendations of the Maekawa Report remained unfulfilled. The agricultural lobby was too powerful to permit the kinds of rationalisation of agriculture recommended, except to some extent in the very long term. Attempts to encourage increased imports of manufactured goods fell foul of myriad hidden obstacles put in place by manufacturing interests, often with the connivance of Government ministries and politicians. The same could be said of the aspiration to encourage increased foreign investment into Japan.

The best that could be said for the impact of the Maekawa Report was that it set an agenda for change that future governments could begin to think about in the drastically altered economic circumstances of the 1990s. It also provided a graphic illustration of the difficulty of bringing about fundamental reform given the strength of policy networks having a vested interest in the status quo.

Management and Co-ordination Agency (Sōmuchō) The Management and Co-ordination Agency was established in 1984 as an external agency of the Prime Minister's Office (*Sōrifu*), with a Minister of State as its Director. This resulted from a recommendation of the Second *Ad Hoc* Administrative Reform Commission that there needed to be stronger and more comprehensive control over the national public service. It replaced the ADMINISTRATIVE MANAGEMENT AGENCY (*Gyōsei kanrichō*), in existence since 1948.

The Agency consisted of the Director's Secretariat, Personnel Bureau (*Jinjikyoku*), Administrative Control Bureau (*Gyōsei kanrikyoku*), Administrative Inspection Bureau (*Gyōsei kansatsukyoku*), Pensions Bureau (*Onkyūkyoku*) and the Statistics Bureau (*Tōkeikyoku*). Other miscellaneous functions were transferred from the Prime Minister's Office itself. These included a Youth Policy Headquarters and a Northern Territories Policy Headquarters, while the Director's Secretariat acquired functions relating to the elderly, and 'regional improvement' (meaning *dōwa* policy, in other words policy towards the *burakumin* minority) [*see also* MINORITIES AND POLITICS].

In the amalgamation of ministries and agencies that took place in January 2001, the Management and Co-ordination Agency joined with the Ministry of Posts and Telecommunications (*Yūseishō*) and the Ministry of Home Affairs (*Jichishō*) to form the Ministry of Public Management, Home Affairs, Posts and Telecommunications, given more succinctly in Japanese as *Sōmushō*.

mass media and politics Japan is conspicuously an information society, so that the consumer of information may feel overwhelmed by what is on offer, rather than having a sense of being deprived. It may seem surprising, therefore, that some have argued that Japanese do not learn all that they should learn through the mass media.

In recent years the popularisation, and 'dumbing down', of the media has occurred in Japan, just as it has in many other countries. Many television programmes in Japan are as puerile and low quality as their counterparts are in the United States, Europe or Australasia. Nevertheless, taking the media as a whole, there is a sustained effort made to report and inform accurately and in depth about what is happening in politics, as well as in other spheres of life.

Japan has a number of quality newspapers, all with a long history. Principal among them are the *Asahi Shinbun*, *Yomiuri Shinbun*, *Mainichi Shinbun*, *Nihon Keizai Shinbun* (*Nikkei Shinbun*) and *Sankei Shinbun*. The *Yomiuri*, which has the highest circulation, sells around 12 million copies daily. The others have lower, but still very large, circulations. The main dailies, *Asahi*, *Yomiuri* and *Mainichi*, publish evening editions over much of the country, as well as morning editions, and distribute to huge subscription lists through tied outlets. The largest of them can afford sufficient journalistic staff to provide virtually saturation coverage of political organisations, issues and events. This includes foreign correspondents, who are stationed around the world in impressive numbers. The *Asahi*, *Yomiuri* and *Mainichi* all produce English language dailies, with on-line access. There is also an independent English language daily, the *Japan Times*.

Two aspects, however, of the way newspapers gather news have been subject to criticism. The first is that a newspaper will assign a particular correspondent to a particular politician, faction, party, bureau, etc., over a long period. Given the norms of mutual obligation current in Japanese society, such a correspondent may find it difficult to report adversely about the people he or she is in such close contact with. There is much anecdotal evidence of journalists virtually living in the houses of politicians so as not to miss any scrap of news. But guests inevitably incur obligations to their hosts. To overcome this problem, newspapers often publish joint articles by a number of journalists attached to different politicians or offices, in order to ensure balance.

The second target of criticism is the institution of journalists' clubs. They have been criticised in particular by correspondents of foreign newspapers, who have been excluded from them even when they speak fluent Japanese. To some extent this situation has been mitigated in recent years. A broader criticism is that the clubs create a cliquish atmosphere and a tendency to process the news through a screen that excludes certain types of news that might embarrass politicians or others to whom journalists may be beholden. For instance, in 1974, when the monthly magazine, *Bungei shunjū*, published a long article by an investigative reporter, Tachibana Takeshi, alleging financial misdemeanours by the Prime Minister, Tanaka Kakuei, the daily press ignored it. It was only when the foreign press published it that the local dailies got into the act.

In relation to this second criticism, however, there is a kind of safety valve in the shape of weekly magazines. These are the rough counterpart of the tabloid press in Britain. Some of them are little more than scandal sheets, but, unlike the 'respectable' dailies, they report stories that are little more than salacious rumours. Irresponsible as many of these magazines are, they ensure that disreputable news should not be swept under the carpet.

So far as television is concerned, the Japan Broadcasting Corporation (NHK, *Nippon hōsō kyōkai*) is a national public broadcaster, roughly the counterpart of the BBC in Britain, with a brief to maintain high standards of broadcasting. Though often affected by pressures from commercial broadcasting, NHK manages to purvey national, local and international news effectively, and broadcasts high-quality feature films and the like. It is sometimes subjected to the criticism of reticence in broadcasting news that might embarrass prominent figures, but such embarrassment more rarely inhibits the commercial broadcasting channels. There, the problem is triviality and lack of concern for important political issues, rather than reluctance to embarrass.

As in other political systems, politicians are concerned to manage the media, much as sections of the media seek to find sensational material about politicians. The mass media and the political system operate in a complex process of interaction with each other, and though this does not always produce ideal results, each side interacts with the other in a relatively sophisticated fashion.

The system as a whole has been resistant to bids for foreign ownership of sections of the media.

Further reading
Feldman (1993)
Freeman (2000)
Krauss (2000)

Matsushita Institute of Government and Management (Matsushita seikei juku) The Matsushita School of Government and Management was founded in 1979 by Matsushita Kōnosuke, founder of Matsushita Electric. The name in English was changed in 1990 from 'School' to 'Institute'. It is located in Chigasaki, south of Tokyo.

The purpose of its founder was to:

give talented young persons the opportunity to realise a better future for themselves and for Japan and for the world [and to provide] a place where the leaders of the future can create clear national and international policies and the programmes for their realisation, that will bring lasting benefit to the citizens of Japan and the world.

The Institute became a focus of media attention from 1993, given that several of those elected to the HOUSE OF REPRESENTATIVES from the recently founded JAPAN NEW PARTY led by HOSOKAWA MORIHIRO were its graduates. The numbers of its graduates with seats in the House of Representatives thereafter gradually increased, and numbered more than 20 following the general elections of June 2000. The average age of those elected was 40. The Institute maintained a policy of political neutrality, but almost all parliamentary members who were its graduates around the turn of the millennium belonged either to the LIBERAL DEMOCRATIC PARTY (LDP) or to the DEMOCRATIC PARTY. They were particularly influential in the latter, as became evident in its leadership reshuffle of September 2002.

The founder's philosophy was both influenced by traditional Japanese ethical ideas (such as pursuit of harmony) and open to innovation, independence of spirit, ambition and diligent study. He promoted the concept of *sunao*, defined as 'accepting life in a constructive way...enabling us to see things as they actually are, without any prejudice or preconceived idea'. He expressed strong concern about Japan's lack of vision and lack of international contribution, despite its economic strength. The School (later Institute) succeeded in establishing itself as an important training ground for significant numbers of young politicians.

Further reading
Kotter (1997)

Middle East, relations with By far the greatest Japanese preoccupation in relation to the Middle East has been oil. The 15-year period of rapid economic growth from the late 1950s to the early 1970s was accompanied by a rapidly increasing dependence on oil to fuel Japan's manufacturing industries. This made sense in narrowly defined economic terms, since the world price of oil up to the early 1970s was low. But when the first (OPEC) oil crisis occurred late in 1973, the Japanese economy faced a most severe crisis. In order to avert the threat of suspension of oil deliveries from the Middle East, the Japanese Government despatched top-level delegations to Middle Eastern countries. It also changed its official stance in relation to the Arab–Israeli dispute from one that had followed US policies favouring Israel to one more respectful of Arab positions on the issues concerned.

The fourfold increase in the price of oil that the oil crisis created hit the Japanese economy hard, though it quickly recovered. During the mid-1970s Japanese decision-makers were much exercised by the need to reduce dependence on sources of oil from the Middle East, by measures of stockpiling, conservation and the search for alternative energy sources. By the time of the second oil crisis of 1979–80, Japan was much better placed to withstand the economic consequences, though the Middle East remained Japan's primary source of oil.

As in other parts of the world that were not a primary Japanese concern (apart, in this case, for the oil factor), Japan's policies towards the Middle East remained low-key until the 1990s. The Japanese Government offered its good offices in search of a solution to the Iran–Iraq War of the 1980s, but this initiative did not bear fruit. Political instability in the region inhibited Japanese commercial interest, though investment took place in areas seen as relatively stable.

The Iraqi invasion of Kuwait in August 1990 put Japan on the spot in terms of what response was most appropriate. In the end the Japanese Government provided $13 billion towards the cost of the United States-led military expedition that was to liberate Kuwait and defeat the Iraqi military early in 1991. The KAIFU Government was unable to overcome a deep-seated pacifist tradition that balked at the idea of sending contingents from the Self-Defence Forces. This seemed strange to Americans and others who noted the continuing importance of Middle Eastern oil to the Japanese economy. Opinion within Japan was in any case divided on the merits of mounting a military operation to defeat Saddam Hussein. But the international reaction to what some overseas described as pusillanimous attitudes on the part of Japan in not participating in the cause of liberating Kuwait had a long-term impact on Japanese public opinion. After the terrorist attacks on New York and Washington on 11 September 2001, the KOIZUMI Government found it far easier than had its predecessor a decade earlier to send contingents to support the international military operation in Afghanistan.

The complex and difficult issues arising from international terrorism based in the Middle East saw Japanese opinion torn between the hard-line 'eradication of terrorism' policies emerging from the Bush administration in Washington and a preference for low-key diplomacy in the pursuit of solutions to disputes. But over the years Japanese Government attitudes to terrorist acts, such as aircraft hijackings, had hardened. In any case, the importance Japan attached to her relationship with the United States was sufficiently strong to make the pursuit of a sharply independent line in Middle Eastern policy unlikely. The

Koizumi Government found itself in a similar situation to that of the Blair Government in the United Kingdom. Both had strong motivation to place the alliance with the United States ahead of other considerations in developing policy on Middle Eastern issues. But whether either would succeed in carrying public opinion with them in support of radical US policies towards the region was open to some doubt [see also UNITED STATES, RELATIONS WITH].

Miki Bukichi Miki Bukichi, born in 1884 in Kagawa, had long experience of pre-war politics, first entering the HOUSE OF REPRESENTATIVES in 1917. After the war, though purged from politics between 1946 and 1951, he was active in the Liberal Party and became its Secretary-General in 1953. But in the midst of a struggle for party leadership between the Prime Minister, YOSHIDA SHIGERU and HATOYAMA ICHIRŌ, Miki, along with Hatoyama, ISHIBASHI TANZAN, KŌNO ICHIRŌ and others broke away and formed the SEPARATISTS' LIBERAL PARTY (Buntō ha Jiyūtō), which did well in the April general elections. Most of its members, including Hatoyama, returned to the Liberal Party in November, but Miki and seven others were not admitted back, and formed the JAPAN LIBERAL PARTY (II) (Nihon Jiyūtō), with the aim of replacing Yoshida with Hatoyama as Prime Minister. During 1954 he worked towards the formation of the Japan Democratic Party (Nihon Minshutō), and in 1955 was central to the creation of a single conservative party, the LIBERAL DEMOCRATIC PARTY (LDP), out of the Liberals and the Democrats [see also CONSERVATIVE PARTIES, 1945–55]. He became a member of the four-man interim ruling council of the new party.

Miki died in 1956.

Miki Takeo Miki Takeo was a member of the House of Representatives for 51 years (1937 to his death in 1988), a politician who sought to reform the institutions and practices of politics, and PRIME MINISTER 1974–6.

Born in 1907 in Tokushima (Shikoku), Miki was educated at Meiji University and at a university in California (three separate universities are given by different sources), entering Parliament in 1937 aged 30. He was an 'unendorsed' candidate in the wartime elections of 1942. After the war he formed the National Co-operative Party (Kokumin Kyōdōtō), and took it into the three party coalition Government headed by KATAYAMA TETSU, where he was Minister of Communications. In the early 1950s he occupied senior positions successively in the NATIONAL DEMOCRATIC PARTY (Kokumin Minshutō) and the REFORMIST PARTY (Kaishintō). In 1955 he was Minister of Transport in the second HATOYAMA Government, and then Secretary-General of the LIBERAL DEMOCRATIC PARTY (LDP) in 1956. Subsequently he served as Economic Planning Agency Director, Director of the Science and Technology Agency, Minister of International Trade and Industry, and Foreign Minister (1966–8). He became Deputy Prime Minister in the TANAKA Government from 1972, but resigned in July 1974 (as did FUKUDA TAKEO), unhappy with Tanaka's leadership.

In the 1960s Miki was active against mainstream LDP opinion, in favour of normalising relations with China, and began to advocate ideas of regional organisation for the Pacific Basin. He founded his own faction (initially with Matsumura Kenzō), which was smaller than most others but stood out for its progressive views. He unsuccessfully contested the LDP presidency on three occasions (1968, 1970 and 1972), but, when Tanaka resigned in December 1974, he finally had his chance. Through the mediation of the party elder, Shiina Etsusaburō, and no doubt influenced by the fear that if snubbed Miki might take his followers out of the party, he was appointed party President and thus PRIME MINISTER.

As Prime Minister, Miki set out with a radical agenda of cleaning up the political world, combating political corruption, reforming the LDP and tightening controls on political donations. He initiated moves towards a primary election system of party members for the LDP presidency. He signalled his belief in the need for education system reform by appointing the educational specialist Nagai Michio as his Education Minister. A major new DEFENCE plan was finalised in 1975, embodying the principle that defence spending should be kept within one per cent of GNP. Heading a minor faction, however, his position within the LDP was rather weak, and in some parliamentary divisions he had to rely on opposition party votes against opposition from the LDP right wing. His attempt to revise the Anti-Monopoly Law ended in failure because of fierce resistance from within the LDP, the bureaucracy and industry [see also FAIR TRADE COMMISSION AND ANTI-MONOPOLY POLICIES]. The biggest test of Miki's leadership began in February 1976, when the LOCKHEED SCANDAL broke, implicating Tanaka. Breaking with LDP precedent, Miki refused to block the investigation, and in July Tanaka was briefly and sensationally arrested. By this time, however, so many in the party were determined to get rid of Miki that he was forced to resign in December. The party's poor showing in the general elections held the same month provided a need for him to 'take responsibility' for the defeat.

The Miki faction was one of the three that abstained in the no-confidence motion that brought down the Ohira Cabinet in 1980. But in the same year Miki handed over leadership of his faction to KŌMOTO TOSHIO, and died, aged 81, in 1988. Most observers have seen him as a conviction politician with progressive views, but a few have emphasised his manipulative side. It seems surprising in retrospect that he remained within a party with so many of whose policies he disagreed. But he understood where power lay.

Further reading
Curtis (1988)
Masumi (1995)
Pempel (1977)
Stockwin (1999)

Ministry of Agriculture, Forestry and Fisheries (MAFF, Nōrinsuisanshō) The origins of this ministry go back to the early Meiji period, but the title 'Ministry of Agriculture and Foresty' (*Nōrinshō*) was applied from 1925, although a different name was used during the Second World War. It was re-established under its 1925 name in 1945, and was soon faced with the upheaval of the Occupation-sponsored land reform. Its most urgent task in the postwar period of severe food shortages was to organise a food control system (*Shokuryō kanri seido, Shokkan seido*), whereby the new class of independent small farmers created by the land reform would deliver rice and other foods to the Government at a guaranteed producer price, for passing on to the consumer.

By the 1960s food shortage had been largely eliminated and the food control system began to create a rice surplus, which during the 1970s grew to unsustainable levels. The ministry was therefore impelled to enforce large-scale reductions in rice production, as well as capping the producer rice price. Even so, the price of rice to the consumer rose to as much as seven times the price at which rice could be obtained on the world market, and until 1994 a total ban was in place on imports of rice for direct consumption.

In the 1970s fisheries policy achieved new salience with the new law of the sea enforcing 200 mile national limits on fisheries. As a reaction to this, the Ministry of Agriculture and Forestry took on fisheries as well, becoming the Ministry of Agriculture, Forestry and Fisheries.

The MAFF is famous in Japan and elsewhere as a ministry that is exceptionally energetic and well organised in protecting its clientele, namely farmers. Indeed some have seen the agricultural politics of Japan as the most clientelistic part of the whole politico-economic system. Two of the most effective methods employed have been the following: First, the ministry maintains a symbiotic relationship with the Agricultural Co-operative Association (*Nōgyō kyōdō kumiai, Nōkyō*). For many years, the *Nōkyō* was the key intermediary between the ministry and the farmers in the administration of the Food Control System, as well as being a powerful pressure group in relation to Government. Second, agriculture has been extremely well represented in Parliament, in part because of electoral malapportionment in favour of the agricultural areas. The 'agricultural tribe' (*Nōgyō zoku*) of LIBERAL DEMOCRATIC PARTY (LDP) parliamentarians works closely with the MAFF and the *Nōkyō* to protect the interests of farmers [see also 'TRIBES' OF PARLIAMENTARIANS].

Despite the powerful position occupied by the MAFF in Government as a whole, the capacity of the agricultural lobby to pressure

Government into maintaining high levels of protection has necessarily declined with the continued exodus from farming into other occupations. The price of entering the World Trade Organization at the conclusion of the Uruguay round of trade negotiations in 1994 was that Japan had to import rice for direct consumption for the first time. Following that episode, farmers received large-scale Government compensation packages. But in July 1999 Parliament passed the Basic Law on Food, Agriculture and Rural Areas (*Shokuryō, nōgyō, nōson kihonhō*), whose effect is to increase the role of market principles in agriculture and reduce the scale of Government protection (George Mulgan, 2000, p. 6). It would, however, be premature to argue that the Ministry of Agriculture and its symbiotically linked interest lobbies have lost their influence. Agriculture remains an interest that no government can afford to ignore.

Further reading
George Mulgan (2000)

Ministry of Construction (Kensetsushō) The Ministry of Construction emerged as such in July 1948, after a series of administrative reorganisations following the breaking up of the Ministry of Home Affairs (*Naimushō*). Essentially the new ministry took over the functions of the National Lands Bureau (*Kokudokyoku*) of the latter. Central functions of the Ministry of Construction have included housing and housing development, roads, rivers, parks, sewerage and drainage. It has exercised a supervisory and guidance role over the construction and real estate industries. In 1974, following the publication of Tanaka Kakuei's prime ministerial plan for the 'Reconstruction of the Japanese Archipelago', the land planning functions of the ministry were hived off to a new NATIONAL LAND AGENCY (*Kokudochō*) under the umbrella of the PRIME MINISTER'S OFFICE (*Sōrifu*).

As of the late 1980s, the central organisation of the ministry consisted of the Minister's Secretariat and five bureaux (*kyoku*) – specialising respectively in construction economics, cities, rivers, roads and housing. There were also eight bureaux covering different regions of Japan, and a number of consultative and investigative commissions (*shingikai*). In addition there were a number of attached facilities including the University of Construction (*Kensetsu Daigaku*).

The Ministry of Construction has been unique among the Ministries of the Japanese Government in treating line officials (*jimukan*) and technical officials (*gikan*) as equal in status. The top position of administrative vice-minister (*jimujikan*) has always alternated between *jimukan* and *gikan*.

Given the nature of its responsibilities, it is hardly surprising that the ministry should take a large slice of the national budget. Indeed its proportion of the budget has been around 10 per cent, while some 70 per cent of total public works have been accounted for by projects devised and controlled by the ministry. The extent and local dispersal of these projects mean extensive involvement with local authorities, and, of course, with construction companies. The extent to which central ministries control projects affecting local interests is a matter of long-standing controversy, and that is particularly so in the case of the Ministry of Construction. In addition the powerful 'construction tribe' (*kensetsu zoku*) of LIBERAL DEMOCRATIC PARTY (LDP) parliamentarians plays an important role in influencing the location, nature and extent of construction projects, so that media attention has come to be focused on allegedly corrupt relationships in the construction area. The ministry has also come under attack from environmentalists in respect of its penchant for concreting the beds of rivers throughout Japan in the interests of flood control. Some ambitious dam construction projects have also attracted intense criticism on environmental grounds. Various types of project have been criticised on the grounds they are justified not in terms of cost–benefit analysis, but in terms of political pay-offs.

The scale of this problem has been seen as so enormous that the term 'Construction State' (*doken kokka*) has been coined to describe it.

In January 2001 the Ministry of Construction was merged with the Hokkaidō Development Agency, the MINISTRY OF TRANSPORT and the NATIONAL LAND AGENCY into the Ministry of Land, Infrastructure and Transport (*Kokudokōtsūshō*).

Further reading
Koh (1989)
McCormack (1996)

Ministry of Economy, Trade and Industry (METI, Keizaisangyōshō) As a result of the administrative reorganisation that took place in January 2001, the MINISTRY OF INTERNATIONAL TRADE AND INDUSTRY, in existence under that name since 1949, became the Ministry of Economy, Trade and Industry. Some of the functions of the former MITI were transferred to the MINISTRY OF THE ENVIRONMENT.

Ministry of Education (Monbushō) The history of the Ministry of Education goes back to 1871, and from the beginning the ministry developed educational structures based on central control. It oversaw the rapid creation of primary schools throughout the country, and more limited development in the tertiary and secondary sectors. By the first decade of the twentieth century it was in full control of textbook authorisation throughout the educational system.

Following Japan's 1945 defeat, the Occupation authorities targeted the Ministry of Education as having been responsible for authoritarian control of schools, and for using them as instruments of militarist indoctrination. Promoting democracy in the education system meant wholesale revision of textbooks and decentralising control of schools. At one stage there was even discussion of abolishing the ministry and replacing it with a 'Ministry of Arts and Sciences' (*Gakugeishō*). Though this did not happen, much of the authority formerly exercised by the ministry over schools was devolved to local Boards of Education, on which labour union representation soon became strong. The status of the ministry was established in a law of June 1949, in which its information function was emphasised.

After the end of the Occupation in 1952, the ministry worked hard to reassert central control, aided by the conservative colouring of post-Occupation governments. Boards of Education became appointive, no longer elective, and, by refusing to negotiate centrally with the militant JAPAN TEACHERS' UNION (*Nikkyōso*), the ministry was able, for the most part, to squeeze its influence out of the system. A textbook accreditation system was re-established by 1956, and was later fought through the courts by those, such as the historian Ienaga Saburō, whose textbooks had been rejected. The ministry was widely accused of censoring reference in textbooks to horrors committed by Japanese forces on the mainland of Asia during the Second World War.

By the 1980s, the control of the ministry over the education system was firm. When, however, NAKASONE became Prime Minister, he established the *Ad Hoc* Council on Education (*Rinji kyōiku shingikai, Rinkyōshin*), with a view to giving more variety of educational provision and freeing up the system from excessive central control. The Council, however, came under the influence of the ministry, and did not live up to Nakasone's expectations for it. Nevertheless, over the longer term the ministry itself has sought to respond to the need, in an increasingly sophisticated society, for a less stereotyped educational system, without giving up too much of its power. Despite the criticism to which the ministry has been long subjected, it should be noted that it has presided over the development of an educational system that has inculcated outstandingly high levels of literacy and numeracy in the vast bulk of the school-age population.

The ministry was divided into a number of bureaux concerned with specific aspects of education, and it also administered the Cultural Agency (*Bunkachō*) as an 'external' bureau. It had responsibility for the National Educational Research Institute (*Kokuritsu kyōiku kenkyūjo*) and the National Science Museum (*Kokuritsu kagaku hakubutsukan*).

In January 2001 it was amalgamated with the Science and Technology Agency (*Kagaku gijutsuchō*) to form the Ministry of Education, Culture, Sports, Science and Technology (*Monbukagakushō*).

Further reading
Aspinall (2001)
Duke (1973)
Hood (2001)
Pempel (1978)
Schoppa (1991)
Thurston (1973)

Ministry of Education, Culture, Sports, Science and Technology (Monbukagakushō) Principal aims of the administrative reorganisation that came into effect in January 2001 were rationalisation of functions and avoidance of overlap. To this end, the MINISTRY OF EDUCATION (*Monbushō*) and the SCIENCE AND TECHNOLOGY AGENCY (*Kagaku gijutsuchō*) were united in a single ministry.

Ministry of the Environment (Kankyōshō) The creation of this ministry in the administrative reorganisation of January 2001 represented an upgrading of the former ENVIRONMENT AGENCY, which had been formed as a political response to a pollution crisis in 1971. Apart from taking over the various functions of the Environment Agency, it also inherited some functions from the former MINISTRY OF INTERNATIONAL TRADE AND INDUSTRY, and from the former MINISTRY OF HEALTH AND WELFARE. The promotion to ministry status indicated how far environmental concerns (both national and international) had become prominent in Government thinking since the 1970s.

Ministry of Finance (MOF, Okurashō [to 2001], Zaimushō [from 2001]) The Ministry of Finance has long had a reputation as the *crème de la crème* of Japanese ministries, recruiting the best and brightest brains, principally from the Law Department of Tokyo University. It bears, of course, central responsibility for the formulation and administration of financial policy, under the Minister of Finance.

The ministry's history can be traced back to 1869, and at least since the beginning of the twentieth century it has occupied a stable position in the Government bureaucracy. It was little affected by the administrative reforms of the Allied Occupation from 1945. Its internal structure has also been unusually static. In the late 1990s, apart from the Minister's Secretariat, the MOF contained the Budget Bureau (*Shukeikyoku*), Tax Bureau (*Shuzeikyoku*), Customs and Tariff Bureau (*Kanzeikyoku*), Finance Bureau (*Rizaikyoku*), Securities Bureau (*Kinyū kikakukyoku*), Banking Bureau (*Ginkōkyoku*) and the International Bureau (*Kokusaikyoku*). 'External' organs include the Mint (*Zōheikyoku*) and the National Tax Agency (*Kokuzeichō*).

The role of the MOF in the post-war period of rapid economic growth can hardly be overestimated. In the post-war years it was much concerned with preventing inflation, exercising investment guidance and controlling the banking system. Concerned with the balance of payments, it took a generally conservative line on financial policy. From the early 1970s, however, international pressures and domestic political imperatives meant that public spending, on welfare, roads and other purposes, rose sharply. The ministry became concerned and put pressure on political leaders to curb public spending, and this led to a regime of general financial discipline during the early to mid-1980s. From the late 1970s the MOF spearheaded a campaign to introduce some form of indirect, VAT-type taxation, against strong popular resistance. Finally it was introduced in 1989, but its introduction was an important factor in bringing down the TAKESHITA Government. The ministry's campaign to raise the level of consumption tax (described as a 'welfare tax') early in 1994 caused difficulties within the HOSOKAWA coalition Government. When the rate of consumption tax was finally raised from 3 to 5 per cent in 1998, the LIBERAL DEMOCRATIC PARTY (LDP) did badly in the subsequent House of Councillors elections, and the Hashimoto Cabinet resigned. A prime concern of the MOF at this time was to provide sufficient funds to be able to cope with the future welfare requirements of a society that was rapidly ageing.

With a mood developing in the 1990s that reform of the political and politico-administrative system was essential, the Ministry of Finance not surprisingly became a target of attack. In particular, its oversight of the banking sector came under criticism, following the collapse of asset values from early in the decade and the huge backlog of bad debts overhanging the banking sector. Compounded by allegations of corrupt behaviour levelled at some of its officials, this situation led to a decline in the reputation of the MOF.

In July 2000, the ministry lost part of its financial system supervision function with the creation of Financial Services (*Kinyūchō*).

Then, in the administrative restructuring that took place in January 2001, the ministry suffered a name change in Japanese from *Okurashō*, which was a prestigious name with long historical antecedents, to the more prosaic *Zaimushō*. Both, however, translate into English as 'Ministry of Finance'. The Ministry had thus come through the financial and economic difficulties of the 1990s into the twenty-first century with its functions somewhat truncated and its prestige diminished. But it was still a key ministry at the very centre of the politico-administrative system.

Further reading
Ishi (2000)
—— (2001)
Kato (1994)

Ministry of Foreign Affairs (Gaimushō) The Ministry of Foreign Affairs has a history going back to 1869, when it was set up just after the overthrow of the Shogunate and establishment of the Meiji regime. It was a powerful ministry from then until the 1920s, but much of its power was usurped by the military from the early 1930s.

During the early Occupation period Japan did not have a foreign policy of its own, so that the Ministry of Foreign Affairs concentrated on liaison with the Occupation authorities and on training future diplomats. With the ending of the Occupation in April 1952, the ministry could fulfil once more the normal functions of a Foreign Ministry. Its structure at that time consisted of the Minister's Secretariat and six bureaux, two of which were regional (one concerned with Asia, one with America and Europe). The other four dealt, respectively, with economics, treaties, international co-operation, and information and culture. Subsequently, the number of bureaux expanded, so that by 2000 they were as follows: Minister's Secretariat, Foreign Policy Bureau (*Sōgō gaikō seisakukyoku*), Asia Bureau (*Ajiakyoku*), North American Affairs Bureau (*Hokubeikyoku*), Latin American and Caribbean Affairs Bureau (*Chūnanbeikyoku*), Europe and Oceanic Affairs Bureau (*Oakyoku*), Middle East and African Affairs Bureau (*Chūkintō Afurikakyoku*), Economics Bureau (*Keizaikyoku*), Economic Co-operation Bureau (*Keizai kyōryokukyoku*), Treaties Bureau (*Jōyakukyoku*) and International Information Bureau (*Kokusai jōhōkyoku*). In addition, the ministry administered embassies in nearly all significant states, as well as numerous consulates around the world, and several missions to international bodies.

In the modern world the conduct of foreign policy in major states is not simply a matter for a foreign ministry. In Japan, as elsewhere, economic ministries in particular have substantive international responsiblities. Representatives of the MINISTRY OF FINANCE, MINISTRY OF ECONOMY, TRADE AND INDUSTRY (formerly MITI) and of other ministries and agencies of Government are to be found in major embassies on a permanent basis. In the Japanese case there is the legacy of a low-key foreign policy approach, which has tended to reduce the influence of the Ministry of Foreign Affairs. Since the ending of the Cold War, however, the ministry has been able to demonstrate the depth of its expertise in a range of foreign policy negotiations, showing that 'low-key' does not mean 'inexpert'. Unlike some other ministries, it is true, the Ministry of Foreign Affairs lacks a significant domestic clientele, thus weakening its clout in inter-ministerial disputes and contests for budgetary resources. This is similar to the situation of foreign ministries in many countries. The Foreign Minister, however, has normally been a very senior LIBERAL DEMOCRATIC PARTY (LDP) politician, and that lends political weight to the ministry. It is, nevertheless, by most international comparisons, inadequately funded and staffed.

Though it is difficult to generalise about the attitudes of the ministry towards foreign policy in general, there is no doubt that it has consistently fought for the integrity of Japan's relationship with the United States (*see* UNITED STATES, RELATIONS WITH). It has maintained a cool view of Japan's Russian neighbour, particularly in view of the Northern Territories dispute, where it takes a hard line [*see also* SOVIET UNION AND RUSSIA, RELATIONS WITH]. Attitudes to China are affected by rivalry between the North American Affairs Bureau and the Asian Affairs Bureau, though the tendency has been to pay more attention to China, while maintaining the primacy of the

US connection [see also CHINA (PRC AND ROC), RELATIONS WITH]. Relations with Europe, and for quite different reasons with the Middle East, have been gaining ground in the ministry's attentions [see also EUROPE, RELATIONS WITH; MIDDLE EAST, RELATIONS WITH].

From the early 2000s, the Ministry of Foreign Affairs faced accusations of corrupt practice on the part of some of its officials. The appointment of Ms TANAKA MAKIKO as Foreign Minister, in April 2001, rapidly raised the profile of this issue, as the new Minister was determined to root out corruption from the ministry. Her own maverick conduct, however, and her well-publicised disputes with Suzuki Muneo, a powerful LDP parliamentarian, led to her dismissal by the PRIME MINISTER, KOIZUMI in January 2002, though a leading ministry official also lost his job and Suzuki left the LDP. She was succeeded as Minister by another woman, Kawaguchi Junko.

Further reading
Drifte (2002)
Hook *et al*. (2001)

Ministry of Health and Welfare (Kōseishō)

The Ministry of Health and Welfare was originally founded in 1938. After the war it received a number of new functions, so that its primary involvement was with medicine, insurance and hygiene. In 1947 it lost its labour-related functions to the newly established Ministry of Labour (*Rōdōshō*). By the late 1980s it consisted of nine bureaux, relating to Health Policy (*Iryō seisakukyoku*), Insurance Medicine (*Hoken iryōkyoku*), Life Hygiene (*Seikatsu eiseikyoku*), Pharmaceutical Matters (*Yakumukyoku*), Society (*Shakaikyoku*), Children and Family (*Jidō kateikyoku*), Insurance (*Hokenkyoku*), Pensions (*Nenkinkyoku*) and Protection (*Engokyoku*). In addition there was the Minister's Secretariat, and an 'external' body, the Social Insurance Agency (*Shakai hoshōchō*). As these titles imply, the ministry exercised a wide range of functions in relation to medical and other types of insurance, pharmaceutical issues and drug control, welfare provision including disaster relief, pensions, population questions, relief for the families of war dead and missing, and welfare for the handicapped. The ministry has been closely involved in efforts to improve welfare systems since the war, particularly with the great improvements that took place from the early 1970s. In the most recent period it has been much exercised by the need to adjust welfare provision in the light of the future requirements of a rapidly ageing society.

Relations between the ministry and the JAPAN MEDICAL ASSOCIATION (*Ishikai*) have often been complex and full of tension.

The ministry received much bad publicity in the 1990s over a 'tainted blood' scandal dating back to the 1980s. When KAN NAOTO was appointed Minister of Health and Welfare in January 1996, he publicly apologised to a large group of relatives of patients who had received non-heat-treated blood products that had been infected with HIV. Many patients had died, but officials had never admitted responsibility. Kan, however, went down on his knees to apologise on behalf of the ministry. This case became a symbol for bureaucratic arrogance and insensitivity [see also HIV-TAINTED BLOOD SCANDAL].

Nevertheless, in the broader picture, the ministry had achieved much in improving systems of welfare.

In January 2001, the Ministry of Health and Welfare was amalgamated with the Ministry of Labour to form the Ministry of Health, Labour and Welfare (*Kōseirōdōshō*).

Further reading
Goodman (2000)

Ministry of Health, Labour and Welfare (Kōseirōdōshō)

This ministry emerged in January 2001, as part of a general reorganisation of ministries and other organs of Government, by bringing together under the same roof the MINISTRY OF HEALTH AND WELFARE (*Kōseishō*) and the MINISTRY OF LABOUR (*Rōdōshō*). The merger was designed to create better co-ordination of welfare and employment policies, particularly in view of the rapidly ageing society. In view of rising unemployment, from extremely low levels to levels that were socially and politically significant by 2001, more active policies were called for in respect of people out of work. It remained to be seen, however, whether concerns central to the former Ministry of Health and Welfare would tend to overwhelm issues of importance to the former Ministry of Labour, which had been considerably weaker.

Ministry of Home Affairs (Ministry of Local Autonomy, Jichishō) The pre-war Home Ministry (*Naimushō*) was one of the most powerful ministries, with extensive control over appointments in local government, in addition to its administration of the police and of elections. The Occupation authorities quickly identified it as one of the central core elements in the wartime regime, and determined to abolish it. The Home Ministry ceased to exist on 31 December 1947. Various functions that had belonged to the Home Ministry were given to other administrative bodies, but, with the introduction of wide-ranging democratic procedures in local government, it was felt that a central co-ordinating body was needed. Thus, in June 1949, the Local Autonomy Agency (*Chihō jichichō*) was established. Shortly thereafter, its powers over local government finances were taken away and placed in a new body called the Local Finance Committee (*Chihō zaisei iinkai*). Then, in August 1952, the Occupation having ended in April, the two were amalgamated into the Local Autonomy Agency (*Jichichō*).

Eight years later, in July 1960, in the immediate aftermath of the Security Treaty revision crisis, the *Jichichō* was upgraded to the *Jichishō*, in other words Ministry of Local Autonomy. This is the only example, since the end of the Occupation, of an agency of the Prime Minister's Department being transformed into a ministry, with the increase in prestige that entailed. Moreover, some time thereafter, the ministry sought to make a point about its antecedents and its current status by naming itself in English 'Ministry of Home Affairs'. This did not, however, indicate any change in its Japanese title, nor was it a translation of the latter.

The ministry had a relatively simple structure, consisting of an Administrative Bureau (*Gyōseikyoku*), Financial Bureau (*Zaiseikyoku*), Taxation Bureau (*Zeimukyoku*) and the Minister's Secretariat. It also had one 'external' body under its wing, the Fire Prevention Agency (*Shōbōchō*). Its powers over local authorities, however, were very extensive indeed, encompassing supervision of their taxation and finance-raising activities. Projects developed by the ministry would require the active involvement of local authorities to carry them out, and this in turn would tend to increase ministry control over those local authorities, since the ministry was their 'supervisory authority'. One example among many was an anti-pollution project in the late 1960s. It was indeed a fairly consistent aim of the ministry to link local authorities into its administrative structure so far as possible, and obstruct the 'encroachment' of other ministries and agencies of the central Government on its 'turf' – in other words, into local administration. According to Masumi, some 40 per cent of its officials were on loan to local authorities at any one time (p. 254). Moreover, considerable numbers of those elected prefectural governors and city mayors had been senior officials of the ministry. This was reminiscent of pre-war days, when the former Home Ministry used to appoint officials to those same positions, at that period without election. In the 2000s, however, it was noticeable that resistance to electing former ministry officials to local executive positions appeared to be growing, and some of them were spectacularly defeated.

In January 2001, the Ministry of Home Affairs was united with the Ministry of Posts and Telecommunications (*Yūseishō*) and the Management and Co-ordination Agency (*Sōmuchō*) to form the Ministry of Public Management, Home Affairs, Posts and Telecommunications (*Sōmushō*).

Further reading
Masumi (1995)

Ministry of International Trade and Industry (MITI, Tsūshō sangyōshō, Tsūsanshō) Widely recognised as one of the most important ministries of Japanese Government, this ministry was long regarded overseas, rightly or wrongly, as 'Notorious MITI' – the ruthless architect of Japan's economic miracle, protector of its domestic market and promoter of its global export drive.

Its origins may be traced back to the Meiji period. In 1881 an Agricultural and Commercial Affairs Ministry was established, but a more direct ancestor of MITI was the Ministry of Commerce and Industry (Shōkōshō) set up in 1925. Its main bureaux dealt respectively with commerce, industry and mines, but it also ran the Patent Office and nationalised Yawata Steel Works. During the Second World War its functions were split between various ministries, but it was re-established in 1945, as was a new body called the Trade Agency (Bōekichō). Then, in the general reorganisation accompanying the Dodge Line, in May 1949, the Ministry of Commerce and Industry was merged with the Trade Agency to form MITI.

MITI's internal organisation had stabilised by the early 1950s to the Minister's Secretariat, nine 'internal' bureaux and three 'external' bureaux. The former were: the Commerce Bureau (Tsūshōkyoku), Enterprise Bureau (Kigyōkyoku), Heavy Industry Bureau (Jūkōgyōkyoku), Light Industry Bureau (Keikōgyōkyoku), Textile Bureau (Senikyoku), Mining Bureau (Kōzankyoku), Coal Bureau (Sekitankyoku), Mining Safety Bureau (Kōzan hoankyoku) and the Public Interest Enterprises Bureau (Kōeki jigyōkyoku). The 'external' bureaux were the Patent Office (Tokkyochō), Small and Medium Industry Agency (Chūshōkigyōchō) and the Industrial Technology Institute (Kōgyō gijutsuin).

The changing character of the economy following the ultra-high economic growth of the 1960s led to a reorganisation under which, in July 1973, a Natural Resources and Energy Agency (Shigen enerugiikyoku) was set up under MITI auspices. In addition, three bureaux with broad responsibilities were introduced, relating to basic industries, machinery and information industries, and consumer goods industries.

By 1999, the single industry bureaux of the earlier years had largely given way to bureaux with broad definitions. These, apart from the Minister's Secretariat, were the Commercial Policy Bureau (Tsūshō seisakukyoku), Trade Bureau (Bōekikyoku), Industrial Policy Bureau (Sangyō seisakukyoku), Industrial Location and Environmental Protection Bureau (Kankyō ritchikyoku), Basic Industries Bureau (Kiso sangyōkyoku), Machinery and Information Industries Bureau (Kikai jōhō sangyōkyoku) and the Consumer Goods Industries Bureau (Seikatsu sangyōkyoku). In addition, the main 'external' organs were the Industrial Science and Technology Agency (Kōgyō gijutsuin), Natural Resources and Energy Agency (Shigen enerugiichō), Patent Office (Tokkyochō) and the Small and Medium Enterprise Agency (Chūshō kigyōchō).

During the years of rapid economic growth up to the early 1970s, MITI exercised great influence on the directions taken by Japanese industry and commerce. As was widely noted abroad, it took a strategic and long-term approach to economic development. Its approach was to promote investment in industrial sectors that it perceived to have a commercial future and allow obsolescent sectors, in which Japan might have a current comparative advantage, to decline. The progress from textiles to consumer electronics to heavy machinery and chemical industries in the 1950s and 1960s owed much to the prompting of MITI. Some observers have doubted the ability of a Government ministry to enforce its will in this regard. But at that period MITI had at its disposal a range of instruments of control that it could mobilise. The Government maintained tight controls over international trade, and could protect the domestic market from undue international competition while applying a range of pressures and persuasion for industries to move into new areas of manufacture, with promising export potential. The ministry did not have a large budget, but its close contacts with industry and leading politicians, its strategic deployment of licences and permissions, and the high quality of its top echelons, made it into a remarkable instrument of economic growth. Its use of 'ADMINISTRATIVE GUIDANCE' (gyōsei shidō), though there were instances where it did not work, was in the main effective in persuading businesses to follow the desired line.

Chalmers Johnson in his influential book *MITI and the Japanese Miracle*, argued that MITI was a key instrument in a 'plan-rational' and 'developmental' State. Unlike Soviet-style planned economies the Japanese planners were not 'Socialist', accepted a role for the market and believed in conforming to long-term market forces. But unlike 'market-rational' economies, there was less emphasis on pluralism and legalism, or, indeed, on the supremacy of Parliament.

More recent observers have suggested that, while Johnson's argument was accurate and insightful for the period from the 1950s to the 1970s, the liberalising measures introduced from the 1960s took away from MITI many of its instruments of control. Moreover, as Japanese companies became international players, they were less inclined to shape their investment plans according to the priorities expressed by MITI. The economy was becoming more complex and Government policy subject to an increasing number of pressures, both domestic and international. MITI had come under intense international criticism for its protection of domestic markets and promotion of exports. Gradually the role of the ministry evolved and it became more sensitive to Japan's international environment. This did not mean, however, that MITI had ceased to be interventionist. Okimoto argues that a range of structural elements in the economy facilitated intervention, where it was seen to be needed. These, which included the vertical linkages between major firms and sub-contracting firms, and the small number of big corporations with commanding market shares, he calls 'access points'.

In the administrative reorganisation of January 2001 the Ministry's name was changed to MINISTRY OF ECONOMY, TRADE AND INDUSTRY (METI, *Keizai sangyōshō*).

Further reading
Johnson (1982)
Okimoto (1989)

Ministry of Justice (Hōmushō) The predecessor of the current Ministry of Justice was established in 1871, also bearing in English the name 'Ministry of Justice', but in Japanese called *Shihōshō*. In the pre-war system there was no separation of powers between the executive and judiciary, so that the ministry had enormous powers over the courts, the public prosecutor's office, and other parts of the legal system. Some nominal curbs on this power were introduced under the 1889 Constitution, but this did not much reduce the ministry's power over the judiciary.

A central principle of the CONSTITUTION OF 1946 was that the executive and judicial powers should be clearly separated. In pursuance of this aim nearly all aspects of judicial administration, including budgetary and personnel matters, were taken away from the Minister of Justice and placed in the hands of the Supreme Court. In 1948 the *Shihōshō* was abolished, and replaced with the Justice Agency (*Hōmuchō*). In 1949 this became the Justice Office (*Hōmufu*) and in 1952 it finally took on the name Ministry of Justice (*Hōmushō*).

The ministry developed a rather complex organisational structure. It had seven internal bureaux, concerned with civil affairs (*minji*), criminal affairs (*keiji*), correctional matters (*kyōsei*), protection (*hogo*), prosecution (*shōmu*), protection of human rights (*jinken yōgo*) and immigration control (*nyūkoku kanri*). In addition, a number of commissions (*shingikai*) report to it, for instance the Central Rehabilitation and Protection Commission (*Chūō kōsei hogo shingikai*). Third, it ran a number of research and training institutes and other institutions, for instance the Correctional Training Institute (*Kyōsei kenshūjo*) and immigration detention centres (*nyūkokusha shuyōjo*). And finally, there were a number of local and 'external' bodies, including local judicial bureaux (*chihō hōmukyoku*), the Public Safety Investigation Agency (*Kōan chōsachō*) and the Public Prosecutor's Office (*Kensatsuchō*).

The ministry's control over such a variety of institutions suggests that it has clawed back at least some of the powers of its predecessor from the pre-war era, and the long tenure of Government office by the LIBERAL DEMOCRATIC PARTY has been accompanied by broadly conservative attitudes prevailing on the Bench. It is, of course, the Supreme Court that recommends appointments of judges, which have to be ratified by Cabinet. How far the Ministry of Justice, in this situation, is able to exert influence over appointments is a matter of some dispute.

The ministry was not substantively affected by the administrative reorganisation undertaken in January 2001, remaining organisationally intact.

Further reading
Oda (1999)

Ministry of Labour (Rōdōshō) Although matters of labour welfare had been handled before 1945 by various ministries, it was not until the Occupation period that labour was recognised as requiring a separate ministry. Both the emergence of a vigorous labour union movement and the introduction of a comprehensive legal framework for labour suggested that labour matters should not be left to the casual attention of ministries whose primary concern it was not.

The left-of-centre KATAYAMA Government was at one with the Occupation authorities in promoting the idea of a new ministry. In September 1947 three bureaux of the MINISTRY OF HEALTH AND WELFARE (Kōseishō) were hived off to form the new Ministry of Labour. These were the Labour Administration Bureau (Rōseikyoku), Labour Standards Bureau (Rōdō kijunkyoku) and Employment Security Bureau (Shokugyō anteikyoku). In addition, two new bureaux were created: the Women and Youth Bureau (Fujin shōnenkyoku) and the Labour Statistics Investigation Bureau (Rōdō tōkei chōsakyoku). A later addition was the Occupational Skills Development Bureau (Shokugyō nōryoku kaihatsukyoku), investigating training facilities. In general, the ministry concerned itself with administering the various laws relating to labour. The Women's Bureau was particularly active in monitoring conditions of female labour, particularly after a new law on labour equality between men and women was introduced in 1985. Women were a higher proportion of officials in the Ministry of Labour than in most ministries, including in higher positions, and the head of the Women's Bureau was normally a woman [see also WOMEN AND POLITICS]. On the other hand, the ministry was seen as a relatively weak player having limited leverage in inter-ministry contests.

Several functions of the ministry were represented in offices set up in every prefecture. The Central Labour Committee (Chūō rōdō iinkai, or Chūrōi), a corporatist structure including representatives of labour, management and the public interest (as well as its local counterparts), was answerable to the Ministry of Labour.

The administrative reorganisation of January 2001 resulted in the Ministry of Labour being reunited with the MINISTRY OF HEALTH AND WELFARE, forming a new Ministry of Health, Labour and Welfare (Kōseirōdōshō). Whether this would result in labour matters being taken more seriously because they were represented by a more powerful ministry, or whether they risked subordination to other issues in that ministry, remained to be seen.

Ministry of Land, Infrastructure and Transport (Kokudokōtsūshō) This ministry was created in the administrative reorganisation of January 2001 out of the Hokkaidō Development Agency, MINISTRY OF TRANSPORT, MINISTRY OF CONSTRUCTION and NATIONAL LAND AGENCY. The purpose of the amalgamation was to allow the deployment and enrichment of social capital to be co-ordinated in as effective a manner as possible. Roads, railways, harbours, rivers and airports were brought within its remit, as well as other kinds of large-scale infrastructure construction project. The large northern island of Hokkaidō was placed under a central ministry, rather than being treated as a special case as before. Whether the unification would reduce the impact of special interests remained to be seen.

At its inception this ministry accounted for some 68,000 officials, 13 'internal' bureaux and four 'external' bureaux. Its budget exceeded ¥10 trillion, and was nearly 80 per cent of the Government's total budget for public works.

The 'internal' bureaux were as follows: the Minister's Secretariat, General Policy (Sōgō seisaku), National Land Planning (Kokudo keikaku), Land and Water Resources (Tochi, mizu shigen), City and Regional Improvement (Toshi, chiiki seibi), Rivers (Kasen), Roads (Dōro), Housing (Jūtaku), Railways (Tetsudō), Cars and Traffic (Jidōsha, kōtsū), Maritime Matters (Kaiji), Harbours (Kōwan) and Airlines (Kōkū). In addition, there were 14 research and training institutes, two miscellaneous institutions and the following four 'external' bureaux: the Seamen's Labour Committee (Sen'in rōdō iinkai), Weather Agency (Kishōchō), Maritime Safety Agency (Kaijō hoanchō) and the Maritime Disaster Adjudication Agency (Kainan shinpanchō).

The Maritime Safety Agency was the largest of these latter, employing over 12,000 officials.

Ministry of Posts and Telecommunications (MPT, Yūseishō) This ministry was launched in 1949, on the basis of the former Ministry of Communications (*Teishinshō*), its principal brief being to run the various functions of the Post Office. These, apart from the postal service, have been the Post Office Savings Bank, and the insurance schemes. In 1952, however, it took over responsibility for Nippon Telegraph and Telephone (NTT, *Nippon denshin denwa kōsha*) from the former Ministry of Electric Communications (*Denki tsūshinshō*). It also assumed responsibility, among other things, for the allocation of broadcasting licences and the regulation of channels.

The revolution in electronic communications that was in full flow by the 1980s enormously increased the responsibilities of the ministry in this field, extending to satellite and cable broadcasting, and a range of new technologies. When the NAKASONE Government decided to privatise NTT, a new regulatory regime was required. This occasioned complex jurisdictional battles between different bureaucratic agencies, most notably MPT and the MINISTRY OF INTERNATIONAL TRADE AND INDUSTRY (MITI). The MPT came well out of these disputes, with its relative power strengthened.

In the 1990s, privatisation of the Post Office became a political issue. The Post Office Savings Bank, with its nation-wide network of branches, accounted for an unusually high proportion of the people's savings. This, in turn, provided the Government with large revenues. Some conservative politicians, most notably KOIZUMI JUNICHIRŌ, made privatisation of the Post Office Savings Bank a major campaign issue, arguing that greater efficiency and rationality needed to be introduced into the management of the bank and allocation of revenues. With his appointment as Prime Minister in April 2001, limited moves in that direction were initiated.

In the administrative reorganisation of January 2001, the Ministry of Posts and Telecommunications was merged with the Management and Co-ordination Agency (*Sōmuchō*) and the Ministry of Home Affairs (*Jichishō*) to form the Ministry of Public Management, Home Affairs, Posts and Telecommunications (*Sōmushō*). The establishment of a Postal Enterprises Agency (*Yūsei jigyōchō*) was envisaged for 2003.

Further reading
Krauss (2000)
Wilks and Wright (1991)

Ministry of Public Management, Home Affairs, Posts and Telecommunications (Sômushô) This Ministry (whose name is snappier in Japanese than in English) was formed from amalgamating the MINISTRY OF POSTS AND TELECOMMUNICATIONS, the GENERAL AFFAIRS AGENCY and the MINISTRY OF HOME AFFAIRS in January 2001. It was the largest of the new ministries, with a total of some 304,000 employees, although about 297,000 of these worked in post offices. Its purpose was given as that of providing more effective administrative support to the PRIME MINISTER and CABINET. In practice, however, it appeared a somewhat unwieldy creation, in which functions having rather little to do with each other were bundled together in a single super-ministry. Some critics dubbed it a 'grotesque monster', and others wondered whether it did not represent a recreation of the pre-war Home Ministry, or perhaps a new and powerful focus for interest politics.

In addition to the Minister's Secretariat, the new Ministry comprised 10 bureaux, dealing with the following functions, which are easy to trace back to the three parent bodies: Personnel and pensions (*Jinji onkyû*), Administrative control (*Gyôsei kanri*), Administrative evaluation (*Gyôsei hyôka*), Local authority administration (*Jichi gyôsei*), Local authority finance (*Jichi zaisei*), Local authority taxation (*Jichi zeimu*), Information and communication policy (*Jôhô tsûshin seisaku*), Comprehensive communications base (*Sôgô tsûshin kiban*), Postal services planning and control (*Yûsei kikaku kanri*), and Statistics *(Tôkei)*. In addition, there were a number of attached institutions, including the General Research Institute into Communications (*Tsûshin sôgô kenkyûjo*), the Postal Services Research Institute (*Yûsei kenkyûjo*), and the Central Election Control Association (*Chûô senkyo kanrikai*). The Ministry had oversight of four 'external' bodies: the FAIR TRADE COMMISSION (*Kôsei torihiki iinkai*), Environmental Pollution Preparation Committee (*Kôgai tô chôsei iinkai*), Postal Services Enterprises Agency *(Yûsei jigyôchô)* and the Fire Prevention Agency *(Shôbôchô).* The Postal Services Agency was scheduled to become the Postal Services Public Corporation (*Yûsei kôsha*) in 2003.

Ministry of Transport (Unyūshō) This ministry was set up towards the end of 1945, inheriting the transport-related functions of the Ministry of Transport and Communications, formed in 1943 out of the Ministry of Communications and the Ministry of Railways. Thus in a sense the 1945 division of functions represented a return to the pre-war status quo, although transport now included many areas apart from railways. Examples of functions that the ministry came to cover include harbours, inland water transport, tourism, mariners' affairs, weather forecasting, air transport, maritime safety and investigation of maritime disasters.

The ministry was thus heavily involved in establishing the physical infrastructure for the rapid economic growth of the 1960s and later. For instance, its involvement in the establishment of the *Shinkansen* network of super-express railway lines linking major cities was central. It has generally been hostile to deregulation – a position that could be interpreted variously as a desire to maintain its jurisdiction and influence, or as a genuine belief that its regulatory regimes protect the public interest. No doubt both these motivations have been present. It has been one of the ministries most heavily penetrated by the political interests of LIBERAL DEMOCRATIC PARTY (LDP) 'tribal' politicians (*zoku giin*) (*see* 'TRIBES' OF PARLIAMENTARIANS). This has been a key factor in the controversial expansion of the *Shinkansen* network, leading to accusations that political advantage, rather than economic rationality, have been driving the expansion.

In January 2001 the Ministry of Transport was amalgamated with the MINISTRY OF CONSTRUCTION, the Hokkaidō Development Agency and the NATIONAL LAND AGENCY, to form the Ministry of Land, Infrastructure and Transport (*kokudokōtsūshō*). The amalgamation was designed to create an approach to all aspects of transport infrastructure that should be more co-ordinated than hitherto.

Minobe Ryōkichi Minobe Ryōkichi was the Governor of Tokyo for twelve years between 1967 and 1989, and the best known of the progressive governors and mayors that dominated urban local government during that period.

Born in 1904, he was the son of Minobe Tatsukichi, whose liberal interpretation of the 1889 Constitution made him vulnerable to attack by ultra-nationalists during the 1930s. His own experience after the war was as an Economics lecturer and civil servant.

Minobe became Governor of Tokyo, with backing from the JAPAN SOCIALIST PARTY and the JAPAN COMMUNIST PARTY, at a time when policies of economic 'growth above all' had created appalling conditions of pollution and overcrowding. He closed the Ginza to motor traffic on Sundays, built pedestrian overpasses and protective barriers, provided free health care for the elderly and facilities for the handicapped. He sought to enhance the quality of life of Tokyo residents and favoured consultative decision-making rather than imposing solutions. Consultation did not always work, as when deciding where to put a rubbish dump, which no city ward would willingly accept. In 1971 he was re-elected with a majority of one and a half million votes over his conservative opponent, the largest majority ever won by a politician in Japan at that time. Later in the decade, however, issues changed and his lustre faded. He was elected with a reduced majority in 1975, but did not stand in 1979.

He died in December 1984, aged 80.

minorities and politics Discussion of minorities in Japan is largely confined to ethnic groups (including some which constitute distinct linguistic groups), and to one group (*Burakumin*) having some characteristics associated with a caste. Interestingly enough, it is not normally applied to religious groups, despite the proliferation of new religious groups since the end of the Second World War. This probably stems from entrenched preference of Government to play down minority issues, because of a commitment to the idea of a homogeneous Japanese people [*see also* HOMO-GENEITY AND POLITICS]. All-inclusiveness and assimilation to a common norm is the ideal, however far it may be from the reality. These aims have been pursued with increasing sophistication.

In terms of prevalent definitions, the largest minority group is what are now called *Burakumin* (literally 'village people'). These people, more numerous in the west of Japan than the east and north, are ethnically wholly indistinguishable from non-*Burakumin* Japanese. Their total numbers today are hard to determine with accuracy, because of reluctance to admit *Buraku* origin through fear of prejudice and discrimination. The figure, however, is probably somewhere between two and three million (between 1.5 and 2.3 per cent of the total population). During the Tokugawa period (early seventeenth century to 1868) certain groups, many of them engaged in occupations seen as polluting, were excluded from mainstream society, which was itself highly segmented and stratified. After the change of regime from Tokugawa to Meiji in 1868, an Emancipation Edict was given in 1871, reclassifying them as 'New Commoners' (*Shin heimin*). This, however, did not end discrimination, and threatened their monopoly of occupations from which they could make money (such as shoemaking). In 1922 a political movement called the Levellers' Society (*Suiheisha*) was founded to combat discrimination.

After Japan's defeat in 1945, the Buraku Liberation League (*Buraku kaihō undō*) succeeded the Levellers' Society. The League quickly became an active campaigner for the interests of the *Burakumin*, and adopted a confrontational approach of forcefully denouncing those (for instance schoolteachers or local officials) whom it believed to be denigrating members of its community, or otherwise fostering discrimination. The political affiliations of the League were, not surprisingly, on the left, particularly with the JAPAN SOCIALIST PARTY (JSP) and JAPAN COMMUNIST PARTY (JCP). JSP–JCP friction within the *Dōwa* (i.e. *Burakumin*) movement during the 1970s caused problems within the political machine of Governor MINOBE RYŌKICHI of Tokyo, and for a while seemed likely to jeopardise his chances of re-election. *Burakumin* continued to be subject to prejudice of various kinds, but this was felt most acutely in relation to marriage and employment. At least in the earlier post-war period, family registers (*koseki*) were open to inspection, so that prospective parents-in-law or prospective employers could check back addresses to see whether the person in question was of *Burakumin* origin. Even after the registers had been closed to general inspection, detective agencies made money by peddling address lists, from which the same information could be obtained.

Addresses were significant because *Burakumin* tended to live in particular areas, sometimes referred to as 'ghettoes'. After the war, these areas were far more impoverished in terms of facilities and standard of living than mainstream areas. From the late 1960s, however, the Government authorities funded ambitious upgrading of the relevant areas, and strove to improve the educational level – and thus employment opportunities – of people within the communities. They have been much more reluctant to create a legal framework penalising discrimination. In Neary's words: 'The government view has been that if living conditions could be improved so that they were as good as average, there would be no need for additional apparatus to ensure equality of treatment' (2002, p. 209).

In contrast to the *Burakumin* in that they are distinct from Japanese ethnically and in appearance, the *Ainu* inhabit almost exclusively the northern island of Hokkaidō. They have their own culture and their own language (unrelated to Japanese), which is in a fragile state, though interest in preserving it has revived. Their numbers, however, are small (Neary estimates 24,000 at maximum) and until relatively recently they suffered from official neglect (and even denial that they existed in any significant sense). Until the late nineteenth century they had been the principal inhabitants of Hokkaidō, but were no match for Japanese when the latter began to colonise the island. A sense of separate *Ainu* identity, linked with a degree of political activism, began to emerge in the 1970s, and some considerable progress in terms of official recognition was reached in the 1990s. *Ainu* activists have made contact with movements representing indigenous minorities in other parts of the world. There is some evidence that international pressure may be responsible for a certain softening of Japanese governmental attitudes towards the *Ainu*.

Okinawans are also sometimes regarded as a minority group, although they are not so clearly a separate ethnic group as are the *Ainu*. Okinawa and the other Ryūkyū islands only became incorporated into Japan in the late nineteenth century, and have a history of semi-independence before that, including political links with China. Okinawan culture and language is distinct from, though related to, the culture and language of mainland Japan, and Okinawans have suffered considerable discrimination over the years. Their numbers, however (over a million), put them in a much stronger political position than the *Ainu*. There is, however, a unique and overwhelming element in the situation of Okinawans. In 1945 a battle of extraordinary savagery was fought between the US and Japanese forces for possession of the islands, and many Okinawans perished. Then between 1945 and 1972 the islands were under the direct administration of the United States, which sequestered large tracts of land on the main island for military bases. Following the reversion to Japan in 1972, the bases remained, and with them much local resentment of the fact that the bulk of US bases in Japan were located in the smallest prefecture. Matters came to a head for various reasons in the 1990s, but neither the US nor the Japanese governments were willing to meet, in any substantial fashion, Okinawan grievances over the bases [*see also* OKINAWA IN JAPANESE POLITICS].

The mixture of factors affecting the Korean minority in Japan is different again from any of the above. Depending on definition, the Korean population in Japan is approaching a million. They are mainly the descendants of Korean labourers who found themselves in Japan at the end of the war. Many stayed in Japan, but, without Japanese nationality, they were excluded from occupations in the public sector and suffered discrimination also in respect of employment in private firms. This forced sufficient numbers into marginal, or even criminal, occupations that discrimination against them was further reinforced. We may recognise here a common syndrome affecting minorities, and elements of it could also be found in relation to other minority groups in Japan. A particular complication of the Korean case was their divided loyalties between separate organisations linked, respectively, to North and South Korea. In the earlier postwar years the organisation linked with the North predominated, not surprisingly reinforcing suspicions about the Korean community within Japanese officialdom. Even as late as the 1990s it was clear that remittances from the proceeds of the ubiquitous *pachinko* (pinball) industry (much of it Korean-owned) helped sustain the fragile North Korean economy. Gradually, however, the influence of these externally linked organisations has declined, and assimilation into mainstream Japanese society has reached advanced levels.

This does not mean, however, that discrimination has been eliminated. Elements of official discrimination have been mitigated (for details, see Neary, 2002, pp. 209–12), including the much resented fingerprinting requirement, and increasing numbers obtain Japanese nationality. Most people of Korean background are now at least third-generation Japanese residents, and marriage between them and Japanese is extremely common. Even so, they continue to suffer discrimination in the employment market, and, unless they obtain Japanese nationality, are barred from positions of responsibility in the public sector (except in one or two progressive prefectures). Without Japanese nationality, they may not vote in elections.

Significant numbers of Chinese live in Japan, though the numbers are much smaller than in the case of Koreans. There have been political problems in the past. For instance, in the 1960s activists of a Taiwan independence movement were based in Japan. Since the 1980s large numbers of Chinese students have been attending Japanese universities, and accusations are made that some of these disappear into the black economy. There are Chinatowns in many big cities, which are popular among Japanese.

The recent appearance of Chinese triad gangs in areas of criminal activity in Japan has caused disquiet, but generally speaking the Chinese minority has maintained a lower profile than the Korean.

Minorities from a number of other countries may be found in Japan. These are of political significance mainly in so far as their presence (or, indeed, their relative absence) throws light on Government thinking about immigration policy. For a time during the boom times of the late 1980s considerable numbers of workers, from various Asian and some Latin American countries, worked in Japan, some as illegal visa over-stayers. A particular legal anomaly permitted the entry of considerable numbers of Iranians, who worked in Japan and remitted much of their wages to their families in Iran. In 1990, new laws were brought in making this more difficult, at least for unskilled labour. But preference in the granting of visas was shown to people from Latin American countries (especially Brazil) of Japanese descent. Most Brazilians in this category were far more Brazilian than Japanese in attitude (and certainly in language), so that the main factor easing assimilation was appearance. The 1990 law also made provision for training of overseas workers, but little was done in other ways to prevent exploitation (for details, *see* Neary, 2002, pp. 213–17).

Government policy remains deeply resistant to the idea of developing a structured immigration programme for the long term. In some ways this is surprising, given the problems Japan will face in future years in caring for rapidly increasing numbers of elderly people, where immigrant labour could make a substantial contribution. Admittedly, to maintain a balanced population structure through immigration would require levels of immigration far beyond anything politically, socially or economically feasible. But Japanese governments have been far more conservative than their European counterparts in respect of permitting people of foreign origin to work and settle in Japan. We may plausibly detect in the mind-set of officialdom a deep-seated concern to maintain social harmony, an intense fear of 'pockets of difference' that might disrupt it, and an elitist desire to retain ultimate control over the paths taken by society as a whole. Too much immigration, just like too much litigation based on principles of human rights, would threaten those aims, in their eyes.

Further reading
Creighton, in Weiner (ed.) (1997)
Neary (1989)
——, in Weiner (ed.) (1997)
—— (2002)
Refsing (forthcoming)
Sellek, in Weiner (ed.) (1997)
Siddle, in Weiner (ed.) (1997)
Taira, in Weiner (ed.) (1997)
Upham (1987)
——, in Gordon (ed.) (1993)
Vasishth, in Weiner (ed.) (1997)
Weiner (ed.) (1997)

Minseitō This transitional party, its untranslatable name deliberately taken from a major party of the pre-war period, was formed in late January 1998 out of the SUN PARTY, FROM FIVE and one personal grouping. In April it merged with various other groups to form the expanded DEMOCRATIC PARTY.

Mishima Yukio Mishima Yukio was a novelist, several of whose novels brought him international acclaim. Even though his tastes were greatly influenced by European art and culture, he came to deplore what he saw as the corruption of Japanese politics and degradation of Japanese culture by foreign influences. In the 1960s he founded a paramilitary group called the Shield Society (*Tate no kai*) [*see also* EXTREMIST MOVEMENTS (RIGHT)]. He designed a uniform for its members and was allowed to train the group using facilities of the Self-Defence Forces. Mishima was known for his ambiguous sexuality and for his body-building exercises, as well as for his far-right-wing views.

On 25 November 1970, Mishima with three other members of the Shield Society entered the Ichigaya (Tokyo) barracks of the Self-Defence Forces, and brandishing swords imprisoned the Inspector-General (*Sōkan*) in his office. Mishima then went out onto the balcony and made an inflammatory speech to the astonished personnel of the Self-Defence Forces, calling for the abolition of the CONSTITUTION OF 1946 and the post-war system of government. He appealed for the Self-Defence Forces to rise up, in the name of the Emperor (*Tennō*) (*see* EMPEROR AND POLITICS), but was met with a derisive response. He then returned to the Inspector-General's office where he and one other member of the Shield Society committed ritual suicide (*seppuku*).

The episode was a huge Japanese and international sensation, but had none of the effects that Mishima appears to have intended, though it greatly boosted sales of his books.

Mitsuzuka Hiroshi Born in 1927 in Sendai, Mitsuzuka Hiroshi graduated as a vet before taking a second degree in Law from Waseda University. He was secretary to a parliamentarian and a Miyagi prefectural councillor, while chairing the 'Miyagi Prefecture New Right Society' as well as aikidō and karate clubs. He entered the HOUSE OF REPRESENTATIVES for Sendai in 1972, and joined the Young Storm Society (*Seirankai*) of right-wing LIBERAL DEMOCRATIC PARTY (LDP) parliamentarians, formed in 1973.

He joined the right-leaning FUKUDA faction of the LDP, and became Minister of Transport (1985–6), Minister of International Trade and Industry (1988–9), later Foreign Minister, and Finance Minister (1997–8). He was also at various times LDP Secretary-General and Chairman of its Policy Affairs Research Council. On the death in May 1991 of ABE SHINTARŌ, who had inherited the Fukuda faction, he became its leader, eventually handing it over to MORI YOSHIRŌ.

Despite his far-right origins, Mitsuzuka was essentially a politician of the LDP mainstream. Only a mainstream politician could occupy four of the main offices of State, and his faction, though conservative, was of the party centre, not of the party fringe. In this he differed from the highly ideological NAKAGAWA ICHIRŌ and ISHIHARA SHINTARŌ, both of whom had been with him in the *Seirankai*. Like many of his kind, he was fundamentally a networking politician, and, as such, was not immune to accusations of engaging on 'money politics'.

Miyamoto Kenji Miyamoto Kenji was the last leader of the JAPAN COMMUNIST PARTY (JCP) to have experienced what life was like as a Communist before 1945.

Born in 1908 in Yamaguchi, Miyamoto graduated from Tokyo Imperial University and became a literary critic, involved in 'proletarian literature'. Between 1932 and her death in 1951 he was married to Miyamoto Yuriko, perhaps the most powerful practitioner of this genre. He joined the (illegal) Communist Party in 1931, being by 1933 a full member of its central executive committee. Late in the same year Miyamoto and his group, suspecting that two members of the party secretariat were police spies, tortured to death one of them (Obata Tatsuo). The other, Oizumi Kenzō, confessed under torture to spying for the police. In the aftermath of this affair Miyamoto and others were arrested, remaining in prison until the end of the war.

Active in the recreated JCP after Japan's defeat, Miyamoto occupied powerful positions in its executive. In 1946 he was leading drafter of a Constitution for a 'People's Republic of Japan'. In the factional struggles that followed the Cominform criticism in January 1950, Miyamoto sided with the radical SHIGA YOSHIO, favouring a shift towards anti-US militancy. Driven underground in June 1950, he resurfaced in the mid-1950s and became Secretary-General in 1958. He broke with Shiga Yoshio in 1964 over the latter's support for the partial nuclear test ban treaty (which the USSR had signed), since China opposed it. But two years later, the JCP under Miyamoto spectacularly severed ties with the Maoist regime, and relations with China were frozen for a generation. Freed from control by either the USSR or China, the party gathered electoral support in the later 1960s and early 1970s, and some in the LIBERAL DEMOCRATIC PARTY came to regard it as a more serious threat than the JAPAN SOCIALIST PARTY. Miyamoto promoted 'modernisation' of the party platform to fit newly prosperous Japan. To counter this 'threat', conservatives publicised the 1930s spy lynching case, damaging Miyamoto's image and JCP popularity (though other factors were involved).

Miyamoto was a member of the HOUSE OF COUNCILLORS between 1977 and 1989, and Chairman of the JCP Central Committee from 1982 to 1997.

Further reading
Beckmann and Okubo (1969)
Central Committee, Japanese Communist Party (1984)
Swearingen and Langer (1952, 1968)

Miyazawa Kiichi A politician at the centre of Government for many years, Miyazawa was close to IKEDA HAYATO, like him a native of Hiroshima and an ex-official of the MINISTRY OF FINANCE. He also inherited, at several removes, the politically moderate Ikeda faction of the LIBERAL DEMOCRATIC PARTY (LDP). But while Ikeda had led Japan at the height of LDP supremacy, Miyazawa's prime ministership ended in his party's fall from office.

Born in 1919, he took the elite course into politics via Tokyo Imperial University and the Ministry of Finance, entering that ministry in 1941. After the war he was on Ikeda's staff when the latter was negotiating with the US Government, first in 1950 in negotiations towards a peace treaty, and in 1953 during the Ikeda–Robertson talks on DEFENCE. During those years he gained deep experience of how to deal with Americans, and perfected his English. His political career began in 1953, when he entered the HOUSE OF COUNCILLORS, but he moved to the HOUSE OF REPRESENTATIVES in 1967. Beginning with the Ikeda Cabinet of the early 1960s he nearly always held a key portfolio, including MITI Minister, Director of the Economic Planning Agency, Finance Minister (several times), Foreign Minister and Chief Cabinet Secretary.

When PRIME MINISTER OHIRA died during the election campaign in 1980, Miyazawa was widely tipped to succeed him, but SUZUKI ZENKŌ (of the same faction as both Ohira and Miyazawa) was chosen instead. During the 1980s it was widely assumed that he had missed his chance, and this seemed confirmed when he was fingered in the RECRUIT SCANDAL of 1988–9. But when the KAIFU Cabinet fell in 1991 in the aftermath of Gulf War controversies, Miyazawa found himself Prime Minister at the age of 72, at a time when the certainties of the Cold War were giving way to more complex international relations. How far foreign events influenced domestic politics is difficult to say, but in 1992–3 Miyazawa faced a critical situation within his own party.

Ironically, it was his inability, in early 1993, to deliver electoral reform that finally induced the defections that had been brewing since the previous year. His Government was brought down by defeat in a no-confidence motion, followed by defeat in general elections in July, leading to the first non-LDP Government in 38 years.

His financial experience was such that five years later, at the time of the Asian economic crisis in 1998, OBUCHI appointed him as his Finance Minister, a position he continued to hold during the MORI administration of 2000–1. When he finally stepped down, he was 81.

Further reading
Curtis (1999)
Stockwin (1999)

Mori Yoshirō A politician from the right wing of the LIBERAL DEMOCRATIC PARTY (LDP), Mori Yoshirō was PRIME MINISTER from April 2000 to April 2001. His popularity declined throughout that period.

Born in 1937 in Ishikawa, he graduated from Waseda University, was known as a college rugby player and became a journalist and secretary to a parliamentarian. At 32, in 1969, he was elected to the HOUSE OF REPRESENTATIVES for a district of Ishikawa. In 1973 he participated in the Young Storm Society (*Seirankai*), a group of right-wing LDP parliamentarians (including NAKAGAWA ICHIRŌ, ISHIHARA SHINTARŌ and WATANABE MICHIO), who entered into a 'blood pledge' (*keppan*) of solidarity. Mori's contribution to a book published by *Seirankai* was concerned entirely with education, and contained the following passage:

> They used to teach stories about the gods and how they created Japan. People now say that we shouldn't teach such stupid things, but whether they are true or false, I think we really ought to teach these romances to our children. Children know whether they are true or false – in any case nobody knows who the real ancestors of the Japanese were – there are lots of dreams embodied in these fables, and children themselves should work out what doesn't fit reality and criticise what is silly about them. The idea is quite wrong that because they believe these stories

they will go wrong when they grow up. After all it's the same in America and Europe, where Jesus Christ is the product of fables.

Ishihara Shintarō *et al.*, *Seirankai: keppan to aikoku no ronri* (Young Storm Society: the Logic of the Blood Pledge and Patriotism), Tokyo, Roman, 1973, p. 128.

Mori became Education Minister in 1983, Minister of Trade and Industry in 1992 and Minister of Construction in 1995. He also held various top party positions (including the secretary-generalship under OBUCHI), and inherited the leadership of the FUKUDA (later MITSUZUKA) faction. Like many LDP politicians, he was implicated in the RECRUIT SCANDAL of the late 1980s. When Prime Minister Obuchi suffered a stroke in April 2000, Mori was chosen to succeed him. He soon met trouble for gaffes such as: 'Japan is a country of the gods with the Emperor at its centre', which reminded some people of pre-war ideology. His reputation fell further when the LDP and its coalition partner the CLEAN GOVERNMENT PARTY (*Kōmeitō*) lost seats at the Lower House general elections of July. Despite electoral losses and declining popular support, he hung on to power and survived a threatened revolt by the reformist, KATŌ KŌICHI, in November. The early months of 2001, however, saw his support decline to the point where his party could no longer sustain him. In February he continued playing golf after being informed that several Japanese had died in a collision between a US submarine and a Japanese trawler, and instances of corruption in his Government kept recurring. His economic policies made little impact. More positively, during the final seven months of his term, talks between Japan and Russia to find a settlement of the disputed 'northern territories' issue came close to a historic breakthrough. This process, however, was abortive since in April he finally resigned and was replaced as Prime Minister by the overwhelmingly popular KOIZUMI JUNICHIRŌ, who also inherited leadership of the Mori faction.

Morita Akio The co-founder, with Ibuka Masaru, of the Sony Corporation, Morita Akio was a legendary business leader, exercising substantial influence over establishment thinking about business and industry. His core belief was that manufacturing industry should be the heart of any economy, and he was sceptical about what he regarded as the extreme short-term perspectives prevalent in the financial sector. He was a persuasive speaker – in English as well as Japanese – and a convinced internationalist who loved to pour scorn on theories stressing Japanese 'uniqueness'. Nevertheless, in the late 1980s he co-authored with the nationalist ISHIHARA SHINTARŌ an anti-American tract entitled *The Japan that Can Say No*, later, however, regretting having done so.

He was born in January 1921, son of a *sake* brewer in Nagoya. In 1946, amidst the ruins of post-war Japan, he founded with Ibuka a company called Tokyo Tsūshin Denki (Tokyo Communication Electrics), and was able eventually to persuade reluctant bureaucrats to allow the company to manufacture transistors on licence from the United States. Transistors proved a spectacular success, and in 1958 Morita gave the company a name with more international resonance – Sony (from *sonus*, the Latin for 'sound'). In 1970 Sony became the first Japanese company to be quoted on the New York stock exchange, and set up its first factory in the United States in 1972. The company also began manufacturing in Britain (South Wales) and elsewhere. The Sony Walkman in the 1970s brought the company further international fame, particularly among the young (though not necessarily their parents). On the other hand, its purchase in the late 1980s of CBS Records and Columbia Pictures at the height of the Japanese 'bubble economy' caused noisy US resentment without much compensating economic benefit.

Morita suffered a severe stroke in December 1993 and died in October 1999.

Further reading
Ishihara and Morita (1989)
Morita (1994)

Murayama Tomiichi Murayama was the first Socialist PRIME MINISTER since 1947. His election amazed most observers, but it had a certain logic, however improbable it might appear. And he lasted for longer than most people expected. His administration was not without achievement, though it proved disastrous for his party.

Born in 1924 in Oita (Kyūshū), Murayama was in local politics before being elected to the HOUSE OF REPRESENTATIVES in 1972. He was on the left of the JAPAN SOCIALIST PARTY (JSP), but was used to dealing with the Liberal Democrats through work in the parliamentary policy committee. Following the formation of the HOSOKAWA coalition Cabinet in August 1993, the JSP forced its Chairman, YAMAHANA, out of office because of the party's defeat in the July elections, and Murayama replaced him. Thus began his unlikely path to Prime Minister. When Hosokawa resigned the following April, Ozawa attempted to weld into one party the disparate parties of the Hosokawa coalition. But his deliberate omission of the Socialists propelled Murayama into talks with LIBERAL DEMOCRATIC PARTY (LDP) leaders. Essentially the Socialists were looking for the highest bidder, and shrewdly the LDP offered a coalition with Murayama as Prime Minister. In June a coalition Government was launched centred on the JSP and the LDP. Both being defenders of vested interests, their alliance was not quite so bizarre as it appeared.

The Murayama Government lasted from June 1994 until January 1996, when Murayama stepped down in favour of the LDP's HASHIMOTO. In that period he tackled with some success compensation for victims of violence, compensation for victims of Minamata disease, and the question of war apology. On the fiftieth anniversary of the defeat, Murayama proffered a clearer apology for Japan's actions than might have come from an LDP Prime Minister. His efforts, however, to have Parliament issue an agreed apology were less successful.

The early months of 1995 saw the GREAT HANSHIN–AWAJI EARTHQUAKE, centred on Kōbe, and the release of sarin gas on the Tokyo underground. In both these cases, Government disaster preparedness was found lacking, and attention was diverted to this issue. Effort was spent revising laws relating to religious sects, given the suspicion that had fallen on the *Aum Shinrikyō* for the sarin gas release (*see* AUM SHINRIKYŌ AND THE POLITICS OF MASS POISONING). Although the earthquake postponed a JSP split, Murayama was forced by his position to abandon traditional JSP opposition to the Self-Defence Forces and the Japan–US Security Treaty – a change that was reluctantly endorsed, *ex-post facto*, by the JSP itself. He also dropped objections to compulsory use of the *kimigayo* anthem and the *hinomaru* flag in schools. The JSP never recovered from this abandonment of its *raison d'être*.

Murayama resigned as Prime Minister and JSP Chairman in January 1996 and retired from politics in 2000.

Further reading
Curtis (1999)
Stockwin (1999)

N

Nakagawa Ichirō Born in 1925 in Hokkaidō, Nakagawa was first elected to the HOUSE OF REPRESENTATIVES for the LIBERAL DEMOCRATIC PARTY (LDP) in 1963. He first came to national attention as a member of the *Seirankai* (Young Storm Society) in 1973. The *Seirankai* was a group of hard-line right wingers in the LDP, who declared their loyalty to the 'Free World' in its struggle against Communism, and called for an improvement in moral standards, including a return to the teaching of strict morality through the education system. They argued vigorously that Japan needed a new Constitution written and endorsed by Japanese, not the current 'peace Constitution', which they argued had been imposed on a defeated Japan by the US occupiers (*see* CONSTITUTION OF 1946). This, of course, was standard right-wing rhetoric, but what attracted media attention was that they entered into a 'blood pledge' (*keppan*) of mutual loyalty.

Nakagawa was also quintessentially an agricultural politician, representing in particular the dairying interests of his sprawling constituency in eastern Hokkaidō, and working for the maintenance of high producer rice prices. In 1977–8 he was Agriculture Minister under the ideologically congenial Prime Minister, FUKUDA TAKEO. He founded his own small right-wing faction within the LDP early in 1980, and his faction was one of the three that abstained in a no-confidence motion against the OHIRA Government in May 1980, thus bringing it down. Ohira's successor, SUZUKI ZENKŌ, appointed him Minister of Science and Technology, possibly to forestall further acts of dissent. In November 1982 Suzuki resigned as LDP President (and Prime Minister). Nagakawa, along with NAKASONE YASUHIRO, KŌMOTO TOSHIO and ABE SHINTARŌ, contested the primary elections for the party presidency. He was only able to stand because the Fukuda faction 'lent' him enough members to give him 50 endorsements from LDP MPs, which they did in order to ensure the minimum of four candidates required for a primary election to be held. His percentage of the vote of party members, however, was a derisory 6.8 per cent.

Some months later he committed suicide for reasons that remain obscure.

Nakasone Yasuhiro Prime Minister between 1982 and 1987, Nakasone Yasuhiro pursued policies of privatisation, financial conservatism, educational reform, reinforcement of military capacities, and consolidation of the security relationship with the United States.

Born in 1918 in Gunma, he graduated from Tokyo Imperial University and entered the Home Ministry. Shortly thereafter the war caught up with him and he served in the navy for the duration. After the defeat in 1945 he briefly returned to the Government BUREAUCRACY but resigned and stood for the HOUSE OF REPRESENTATIVES in the general elections of April 1947. He was elected under the label of the DEMOCRATIC PARTY (I) for a constituency in Gunma that he went on to represent for more than fifty years.

During the Occupation period Nakasone campaigned on issues relating to national sovereignty, and was critical of YOSHIDA

SHIGERU, whom he regarded as a Prime Minister too ready to do the bidding of General MacArthur. In January 1951, as a young parliamentarian, he presented a 28-page petition to MacArthur, having previously sent copies to leading politicians in the United States. In it, he criticised the Occupation for going on too long, and called for rapid independence for Japan, including granting of the right to determine her own DEFENCE policy without external interference.

Nakasone remained on the anti-Yoshida side of the conservative camp, and joined the faction of KŌNO ICHIRŌ. After the amalgamation of conservative groups into the LIBERAL DEMOCRATIC PARTY (LDP) in 1955, he began to promote the idea of a popularly elected PRIME MINISTER. He believed that the current system whereby the Prime Minister was elected by Parliament tended to perpetuate bureaucratic dominance. The proposal was not widely accepted, but brought him to popular attention. His first Cabinet post, that of Director of the SCIENCE AND TECHNOLOGY AGENCY, came in 1959, so that he became a member of the KISHI Cabinet. During the SECURITY TREATY REVISION CRISIS of 1960, he argued from an early stage for postponement of the Eisenhower visit.

In 1966, following the death of Kōno Ichirō, he inherited the bulk of the Kōno faction, and as faction leader proved adept at ducking and weaving in the constant game of factional advantage. He became Minister of Transport in the SATŌ Government from 1976, Director of the DEFENCE AGENCY in 1970, and Minister of International Trade and Industry in the first TANAKA Government in 1972. The second of these positions enabled him to express relatively radical views on defence, and brought him to international attention. As Director of the ADMINISTRATIVE MANAGEMENT AGENCY in the Suzuki Cabinet from 1980, he put in place the Second Extraordinary Administrative Reform Commission, which concentrated on retrenchment of Government spending.

In November 1982, strongly backed by Tanaka Kakuei, Nakasone became Prime Minister. His first administration contained a high proportion of ministers belonging to the Tanaka faction. Gradually, however, he came to dominate the Government, making extensive use of personal advisers and special commissions that he had set up. He set his Government a number of tasks. One was privatisation of public enterprises. Of these, the most important was the Japan National Railways (*Kokutetsu*), whose finances were in severe deficit. They were split up into a number of regional companies, and the opportunity was taken to weaken the once powerful railway unions. Another was the field of telecommunications, where the monopoly position of NTT (Nippon Telephone and Telegraph) was degraded and competition admitted.

Another area was defence. With his background as a defence enthusiast, Nakasone sought so far as he was able to push back the boundaries of what was possible in terms of defence policy. He breached the ceiling of 1 per cent of GNP for defence spending, though spending soon sank below the ceiling again. He permitted sale of military-related technology to the United States, though not to great effect, and he emphasised the 'common destiny' of Japan and the United States. He controversially visited the Yasukuni Shrine in Tokyo in his official capacity [*see also* RELIGION AND POLITICS]. Throughout the 1980s defence spending was increasing to a marked extent, so that by the end of the decade Japan had impressive defence capacity. Much of this was Nakasone's doing.

The economic side of Japan–United States relations needed concentrated attention while he was Prime Minister [*see also* UNITED STATES, RELATIONS WITH]. The Plaza Accords in 1985 led to a substantial appreciation of the yen against the dollar, while the MAEKAWA REPORT (which he commissioned) recommended wholesale dismantling of Government regulation of industry and commerce. Few of its recommendations, however, were implemented.

Nakasone set up a major commission on education reform, but came up against determined resistance from the MINISTRY OF EDUCATION, which was unhappy about his idea of applying free market principles to education.

As a unifying slogan to encapsulate his programme of reforms, he used the phrase 'settling accounts with post-war politics' (*sengo seiji no sōkessan*). Clearly, one of his main aims was also to establish a sense of national prestige, and he contributed to this by the good rapport he was able to establish with Ronald Reagan, Margaret Thatcher and other world leaders.

While he was Prime Minister, he faced two Lower House general elections (1983 and 1986). The first, in the aftermath of the Tanaka Lockheed verdict [*see also* LOCKHEED SCANDAL], was a poor result for the LDP, but the second, being a double election (for both houses), was a great victory for Nakasone, and strengthened his regime. It is surprising, therefore, that in 1987, after he broke an election promise to reveal that a VAT tax was to be introduced, his popularity rapidly fell, and he ceased to be Prime Minister in November 1987, to be replaced by TAKESHITA NOBORU.

Nakasone, like most other leading LDP politicians, was damaged by the RECRUIT SCANDAL of 1988–9. He handed over leadership of his faction to WATANABE MICHIO in February 1990, but remained in Parliament.

Further reading
Curtis (1999)
Nakasone (1999)
Stockwin (1999)

Narita Tomomi Born in 1912, Narita first entered the HOUSE OF REPRESENTATIVES for the JAPAN SOCIALIST PARTY (JSP) in 1947, and was then elected for his home constituency in Kagawa at every election up to and including that of 1976. When the party split in 1951 over the peace settlement, he joined the Left Socialist Party, where he was a member of the SUZUKI faction, as he was in the reunited JSP from 1955. After EDA SABURŌ launched 'structural reform' in 1960–1, Narita became his closest lieutenant in promoting it. Gradually, however, it became clear that he was less committed to Eda's reformist ideas than was Eda himself. When Eda was forced to resign at the party Congress in November 1962, Narita was elected Secretary-General in his stead, beating the Sasaki faction candidate, Yamamoto Kōichi. When KAWAKAMI resigned as Chairman in 1965 and was succeeded by Eda's leftist rival, Sasaki, Narita stayed on as Secretary-General, and moved somewhat towards the Sasaki approach. In August 1967 Sasaki and Narita both resigned their positions over a row about health insurance law revision, and were replaced, respectively, by KATSUMATA SEIICHI and Yamamoto Kōichi. A year later, however, the Katsumata leadership collapsed, and after tortuous factional struggles Narita was elected party Chairman, with Eda as his Secretary-General. Their approaches had diverged, however, and in November 1970 Eda unsuccessfully challenged Narita for the Chairmanship. ISHIBASHI MASASHI succeeded him as Secretary-General.

The Narita–Ishibashi partnership lasted until 1977, gave marginally more stability to the party, and coincided with modest improvements in JSP electoral fortunes. Both Narita and his deputy strove to distance themselves from factional struggles in order to hold the party together. Nevertheless, Eda on the right and the Socialism Association (*Shakaishugi Kyōkai*) on the left continued to tear the party in opposite directions. When Eda and his group defected from the JSP in 1977, Narita stepped down as Chairman and retired from politics. Though scarcely an inspiring leader, he considered politics to be the art of the possible, and came to look askance at Eda's fervent modernising campaigns on the grounds that they risked destroying the party.

Further rading
Hrebenar (2000)
Johnson (2000)

National Co-operative Party (Kokumin Kyōdōtō) *see* conservative parties, 1945–55

National Democratic Party (NDP, Kokumin Minshutō) *see* conservative parties, 1945–55

National Labour Union Alliance (Zenkoku Rōdō Kumiai Sōrengō, Zenrōren II) This was a national labour centre set up in November 1989 in disagreement with the stated aims of the JAPANESE TRADE UNION COUNCIL (*Rengō*), when the latter was set up in a merger of the major pre-existing union federations earlier the same year. Its leaders castigated *Rengō* for perpetuating what they saw as the heinous Japanese right-wing tradition of 'labour–management co-operation'.

National Labour Union Liaison Council (Zenkoku Rōdō Kumiai Renraku Kyōgikai, Zenrōren I) Zenrōren was founded in March 1947 as a loose organisation to maintain linkages between the fractions union federations of left and right – respectively the CONGRESS OF INDUSTRIAL UNIONS (*Sanbetsu Kaigi*) and the ALL-JAPAN GENERAL FEDERATION OF LABOUR UNIONS (*Sōdōmei*) – in the aftermath of the banned general strike that had been scheduled for 1 February. Communist influence in it, however, was strong, so that the anti-Communist *Sōdōmei* federation left the Liaison Council in June 1948. A secondary influence within it was that of the *Mindō* movement (Democratisation Leagues), which was seeking to combat Communist influence.

Zenrōren ceased to exist in 1950, around the time that the General Council of Japanese Trade Unions (*Sōhyō*) was formed.

Further reading
Cole et al. (1966)
Levine (1958)

National Land Agency (Kokudochō) The National Land Agency was established in July 1974 as an external agency of the PRIME MINISTER'S OFFICE (*Sōrifu*), headed by a Minister of State as Director. It took over the land planning functions of the MINISTRY OF CONSTRUCTION (*Kensetsushō*). It was originally set up with the specific political purpose of putting into practice the recommendations of Prime Minister TANAKA's plan for the 'Reconstruction of the Japanese Archipelago', though there were much older precedents for an overall land planning agency of Government. It was staffed, in order of numbers, by officials transferred from the ECONOMIC PLANNING AGENCY (*Keizai kikakuchō*), the MINISTRY OF CONSTRUCTION and Capital Region Preparation Committee (*Shutoken seibi iinkai*). Its organisation consisted of a Director's Secretariat, Planning and Adjustment Bureau, Land Bureau, Capital Region Preparation Bureau, Regional Development Bureau and Fire Prevention Bureau.

In January 2001 it was amalgamated with the Ministry of Construction, MINISTRY OF TRANSPORT and Hokkaidō Development Agency to form the MINISTRY OF LAND, INFRASTRUCTURE AND TRANSPORT (*Kokudokōtsūshō*).

National Liaison Council of Independent Unions (Chūritsu Rōdō Kumiai Renraku Kaigi, Chūritsu Rōren) This federation of largely private sector unions was founded in 1956 in the aftermath of the split within the GENERAL COUNCIL OF JAPANESE TRADE UNIONS (*Sōhyō*) and the formation of the ALL-JAPAN TRADE UNION CONGRESS (*Zenrō Kaigi*). Its guiding philosophy was based on the idea of neutrality between left and right factions in the union movement and the aim of once more unifying the movement. It made some progress in this direction in the late 1970s and early 1980s, organising joint campaigns with other union groups. It dissolved in November 1987 with the formation of the JAPANESE TRADE UNION COUNCIL (*Rengō*). Shortly before its dissolution it accounted for 10 industrial unions and 1,640,000 unionists.

Further reading
Kume (1998)

National Liaison Council of Labour Unions (Zenkoku Rōdō Kumiai Renraku Kyōgikai, Zenrōkyō) With the amalgamation of the remaining GENERAL COUNCIL OF JAPANESE TRADE UNIONS (*Sōhyō*) unions into the JAPANESE TRADE UNION COUNCIL (*Rengō*) in December 1989, Ota Kaoru, Iwai Akira and others prominent in the leadership of *Sōhyō* since the mid-1950s decided to create a Liaison Council, separate from both the 'accommodationist' *Rengō* and the Communist-dominated NATIONAL LABOUR UNION ALLIANCE (*Zenrōren*). It aimed to further the *Sōhyō* aims of improving wages and conditions, promoting peace and democracy and confronting both Government and capital. *Zenrōkyō* was not conceived of as an exclusive national centre, and dual affiliation of constituent unions was permitted. At the time of its foundation it consisted of 38 constituent organisations having a combined total of some 500,000 members.

National Party (Kokumintō) *see* conservative parties, 1945–55

National Personnel Authority (NPA, Jinjiin)
The National Personnel Authority was a new administrative organ set up during the Allied Occupation in order to rationalise personnel recruitment and management within the public service as a whole. Whereas hitherto each ministry had run its own personnel policy with minimal interference from outside, the aim was now to standardise procedures, pay and conditions in the interests of democratisation and accountability.

The Authority was launched in 1948, as the result of the recommendations of the Hoover Mission (US Personnel Advisory Mission to Japan), and as part of the National Public Service Law enacted by the ASHIDA Government. Despite determined pressure from the CABINET and the bureaucracy, the NPA was set up as a full agency of Cabinet. It was given full authority to ensure that the standards set in the National Public Service Law should be met. Its budget was also protected.

Despite these auspicious beginnings, the NPA proved to be much weaker than envisaged by the Occupation. From the outset, it met concerted resistance from established ministries and agencies of Government, which had been used to organising their own personnel affairs. Tsuji lists the purposes of the NPA as 'democratising the old bureaucracy, keeping party politics out of personnel administration, guaranteeing impartiality in civil service appointments, and promoting administrative efficiency'. In practice, however, it has had to cope with fierce opposition. This comes principally from ministries determined to preserve as much as possible of their authority. But it also comes from the LIBERAL DEMOCRATIC PARTY that, being semi-permanently in power, tends to subvert the principle of political neutrality of civil servants. Also the public service unions resent being deprived of the right to collective bargaining, which means that the NPA is the body that recommends to Government changes in their wages and conditions.

Gradually, the NPA has become accepted within the Government BUREAUCRACY in its role of making regular recommendations so as to keep public service remuneration within the parameters of what can be expected in the private sector. Since it was established, the notion of promotion by merit has made progress in the public service, as has the principle of examinations. But there is still very little lateral movement between ministries, and individual ministries retain substantial control over their own promotion procedures. To some extent, these problems of the vertical structure of the Government bureaucracy have been addressed with the ADMINISTRATIVE REORGANISATION that took place in January 2001.

Further reading
Kim (1988)
Koh (1989)
Tsuji (ed.) (1984)

National Public Safety Committee (Kokka Kōan iinkai) This Committee was set up in 1948 as a consultative body to control and manage the police force. From the start it was made ultimately responsible to the PRIME MINISTER. The Police Law that was ratified in 1954 provided that a Minister of State should chair the Committee, and in addition to the Chairman there should be five members. Its task was to supervise the newly established Police Agency (*Keisatsuchō*). It was to oversee police training and information, criminal identification and crime statistics as well as police equipment. Some observers maintained, however, that real power over the police lay in the Police Agency, and that the Committee's role was inclined to be nominal or honorary.

With the implementation of ADMINISTRATIVE REORGANISATION in January 2001, the Committee became answerable to the Prime Minister by way of the CABINET OFFICE (*Naikakufu*).

nawabari (roping off spheres of jurisdiction)
This term is commonly used to denote demarcation of jurisdiction, territory or 'turf', typically between different bureaucratic agencies. Such demarcation disputes (*nawabari arasoi*) are a commonly recognised phenomenon in bureaucracies throughout the world, but some have argued (or assumed) that it is particularly prevalent in Japan. Weight is given to this view by the unusual stability of bureaucratic structures in Japanese Government until the ADMINISTRATIVE REORGANISATION of January 2001, by 'vertical administration' and by lack of lateral movement of officials from one ministry

or agency to another. *Nawabari* may plausibly be regarded as the other side of the coin of institutional loyalty. Whether institutional loyalty is to be explained as a cultural expression, or as the result of entrenched structures rewarding loyalty, is a chicken-and-egg question. Cultural factors privileging loyalty may explain the structures, which in turn reward loyalty to those structures.

The *nawabari* phenomenon has come under intense criticism since the 1990s. Some saw it as in part responsible for the poor co-ordination of relief services after the GREAT HANSHIN–AWAJI EARTHQUAKE. It was also regarded as responsible for inefficient duplication of services, where different agencies were competing with each other. The reorganisation of central Government administration put into place in January 2001 involved an attempt to break down entrenched institutional loyalties through amalgamation of ministries and rationalisation of functions. Other innovations, such as sub-contracting of some functions to the private sector, increasing the number of lateral postings, and external vetting of performance, have been attempted in an attempt to break down the kind of institutional exclusiveness leading to *nawabari*. At the time of writing in 2002, some progress had been made, but the results were mixed.

nemawashi (digging round the roots, preparing the ground) This word derives from the practice of carefully digging around the roots of a tree prior to replanting it elsewhere. Metaphorically, it means preparing the ground for a decision by extensive consultation with interested parties.

This points to a phenomenon of great significance in Japanese politics. 'Debate' in some prefectural councils (assemblies) is literally scripted in advance, and there is very little departure from a written script that has been previously prepared. Proposals of a particular government ministry are put to the relevant division of the LIBERAL DEMOCRATIC PARTY (LDP) Policy Affairs Research Council (PARC) before going to the relevant standing committee of the HOUSE OF REPRESENTATIVES. Within the PARC there is normally little debate, because the ministry has conducted *nemawashi* with all the PARC members beforehand. Another example is provided by meetings of CABINET. These are notoriously short and perfunctory in most (though not all) cases. The reason is that they are preceded by meetings of the Conference of Administrative Vice-Ministers (*jimu jikan kaigi*), in which the administrative heads of each full ministry and agency of Government establish an agreed position on the matters coming up for decision in Cabinet. But even these meetings can be quite perfunctory, because an intensive *nemawashi* process has been conducted beforehand. Since the advent of coalition Government from the 1990s the LDP's coalition partners have to be brought into the decision-making process, but this essentially means an extension of the *nemawashi* process to include them.

A central principle exemplified by *nemawashi* is that if all parties to a decision are extensively consulted beforehand and feel that they have had a part in the decision-making, they will be committed to that decision once it is taken. An obvious disadvantage is that it slows down the process of taking decisions, particularly when there are many participants. On the other hand, in principle at least, it should lead to rapid and effective implementation of the decision taken because of the extent of commitment that has been created. It can cause problems in international negotiations, where the Japanese side comes with a position established through *nemawashi*, but which is difficult to change without further extensive internal consultation. The negotiation process thus becomes asymmetrical, since the foreign negotiators have greater freedom to decide.

The rights and wrongs of *nemawashi* are somewhat complex. The prefectural council example given above sounds undemocratic because it appears to stifle real (as distinct from superficial) debate. On the other hand, in the sense that the interested parties have been consulted, it cannot be regarded as the imposition of decision from above. Indeed, the criticisms of Japanese decision-making procedures conducted since the 1990s suggest that the problem lies more in *nemawashi*-induced immobilism (too many interests having to be consulted and maintaining a stranglehold over decision-making) than in absence of democracy as such. Finally, however, it has negative implications for political transparency, as critics have been increasingly pointing out.

Nemawashi has its parallels in other advanced industrial democracies, but in Koh's words 'very few can rival Japan in the thoroughness with which such preparatory work is carried out'. Decision-making, like transplanting trees, is a delicate process.

Further reading
Koh (1989)

New Frontier Party (NFP, Shinshintō) Originally called the 'New New Party' (also *Shinshintō* but with one different character), the New Frontier Party at its height in 1995 commanded a higher proportion of parliamentary seats than any other Opposition party since 1955. Quintessentially an OZAWA creation, it had been conceived originally as an amalgam of the parties that had participated in the HOSOKAWA coalition. From his experience of that coalition, however, Ozawa had become hostile to the Socialists, and sought to exclude them from an abortive attempt at party building attempted during the HATA Government period. This was a fateful decision, because it in effect pushed the Socialists and NEW PARTY HARBINGER (*Sakigake*) into the arms of the LIBERAL DEMOCRATIC PARTY (LDP).

What was to become the New Frontier Party was launched in December 1994. It was an amalgam of nine different parties and groupings, including most importantly Ozawa's own JAPAN RENEWAL PARTY (*Shinseitō*), the Buddhist CLEAN GOVERNMENT PARTY (CGP, *Kōmeitō*), Hosokawa's JAPAN NEW PARTY (*Nihon shintō*), and the long-established DEMOCRATIC SOCIALIST PARTY (*Minshatō*) based on moderate labour unions. Particularly important from Ozawa's point of view was the adherence of the CGP because of its proven organisational ability (based on the *Sōka Gakkai* lay Buddhist organisation) and financial strength. But if the CGP provided organisation and funding, it was also a most imperfectly assimilated element in the new party. Indeed, its Upper House contingent never joined the NFP, while its local branches maintained a substantial measure of autonomy (especially financial) even though technically merged into the NFP.

Ozawa was determined to pursue the aim of a party political system where power would alternate between two major parties. To this end, he set up what he termed 'tomorrow's Cabinet', on the model of shadow cabinets in Britain and elsewhere. The first leader of the NFP was the former Prime Minister, KAIFU TOSHIKI, but in December 1995 Ozawa himself was elected leader through a system of election whereby any member of the public could vote on payment of a small fee. The NFP had a notable success in the HOUSE OF COUNCILLORS elections of July 1995, but actually lost seats in the Lower House elections of October 1996. Thereafter, it suffered the defections of the HATA group (December 1996) and the Hosokawa group (June 1997), both apparently resentful at what they saw as Ozawa's autocratic style of leadership. By the second half of 1997 it was plain that the party was failing, and at the end of December Ozawa announced its dissolution.

The idea of combining elements out of the LDP stable with those originating in the *Sōka Gakkai* was highly original, and, although it eventually failed, it foreshadowed a later rather durable coalition between the reconstituted CGP and the LDP itself. What failed comprehensively, however, was Ozawa's cherished aim of using the NFP to foster two-party alternating government based on real policy choices. Apart from anything else, the NFP was hardly a radical alternative to the LDP. For instance, in the summer of 1995, the party abstained *en masse* from voting on a parliamentary resolution to apologise for the behaviour of Japanese armed forces in Asia during the Second World War.

Further reading
Curtis (1999)
Stockwin (1999)

New Liberal Club (NLC, Shin Jiyū Kurabu)
The New Liberal Club was a group that broke from the LIBERAL DEMOCRATIC PARTY (LDP) in June 1976 in protest against the LOCKHEED SCANDAL. Five Lower House members and one from the Upper House, led by KŌNO YŌHEI (son of KŌNO ICHIRŌ), defected, but the group won 17 seats in the Lower House elections of December 1976.

The party roundly criticised LDP decay and corruption, and argued for a new conservatism that would combine free market economics with concern for social justice, the environment and land use, reduce the power of Government BUREAUCRACY, promote education (*see* EDUCATION AND POLITICS), and protect the family (*see* FAMILY AND POLITICS). They supported the Japan–US Mutual Security Treaty, advocated a peace treaty with China, and opted out of promoting constitutional revision, declaring it too divisive.

In the late 1970s they occupied a pivotal parliamentary position, given a paper-thin LDP majority, and with other opposition parties were able to insist on tax cuts in the 1977 budget. Their initial electoral successes, however, proved ephemeral. Co-operation with other opposition parties led their Secretary-General, Nishioka Takeo, to defect in 1979 and return to the LDP. The NLC only won four seats in the October 1979 Lower House elections, though they improved to 12 in the elections of June 1980. In the elections of December 1983, with NAKASONE now Prime Minister, the NLC won only eight seats, but the LDP found itself once again with a bare majority. Nakasone therefore invited the NLC to enter into a coalition government, and gave it one position in Cabinet. After the double elections of July 1986 bestowed on the LDP a thumping majority, nearly all of the NLC defectors were reabsorbed into the LDP.

Even though this first LDP split failed, it represented a – largely urban – agenda of reform, which others would take up in the 1990s.

Further reading
Curtis (1988)

New Party Amity (Shintō Yūai) With the collapse of the NEW FRONTIER PARTY (NFP) in December 1997, former members of the DEMOCRATIC SOCIALIST PARTY within the NFP briefly formed themselves as the New Party Amity. The name *Yūai* was reminiscent of the *Yūaikai*, Japan's first labour union, around the time of the First World War. In April 1998, however, it merged with the expanded DEMOCRATIC PARTY.

New Party Future (Shintō Mirai) In April 1994, a group of five parliamentarians, led by Kano Michihiko, defected from the LIBERAL DEMOCRATIC PARTY and formed the New Party Future. This group was absorbed into the NEW FRONTIER PARTY (*Shinshintō*) on its formation in December 1994, but, when that party split apart just three years later, Kano and his group formed a discrete (though temporary) party called VOICE OF THE PEOPLE (*Kokumin no Koe*). It is not clear how far the motives of this group related to policy and how far to opportunism in times of political instability.

New Party Harbinger (NPH, Shintō Sakigake) Following the failure of MIYAZAWA KIICHI, as Prime Minister, to introduce reform of the electoral system early in 1993 (*see* ELECTION SYSTEMS), two quite separate groups defected from the LDP. Chronologically the first, but also much the smaller, of these was the group led by Takemura Masayoshi, which went on to form the New Party Harbinger. (The second was the HATA–OZAWA group that formed the JAPAN RENEWAL PARTY.) It won 13 Lower House seats in the general elections of July 1993, and participated in the HOSOKAWA coalition Government formed on 9 August.

Early expectations of a merger between the NPH and Hosokawa's Japan New Party were dashed by a rift that emerged early in 1994 between Takemura and Hosokawa over proposals to increase consumption tax from 3 to 7 per cent. Following Hosokawa's resignation and the brief interlude of the Hata Government, the NPH joined in a three-way coalition with the LIBERAL DEMOCRATIC PARTY (LDP) and JAPAN SOCIALIST PARTY under the Socialist MURAYAMA as Prime Minister. Takemura became Minister of Finance for a while. But in the next Lower House elections of October 1996 the NPH lost all but two of its seats, and although, together with the rump of the Socialist Party, it remained in coalition with the LDP, it did not receive any Cabinet positions. The party dissolved late in 1998.

New Party Peace (Shintō heiwa) When the NEW FRONTIER PARTY collapsed in December 1997, one of the six new parties to emerge from its ruins was the New Party Peace, consisting of most of the former CLEAN GOV-

ERNMENT PARTY (*Kōmeitō*) members of the Lower House. This proved to be the first stage in reconstructing the CGP, whose dispersed elements were brought back together into a single party in 1998.

New Politics Club (Shinsei Club) *see* conservative parties, 1945–55

New Socialist Party (NSP, Shinshakaitō)
The New Socialist Party was formed on 1 January 1996 by five defectors from the JAPAN SOCIALIST PARTY (JSP), led by Yatabe Osamu of the HOUSE OF COUNCILLORS. The party was set up in protest against the dilution by the JSP of its pacifist spirit while Murayama was Prime Minister (June 1994–January 1996). On peace issues its platform read:

> We seek to defend the Constitution, and spread the spirit of article 9 throughout the world. We wish to make clear the nation's responsibility for former aggression and war, to make apology and compensation for the victims, and to implement correct education about history. We aim to reduce and eliminate US military bases in Japan, and by the start of the 21st century create an Okinawa and Japan free of bases. We aim at renunciation of war and unarmed neutralism, and will promote a general reduction in the Self Defence Forces and international co-operation for disarmament. We shall create a framework for peace maintenance in Asia and the Pacific, abolish the Japan–US Security Treaty, and conclude a treaty of peace and friendship. Aiming at the elimination of nuclear weapons, we shall attempt to create a non-nuclear zone in North-East Asia. We shall promote a democratic and fair reform of the United Nations.

The platform also attacked the handling of taxation and financial issues, promoted the interests of lower income groups, women (*see* WOMEN AND POLITICS) and minorities (*see* MINORITIES AND POLITICS), advocated radical reform of bureaucratic practice and called for single-member parliamentary constituencies to be scrapped.

At the 1996 and 2000 Lower House elections, and the 1998 and 2001 Upper House elections, the NSP failed to have any of its candidates elected. Thus after 2001 it had no parliamentary representation.

Nikaidō Susumu Nikaidō Susumu was a Kagoshima (Kyūshū) politician, born in 1909, whose failed attempt to challenge NAKASONE in 1984 came close to splitting the LIBERAL DEMOCRATIC PARTY (LDP).

He was first elected to the House of Representatives for a Kagoshima district in the first post-war elections of 1946. He went on to win 16 of the 19 elections between then and the last one he contested, in 1993. A member of the LDP from its formation in 1955, he became a strong supporter of TANAKA KAKUEI, and extremely active within his faction. He held two minor Cabinet positions in 1966–7 (Director of the Hokkaidō Development Agency and Director of the Science and Technology Agency), but then was Tanaka's Chief Cabinet Secretary in 1972–4, and, as such, played an important role in negotiations for normalising relations with China. After the fall of the Tanaka Government he held certain party positions, but never major offices of state.

He thus arrived with an insubstantial administrative background at the episode that made him famous. In 1984 FUKUDA TAKEO, SUZUKI ZENKŌ, KŌMOTO TOSHIO and others backed him in a bid for the party presidency to replace Nakasone, who was seeking a second two-year term. The idea was to have him form a Government with the support of the CLEAN GOVERNMENT PARTY (*Kōmeitō*) and DEMOCRATIC SOCIALIST PARTY (*Minshatō*). The plotters had held talks with the leaders of those two parties, and, had the scheme succeeded, it would presumably have split the LDP and led to a centrist coalition Government. Tanaka, however, vetoed the plan. When Takeshita later took over leadership of the Tanaka faction, Nikaidō held aloof.

Further reading
Masumi (1995)

Nishio Suehiro One of the few labour and Socialist party leaders from the pre-war period who was genuinely working class, Nishio was also among the most able of them.

Born in Kagawa (Shikoku) in 1891, he left

school at an early age to work in Osaka, and by 1915 was already involved with the labour movement. Subsequently he led a series of unions and was involved in many disputes. In 1926, already showing the anti-Marxist attitudes that marked him out among unionists, he helped found the Social Masses Party (*Shakai Minshūtō*), which remained the basis of his group identification well into the post-war period. In 1928 he was first elected to Parliament for an Osaka constituency, which continued to return him over many successive elections. In 1938 he was expelled from the house because of an intervention during a debate on the Government's universal conscription legislation. Though supporting the bill, he referred to its promoters as 'like Hitler, like Mussolini, *like Stalin*'.

After the war he participated in the founding of the JAPAN SOCIALIST PARTY (JSP), and was the principal 'force behind the throne' in the KATAYAMA coalition Government of 1947, where he was Minister of State and Chief Cabinet Secretary. During the ASHIDA Government, however, he was accused of complicity in the SHŌWA DENKŌ SCANDAL, from which it took several years to clear his name. Seriously unhappy with the left-wing influence over the unified JSP in the charged atmosphere of the late 1950s, he pulled his 'Social Masses' faction out of the party in 1959–60, followed by some members of the 'Japan Labour' faction of KAWAKAMI. This led to the founding of the DEMOCRATIC SOCIALIST PARTY (DSP, *Minshu Shakaitō*, later *Minshatō*) in 1960. The political philosophy of the DSP was based on welfare state notions derived from the British Labour Party, and it was solidly anti-Communist. Organisationally, it was close to the ALL-JAPAN TRADE UNION CONGRESS (*Zenrō*), later JAPAN CONFEDERATION OF LABOUR (*Dōmei*), which had split from the GENERAL COUNCIL OF JAPANESE TRADE UNIONS (*Sōhyō*) in 1954. Relations between the two sides of the labour movement were bitter at this time, and this was reflected in relations between the two Socialist Parties. The DLP did less well electorally than its founders had expected, but was a durable minor party. Nishio was Chairman from 1960 to 1967, when he stepped down. He retired from politics in 1972 and died in 1981.

Further reading
Cole *et al.* (1966)
Stockwin (1968)
Totten (1966)

'Nixon shocks', 1971 In the summer of 1971 Satō Eisaku had been Prime Minister for more than six years, and the Japanese economy had been growing at an average rate of around 10 per cent since the late 1950s. An anticipated crisis over the term of the Japan–US Security Treaty had been averted the previous year, but the United States was bogged down in Vietnam. Relations between Japan and the United States had come under strain owing to a textile trade dispute that owed more to attempts by President Nixon and Prime Minister Satō to reward their domestic constituencies than to the economic importance of the issue. Satō had loyally backed US policies on China, and worked to block recognition of Beijing as the legitimate Government of China (which would delegitimise Taipei). But the poor personal relations between Nixon and Satō resulting from the textile dispute, and concern on the US side about the growing strength of the Japanese economy, fuelled US distrust of Japan. Meanwhile, a mood was beginning to develop among Japanese policy makers that Japan faced isolation in world affairs [*see also* UNITED STATES, RELATIONS WITH; CHINA (PRC AND ROC), RELATIONS WITH].

In these circumstances, policy-makers in Tokyo reacted with disbelief to the news they received on 16 July 1971, that President Nixon planned to visit Beijing the following year. It was less the news of his planned visit that caused such shock, as the fact that the message reached the Japanese Prime Minister only a few minutes before a formal announcement was made simultaneously in Washington and Beijing. This lack of consultation on such a key matter by their ally and protector created reactions of anxiety and insecurity. A change of policy on China by the United States could perhaps have been anticipated, but nobody imagined the United States would not consult.

Then on 15 August (a significant date in the Japanese calendar), President Nixon announced suspension of the convertibility of the $US into gold, together with a temporary 10 per cent surcharge on imports into the United States. A principal purpose of these measures was to force Japan to revalue the yen, which had been pegged at ¥360 to the $US since 1949. The Bank of Japan tried to resist this for a while, but soon had to revalue and, ultimately, to adopt floating exchange rates.

These actions by the US President quickly undermined the credibility of the Japanese Prime Minister, who had been resisting strong domestic pressure (including pressure from within the LIBERAL DEMOCRATIC PARTY) for a more flexible policy towards recognition of Beijing, in deference to US policy. In the following July he ceased to be Prime Minister, his successor being TANAKA KAKUEI, who negotiated diplomatic recognition of Beijing within three months.

Further reading
Fukui, in Pempel (ed.) (1977)
Masumi (1995)

Nosaka Sanzō With TOKUDA KYŪICHI, Nosaka (pseudonyms: Okano Susumu, Lin Che) was one of the two principal JAPAN COMMUNIST PARTY (JCP) leaders between 1945 and 1950. Unlike the incandescent Tokuda, he was a sophisticated intellectual with an acute strategic sense.

Born in 1892 in Yamaguchi, Nosaka graduated from Keiō University and worked for the *Yūaikai* labour union before going in 1919 to the London School of Economics, where he researched labour movements under Clement Attlee. Active in British labour politics, he joined the British Communist Party in 1920, but was expelled from Britain in 1921, returned to Japan via various countries in 1922, and joined the new (illegal) JCP. He was in prison in 1923 and again arrested in 1928, along with Tokuda and many others. He was able to negotiate his release in 1930 (ostensibly for eye treatment), and in 1931 managed to leave Japan for Moscow, his base for the next nine years. There he became a member of the Comintern Presidium, gaining unique access to Communist leaders from around the world, and seeking in vain to infiltrate activists into Japan. In 1940 he joined Mao Zedong in the caves of Yenan, where he was based until his return to Japan in 1946.

Nosaka reappeared dramatically at a JCP rally in Tokyo in January 1946. He was elected to the HOUSE OF REPRESENTATIVES for a Tokyo constituency in the general elections of 1946, 1947 and 1949. Occupying key positions in the party executive, he pioneered a relatively moderate line for the JCP, projecting the image of a 'lovable Communist Party'. This came to an end in 1950 with the Cominform criticism of the JCP leadership, and he was forced underground when the Occupation applied its purge edict to Communist leaders. He re-emerged in 1955 and was elected to the HOUSE OF COUNCILLORS in 1956 for Tokyo, retiring in 1977. He was Chairman of the JCP Central Committee between 1958 and 1982, so that he presided over the resurgence in JCP fortunes that occurred in the late 1960s and early 1970s.

In 1992, aged 100, Nosaka admitted the claim in a weekly magazine that in 1939 he had denounced his comrade Yamamoto Kenzō to the Comintern on suspicion of spying, which led to Yamamoto being shot on Stalin's orders. The JCP stripped him of his position of Emeritus Chairman, and later expelled him from the party. He died in 1994.

Further reading
Beckmann and Okubo (1969)
Central Committee, Japanese Communist Party (1984)
Swearingen and Langer (1952, 1968)

nuclear issues The atomic bombing of Hiroshima and Nagasaki on 6 and 9 August 1945 places Japan in a quite different category from any other nation in respect of nuclear issues. Even though, with time, nuclear sensitivities have tended to decline, Governments are acutely aware of the capacity of public opinion to react forcefully were there to be a real erosion of the State's stance against nuclear weapons. Nevertheless, Government policy regarding nuclear weapons is hardly exemplary from the perspective of an activist for nuclear disarmament. During the Cold War period, Japan was an integral part of a US-led international security system whose strategic doctrines included the maintenance, and in conceivable circumstances the use, of nuclear weapons. Since the ending of the Cold War, though the location of a hypothetical enemy has become rather less clear, the structure of military cooperation between Japan and the United States has been strengthened rather than weakened, and the nuclear overtones of the alliance still remain.

Nuclear policy resolves itself into policy on nuclear weapons and policy on nuclear energy. Whereas the 'nuclear allergy' of the Japanese population regarding nuclear weapons has been extremely strong, attitudes towards the generation of power through nuclear power stations have been ambivalent. In Hayden Lesbirel's phrase, most of the objection to nuclear power stations has been based on a NIMBY (not in my backyard) syndrome, rather than on a principled concern with the issues involved. Moreover, Japan's extreme lack of indigenous sources of energy (especially fossil fuels) has acted as a powerful counter-argument to those who object to the harnessing of nuclear energy on the grounds of the potential dangers involved. Arguments based on the proposition that Japan was chronically resource-poor (and therefore internationally vulnerable) were marshalled to good effect in favour of the nuclear energy option in the aftermath of the first oil crisis of 1973–4.

During the Occupation, discussion of the atomic bombing of Hiroshima and Nagasaki was subject to stringent censorship regulation. This, not surprisingly, resulted in a sudden outpouring of controversy about nuclear weapons as soon as the Occupation ended in 1952. A US research project on victims of the atomic bombs, to determine the effects of radiation, caused intense resentment in Hiroshima, Nagasaki and elsewhere, in part because no treatment was offered. The early 1950s were, in any case, a period of great international tension. The Korean War was still being fought, while Japan was under severe US pressure to rearm. The left in Japan was developing what was to become a powerful political appeal against too close a security relationship with the United States, and in particular against nuclear weapons. Domestic tensions over defence issues generally, and nuclear weapons in particular, were greatly exacerbated while KISHI NOBUSUKE was Prime Minister between 1957 and 1960. Kishi – who of course wished to revise the CONSTITUTION OF 1946 – argued publicly that the possession of nuclear weapons by Japan would not be unconstitutional so long as they were used for defensive (he may have meant 'deterrent') purposes. His period in office culminated in the worst political crisis of the post-war period, over revision of the Japan–US Security Treaty (see SECURITY TREATY REVISION CRISIS).

In March 1954 an event occurred that was rather little noticed on the other side of the Pacific, but galvanised opinion against nuclear weapons in Japan. The Americans tested a hydrogen bomb at Bikini atoll in the Pacific. Fishermen in a fishing boat outside the declared exclusion zone were showered with radioactive ash from the explosion, and one of them later died. In the charged atmosphere of the time it did not seem too much of an exaggeration when the episode was widely portrayed as 'the third atomic bombing of Japan'. In direct reaction to the Bikini incident an anti-nuclear petition was organised by housewives in Tokyo, and the petition was ultimately signed by tens of millions of people throughout Japan. It was from this initiative that the Movement against Atomic and Hydrogen Weapons (*Gensuikyō*) was born [see also PACIFIST AND ANTI-NUCLEAR MOVEMENTS].

During the 1960s the salience of the nuclear weapons issue was reduced for a while in the non-confrontational policies of IKEDA HAYATO, Prime Minister 1960–4. When China for the first time tested a nuclear weapon at Lop Nor in November 1964, the governmental reaction in Japan was muted, despite the protests of some defence hawks such as Genda Minoru. But with the prime ministership of SATŌ EISAKU (1964–72), overlapping with the Vietnam War, the Government was constrained to look at its position on nuclear weapons once again. It is clear that the option of acquiring nuclear weapons was actively considered, in secret, in Government circles in the late 1960s, but in the end rejected. This was a period of rising tensions in East Asia both because of the Vietnam War and because the People's Republic of China was in the throes of the Great Proletarian Cultural Revolution. Chinese leaders were now inclined to issue extremist statements, though Chinese foreign policy remained cautious [*see also* CHINA (PRC AND ROC), RELATIONS WITH].

The nuclear issue had to be considered also in relation to the return of Okinawa to Japanese sovereignty (*see* OKINAWA IN JAPANESE POLITICS), which had a high priority position on Satō's policy agenda. After lengthy and difficult negotiations, Satō secured an agreement that the United States would return Okinawa to Japanese control, with nuclear weapons removed from US bases on the island. It was revealed many years later that a secret protocol to the agreement provided that Japan would allow such weapons to be brought back in case of an international emergency.

With the Okinawa agreement signed and sealed, Parliament resolved, in 1971, that Japan would abide by three non-nuclear principles, not to manufacture, stockpile or introduce nuclear weapons onto Japanese soil. (These principles had actually been formulated by the Government in 1967.) It seems that this was a major factor in the award to Satō of the Nobel Peace Prize in 1974. There was a problem, however, with the third of these principles, 'introduction' (*mochikomi*). It struck most observers as hardly credible that US naval vessels docking at Japanese ports would somehow offload the nuclear weapons they were undoubtedly carrying before entering port. It was the custom for the two governments to conduct a charade before a docking was scheduled. The Japanese Government would ask whether the vessel was nuclear-armed or not, and the Americans would reply 'no comment'. Occasionally a retired US admiral or ambassador would make a statement indicating the reality of the situation, and this would stir up a controversy in Japan. But the charade was maintained over many years. When, in the 1980s, the New Zealand Prime Minister, David Lange, refused any more to engage in a similar charade, the Americans took sharp retaliatory action. Much of the motivation for this seems to have been in order to prevent this 'New Zealand disease' infecting Japan.

Japan signed the Nuclear Non-Proliferation Treaty (NPT, *Kaku hikakusan bōshi jōyaku*) in 1970, but did not ratify it until 1976, during the period of the centrist Miki administration. The NPT critics emphasised that the Treaty was defective in failing to place nuclear disarmament obligations on the five nuclear powers. But in fact, elements, largely within the BUREAUCRACY, were holding out against ratification in order to preserve the possibility of a nuclear option for Japan. Once the treaty was ratified, of course, such a possibility was precluded so long as Japan remained bound by it.

Since the 1970s the Japanese Government has worked consistently in international fora, though mostly in a low-key manner, in the cause of nuclear disarmament. Its reactions towards nuclear testing by India and Pakistan have been particularly sharp. When India exploded a nuclear device in 1974, the Japanese HOUSE OF REPRESENTATIVES responded with a unanimous resolution condemning it. Then when both India and Pakistan engaged in nuclear weapons testing in 1998, the HASHIMOTO Government responded by imposing quite extensive economic sanctions on both, as well as taking other action. This was justified in terms of Japan's normal anti-nuclear positions, but also on the grounds that the two states had offended against provisions of its ODA Charter. Jain, however, argues that Hashimoto was also motivated by a need to demonstrate international leadership in circumstances of economic and political difficulty (Jain, in Inoguchi and Jain (eds), 2002, pp. 268–9).

Japan has sometimes been accused of maintaining a 'victim consciousness' as a result of the Hiroshima and Nagasaki experience, and this is linked with the accusation of unwillingness to come to terms with Japanese atrocities during the Asia–Pacific War. However this may be, anti-nuclear sentiment has penetrated deep into the consciousness of Japanese people. Governments have responded to nuclear weapons issues with some inconsistency and much lack of resolution, lending weight to the accusation that Japanese foreign policy tends to be 'reactive'. This is, however, hardly surprising given that any Japanese Government is torn between competing pressures – from the United States for greater military co-operation and nuclear permissiveness, on the one hand, and from large sections of public opinion for a more assertive anti-nuclear diplomacy, on the other.

It remains to be seen whether pressures from the Bush Administration, sceptical of international regimes of nuclear control, will destabilise the delicate balance of nuclear policy in Japan.

Further reading

Hook *et al.* (2001)
Inoguchi and Jain (eds) (2000)
Lesbirel (1998)
Welfield (1970)
—— (1988)

O

Obuchi Keizō Prime Minister between July 1998 and April 2000, Obuchi Keizō has been described by Curtis as 'a consummate political insider'. He rarely took clear public stands on political issues, he made a virtue out of modesty, but, like his mentor TAKESHITA NOBORU, he knew the political system inside out, and was skilled at exploiting his network of connections in many fields.

He was born in June 1937 and died in May 2000. His father was a politician, and it was his father's death that brought him into politics as a member of the Lower House in the general elections of 1963 at the unusually early age of 26. His constituency was in Gunma Prefecture, which had produced the much more famous figures of FUKUDA and NAKASONE. Overshadowed by them he may have been, but he remained in Parliament continuously for the next 37 years.

As a member of the dominant TANAKA (later Takeshita) faction of the LIBERAL DEMOCRATIC PARTY (LDP), he filled several Cabinet positions, heading the PRIME MINISTER'S OFFICE, directing the OKINAWA DEVELOPMENT AGENCY, being Chief Cabinet Secretary (while Takeshita was Prime Minister) and Foreign Minister under HASHIMOTO between 1996 and 1998. He first became widely known, however, in 1992–3, when the HATA–OZAWA group defected from the Takeshita faction (and later from the LDP), leaving him in charge of the rump of the faction that stayed inside the party.

After Hashimoto resigned as PRIME MINISTER in July 1998, Obuchi, relying on insider votes, beat off challenges from the more widely popular KOIZUMI and KAJIYAMA, to become LDP President and thus Prime Minister. Both as Foreign Minister and then as Prime Minister, he proved rather more adept than expected. In the former post he negotiated Japanese adherence to the land mines treaty, and the Security Guidelines Agreement with the United States. In the latter, he was able to bring Ozawa's LIBERAL PARTY (III) into a coalition with the LDP in November 1998, and later enticed the CLEAN GOVERNMENT PARTY (*Kōmeitō*) to enter the coalition as well. Backed by this 'grand coalition', he was able to pass surprisingly easily a number of controversial bills during 1999, including a wiretapping bill, bills legitimising the raising of the national flag and singing of the national anthem in schools, and bills relating to the Japan–US Guidelines Agreement. Facing a severe banking crisis, he negotiated a rescue programme for city banks against widespread opposition at the expenditure of public money that this entailed.

In April 2000 the withdrawal from the coalition of much of the Liberal Party immediately preceded his severe stroke, which ended his career. He died a few weeks later.

Further reading
Curtis (1999)

Ohira Masayoshi Born in 1910 in Kagawa (Shikoku), Ohira was a Finance Ministry official turned politician. Like his junior, MIYAZAWA KIICHI, he was inspired by IKEDA HAYATO, for whom he worked in the late 1940s, and in the 1970s led the LIBERAL DEMOCRATIC PARTY (LDP) faction founded by

Ikeda in the 1950s. He was regarded as moderate in conservative politics, and his ponderous manner masked an exceptional intellect.

His career in the MINISTRY OF FINANCE began in 1936, and he was first elected to the HOUSE OF REPRESENTATIVES from Kagawa for the Liberal Party in 1952. From 1960 he occupied a succession of senior Cabinet positions. He was Chief Cabinet Secretary, then Foreign Minister, under Ikeda, Minister of International Trade and Industry under SATŌ, Foreign Minister again under TANAKA, and Finance Minister under MIKI. During the long Satō prime ministership (1964–72), he forged close links with Tanaka Kakuei, so that, when in the 1970s they were both heading their own factions, they together constituted a formidable voting bloc, directed in particular against the interests of FUKUDA TAKEO. Their combined strength was demonstrated sharply in 1978, when their recruitment of local members to vote in primary elections for the LDP presidency ensured victory for Ohira and defeat for the incumbent party President and Prime Minister, Fukuda.

Ohira, as Prime Minister between 1978 and 1980, faced a hostile campaign from Fukuda and his supporters. This led to the 40-day crisis after the general elections of October 1979, when the party could not agree on its candidate for Prime Minister. Thus the names of both Ohira and Fukuda went forward to be voted on in Parliament. Although Ohira narrowly won that contest, in June 1980 he lost a no-confidence motion, after the Fukuda, Miki and NAKAGAWA factions abstained. This brought down his Government, he suffered a heart attack and later died during the election campaign, but the LDP, no doubt receiving a sympathy vote for its dead leader, went on to increase its majority.

During his prime ministership Ohira set up a number of commissions, on foreign and defence policy in particular, whose conclusions anticipated reforms by later administrations, notably that of Nakasone. The notion of 'comprehensive security' emerged under his guidance. On one issue he miscalculated: before the October 1979 elections, he hinted that his Government might need to bring in a VAT-type of indirect taxation. This probably contributed to the relatively poor LDP results at those elections and encouraged opposition to his leadership.

Further reading
Curtis (1988)
Satō *et al.* (1990)
Stockwin (1999)

Okinawa Development Agency (Okinawa Kaihatsuchō) With the return to Japan of Okinawa and the surrounding Ryūkyū islands in 1972, the Okinawa Development Agency was set up as an external agency of the PRIME MINISTER'S OFFICE (*Sōrifu*), with a Minister of State as its Director. It had been preceded by the Okinawa and Northern Territories Policy Agency (*Okinawa Hoppō Taisakuchō*), but, with its return to Japan, Okinawa was given its own agency.

The scale of the agency was relatively small, it was largely based in Okinawa itself, and its sections shadowed the MINISTRY OF FINANCE, MINISTRY OF AGRICULTURE, FORESTRY AND FISHERIES, MINISTRY OF ECONOMY, TRADE AND INDUSTRY, MINISTRY OF TRANSPORT and MINISTRY OF CONSTRUCTION.

The Second *Ad Hoc* Administrative Reform Commission in the 1980s recommended that the Okinawa Development Agency, the Hokkaidō Development Agency and the NATIONAL LAND AGENCY be amalgamated into a single body, but this was not acted upon. In the administrative reorganisation of January 2001, though the last two were put together with the ministries of Transport and Construction into a single new Ministry, the Okinawa Development Agency was rather oddly united with the Prime Minister's Office (*Sōrifu*) and ECONOMIC PLANNING AGENCY (*Keizaikikakuchō*) to form the CABINET OFFICE (*Naikakufu*).

Okinawa in Japanese politics Okinawa and the Ryūkyū group of islands, situated to the south of the main Japanese islands, were captured from Japan by the US forces in 1945 in one of the bloodiest battles of the Asia–Pacific War. Following the Japanese surrender on 15 August, the United States retained control of Okinawa, which was developed as a series of US military bases.

Before the war Okinawa had been a Japanese prefecture, but its history had been different from that of mainland Japan. Until the 1870s it had had a semi-independent status, maintaining links with China, as with the south-western Japanese *han* (fief) of Satsuma (now Kagoshima). Okinawans, who spoke their own language, related to but not mutually comprehensible with Japanese, were often looked down on as inferior in the rest of the country [*see also* MINORITIES AND POLITICS].

Between 1945 and 1972 Okinawa was directly administered by the United States, through a form of military administration. Japan, however, was accorded what was termed 'residual sovereignty', which could be interpreted to mean that full sovereignty would eventually be returned to Japan. 'Residual sovereignty' was from time to time used as a combination of carrot and stick to ensure Japan complied with US wishes on other issues. For instance, in 1956 John Foster Dulles effectively scuppered the prospect of a settlement over the southern Kurile islands (and thus a peace treaty between Japan and the USSR), by threatening to withdraw Japan's 'residual sovereignty' over Okinawa [*see also* SOVIET UNION AND RUSSIA, RELATIONS WITH].

In the second half of the 1960s SATŌ EISAKU, as Prime Minister, made return of Okinawa the most important aim of his administration, declaring that the post-war period would not have ended until Okinawa reverted to Japan. Irredentist sentiment both in Japan proper and in the islands themselves built up to great intensity in this period. US administrations were not entirely averse to conceding this, provided that they would retain their bases. They were also keen to use the Japanese irredentist claim in order to extract concessions from Japan for greater Japanese co-operation with the US security effort in North-East Asia. Satō agreed to a statement that the security of Korea was of 'great importance' to Japan, and that the security of Taiwan was of 'importance' to her.

The most difficult part, however, of any Okinawan settlement was the presence of nuclear weapons on US bases there. The Japanese Government, committed as it was to maintaining Japan free of nuclear weapons [*see also* NUCLEAR ISSUES], considered it unacceptable to have Okinawa return to Japanese sovereignty without these weapons being removed. After much hard bargaining, the Nixon Government in 1969 agreed to return Okinawa to Japan with the nuclear weapons removed, and in 1972 Okinawa Prefecture was re-established. In the 1990s it was discovered that a secret protocol to the agreement had provided that in case of war emergency nuclear weapons might be brought back to US bases in Okinawa.

In September 1995 three US servicemen raped a young Okinawan schoolgirl. This caused outrage in Okinawa and throughout Japan, and resulted in an upsurge of anti-American sentiment to an extent that had not been seen for many years. The Governor of Okinawa Prefecture, Ota Masahide, agitated to have the US bases reduced in number and size, if possible to be located in other parts of Japan, and, if not, abolished altogether. It so happened that a number of leases for land used for bases needed to be renewed by 1997. Governor Ota, who was a doughty fighter for Okinawan interests, refused to sanction renewal of the leases. This placed the HASHIMOTO and Clinton administrations in a dilemma, because no other Japanese prefecture would accept relocated bases, and the two Governments were in the process of negotiating the Guidelines Agreement to strengthen the provisions of the Mutual Security Treaty. In the end Hashimoto decided to override the Governor's veto – as he was legally permitted to do – and sanction the renewal of the bases [*see also* UNITED STATES, RELATIONS WITH]. Subsequently, some relocation of bases took place to less sensitive areas of Okinawa island itself.

There is little doubt that the presence of US bases on Okinawa caused deep and lasting resentment. Memories of the way Okinawans had been treated during the battle of Okinawa in 1945, and their second-class citizenship during the long years of US military rule, were etched into their consciousness. Their prefecture was small, and the bases took up a substantial proportion of the land area of the main island. Okinawans, however, faced the problem that theirs was a relatively poor and peripheral prefecture, and the bases brought in much needed revenue, particularly for some outlying communities. Opinion, therefore, tended to divide between those who wanted to campaign for the removal of the bases and take the economic consequences, and those who preferred to maintain the economic benefits while putting up with the nuisance of the bases. It was tension between these two kinds of view that led to the defeat of Ota Masahide in November 1998 and his replacement as Governor by Inamine Keiichi, who was somewhat more accommodating to Tokyo.

A further issue relating to Okinawa was that the Senkaku islands (known in Chinese as Tiaoyutai) were considered part of Okinawa Prefecture, but both China and Taiwan claimed ownership of them. Although there was a tacit understanding that this issue would be kept low-key, it flared up from time to time. But so far as China and Taiwan were concerned, in the eyes of many Okinawans they represented an opportunity to diversify trading activities. Rather than being a somewhat neglected periphery of Japan, Okinawa might strengthen its economic links with the two Chinas and use this to obtain greater leverage with the Government in Tokyo. Those with historical imagination even reminisced about the period before the 1870s when Okinawa had a degree of independence.

Further reading
Hook *et al.* (2001)
Inoguchi and Jain (eds) (2000)
Kerr (1958)
Stockwin (1999)

omote-ura (surface–background) This bipolar expression is related to *tatemae-honne* and *uchi-soto*, but is not identical to either. Like other such expressions, it has complex connotations. For instance the *kanji* (Chinese characters) for *omote-ura* may also be read *hyōri*. Thus *hyōri no aru hito* (literally 'somebody who has surface and background') means somebody who is two-faced, double-dealing or treacherous. By contrast, *hyōri no nai hito* ('somebody who lacks surface and background') means a person who is straight, single-hearted, honest or faithful. Essentially *omote-ura* is used to underline the structural difference between behaviour on the surface or in the open against behaviour in the background or behind the scenes. In the Japanese political context what occurs at the level of *omote* is what happens in public, at the official level, while what happens in the *ura* is hidden from view. However common this may be in politics we should remember that in ordinary speech, this combination of *kanji* carries a pejorative connotation.

No doubt such a distinction exists in politics practically everywhere, but it assumes particular importance in the politics of Japan given the high value attached to inter-personal harmony and surface tranquillity. The author once attended a session of a prefectural council in provincial Japan where almost the whole session had been scripted in advance, and the questions and answers actually given could be read from a script that the author was provided with by council officials. That was the *omote*, but undoubtedly much discussion and hard bargaining had occurred previously in the *ura* [*see also* LOCAL GOVERNMENT AND POLITICS].

We normally associate the *omote* with harmony and surface agreement, but Ishida points out that *omote* and *ura* can also operate in reverse, so that groups may harangue each other and call each other names in the *omote* while doing deals in the *ura*. It is true that such behaviour is not confined to Japan, and one is reminded of the Communist unionist (played by Peter Sellers) doing backstage deals with a crooked employer in the British film, *I'm All Right Jack*. But we might tentatively generalise that Japanese political culture creates a propensity for behaviour of this type.

Further reading
Hendry (1995)
Ishida, in Krauss *et al.* (1984)

Ono Banboku Born in 1890 in Gifu, Ono Banboku was an important leader in conservative politics of the first two post-war decades. Famed for his practice of **giri-ninjō**, he was leader of a 'party-man' faction, as distinct from factions dominated by former bureaucrats.

He developed extensive political experience in the 1920s and 1930s, first as a member of the Tokyo Municipal Assembly and then, from 1932, as a *Seiyūkai* member of the House of

Representatives. He was actively involved in the politics of the Liberal Party from 1945, but was out of politics between 1948 and 1951, charged with – but eventually acquitted of – involvement in the SHŌWA DENKŌ SCANDAL. Following his acquittal he occupied various senior positions, including that of speaker of the Lower House. With the formation of the LIBERAL DEMOCRATIC PARTY in 1955, he was leader of one of its eight powerful factions (see FACTIONS WITHIN POLITICAL PARTIES), and a member of its four-man interim ruling council. He was party Vice-President from 1957 until his death in 1964.

In 1959 Ono received the backing of the PRIME MINISTER, KISHI NOBUSUKE, to be his successor. In the event, however, he lost to IKEDA HAYATO in the factional manœuvrings following Kishi's resignation in July 1960. Nevertheless, his skill in factional leadership and manipulation was legendary.

Further reading
Curtis (1988)
Kohno (1997)

oyabun-kobun relationships In Japanese, *oya* means 'parent', *ko* means 'child', and *bun* means 'part', thus 'taking the part of'. It is sometimes written *oyakata-kokata*, where *kata* means much the same as *bun*. The meaning is roughly 'boss–henchman', but the words used bring a strong quasi-familial element into the expression. Relationships between an *oyabun* and his *kobun* are widely described in *yakuza* (gangster)-type organisations, which bear some comparison with the Italian Mafia. The *oyabun* is certainly the boss, commanding the loyalty of his various *kobun*, but he is also expected to be magnanimous to them, rather like vertical relationships in a traditional family (see FAMILY AND POLITICS). The term has also been widely used in connection with traditional artisan and craft activities, where relationships are hierarchical. It is also employed to indicate the nature of the labour gang system among day labourers.

In politics, the term has taken on derogatory connotations, but still may be met with in the mass media to describe factional-type relationships within political parties and other political organisations. If a faction leader (see FACTIONS WITHIN POLITICAL PARTIES) is described as an *oyabun* this implies that he is a particularly traditional – even feudal – kind of leader. A leader considering himself modern would be annoyed by such a description. In the more traditional parts of Japan, however, *oyabun-kobun* relationships are seen as providing protection in environments regarded as potentially threatening.

Further reading
Bennett and Ishino (1963)
Hendry (1995)

Ozawa Ichirō If breaking the mould of politics makes a politician significant, Ozawa Ichirō may be regarded as the most remarkable Japanese politician of the post-Cold War period. Such a judgement, however, like the man himself, remains controversial. It was he, above all others, who brought down the LIBERAL DEMOCRATIC PARTY (LDP) Government in August 1993 and substituted a multi-party coalition Government dedicated to wholesale reform of the system of governance. But subsequently, actions taken by Ozawa himself contributed to the failure of this experiment and enabled the LDP gradually to claw its way back to a dominant political position. Those observers (not excluding the present writer) who thought that the genie had finally escaped from the bottle found it stuffed back in again. Then Ozawa's attempt to build an alternative party of Government, after initial successes, foundered on personality clashes and organisational incompatibilities. His next approach was to head a small party of personal supporters, which he led into coalition with the LDP and out again, splitting his own party on quitting the coalition. But all the time Ozawa maintained a clear vision of what was wrong with Japanese politics and Government, and what ought to be done to correct it.

Ozawa, born in 1942, was educated at Keio University and first entered the HOUSE OF REPRESENTATIVES at the general elections of 1969, 'inheriting' his father's seat in Iwate after the latter's death. He joined the TANAKA faction and became close to Tanaka, occupying influential posts within the LDP from the early 1980s. He was briefly Home Affairs Minister between December 1985 and July 1987, and during the 1980s gained extensive experience in party organisation and in international negotiations. During this period he gained a reputation for the kind of back-stage dealing associated with his mentors, Tanaka, TAKE-SHITA and KANEMARU.

His real break came when he was appointed Secretary-General of the LDP with the establishment of the KAIFU Government in August 1989. As such, he was virtually the force behind the throne in that Government, given the weak power base of the Prime Minister. During his tenure, he had to try to orchestrate a Japanese response to the Gulf crisis and war of 1990–1. The experience made an enormous impression upon him. Even though a total of $13 billion was eventually contributed to the financing of the US-led expedition to liberate Kuwait, Japan met with international opprobrium for not contributing troops [*see also* MIDDLE EAST, RELATIONS WITH]. An attempt to bring in legislation permitting this failed in November 1990, against pacifist reservations from opposition parties. Even though a similar bill was eventually passed in July 1992, by that time Ozawa was no longer Secretary-General. In an attempt to curry favour with the CLEAN GOVERNMENT PARTY (CGP, *Kōmeitō*) and persuade it to support a peace-keeping operations bill, he had promoted a new candidate for Governor of Tokyo in April 1991, against the incumbent Governor, who was unpopular with the CGP. But that Governor refused to stand down and was comfortably re-elected. Ozawa resigned to take responsibility for this fiasco, but his stratagem did convince the CGP to support the PKO bill in 1992.

On 23 June 1993, after the passage of a no-confidence motion against the MIYAZAWA Government, Ozawa, with HATA TSUTOMU, formed a new party, the JAPAN RENEWAL PARTY (*Shinseitō*). The party did well in the July general elections, which left the LDP short of a majority. It was to a great extent Ozawa's vision and organisational ability that led to the creation of the HOSOKAWA eight-party coalition Cabinet on 9 August. Even though the Hosokawa Government proved unwieldy and fractious, its programme of deregulation, decentralisation and electoral system reform was deeply inspired by Ozawa's advocacy. Ozawa seems to have believed that only by depriving the LDP of power for a long period, could real reform of the political system be effected. This purpose, however, was confounded when Hosokawa resigned in April 1994 and during the brief Hata Government that followed Ozawa sought to create a party amalgamating the parties of the Hosokawa coalition *except the Socialists*. This led to a deal between the Socialists and the LDP, and less than a year after it had been expelled from office the LDP was once more in power. Ozawa in retrospect recognised that his exclusion of the Socialists was a mistake that had had dire consequences for his project of political system reform.

His next step was to form (in December 1994) the NEW FRONTIER PARTY (NFP, *Shinshintō*). It had some initial successes, but personality clashes and problems of organisation led to its collapse into several fragments just three years later. The NFP was an attempt to create a party that might win enough seats in Parliament to replace the LDP in Government. Although it never managed this, it came closer than any party had done since 1955.

Ozawa's third party-building exercise resulted in the formation of the LIBERAL PARTY (III) (*Jiyūtō*) in January 1998. Unlike the NFP it was much less an amalgam of differing groups than a group of Ozawa followers. It had little chance of ever being able to challenge for office (except in a coalition), but Ozawa wished it to be a source of political ideas. Between January 1999 and April 2000 the Liberal Party was in a coalition Government with the LDP (and latterly also with the CGP), but in April Ozawa decided to withdraw the Liberal Party from the coalition after a series of disagreements about policy. Nearly half its parliamentarians, however, refused to follow, and formed a new party they called the CONSERVATIVE PARTY (*Hoshutō*). Ozawa was left with a shrunken party, but its electoral performance in subsequent elections was respectable.

Ozawa's views are difficult to summarise, and his motives sometimes obscure. Observers variously regard him as a power-hungry politician seeking to change the system to his own advantage, a right-wing ideologue with militaristic intentions for Japan, a grand strategist but a poor tactician, a politician with a proven capacity to alienate potential or actual allies, a wrecker rather than a builder, or a political reformer with a valuable vision for Japan's future. Sympathetic pessimists might see him as a Cassandra figure, telling truths about what is wrong with the system, but to whom few now listen. No doubt, he has been poorly served by a preference for the kind of high-risk *démarche* that has spectacular results if it succeeds, but often ends in failure. But he would argue in face of such criticism that the time is past for the traditional arts of consensus-building and networking with vested interests because the system is so desperately in need of reform.

The reforms that he advocates are those of the moderate – not the extreme – right wing. He argues for a more deregulated, market-oriented economy, in which individual effort will be rewarded and where individuals take responsibility for their actions. He presses for increased executive power in Government, especially the power of the PRIME MINISTER, while improving accountability and ensuring that Government officials are public servants rather than bureaucrats. He thinks that small government is a good thing, while realistically admitting that the State performs necessary functions. He wants Japan to become a 'normal State', in the sense that the State should shoulder its burden of responsibility – including responsibility for security – in world affairs. But he endorses maintaining security relations with the United States and is not an advocate of independent Japanese military policy [*also* UNITED STATES, RELATIONS WITH]. He believes that the CONSTITUTION OF 1946 needs some revisions, but sees merits in parts of the current document. Finally, he takes much inspiration from the way the British political system works, particularly what he regards as its clear lines of responsibility and accountability.

Even though Ozawa the politician has been shunted rather to the sidelines of politics, Ozawa's political vision has developed surprising resonance in the vacuum of clear political ideas that has followed the ending of the Cold War.

Note: I have profited from discussions with Mr Oka Takashi in writing this entry, but responsibility for the opinions expressed is mine.

Further reading
Christensen (2000)
Curtis (1999)
Ozawa (1994)

P

pacifist and anti-nuclear movements Japan being the first and only nation in history to have suffered nuclear bombing of her cities, it is not surprising that opposition to nuclear weapons is strong and widespread within the Japanese population. It is widely assumed that anti-nuclear sentiment reached its height in the 1950s and 1960s, and declined thereafter. But it is worth noting that as late as 1982 anti-nuclear organisations in Japan were able to send a petition with 80 million signatures to the Second Special Session on Disarmament of the United Nations, and in the same year an anti-nuclear rally in Tokyo attracted over 400,000 participants (Hook *et al.*, 2001, p. 327).

NUCLEAR ISSUES have thus loomed large in Japanese politics. Japan is unique among top economic powers in having renounced possession of nuclear weapons, although in a sense her position is compromised by being party to a set of security arrangements with the United States that are premised on nuclear deterrence. In international fora, Japanese governments often show ambivalence on nuclear disarmament issues because an uncompromising anti-nuclear stance might be seen to conflict with commitment to the Japan–US Security Treaty.

During the Occupation, most open discussion of nuclear issues was suppressed, so that it was impossible to organise an anti-nuclear movement. But when the Occupation ended in 1952, the August issue of the *Asahi Graph* was devoted to the nuclear question. Around the same time a woman called Maruki Iri set up an exhibition about the effects of nuclear bombing. Concern rapidly mounted.

In March 1954 a Japanese fishing boat, the Lucky Dragon No. 5 (*Daigo fukuryū maru*), was showered with radioactive ash from a US nuclear test at Bikini atoll in the Pacific, and one of the crew members, Kuboyama Aikichi, subsequently died. Concern about the general issue and about pollution of fish stocks by radioactivity led a group of Tokyo housewives to organise an anti-nuclear petition, which was ultimately signed by over 33 million people. This, in turn, led in September 1955 to the formation of the Japan Council against Atomic and Hydrogen Weapons (*Gensuikyō*). In the late 1950s *Gensuikyō* served as the focus for the movement against nuclear weapons, and held rallies at Hiroshima on 6 August each year.

In the charged domestic and international atmosphere of the time, pacifist and anti-nuclear movements could not long remain unentangled in partisan politics. When *Gensuikyō* was first set up, it included representatives of all major parties. By the late 1950s, however, it was moving steadily towards the left, and by 1960 those on the conservative side of the political fence had mostly gone. In 1961 a small group close to the newly founded DEMOCRATIC SOCIALIST PARTY (*Minshatō*) broke away and founded its own organisation. The years 1961–2 saw a vicious conflict develop within *Gensuikyō* between the JAPAN SOCIALIST PARTY (JSP, *Nihon Shakaitō*) and the JAPAN COMMUNIST PARTY (JCP, *Nihon Kyosantō*) for control of the organisation.

The main issue was nuclear testing. France had tested a nuclear weapon in 1960, becoming the fourth nuclear power after the United States, the USSR and the United Kingdom. For a while, the Soviet Union had been observing a nuclear testing moratorium, but in October 1961 it broke the moratorium. Representatives of the JCP, which had become the leading force within *Gensuikyō*, supported the Soviet action, on the ground that it was a 'peace force', needing to defend itself against US 'imperialism'. Representatives of the JSP fiercely disputed this, arguing that nuclear testing by whatever state was unacceptable, since it increased levels of radioactivity and accelerated the development of nuclear weapons, which could lead to nuclear war. The Socialist leader, EDA SABURŌ, stated that the party's ultimate aim was 'to abolish the balance of terror, ban nuclear weapons and achieve total disarmament, thus rooting out the very essence of power politics'.

Things came to a head in Hiroshima in August 1962, when Communists and Socialists clashed physically at the *Gensuikyō* annual Congress, and the Socialists walked out of the Congress. There were further clashes in 1963 over the Partial Nuclear Test Ban Treaty, by which time the Sino-Soviet dispute was already in evidence, and having an impact on Japanese politics. The JSP and the GENERAL COUNCIL OF JAPANESE TRADE UNIONS (*Sōhyō*) supported the Treaty, but the JCP opposed it, since that party had shifted to a pro-China line. China, which had refused to sign the Treaty, and was moving towards its own nuclear testing, represented for the JCP the 'peace forces'. At the ninth *Gensuikyō* annual Congress in 1963 delegates from the USSR and the PRC attended and publicly clashed on the platform of the Congress. The final denouement of this process came in 1965, with the formation of a breakaway organisation, the Japan National Congress against Atomic and Hydrogen Weapons (*Gensuikin*), backed by the JSP and *Sōhyō*. This left *Gensuikyō* entirely under the control of the JCP. Ironically, in the following year (1966), relations between the JCP and China were traumatically severed, but this did not result in any coming together of the two sides of the anti-nuclear weapons movement. Even in 2002, when the issues that drove them apart had long since ceased to be relevant, they maintained separate organisations, though they were now prepared to co-operate with each other.

The extreme politicisation of the anti-nuclear weapons movement in the early 1960s took much of the steam out of what had been a dynamic popular cause in the 1950s and alienated the politically uncommitted. As Yamamoto Mari has shown (2002), there was a great deal of spontaneity in the development of popular pacifism in the first years after the ending of the Occupation, with women playing a major part. To some extent this continued into later decades, and, as we have seen, there was a major revival of anti-war activity in the early 1980s. The timing was not entirely coincidental, since this period coincided with the early stages of what some have called the 'Second Cold War'. In this period the role of religious organisations in pursuit of pacifist aims had become substantial. Apart from specific religious groups, the *Shinkyōren* (New Union of Japanese Religious Organisations) was active. Another organisation that made waves in the 1980s and early 1990s was the NPT [Non-Proliferation Treaty] Research Association. Rather surprisingly, this association actively opposed extension of the NPT in 1995, on the ground that it left in place the weapons of the nuclear-have powers (Hook *et al.*, 2001, p. 327).

Pacifist and anti-nuclear weapons movements have never been in a commanding position politically in Japan since the 1950s, and their impact was severely curtailed by their destructive involvement in conflictual party politics of the left. Nevertheless, they undoubtedly represented an underlying stratum of opinion that governments ignored at their peril. In the post-Cold War world, and now in the new millennium, the shape of the international system has radically changed. But the question of how to avoid war – and particularly nuclear war – has not gone away. Now that Japan is gradually becoming more of an active participant in world affairs, pacifist and anti-nuclear movements remain active and have a contribution to make, not just within Japan itself, but also on the international stage.

Further reading
Braddick (1997)
Hook *et al.* (eds) (2001)
Inoguchi and Jain (eds) (2000)
Stockwin (1968)
Yamamoto (2003)

parties Japanese politics is heir to a remarkably rich culture of parties. A study published in 1985 gave entries on 176 parties that had existed at various times since the 1870s. Some of these were short-lived, and some of them were locally based, but many of them were more substantial. During the decade from 1992 – a period of political instability – more than 25 new parties were formed, though many of these did not exist long enough to contest elections. The role of parties under the Meiji Constitution of 1889 was more circumscribed than under the CONSTITUTION OF 1946, when they became beneficiaries of extensive constitutional guarantees, undertaking a central political role.

In the pre-war system, parties at national level contested regular elections for the HOUSE OF REPRESENTATIVES, but this was the only elective house and enjoyed limited powers within the system as a whole. Although during the 1920s there was a series of party Cabinets, a more common pattern was that of the 'transcendental' Cabinet. The latter was a Cabinet that neither consisted predominantly of party members, nor was obliged to resign if defeated in the House of Representatives. Party Cabinets were the reverse, on both counts. In the early years from 1889, the suffrage was extremely limited, and elections were largely of interest to local elites, but the electorate was gradually enlarged, and in 1925 males over the age of 25 were granted the vote. By this time the *Seiyūkai* party possessed a nation-wide organisation of local branches based largely on local notabilities, and other major parties followed suit. Its form of party organisation was inherited almost intact by post-war conservative parties, including the LIBERAL DEMOCRATIC PARTY (LDP) formed in 1955. These included the method of electing a party president by the party congress (but, more often than not, by unanimous vote for a candidate selected by the central executive), the committee structure of the Policy Affairs Research Council, close financial links with leading business firms, and internal factionalism. The other major pre-war conservative party, *Kenseikai* (*Minseitō* from 1927), had a very similar structure. It pioneered the practice of regular meetings of top party leaders, which became formalised in the post-war LDP in the shape of meetings between the party President, the Executive Committee Chairman, and the Secretary-General, as well as chairmen of various PARC committees.

Another area of continuity between pre-war and post-war conservative parties lies in occupational composition of their parliamentary members. According to Fukui, in the early 1920s the bulk of parliamentarians affiliated with the *Seiyūkai* and the *Kenseikai* were previously local politicians, Government officials, businessmen, lawyers and journalists. There were, however, more former local politicians in the *Kenseikai* (close to 50 per cent), and more former Government officials, businessmen and lawyers in the *Seiyūkai*. When we come to the 1960s, around a quarter of LDP parliamentarians had a local politics background, a similar proportion a bureaucratic background, about a fifth were former businessmen, and there were smaller but still significant numbers of lawyers and journalists.

Continuity is also highly significant between pre-war Socialist and social democratic parties and the post-war JAPAN SOCIALIST PARTY (JSP). The best-known feature of continuity here is that of the ideological divisions that divided the party for many years after the war. But, in addition, close organisational linkages with labour unions, and a real decision-making role given to the party congress are features that can be traced back to the pre-war period. So far as the post-war JAPAN COMMUNIST PARTY (JCP) is concerned, it was profoundly influenced by the clandestine, incarcerated and exiled lives of its membership before 1945.

The most common way of categorising political parties is on an ideological spectrum from right to left. Thus taking Japanese parties between 1945 and 1993, the LDP would be the furthest to the right, the DEMOCRATIC SOCIALIST PARTY (DSP) and the CLEAN GOVERNMENT PARTY (CGP) would be in the centre, the JSP would be on the left and the JCP on the far left. Such a unidimensional categorisation, however, fails to take account of ideological overlap between parties, and the fact that both the LDP and JSP, in particular, contained within them a wide ideological spectrum. Moreover, by the 1990s divisions over policy could best be understood in a multi-dimensional framework. For instance, the axis of division between big government and small government did not necessarily coincide with the axis of division between peace advocacy and 'normal State' advocacy.

A different framework for understanding how the parties differ from each other is in terms of organisation type. We propose six categories:

Dominant party type

The LDP is the sole exemplar of this type. It was essentially the sole party in power between 1955 and 1993, then out of power for nine months, followed by several years in which it was the dominant party in coalition governments. This meant, in effect, that its party organisation was intimately bound up with that of Government ministries and a variety of interest groups. Choosing the party leader was tantamount to choosing the Prime Minister. Sub-committees of PARC mirrored committees of the two houses of Parliament, as well as the various ministries. Appointment to party positions and to Cabinet positions were considered as a package. One of the principal functions of factions (*habatsu*) has been to secure for their members the maximum number of Cabinet and party positions, taking the two things together (*see* FACTIONS WITHIN POLITICAL PARTIES). 'TRIBAL' PARLIAMENTARIANS (*zoku giin*) of the LDP, in conjunction with relevant Government officials and interest group representatives, act as powerful policy sub-communities. In short, the LDP acts as an entrenched part of the Government structure, not simply as a party contesting elections. In its electoral organisation, however, it has been highly decentralised, relying on district candidates and their personal support groups (*kōenkai*) to bring out the vote. On the other hand, central party organisation has been effective in policing candidate selection.

Social democratic party type

These include principally the JSP (later Social Democratic Party) and the DSP up to the 1990s. Four characteristics of their organisational structure stand out. One is that the annual party congress was a genuine decision-making body, both in relation to basic policy and in relation to appointments. Second, the organisation of electoral campaigns was heavily dependent on sympathetic labour unions. And third, electoral organisation centred on individual candidates rather than being organised by the central party machine. Thus, typically, a candidate in an electoral district would have close relationships with a local union branch (sometimes having been an official of that branch), and would work closely with that branch in pursuit of votes. Some candidates, on the other hand, based their campaigns on citizens' movements (*shimin undō*). A fourth characteristic was that the party leadership did not attempt to suppress factionalism, but, rather, to balance the interests and views of the factions in the interests of party harmony. The DEMOCRATIC PARTY, founded in 1996, took on some, but not all, of the characteristics of this type.

Religious-based party type

The CGP is the only substantial party based on a religion. Even though the parent body, *Sōka Gakkai*, and the CGP formally separated their organisations in 1970, links remain close. The party organisation is hierarchical, and, so far as possible, factionalism is suppressed. The party maintains remarkable voting discipline over its voters (the great majority of whom are *Sōka Gakkai* members), directing them on which candidate to vote for in such a way as to optimise the effectiveness of the CGP vote. Candidates are concentrated in winnable seats. The CGP has proved hard to assimilate (as shown by the NEW FRONTIER PARTY experience), but has not been averse to entering into coalition governments.

Communist party type

This party has been unique in Japan in organising itself along the lines of democratic centralism, whereby views are supposed to filter upwards from the rank and file, but, when a decision is made, this is absolutely binding on the membership as a whole. The party has therefore suppressed (or sought to suppress) factional dissidence. Elections are also organised by the central party organisation, which allocates candidates to electoral districts. Unlike virtually all other parties, little weight is placed on local ties, of family, residence, etc., when choosing candidates. Differing from other minority parties, the JCP fields candidates in nearly all districts, including many that are hopeless. The purpose is to maintain the commitment of local party members, but it has the added effect of boosting the party's total national vote. Some loosening of this centralised organisational structure has occurred, but much of it still remains in place. Finally, great emphasis has been placed, since the 1960s, upon the building up of membership and on involving the members in close relations with the party. This creates dynamism, and helps with finances, as do sales of party publications. Unlike the CGP, with which it has some organisational similarities, it is extremely reluctant to enter into close co-operation with other parties. There are some signs that this might now be changing.

Transitory party type

At certain stages in Japanese party development, a rash of new parties appear, many of which soon disappear again. In the 1990s parties came and went so rapidly, that some parliamentarians did not bother to have new business cards made indicating a fleeting party affiliation. Most of these parties were splinters from larger parties, with few members, having minimal organisational structure. Few of them ever contested an election, and they hardly existed outside Parliament, except in the sense that the local electoral organisations of their individual members would be nominally incorporated into the new party.

Minor party type

A few minor parties, such as the Sports Peace Party, the Salary Man New Party, the Taxpayers' Party and the Welfare Party, have gained parliamentary representation. But this has been largely in the proportional representation constituency of the House of Councillors since its creation in 1982. Loose groupings of Independents, such as the Second Chamber Club (or in the 1950s the Green Breeze Society), have also gained representation, as well as local parties in Okinawa (in local districts). In addition, considerable numbers of minor parties have unsuccessfully contested the PR constituency. In the 1992 Upper House elections, these included (in descending order of votes) the Old People's Welfare Party, Pensions Party, New Liberal Party, Breeze Association, Motor New Party, Hope, Discovery Politics, All Japan Drivers' Club, People's New Party, People's Party, Progressive Liberal League, Environment Party, Education Party, Commoners' Party, Small and Medium Enterprise Livelihood Party, Japan Social Reform Party, Japan National Political League, Japan *Sake* Lovers' Party, Cultural Forum, UFO Party, International Political League, Freedom of Expression Party, Odds and Sods Party (*Zatsumintō*), Heisei [era] Renovation Party, Free Work Union, Global Restoration Party, Political Corporation Tranquillity Society, World Pure Spirit Association, Great Japan True Path Society. None of these groups gained 1 per cent of the total vote, but between them they won 6.08 per cent. Minor parties of this kind regularly contest local districts in Tokyo and Osaka, but very little elsewhere.

Further reading
Christensen (2000)
Curtis (1971)
—— (1999)
Fukui (1970)
—— (ed.) (1985)
Hrebenar (2000)
Pempel (ed.) (1990)
Stockwin (1968)
—— (1999)
Thayer (1969)

pressure groups (atsuryoku dantai) The Japanese political system, like the systems of other comparable countries, embodies a vigorous culture of pressure groups, interest groups and lobby groups (henceforth, pressure groups). Groups seeking to influence government policy have proliferated in Japan since the Occupation period. But in the wartime and pre-war periods the activities of pressure groups were circumscribed by the official requirement that they serve the interests of the

State. The notion of lobbying on behalf of sectional interests was regarded with opprobrium and risked attracting the attention of the prosecuting authorities. Even though such activity went on extensively behind the scenes, the notion that pressure group activity, by its very nature, was selfish, narrow and unpatriotic, carried over into the post-war period and was widely reflected in the mass media.

The CONSTITUTION OF 1946 guaranteed freedom of political activity, and thus unambiguously legitimised the formation and operation of pressure groups. Article 21 of the Constitution states: 'Freedom of assembly and association as well as speech, press and all other forms of expression are guaranteed.' Even though the Occupation, with its purging, first of rightists, then of Communists, and by its extensive censorship, did not consistently uphold this provision, article 21 effectively opened the floodgates to pressure group formation and activity that has continued to this day.

Japanese pressure groups could be categorised in various ways. One way would be in terms of resources and access to central power structures. Another would be by size and character of membership, and degree of organisation of membership. Third, we might concentrate on degree of ability to mobilise votes in favour of one political party or another. Fourth, there is the question whether the group in question is lobbying in the narrow interests of its members or in terms of larger issues of principle, affecting the community (or communities) as a whole. Fifth, we could distinguish groups that tend to co-operate with the authorities and influence them through contact and negotiation, from those that prefer (or are forced into) a confrontational approach. Sixth, we might separate those groups that take on the character of a 'movement', more or less loosely uniting many local groups, from groups that are tightly organised. And finally, we could look at different periods of political history since the war to see which kinds of pressure group tended to emerge in different periods.

Access to central power structures is a crucial indicator of probable success in influencing policy. If, as in Japan, central power structures have been relatively stable, access for certain groups can bring dividends on a long-term basis. Perhaps the most conspicuous have been those pressure groups representing the *zaikai* (business world), particularly the FEDERATION OF ECONOMIC ORGANISATIONS (*Keidanren*) and the JAPAN FEDERATION OF EMPLOYERS' ASSOCIATIONS (*Nikkeiren*) – now united into the JAPAN FEDERATION OF ECONOMIC ORGANISATIONS. Particularly in the case of *Keidanren*, there has been a degree of incorporation into the ruling structure itself, as shown, for instance, by the fact that *Keidanren* representatives have been stationed in Japanese embassies in important countries. Even more conspicuous is the example of the Agricultural Co-operative Association (*Nōkyō*), which is perhaps the most interesting of all Japanese pressure groups. Normally treated as a pressure group, *Nōkyō* from early in the post-war period co-operated closely with the Ministry of Agriculture and Forestry (*see* MINISTRY OF AGRICULTURE, FORESTRY AND FISHERIES) in the administration of the rice price support scheme and other schemes aimed at stabilising the return to farmers from their products. In a real sense it was incorporated into central government structure, while also lobbying (as a pressure group should) in favour of farmers' interests, and, for good measure, running a range of services for farmers in the manner of a conglomerate firm [*see also* AGRICULTURAL POLITICS AND THE AGRICULTURAL CO-OPERATIVE ASSOCIATION]. In any case, the groups constituting this category have deployed exceptional resources and have enjoyed unusual access to stable Government structures. In the recent period, however, of change and instability, such massive groups have gradually lost influence.

Our second issue relates to membership and its organisation. Some labour unions in the earlier post-war years had huge memberships. In the General Council of Japanese Trade Unions (*Sōhyō*), for instance, there were between three and four million members. The religious group *Sōka Gakkai*, which from some perspectives may be considered a pressure group, claims more than ten million members. In this latter case, the group exercises an extraordinary level of discipline over its members, particularly in directing them how to vote. But for these groups, degree of effectiveness depended less on membership and discipline, than on whether they could gain real access to central power. The *Sōka Gakkai* was able to achieve this from the late 1990s by having its spin-off CLEAN GOVERNMENT PARTY (*Kōmeitō*) join a coalition Government as a junior partner to the LIBERAL DEMOCRATIC PARTY (LDP).

The third question concerns mobilisation in favour of particular parties. Many pressure groups have deliberately sought to mobilise votes for the LDP, partly perhaps because of sympathy with its aims, but more importantly because it is obvious that this is where power lies and where it will no doubt continue to lie. The former JAPAN CONFEDERATION OF LABOUR (*Dōmei*) labour federation mobilised its votes in favour of the small DEMOCRATIC SOCIALIST PARTY (*Minshatō*), with only a slight hope that its favoured party would gain access to power (as eventually, but briefly, happened during the period of the Hosokawa Government). By contrast, certain kinds of pressure group steer clear of links with political parties altogether. These include many citizens' movements and environmental groups that regard parties as essentially corrupt. They have also included extremist movements on the far left, for instance groups participating in the struggles against the Narita Airport.

Fourth, there is a significant distinction between pressure groups narrowly concerned with its members' interests and those whose vision is much wider. Examples of the former would be professional groups, representing doctors [see also JAPAN MEDICAL ASSOCIATION], dentists or lawyers, which, though they may engage in rhetoric glorifying the wider good, are essentially seeking to further the interests of their members. The latter would be exemplified by various groups campaigning against nuclear weapons [see also PACIFIST AND ANTI-NUCLEAR MOVEMENTS], or in favour of environmental protection [see also ENVIRONMENTAL POLITICS], or human rights. But in the Japanese case, it has proved difficult to sustain nation-wide movements promoting generalised ideas. Many Japanese seem more comfortable with local or issue-specific groups, which campaign, for instance, against locating a power plant in a particular locality.

The fifth division that we may draw is between groups co-operating with Government and groups confronting it. Those in the former category are legion, whereas the latter category includes left-wing labour unions maintaining ideological objections to Government policy. An example of the latter would be the JAPAN TEACHERS' UNION (JTU, *Nikkyōso*), which until the end of the 1980s consistently confronted (and was confronted by) the MINISTRY OF EDUCATION (*Monbushō*). Interestingly, however, the JTU is one of several examples of the Government practice of seeking gradually to embrace – and thus neutralise – dissident and critical groups. In 1990 the JTU split, and the larger of the unions to emerge from the split adopted a set of policies and attitudes far more co-operative with the ministry than hitherto. This may be described as the 'ripples in the pond' effect, with Government making sure that its influence washes over a wider and wider range of groups. Of course the ripples may not reach right to the edge of the pond, but those areas that the ripples fail to reach are marginalised.

The sixth distinction is between groups that are tightly organised and those that are loose umbrella organisations embracing many fragmented groups. If the *Sōka Gakkai* is an example of the former, the latter would include the concept of the Citizens' Movement, which, though it hardly exists in terms of central organisation, serves to unite under a common set of broad principles a host of local and issue-specific groups.

Finally, the history of the emergence and evolution of pressure groups since the war reflects changing social, political and economic reality, and consequent changes of priority. From the end of the war until around 1960 huge numbers of pressure groups emerged, but the most conspicuous of them represented capital, labour or agriculture in a resurgent capitalist economy. *Keidanren*, *Sōhyō* and *Nōkyō* are type cases from this period, as well as professional groups. In the 1960s and into the 1970s, rapid economic growth was transforming society. Radical and independent-minded student movements, as well as movements concerned with the environment, quality of life and defence of the Peace Constitution were active, while consumers' movements, groups advocating improvements to welfare, citizens' movements and the closely related residents' movements also made their appearance. In the 1980s and 1990s, groups promoting the interests of local regions, seeking to establish links with foreign cities, or concerned with the rights of minorities, begin to be significant, while charitable groups and CONSUMER GROUPS organising the production and sale of organic food become conspicuous. That is not to say that the older groups had disappeared, merely that groups were diversifying and sharpening their focus, as society became more sophisticated.

One result of the 'ripples in the pond' effect, mentioned above, has been to reduce the areas of manœuvre available to Government, given that so many interests have been brought into its ambit, and these interests need to be satisfied. To keep a large coalition of interests together in this fashion violates the principle of the 'minimum winning coalition' whereby a given quantity of largesse is distributed to the smallest number of participants necessary to security a majority. With even labour unions and other groups now within the fold, it is difficult to reform and streamline government structures to permit needed radical solutions to severe economic problems.

Further reading
Calder (1988)
George, in Stockwin *et al.* (1988)
George Mulgan (2000)
Lam (1999)
LeBlanc (1999)

Prime Minister (Sōri daijin, Sōri, Shushō)
Between Higashikuni in 1945 and Koizumi in 2002, 27 men (no women) have been Prime Minister of Japan. Of these only one, Yoshida, occupied the position for two separate periods. By comparison, in Britain from Attlee to Blair, 10 men and one woman have been Prime Minister, with Wilson taking the position at two separate periods. And in Australia, from Chifley in 1945 to Howard in 2002, 10 men have been Prime Minister, with no repeats.

This contrast in the turnover rate between Japan and other comparable countries is significant and indicates a structural difference. At first sight it seems surprising that a political system where one party has been dominant over a very long period should have produced more than twice the number of prime ministers than systems where changes of party in power occur from time to time. In order to understand why this should be so, it is worth considering a small number of exceptions to the rule of a short-term Prime Minister.

The longest period ever served by a Prime Minister under the CONSTITUTION OF 1946 was the seven years and eight months of SATŌ EISAKU between November 1964 and July 1972. Satō succeeded IKEDA HAYATO, who, had he not had to resign from illness in November 1964, would have had an excellent chance of surviving as Prime Minister until at least 1966, which would have given him a six-year term. Ikeda's predecessor, Kishi Nobusuke, served for three years and five months, and would no doubt have served longer had it not been for the traumatic events of May–July 1960. The length of Satō's term, however, was truly exceptional and reflected fortuitous circumstances. Three of his most formidable factional rivals, Ikeda, ONO and KŌNO, died within his first year in office. This enabled him to consolidate an alliance of LIBERAL DEMOCRATIC PARTY (LDP) factions that he was able to dominate. Though others challenged him every two years or so in elections for the LDP presidency, his factional strength enabled him to prevail. He also benefited from rapid economic growth and strong US backing, as well as showing a canny sense of political strategy. In 1971–2 world events undermined his authority, and ended his prime ministership.

The second example is YOSHIDA SHIGERU, who was Prime Minister in his second term in the eventful period between October 1948 and December 1954 (six years and two months). The reasons for his political longevity were similar to those in the previous example, namely that he was able to dominate his own party, which had the numbers in Parliament, enjoyed US backing and was a tough and effective strategist. During his last two years, however, with the Occupation over and previously purged politicians returning to political activity, his power base was gradually weakened and he was eventually forced out of office.

The third case, that of NAKASONE YASUHIRO, is more complicated. He became Prime Minister in November 1982 largely because of the preferences of TANAKA KAKUEI and his dominant faction. Because of the aftermath of the LOCKHEED SCANDAL, it was difficult for Tanaka or one of his close associates to aspire to the top position, but he could act as kingmaker. The Tanaka faction dominated Nakasone's early cabinets, but he gradually consolidated his own power and won a handsome victory in the 1986 Lower House elections. He was highly popular with the US Government and won electoral backing for his attempts at activist leadership on a range of issues. But in the end his power base dissolved in the 'revolving chairs' atmosphere of LDP politics and his tenure of the top post came to an end after he had been Prime Minister for almost five years.

When we break it down, we find that the length of prime ministerial tenure differs greatly depending on the period (see Table 32).

It will be seen from Table 32 that prime ministers were very frequently replaced in the unstable period to 1948. Then between 1948 and 1972 the average length of tenure approached four years. In the decade between 1972 and 1982 a two-year term became the norm. Nakasone in the 1980s was unique for the period in enjoying five years. From 1987, again reflecting political instability, the average tenure of the position was less than eighteen months. (See Table 33.)

The reasons for prime ministerial departure were various. None departed because of death, though Ikeda, OHIRA and OBUCHI all died rather soon after their departures. Of these Ikeda and Obuchi left because of serious illness. ISHIBASHI also resigned because of illness, but recovered subsequently. Ill health was also a factor in HATOYAMA's resignation. Higashikuni was regarded as a brief stopgap following the defeat. Those resigning in part because of scandals affecting themselves or their governments included ASHIDA, Tanaka, TAKESHITA, UNO and HOSOKAWA. Ohira resigned and dissolved the House of Representatives, having lost a no-confidence motion (he died during the election campaign). KISHI resigned following the severe political crisis over revising the Japan–US Security Treaty (see SECURITY TREATY REVISION CRISIS). Takeshita and MORI left in part because their electoral popularity had fallen to catastrophic levels. HATA resigned because he lacked a majority in the House of Representatives. Those leaving office because of adverse results in a general election were surprisingly few. They included SHIDEHARA, Yoshida (after his first administration), MIYAZAWA and HASHIMOTO. (In Hashimoto's case the LDP had done badly in an Upper House election, but still had a majority in the Lower House.) KATAYAMA and MURAYAMA (both Socialists) resigned because of problems, or changes in the balance of power, in coalition governments. Yoshida resigned for the second time in 1954 essentially because he had been beaten in a power struggle with his old rival, Hatoyama, but also because the business world was threatening to deprive him of funds. Those resigning in part or wholly because of factional struggles within the LDP included Kishi, Satō, Tanaka, MIKI, FUKUDA, Ohira, SUZUKI, Nakasone, KAIFU and to some extent Mori. Of these Fukuda had lost newly instituted primary elections for the LDP presidency to Ohira.

The relative shortness of prime ministerial tenure since the 1970s reflects a determination on the part of LDP factions to prevent particular leaders becoming too dominant (see FACTIONS WITHIN POLITICAL PARTIES). The institution of the party presidential election every two years has had the effect of ensuring that the party President will rotate in such a way as to balance factional interests. Only one LDP President, KŌNO YŌHEI in the mid-1990s, has been party President but not Prime Minister, and that because during his tenure the LDP was out of power. Once it was becoming plain, in the later months of 1995, that the LDP was close to recovering for itself the post of Prime Minister, Kōno was removed in favour of Hashimoto through the device of a party presidential election.

An obvious corollary of short tenure is relative lack of power. The recent creation of the CABINET OFFICE (*Naikakufu*) is part of a

Table 32 Length of prime ministerial tenure

Name of Prime Minister	Dates in office	No. of months in office
Higashikuni	August–October 1945	2
Shidehara	October 1945–May 1946	7
Yoshida	May 1946–June 1947	13
Katayama	June 1947–May 1948	11
Ashida	March–October 1948	7
Yoshida	October 1948–December 1954	74
Hatoyama	December 1954–December 1956	24
Ishibashi	December 1956–February 1957	2
Kishi	February 1957–July 1960	41
Ikeda	July 1960–November 1964	52
Satō	November 1964–July 1972	92
Tanaka	July 1972–November 1974	29
Miki	December 1974–December 1976	24
Fukuda	December 1976–December 1978	24
Ohira	December 1978–July 1980	19
Suzuki	July 1980–November 1982	28
Nakasone	November 1982–November 1987	60
Takeshita	November 1987–June 1989	19
Uno	June–August 1989	2
Kaifu	August 1989–November 1991	27
Miyazawa	November 1991–August 1993	21
Hosokawa	August 1993–April 1994	8
Hata	April–June 1994	2
Murayama	June 1994–January 1996	18
Hashimoto	January 1996–June 1998	30
Obuchi	July 1998–April 2000	21
Mori	April 2000–April 2001	12
Koizumi	April 2001–	

movement to increase the power of the Prime Minister and CABINET to control policy-making. Policy-making structures within the LDP have to a great extent weakened the power of the Prime Minister and taken away much of his ability to control the policy agenda. The powers given to the Prime Minister by the 1946 Constitution are extensive. Article 67 provides that: 'The Prime Minister shall be designated from among the members of the Diet [Parliament] by a resolution of the Diet. This designation shall precede all other business.' According to article 68, he appoints Ministers of State, and 'may remove Ministers of State as he chooses'. Article 72 gives him the power 'representing the Cabinet [to submit] bills, reports on general national affairs and foreign relations to the Diet and [to exercise] control and supervision over various administrative branches'. According to article 74: 'All

Table 33 Average length of tenure

Years (months)	No. of prime ministers	Average tenure
1945–8	5	8
1948–72	6	47
1972–82	5	25
1982–7	1	60
1987–2001	10	16

laws and Cabinet orders shall be signed by the competent Minister of State and countersigned by the Prime Minister.'

It is the substantial 'hollowing out' of these powers that the recent reforms are attempting to overcome.

Further reading
Curtis (1999)
George Mulgan (2002)
Hayao (1993)
Shinoda (2000)
Stockwin (1999)

Prime Minister's Office (Sōrifu) In 1947 the Prime Minister's Agency (Sōrichō), which had been set up in 1947, was transformed into the Prime Minister's Office (Sōrifu).

An important function of the Prime Minister's Office was to give some flexibility to the overall administrative structure of Government without having to establish new full-blown ministries. Whereas the number of ministries was restricted (whether by law or by custom), it was possible to increase the number of 'external agencies' of the Prime Minister's Department to meet changing needs. Moreover, because there was no concept of an inner Cabinet and all Ministers of State were members of Cabinet, directors of these agencies were designated ministers without portfolio. Thus an agency could have the power equal to that of a ministry, though, as in the case of the DEFENCE AGENCY, the fact that it was not actually called a 'ministry' indicated that it had a problematic legacy. Between around 1952 and the 2001 reorganisation, there was only one case of a Prime Minister's Office Agency being promoted to ministry status. That was when the Local Autonomy Agency (*Jichichō*) became the Ministry of Local Autonomy (also called in English 'MINISTRY OF HOME AFFAIRS') in 1960.

The 'external agencies' were: MANAGEMENT AND CO-ORDINATION AGENCY (*Sōmuchō*), Hokkaidō Development Agency (*Hokkaidō kaihatsuchō*), Defence Agency (*Bōeichō*), ECONOMIC PLANNING AGENCY (*Keizai kikakuchō*), SCIENCE AND TECHNOLOGY AGENCY (*Kagaku gijutsuchō*), ENVIRONMENT AGENCY (*Kankyō-chō*), OKINAWA DEVELOPMENT AGENCY (*Okinawa kaihatsuchō*) and NATIONAL LAND AGENCY (*Kokudochō*). The IMPERIAL HOUSEHOLD AGENCY (*Kunaichō*) was also an 'external agency' of the Prime Minister's Office, but without a separate Minister of State, because the Prime Minister assumed this portfolio. In addition, the following commissions and committees fell under the Office's jurisdiction: FAIR TRADE COMMISSION (*Kōsei torihiki iinkai*), Public Safety Committee (*Kokka kōan iinkai*) and Pollution etc. Preparation Committee (*Kōgai tō chōsei iinkai*). Of these only the Public Safety Committee was headed by a Minister of State.

The 'internal functions' of the Prime Minister's Office were reduced in 1984 when the Statistics Bureau (*Tōkeikyoku*) and the Pensions Bureau (*Onkyūkyoku*) were shifted to the newly created Management and Co-ordination Agency. The Minister's Secretariat, however, and the Decoration Bureau (*Shōkunkyoku*) – issuing awards for merit – remained.

In the administrative reorganisation that took place on 6 January 2001, the Prime Minister's Office joined with the ECONOMIC PLANNING AGENCY and the OKINAWA DEVELOPMENT AGENCY to form the CABINET OFFICE (*Naikakufu*).

Further reading
Shinoda (2000)

R

Recruit scandal (1988–9) In terms both of its scale and of its political consequences, the Recruit scandal was perhaps the most serious since the war. It came to be regarded as the type case of 'structural corruption'.

The Recruit Co. Ltd. was a middle-ranking company engaged in providing information about job vacancies for job seekers, and about potential recruits (students etc.) for companies wishing to recruit new staff. It was a company with a determination to expand and was moving into a wide range of information services at a time when computers were beginning to be widely available. In June 1988 a journalistic investigation in Kawasaki City, just south of Tokyo, found that the Recruit Co. had been floating subsidiary companies and trading in their unlisted shares. It was discovered that, after the floating of a company called Recruit Cosmos, unlisted shares had been distributed to a large number of influential people, including parliamentarians from various parties, Cabinet ministers, Government officials, newspaper proprietors, officials of NTT (Nippon Telephone and Telegraph) and so on.

In October 1988 the Tokyo Prosecutor's Office began an investigation and arrested several people, including the Chairman of the Recruit Co., Ezoe Hiromasa. Ezoe was an extremely ambitious young businessman, determined to propel his company into the first rank. He had the drive and skill to exploit the insatiable need of politicians and others for funding, in order to gain influence rapidly.

The political repercussions of the Recruit affair were extensive. It was found that Ezoe had targeted practically the whole political class, including members of both Government and opposition parties. Among Government leaders, the former Prime Minister, NAKASONE YASUHIRO, the LIBERAL DEMOCRATIC PARTY (LDP) Secretary-General, ABE SHINTARŌ, the current Minister of Finance, MIYAZAWA KIICHI, and the Prime Minister, TAKESHITA NOBORU, were found to have received large quantities of unlisted shares in Recruit Cosmos, able to be sold at a profit once the shares were listed on the stock exchange. Miyazawa had to resign his Cabinet position, Nakasone temporarily left the LDP, but the most severe effects were suffered by Takeshita – already in trouble over other issues – who in April 1989 was forced to resign as Prime Minister. Takeshita's former secretary, who had been responsible for the transactions with Recruit, committed suicide. Only two politicians, one from the LDP and one from the CLEAN GOVERNMENT PARTY (*Kōmeitō*) received punishment as the result of judicial process. For a case to be successful, it was necessary to prove that a gift of money or shares had been traded for favourable treatment in relation to legislative initiatives. In most cases, this was exceedingly difficult to prove.

The Recruit scandal focused popular attention on issues of structural corruption, and was a major factor leading to a tightening of the anti-corruption laws several years later, in 1994.

Further reading
Curtis (1999)
Mitchell (1996)

Reform Club (Kakaku kurabu) After the NEW FRONTIER PARTY dissolved at the end of 1997, one of the resultant splinter groups was the Reform Club, led by Ozawa Tatsuo. This was essentially a personal leader–follower grouping. Its members subsequently dispersed.

Reformist Party (Kaishintō) *see* conservative parties, 1945–55

religion and politics Religion has not played a defining part in Japanese politics since 1945 in the way that it has in certain other countries. There is no equivalent, for instance, of Christian Democratic parties, as in some European countries, or of an Islamic party, as in Turkey. Even in England, the Church of England used to be referred to, semi-seriously, as 'the Conservative Party at prayer', and the roots of the British Labour Party were seen by some historians as owing much more to Methodism than to Marxism. Japan emphatically has no equivalent of the violent religious divide that exists in Northern Ireland, where in Belfast Protestants and Catholics have had to be protected from each other by building a wall (of bricks and mortar!) between them. Many Japanese express perplexity at the intensity of this religious divide, and wonder why it should not be easy to reach a consensus between the two communities. Such perplexity comes naturally from a religious environment in which it is normal for the same person to be married according to Shintō rites and to be buried according to the rites of Buddhism – a situation that incidentally has parallels elsewhere in East and South-East Asia.

This does not mean, however, that religious considerations are absent from politics, though to what degree, to what effect and through what mechanisms they are projected into the political arena is less clear. The relationship between religion and politics in Japan is indeed a seriously under-researched area.

As a broad generalisation it is perhaps reasonable to argue that Japanese society in 2002 has reached a comparable level of secularisation to that of the United Kingdom or France. But whereas in those two countries it is relatively easy to measure the extent of religious adherence by such indicators as percentage of the population regularly attending church, no such clear indicators exist in the Japanese case. There is a relatively high level of superficial religious observance. Very large numbers of people from time to time visit Shintō shrines and Buddhist temples. It is common to write prayers on pieces of paper and tie them to sacred trees at shrines. *Omikuji*, or written oracles, are commonly purchased at shrines and their messages taken note of. But the attitudes of those receiving them appear to have much in common with those of the readers of astrology columns in European popular newspapers. There is a major fortune-telling industry in Japan. In 1990 the present writer counted no less than eight pages of advertisements for fortune-tellers (*uranai*) in the yellow pages of Sapporo, a city of slightly over a million people.

By far the most serious occasion for religious observance is death, and this is almost entirely the preserve of Buddhism. The tradition of respect for ancestors remains strong, though it has weakened by comparison with that still to be found in South Korea. Some households maintain a Buddhist altar (*butsudan*), sacred to the family ancestors. Many also keep a Shintō 'god shelf'. Funeral rituals can be elaborate and are strictly observed. Many families living in cities make annual pilgrimages to their ancestral villages to tend the graves of their ancestors. Even though these take on the atmosphere of family outings to the countryside, the cleaning and tidying of graves is taken very seriously.

Broadly speaking, however, religious doctrine, in so far as it exists in the 'traditional' religions, is regarded with rather little interest by most of those who nevertheless observe certain rituals. Buddhism, of course, has a complex doctrinal history, but Shintō, with its concern for ritual purification, is far more a matter of observance than of doctrine.

An exception must be made here for many of the 'new' religions – those that emerged soon after (or in some cases before) the Asia–Pacific War, and the 'new new' religions that have appeared since the 1980s. The proliferation of new sects in Japan since the war is remarkable, and may perhaps best be compared with similar phenomena in the United States. In the Japanese case, however, there is a particular reason why such a religious flowering should have taken place after the war. From the Meiji period until 1945 Shintō (the Way of the Gods) was transformed into a State religion, with the *Tennō* at its head [*see also* EMPEROR AND POLITICS]. Previously it had been little more than folk religion, worshipping spirits in the trees and the rocks. One of the early acts of the Allied Occupation was to 'disestablish' Shintō and to write into the new Constitution the principle of separation of religion and the State (*see* CONSTITUTION OF 1946). The *Tennō* was also persuaded to renounce his 'divinity' in 1946. Thus, the post-war era began with the formal abolition of the officially sponsored system of nationalistic religious belief in which the population had been indoctrinated up to that time. In its place came what was often described as a 'spritual vacuum', and into it flowed amazing ingenuity and inventiveness in the creation of new sects. The proliferation of sects was facilitated by a new law that made it relatively easy to register a new religion. Indeed, the original version of the law (until it was amended) made it so easy that hotels in hot spring resorts were registering as religions in order to benefit from tax breaks.

The formal separation of religion from the State caused problems from time to time in respect of practices that nobody had earlier thought to question. Technically speaking, the provision by a local authority of funding towards the upkeep of a shrine was in breach of the Constitution. Yet it seemed perfectly natural in the traditional Japanese social context. Shintō ceremonies in association with the accession of a new Emperor (*Tennō*) also had to be designed with great finesse to avoid the accusation of unconstitutionality. A complaint by the Christian widow of a deceased member of the Self-Defence Forces that his enshrinement in a Shintō shrine breached his constitutional rights had merit in constitutional terms but appeared to contradict traditional practices.

Much the most successful of the new sects in the 1950s and 1960s was a Buddhist group that had started life just before the war as a society to reform education. This was the *Sōka Gakkai*, whose name roughly translates as 'Value Creation Association'. Under charismatic leadership after the war, it had great success in appealing mainly to underachieving and underprivileged urban dwellers. It derived inspiration from a thirteenth-century monk, Nichiren, and was aggressive in its proselytising style. By the 1960s it was claiming more than ten million members, or a little less than 10 per cent of the total population. Unlike nearly all other Japanese religious groups, the *Sōka Gakkai* was intolerant of other religions. Given the Japanese tradition of religious tolerance, this was shocking to many non-members, and early observers of this group feared that it would develop in ultra-nationalist or extreme right-wing directions. Such fears were fuelled by its organisational structure, which was rigidly top-down and based at its lowest extremity on a small cell-like unit called a *kumi* (group). It also employed techniques of 'encapsulating' its members in a near-exclusive control by the organisation. Its proselytising techniques could be aggressive. In fact, however, it proved to be politically rather moderate, if broadly conservative.

In terms of religion and politics, the *Sōka Gakkai* employed a unique method of linking the two. It founded its own political party, the CLEAN GOVERNMENT PARTY (*Kōmeitō*), in 1964. Apart from the period 1994–8, when it had partially dissolved its separate identity into the NEW FRONTIER PARTY (*Shinshintō*), it remained a substantial minority party, normally winning between 30 and 55 seats in elections to the House of Representatives. Since November 1998 it has been in coalition with the LIBERAL DEMOCRATIC PARTY in Government.

No other religious group has attempted to form a political party (whereas *Aum Shinrikyō* formed its own 'government'; *see* AUM SHINRIKYŌ AND THE POLITICS OF MASS POISONING), though a socially and politically conservative group called *Seichō no ie* (House of Growth) unsuccessfully ran a number of its members as Independents in the July 1974 House of Councillors elections. TAMAKI KAZUO, an executive member of *Seichō no ie*, was a prominent representative of religious organisations in the House of Councillors between 1965 and his death in 1987. In general, religious groups constitute a significant – though dispersed –

political force at local district level. Many political candidates feel that they cannot afford to ignore the demands of religious groups, and seek to incorporate them into their networks of support.

In the 1990s the politics of religion took an alarming new turn with the release of poison gas by the *Aum Shinrikyō* in the Tokyo subway system in 1995. One issue that came to public notice in the aftermath of this affair was the fact that the police had been seriously inhibited in pursuing the sect (which was earlier under suspicion for a series of murders and violent acts) by laws that appeared unduly to favour the rights of religious groups, however antisocial they might be. In October 1995, despite strong objections from the *Sōka Gakkai*, a Religious Corporate Body Law (*Shūkyō hōjin hō*) was introduced into Parliament, resulting eventually in a somewhat modified version of the law being passed.

It seems that the widespread revulsion against the acts of the *Aum Shinrikyō* caused a reaction against religious groups in general (particularly those that were new and extreme). On the other hand, it is worth noting that the *Aum Shinrikyō* was never suppressed or ordered to disband, and under a new name (*Aleph*) was able to recruit small numbers of new members into the new millennium.

A final point remains to be made about Christianity in Japan. Avowed Christians amount to a little more than 1 per cent of the total population of Japan, and the proportion is static. The only 'Christian' sect that is to any extent expanding its membership is the Jehovah's Witnesses, who no doubt appeal to a certain millennial sentiment on the fringes of Japanese society. On the other hand, the influence of Christianity in the intellectual and political elite is somewhat greater than the bald figures of membership might suggest. Two Prime Ministers since 1945, KATAYAMA TETSU and OHIRA MASAYOSHI, have been Christians, though it is unclear whether their religious beliefs influenced their policies to any significant extent. The JAPAN SOCIALIST PARTY was undoubtedly influenced by Christianity alongside Marxism, though it would be difficult to trace exactly how much effect this in fact exercised. In this respect an interesting parallel might be drawn with the British Labour Party, though it would be perilous to develop the analogy too far. The idea that Christianity is monotheistic and universalist, whereas Japanese religion is typically polytheistic and particularistic, has some substance, and is put forward mainly by those who concern themselves with the integrity of Japanese culture, narrowly defined. In any case mainstream non-Christian religions in Japan have gradually been evolving towards a more universalist view of the world, emphasising, for example, the need for charity on an international, not just a local, plane.

The influence of religion on Japanese politics has thus been complex and far from insignificant, but the bedrock of society – and thus of politics – as Japan moves into the new millennium should be regarded as predominantly secular rather than religious.

Further reading
Bocking (1996)
Crump (1992)
Hendry (1995)
Reader (1991)
—— (2000)
Stockwin (1999)
White (1970)

ringi (circulation of proposals within a ministry) This is a formalised way of arriving at decisions within a ministry or agency of Government. (*Ringi* may also be found in the private sector). It is often referred to as *ringisei* (*ringi* system), while the document being circulated is a *ringisho*. Much attention has been focused on this system since at least the 1960s, because of the perception that *ringisho* were drafted by junior officials, who appeared to exercise unusual power, then circulated in a set order from junior to senior in a succession of divisions of the same bureaucratic agency. Tsuji and others argued that it was a formalised system designed to spread responsibility and ensure that relevant views and perspectives within the agency were taken into account (a kind of NEMAWASHI process). On the other hand its disadvantages were that it retarded decisions, made it easy to veto aspects of proposals and inhibited political input by ministers or even senior officials.

More recent work on *ringi*, however, has shown that the system has become much less rigid and stereotyped than the above implies. When a proposal is being considered, much informal communication, and particularly early consultation with senior officials, takes place, and *ringisho* are often *ex post facto* formalisations of decisions already taken informally. Enhanced political input into decision-making makes it difficult to hide behind the *ringi* process in an attempt to bury, emasculate or delay decisions that politicians favour. Nevertheless, it remains one weapon in the bureaucratic armoury that may be used judiciously to defend in-house positions against attack from the outside. It is also still widely used for routine proposals that are not politically controversial.

Further reading
Koh (1989)
Tsuji, in Ward (ed.) (1968)

S

Sagawa Kyūbin scandal (1992) *Sagawa Kyūbin* was a parcel delivery company that became the focus of media attention in 1992. The starting point of the scandal associated with its name was a press allegation, soon confirmed by the company, that the leading LIBERAL DEMOCRATIC PARTY (LDP) politician, KANEMARU SHIN, had failed to report, as required by law, a donation of 500,000,000 from the *Sagawa Kyūbin* company.

Kanemaru was fined a small sum (200,000) for this misdemeanour, but the press unearthed the fact that in 1987 he had asked the President of the company to make contact with an ultra-rightist organisation. The rightists had been publicly praising Kanemaru's close factional associate, TAKESHITA NOBORU, with a view to discrediting him by demonstrating his association with the far right. The intervention had been successful in its aim, but in the process a gangster group had been involved and Kanemaru had personally thanked the head of this group.

In September 1992 Kanemaru's house was raided by police investigating *Sagawa Kyūbin*. The police found enormous amounts of money and gold bars.

Public reaction against the derisory fine, his connections with gangsters, and plain evidence of corrupt dealing resulted in Kanemaru's departure from politics. The political ramifications were profound, since the affair was a principal cause of the split in the Takeshita faction that in turn led to defections from the LDP and its eviction from office the next year, ushering in a period of coalition governments.

Further reading
Curtis (1999)

Sasaki Kōzō Sasaki Kōzō was a left-wing member of the JAPAN SOCIALIST PARTY (JSP), who served as Chairman between May 1965 and August 1967.

Born in 1900 in northern Japan (and famous for his Tōhoku accent), he was on the Marxist left of the JSP in the post-war period, and seemed the natural successor to SUZUKI MOSABURŌ, who dominated the left-wing Socialists throughout the late 1940s and the 1950s. But after the assassination of ASANUMA INEJIRŌ during the general election campaign in November 1960, EDA SABURŌ, a member of the same faction as Sasaki, was able to make a bid for party leadership using his theories of 'structural reform' and proclaiming the 'Eda vision'. Sasaki, allied with Professor Sakisaka's Socialism Association and with the sympathy of the General Council of Japanese Trade Unions (*Sōhyō*) leadership, was able to defeat Eda's proposals at the party Congress held in November 1962.

After a series of complicated factional struggles, Sasaki was elected Chairman in May 1965, and the next year successfully fought off a challenge from Eda. For a short while he held a dominant position in the party. In 1967, however, the leadership negotiated a compromise with the LDP over health insurance law revision, but the compromise was repudiated by the Association of JSP Parliamentarians. Sasaki and his deputy, NARITA TOMOMI, promptly resigned, but to prevent the possibility of Eda taking over, the Sasaki and Katsumata factions negotiated a deal whereby KATSUMATA SEIICHI would become the next Chairman.

Sasaki's period as Chairman illustrates the wisdom that radicalism in power is often tempered by confrontation with reality. Not only did Sasaki do a deal with the LDP over health insurance, but also he found himself having to confront radicals associated with his own party in an atmosphere of rising tension caused by the Vietnam War. His behaviour exhibited the pragmatism of a faction boss, a term that ultimately describes him better than 'ideologist'.

Sasaki died in December 1985, aged 85.

Satō Eisaku Satō Eisaku was Japan's longest-serving Prime Minister in a continuous stretch, between November 1964 and July 1972, aided by rapid economic growth.

Born in 1901 in Yamaguchi (formerly the Chōshū domain), he was the younger brother of KISHI NOBUSUKE (who had been adopted into a different family). After graduation from Tokyo Imperial University, he entered the Railways Ministry, where he rose to a senior position. After the war he became Administrative Vice-Minister of the MINISTRY OF TRANSPORT, but in 1948 was picked out by the Prime Minister, YOSHIDA SHIGERU, to be Chief Cabinet Secretary in his second administration. He stood for Parliament in the 1949 elections for a Yamaguchi constituency, and was elected as a member of Yoshida's Democratic Liberal Party. Regarded (with IKEDA HAYATO) as a most brilliant pupil of the 'Yoshida School', he went on to fill senior posts in that party and its successor, the LIBERAL DEMOCRATIC PARTY (LDP). He was also successively Minister for Posts and Telecommunications, Minister of Construction, Minister of Finance and Minister of International Trade and Industry. In 1954 his career was threatened by an investigation into a SHIPBUILDING SCANDAL. But Yoshida protected him and he avoided arrest, though he was forced to resign his current position of party Secretary-General.

A decade later, in July 1964, he challenged Ikeda Hayato for the LDP presidency, but was narrowly defeated. Then in November Ikeda retired because of ill health and Satō was elected party President and Prime Minister in his stead. As Prime Minister, he had a number of significant achievements. In 1965 he negotiated a Basic Treaty between Japan and the Republic of Korea, negotiations having been bogged down for many years in mutual vilification [see also KOREA (ROK AND DPRK), RELATIONS WITH]. Exercising great skill over timing, he engineered legislation that effectively put a stop to the student revolt of the late 1960s, by requiring universities to exercise control over student disruption [see also EDUCATION AND POLITICS; STUDENT POLITICAL MOVEMENTS]. He negotiated an agricultural compensation law that slowed the inexorable rise in agricultural subsidy [see also AGRICULTURAL POLITICS AND THE AGRICULTURAL CO-OPERATIVE ASSOCIATION]. He skilfully avoided a second 'Security Treaty crisis', given the need for a renewal of the 1960 Treaty in 1970 [see also SECURITY TREATY REVISION CRISIS]. But perhaps his most significant achievement was to secure the return to Japan in 1972 of Okinawa and the other Ryūkyū islands from US military control. Soon after arriving in office, Satō made the statement: 'Until Okinawa returns to Japan, the post-war period will not have ended.' It was difficult to negotiate the reversion of Okinawa during the Vietnam War, given its importance as a base of US operations in pursuit of that war. The Americans were concerned about the nuclear aspect of reversion, considering Japanese aversion to having nuclear weapons on Japanese soil. In the end, Satō secured the reversion of Okinawa with nuclear weapons removed, even though many years later it was revealed that, under a secret agreement between the two governments, the United States was permitted to reintroduce nuclear weapons to Okinawa 'in case of emergency' [see also OKINAWA IN JAPANESE POLITICS].

In talks with President Lyndon Johnson, and later with President Richard Nixon, Satō committed Japan – at least in rhetoric – to a somewhat more active role in the defence of the region, with particular reference to Korea and Taiwan. This was *quid pro quo* for reversion of Okinawa, but he also set out a doctrine on nuclear weapons: 'not to manufacture, stockpile or introduce' nuclear weapons.

Even though 'introduce' later generated controversy, since nuclear weapons plainly entered Japan on board US naval vessels, the non-nuclear principles were to be a factor behind the award of the Nobel Peace Prize to Satō in 1974 [see also NUCLEAR ISSUES].

Satō's exceptional longevity as Prime Minister is in part explained by political skill and by an extraordinarily favourable economic environment. But luck was also on his side. During his first year in post three of his most effective factional rivals, Ikeda Hayato, KŌNO ICHIRŌ and ŌNO BANBOKU, died. Their successors were weak and untried. Thenceforth he and his faction were able to dominate the LDP, and largely dictate its personnel policies. Eventually, however, he was brought down by external factors. In July 1971, President Nixon announced – without prior reference to the Japanese Government – that he would visit Beijing. In August, he broke the link between the US dollar and gold, and imposed a temporary surcharge of 10 per cent on imports. Satō's pro-United States policy of not recognising the PRC was undermined by the first of the two 'NIXON SHOCKS', and his cheap yen policy was wrecked by the second. Relationships between Nixon and Satō had in any case deteriorated because of an acrimonious dispute over trade in textiles, where both men were seeking to appease domestic constituents. By July 1972 Satō's position had deteriorated to the point where he was forced to step down in favour of TANAKA KAKUEI.

He died in 1975.

Science and Technology Agency (Kagaku gijutsuchō) In May 1956, just as Japan's economic development was beginning to accelerate, the Government established the Science and Technology Agency as an external agency of the PRIME MINISTER'S OFFICE, with a Minister of State as its Director.

It was given the general function of planning and implementing science-related policy, as well as helping other ministries and agencies co-ordinate their efforts in the field. In addition, it was given special responsibility for nuclear energy, space research and international scientific co-operation. A number of consultative bodies (*shingikai*) reported to it, and it controlled several important research institutes, such as the Nuclear Energy Research Institute (*Genshiryoku kenkyūjo*), and the Space Research Enterprise (*Uchū kaihatsu jigyōdan*). It was sometimes criticised for the alleged shallowness of its links with industry.

In the comprehensive reform of the Government administrative structure that occurred in January 2001, the agency was united with the Ministry of Education (*Monbushō*) to form the Ministry of Education, Culture, Sports, Science and Technology (*Monbukagakushō*).

Security Treaty revision crisis, 1960 A principal aim of the KISHI Government (1957–60) was to revise the Japan–US Security Treaty, signed in October 1951 at the time of the San Francisco Peace Treaty. Japan by this time, having been admitted to the United Nations in 1956 (see UNITED NATIONS, RELATIONS WITH), was consolidating her position once again as a full member of the comity of nations. The Government therefore thought it appropriate to negotiate with the United States for a more equal Treaty, appropriate to Japan's new status. To be able to negotiate a new Treaty was itself important, in that it would be freely negotiated, not a product of limited Japanese sovereignty during the Occupation. The 'internal disturbance' clause of the 1951 Treaty, whereby US forces could intervene, at the request of the Japanese Government, to put down externally instigated (read 'Communist') riots or disturbances, was removed. In addition, Japan was no longer forbidden to grant any military-related facilities to a third power without US permission. A 'prior consultation' clause was also introduced, whereby the United States and Japan would consult before major changes in deployment, equipment and use of bases were carried out. What this 'prior consultation' meant in practice – did it give Japan a veto? – was much debated in Parliament, as was the meaning of 'Far East' in the phrase 'peace and security of the Far East', occurring three times in the new Treaty. Much of the opposition stemmed from concern that Japan might be dragged into wars that did not directly affect her interests.

Talks between the two governments began in 1958 and Prime Minister Kishi and President Eisenhower signed the revised Treaty in Washington in January 1960. The Socialist and

Communist Parties, much of the labour union movement (see LABOUR UNIONS), STUDENT POLITICAL MOVEMENTS, intellectuals and sections of the mass media opposed the process of revision because it meant the perpetuation of exclusive defence arrangements with the United States, the maintenance of US military bases on Japanese soil, and a situation that could be in breach of the 1946 'Peace Constitution' (see CONSTITUTION OF 1946). Many mass demonstrations took place but much of the population was apathetic.

In the summer of 1960, however, the issue took on an entirely new complexion. A US U2 spy plane was shot down over the USSR, worsening East–West tensions. President Eisenhower had planned a trip to Asian capitals and to Moscow, but now had to cancel his trip to Moscow, so that, when he visited Tokyo, it would be as part of a round of anti-Communist Asian capitals, such as Seoul and Taipei. Anti-Government, and anti-Kishi, demonstrations increased in volume and frequency, and Opposition parties (principally the Socialists) were obstructing parliamentary business in protest against the Treaty. Kishi had unwisely created a deadline for himself by inviting the US President to Tokyo on 19 June. This meant that the Treaty had to be approved by the HOUSE OF REPRESENTATIVES a month earlier, by midnight on 19 May, so that it would automatically be passed by the HOUSE OF COUNCILLORS on 19 June, and Kishi could present Eisenhower with a ratified Treaty.

Socialist parliamentarians and their muscular secretaries, fully aware of Kishi's deadline problem, spent several hours late on 19 May preventing the Speaker from leaving his office to put an extension of the session to the vote. Kishi reacted by calling police into the Parliament building to remove them. When the Speaker was freed, two votes were held, with only Liberal Democrats present, first to extend the session and second to ratify the Treaty.

This stratagem proved a two-edged sword for Kishi. The Treaty was duly ratified a month later by the House of Councillors. But the scale of the demonstrations mounted, since to worries about the implications of the revised Treaty were added deep concern about the integrity of democratic procedures, challenged – in the eyes of many demonstrators – by the introduction of police into Parliament. Eisenhower's press secretary, Hagerty, was threatened by a mob and had to be rescued by helicopter on 10 June. A huge demonstration on 15 June led to widespread violence and the death of a woman student, Kanba Michiko, who was trampled in the crush. Kishi was forced to cancel the visit of the US President, and, shortly after ratification of the Treaty, resigned as LIBERAL DEMOCRATIC PARTY (LDP) President and Prime Minister. Some factions within the LDP had used his discomfiture to their advantage. He later was injured in a bizarre stabbing by an extreme rightist.

The Security Treaty revision crisis did not prevent the new Treaty coming into force, and entrenching the security relationship between Japan and the United States. But its impact on Japanese politics as a whole was profound. The years up to 1960 had seen increasing tensions as extreme conservative politicians from the wartime era, such as Kishi, sought to challenge important elements in the Occupation settlement and were confronted by an increasingly militant and disaffected left wing. The 1960s crisis brought these tensions to a head, and a tacit consensus emerged that it was vital to lower the political temperature. Kishi's successor, IKEDA HAYATO, deliberately played down contentious issues of domestic politics and foreign policy, preferring instead to concentrate on economic programmes that were easy to bring to fruition because of the rapid pace of economic growth. Several decades were to pass before political leaders were prepared to grasp the nettle of political issues such as the Constitution, DEFENCE policy and the security relationship with the United States [see also UNITED STATES, RELATIONS WITH]. Critics of this approach complained that, by shelving questions of this kind, policy was allowed drift, but those who welcomed it pointed to the arrival of economic prosperity accompanied by a degree of political stability that Japan had hardly known in her recent history.

Further reading

Masumi (1995)
Packard (1966)
Stockwin (1999)

Separatists' Liberal Party (Buntōha Jiyūtō)
see conservative parties, 1945–55

Shidehara Kijūrō Shidehara Kijūrō was a distinguished diplomat and statesman of the pre-war period, who after the defeat became PRIME MINISTER from October 1945 to April 1946.

Born in 1872 in Osaka, he graduated from Tokyo Imperial University, and joined the Foreign Ministry, where he rose rapidly. From 1919 he was Ambassador to the United States. He served two terms as Foreign Minister (1924–7 and 1929–31), and lent his name to the concept of 'Shidehara diplomacy', which meant conciliatory policies towards China and a general 'Anglo-American' foreign policy orientation.

Chosen as Prime Minister in October 1945, he presided over the early radical reforms of the Allied Occupation, in circumstances of extreme socio-economic disruption. At first he did not take seriously the need to revise radically the Meiji Constitution. But he later claimed to have suggested to General MacArthur (after the General's determination to write a new Constitution became apparent) that the new Constitution should include a 'no war' clause, and that he was therefore the inspirer of article 9 (see CONSTITUTION OF 1946). Though MacArthur in his memoirs lent credence to this, it has not convinced all historians.

After the April 1946 general elections, he was replaced as Prime Minister by his Foreign Minister, YOSHIDA SHIGERU. He died in 1951.

Further reading
Dower (1999)

Shiga Yoshio Shiga Yoshio was born in the same town in Yamaguchi as NOSAKA SANZŌ, though nine years later (1901).

As a student at Tokyo Imperial University in the early 1920s, Shiga became involved with left-wing movements, and joined the JAPAN COMMUNIST PARTY (JCP), though not at its foundation in 1922. He contributed to the movement largely through his journalism and application of Marxist theory to Japanese conditions. With TOKUDA KYŪICHI, he was arrested in 1928 and remained in prison until 1945, being one of the few Communist prisoners who over 18 years locked up refused to recant. Between 1945 and 1950 he was editor of the party journal *Red Flag* (*Akahata*). He was elected to the HOUSE OF REPRESENTATIVES for an Osaka constituency in the 1946 general elections, failed to be elected in 1947, but was elected again in 1949.

When, in January 1950, the Cominform criticised the JCP for excessive softness, Shiga, along with MIYAMOTO KENJI, attacked Tokuda and Nosaka for trying to brush off the criticism, and called for a more radical, militant, anti-American line. A period of intense factional conflict ensued between the 'mainstream' (Tokuda/Nosaka) group and the 'internationalists' (Shiga/Miyamoto) group. In June 1950 Shiga, with much of the leadership, was purged by the Occupation authorities. A degree of reconciliation was effected, and Shiga returned to party office in 1951 though the JCP could not operate openly until later.

Hardly any Communists were elected to Parliament in the 1950s, but Shiga was returned to the Lower House in 1955, 1958 (the only Communist elected), 1960 and 1963, for the first constituency of Osaka. In 1964 the JCP leadership, inclining towards a pro-China line, opposed the partial nuclear test ban treaty that the USSR had ratified. Shiga, preferring the Soviet position, voted against the party line in Parliament, and was expelled from the party. He founded the Voice of Japan Communist Party, which never achieved electoral success.

Shiga died in 1989.

Further reading
Beckmann and Okubo (1969)
Central Committee, Japanese Communist Party (1984)
Stockwin (1965)
Swearingen and Langer (1952, 1968)

Shigemitsu Mamoru Born in 1887 in Oita, Shigemitsu Mamoru graduated in Law from Tokyo Imperial University, and became a diplomat. In 1929 he was appointed Consul-General in Shanghai, and spent the next few years in China. In 1932 he lost a leg in a bomb attack by a disaffected Korean. The next year, however, he was appointed Vice-Minister – the most senior position in the Foreign Ministry. In

1936 he became Ambassador to the USSR, and in 1938 to the United Kingdom. He was Foreign Minister under Tōjō, and later under Koiso, between 1943 and 1945, being one of the Japanese delegates to sign the surrender document on board the USS Missouri on 2 September 1945.

Shigemitsu was Foreign Minister again in the brief Higashikuni Cabinet that immediately followed the defeat. He worked hard behind the scenes to protect the position of the Emperor (*Tennō*). At the Tokyo war crimes trials from 1946, Shigemitsu was sentenced to seven years' imprisonment, but in 1950 he was freed.

With Japan once again independent, Shigemitsu resumed an active political life. In 1952 he was elected President of the Reformist Party (*Kaishintō*), and in 1954 became Vice-President of the newly formed Japan Democratic Party (*Nihon Minshutō*). With the formation of the first Hatoyama Cabinet in 1954, he was chosen as Deputy Prime Minister and Foreign Minister [*see also* CONSERVATIVE PARTIES, 1945–55]. He played a role in the Japan–Soviet normalisation talks in 1956 [*see also* SOVIET UNION AND RUSSIA, RELATIONS WITH]. He died in 1957 aged 70.

Further reading
Dower (1999)

Shii Kazuo In an effort to rejuvenate the superannuated image of the JAPAN COMMUNIST PARTY (JCP) at a time when world Communism appeared to be collapsing, Shii Kazuo was appointed Secretary-General (the third-ranking position) in 1990. Born in 1954, he graduated from Tokyo University, entered the JCP organisation and was responsible for youth and student affairs. He was highly articulate and media-friendly. First elected to the HOUSE OF REPRESENTATIVES at the 1993 general elections for a Chiba constituency, he was returned for the South Kantō regional bloc in the elections of 1996 and 2000. With the retirement of MIYAMOTO KENJI in 1997, Shii became number two in the party to the Chairman, FUWA TETSUZŌ. In September 1998, after good results in the Upper House elections, he announced that if the LIBERAL DEMOCRATIC PARTY failed to obtain a clear majority in subsequent general elections, the JCP might modify its policies opposing the Japan–US Security Treaty prior to discussing a possible coalition with other parties. This departure from uncompromising JCP independence apparently cost the party votes at later elections.

Shinsanbetsu (New Sanbetsu) *Shinsanbetsu* was a small but significant union federation, formed by Hosoya Matsuta as a splinter from the Communist-dominated Congress of Industrial Unions (*Sanbetsu kaigi*). Hosoya had been a founder-member of *Sanbetsu kaigi*, but objected to the Communist interpretation of the SCAP order banning the general strike set for 1 February 1947. *Shinsanbetsu* was born as a federation in 1949, with Hosoya as its leader. Its position was independent of the JAPAN COMMUNIST PARTY, but still on the Marxist left. In the early years of the General Council of Japanese Trade Unions (*Sōhyō*) (1950–1) *Shinsanbetsu* exercised a crucial influence in pushing *Sōhyō* towards the left on a number of issues, thus strengthening the hand of its radical Chairman, Takano Minoru. These included opposition to membership of the International Confederation of Free Trade Unions, support for a neutralist foreign policy and criticism of a 'weak-kneed' approach towards the Occupation-sponsored purge of Communist unionists.

Shinsanbetsu remained in existence until October 1988, when it joined the emergent Japanese Trade Union Council (*Rengō*).

shipbuilding scandal (Zōsen gigoku) (1954)
This scandal probably accelerated the demise of the long-running YOSHIDA Government, and temporarily affected the careers of several close Yoshida supporters. His action in protecting his acolytes against accusations of corruption was one of the most controversial aspects of the affair.

After the 1953 truce in effect ended the Korean War, the boom that the war had created in Japan collapsed, adversely affecting the shipbuilding industry. Elements in the industry responded to this by agitating for Government assistance, and in 1953 a law was passed to provide preferential treatment for the industry. The methods used to obtain this outcome included substantial monetary contributions to both politicians and Government officials. The prosecutors were able to find plenty of hard evidence about what had been going on, and since the payment of money to obtain favourable legislative treatment constitutes a bribe, they sought to bring the culprits to book.

The difficulty was that the presumed culprits included several high-flying politicians, of whom some were top pupils of the 'Yoshida school'. Of these, both SATŌ EISAKU and IKEDA HAYATO were future Prime Ministers, destined successively to be at the head of the Government for a full 12 years from 1960. Ikeda was exonerated, but Satō was not. Yoshida, still Prime Minister in 1954 when the cases came for trial, was determined to save Satō, his star pupil, who enjoyed immunity from prosecution while Parliament was sitting. Yoshida persuaded his Minister of Justice not to ask the HOUSE OF REPRESENTATIVES to waive his immunity from arrest. The Minister complied, but promptly resigned, and the Government then survived a motion of no confidence. At the end of the year, Satō was ultimately arrested during a parliamentary recess, and put on trial, but was released two years later because of a general amnesty.

The shipbuilding scandal damaged the Yoshida Government, and contributed to its fall. If it had a positive effect, it was that the business world went on to ensure that political funding would be placed within a more stable institutional framework. Many years were to pass, however, before the phenomenon of money for political favours was tackled with the vigour that was required.

Further reading
Masumi (1985)
Mitchell (1996)

Shōwa Denkō scandal (1948) Between June 1947 and October 1948 Government was in the hands of a three party coalition led, successively, by the JAPAN SOCIALIST PARTY Chairman, KATAYAMA TETSU, and the DEMOCRATIC PARTY Chairman, ASHIDA HITOSHI. It was a turbulent period, in which political corruption flourished, and interest groups affected by the radical changes of the time did not hesitate to take extreme measures to have their demands heard. The proposals of the Katayama Government for nationalising the coal-mining industry had actually been followed by an unsuccessful plot to murder Cabinet ministers. Prominent politicians, including the Deputy Prime Minister in the Ashida Cabinet, NISHIO SUEHIRO, were caught up in an unrelated bribery scandal, and Nishio had to resign, though he was acquitted. The young TANAKA KAKUEI, who was to be Prime Minister between 1972 and 1974, was given a six months' prison sentence, quashed on appeal.

In this charged political atmosphere, not long into the tenure of the Ashida Cabinet, the *Shōwa Denkō* (Shōwa Electric) scandal broke. The circumstances of this affair were complicated, but in essence Hinohara Setsuzō, President of *Shōwa Denkō* (a chemical fertiliser company), had distributed very large sums of money to numbers of Government officials and politicians. His aim was to take over various firms that were being broken up in the Occupation's anti-conglomerate drive. Accusations of receiving bribes from the company were directed both at the Prime Minister, Ashida, and also at Nishio, as well as several others. FUKUDA TAKEO, at that time heading the Budget Bureau of the MINISTRY OF FINANCE, and later Prime Minister between 1976 and 1978, was one of several others arrested in connection with the affair.

An unusual aspect of the affair was that it pitted the SCAP Government Section against the Staff Section G2, led by Major General Charles Willoughby. Some writers have regarded the affair as involving an attempt by G2 to discredit the liberal Colonel Charles Kades, of the Government Section, and to get rid of Ashida and his coalition Government. If this is the case, Willoughby succeeded.

The political repercussions of the *Shōwa Denkō* scandal were profound. The Ashida Government fell in October 1948, and was succeeded by the second Yoshida administration, which lasted for more than six years and oversaw the transition from Occupation to the return of independence. In the general elections of January 1949, the three parties of the coalition Government were badly defeated, and in particular the Socialists suffered a crushing reverse (though they later recovered). The change from a left-of-centre coalition Government to one balanced towards the right wing mirrored the shift in priorities of the Occupation from democratising and demilitarising Japan, to creating a strong ally amidst the gathering clouds of the Cold War. Even though the details of the *Shōwa Denkō* scandal remain murky, the opportunity it provided for political manipulation by both Japanese and Americans should not be underestimated.

Further reading
Masumi (1985)
Mitchell (1996)

Social Democratic League (SDL, Shakai minshu rengō, Shaminren) The Social Democratic League (sometimes also known in English as the Social Democratic Federation, or the United Social Democratic Party) was initiated in 1977 by EDA SABURŌ who had decided that, instead of trying to reform the Japan Socialist Party (JSP) from within, he could better found a new party to stimulate rethinking in the centre-left. Initially called the Socialist Citizens' League (*Shakai Shimin Rengō, Shashiren*), its name was changed after Eda unexpectedly died just after he had left the JSP. The mantle thus fell on his son, EDA SATSUKI, who created the SDL along with KAN NAOTO and others. Another group of defectors, including the broadcaster, Den Hideo, joined it soon after its formation.

Never more than a mini-party, it began with six parliamentarians across the two houses, and remained more or less at that level throughout its existence. It had, however, a high profile, and sought to bring about co-operation between parties of the centre-left. Until 1985, its 'representative' (i.e. leader) was Den Hideo, but then Eda Satsuki replaced him. Its platform was based on ideas of modernised social democracy.

In 1992 Eda organised a discussion group called 'Sirius', as a kind of SDL extension. The party participated in the HOSOKAWA coalition Government (in which Eda was Minister of Science and Technology) from August 1993, but in 1994, 'our mission accomplished', in the words of one of its parliamentarians, the party dissolved and its members dispersed.

social welfare (shakai fukushi) The provision of social welfare in Japan has been an arena for the clash of ideologies. On the one hand, there is the idea of 'traditional' welfare, based on family, company and local community, cheap to provide, with minimal State expenditure, and rooted in conservative moral values. On the other hand, the influence has been felt of comprehensive and egalitarian systems of welfare, with substantial financial and organisational commitment from the State. The first has been put forward as a quintessentially Japanese method of welfare provision, and the second as a Western method. But this form of designation, contrasting a 'Japanese' with a 'Western' approach, contains a considerable degree of ideological manipulation.

Such welfare provision as existed before the Asia–Pacific War tended to serve the aims of control by the State as much as that of relieving distress or alleviating poverty. During the period of the Allied Occupation, some attempts were made to introduce more comprehensive systems, but neither the finances nor the instincts of the Japanese Government were conducive to this taking place except to a limited extent. Meanwhile, an institution inherited from the pre-war period was renamed and developed. This was the institution of welfare commissioners (*minsei iin*). These have continued to expand in numbers, and, according to Roger Goodman, there were 190,000 of them by the late 1990s (Goodman *et al.*, 1998, p. 144). They are unpaid (apart from some reimbursement of expenses), largely untrained, more commonly male than female, typically in late middle age or even older, and respected in the local community. A typical welfare commissioner gives 90 days' service a year. By contrast, local government welfare officials (*Shakai fukushi shūji*) do not exceed 15,000 throughout the country (Goodman, ibid.) and have to rely on the welfare commissioners to make home visits and do most follow-up work.

During the 'economic miracle' period of the 1960s minimal State welfare provision was made tolerable by the fact that unemployment hardly existed. Moreover, divorce rates were extremely low, meaning that there were few broken homes. Illegitimacy was (and is) a rarity, and single-parent families uncommon (mainly resulting from the premature death of one parent). The population was also predominantly young. Towards the end of that period, however, political pressure and a need for the LIBERAL DEMOCRATIC PARTY to attract new support led to the placing of much greater emphasis on State welfare provision by the TANAKA Government. The year 1973 was designated 'Year One of Welfare' (*fukushi gannen*). Shortly thereafter, the first oil crisis brought economic growth to a juddering halt, and, though it was to resume later in the decade, this experience exerted a profoundly negative impact on Government attitudes towards spending money on welfare schemes.

It was hardly coincidental that the late 1970s and early 1980s saw the 'Japanese' welfare approach put forward as a model deserving of study and emulation. One Japanese writer even described Japan as a 'Welfare Super-Power' (Nakagawa, 1979), and Ezra Vogel, in his *Japan as Number One* (1979), lauded Japanese welfare policy. Within Japan itself reliance on family, workplace and local community were trumpeted as the best way of preventing the disease of welfare dependence, and Western systems of welfare provision, based on entitlement and high levels of expenditure by the State, were regularly denigrated.

With the downturn in the Japanese economy from the early 1990s, unemployment began to rise and 'traditional' methods of welfare provision began to seem less adequate to cope with increasing levels of social distress. Moreover, the age profile of the population was rapidly shifting towards the older age groups – a phenomenon that concerned policy-makers more and more urgently. The abortive attempt of the HOSOKAWA coalition Government early in 1994 to bring in a 'welfare tax' (*fukushi zei*) was actually the product of a strategy by the MINISTRY OF FINANCE. But it reflected a concern that the tax base was likely to be inadequate to cope with increasing welfare demands over the coming decades. This did not mean that 'traditional' methods were likely to be abandoned, since the need to avoid excessive welfare dependence would increase rather than decrease with the ageing society. But political pressures for approaches that would at least supplement 'traditional' methods by State provision were to some extent increasing.

Further reading
Campbell (1992)
Collick, in Stockwin et al. (1988)
Goodman *et al.* (1998)
Nakagawa (1979)
Vogel (1979)

South Asia, relations with The attention paid in Japan to the nations of South Asia (India, Pakistan, Bangladesh, Sri Lanka, Nepal, Bhutan, Maldives) is far less than that paid to South-East Asian nations. Similarly, Japan has ranked low in the attention scale of South Asian countries, their governments, business communities and intellectuals. The contrast with South-East Asia is surprising, given the fact that India, in particular, had a remarkably favourable view of Japan after 1945, and worked hard to help secure Japanese membership of the United Nations in 1956. In much of South-East Asia, by contrast, relations with Japan at the end of the war were extremely antagonistic; yet close linkages soon developed.

Speaking broadly, the following factors may be cited to explain the relative thinness of relations between South Asian countries and Japan. First, Cold War logic by the early 1950s had tied Japan firmly into the United States-led anti-Communist camp, whereas India, by far the largest state in South Asia, hovered between non-alignment and close relations with the Soviet Union. Although the JAPAN SOCIALIST PARTY was inspired in the 1950s by the Nehru brand of non-alignment (or neutralism), this was not to the liking of the mainstream LIBERAL DEMOCRATIC PARTY, which occupied the Government benches in Parliament from 1955.

Second, South Asian countries (but again, particularly India) developed economic policies from the 1950s seeking autarchic goals rather than a free and open trading regime. For Japanese firms, doing business in the circumstances was a bureaucratic and painful experience. But the policies also tended to inhibit development, which made economic interaction with these countries doubly unattractive.

Third, most South Asian countries came to be regarded in Japan as politically unstable.

Sudden changes of policy resulting from shifts in the political landscape were seen among Japanese businessmen as introducing unacceptable uncertainty into the business environment. Kalam (in Jain (ed.), 1996, pp. 129–32) gives the example of the demand by a new Government in Bangladesh to renegotiate a fertiliser contract, recently signed by the preceding Government.

Fourth, regional inter-state (and in some cases, intra-state) conflicts were seen as dangerous and unpredictable. There has been a particularly sharp reaction in Japan against the recent nuclear weapons programmes (and tests) of both India and Pakistan, and for the potential for nuclear war presented by the long-running conflict in Kashmir. For obvious reasons, anti-nuclear feeling in Japan runs very deep [*see also* NUCLEAR ISSUES].

Fifth, within South Asia itself, and despite not inconsequential trade with Japan, serious interest in Japan has been, at least until rather recently, at remarkably low levels. The cultural factors that tend to link Japan with other East and South-East Asian countries are largely missing, and, for reasons already suggested, the Japanese commercial presence in South Asian countries, which might have stimulated such interest, has not been extensive.

Finally, some have argued that cultural factors play a significant role in the shallow nature of the relationship. Although Buddhism is central to the culture of Japan, it has largely disappeared from South Asia, except for its southern and northern peripheries (Sri Lanka, Bhutan and to some extent Nepal). The kinds and extent of religious divisions in the region are largely outside the Japanese experience. The caste system in India also creates problems of comprehension. The larger South Asian countries are multi-lingual, multi-confessional and multi-ethnic to an extent that is far beyond Japanese experience within Japan. People differ fundamentally in other ways as well. A German priest, long resident in Japan, once told the present writer that, in his experience, the two most difficult problems for a chairman in international conferences were to persuade Japanese to talk, and Indians to stop talking. The Japanese social anthropologist, Nakane Chie, published an influential book in 1970 entitled *Japanese Society*. She told the present writer that she had developed the idea for the book during a stay in India, where she was able to study members of the Japanese expatriate community. She noticed the extreme contrast in their modes of behaviour from those in Indian society. On the other hand, the operation of personal factions in Japanese and Indian political parties suggests remarkable similarity (Stockwin, 1970).

Since the 1990s, and following the ending of the Cold War, the geo-strategic situation of South Asia has changed and become more complex. India has put in place more outward-looking economic policies, which have been reflected in modest increases in economic interaction with Japan. The Indian economy was growing at around 6 per cent per annum in 2002. But the unstable situation over Kashmir, with its nuclear overtones, can only do harm to the relationship of Japan with South Asian countries in general, and India and Pakistan in particular.

Further reading
Jain (ed.) (1996)
Jain, in Inoguchi and Jain (eds) (2000)
Nakane (1970)
Panda and Ando (eds) (1997)
Stockwin (1970)

South-East Asia, relations with Japan, since the end of the Asia–Pacific War, has been constrained in its relations with South-East Asia for two main reasons. One is the memory of Japanese occupation during the war, and the other is Japan's relationship with the United States. Of these the second is a more important factor than the first.

The Japanese occupation was often brutal, and had many terrible effects throughout the region, but its duration was relatively short. Korea and China, as Lam Peng Er points out (2000, p. 254), suffered for much longer periods from Japanese colonialism than did the nations of South-East Asia, and were bitter about it for longer. Japan's bilateral relations with the United States, by contrast, remain the central pillar of Japanese foreign policy, and create limits beyond which any Japanese initiative aimed at South-East Asia may not venture. As a means to solving the Asian economic crisis that broke out in 1997, the Japanese Government proposed an Asian Monetary Fund (AMF), but this provoked such sharp criticism from the US Government that it had to be dropped.

During the 1950s Japan entered into bilateral aid agreements with several states of the region, though formally described as reparations. Most of these were geared, through various means, towards the supply of Japanese manufactured goods, and thus facilitated Japanese economic re-entry into the region on a large scale. It was particularly important, at that period, for Japanese manufacturing industry to be able to trade with countries to the south of Japan, since until the 1970s little economic interaction was possible with China. Japan attempted few political initiatives, though the abortive attempt of the Ikeda Government to mediate in the *konfrontasi* dispute between Indonesia and the newly created Malaysia in the early 1960s should be noted.

The Vietnam War tested both the Japan–US relationship and the stability of domestic politics in Japan itself. While SATŌ EISAKU was Prime Minister, however, Japanese Government policy was to support the US war effort in Vietnam in almost all its aspects. A key factor in Satō's calculations was his determination to have Okinawa returned to Japan, and to achieve this he needed to show steadfast loyalty to the US cause.

Once the Vietnam War was out of the way, it became rather easier for Japan to take its own initiatives in relation to the region. But a reminder that the region was less than complacent about Japanese economic penetration came in January 1974. The Prime Minister, TANAKA KAKUEI, making an official tour of South-East Asian nations, was confronted by widespread protests and rioting, most seriously in Jakarta.

An important development in South-East Asia was the formation of the Association of South-East Asian Nations (ASEAN) in 1967, and its gradual development into a cohesive regional bloc. In the late 1970s Japan and ASEAN set up structures for discussion and interaction between them. But the most important development of the 1970s was the announcement of the 'Fukuda Doctrine' by the Prime Minister, FUKUDA TAKEO, in 1977. The Doctrine was couched in general terms about regional friendship, but most importantly it ruled out a major regional military role for Japan, and proposed that Japan should act to facilitate relations between ASEAN and the Indochina states.

Complex local and international conflicts concerning the Indochina states throughout the 1980s made this last ideal difficult to fulfil. During the 1990s, however, Japan played an active diplomatic role in relation to Cambodia, including taking part in the UN peace-keeping mission there after the Peace-Keeping Operations (PKO) bill finally passed into law in Tokyo in 1992. The gradual improvement in Cambodian stability (though there have been serious setbacks along the way) since 1990 owes much to Japanese diplomacy in co-ordination with ASEAN.

Another South-East Asian state, Myanmar (Burma), has been the focus of quiet but intensive Japanese diplomacy to try to break the logjam between the democratically elected leader, Aung San Suu Kyi, and the ruling military junta. The Burmese example, however, appears to demonstrate the limits of a Japanese diplomacy based on the idea that quiet mediation combined with an inclination to assist economic development will eventually create an improved political situation. In the Burmese case, the junta maintains its iron grip on the country and there has been little effective economic development.

There have been a number of initiatives to establish regional organisations covering East and South-East Asia, with Japanese participation. The most durable of these has been Asia Pacific Economic Co-operation (APEC), founded in 1980 on Japanese initiative, but with Australian sponsorship. It is also the regional organisation with the widest spread, since its membership extends to the eastern side of the Pacific. A principal aim of APEC has been to seek and promote multilateral solutions to economic problems, rather than bilateral solutions that leave some states out in the cold. From the early 1990s, the US role in APEC has been dominant, so that it has taken on a strong colouring of liberal free market economics.

Partly based on unhappiness about US ideological leadership of APEC, Malaysia proposed in 1991 an East Asian Economic Council (EAEC), specifically excluding those states of APEC deemed to be external to the region, notably the United States, Australia and New Zealand. This posed a dilemma for Japan, since the EAEC concept envisaged Japan taking a leadership role, but, had Japan preferred EAEC to APEC, this would have risked jeopardising her relationship with the United States. In the end EAEC was allowed to develop within the framework of APEC, making things easier for Japan. As Hook et al. (2001) comment, Japan

> can push an agenda within APEC of considering the interests of ASEAN and the other East Asian countries in the face of US demands for liberalization by stressing the need for economic development assistance and staged changes to accompany this process. On the other hand, the APEC framework, most vitally, keeps the US engaged in the region.

One regional body where Japan has taken a leadership role is the Asian Development Bank (ADB), whose disbursement of funds has been heavily concentrated in the South-East Asian area.

Whereas Japan has tended towards reticence on matters of military security, relying on the Japan–US Mutual Security Treaty for its own security and appearing less concerned with the security of the region, there has been one important Japanese initiative in this field. This is the Asian Regional Forum (ARF), proposed by Japan in 1991 and established in 1994. It is not yet a substantial player in regional security matters, but some observers (e.g. Lam, 2000, p. 257) regard it as having potential. As a specifically Japanese initiative in the security area, it merits attention.

Economically, Japan is dominant in South-East Asia. Its GNP amounts to more than half that of the whole of Asia (however defined), and Japanese companies are an integral part of the economies of most South-East Asian states. This contrasts with Japanese reticence on political and diplomatic issues, although the effectiveness of Japanese low-key diplomacy in some trouble spots should not be underestimated. In recent years, Japan has had to tread a fine line between her all-important relationship with the United States and her aspirations for a possible future role as regional leader. The stagnation of the Japanese economy over the past decade has slowed down possible developments in the latter direction. Nevertheless, Japan remains an economic giant in the region, and, as Lam speculates (p. 264), in conceivable future circumstances South-East Asians might come to regard Japan as a useful political and strategic counterweight to China.

Further reading
Drifte (1998)
Hook *et al.* (2001)
Lam, in Inoguchi and Jain (2000)
Nishihara (1975)
Wihtol (1988)

Soviet Union and Russia, relations with
There have been few periods in their interactions since the late nineteenth century when relations between Japan and its huge northern neighbour could be said to be friendly. Before the nineteenth century, the two scarcely came into contact. This changed, however, when both began to develop and expand their territories. Since the native peoples (*Ainu* and related groups) were few in number and had no military capacity, both Japanese and Russians regarded these lands as empty, to be occupied and exploited at will. The disputed territories comprised the large island of Sakhalin (Karafuto in Japanese), due north of Hokkaidō, and the island chain (called Kuriles by the Russians, and Chishima, or 'thousand islands', by the Japanese) linking eastern Hokkaidō with the Kamchatka peninsula. Between the 1870s and 1945, the official border between Russian and Japanese territory changed several times.

Moreover, the interests of the two sides clashed on the north-east Asian mainland. In 1904–5 Russia and Japan fought a major war, the Russo-Japanese War, which resulted in Japanese victory. This was noted around the world, and enhanced Japan's reputation as the first Asian state in modern times to defeat a European power in battle. Following the Bolshevik Revolution of October 1917, Japanese forces invaded eastern parts of Siberia, and were only withdrawn some four years later. Then between May and September 1939 Japan and the Soviet Union fought a small but vicious war at a Manchurian–Mongolian border area called Nomonhan. During the Asia–Pacific War of 1941–5, the two states were bound by a Neutrality Pact concluded in 1941. But in the last week of the war Stalin broke the Neutrality Pact and conducted a blitzkrieg invasion of mainland and island areas controlled by Japan. Many Japanese were taken prisoner, and of those who survived a great number remained incarcerated in Siberia for the next decade.

Soviet actions at the end of the war came to be regarded in Japan as a great betrayal, and negatively affected Japanese perceptions of their northern neighbour over a very long period indeed. Japan avoided the German fate of Soviet participation in a divided Occupation, but the Soviet Union did not sign the San Francisco Peace Treaty of 1951, and technically, therefore, a state of war persisted between Japan and the USSR. YOSHIDA's successor as Prime Minister, HATOYAMA ICHIRŌ, concluded in 1956 an agreement with the Soviet Union to normalise diplomatic relations, but was unsuccessful in bringing about a peace treaty. The principal issue frustrating conclusion of a peace treaty was a territorial dispute that still remains unresolved 46 years later, in 2002.

The territorial dispute is complex and needs to be described in some detail. The islands in dispute were (and are) Etorofu (Russian, Iturup), the largest of the Kuriles and the most northerly island under dispute; Kunashiri (Russian, Kunashir), immediately south-west of Etorofu; Shikotan, a much smaller island due south of the southern tip of Etorofu; and the Habomai group of very small islands between Shikotan and the Nemuro peninsula in Hokkaidō. As the Japanese side was able to point out, none of these territories had ever been Russian before 1945. Between the Treaty of Shimoda in 1855 and the Treaty of St Petersburg in 1875, the boundary between Russia and Japan was placed in the strait between Etorofu and the island to its north-east, Uruppu (Russian, Urup). The latter treaty had ceded to Japan the rest of the Kurile chain, including Shimushu island just off the coast of Kamchatka. Moreover, there was a further distinction between Etorofu and Kunashiri, on the one hand, and Shikotan and the Habomai group, on the other. Whereas the first two were plainly part of the Kurile chain, the latter two were not, and indeed had been administered up to 1945 as part of Hokkaidō proper. A Japanese Government document of 1946 discovered by Hara in the Australian archives makes this distinction clearly (Hara, 1998, pp. 24–33), in contrast to later official positions lumping all four territories into the same category. During the negotiations leading to the San Francisco Peace Treaty, the Yoshida Government publicly claimed the return of the Habomai group and Shikotan (or, as it was sometimes put, the Habomai group including Shikotan), but at this stage Etorofu and Kunashiri did not appear to be in dispute.

In the negotiations between the two governments held in 1955 and 1956, the Japanese position eventually developed into a four-island claim. But this was not entirely on Japanese initiative. By the summer of 1956 the Japanese Foreign Minister, SHIGEMITSU MAMORU, and Soviet Foreign Minister, Dmitry Shepilov, were close to an agreement on a peace treaty, involving the return to Japan of Shikotan and the Habomais. But in August 1956, the US Secretary of State, John Foster Dulles, issued a statement warning Japan that concessions to the USSR on the territorial issue would risk jeopardising Japan's eventual claim for the return of Okinawa. In the aftermath of the Dulles statement, the Japanese Government felt obliged to pursue a claim for Etorofu and Kunashiri, as well as Shikotan and Habomai, thus wrecking the prospects for a peace treaty for more than one generation. Dulles's primary motivation was to use the Okinawa issue to frustrate any kind of rapprochement between Japan and the USSR. Indeed, it seems very likely, as Hara argues (p. 44), that had the Soviet negotiators agreed to return all four islands, the US Government would have pressured Japan to hold out for the return of other territory lost by Japan in 1945, including the northern Kuriles and perhaps the southern part of Sakhalin.

Subsequently the official Japanese position was that all four islands should be returned to Japan. Between 1956 and 1960 the Soviet offer to return Shikotan and Habomai on conclusion of a peace treaty apparently still stood. But around the time of the Security Treaty revision crisis in 1960 Nikita Khrushchev placed a further condition on the return of these islands, namely that Japan should renounce the Security Treaty. Subsequently, the territorial dispute became stalemated, with successive Soviet leaders holding that no territorial issue existed, whereas Japanese governments maintained their four-island claim. Some hope of a breakthrough seemed possible with an official visit to Japan by Gorbachev in 1991, but by that time the Soviet leader's domestic position had weakened to the point where he could not risk alienating nationalist sentiment by ceding territory to Japan. Given that, had he done so, the Soviet Union would probably have benefited in a big way from favourable economic treatment by Japan, it seems possible that his judgement may have been at fault in not conceding.

Various developments took place in the 1990s, the most important of which was an agreement in 1997 between Prime Minister HASHIMOTO and President Yeltsin to settle outstanding issues by 2000. But 2000 came and went, and the territorial dispute remained unresolved.

The territorial issue is important because it created a recurrent irritant that perpetuated unfriendly attitudes on both sides based on history, ideology and geo-politics. No doubt this was the long-term situation Dulles was aiming at when he made his unhelpful intervention in 1956. In the Soviet period there were, it is true, fluctuations in the degree of coolness between the two sides. The early 1970s saw a slight thaw, and that was a period in which a major oil pipeline scheme was under discussion, though it was to come to nothing. The late 1970s and early 1980s, however, included a number of episodes that turned mere coolness into heavy frost. These included the Soviet invasion of Afghanistan in 1979, and the shooting down of a Korean airliner, with many Japanese passengers on board, that had strayed over Soviet air space in September 1983. Violations of Japanese air space by Soviet military aircraft averaged more than 300 per year.

The collapse of the Soviet Union at the end of 1991 led to some improvements in relations between Japan and the new Russia. Japan's northern neighbour could no longer so easily be classified as an 'enemy', and US pressure to stay aloof was removed. But chaotic economic conditions in Russia hardly encouraged major investment initiatives in Russian industries by Japanese firms. What it did do was to open up links on a modest but still significant scale between Japan and Russian territories to her north. Enterprising businessmen, for instance, set up a rather lucrative industry selling Japanese second-hand cars in nearby coastal areas of Russia. Travel between the two countries became much easier. Some of the antagonisms of the past began to dissipate. The security pressure felt over four decades by Japan from Soviet armed forces to her north disappeared. But, unaccountably, there was still no solution to the territorial dispute over a few rocky islands on the edge of the northern Pacific. This seems a triumph of nationalistic pride on both sides over common sense and neighbourly feelings. Ironically, exceptional progress was made towards solving this issue during the last seven months of the otherwise unpromising Mori administration that ended in April 2001. Mori's successor, Koizumi, failed to follow through the initiatives taken, and the talks came to nothing. Rozman, however, argues in a 2002 article that the prospects for a settlement may be improving.

Further reading

Braddick, in Inoguchi and Jain (eds) (2000)
Hara (1998)
Hellmann (1969)
Ivanov and Smith (eds) (1999)
Rozman (1992)
—— (2002)
Vishwanathan (1973)
Welfield (1988)

Sports Peace Party (Supōtsu heiwatō) The former all-in wrestler, 'Antonio' Inoki, founded this mini-party in the late 1980s. Inoki was first elected from the proportional representation constituency of the House of Councillors in July 1989, his party gaining just under a million votes, or 1.77 per cent of those voting.

Late in 1990, Inoki rescued 39 Japanese nationals held against their will in Iraq by the Government of Saddam Hussein. Although he did not stand in July 1992, his party gained 3.06 per cent of the vote, and one candidate was elected. In 1995 and 1998, however, the party polled 1.33 and 0.85 per cent of the vote, and failed to elect any candidate. It did not contest the 2001 elections.

student political movements From early in the post-war period, political activism by student organisations was a highly visible feature of Japanese politics. The causes espoused by student activists were for the most part closely related to the issues motivating left-of-centre political parties. These included defence of the earlier, democratising and demilitarising, reforms of the Allied Occupation, opposition to 'feudal practices' in politics, the economy and social life, defence of the interests of workers against oppression from 'monopoly capital', and opposition to what was termed 'American imperialism'. This last became in many ways the most important aim for much of the student movement of the 1950s and 1960s. The other side of the coin of combating 'imperialism' in its American variety came to be defence of the peace CONSTITUTION OF 1946. The decade from 1950 to 1960 saw the gradual incorporation of an internationally weak Japan into the US anti-Communist security structure in East Asia. This meant forming the Self-Defence Forces (1954) [see also DEFENCE], creating (1951–2), then revising (1960) the Japan–US Security Treaty, and perpetuating the presence of US forces on Japanese soil [see also UNITED STATES, RELATIONS WITH].

Within the broad lines of these political attitudes a turbulent political environment had developed between, and indeed within, political parties of the left. Factional rivalries were fought out, in which ideological issues were used as ammunition. Organisational rivalry between the JAPAN COMMUNIST PARTY (JCP) and JAPAN SOCIALIST PARTY (JSP) was particularly intense. Given the potential organisational strength of the student movement, the control of it was a valuable prize.

The main national student organisation in the 1950s was the All-Japan Federation of Student Self-Governing Associations (*Zengakuren*). In the middle of the decade this largely worked under the auspices of the JCP, but in 1958 the bulk of its membership, finding JCP control too bureaucratic and constraining, broke away from party control. It was this, more or less politically independent, *Zengakuren* that mobilised many thousands of students from various campuses in the SECURITY TREATY REVISION CRISIS of 1959–60. They mounted massive demonstrations on a number of famous occasions, alongside the massed ranks of labour unionists and others.

The *Zengakuren* was in essence an umbrella organisation for a large number of small groups of students from particular universities, professing various political outlooks, mostly, however, within a broad Marxist framework. The movement was extremely fluid and decentralised, but none the less effective for that. Some of its leaders were impressively able, and made their mark in brilliant careers later in life. It was largely non-violent, and indeed such violence as occurred was perpetrated against it by groups of ultra-rightists. Nevertheless, the sheer scale of the whole movement (of which the students were a large part) was such that ultimately the Eisenhower visit had to be cancelled and KISHI was forced out of office. One student died, a woman called Kanba Michiko, who was trampled underfoot during a major demonstration.

In the immediate aftermath of the crisis, groups of students returned to their home towns and villages, determined to spread the message of resistance to American 'imperialism' and defence of the pacifist message of the Constitution. This was known as the 'Return Home Movement' (*Kikyō undō*). The students involved encountered the entrenched conservatism of rural and small-town Japan, and learned that changing people's attitudes, particularly those of the older generation, was much less easy than they had thought.

In the late 1960s the Vietnam War brought into being an atmosphere of protest in universities around the world. From 1968 Japanese university campuses exploded in an extraordinary outpouring of radical student activity. Once again, the movement was not centrally controlled, but rather consisted of numerous small groups concentrated in particular universities. Again, the personality and leadership ability of particular leaders was a crucial factor. Left-wing political parties, it is true, had their own student wings, which were part of the broader movement, but there was a strong sense of anarchism in the way the movement developed. The Great Proletarian Cultural Revolution in China served as an inspiration for some student groups, and the influence of Maoism was widespread [see also CHINA (PRC AND ROC), RELATIONS WITH].

At the same time as international protest over the Vietnam War, and protest with a domestic focus against the policies of the Satō Government, issues local to particular universities played a considerable part. Student revolt in Tokyo University – regarded as the most elite university in the land – actually began in the Medical Faculty, as a protest against an 'intern' system regarded as exploitative and feudalistic. With great speed, however, the movement spread throughout the student body and developed an ideological agenda far removed from the issues that had sparked it off. Television audiences around the world were shown footage of the police siege of the Yasuda Hall (*Yasuda kōdō*), at that time the principal administrative building of the University's Hongō campus. In an effort to dislodge the students that had invaded the building, the police were seen 'bombing' it with tear gas canisters dropped from helicopters. The situation became so serious that the university had to be closed for several months and one year's student entry was cancelled.

A positive long-term effect of campus protest in the late 1960s and early 1970s was that university authorities came to listen more carefully to student interests and views, and to some extent mechanisms were set up through which these could be formally expressed. In addition, the Government had been placed on notice that too close a relationship with US military aims risked causing serious social disruption. A much more negative effect – apart from the great disruption to normal university activities caused by the crisis – was that a few groups emerged from the movement so disillusioned with peaceful protest that they embarked on a career of violence [see also EXTREMIST MOVEMENTS (LEFT)].

After the early 1970s universities quickly returned to normal, and protest groups for the most part lost membership and scaled down their activities. By the 1980s it was the political and social conservatism of most students that caused wringing of hands by observers, rather than their radicalism. By the 1990s unhappy students were more likely to take refuge in religion rather than politics, and sects such as the Unification Church (colloquially known as the Moonies) were active on many campuses. Most students, however, were secular, materialistic and relatively non-political.

Further reading
Krauss (1974)

Sun Party (Taiyōtō) Although OZAWA ICHIRŌ and HATA TSUTOMU had worked closely together for several years (but most notably in 1992–3 when they split the TAKESHITA faction, formed the JAPAN RENEWAL PARTY, and broke away from the LIBERAL DEMOCRATIC PARTY), relations between them became increasingly tense during the first two years of the NEW FRONTIER PARTY (NFP). Thus, in December 1996, Hata, with twelve of his close associates, left the NFP and formed the Sun Party – surely the most attractively named of the various new parties formed at this period. Its politics were somewhat to the left of the mainstream of the NFP, and, after the break-up of the latter at the end of 1997, Hata and most of his associates joined the Minseitō in late January 1998, and, in April, the DEMOCRATIC PARTY.

Supreme Court power of judicial review In the 1889 Constitution, the courts had no power of judicial review. Such a power, however, was granted to the Supreme Court (*Saikō saibansho*) in the CONSTITUTION OF 1946. Article 81 of the Constitution states: 'The Supreme Court is the court of last resort with power to determine the constitutionality of any law, order, regulation or official act.' Judicial review, therefore, was a post-war innovation, plainly inspired by practice in the United States. The Japanese Supreme Court took time to become used to the exercise of this new power, which it has used extremely sparingly.

The theory and practice of judicial review bears on the question of separation of powers between the judiciary, legislature and executive. In the United States, this is a central feature of the political system. In Japan, by contrast, the idea of separating powers in the US sense had been largely absent until the 1946 Constitution. The Supreme Court therefore had to feel its way in uncharted territory. One of its first challenges, following the return of Japanese independent statehood with the San Francisco settlement in 1952, was to decide whether it should exercise its power of judicial review in relation to the constitutionality of the National Police reserve, which preceded the Self-Defence Forces. In the Suzuki case of that year, the Supreme Court decided that it could act on matters of constitutionality 'only where a concrete dispute exists between specific parties'. Interestingly, it justified this position on separation-of-powers grounds, arguing that, unless it confined its use of judicial review to cases of specific dispute, it would risk usurping too much power rightly belonging to the other two branches.

In similar vein, the Supreme Court has resorted on various occasions to the doctrine of the 'political question', ruling out of its jurisdiction 'sensitive political issues', since, unlike CABINET or Parliament, 'the courts cannot bear political responsibility'. It should be noted that this self-denying stance is highly controversial, with some arguing that the Court should be more proactive when fundamental rights are concerned (Oda, 1999, pp. 40–1). In the 1959 Sunakawa decision the Supreme Court used the doctrine of the 'political question' to overturn a judgment of the Tokyo District Court arguing that the Japan–US Security Treaty and its Administrative Agreement were unconstitutional under the terms of article 9 of the Constitution. In several rather similar cases relating to military base extensions in Hokkaidō in the 1970s and 1980s, the Supreme Court managed to avoid the issue of constitutionality.

There have, however, been five cases (up to 1999) where the Supreme Court has declared unconstitutional specific legal provisions. Of these, the first one is the most interesting, because it bears on a discrepancy between traditional cultural and modern universalistic norms. This was the Aizawa patricide case of 1973. The pre-war criminal code provided more severe penalties for murder of a lineal ascendant (father, grandfather) than for 'ordinary' murder. This was based on Confucian principles of reverence for ancestors, but it clashed with the constitutional principle of equality of rights before the law. Whereas in 1950 the Supreme Court had refused to find the provision contrary to the Constitution, in 1973 it found it unconstitutional. But owing to political opposition among conservatives within the LIBERAL DEMOCRATIC PARTY, the law was not changed until 1994.

The other cases may be briefly summarised. The following were declared unconstitutional: in 1962 a provision of the Customs Law; in 1975 provision of the Pharmaceutical Law controlling the location of chemists' shops; and in 1987 a provision of the Forestry Law. Finally, there were several Supreme Court judgments declaring unconstitutional wide differences in the value of a vote between different electoral districts, though in each case the Court stopped short of seeking to invalidate a previous election. But the pressure thus placed on Parliament by the Court did eventually result in some (inadequate) remedial action. It is interesting that, in these cases concerning inequality in the value of votes, the Supreme Court was prepared to step into an area of controversy that was politically sensitive. But the history of the interaction between the judicial and legislative branches on issues of electoral malapportionment (the 'negative gerrymander') indicated that the effective power of the Court was quite limited.

The evidence strongly suggests that the power of judicial review under article 81, though not quite a dead letter, is a mere shadow of its US counterpart.

Further reading
Beer (ed.) (1992)
Beer and Itoh (1996)
Oda (1999)

Suzuki Mosaburō Suzuki Mosaburō was a charismatic Socialist politician, and a central figure in Japanese-style left-wing Socialism throughout the 1950s.

Born in 1893, he graduated from Waseda University and became a journalist, being much influenced by the Bolshevik Revolution of 1917 and the Marxism that inspired it. He sought, however, a peaceful road to proletarian revolution in Japan, and did not join the JAPAN COMMUNIST PARTY, founded clandestinely in 1922, entering instead the complex world of proletarian-Socialist parties in 1928. In 1937 he and several hundred others were arrested in the 'popular front incident', having founded in the same year the Japan Proletarian Party, which had a clear (and thus illegal) Marxist colouring.

After the war he joined the newly formed JAPAN SOCIALIST PARTY (JSP), entering Parliament in 1946. But as Chairman of the Lower House budget committee in February 1948 he was instrumental in forcing the resignation of the Socialist-led KATAYAMA Cabinet, when his committee rejected a Government deal over the pay of civil servants. With the JSP moving towards the left after the fall of that Government, he became its Secretary-General in 1948 and Chairman in 1951. When the JSP split over the peace settlement in October of the same year, he became Chairman, first of the Left Socialist Party, then of the reunited JSP from October 1955, until he stood down in favour of his deputy, ASANUMA, in March 1960. With left-wing Socialism gaining ground throughout the 1950s, Suzuki was a major political figure of that era.

He wrote about his career in a book entitled *Half the Life of a Socialist* (*Aru shakaishugisha no hansei*), but the title included a pun, since when spoken it could also mean 'Reflections of a Socialist'. Suzuki died in September 1970.

Suzuki Zenkō Suzuki Zenkō was the only LIBERAL DEMOCRATIC PARTY (LDP) Prime Minister to have been a former Socialist, and the only one to represent fisheries' interests. Though Prime Minister for two years (1980–2), his performance was as undistinguished as his appointment was unexpected, and he may be regarded as a transitional leader.

Born in 1911 in Iwate, he was a JAPAN SOCIALIST PARTY parliamentarian from 1947, but defected with Hirano Rikizō's agricultural faction, and was elected to Parliament from Yoshida's Democratic Liberal Party (*Minshu Jiyūtō*) in 1949. He attained ministerial rank in the 1960s, and was Chief Cabinet Secretary under IKEDA HAYATO. He occupied senior party positions in the late 1960s and early 1970s, as well as chairing various policy commissions. He was Minister of Agriculture and Forestry in 1996–7 under FUKUDA TAKEO.

Suzuki was chosen – apparently on TANAKA's initiative – to succeed the late OHIRA MASAYOSHI as LDP President and Prime Minister in July 1980. His surprise appointment reflected a desire to avoid the kinds of factional disruption of intra-LDP harmony that had occurred in the previous few years. His Government was not outstanding in handling policy issues. In May 1981, on an official visit to the United States, he signed a policy statement with the Americans that referred to the 'alliance relationship' between the two countries. Back home he questioned whether Japan was really in an 'alliance' with the United Staes – something having constitutional implications. This episode led to the resignation of his Foreign Minister, ITŌ MASAYOSHI. On the other hand the period of his Government saw the beginning of certain initiatives that came to fruition under NAKASONE: most notably the Second Extraordinary Administrative Reform Commission (*Dai Niji Rinchō*).

After Ohira's death, Suzuki led the faction Ohira (and originally Ikeda) had headed, but the last general election he contested was that of 1986. In 1990 he retired from politics, aged 79.

Further reading
Curtis (1988)
Masumi (1995)
Stockwin (1999)

T

Takeiri Yoshikatsu Takeiri Yoshikatsu was Chairman of the CLEAN GOVERNMENT PARTY (CGP, *Kōmeitō*) (founded 1964) from February 1967 until December 1986, when he was replaced by YANO JUNYA.

Takeiri was born in 1926 in Nagano, and by the early 1960s was a senior executive of the *Sōka Gakkai*, the parent organisation of the CGP. He was elected for a Lower House Tokyo constituency in the elections between 1964 and 1986. Until 1970 the CGP was essentially the political arm of the *Sōka Gakkai*, but in that year a scandal forced the two organisations to separate, at least nominally.

In 1971 Takeiri led a CGP delegation to Beijing and met the top Chinese leaders. This initiated a crucial chain of events leading to normalisation of Japan–China relations in 1972. Takeiri had developed close links with Tanaka Kakuei, and, when Tanaka became Prime Minister in July 1972, he acted as much the most important of several informal intermediaries linking Tanaka and the Chinese leadership. Takeiri was in effect negotiating on Tanaka's behalf [*see also* CHINA (PRC AND ROC), RELATIONS WITH].

Under Takeiri relations between the CGP and the JAPAN COMMUNIST PARTY (JCP) – two parties contesting a very similar socio-economic constituency – were hostile. When, in 1975, the *Sōka Gakkai* chairman, Ikeda Daisaku, attempted a reconciliation with the JCP, Takeiri fiercely rejected his initiative.

The Tanaka–Takeiri connection persisted and was carefully cultivated by Tanaka. Takeiri was party to the attempt in 1984 to replace NAKASONE as Prime Minister by NIKAIDŌ SUSUMU, which would have meant splitting the LIBERAL DEMOCRATIC PARTY and forming a centrist coalition Government. The plan was eventually vetoed by Tanaka, and Takeiri was criticised within the CGP for this 'unauthorised' initiative, weakening his position within the party.

On 28 September 1998, Takeiri was severely criticised in the *Kōmei Shinbun* for reminiscences he had published in the *Asahi Shinbun* concerning his relations with the *Sōka Gakkai* during his period as party Chairman.

Takeiri was a pragmatic politician, who had considerable success in establishing and consolidating the CGP as a centrist party over the first two decades of its existence.

Further reading
Hrebenar (2000)
Pempel (ed.) (1977)

Takeshita Noboru Takeshita Noboru was often regarded as embodying Japan's tradition of clientelist politics, but it might be more accurate to see him as representative of the specific traditions established by the faction of TANAKA KAKUEI, dominant in the LIBERAL DEMOCRATIC PARTY (LDP) from the 1970s into the 1990s.

He was born in rural Shimane in February 1924 and died in June 2000. He was elected to local political office in 1951 and became a member of the HOUSE OF REPRESENTATIVES in 1958 at the age of 34. He rose quickly within the LDP, being Chief Cabinet Secretary under SATŌ EISAKU and Minster of Construction under TANAKA KAKUEI. In 1978, as Head of the LDP Organisation Bureau, he played a leading role in shaping the primary elections for party President in favour of OHIRA MASAYOSHI and against the incumbent Prime Minister, FUKUDA TAKEO. As Minister of Finance in 1985 he was the leading negotiator of the Plaza Accords, which arguably set the stage for the 'bubble economy' of the late 1980s. In the same year he took over leadership of the Tanaka faction after Tanaka's stroke, having a little earlier formed a 'study group' within the faction, indicating a leadership challenge. Most, though not all, of the faction members stayed with it under the new leader.

In October 1987 he replaced NAKASONE YASUHIRO as LDP President and thus Prime Minister, being the first leader of the party's dominant faction to assume the supreme office since Tanaka himself 13 years earlier. While in office he liberalised imports of beef and citrus fruits, and introduced a 3 per cent 'consumption tax', both of which policies proved unpopular. The sharp decline in his popularity was further stimulated by the Recruit stocks for favours scandal (see RECRUIT SCANDAL) in 1988–9, and he was forced to resign in June 1989.

Until close to the end of his life, he was a central figure in the dominant faction of the dominant party. His eldest daughter was married to the son of KANEMARU SHIN, and relatives had married into the top of the construction industry. During the party presidential election campaign of 1987 Takeshita found that a gangster organisation was giving him public support, in an attempt to smear his reputation. Kanemaru, using the head of the *Sagawa Kyūbin* parcel delivery company as intermediary, persuaded the gangster group to desist (see SAGAWA KYŪBIN SCANDAL). He followed this up with a personal visit to the group's leader, to thank him. Contacts between conservative politicians and gangsters are, however, highly controversial, and, when this story was reported in the press, it caused outrage. Kanemaru, for this and other reasons, was forced out of politics, and the Takeshita faction split, leading to a split in the LDP itself. Takeshita's reputation was also harmed, but he was able to play the elder statesman during the 1990s.

Takeshita pursued the politics of personal connections, financial dealing and electoral distribution of benefits, but was rarely explicit about where he stood on policy issues. His style of politics was effective in the earlier postwar years, but increasingly criticised in the more complex environment of Japan after the 1980s.

Further reading
Curtis (1999)

Tamaki Kazuo Born in Wakayama in 1923, Tamaki Kazuo graduated from Takushoku University, and entered the HOUSE OF COUNCILLORS in the elections of 1965. A politician of right-wing views, he was an executive member of the religious group, House of Growth (*Seichō no ie*), which professed highly conservative social values [see also RELIGION AND POLITICS].

Tamaki was elected for the LIBERAL DEMOCRATIC PARTY from the national constituency of the House of Councillors for six-year terms in 1965, 1971 and 1977. In 1965 he was placed third (out of 50 elected), with 854,473 votes, in 1971 eleventh with 719,017 votes and in 1977 fourth with 1,119,598 votes. This indicated the strength of his kind of conservative religious thinking, with its emphasis on a stern morality, and hostility to post-war 'American-imposed' values, in sections of the electorate. He was a member of the Young Storm Society (*Seirankai*) on its foundation in 1973, and became the representative of a syndicate of religious groups in Parliament. Surprisingly, perhaps, he had close links with Australia.

In 1983 he moved to the HOUSE OF REPRESENTATIVES, being elected for a Wakayama constituency at the top of the poll, a feat he repeated in 1986. But he died in January 1987, aged 64.

Tanabe Makoto Born in 1922, Tanabe Makoto succeeded DOI TAKAKO as Chair of the JAPAN SOCIALIST PARTY (JSP) in July 1991, when the electoral boom of 1989–90 was already fading.

A post office worker involved in labour unionism after the war, he was in local politics before entering the HOUSE OF REPRESENTATIVES in 1960 for a Gunma constituency.

Within the JSP he served as Parliamentary Policy Committee Chairman, and then Secretary-General (1983–6). He was a skilled political networker. His contacts outside the JSP paid off when in September 1990 he and KANEMARU SHIN of the LIBERAL DEMOCRATIC PARTY together visited North Korea. This was an exercise in informal diplomacy that displeased both the South Koreans and the Japanese Foreign Ministry. Nevertheless, Kanemaru and Tanabe secured the release of the crew of a fishing boat held in custody in North Korea since 1983 [see also KOREA (ROK AND DPRK), RELATIONS WITH].

Tanabe was JSP Chairman between July 1991 and December 1992, when YAMAHANA SADAO replaced him. During that period he sought to modernise the party's policies and appeal, but found it difficult to prevail in the face of entrenched attitudes. His regime preceded the bitter-sweet experience of 1993, combining electoral defeat with entry into Government.

Tanaka Kakuei Tanaka Kakuei was a remarkable politician. PRIME MINISTER for less than two and a half years, he nevertheless had a huge influence on the way Japanese politics was conducted between the early 1970s and the early 1990s. In some ways his influence grew after he ceased to be Prime Minister, even though he was repeatedly dogged by accusations of corruption.

He was born in May 1918, in a farming district of Niigata Prefecture, on the Japan Sea coast. His family was far from wealthy, and he had to leave school at 15 to work on a construction site. He did various jobs over the next few years and acquired some education through night school. A spell in the army between 1939 and 1941 ended with his discharge through illness. During the war he built up his own construction company to be one of the largest in Japan. He was elected to Parliament in 1947 for YOSHIDA's Liberal Party, and, after a failed attempt the previous year, received his first full CABINET position in 1957, and became IKEDA's Minister of Finance in July 1962. He remained in that position until June 1965, when the new Prime Minister, SATŌ, to whose faction he belonged, made him LIBERAL DEMOCRATIC PARTY (LDP) Secretary-General.

He retained that position for several years, using it to build up his party power base. In 1971, he moved from the key party post to a central position in Cabinet, that of Minister of International Trade and Industry.

In July of the following year, he became Prime Minister at the young age for Japan of 55. Unlike his elite ex-bureaucrat predecessors, KISHI, Ikeda and Satō, he had little formal education, though he was an impressive graduate of the 'university of life'. Though without experience as a Government official, he was adept at motivating officials, was known for his astonishing memory, and for his refreshingly direct and informal approach both to people and to problems. The press called him the 'computerised bulldozer'. To become Prime Minister, he had worked hard to defeat Satō's putative successor, FUKUDA TAKEO, another high-status former official. He had inherited the bulk of the former Satō faction and obtained the support of the faction led by OHIRA MASAYOSHI, who became his Foreign Minister.

Once in office, Tanaka concentrated on three principal tasks. The first was to transfer Japan's diplomatic relations with 'China' from Taipei to Beijing. This was an issue that had divided Japanese political opinion (including opinion within the LDP) for years, and by 1972 was perhaps the most divisive issue politicians faced. Satō had stuck closely to the US pro-Taiwan line, so that, when President Nixon suddenly announced in July 1971 that he would visit Beijing, Satō's long-held position became vulnerable. Tanaka, therefore, was following a gathering trend when he decided to reverse Japan's China policy in favour of Beijing. Amazingly, mobilising his own task force, he was able to establish diplomatic relations with the People's Republic of China at the early date of 30 September 1972 [see also CHINA (PRC AND ROC), RELATIONS WITH].

In the second task he was less successful, partly because of unfortunate timing. Determined to reduce urban overcrowding and pollution by dispersing industry to new industrial zones in the countryside, he inadvertently fuelled a speculative land boom, and exacerbated an already accelerating inflation. His expansionary policies were further knocked off course by the first oil crisis of 1973–4.

His third task was to improve general welfare provision, in which Japan had lagged behind other advanced countries. Here he was reacting to a steady decline in LDP electoral support since the 1950s. The year 1973 is often referred to as the 'birth year of welfare'. Unfortunately, generous policies on welfare would also in the long term have an inflationary effect [see also SOCIAL WELFARE].

In October 1974 the journal, *Bungei Shunjū*, published an article alleging irregular financial transactions by Tanaka. This was publicised by foreign journalists, and only then did the Japanese press run the story. It led to his resignation at the end of November, and his public image was linked thenceforth with dubious finance. In February 1976 the LOCKHEED SCANDAL broke, as a result of testimony to the US Senate Foreign Relations Committee. Tanaka and others were accused of taking bribes from the Lockheed Corporation for the sale of Tristars to All Nippon Airways. Tanaka was briefly arrested in July, his successor, MIKI TAKEO, would not allow a cover-up, and court proceedings lasted until October 1983, when he was pronounced guilty and given a suspended sentence.

The final phase of his career was perhaps the most bizarre. He resigned from the LDP, but continued to lead his own faction within it, ensuring that it grew to become the largest faction in the party. He remained well connected and widely influential, while inside the party he made sure that Ohira, Suzuki and Nakasone should each in turn become Prime Minister. It was largely owing to his influence that throughout the 1980s and into the 1990s one faction dominated the direction of the ruling party.

Tanaka suffered a severe stroke in February 1985, and retired from politics. He died in December 1993. His daughter, TANAKA MAKIKO, succeeded him in the same constituency, and also became known as a political maverick.

Further reading
Curtis (1988)
—— (1999)
Masumi (1995)

Stockwin (1999)
Tanaka (1973)

Tanaka Makiko Daughter of the former PRIME MINISTER, TANAKA KAKUEI, she was the first woman to become Foreign Minister.

Born in 1944 in Niigata, she graduated from Waseda University, and became deputy director of a bus company. In July 1993 she was elected for the first time to the House of Representatives for her father's old constituency in Niigata, standing as an Independent. She later joined the LIBERAL DEMOCRATIC PARTY (LDP) and was appointed Director of the SCIENCE AND TECHNOLOGY AGENCY in the first Murayama Government, from June 1994 until August 1995. In this position she showed some propensity to quarrel with her officials, as happened in her later tenure of the Foreign Ministry portfolio.

She did well in the 1996 and 2000 Lower House general elections, easily beating all comers in a newly created single-member constituency in Niigata. Over this period she was becoming well known nationally, and her forthright comments on television concerning a range of matters made her extremely popular.

When KOIZUMI JUNICHIRŌ became Prime Minister in April 2001, he made Tanaka Makiko his Foreign Minister, thus adding to the already high levels of popularity he was enjoying as a 'new broom' Prime Minister. She soon, however, became embroiled in controversy over a range of matters. She publicly criticised plans of the new Bush administration in the United States to set up a new version of 'star wars'. She was on bad terms with some of the senior officials of her ministry, and she sought to interfere in ministry personnel appointments, in order to root out what she saw as endemic corruption among her officials. Things came to a head in January 2002, when she clashed with a LDP politician from Hokkaidō called Suzuki Muneo, over a conference on aid to Afghanistan, from which she claimed some aid agencies had been excluded for criticising Government policy. The Prime Minister dismissed her from her post, though a leading Foreign Ministry official also lost his job, and two months later, Suzuki was forced out of the LDP. Without his popular Foreign Minister, Koizumi's popularity ratings sank precipitately. She resigned her parliamentary seat in August 2002.

tatemae-honne (public position and real intention) Social anthropologists in particular have made extensive use of the dichotomy between *tatemae* and *honne* in formulating theories of Japanese society. *Tatemae* is a difficult word to translate, having various meanings in Japanese, but the relevant meaning is 'public position' or 'set of principles'. *Honne* may be translated as 'real intention', implying pragmatic attitudes in concrete situations. The implication is that these two things do not necessarily coincide. Outside Japan, of course, everyone is familiar with situations where people profess grand principles but behave in a manner divergent from those principles.

Where these terms appear to have a particular Japanese connotation is that the harmony of society (or the harmony of the group) is greatly valued, and may well be seen as a value that should over-ride broad principles. Therefore, since principles are also important, situations arise where principles are expressed (*tatemae*) but social conformity is a more powerful motivation and dictates adherence to standards of behaviour (*honne*) that may substantially differ from those stemming from the principles. Much Western thinking, based on ideas of universalism, would deplore an *institutionalised* divergence between principles and actual behaviour. But Japanese thinking, more inclined to particularism or 'situational ethics', and valuing social harmony, tends to see it as more or less acceptable. Indeed, where making people feel uncomfortable (or, to vary the vocabulary, making people 'lose face') is avoided wherever possible, it makes sense to embroider the truth with high-flown principles and oblique expression, rather than to tell the unvarnished truth in a crude manner. At least, that makes sense in a society where it is generally expected that a distinction will be made between *tatemae* and *honne*.

Hendry throws light on the *tatemae/honne* distinction by her use of the metaphor of wrapping. Just as Japanese department stores routinely wrap goods beautifully in several layers of wrapping material, so the *honne* is beautifully wrapped in layers of *tatemae*. An aesthetic phenomenon becomes a metaphor for a fundamental characteristic of social behaviour.

The implications of this for politics are significant. A gap between principles and practice may well exist in politics everywhere, but in Japan it seems particularly marked, and even accepted as the norm. One example, which we have discussed in the ***uchi-soto*** entry, is furnished by the phenomenon of *kokutai seiji*, that is, the politics of the Parliamentary Management Committees (*kokkai taisaku iinkai*, or *kokutai*). In these committees, which exist in both Houses of Parliament, representatives of parties, which on matters of principle are strongly opposed to each other, in practice co-operate to ensure the smooth running of the parliamentary timetable. A more general example relates to the failure of opposition parties over the long term to mount a credible opposition to the LIBERAL DEMOCRATIC PARTY (LDP). The *tatemae* of opposing and seeking to replace the current Government jostles with the *honne* of 'getting with the strength', in other words of seeking to join the ruling party in a coalition arrangement, or at least picking up crumbs from its patronage table.

Here, however, we need to end on a note of caution. It is crucially important not to take the *tatemae/honne* distinction too far as an explanatory variable. Examining the first example in the paragraph above, we can find quite frequent cases where it proved impossible to patch up an agreement in the *kokutai*, and where the JAPAN SOCIALIST PARTY employed highly obstructive filibustering tactics, including 'COW WALKING' (*gyūho*) through the voting lobbies. In the second example, alternative explanations of the failure of opposition parties to mount credible opposition to the LDP may be found in poor organisation, uninspired leadership and, since the end of the Cold War, a drastic shortening of the ideological distance between party platforms. In both examples we should be sensitive to the time dimension. During the 1950s, for instance, social harmony took a back seat to tumultuous ideological confrontation. But it is politically significant that in the Japanese socio-political context the unvarnished expression of *honne* is often filtered through concerns about social relationships, and diverted into the innocuous if vacuous world of *tatemae*.

Further reading
Hendry (1993)
—— (1995)
Ishida, in Krauss *et al.* (1984)

Tokuda Kyūichi With NOSAKA SANZŌ, Tokuda Kyūichi was one of the two leading Communists of the immediate post-war period.

Born in desperate poverty in Okinawa in 1894, he studied law and helped found Japan's first (illegal) Communist Party in 1922. In the 1920s he travelled to Shanghai and Moscow, and was involved in writing various theses for the JAPAN COMMUNIST PARTY (JCP). Having spent eight months in prison in 1926–7, he was arrested in 1928 and remained in prison until October 1945, refusing to renounce his Marxist beliefs unlike some of his colleagues. After his release he became Secretary-General of the recreated JCP in December 1945. He was elected to the HOUSE OF REPRESENTATIVES for a Tokyo constituency in the general elections of 1946, 1947 and 1949. In June 1950 he was driven underground when the Occupation purged the Communist leadership. He disappeared completely from view, and in 1953 died in Beijing, though his death was not announced until 1955.

Tokuda was an emotionally committed revolutionary and inspirational leader, who commanded devotion among his followers in the turbulent conditions of post-war Japan.

Further reading
Beckmann and Okubo (1969)
Central Committee, Japanese Communist Party (1984)
Swearingen and Langer (1952, 1968)

'tribes' of parliamentarians (zoku) *Zoku* is a Japanese word meaning 'tribe'. It is important to distinguish it from *habatsu*, usually translated 'faction' (*see* FACTIONS WITHIN POLITICAL PARTIES). Whereas *habatsu* means a cohesive group within a party (or other organisation) concerned principally with power broking, the channelling of funds and distribution of posts, and to a more minor extent with policy, *zoku* has come to mean a group within a party, specialising in a particular policy area. Parliamentarians belonging to *zoku* are known collectively as *zoku giin*. Since the LIBERAL DEMOCRATIC PARTY (LDP) has been politically dominant, *zoku* have almost been confined to that party.

Inoguchi and Iwai, in their 1987 study of *zoku*, give data on 11 separate *zoku* (see Table 34).

Zoku are cross-factional, though, in some, members of one faction are concentrated. For instance, according to Inoguchi and Iwai, 22 out of 32 members of the construction *zoku* (69 per cent), and 18 out of 32 members of the postal *zoku* (56 per cent) belonged to the TANAKA faction. This indicates the extent of that faction's involvement in the construction industry and the Post Office. It is also worth noting that 13 out of the 22 members of the finance *zoku* (59 per cent) were ex-officials of the MINISTRY OF FINANCE.

The term *zoku* began to be used in the 1970s, but it was not until the 1980s that it became a focus of attention among political observers. There were policy-oriented groups within the LDP back in the 1960s. These

Table 34 Eleven separate *zoku*

Zoku	No. of members
Commerce and Industry	41
Agriculture and Forestry	37
Fisheries	9
Transport	25
Construction	32
Welfare	24
Labour	18
Education	21
Postal	32
Finance	22
Defence	21

> *Source*: Inoguchi Takashi and Iwai Tomoaki, '*Zoku giin' no kenkyū: Jimintō seiken o gyūjiru shuyakutachi* [A Study of 'Tribal Parliamentarians': The Leaders Who Control the LDP Regime]. Tokyo, Nihon keizai Shinbunsha, 1987.

included, for instance, rival groups on opposite sides of the debate about China policy: the 'Asia group' that wished to maintain diplomatic relations with the Republic of China on Taiwan, and the 'Asia–Africa group' that favoured establishing closer links (including diplomatic relations with the People's Republic of China) [*see also* CHINA (PRC AND ROC), RELATIONS WITH]. These, however, were general policy groups, though they may have had links with vested interests. As Curtis points out, however, *zoku* are groups representing special interests that needed to be incorporated into LDP policy-making. Specialist *zoku* were therefore formed as political link-groups between the interests themselves and the relevant sections of the Government bureaucracy. These linkages are often referred to, on the US model, as 'iron triangles', and they may be seen as a method of incorporating significant interests into the LDP-bureaucracy structure of governance.

Almost all the *zoku* listed above mirror the concerns of a particular ministry. But since the 1980s new *zoku* have formed around a more narrow interest, such as that of the tobacco industry. The unstable politics of the mid-1990s, and weakening of LDP dominance during that period, led to a decline in the strength of *zoku*, but, with the stabilising of LDP dominance since around 1998, they have once more emerged as important elements in policy-making.

Further reading
Curtis (1999)
Stockwin (1999)

Tupac Amaru Embassy Hostage crisis (Peru), 1996–7 On 17 December 1996, 14 armed members of the Tupac Amaru Revolutionary Movement (MRTA), posing as waiters at a reception given by the Ambassador, occupied the Japanese Embassy in Lima, Peru. They took hostage 72 people, including 24 Japanese, at the start of a siege that was to last 127 days.

The Peruvian President at the time was Alberto Fujimori, himself of Japanese parentage and well known in Japan. The Japanese Prime Minister, HASHIMOTO RYŪTARŌ, took a tougher line than some of his predecessors, who had been faced with aircraft hijackings in which Japanese citizens had been taken hostage, but where negotiations had led to the release of hijackers. Intensive interaction took place between the Japanese and Peruvian governments concerning the handling of the crisis. Knowing the sensitivity of Japanese public opinion on this kind of issue, the Japanese Government publicly emphasised the need for a peaceful resolution of the siege. In practice, however, it was clear that President Fujimori, who had employed military means to suppress the *Sendero Luminoso* (shining path) guerrillas, was prepared to contemplate a violent solution.

After negotiations with the guerrillas had been tried repeatedly and proved fruitless, Peruvian special forces blasted their way into the embassy through drainage tunnels on 22 April 1997. Hostages had been able to inform the authorities that at certain times of day the hijackers played mini-football on the ground floor of the embassy, which had the effect of separating them from the hostages. The special forces killed all 14 guerrillas. One Peruvian hostage and two of the special forces died in the attack. All the Japanese hostages, including the Ambassador, Aoki Morihisa, were saved, though some were injured.

The Ambassador later caused controversy by holding a press conference in which he neglected to apologise, as Japanese custom demands, for possible lapses in security that had made the hijacking possible. He was moved to other duties in the MINISTRY OF FOREIGN AFFAIRS.

The response of Hashimoto to the ending of the crisis was to thank President Fujimori, but to express mild regret – no doubt with public opinion in mind – that the Japanese Government had not been informed in advance of the planned operation. Apart from its dramatic impact, this episode is important in that it marked a distinct toughening of Japanese Government attitudes towards terrorism.

U

uchi-soto (inside-outside) This is an important cultural concept relevant to understanding certain aspects of Japanese politics. *Uchi* literally means 'inside' while *soto* means 'outside'. In compounds, the *kanji* (Chinese character) for 'inside' can also be read *nai*, as in *naibu* (the interior) or *nairiku* (inland, inland territory). *Soto* in compounds can be read *gai*, as in *gaijin* (foreigner), *gaikoku* (foreign country) or *igai* (with the exception of, apart from). *Uchi-soto* can also be read *naigai* (internal and external, domestic and foreign).

Thus these are everyday words used in common speech, with a variety of idiomatic compounds and usages. Social anthropologists such as Hendry, however, emphasise the particular significance of the *uchi-soto* distinction in the context of fundamental relationships within society. In the arrangement of the Japanese house, a conceptual distinction is made between the inside of the house (*uchi*) and the outside of it (*soto*). This is symbolised by the universal practice of taking one's shoes off in the *genkan* (porch) before entering the house proper. Ohnuki-Tierney and others see this as reflecting embedded notions of purity. The outside is by definition impure, dirty, germ-ridden. The inside is, by contrast, a place of purity, which must be kept clean, both physically and symbolically, and may not be polluted by shoes that have been in contact with external impurities. We should remember that the Shintō religion is centrally concerned with purity and purification.

It is widely argued that, by extension, Japanese people are acutely aware of *uchi-soto* distinctions in society itself. The family, the work group, the company, the guild of craftsmen, the political faction (*habatsu*) are, in this argument, expressions of such distinctions (*see* FACTIONS WITHIN POLITICAL PARTIES). Relations with the *uchi* are close, warm, informal, affective, whereas relations with the *soto* are more distant, cool, polite, businesslike and, in some circumstances, hostile. The Japanese language makes complex and subtle distinctions between levels of politeness, so that the difference in behaviour is clearly marked. On the other hand, the *uchi* is not impermeable. In certain situations (marriage being the most obvious example in the case of the family) outsiders – even foreigners – are welcomed into the *uchi*. But those within an *uchi* must conform to the norms of that *uchi*. Behaviour appropriate to relations with the *soto* will not be appreciated, nor will *uchi*-type behaviour in the *soto*. It is important not to over-simplify the case, because *uchi* and *soto* are not rigidly separated from each other. Indeed some prefer the metaphor of concentric circles to express differing levels of *uchi-soto* relationships. Though the social connotations are not identical, the difference in French between '*tutoyer*' and '*vouvoyer*' may be borne in mind.

The implications for understanding political behaviour are obvious. The pervasive tendency to form factions within parties and other types of political organisation may be explained in terms of rational choice. But such explanations fail to account for the organic and durable character of many *habatsu*-type organisations in politics. Relationships within LDP *habatsu*, for example, appear to be much more than simply contractual.

To this, however, it may be objected that if politics is composed of many *uchi* groups regarding other groups as *soto*, then the system risks falling apart, but this has plainly not happened. Ishida has an ingenious explanation for why it has not. He employs another bipolar expression: OMOTE-URA (surface–background). *Omote* behaviour in relation to a person's *soto* might involve a show of hostility and intransigence. But in the *ura* (behind-the-scenes) sphere of activity rival groups may well negotiate quite happily together. A good example of this might be relations between the LIBERAL DEMOCRATIC PARTY and the JAPAN SOCIALIST PARTY in the management of parliamentary business from the 1960s. Whereas on the surface and in rhetoric, their relations were hostile, behind the scenes they were co-operating to make the parliamentary system work.

It is important to regard the *uchi-soto* distinction neither as a total explanation of political behaviour, nor as entirely unique to Japan. Japanese politics is routinely affected by pragmatic considerations, and insider–outsider relationships are common to most societies throughout the world. Nevertheless, the particular connotations, in the Japanese context, of this distinction help understand otherwise puzzling aspects of political behaviour.

Further reading
Creighton, in Weiner (ed.) (1997)
Hendry (1995)
Ishida, in Krauss, *et al.* (1984)
Ohnuki-Tierney (1984)

United Nations, relations with Japan was not admitted to membership of the United Nations (UN) until 1956, following extensive international diplomacy that eventually overcame opposition from the Soviet Union. As a member, Japan routinely emphasised her commitment to the UN and to the internationalist ideas for which the world body stood. This fitted in well with the anti-war pledge embodied in the CONSTITUTION OF 1946, and with the strong pacifist sentiments that had permeated much of the Japanese population by the late 1950s. Of course, the reality was that in matters of defence Japan was closely tied to the United States by bilateral treaty, but the UN ideal remained strong as rhetoric and as a means of convincing domestic opinion and neighbouring countries of Japan's pacifist and benevolent intentions.

In the earlier years of Japanese membership, Japan in the UN played an unassertive role, and generally supported the United States in its voting behaviour. Gradually, the Japanese contribution to the UN budget increased as a proportion of the total UN budget, and in the 1980s helped sort out a crisis precipitated by a refusal by the United States to continue its financial contributions to the world body. Japan also became more independent in its voting choices in the General Assembly.

Japan was several times a non-permanent member of the UN Security Council, but permanent membership became a consistent aim of Japanese diplomacy from early in the 1990s. This was widely supported in the UN, but faced two principal obstacles. The first was that however logical it might seem to reform a structure reflecting the international realities of 1945, the issues raised for the UN went far beyond simply admitting Japan. Several other states felt they had an equal claim to join the five permanent members, and there was no question of existing permanent members stepping down to accommodate new ones. Moreover, if the veto were retained for permanent members, the more such members there were, the less flexibility the Security Council would have.

The second problem for Japan was that her constitutionally derived inhibitions on overseas deployment of troops could be regarded overseas as an obstacle to obtaining a central position in the Security Council, whose mission it was to mount peace-keeping missions in areas of conflict. With the passage in July 1992 of the Peace-Keeping Operations (PKO) bill, Japan began to participate in a series of UN peace-keeping missions around the world. Even so, tight restrictions were maintained on what tasks they were allowed to perform. But if the Gulf crisis of 1990–1 led to the PKO bill, the terrorist attacks on New York and Washington of 11 September 2001 further extended the boundaries of what was permissible. Legislation passed in the aftermath of those events made possible low-key Japanese participation in the United States-led mission against terrorism based on Afghanistan.

Japan learned from the Gulf crisis that chequebook diplomacy (to the tune of $US13 billion) was not sufficient to assuage influential opinion overseas, which insisted on troops on the ground. After September 2001, the Japanese Government showed it had assimilated that lesson. Nevertheless, another strand of argument deployed over a long period in favour of the Japanese bid for permanent membership of the UN Security Council was to demonstrate the efficacy of deploying diplomatic, rather than military, means in seeking solutions for international conflicts. In the aftermath of 11 September, which led to a United States-dominated 'war against terrorism', such an approach became unfashionable. But the alternative (or complementary) approach, of settling disputes through patient diplomacy conducted by experienced negotiators, also has a part to play, and here Japan has a surprising amount to offer.

Further reading
Dore (1997)
Drifte (2000)
Searight, in Vogel (ed.) (2002)
Tanaka (2002)

United States, relations with There is no country with which Japan's relationship has been more important than the United States since 1945. Indeed, it is difficult to exaggerate the comprehensive significance for Japan of her linkages with her powerful trans-Pacific neighbour. The story has an epic quality to it. The United States, in 1853, began the process of prizing open Japan's hermit state, when Commodore Perry sailed his 'black ships' into Edo Bay. Even though Europeans, more than Americans, influenced Japan between the 1860s and the 1920s, by the 1930s events were moving towards a titanic struggle between the United States and Japan. In December 1941 Japanese bombers destroyed the US fleet at Pearl Harbour, remembered in the United States as a 'Day of Infamy'. In August 1945 the United States destroyed Hiroshima and Nagasaki, incinerating and irradiating children, women and men, in the first use of nuclear weapons in warfare. Between those two months the armed forces of the two sides fought each other in a series of battles across the Western Pacific, where little quarter was given.

After the defeat of Japan on 15 August 1945, the United States became overwhelmingly the dominant power in an Allied Occupation that lasted until the coming into force of the San Francisco Peace Treaty in April 1952. The Occupation turned out to be far more than a mere holding operation. The Americans, under the formidable leadership of General Douglas MacArthur, had little compunction about seeking to reform Japanese institutions and practices along liberal, democratic lines. They stripped away the powers of the Emperor (*Tennō*) (*see* EMPEROR AND POLITICS) and his advisers (while retaining him as a figurehead), and placed sovereignty in the hands of the people, to be exercised through their elected representatives. They were also determined to prevent a recurrence of Japanese militarism, and to that end gave the new Constitution a strongly pacifist colouring (*see* CONSTITUTION OF 1946). In the event, these policies came to be modified with the advent of the Cold War, which from the US point of view required that Japan be transformed into an ally strong enough to render assistance in the gathering global struggle. Products of this change of tack were a shift in US support from left-of-centre to right-of-centre forces in Japanese politics, the introduction of a US–Japan Security Treaty, and the eventual birth of quasi-armed forces under the euphemism 'Self-Defence Forces'.

In many ways the Occupation may be judged a success, though it is a gross oversimplification to regard it as simply a case of the US occupiers imposing Western solutions upon an Eastern society. First of all, there is a case for regarding the Occupation (and even the new Constitution, the first draft of which was written by Americans) as a joint production, in which Japanese participated actively. Certainly there was Japanese obstruction and subtle subversion of Occupation initiatives, but there was also much constructive participation in the reforms. What emerged from the Occupation experience was neither entirely what the

Americans had been seeking nor a reversion to the pre-war system. Rather, a new system of governance eventuated that had reached maturity by the early 1960s. It may be seen as an amalgam of Occupation reformism and a kind of statist approach inherited from before the war. The character of this system was later to cause sharp divisions of interpretation between those who saw Japan as having evolved a liberal democratic system that knew how to create and sustain economic growth, and 're-visionists' who saw it as quite different from Western systems, self-serving and potentially dangerous [see also THEORIES OF JAPANESE POLITICS].

With the recovery of full independence by Japan in 1952, the United States had to deal with a newly re-emerging state whose future direction seemed difficult to predict. Japanese politics in the 1950s were seriously unstable, and, although by the middle of that decade the economy had recovered from the war, the average standard of living remained low. In these circumstances, the United States consistently cultivated Japan as a Cold War ally whose territory was strategically placed to provide a chain of military bases that the Americans could use to 'contain' Communism in Asia. This chain extended to the island of Okinawa, which remained under direct US administration until 1972 (see OKINAWA IN JAPANESE POLITICS). The security relationship was contained within the framework of the Security Treaty, the 1951 version of which permitted US interference in domestic Japanese politics in case of insurrection, as well as exhibiting other clear inequalities. Successive Japanese prime ministers had little choice but to accept a subordinate relationship, since they needed US help to normalise the Japanese position within international organisations and the international trading regime. Japan was not admitted to the United Nations until 1956 (see UNITED NATIONS, RELATIONS WITH), and it was not until the mid-1960s that she had attained full status in the IMF, the GATT and the OECD. YOSHIDA went along more or less willingly with this status discrimination (though successfully resisting US pressure to rearm on a massive scale), whereas HATOYAMA, by negotiating with the USSR, signalled an aspiration for greater foreign policy independence.

KISHI NOBUSUKE, a right winger and visceral anti-Communist, challenged the status quo in a different fashion, by proposing a revision of the Security Treaty to establish a more equal framework for the security relationship. He succeeded in revising the Treaty, but at the cost of precipitating the worst political crisis since the war, and his own political demise [see also SECURITY TREATY REVISION CRISIS]. The crisis prompted a US reassessment of its relationship with Japan, following an influential article by the Harvard Professor, Edwin Reischauer, entitled: 'The Broken Dialogue with Japan'. President Kennedy subsequently appointed Reischauer US Ambassador in Tokyo, with a brief to re-establish the dialogue that had been broken. Japan by now had entered into its period of ultra-rapid economic growth. The United States was contributing to it by ensuring the persistence of a benign international trading regime, favourable to the expansion of Japanese exports, while tolerating severe barriers to foreign penetration of the Japanese domestic market.

Between the late 1950s and the early 1970s the Japanese economy was transformed. Whereas in the 1950s it was too small to matter greatly to the international economy as a whole, by the 1970s Japan had become a major economic force. The change was reflected in more critical attitudes from the United States. In the 1950s and for much of the 1960s the United States had tolerated mercantilist policies by Japan in the interests of securing a strong ally in the Cold War. By the early 1970s, however, the mood in Washington had changed, and Japan was coming increasingly to be seen as a threat to US economic interests. Between 1969 and 1971 the two sides engaged in a bad-tempered confrontation over textiles. This dispute was more severe than was justified by an objective assessment of the textile industry's weight in either economy, but both Prime Minister SATŌ EISAKU and President Richard Nixon had made promises to their respective textile lobbies, which were important for each of them politically. In the end, acute personal distrust between the two men exacerbated the difficulty of finding a solution.

In July and August 1971, President Nixon administered what came to be known in Japan as the 'NIXON SHOCKS'. In July, without prior consultation with the Japanese Government, the President announced that he would visit the People's Republic of China. This dealt a blow to Satō's credibility that led to his replacement as Prime Minister a year later. Then in August, a second shock announcement came from Washington, ushering in a raft of economic measures designed, in large part, to force Japan to revalue the yen. The new policy brought to an end the Bretton Woods system of fixed exchange rates, under which Japan had enjoyed a rate of 360 yen to the US dollar since the late 1940s.

The early 1970s were a turning point in Japan–US relations in another sense as well. During the two previous decades domestic Japanese opinion had been polarised over the security relationship between the two countries, and related issues. Matters had come to a head in the 1960 Security Treaty revision crisis, and then calmed somewhat. But in the latter half of the 1960s the Vietnam War thrust security issues once more into the forefront of debate. Whether Japan should recognise the Government in Taipei or that in Beijing as the Government of 'China' became increasingly controversial within the framework of the US–Japan relationship, essentially because of Vietnam. The fact that Satō had loyally supported the US policy of keeping the PRC out of the United Nations, but then found his whole position undermined by President Nixon in July 1971 was particularly traumatic for ruling circles in Japan. But the response in Japan was positive and resourceful. Satō's successor as Prime Minister, TANAKA KAKUEI, negotiated a diplomatic recognition agreement with Beijing within three months of taking over [see also CHINA (PRC AND ROC), RELATIONS WITH].

Two other issues, by contrast, were resolved more smoothly between Japan and the United States. The revised Security Treaty was due to run for ten years, after which it could be terminated if either side gave a year's notice of termination. During the late 1960s, many feared a repeat performance in 1970 of the severe crisis that had occurred in 1960. This, however, was avoided by the simple expedient of both sides agreeing not to seek the ending of the Treaty.

The other issue was Okinawa (see OKINAWA IN JAPANESE POLITICS). The Vietnam War turned this into a particularly volatile issue in domestic Japanese politics, because of the use made of US bases in Okinawa to pursue the war in Vietnam. Since 1945 Okinawa and the surrounding Ryūkyū islands had been under direct US administration, though Japan was granted an ill-defined 'residual sovereignty'. John Foster Dulles had even threatened withdrawal of 'residual sovereignty' when the Hatoyama Government seemed to him to be making unnecessary territorial concessions to the Russians in the Japan–Soviet negotiations of 1956 [see also SOVIET UNION AND RUSSIA, RELATIONS WITH]. In the 1960s, the desire for Okinawa to revert to full Japanese sovereignty turned into a major political issue. Satō invested the reversion of Okinawa with enormous political significance by relating it to the task of 'ending the post-war period'. With much difficulty and great determination, he was able to negotiate its return to Japan, to take effect in 1972. He had to make important concessions, notably an acknowledgement of the importance of Korea and Taiwan to Japanese security. On the ticklish issue of nuclear weapons, he secured their removal from US bases on Okinawa, thus placing Okinawa in the same condition as the Japanese mainland (*hondo nami*). He was committed to the three non-nuclear principles, that Japan should not 'manufacture, stockpile or introduce' nuclear weapons in or into its territory, which, from 1972, would include Okinawa Prefecture. Many years later, however, a secret agreement was revealed that would permit their relocation on Okinawa in case of emergency. The third non-nuclear principle, that of 'introduction' (*mochikomi*), was later to prove controversial given the virtually universal belief (never formally acknowledged) that nuclear weapons remained on US naval vessels docking at Japanese ports. The two governments had an agreement 'neither to confirm nor deny' whether their ships had nuclear weapons on board when in port. This phrase was to cause recurrent boredom among Government spokesmen and journalists alike [see also NUCLEAR ISSUES].

With the reversion of Okinawa, 'automatic' renewal of the Security Treaty, and a change of policy in favour of the PRC by both the United States and Japan, the three most contentious political issues of the 1960s lost much of their salience. This was true even though the Vietnam War did not end until 1975. In their place, events were to throw economics into the forefront of debate. The OPEC oil crisis of 1973–4 faced Japan initially with the threat of losing much of her oil supply and then with a quadrupling of the price of oil. Economic growth came to a sudden halt and for a few months inflation was in double figures. This made the problem of resource dependence a central concern, and led to essays in resource diplomacy, diversification of energy sources, stockpiling and conservation.

Much slower economic growth by Japan during the 1970s took some heat out of the kinds of economic dispute with the United States that had been emerging at the beginning of that decade. In the 1980s, however, disputes became much more frequent and divisive, as the Japanese economy grew rapidly again without the degree of market opening that the Americans desired. In the first half of the decade the yen appeared to be seriously undervalued, giving Japan a significant advantage in exports. This was corrected by the Plaza Accords of 1985, which lowered the value of the US dollar in relation to the yen and other currencies. The strong yen, however, prompted many Japanese companies to restructure and cut costs to the extent that they continued to be highly competitive in export markets. The late 1980s were also a period in which Japanese overseas investment greatly increased, prompting some US protests at Japanese takeovers of some of their high-profile companies and institutions.

In 1986 the two sides signed a Semiconductor Trade Agreement that was supposed to admit foreign firms into the highly regulated Japanese semiconductor industry. More general negotiations, called the Structural Impediments Initiative, were conducted between 1988 and 1989, with a view to correcting (from the US point of view) difficulties faced by foreign firms in the form of tight linkages between *keiretsu*-type firms and exclusive distribution networks. The basic problem here was that US assumptions about free market access were confronted by the Japanese practice of in-group network preference.

The 1980s also saw important developments in security relations between the two countries. Japanese DEFENCE spending grew steadily throughout the decade by some 6.5 per cent per annum. The OHIRA Government (1978–80) had devised the notion of 'comprehensive security', bringing areas such as overseas development aid under the rubric of security policy. But during the 1980s, the balance within the LDP and the Government shifted to some extent in favour of those preferring more positive approaches to defence and security, including closer interaction with the United States. NAKASONE YASUHIRO, Prime Minister from 1982 to 1987, was ideologically committed to a greater defence effort, and he established close links with President Reagan. For the first time since the 1950s, Japanese spending on defence broke the ceiling of 1 per cent of GNP, though this level was not long maintained. Nakasone also authorised the transfer to the United States of Japanese innovations in military technology (previously banned under a policy of no armaments exports), but the amount of technology transferred in this way remained limited. The attempted co-development of a new fighter aircraft, the FSX, proved extraordinarily contentious, and the end product was expensive and unimpressive.

Adapting a phrase much used by his predecessor, Satō Eisaku, Nakasone frequently spoke of 'settling accounts with the post-war period'. It should be noted that this was not entirely a pro-United States slogan, since in certain areas of policy, such as education, it meant drastically modifying structures inherited from the Occupation. But in the defence and foreign policy sphere Nakasone generally found it expedient to co-operate with the United States.

One issue straddling the late 1980s and early 1990s was the GATT Uruguay round, which led in 1994 to the World Trade Organisation (WTO), with Japan as a member. This meant the first breach in Japan's rigid protection of its rice market. Reluctantly, some imports of rice were permitted, following intense pressure from the United States. It did not, however, mean a wholesale freeing of agriculture from protection, given the continued strength of the agricultural lobby [*see also* INTERNATIONAL ORGANISATIONS AND JAPAN].

The 1990s saw a shift in favour of the United States in the economic relativities between the two countries. The US economy entered a long period of rapid development on the back of the information technology revolution, while the Japanese economy stagnated after the collapse of its 'bubble' in 1991. It was, of course, the first decade following the end of the Cold War, so that the international background to US–Japan relations had drastically changed. They had, however, changed much less in East Asia than in other parts of the world. The Korean peninsula remained divided, with a Stalinist regime still in place in the north. China had opened up economically but was still run by the Chinese Communist Party. With the disappearance of any serious threat from the Soviet Union (or its successor state, the Russian Republic), some observers thought that the rationale of the Japan–US Mutual Security Treaty had gone, and that it was destined to disappear. In fact, however, it was strengthened by the Guidelines Agreement of 1997. Despite a serious crisis over Okinawa, following the rape of a child by US servicemen in 1995, the Clinton and Hashimoto administrations confirmed the status of Okinawa as the linchpin of their security relationship.

In the 1980s, Japanese frequently complained of US 'Japan-bashing'. In the 1990s, and into the 2000s, the complaint is rather about 'Japan-passing', meaning essentially a US propensity for taking the rapidly expanding Chinese economy more seriously than the rather stagnant economy of Japan. This was symbolised by a visit by President Clinton to China, when he failed to drop into Japan on the way. After the Asian economic crisis began in 1997, a Japanese proposal to form an Asian Monetary Fund to help resolve the crisis was speedily repudiated by Washington, and therefore dropped by Tokyo. Even though the Bush administration may have redressed the balance to some extent back towards Japan, it seems unlikely that the United States will soon take Japan so seriously, in either a positive or a negative sense, as it was having to do before 1991. The KOIZUMI Government passed legislation, following 11 September 2002, to permit contingents of the Self-Defence Forces to join operations such as that being mounted by the United States and its allies in Afghanistan. It would be difficult, however, to regard the Japanese contribution as much more than token.

It is difficult to predict the future of the US–Japan relationship from the perspective of 2002. In some senses, the structures inherited from the early 1950s remain intact and have even been strengthened. Much the same problems and disputes are still played out between the two countries. But the power structures in the East Asian region are changing, so that the relationship will need to exhibit flexibility and a degree of innovation in order to survive as a force for international stability.

Further reading
Barnds (1979)
Buckley (2002)
Curtis (ed.) (1993)
Destler *et al.* (1979)
Dower (1999)
Drifte (1998)
Gourevitch *et al.* (1995)
Hook *et al.* (2001)
Inoguchi (1991)
Langdon (1973)
Prestowitz (1988)
Reischauer (1960)
Vogel (ed.) (2002)
Weinstein (1978)
Welfield (1988)

Uno Sōsuke Born in 1922, Uno Sōsuke was briefly PRIME MINISTER in 1989.

Known as a writer of *haiku* and author of a book on his experiences as a prisoner of war in Soviet Siberia after 1945, he was neither a faction leader nor had he held a senior position in the LIBERAL DEMOCRATIC PARTY (LDP). He had, however, been secretary to KŌNO ICHIRŌ, followed by entry into Parliament in 1960, close relations with

NAKASONE YASUHIRO, and a number of Cabinet positions. These included serving as Defence Agency Director under TANAKA KAKUEI in 1974, and Foreign Minister under TAKESHITA NOBORU in the late 1980s.

Uno succeeded the discredited Takeshita when he stepped down as Prime Minister in June 1989. But the change did little to stop the rot, and in July the LDP lost its majority in the HOUSE OF COUNCILLORS elections for the first time in the history of that house. In addition, Uno's mistress had gone public with complaints about his meanness, so that he was quickly replaced after the elections by KAIFU TOSHIKI.

He died in 1998.

V

Voice of the People (Kokumin no koe) Following the dissolution of the NEW FRONTIER PARTY at the very end of 1997, one of the six party groupings to emerge was Voice of the People, led by Kano Michihiko. It was essentially a leader–follower grouping, and by the end of January 1998 had merged with the SUN PARTY and FROM FIVE into the MINSEITŌ.

W

Wada Hiroo Wada Hiroo, born in 1903, was an atypical Socialist of the post-war period. With KATSUMATA SEIICHI, Sata Tadataka and others of left-wing opinions, he had been an official of the Government's Planning Board, until, following the exposure of the Sorge spy ring in 1941, his group was accused of Communist inclinations and its members were imprisoned. After the war he returned to a senior post in the Ministry of Agriculture (*see* MINISTRY OF AGRICULTURE, FORESTRY AND FISHERIES), and then in April 1946 became Minister of Agriculture in the first YOSHIDA administration. When the KATAYAMA coalition Government was formed in June 1947, Wada became Director-General of the Economic Stabilisation Board, and an important pipeline to the bureaucracy for the Socialists in the coalition.

In 1949 he joined the JAPAN SOCIALIST PARTY (JSP), and when it split over the peace settlement in 1951 he joined the Left Socialist Party and became leader of one of its four factions (*see* FACTIONS WITHIN POLITICAL PARTIES), other members including Katsumata and Sata. This core group derived its solidarity from the Planning Board experience, but the faction recruited members of differing backgrounds, and maintained a wide range of labour union contacts. There was no doubting the left-wing credentials of Wada and his faction, but their reputation was that of policy-oriented intellectuals. For that very reason they aroused some distrust among other left wingers in the party, particularly of the SUZUKI faction, which regarded them as power rivals.

In the 1950s Wada fought hard against the developing security arrangements with the United States, and became Secretary-General of the Left Socialist Party in January 1954. After the party reunited in October 1955, he occupied various positions, and was important in the struggles against the revised Security Treaty in 1958–60 (*see* SECURITY TREATY REVISION CRISIS). In the early 1960s, as Chairman of the JSP Foreign Policy Bureau, he played a key role in developing the party's advocacy of 'positive neutrality' in world affairs, resisting the tendency to pull it towards a pro-Soviet interpretation. In January 1966 he resigned his party vice-chairmanship because of ill health and died in 1967.

Further reading
Cole *et al.* (1966)
Stockwin (1968)
Totten (1966)

Watanabe Michio Watanabe Michio was a right-wing LIBERAL DEMOCRATIC PARTY (LDP) politician who took over the NAKASONE faction in the late 1980s, had the earthy populist manner of a faction boss, and aspired in vain to become PRIME MINISTER.

Born in Tochigi in 1923, he worked in a tax office and was a local councillor before entering the HOUSE OF REPRESENTATIVES in 1963 for a Tochigi constituency. He joined the Nakasone faction of the LDP, and from 1973 was a leading member of the Young Storm Association (*Seirankai*) of right-wing activists, where he showed strong concern for economic issues. He was successively Minister of Health and Welfare (1976–7), Agriculture Minister (1978–9), Finance Minister (1980–2) Minister of International Trade and Industry (1985–6, under Nakasone), Deputy Prime Minister and Foreign Minister (1991–3, under Miyazawa), and also held senior party positions.

In February 1990, Watanabe became leader of the former Nakasone faction. In August 1990 he proposed sending minesweepers to the Gulf as an earnest of Japan's good intentions towards the United States. When the MIYAZAWA Government resigned in August 1993, KŌNO YŌHEI beat Watanabe in a contest for the LDP presidency by 208 votes to 159 in a ballot of LDP parliamentarians, his image of a traditional party boss limiting his appeal. Next April, however, when the Hosokawa Government had just collapsed, OZAWA tried to tempt Watanabe out of the LDP to become Prime Minister in a non-LDP administration. Watanabe could not persuade many of his faction members to follow him out of the safety of the LDP into an unknown electoral future. He therefore missed his chance of becoming Prime Minister, but may have saved the LDP from ultimate collapse. It was a close call, but the party was back in power in a coalition with the Socialists and NEW PARTY HARBINGER (*Sakigake*) a few weeks later.

At this stage Watanabe's health was deteriorating, and he died in September 1995.

Further reading
Curtis (1999)

women and politics The justification for including an entry on 'women and politics' but no entry on 'men and politics' is that, until the late 1980s, women in politics were a comparative rarity, and men dominated the scene. The JAPAN COMMUNIST PARTY (JCP) was the only party to favour women candidates as a matter of policy, so that the number of women in Parliament tended to fluctuate with the fortunes of that party. Since then, women have come to participate rather more. Even so, had this *Dictionary* been subtitled 'Men and politics', it would not have been far wide of the mark.

Before 1946 women did not have the vote, and were banned from participation in politics.

The new dispensation after the war gave the vote to both females and males over the age of 20, and allowed women to stand for election to Parliament and at local level. Nevertheless, social inhibitions remained and actual behaviour was slow to change. In one area, however, female participation actually exceeded that of men by the late 1960s. This was in the turnout rates for general elections to the House of Representatives, as may be seen on Table 35, which gives the turnout figures up to the 1980 elections.

The number of women elected to the House of Representatives until the 1990s was rarely above ten. For instance, in the elections held in June 1980, 28 women stood as candidates, of whom nine were elected (seven Communists and two Socialists). The number of seats totalled 511, so that 1.8 per cent of the membership was women. In the 1990 elections, the number had risen slightly, to 12, out of 512 seats (2.3 per cent). But with a changed electoral system, in 1996, the proportion had doubled, being 23 out of 500, or 4.6 per cent. Moreover, though the numbers were still small, there was now a greater spread across the parties (LDP 4, NFP 8, DPJ 3, JCP 4, SDP (JSP) 3, Independent 1).

In the House of Councillors, the existence of a national (latterly proportional representation) constituency made it easier for high-profile women to be elected. For instance, in the 1980 House of Councillors elections the veteran human rights and anti-corruption campaigner, Ichikawa Fusae, topped the poll with 2,784,998 votes, and four women were among the seven candidates obtaining the highest number of votes. But the election of DOI TAKAKO in 1986 as the first woman to head a Japanese political party (JAPAN SOCIALIST PARTY (JSP)) ushered in the 'Madonna policy' whereby women were actively sought as candidates for that party. The policy was spectacularly successful in the Upper House elections of July 1989. Even though the star of Doi Takako was soon to fade after 1990, it seems likely that her emergence, for a while at least, inspired a number of women to contemplate a political career. In 1996 the JSP (now called Social Democratic Party) split and the rump of

Table 35 Turnout rates for general elections to the House of Representatives

Date of election	Turnout (%)	Turnout (men)	Turnout (women)
April 1947	67.95	74.87	61.60
January 1949	74.04	80.74	67.95
October 1952	76.43	80.46	72.76
April, February 1955	75.84	79.95	72.06
May 1958	76.99	79.79	74.42
November 1960	73.51	76.00	71.22
November 1963	71.14	72.36	70.02
January 1967	73.99	74.75	73.28
December 1969	68.51	67.85	69.12
October 1972	71.76	71.01	72.46
December 1976	73.45	72.81	74.05
October 1979	68.01	67.42	68.56
June 1980	74.57	73.72	73.56

the party was reduced to marginal significance. Nevertheless, it is worth noting that of the 19 of its candidates elected in the 2000 elections for the House of Representatives, a majority (10) were women.

The first Cabinet position to be allocated to a woman was the Health and Welfare portfolio, occupied by Nakayama Masa in the first Ikeda Cabinet between July and December 1960. There was then a 30-year gap before Moriyama Mayumi and Takahashi Sumiko were placed in charge, respectively, of the ENVIRONMENT AGENCY and the ECONOMIC PLANNING AGENCY in the first Kaifu Cabinet in 1990. This, however, was plainly a riposte to the Doi 'Madonna' strategy. With the election of the non-LIBERAL DEMOCRATIC PARTY (LDP) Hosokawa Cabinet in August 1993 no less than three women were appointed to the Education, Economic Planning and Environment portfolios, respectively. This set a pattern in which it became less outré than before to have a small number of women as Cabinet ministers. But it was not until the formation of the Koizumi Cabinet in April 2001 that a major ministry, that of Foreign Affairs, was headed by a woman, TANAKA MAKIKO. The experience was not a happy one, however, and the Prime Minister dismissed her in January 2002. She was, though, succeeded by another woman, Kawaguchi Junko. In the bureaucracy, similarly, the number of women in senior positions has been extremely small. The Ministry of Labour, by contrast (before the amalgamations of January 2001), has often been headed by a woman.

In 1985 legislation was passed through Parliament nominally providing for equal remuneration and treatment of women and men in the workforce. The legislation was flawed, and easy to evade, but it set a certain benchmark for the treatment of women in work, and this had some long-term effect. The relative economic stagnation since the early 1990s has hurt women in the sense that they tend to lose their jobs before men do. But in certain kinds of urban, high-skilled occupation in the tertiary sector, woman have gained some dominance. More specifically in the political domain, at local level women are active, and often dominant, in citizens' movements concerned with particular problems of the environment and the quality of life. They also are extremely active in the educational sphere, through parent–teacher associations and the like. Many of the women who enter local or national politics come from this kind of background, though there are important exceptions.

Further reading

Gelb and Estevez-Abe (1998)
Iwao (1991)
Kondo (1990)
LeBlanc (1999)
Osawa (1998)
Pharr (1981)
Roberts (2000)

Y

Yamahana Sadao Born in 1936 in Tokyo, Yamahana was the son of a leading JAPAN SOCIALIST PARTY (JSP) parliamentarian, Yamahana Hideo, who in the debates over revision of the Japan–US Security Treaty in 1960 did much to embarrass the Kishi Government with his persistent and acute questioning (*see* SECURITY TREATY REVISION CRISIS).

Trained as a lawyer, and advising labour unions on legal matters, Yamahana was first elected to the HOUSE OF REPRESENTATIVES for the JSP in 1976 representing an outer Tokyo constituency. He became Secretary-General of the party in 1991, and Chairman in December 1992. This proved to be a crucial time to lead the party, since he could play a major role in the construction of the HOSOKAWA coalition Cabinet from August 1993. The JSP was essential to the coalition, and Yamahana bargained skilfully to bring the party on board. In the July general elections, however, the party had lost nearly half of its seats in favour of new parties led by OZAWA, Hosokawa and Takemura. Thus, at the JSP national congress in September he had to take responsibility for the defeat by resigning his chairmanship in favour of MURAYAMA TOMIICHI. He remained, however, Minister in charge of political reform, and played a crucial role in reforming the electoral system.

With the formation of the LDP/JSP/NPH coalition Government in June 1994, Yamahana found himself in a coalition he did not really approve of, and a Government led by Murayama. Whereas Yamahana was on the right wing of the JSP, Murayama was on its traditional left wing, so that ideological differences were added to personal rivalry. In January 1995, Yamahana was about to lead much of the JSP right wing out of the party, but this was aborted by the Kōbe earthquake on 17 January (*see* GREAT HANSHIN–AWAJI EARTHQUAKE). It was not until September 1996, in advance of the October general elections, that the right wing defected, helping found the DEMOCRATIC PARTY, and reducing the JSP to minor party status. Yamahana joined the Democratic Party, but did not lead it.

Further reading
Stockwin (1999)

Yamasaki Taku Born in 1936 in Fukuoka, Yamasaki Taku was one of the YKK group (including also KATŌ KŌICHI and KOIZUMI JUNICHIRŌ), regarded as the up-and-coming new leaders in the 1990s.

He graduated from Waseda University, was briefly in local politics and was first elected to the HOUSE OF REPRESENTATIVES for a Fukuoka constituency in 1972. Up to and including the elections of 2000, he had never been defeated. Initially a member of the Young Storm Association (*Seirankai*) of right-wing activists founded in 1973, he was later a mainstream (NAKASONE faction) conservative rather than a member of the extreme right.

Over time he occupied a number of prominent positions in the LIBERAL DEMOCRATIC PARTY (LDP), including those of Deputy Secretary-General, Parliamentary Policy Committee Chairman and Policy Affairs Research Committee Chairman. He also held a number of positions in Cabinet, including those of Deputy Cabinet Secretary, Director of the DEFENCE AGENCY and Minister of Construction.

After the death in September 1995 of WATANABE MICHIO, who had inherited the leadership of the Nakasone faction, LDP factions (see FACTIONS WITHIN POLITICAL PARTIES), which had tended to atrophy in the confused atmosphere of the mid-1990s, began to reassert themselves. By 1999, Yamasaki had his own faction, largely formed from former Watanabe faction members. It was the fifth largest out of seven factional groupings in the party.

Yano Junya Yano Junya became Secretary-General of the CLEAN GOVERNMENT PARTY (Kōmeitō) (founded 1964) in February 1967. Born in Osaka in 1932, he was first elected to the HOUSE OF REPRESENTATIVES for an Osaka constituency in 1967. He was also an official of the Sōka Gakkai until a scandal in 1970 forced the (nominal) separation of the two organisations [see also RELIGION AND POLITICS].

He worked closely with Chairman TAKEIRI YOSHIKATSU until the latter's retirement in 1986, the two forming an exceptionally stable leadership pair. He then became party Chairman, until he was himself replaced by ISHIDA KŌSHIRŌ in 1989.

YKK YKK was a term widely used in the 1990s to designate three up-and-coming LIBERAL DEMOCRATIC PARTY (LDP) leaders, YAMASAKI TAKU, KATŌ KŌICHI and KOIZUMI JUNICHIRŌ.

Yoshida Shigeru A towering political figure who shaped the history of Japan following her defeat in 1945, Yoshida Shigeru was a shrewd, far-sighted and complex politician.

His pre-war career was as a diplomat. Born in 1878 of a Kōchi family and adopted into the Yoshida family of Yokohama, he graduated from Tokyo Imperial University and entered the diplomatic service in 1906. He had a succession of foreign postings, including several in China and in Europe. He was Vice-Minister for Foreign Affairs between 1928 and 1931, and in the 1930s was Ambassador to Rome, and later to London. At this time he was regarded as a member of the 'Anglo-American faction' of Japanese diplomacy. During the war he co-operated with the former Prime Minister, Konoe Fumimaro, in efforts to bring the war to a speedy conclusion and thus save the Emperor system (see EMPEROR AND POLITICS). These efforts cost him a spell in prison early in 1945.

After the war he became Foreign Minister in the SHIDEHARA Cabinet formed in October 1945. He was elected to Parliament in the first post-war elections of April 1946, became President of the Japan Liberal Party (in place of HATOYAMA ICHIRŌ, whom the Americans had purged), and PRIME MINISTER. His first administration only lasted a year, since the elections of April 1947 led to the formation of the KATAYAMA coalition Cabinet, which Yoshida's party did not join. Many of the reforms being promoted by the Occupation were put in place during the first Yoshida Government, including the new Constitution. Following the collapse of first the Katayama, then the ASHIDA, coalition governments, Yoshida returned to power in October 1948, and his party (now called the Democratic Liberal Party [Minshu jiyūtō]) won an overall majority in the House of Representatives in the January 1949 general elections.

Yoshida was Prime Minister continuously from October 1948 until December 1954. He represented his country at the peace settlement, whereby Japan regained her independence in April 1952. He was at the helm when the economic retrenchment policies of the Dodge Line were administered, and he co-operated enthusiastically with the anti-union policies that these entailed. The Korean War broke out on his watch also, so that he had to cope with General MacArthur's requirement to form a National Police Reserve to replace US forces sent to Korea. It also led to the 'red purge' that targeted Communists and their sympathisers. In general, while Yoshida was in charge, policies moved away from the democratising reforms of the early Occupation period towards a more conservative approach. How much of this represented changing US priorities and how much Yoshida's own initiatives is obscure, but much of the change did not go against the grain so far as he was concerned. As a political leader he was deeply conservative, inclined to be autocratic in his methods, and sceptical of reforms that tended to place power in the hands of the people.

On the other hand, he was no militarist, and resisted pressure from John Foster Dulles in the early 1950s to embark upon a massive programme of rearmament. Yoshida's position – for which he received some support from MacArthur – was that for Japan to rearm on the scale proposed would jeopardise economic recovery, alarm neighbouring countries and risk serious political instability at home. Out of this confrontation emerged what later came to be called the 'Yoshida Doctrine', namely that Japan should maintain a close security linkage with the United States, but should only built up her DEFENCE capacity at a modest pace and with strict limits observed. He accepted the Japan–US Security Treaty signed simultaneously with the San Francisco Peace Treaty in October 1951, and later the transformation of the National Police Reserve through stages into the Self-Defence Forces (*jieitai*) in 1954 (together with the Mutual Security Agreement – MSA – in the same year). Nevertheless, he carefully distanced himself from US official attempts to draw Japan more closely than he considered necessary into a Cold War alliance. In particular, he maintained some reserve about US hostility to China. Even though he went along with US pressure to sign a separate peace treaty with Taiwan (as the 'Republic of China'), his pre-war experience as a diplomat in China suggested to him that the People's Republic would in the end prove more Chinese than Communist [*see also* UNITED STATES, RELATIONS WITH; CHINA (PRC AND ROC), RELATIONS WITH].

Yoshida's political position began to weaken after the Occupation ended, and purged politicians returned to political life. As Prime Minister and President of his party, he had promoted politicians who, like him, were former Government officials, whereas most of those returning to politics from Occupation limbo were party politicians, pure and simple. Yoshida came under attack for 'bureaucratic politics', for 'one-man rule' and for bending too easily to the wishes of the United States. This last accusation was hardly fair, since he had been playing a subtle game with the Americans. But his attackers on the right wanted more openly nationalistic policy agenda, including the writing of a new Constitution – an issue where Yoshida was much more ambivalent than they. Another important factor was personal rivalry between Yoshida and Hatoyama Ichirō. When the latter had been purged in 1946, and Yoshida replaced him, Yoshida was said to have promised to hand over the leadership to Hatoyama once the latter was released from the purge. Yoshida, however, denied this, and in any case did not act on it.

Two successive elections shortly after the end of the Occupation weakened Yoshida's position, and some high-handed actions by him (including protecting his protégés accused of involvement in a SHIPBUILDING SCANDAL) increased the determination of his rivals to replace him. A lengthy foreign trip late in 1954 provided ample occasion for sharpened attacks on him in Parliament, and he was forced to resign in December.

After ceasing to be Prime Minister, he came to be treated as an elder statesman, and his influence was prolonged into the 1960s while his disciples IKEDA HAYATO and SATŌ EISAKU were successively Prime Minister. On his death in 1967, aged 89, he was given a state funeral (the first since the war).

Further reading
Dower (1979)
Masumi (1985)
Stockwin (1999)
Welfield (1988)
Yoshida (1961)

BIBLIOGRAPHY

Reference books

The Cambridge Encyclopedia of Japan. Richard Bowring and Peter Kornicki (eds), Cambridge, Cambridge University Press, 1993.
Japan: An Illustrated Encyclopedia. 2 vols. New York, London and Tokyo, Kodansha, 1993.
Political Parties of Asia and the Pacific. Haruhiro Fukui (Editor-in-Chief). 2 vols. Westport, CT and London, Greenwood Press, 1985 (Vol. 2 covers Japanese parties).

Periodicals

Asian Survey. Berkeley, CA, University of California Press. Six issues annually.
Japan Forum. London, Routledge, for the British Association of Japanese Studies. Three issues annually.
Japan Review of International Affairs. Tokyo, Japan Institute of International Affairs. Four issues annually.
Japanese Journal of Political Science. Cambridge, Cambridge University Press. Two issues annually.
Japanese Studies. Carfax Publishing for the Japanese Studies Association of Australia. Two issues annually.
Journal of Japanese Studies. Seattle, WA, Society for Japanese Studies. Two issues annually.
Pacific Affairs. Vancouver, University of British Columbia. Four issues annually.
Pacific Review. London, Taylor & Francis for the Centre for the Study of Globalisation and Regionalisation, University of Warwick.
Social Science Japan Journal. Tokyo, Cary, NC, and London, Oxford University Press for the Institute of Social Science, University of Tokyo. Four issues annually.

Books, articles, theses and papers

Abe, Hitoshi, Muneyuki Shindō and Sadafumi Kawato (trans., with an Introduction, by James W. White), *The Government and Politics of Japan*. Tokyo, University of Tokyo Press, 1994.
Abegglen, James C., *Japanese Factory: Aspects of its Social Organization*. Glencoe, IL, The Free Press, 1958.
Allinson, Gary D. and Yasunori Sone, *Political Dynamics in Contemporary Japan*. Ithaca, NY, and London, Cornell University Press, 1993.
Ampiah, Kweku, *The Dynamics of Japan's Relations with Africa: South Africa, Tanzania and Nigeria*. London and New York, Routledge, 1997.
Apter, David E. and Nagayo Sawa, *Against the State: Politics and Social Protest in Japan*. Cambridge, MA, and London, Harvard University Press, 1984.
Arase, David, *Buying Power; The Political Economy of Japan's Foreign Aid*. Boulder, CO, and London, Lynne Rienner, 1995.
Aspinall, Robert W., *Teachers' Unions and the Politics of Education in Japan*. Albany, NY, State University of New York Press, 2001.
Babb, James, *Business and Politics in Japan*. Manchester and New York, Manchester University Press, 2001.
Baerwald, Hans H., *Japan's Parliament*. London, Cambridge University Press, 1974.
——, *Party Politics in Japan*. Boston, London and Sydney, Allen and Unwin, 1986.
Bailey, F.G., *Stratagems and Spoils: A Social*

Anthropology of Politics. Oxford, Basil Blackwell, 1969.

Bailey, Paul J., *Postwar Japan: 1945 to the Present.* Oxford and Cambridge, MA, Blackwell, 1996.

Barnds, William J. (ed.), *Japan and the United States: Challenges and Opportunities.* New York, New York University Press, 1979.

Beasley, W.G., *The Modern History of Japan.* London, Weidenfeld & Nicolson, 1963, and later edns.

Beckmann, George M. and Okubo Genji, *The Japanese Communist Party, 1922–1945.* Stanford, CA, Stanford University Press, 1969.

Beeman, Michael L., *Public Policy and Economic Competition in Japan: Change and Continuity in Antimonopoly Policy, 1973–1995.* London and New York, Routledge, 2002.

Beer, Lawrence (ed.), *Constitutional Systems in Late Twentieth Century Asia.* Seattle and London, University of Washington Press, 1992.

Beer, Lawrence W. and Hiroshi Itoh, *The Constitutional Case Law of Japan, 1970 through 1990.* Seattle and London, University of Washington Press, 1996.

Benedict, Ruth, *The Chrysanthemum and the Sword.* Houghton Mifflin, 1946; Tokyo, Tuttle, 1954.

Bennett, John W. and Iwao Ishino, *Paternalism in the Japanese Economy.* Minneapolis, University of Minnesota Press, 1963.

Bergamini, David, *Japan's Imperial Conspiracy: How Emperor Hirohito led Japan into War against the West.* London, Heinemann, 1971.

Blaker, Michael K., *Japan at the Polls: The House of Councillors Election of 1974.* Washington, DC, American Enterprise Institute for Public Policy Research, 1976.

Bocking, Brian, *A Popular Dictionary of Shinto.* Richmond, Curzon Press, 1996.

Bouissou, Jean-Marie and Paolo Pombeni, 'Grandeur et décadence de la "partitocracie redistributive régulée". L'évolution du système politique au Japon et en Italie depuis la guerre', *Revue Française de Science Politique*, 51, 4 (Août 2001).

Braddick, Christopher W., 'Japan and the Sino-Soviet Alliance, 1950–1964'. D. Phil. Thesis, Faculty of Social Sciences, University of Oxford, 1997.

——, 'The Waiting Game: Japan–Russia Relations', in Takashi Inoguchi and Purnendra Jain (eds), *Japanese Foreign Policy Today.* Basingstoke and New York, Palgrave, 2000.

Bridges, Brian, *Japan and Korea in the 1990s: From Antagonism to Adjustment.* Aldershot, Edward Elgar, 1993.

——, *Europe and the Challenge of the Asia–Pacific.* Cheltenham, Edward Elgar, 1999.

Buck, James H. (ed.), *The Modern Japanese Military System.* Beverly Hills and London, Sage Publications, 1975.

Buckley, Roger, *The United States in the Asia–Pacific since 1945.* Cambridge, New York and Melbourne, Cambridge University Press, 2002.

Calder, Kent E., *Crisis and Compensation: Public Policy and Political Stability in Japan, 1949–1986.* Princeton, NJ, and Guildford, Princeton University Press, 1988.

——, *Strategic Capitalism: Private Business and Public Purpose in Japanese Industrial Finance.* Princeton, NJ, and Chichester, Princeton University Press, 1993.

Campbell, John C., *How Policies Change: The Japanese Government and the Aging Society.* Princeton, NJ, Princeton University Press, 1992.

Carlile, Lonny E. and Mark C. Tilton (eds), *Is Japan Really Changing its Ways? Regulatory Reform and the Japanese Economy.* Washington, DC, Brookings Institution Press, 1998.

Central Committee, Japanese Communist Party, *Sixty-Year History of Japanese Communist Party, 1922–1982.* Tokyo, Japan Press Service, 1984.

Chapman, J.W.M., R. Drifte and I.T.M. Gow, *Japan's Quest for Comprehensive Security.* London, Frances Pinter, 1983.

Christensen, Ray, *Ending the LDP Hegemony: Party Cooperation in Japan.* Honolulu, University of Hawai'i Press, 2000.

Cole, Allan B., George O. Totten and Cecil H. Uyehara, *Socialist Parties in Postwar Japan.* New Haven and London, Yale University Press, 1966.

Collick, Martin, 'Social Policy: Pressures and Responses', in J.A.A Stockwin, Alan Rix, Aurelia George, James Horne, Daiichi Itō and Martin Collick., *Dynamic and Immobilist Politics in Japan.* London, Macmillan, 1988.

Colton, Kenneth E., 'The Conservative Political Movement', in *The Annals of the American Academy of Political and Social Science*

(special issue on 'Japan since Recovery of Independence'), November 1956.
Cox, Gary W. and Frances Rosenbluth, 'Anatomy of a Split: The Liberal Democrats of Japan', *Electoral Studies*, 14, 4 (1995).
Creighton, Millie, '*Soto* Others and *Uchi* Others: Imaging Racial Diversity, Imagining Homogeneous Japan', in Michael Weiner (ed.), *Japan's Minorities*. London and New York, Routledge, 1997.
Crump, Thomas, *The Death of an Emperor: Japan at the Crossroads*. London, Constable, 1989.
——, *The Japanese Numbers Game: The Use and Understanding of Numbers in Modern Japan*. London and New York, Routledge, 1992.
Cummings, William K., *Education and Equality in Japan*. Princeton, NJ, Princeton University Press, 1980.
Curtis, Gerald L., *Election Campaigning Japanese Style*. New York, Columbia University Press, 1971.
——, *The Japanese Way of Politics*. New York, Columbia University Press, 1988.
—— (ed.), *Japan's Foreign Policy after the Cold War: Coping with Change*. New York, M.E. Sharpe, 1993.
——, *The Logic of Japanese Politics*. New York, Columbia University Press, 1999.
Dale, Peter N., *The Myth of Japanese Uniqueness*. London and New York, Routledge, 1986 and later edns.
Denoon, Donald, Mark Hudson, Gavan McCormack and Tessa Morris-Suzuki (eds.), *Multicultural Japan: Palaeolithic to Postmodern*. Cambridge and New York, Cambridge University Press, 2001.
Destler, I.M., Haruhiro Fukui and Hideo Sato, *The Textile Wrangle: Conflict in Japanese-American Relations, 1969–1971*. Ithaca and London, Cornell University Press, 1979.
Dixon, Karl H., 'The Extreme Right in Contemporary Japan'. Doctoral Thesis, The Florida State University, 1975.
Donnelly, Michael W., 'Setting the Price of Rice: A Study in Political Decisionmaking', in T.J. Pempel (ed.), *Policymaking in Contemporary Japan*. Ithaca and London, Cornell University Press, 1977.
Dore, Ronald P., *City Life in Japan*. London, Routledge and Kegan Paul, 1958.
——, *Land Reform in Japan*. London, New York and Toronto, Oxford University Press, 1959.
——, *British Factory Japanese Factory: The Origins of National Diversity in Industrial Relations*. London, Allen & Unwin, 1973.
——, *Taking Japan Seriously: A Confucian Perspective on Leading Economic Issues*. London, Athlone, 1987.
——, *Japan, Internationalism and the UN*. London and New York, Routledge, 1997.
Dore, Ronald P. and Hugh Whittaker, *Social Evolution, Economic Development and Culture: Selected Writings of Ronald Dore*. Cheltenham and Northampton, MA, Edward Elgar, 2001.
Dower, John, *Empire and Aftermath: Yoshida Shigeru and the Japanese Experience, 1878–1954*. Cambridge, MA, Harvard University Press, 1979.
——, *Embracing Defeat: Japan in the Aftermath of World War II*. London, Penguin, 1999.
Drifte, Reinhard, *Japan's Foreign Policy for the 21st Century: From Economic Power to What Power?* Basingstoke and London, Macmillan; New York, St Martin's Press, 1998.
——, 'Japan and the European Union', in Takashi Inoguchi and Purnendra Jain (eds), *Japanese Foreign Policy Today*. Basingstoke and New York, Palgrave, 2000.
——, *Japan's Quest for a Permanent Security Council Seat: A Matter of Pride or Justice*. Basingstoke, Macmillan, 2000.
——, *Japanese Security Relations with China since 1989: From Balancing to Bandwagoning*. London and New York, Routledge, 2003.
Drysdale, Peter, 'Australia's Relationship with Japan after the Koizumi Visit', *APEC Economies Newsletter*. Canberra, ANU/AJRC, 6, 6 (June 2002).
Drysdale, Peter and Hironobu Kitaoji (eds), *Japan and Australia: Two Societies and their Interaction*. Canberra, London and Miami, Australian National University Press, 1981.
Duke, Benjamin C., *Japan's Militant Teachers*. Honolulu, University Press of Hawai'i, 1973.
Economist, *Consider Japan*. London, Duckworth, 1963.
Feldman, Ofer, *Politics and the News Media in Japan*. Ann Arbor, MI, University of Michigan Press, 1993.
Flanagan, Scott C., Shinsaku Kohei, Ichiro Miyake, Bradley M. Richardson and Joji

Watanuki, *The Japanese Voter*. New Haven and London, Yale University Press, 1991.

Foster-Carter, Aidan, 'The Democratic People's Republic of Korea (North Korea): Foreign Relations', in *The Far East and Australasia 2002*. 33rd edn. London, Europa Publications, 2002, pp. 628–32.

Freeman, Laurie Anne, *Closing the Shop: Information Cartels and Japan's Mass Media*. Princeton, NJ, Princeton University Press, 2000.

Fukui, Haruhiro, *Party in Power: The Japanese Liberal-Democrats and Policy-Making*. Canberra, Australian National University Press, 1970.

——, 'Tanaka Goes to Peking: A Case Study of Foreign Policymaking', in T.J. Pempel (ed.), *Policymaking in Contemporary Japan*. Ithaca and London, Cornell University Press, 1977.

—— (editor-in-chief), *Political Parties of Asia and the Pacific*. 2 vols. Westport and London, Greenwood Press, 1985.

Fukutake, Tadashi (trans., with a Foreword, by Ronald P. Dore), *The Japanese Social Structure: Its Evolution in the Modern Century*. Tokyo, University of Tokyo Press, 1982.

Gelb, Joyce and Margarita Estevez-Abe, 'Political Women in Japan: A Case Study of the Seikatsusha Network Movement', *Social Science Japan Journal*. 1, 2 (October 1998).

George, Aurelia, 'Japanese Interest Group Behaviour: An Institutional Approach', in J.A.A. Stockwin et al., *Dynamic and Immobilist Politics in Japan*. Basingstoke and London, Macmillan, 1988.

George Mulgan, Aurelia, 'Agriculture and Fisheries', in Patrick Heenan (ed.), *The Japan Handbook*. Chicago and London, 1998.

——, *The Politics of Agriculture in Japan*. London, Routledge, 2000.

——, *Japan's Failed Revolution: Koizumi and the Politics of Economic Reform*. Canberra, Asia–Pacific Press, 2002.

George, Timothy, *Minamata: Pollution and the Struggle for Democracy in Postwar Japan*. Cambridge, MA, and London, Harvard University Press, 2001.

Gilson, Julie, *Japan and the European Union: A Partnership for the Twenty First Century*. London, Macmillan, 2000.

Goodman, Roger, *Children of the Japanese State: The Changing Role of Child Protection Institutions in Contemporary Japan*. Oxford and New York, Oxford University Press, 2000.

Goodman, Roger, Gordon White and Huck-ju Kwon, *The East Asian Welfare Model: Welfare Orientalism and the State*. London and New York, Routledge, 1998.

Gordon, Andrew, 'Contests for the Workplace', in Andrew Gordon (ed.), *Postwar Japan as History*. Berkeley, Los Angeles and Oxford, University of California Press, 1993.

—— (ed.), *Postwar Japan as History*. Berkeley, Los Angeles and Oxford, University of California Press, 1993.

Gourevitch, Peter, Takashi Inoguchi and Courtney Purrington (eds), *United States–Japan Relations and International Institutions after the Cold War*. University of California, San Diego, 1995.

Haley, John, 'Weak Law, Strong Competition, and Trade Barriers: Competitiveness as a Disincentive to Foreign Entry into Japanese Markets', in Kozo Yamamura (ed.), *Japan's Economic Structure: Should it Change?* Seattle, Society for Japanese Studies, 1990.

Hara, Kimie, *Japanese–Soviet/Russian Relations since 1945: A Difficult Peace*. London and New York, Routledge, 1998.

Hayao, Kenji, *The Japanese Prime Minister and Public Policy*. Pittsburgh, PA, University of Pittsburgh Press, 1993.

Heenan, Patrick (ed.), *The Japan Handbook*. Chicago and London, Fitzroy Dearborn, 1998.

Hellmann, Donald C., *Japanese Domestic Politics and Foreign Policy: The Peace Agreement with the Soviet Union*. Berkeley, University of California Press, 1969.

——, *Japan and East Asia*. New York, Praeger, 1972.

Henderson, Dan Fenno (ed.), *The Constitution of Japan: Its First Twenty Years, 1947–67*. Seattle and London, University of Washington Press, 1968.

Hendry, Joy, *Marriage in Changing Japan*. Rutland, VT, and Tokyo, 1979.

——, *Marriage in Changing Japan*. London, Croom Helm, 1981.

——, *Wrapping Culture: Politeness, Presentation, and Power in Japan and Other Societies*. Oxford, Clarendon Press, 1993.

——, *Understanding Japanese Society* (second edn), London and New York, Routledge, 1995, and third edition forthcoming, 2003.

Hollerman, Leon, *Japan, Disincorporated: The*

Economic Liberalization Process. Stanford, CA, Hoover Institution Press, 1988.

Hood, Christopher P., *Japanese Education Reform: Nakasone's Legacy.* London, Routledge, 2001.

Hook, Glenn D., Julie Gilson, Christopher W. Hughes and Hugo Dobson, *Japan's International Relations: Politics, Economics and Security.* London and New York, Routledge, 2001.

Hook, Glenn D. and Gavan McCormack, *Japan's Contested Constitution.* London and New York, Routledge, 2001.

Hrebenar, Ronald J., *The Japanese Party System.* Boulder, CO, and Oxford, Westview Press, 1986, 1992.

——, *Japan's New Party System.* Boulder, CO, and Oxford, Westview Press, 2000.

Ike, Nobutaka, *Japanese Politics: An Introductory Survey.* New York, Knopf, 1957.

Inoguchi, Takashi, *Japan's International Relations.* London, Pinter; Boulder, CO, Westview, 1991.

——, *Japan's Foreign Policy in an Era of Global Change.* London, Pinter, 1993.

Inoguchi, Takashi and Purnendra Jain (eds), *Japanese Foreign Policy Today.* Basingstoke and New York, Palgrave, 2000.

Inoguchi, Takashi and Daniel I. Okimoto (eds), *The Political Economy of Japan: The Changing International Context.* Stanford, CA, Stanford University Press, 1988.

Ishi, Hiromitsu, *Making Fiscal Policy in Japan: Economic Effects and Institutional Settings.* Oxford and New York, Oxford University Press, 2000.

——, *The Japanese Tax System* (third edn). Oxford and New York, Oxford University Press, 2001.

Ishida, Takeshi, 'Conflict and its Accommodation: *Omote-ura* and *uchi-soto* Relations', in Ellis S. Krauss, Thomas P. Rohlen and Patricia G. Steinhoff, *Conflict in Japan.* Honolulu, University of Hawai'i Press, 1984.

Ishihara, Shintarō and Akio Morita (trans. Frank Baldwin), *The Japan that Can Say No,* New York and London, Simon & Schuster, 1991.

Ishikawa Masumi, 'New Heights, Louder Message: Abstentions in Japan's National Elections, 1993–95', in Purnendra Jain and Takashi Inoguchi (eds), *Japanese Politics Today: Beyond Karaoke Democracy.* Melbourne, Macmillan Education Australia, 1997.

Itoh, Hiroshi and Lawrence W. Beer, *Selected Supreme Court Decisions, 1961–70.* Seattle, University of Washington Press, 1978.

Ivanov, Vladimir I. and Karla S. Smith (eds), *Japan and Russian in Northeast Asia: Partners in the 21st Century.* Westport, CT, and London, Praeger, 1999.

Iwao, Sumiko, 'The Quiet Revolution: Japanese Women Today', *Japan Foundation Newsletter,* XIX, 3 (December 1991).

Jain, Purnendra, *Local Politics and Policymaking in Japan.* New Delhi, Commonwealth Publishers, 1989.

—— (ed.), *Distant Asian Neighbours: Japan and South Asia.* New Delhi, Sterling Publishers Private Ltd, 1996.

—— (ed.), *Australasian Studies of Japan: Essays and Annotated Bibliography (1989–96).* Rockhampton, Central Queensland University Press, 1998.

——, 'Japan and South Asia: Between Cooperation and Confrontation', in Takashi Inoguchi and Purnendra Jain (eds), *Japanese Foreign Policy Today.* Basingstoke and New York, Palgrave, 2000.

Jain, Purnendra and Takashi Inoguchi (eds), *Japanese Politics Today: Beyond Karaoke Democracy.* Melbourne, Macmillan Education Australia, 1997.

Johnson, Chalmers, *MITI and the Japanese Miracle.* Stanford, CA, Stanford University Press, 1982.

Johnson, Stephen, *Opposition Politics in Japan: Strategies under a One-Party Dominant Regime.* London and New York, Routledge, 2000.

Kataoka, Tetsuya, *The Price of a Constitution: The Origin of Japan's Postwar Politics.* New York and London, Crane Russak, 1991.

—— (ed.), *Creating Single-Party Democracy: Japan's Postwar Political System.* Stanford, CA, Hoover Institution Press, 1992.

Kato, Junko, *The Problem of Bureaucratic Rationality: Tax Politics in Japan.* Princeton, NJ, Princeton University Press, 1994.

——, 'Withering Factionalism? The Future of Japanese and Italian Partisan Politics', in Michèle Schmiegelow (ed.), *Democracy in Asia.* Frankfurt, Campus Verlag and New York, St Martin's Press, 1997.

Kawai, Kazuo, *Japan's American Interlude.* Chicago, University of Chicago Press, 1960.

Kawanishi, Hirosuke, *Enterprise Unionism in*

Japan. London and New York, Kegan Paul International, 1992.

Keddell, Joseph P., *The Politics of Defense in Japan*. New York, M.E. Sharpe, 1992.

Kelly, William W, 'Finding a Place in Metropolitan Japan: Ideologies, Institutions, and Everyday Life', in Andrew Gordon (ed.), *Postwar Japan as History*. Berkeley and Los Angeles, University of California Press, 1993.

Kerr, George H., *Okinawa: The History of an Island People*. Rutland, VT, and Tokyo, Tuttle, 1958.

Kersten, Rikki, 'Japan and Australia', in Inoguchi Takashi and Purnendra Jain, *Japanese Foreign Policy Today*. Basingstoke and New York, Palgrave, 2000.

Kim, Paul S., *Japan's Civil Service System: Its Structure, Personnel and Politics*. Westport, CT, and London, Greenwood Press, 1988.

Kinmonth, Earl, 'Can Japan Squeeze into One Middle Class or Not?', *Japan Times*, 17 March 1985.

Kisala, Robert J. and Mark R. Mullins (eds), *Religion and Social Crisis in Japan: Understanding Japanese Society through the Aum Affair*. Basingstoke and New York, Palgrave, 2001.

Kobayashi, Naoki, 'The Small and Medium-Sized Enterprises Organization Law', in Hiroshi Itoh (trans. and ed.), *Japanese Politics: An Inside View*. Ithaca, NY, and London, Cornell University Press, 1973.

Koh, B.C., *Japan's Administrative Elite*. Berkeley, Los Angeles and Oxford, University of California Press, 1989

Kohno, Masaru, *Japan's Postwar Party Politics*. Princeton, NJ, Princeton University Press, 1997.

Koike, Kazuo, *The Economics of Work in Japan*. Tokyo, LTCB International Library Foundation, 1991.

Kondo, Dorinne K., *Crafting Selves: Power, Gender and Discourses of Identity in a Japanese Workplace*. Chicago, University of Chicago Press, 1990.

Kosai, Yutaka, 'The Politics of Economic Management', in Kozo Yamamura and Yasukichi Yasuba (eds), *The Political Economy of Japan; Volume 1, The Domestic Transformation*. Stanford, CA, Stanford Univesity Press, 1987.

Koseki, Shōichi, *The Birth of Japan's Postwar Constitution*. Boulder, CO, Westview Press, 1997.

Kotter, John P., *Matsushita Leadership: Lessons from the 20th Century's Most Remarkable Entrepreneur*. New York, Free Press, 1997.

Krauss, Ellis S., *Japanese Radicals Revisited: Student Protest in Postwar Japan*. Berkeley and Los Angeles, University of California Press, 1974.

——, *Broadcasting Politics in Japan: NHK and Television News*. Ithaca, NY, Cornell University Press, 2000.

Krauss, Ellis S., Thomas P. Rohlen and Patricia G. Steinhoff, *Conflict in Japan*. Honolulu, University of Hawai'i Press, 1984.

Kume, Ikuo, *Disparaged Success: Labor Politics in Postwar Japan*. Ithaca, NY, Cornell University Press, 1998.

Kyogoku, Jun-ichi (trans. Nobutaka Ike), *The Political Dynamics of Japan*. Tokyo, University of Tokyo Press, 1987.

Lam, Peng-Er, *Green Politics in Japan*. London and New York, Routledge, 1999.

——, 'Japanese Relations with Southeast Asia in an Era of Turbulence', in Takashi Inoguchi and Purnendra Jain (eds), *Japanese Foreign Policy Today*. Basingstoke and New York, 2000.

Langdon, Frank C., *Politics in Japan*. Boston and Toronto, Little, Brown, 1967.

——, *Japan's Foreign Policy*. Vancouver, University of British Columbia Press, 1973.

Large, Stephen S., *Emperor Hirohito and Showa Japan: A Political Biography*. London and New York, Routledge, 1992.

LeBlanc, Robin M., *Bicycle Citizens: The Political World of the Japanese Housewife*. Berkeley, Los Angeles and London, University of California Press, 1999.

Leiserson, Michael, 'Factions and Coalitions in One-Party Japan: An Explanation Based on the Theory of Games', *American Political Science Review*, 62 (1968).

Lesbirel, S. Hayden, *NIMBY Politics in Japan: Energy Siting and the Management of Environmental Conflict*. Ithaca and London, Cornell University Press, 1998.

Levine, Solomon B., *Industrial Relations in Postwar Japan*. Urbana, IL, University of Illinois Press, 1958.

Lie, John, *Multiethnic Japan*. Cambridge, MA, Harvard University Press, 2001.

Lincoln, Edward, *Arthritic Japan: The Slow Pace of Economic Reform*. Washington, DC, Brookings Institution, 2001.

McCormack, Gavan, *The Emptiness of Japa-*

nese Affluence. New York, M.E. Sharpe, 1996.

McKean, Margaret A., *Environmental Protest and Citizen Politics in Japan*. Berkeley, Los Angeles and London, University of California Press, 1981.

Maclachlan, Patricia L., *Consumer Politics in Japan: The Institutional Boundaries of Citizen Activism*. New York, Columbia University Press, 2002.

McVeigh, Brian J., *The Nature of the Japanese State: Rationality and Rituality*. London and New York, Routledge, 1998.

Maki, John M., *Court and Constitution in Japan: Selected Supreme Court Decisions, 1948–60*. Seattle, University of Washington Press, 1964.

—— (trans. and ed.), *Japan's Commission on the Constitution: The Final Report*. Seattle and London, University of Washington Press, 1980.

Maruyama, Masao (Ivan Morris, ed.), *Thought and Behaviour in Modern Japanese Politics*. London and New York, Oxford University Press, 1963.

Mason, R.H.P., *Japan's First General Election, 1890*. Canberra, Australian National University Press, 1969.

Masumi, Junnosuke (trans. Lonny E. Carlile), *Postwar Politics in Japan, 1945–1955*. Institute of East Asian Studies, University of California, Berkeley, 1985.

—— (trans. Lonny E. Carlile), *Contemporary Politics in Japan*. Berkeley, Los Angeles and London, University of California Press, 1995.

Maswood, S. Javed, *Japan in Crisis*. Basingstoke and New York, Palgrave, 2002.

Metraux, Daniel, 'Religious Terrorism in Japan: The Fatal Appeal of Aum Shinrikyō', *Asian Survey*, 35, 12 (1995).

Mitchell, Richard, *Political Bribery in Japan*. Honolulu, University of Hawai'i Press, 1996.

Miyaoka, Isao, *The International Construction of Legitimacy:Its Impact on Japan's Wildlife Protection*, Palgrave-Macmillan, forthcoming, 2003.

Mochizuki, Mike, 'Public Sector Labor and the Privatization Challenge: The Railway and Telecommunications Unions', in Gary D. Allinson and Yasunori Sone, *Political Dynamics in Contemporary Japan*. Ithaca, NY, and London, Cornell University Press, 1993.

—— (ed.), *Toward a True Alliance: Restructuring US-Japan Security Relations*. Washington, DC, Brookings, 1997.

Moore, Ray A. and Donald L. Robinson, *Partners for Democracy: Crafting the New Japanese State under MacArthur*. Oxford and New York, Oxford University Press, forthcoming, 2002.

Morikawa, Jun, 'The Anatomy of Japan's South African Policies', *The Journal of Modern African Studies*. 22, 1 (1984).

Morita, Akio, with Edwin M Reingold and Mitsuko Shimomura, *Made in Japan*. London, Harper Collins, 1994.

Morris, David, 'The Internal Roles and Functions of Kōmoto Faction Liberal Democratic Party Members', *Japan Forum*, 1, 2 (October 1989).

Morris, Ivan I., *Nationalism and the Right-Wing in Japan: A Study of Post-War Trends*. London and New York, Oxford University Press, 1960.

Mouer, Ross and Yoshio Sugimoto, *Images of Japanese Society*. London and New York, Routledge and Kegan Paul, 1986.

Murakami, Haruki, *Underground: The Tokyo Gas Attack and the Japanese Psyche*. London, Harvill, 2000.

Murakami, Yasusuke, 'The Age of New Middle Mass Politics: The Case of Japan', *Journal of Japanese Studies*, 8, 1 (winter 1982).

Muramatsu, Michio (trans. Betsey Scheiner and James White), *Local Power in the Japanese State*. Berkeley, CA, Los Angeles and London, University of California Press, 1988, 1997.

——, 'Patterned Pluralism under Challenge: The Policies of the 1980s', in Gary D. Allinson and Yasunori Sone, *Political Dynamics in Contemporary Japan*. Ithaca, NY, and London, Cornell University Press, 1993.

Muramatsu, Michio, Farrukh Iqbal and Ikuo Kume (eds), *Local Government Development in Post-war Japan*. Oxford, Oxford University Press, 2001.

Muramatsu, Michio and Ellis S. Krauss, 'The Conservative Policy Line and the Development of Patterned Pluralism', in Kozo Yamamura and Yasukichi Yasuba (eds), *The Political Economy of Japan; Volume 1, The Domestic Transformation*. Stanford, CA, Stanford University Press, 1987.

Nakagawa, Yatsuhiro, 'Japan, the Welfare Super-Power', *Journal of Japanese Studies*, 5, 1 (1979).

Nakane, Chie, *Japanese Society*. London, Penguin, 1970.
Nakano, Kōichi, 'Becoming a "Policy" Ministry: The Organization and *Amakudari* of the Ministry of Posts and Telecommunications', *Journal of Japanese Studies*, 24, 1 (winter 1998).
Nakasone, Yasuhiro (trans. and annotated by Lesley Connors), *The Making of the New Japan: Reclaiming the Political Mainstream*. Richmond, Curzon, 1999.
Neary, Ian J., *Political Protest and Social Control in Pre-War Japan: The Origins of Buraku Liberation*. Manchester, Manchester University Press, 1989.
——, 'Burakumin in Contemporary Japan', in Michael Weiner (ed.), *Japan's Minorities*. London and New York, Routledge, 1997.
——, *The State and Politics in Japan*. Cambridge, Polity Press; Malden, MA, Blackwell, 2002.
Newland, Kathleen (ed.), *The International Relations of Japan*. Basingstoke and London, Macmillan, 1990.
Nishihara, Masashi, *The Japanese and Sukarno's Indonesia: Tokyo–Jakarta Relations, 1951–1966*. Honolulu, University Press of Hawaii, 1975.
Nonaka, Naoto, 'Characteristics of the Decision-making Structure', in Otake Hideo, *Power Shuffles and Policy Processes: Coalition Government in Japan in the 1990s*. Tokyo and New York, Japan Center for International Exchange, 2000.
Norgren, Tiana, 'Abortion before Birth Control: The Interest Group Politics behind Postwar Japanese Reproduction Policy', *Journal of Japanese Studies*, 24, 1 (winter 1998).
Oda, Hiroshi, *Japanese Law* (second edn). Oxford and New York, Oxford University Press, 1999.
Ohnuki-Tierney, Emiko, *Illness and Culture in Contemporary Japan: An Anthropological View*. Cambridge, Cambridge University Press, 1984.
Okimoto, Daniel I., *Between MITI and the Market: Japanese Industrial Policy for High Technology*. Stanford, CA, Stanford University Press, 1989.
Osawa, Mari, 'The Feminization of the Labour Market', in Banno Junji (ed.), *The Political Economy of Japanese Society*. Vol. 2. Oxford, Oxford University Press, 1998.
Otake, Hideo, *Power Shuffles and Policy Processes: Coalition Government in Japan in the 1990s*. Tokyo and New York, Japan Center for International Exchange, 2000.
Ozaki, Robert S. and Walter Arnold, *Japan's Foreign Relations: A Global Search for Economic Security*. Boulder, Co, and London, Westview Press, 1985.
Ozawa, Ichirō, *Blueprint for a New Japan*. Tokyo, Kodansha International, 1994.
Packard, George R., *Protest in Tokyo: The Security Treaty Crisis of 1960*. Princeton, NJ, Princeton University Press, 1966.
Panda, Rajaram and Kazuo Ando (eds), *India and Japan: Multi-Dimensional Perspectives*. New Delhi, Japan Foundation, 1997.
Parker, L. Craig, Jr, *The Japanese Police System Today: A Comparative Study*. New York, M.E. Sharpe, 2001.
Passin, Herbert, 'The Legacy of the Occupation – Japan', *Occasional Papers*, New York, East Asian Institute, Columbia University, 1968.
Pempel, T.J. (ed.), *Policymaking in Contemporary Japan*, Ithaca and London, Cornell University Press, 1977.
——, *Patterns of Japanese Policy-making: Experiences from Higher Education*. Boulder, CO, Westview Press, 1978.
——, *Policy and Politics in Japan: Creative Conservatism*. Philadelphia, Temple University Press, 1982.
—— (ed.), *Uncommon Democracies: The One-Party Dominant Regimes*. Ithaca and London, Cornell University Press, 1990.
——, *Regime Shift: Comparative Dynamics of the Japanese Political Economy*. Ithaca, NY, and London, Cornell University Press, 1998.
Pempel, T.J. and Keiichi Tsunekawa, 'Corporatism without Labor? The Japanese Anomaly', in Phillippe C. Schmitter and Gerhard Lehmbruch (eds), *Trends toward Corporatist Intermediation*. Beverly Hills, CA, Sage, 1979.
Pharr, Susan J., *Political Women in Japan: The Search for a Place in Political Life*. Berkeley, Los Angeles and London, University of California Press, 1981.
Prestowitz, Clyde V., *Trading Places: How America Allowed Japan to Take the Lead*. Tokyo, Tuttle, 1988.
Quigley, Harold S. and John E. Turner, *The New Japan: Government and Politics*. Minneapolis, University of Minnesota Press, 1956.
Ramseyer, J. Mark and Frances McCall Rosen-

bluth, *Japan's Political Marketplace*. Cambridge, MA, and London, Harvard University Press, 1993.

Reader, Ian, *Religion in Contemporary Japan*. Basingstoke, Macmillan, 1991.

——, *Religious Violence in Contemporary Japan: The Case of Aum Shinrikyō*. Richmond, Curzon, 2000.

Reed, Steven J., *Japanese Prefectures and Policymaking*. Pittsburgh, University of Pittsburgh Press, 1986.

——, *Creating a New Party System: Electoral Politics in Japan from 1993*. London and New York, RoutledgeCurzon, forthcoming 2003.

Refsing, Kirsten, 'Ainu', *Encyclopaedia of Asia*. New York, Scribners, forthcoming.

Reischauer, Edwin O., 'The Broken Dialogue with Japan', *Foreign Affairs*, 39, 1 (October 1960).

Richardson, Bradley, *The Political Culture of Japan*. Berkeley, CA, University of California Press, 1974.

——, *Japanese Democracy: Power, Coordination and Performance*. New Haven and London, Yale University Press, 1997.

Rix, Alan, *Coming to Terms*. Sydney, Allen & Unwin, 1986.

——, *Japan's Foreign Aid Challenge: Policy Reform and Aid Challenge*. London and New York, Routledge, 1993.

——, *The Australia–Japan Political Alignment*. London, Routledge, 1999.

Roberts, Glenda, Mari Osawa, Susan Orpett Long and Phyllis Braudy Harris, Karen Shire, Chunghee Sarah Soh (separate articles under the title 'Gendering Contemporary Japan'), *Social Science Japan Journal*, 3, 1, April 2000.

Roesgaard, Marie H., *Moving Mountains: Japanese Education Reform*. Aarhus, Aarhus University Press, 1998.

Rohlen, Thomas P., *Japan's High Schools*. Berkeley, CA, University of California Press, 1983.

Rose, Caroline, *Interpreting History in Sino-Japanese Relations: A Case Study in Political Decision Making*. London and New York, Routledge, 1998.

Rosecrance, Richard N., *Australian Diplomacy and Japan 1945–1951*. London, Melbourne University Press, 1962.

Rothacher, Albrecht, *Economic Diplomacy between the European Community and Japan 1959–1981*. Aldershot, Gower, 1983.

Rozman, Gilbert, *Japan's Response to the Gorbachev Era, 1985–1991: A Rising Superpower Views a Declining One*. Princeton, NJ, Princeton University Press, 1992.

——, 'A Chance for a Breakthrough in Russo-Japanese Relations: Will the Logic of Great Power Relations Prevail?', *Pacific Review*, 15, 3, 2002.

Sako, Mari and Hiroki Satō, *Japanese Labour and Management in Transition*. London and New York, Routledge, 1997.

Samuels, Richard J., *The Business of the Japanese State: Energy Markets in Comparative and Historical Perspective*. Ithaca and London, Cornell University Press, 1987.

Satō, Seizaburō, Ken'ichi Koyama and Shunpei Kumon (trans. William R. Carter), *Postwar Politician: The Life of Former Prime Minister Masayoshi Ōhira*. Tokyo and New York, Kodansha International, 1990.

Scalapino, Robert A., *Democracy and the Party Movement in Prewar Japan: The Failure of the First Attempt*. Berkeley and Los Angeles, University of California Press, 1953, 1975.

——, *The Japanese Communist Movement, 1920–1966*. Berkeley and Los Angeles, University of California Press, 1967.

——, (ed.), *The Foreign Policy of Modern Japan*. Berkeley, Los Angeles and London, University of California Press, 1977.

Scalapino, Robert A. and Junnosuke Masumi, *Parties and Politics in Contemporary Japan*. Berkeley, CA, University of California Press, 1962.

Schaede, Ulrike, 'The "Old Boy" Network and Government-Business Relationships in Japan', *Journal of Japanese Studies*, 21, 2 (summer 1995).

Schoppa, Leonard J., *Education Reform in Japan: A Case of Immobilist Politics*. London, Routledge, 1991.

——, *Bargaining with Japan: What American Pressure Can and Cannot Do*. New York, Columbia University Press, 1997.

Schreurs, Miranda A., 'Domestic Institutions and International Environmental Agendas in Japan and Germany', in Miranda A. Schreurs and Elizabeth C. Economy (eds), *The Internationalization of Environmental Protection*. Cambridge, Cambridge University Press, 1997.

Searight, Amy E., 'International Organizations', in Steven K. Vogel (ed.), *US–Japan*

Relations in a Changing World. Washington, DC, Brookings Institution Press, 2002.
Sellek, Yoko, 'Nikkeijin, the Phenomenon of Reverse Migration', in Michael Weiner (ed.), Japan's Minorities. London and New York, Routledge, 1997.
Shimazu, Naoko, Japan, Race and Equality: The Racial Equality Proposal of 1919. London and New York, Routledge, 1998.
Shinoda Tomohito, Leading Japan: The Role of the Prime Minister. Westport, CT, and London, Praeger, 2000.
Shinoda, Toru, 'Heisei Labour Politics: A Long and Winding Road', in Purnendra Jain and Takashi Inoguchi (eds), Japanese Politics Today: Beyond Karaoke Democracy? Melbourne, Macmillan Educational Australia, 1997.
Siddle, Richard, 'Ainu, Japan's Indigenous People', in Michael Weiner (ed.), Japan's Minorities. London and New York, Routledge, 1997.
Sissons, D.C.S., 'Immigration in Australian-Japanese Relations', in J.A.A. Stockwin (ed.), Japan and Australia in the Seventies. Sydney, Angus & Robertson, 1972.
——, 'Japan', in W.J. Hudson (ed.), Australia in World Affairs, 1971–1975. Sydney, London and Boston, MA, George Allen & Unwin, 1980.
Soderberg, Marie (ed.), Chinese–Japanese Relations in the Twenty-First Century. London and New York, Routledge, 2002.
Steiner, Kurt, Local Government in Japan. Stanford, CA, Stanford University Press, 1965.
Steiner, Kurt, Ellis S. Krauss and Scott C. Flanagan, Political Opposition and Local Politics in Japan. Princeton, NJ, Princeton University Press, 1980.
Steslicke, William, Doctors in Politics: The Political Life of the Japan Medical Association. New York and London, Praeger, 1973.
Steven, Rob, Classes in Contemporary Japan. Cambridge and New York, Cambridge University Press, 1983.
Stockwin, J.A.A., 'The Japan Communist Party in the Sino-Soviet Dispute – from Neutrality to Alignment?', in J.D.B. Miller and T.H. Rigby (eds), The Disintegrating Monolith: Pluralist Trends in the Communist World. Canberra, Australian National University, 1965.
——, The Japanese Socialist Party and Neutralism: A Study of a Political Party and its Foreign Policy. Melbourne, Melbourne University Press, 1968a.
——, 'Is Japan a Post-Marxist Society?', Pacific Affairs, XLI, 2 (summer 1968b).
——, 'A Comparison of Political Factionalism in Japan and India', Australian Journal of Politics and History, XVI, 3 (December 1970).
——, 'The Ultra-Right in Japanese Politics', World Review, 11, 2 (July 1972).
——, 'Dynamic and Immobilist Aspects of Japanese Politics', in J.A.A. Stockwin, Alan Rix, Aurelia George, James Horne, Daiichi Itō and Martin Collick, Dynamic and Immobilist Politics in Japan. Basingstoke and London, Macmillan, 1988.
——, 'Factionalism in Japanese Political Parties', Japan Forum, 1, 2 (October 1989).
——, 'On Trying to Move Mountains: The Political Career of Doi Takako', Japan Forum, 6, 1 (April 1994).
——, Governing Japan: Divided Politics in a Major Economy. Oxford and Malden, MA, Blackwell, 1999.
Stockwin, J.A.A., Alan Rix, Aurelia George, James Horne, Daiichi Itō and Martin Collick, Dynamic and Immobilist Politics in Japan. Basingstoke and London, Macmillan, 1988.
Storry, Richard, A History of Modern Japan. London, Penguin, 1960, and later edns.
Swearingen, Rodger and Paul Langer, Red Flag in Japan: International Communism in Action, 1919–1951. Boston, MA, Harvard University Press, 1952. New York, Greenwood Press (Reprint), 1968.
Taira, Koji, 'Troubled National Identity: The Ryukyuans/Okinawans', in Michael Weiner (ed.) Japan's Minorities. London and New York, Routledge, 1997.
Tanaka, Akihiko, The New Middle Ages: The World System in the 21st Century. Tokyo, LTCB International Library Trust and International House of Japan, 2002.
Tanaka, Kakuei, Building a New Japan: A Plan for Remodelling the Japanese Archipelago. Tokyo, Simul Press, 1973.
Tatebayashi, Masahiko, 'The Reform of Public Corporations', in Otake Hideo (ed.), Power Shuffles and Policy Processes: Coalition Government in Japan in the 1990s. Tokyo and New York, Japan Center for International Exchange, 2000.
Thayer, Nathaniel B., How the Conservatives

Rule Japan. Princeton, NJ, Princeton University Press, 1969.

Thurston, Donald R., *Teachers and Politics in Japan.* Princeton, NJ, Princeton University Press, 1973.

Tilton, Mark, *Restrained Trade: Cartels in Japan's Basic Materials Industries.* Ithaca, NY, Cornell University Press, 1996.

Tipton, Elise K., *Modern Japan: A Social and Political History.* London and New York, Routledge, 2002.

Totten, George O., *The Social Democratic Movement in Prewar Japan.* New Haven and London, Yale University Press, 1966.

Totten, George O. and Tamio Kawakami, 'The Functions of Factionalism in Japanese Politics', *Pacific Affairs*, 38 (summer 1965).

Toyonaga, Ikuko, 'The Battle of the Breakup of NTT', in Otake Hideo (ed.), *Power Shuffles and Policy Processes: Coalition Government in Japan in the 1990s.* Tokyo and New York, Japan Center for International Exchange, 2000.

Tsuji, Kiyoaki, 'Decision-Making in the Japanese Government: A Study of *Ringisei*', in Robert E. Ward, *Political Development in Modern Japan.* Princeton, Princeton University Press, 1968.

——, *Public Administration in Japan.* Tokyo, University of Tokyo Press, 1984.

Tsujinaka, Yutaka, 'Rengo and its Osmotic Networks', in Gary D. Allinson and Yasunori Sone, *Political Dynamics in Contemporary Japan.* Ithaca, NY, and London, Cornell University Press, 1993.

Tsuzuki, Chushichi, *The Pursuit of Power in Modern Japan 1825–1995.* Oxford and New York, Oxford University Press, 2000.

Upham, Frank K., *Law and Social Change in Postwar Japan.* Cambridge, MA, and London, Harvard University Press, 1987.

——, 'Unplaced Persons and Movements for Place', in Andrew Gordon (ed.), *Postwar Japan as History.* Berkeley, Los Angeles and Oxford, University of California Press, 1993.

Uriu, Robert, *Troubled Industries: Confronting Economic Change in Japan.* Ithaca and London, Cornell University Press, 1996.

Van Wolferen, Karel, *The Enigma of Japanese Power: People and Politics in a Stateless Nation.* London, Macmillan, 1989.

Vasishht, Andrea, 'The Chinese Community: A Model Minority', in Michael Weiner (ed.), *Japan's Minorities.* London and New York, Routledge, 1997.

Vishwanathan, Savitri, *Normalization of Japanese-Soviet Relations.* Tallahassee, FL, Diplomatic Press, 1973.

Vogel, Ezra F., *Japan as Number One.* Cambridge, MA, and London, Harvard University Press, 1979.

Vogel, Steven K. (ed.), *US–Japan Relations in a Changing World.* Washington, DC, Brookings Institution Press, 2002.

Wade, Robert, *Governing the Market: Economic Theory and the Role of Government in East Asian Industrialization.* Princeton, NJ, Princeton University Press, 1990.

Ward, Robert E., 'Political Modernization and Political Culture in Japan', *World Politics*, XV, 4, July 1963.

——, 'The Commission on the Constitution and Prospects for Constitutional Change in Japan', *Journal of Asian Studies*, XXIV, 3 (May 1965).

——, *Japan's Political System.* Englewood Cliffs, Prentice Hall, 1967, 1978.

—— (ed.), *Political Development in Modern Japan.* Princeton, NJ, Princeton University Press, 1968.

Waswo, Ann, *Modern Japanese Society, 1868–1994.* Oxford and New York, Oxford University Press, 1996.

——, *Housing in Postwar Japan: A Social History.* London and New York, Routledge Curzon, 2002.

Watanabe, Osamu, 'The Sociology of *jishuku* and *kichō*: The Death of the *Shōwa Tennō* as Reflection of the Structure of Contemporary Japanese Society', *Japan Forum*, 1, 2 (October 1989).

Weiner, Michael (ed.), *Japan's Minorities.* London, Routledge, 1997.

Weinstein, Franklin B. (ed.), *US–Japanese Relations and the Security of East Asia: The Next Decade.* Boulder, CO, Westview Press, 1978.

Welfield, John, *Japan and Nuclear China: Japanese Reactions to China's Nuclear Weapons.* Canberra, Australian National University Press, 1970.

——, *An Empire in Eclipse: Japan in the Postwar American Alliance System.* London, Athlone, 1988.

White, James, *Sokagakkai and Mass Society.* Stanford, CA, Stanford University Press, 1970.

Wihtol, Robert, *The Asian Development Bank and Rural Development: Policy and*

Practice. Basingstoke and London, Macmillan, 1988.

Wilks, Stephen and Maurice Wright (eds), *The Promotion and Regulation of Industry in Japan*. Basingstoke and London, Macmillan, 1991.

Williams, David, 'Reporting the Death of the Shōwa Emperor', *Nissan Occasional Paper*, 14 (1990).

——, *Japan Beyond the End of History*. London and New York, Routledge, 1994.

Williams, Noel, *The Right to Life in Japan*. London and New York, Routledge, 1997.

Yamamoto, Mari, 'The Rebirth of a Nation: Popular Pacifism and Grassroots Revolt in Postwar Japan'. D. Phil. Thesis, Faculty of Modern History, University of Oxford, 2003.

Yamamura, Kozo and Yasukichi Yasuba, *The Political Economy of Japan: The Domestic Transformation*. Stanford, CA, Stanford University Press, 1987.

Yoneyama, Shoko, *The Japanese High School: Silence and Resistance*. London and New York, Routledge, 1999.

Yoshida, Shigeru (trans. Yoshida Kenichi), *The Yoshida Memoirs: The Story of Japan in Crisis*. London, Heinemann, 1961.

JAPANESE LANGUAGE BIBLIOGRAPHY

Reference and periodical works

朝日年間 (Asahi nenkan, Asahi Yearbook), 朝日新聞社 (Asahi Newspaper Company), 1946–2000 (ceased production with 2000 issue).

国会便覧 (Kokkai binran, Parliamentary Handbook), 日本政経新聞社 (Japan Politics and Economics Newspaper Company), two or three times per year.

LEVIATHAN, 木鐸社 (Bokutakusha), twice yearly.

日本近代史辞典 (Nihon kindai shi jiten, Dictionary of Modern Japanese History), 京都大学文学部国史研究室、日本近代史辞典編集委員会 (Kyoto University Faculty of Literature National History Research Office and Dictionary of Modern Japanese History Editorial Committee), 1958 and later editions.

日本政治学会年報 (Nihon seiji gakkai nenpō, Japan Political Science Association Yearbook), 岩波書店 (Iwanami Bookshop), annual.

日本政治辞典 (Nihon seiji jiten, Dictionary of Japanese Politics), 高橋正則 (Takahashi Masanori), 国書刊行会, 1980.

政治学辞典 (Seijigaku jiten, Encyclopedia of Political Science). 猪口孝 (Inoguchi Takashi), 大澤真幸 (Osawa Masachi), 岡沢憲芙 (Okazawa Norio), 山本吉宣 (Yamamoto Yoshinobu), Steven R. Reed (eds), 弘文堂 (Kōbundō), 2000.

政治家の通信簿 (Seijika no tsūshinbo, Politicians' Political Record Book), 日本有権者連盟 (Japan League of Electors), 四ツ谷ラウンド (Yotsuya Round), 1996.

戦後史大辞典 (Sengo shi dai jiten, Encyclopedia of Postwar Japan 1945–1990). 佐々木毅 (Sasaki Takeshi), 鶴見俊輔 (Tsurumi Shunsuke), 富永健一 (Tominaga Kenichi), 中村正則 (Nakamura Masanori), 正村公宏 (Masamura Kimihiro), 村上陽一郎 (Murakami Jōichirō) (eds), 三省堂 (Sanseidō), 1991.

読売年間 (Yomiuri nenkan, Yomiuri Yearbook), 読売新聞社 (Yomiuri Newspaper Company), 2001–2002 (earlier issues also available).

Monographs

福元健太郎 (Fukumoto Gentarō), 日本の国会政治、全政府立法の分析 (Nihon no kokkai seiji: zen seifu rippō no bunseki, Japanese Parliamentary Politics: Analysis of Parliamentary Legislation), 東京大学出版会 (Tokyo University Press), 2000.

堀要 (Hori Kaname), 日本政治の実証分析 (Nihon seiji no jisshō bunseki, An Empirical Analysis of Japanese Politics), 東海大学出版会 (Tōkai University Press), 1996.

猪口孝 (Inoguchi Takashi), 岩井奉信 (Iwai Tomoaki), 「族議員」の研究, 自民党政権を牛耳る主役たち (A Study of "Tribal Parliamentarians": The Leading Actors Controlling Liberal Democratic Party Power). 日本経済新聞社 (Nihon Keizai Newspaper Company), 1987.

石川真澄 (Ishikawa Masumi), 広瀬道貞 (Hirose Michisada), 自民党〜長期支配の構造 (The Liberal Democratic Party – The Structure of Long Term Control), 岩波書店 (Iwanami Shoten), 1989.

石川真澄 (Ishikawa Masumi), この国の政治 (Kono kuni no seiji, This Country's Politics). 労働旬法社 (Rōdōjunpōsha), 1997.

蒲島郁夫 (Kabashima Ikuo), 政権交代と有権者の態度変容 (Seiken kotai to yūkensha no taido henyō, Alternation in Power and

Attitude Change among Electors), 木鐸社 (Bokutakusha), 2000.

佐藤誠三郎 (Satō Seizaburō), 松崎哲久 (Matsuzaki Tetsuhisa), 自民党政権 (Jimintō seiken, The Liberal Democratic Party Regime). 中央公論社 (Chūōkōronsha), 1986.

田中明彦 (Tanaka Akihiko), 安全保障、戦後50年の模索 (Anzen hoshō, sengo 50 nen no mosaku, Security, comprehending the 50 years since the end of the war). 読売新聞社 (Yomiuri Newspaper Company), 1997.

渡辺昭夫 (Watanabe Akio), アジア、太平洋の国際関係と日本 (Ajia, Taiheiyo no kokusai kankei to Nihon), 東京大学出版会 (Tokyo University Press), 1992.

渡辺治 (Watanabe Osamu), 政治改革と憲法改正、中曽根康弘から小沢一郎へ (Seiji kaikaku to kenpō kaisei, Nakasone Yasuhiro kara Ozawa Ichirō e, Political Reform and Constitutional Revision: From Nakasone Yasuhiro to Ozawa Ichiro), 青木書店 (Aoki Bookshop), 1994.

山口二郎 (Yamaguchi Jirō), 危機の日本政治 (Kiki no Nihon seiji, Japanese Politics in Crisis), 岩波書店 (Iwanami Bookshop), 1999.

INDEX

Page numbers in **bold** refer to main subject entries.

Abe Shintarō **1**, 21, 51, 105, 121, 139, 177, 181, 213
Abegglen, James C. xxviii, xxx
abortion 93, 125
accountability xvii, xxiv-xxv, xxviii
activism, political *see* extremist movements; nuclear issues; social movements; student political movements
administration, government 1–5, 17–19, 106, 185–6
administrative guidance (*Gyōsei shidō*) **1–2**, 169
  former and new ministries and agencies, 3–4
  'iron-triangles' business/LDP interests 242
  reorganisation (2001) **2–3**, 18–19, 22, 41, 81, 170, 171, 172, 173, 185–6, 196, 212, 220
  separation from party politics 185
  see also bureaucracy
Administrative Management Agency **2**, 182
Administrative Reform Commission **2**, 182
Administrative Vice-Minister **3–5**
Afghanistan 98, 99, 160, 231, 239, 249
Africa, relations with **5–6**
Agricultural Co-operative Association (*Nōkyō*) **6–8**, 61, 162, 207, 219
agriculture xviii, 162–3
  Basic Law on Food, Agriculture and Rural Areas 163
  Land Reform (post-War) 6, 162
  politics of **6–8**, 149, 157, 162–3, 207, 219, 248
Ainu 174, 229
Akao Bin 87
Akashi Yasushi 120
All-Japan Council of Private Sector Trade Unions **8**, 130
All-Japan Council of Teachers' and Staff Unions **8**, 49, 129
All-Japan General Federation of Labour Unions **8–9**, 43, 184
All-Japan Trade Union Congress **9**, 43, 103, 124, 184, 190
Allied Occupation *see* history, Allied Occupation; Occupation policy
amakudari xxxiii, 3, **9–10**
Amami Oshima 50
Amano Mitsuharu 51, 52
Ampiah, Kweku 5–6
anarchism 30, 85, 233
anti-Americanism 40, 43–4, 87, 179, 181, 189, 197, 203, 221, 222, 232, 239 *see also* Security Treaty revision crisis
Aoki Morihisa 242
Aoshima Yukio 55
apathy, political xiii, 221
Apter David E. 86
Arafune Seijūrō 16
aristocracy 79
army *see* defence
Asahara Shōkō 12–13
Asanuma Inejiro **10–11**, 43–4, 87, 128, 136, 218, 235
Ashida Hitoshi **11**, 27, 28, 32–3, 71, 123, 185, 190, 210, 211, 224, 257
Asia
  Asia-Europe Meeting (ASEM) (1996) 83

economic crisis 68, 107, 118
  Japan and x, 166
Asia, South, relations with **226–7**
Asia, South-East
  Asia Pacific Economic Co-operation (APEC) 228
  Association of South-East Asian Nations (ASEAN) 228
  Fukuda doctrine 228
  relations with xiii, 97, 102, 117, 118, 137, **227–9**
  war, occupation of 227
Asian Development Bank 96, 117–8, 229
Asian Monetary Fund proposal 249
Asian Regional Forum 229
Aspinall, Robert W. 49
Association of Friends 63
Asukata Ichio **11–12**, 119
atomic weapons 191–4, 202–4, 226
  Bikini atoll tests 192, 202
  bombing of Hiroshima and Nagasaki 192–3, 202, 203, 246
  Chinese testing 192, 203
  government policy 192, 193, 202–3
  Japan Council against Atomic and Hydrogen Weapons 192, 203
  Japan National Congress against Atomic and Hydrogen Weapons 203
  Okinawa 193, 197, 219, 247–8
  Partial Nuclear Test Ban Treaty 203, 222
  U.S. navy docking in Japan 193, 220, 247–8
  see also nuclear issues; Nuclear Non-Proliferation Treaty; pacifism; weapons
Aum shinrikyō **11–12**, 37, 85, 87, 215, 216
  mass poisoning (1995) **11–12**, 106, 180, 216
Aum Supreme Truth Religion *see Aum shinrikyō*
Australia 13–14, 209
  relations with **13–15**, 228, 229
  trade and markets 13–14
  'White Australia Policy' 13, 14
authoritarianism x, xxiv, xxv, 33
authority xiii, xxv
  see also culture; political culture
autonomy, individual 2
Ayukawa Yoshisuke 126

Baerwald, Hans H. 95
Bailey, Frederick G. 96
Bangladesh 226, 227
banks and banking xx–xxi, 96, 117–8, 165, 195, 229
Beer, Lawrence W. 32
Benedict, Ruth 104
Bergamini, David 79
Bhutan 226, 227
birth rate 93
Bix, Herbert 79–80
'Black Mist' (*kuroi kiri*) scandals (1966–7) **16–17**
Blair, Tony 99, 209
bōryokudan 88
Bouissou, Jean-Marie xxxvi
bribery *see* corruption
Buddhism 25–6, 214, 215, 227
budget 113
Buraku Liberation League 174
Burakumin 173–4
bureaucracy xix, xxi, xxxii, xxxiii, 1–5, 9–10, **17–19**, 185–6, 189
  Allied Occupation and 17, 185
  amakudari, practice of xxxiii, 3, **9–10**
  bureaucrats in party politics xix, xxxvi, 148, 153, 185, 204, 238, 241
  dominance of xxx–xxxi, xxxiii, xxxvi, 5, 17, 182, 188
  habatsu (bureaucrat-party man) 90
  nawabari (demarcation between agencies) **185–6**
  nemawashi (consultation process) 5, **186–7**, 216
  reorganisation of 2001 xxxv, 2–3, 18–19, 117
  ringi system (decision-making) **216–7**
  women in 254
  see also administration, government
Burma *see* Myanmar
Bush, George W. 143, 194, 239
business 94–5, 179
  government involvement and 1–2, 16–17, 94–5, 149, 168–70, 210, 223–4
  interest groups **19**, 23
  monopolies and cartels 91–2, 135, 162, 182
  political funding scandals 223–5
  small and medium enterprises 126–7
  zaikai (Big Business) 16, 94
  see also corporatism; pressure groups

Cabinet xvii, 5, **20–3**, 186, 187, 204, 210–11
  administrative reorganisation 2–3, 18–19, 21–2, 212
  comparison to British-type system 20–1, 187
  Constitution of 1946 and 31
  establishment of 20
  Prime Minister's Office and 212
  women in 254
Cabinet Legislation Bureau **22**
Cabinet Office 3, 5, **22–3**, 46, 117, 210–11, 212
Cabinet Secretariat 4, **23**
Calder, Kent E. xxxv
Cambodia 228
campaigning *see* electoral behaviour
Campbell, John C. 125
capital punishment 37
censorship 164, 207
Chiang Kai Shek xvii
Chiba 51
China, People's Republic of x, xvii, **23–5**, 198, 229
  Cultural Revolution 192–3, 233
  Japan and xiv, xvi **23–5**, 41, 43–4, 87, 97, 99, 100, 101, 116, 119, 120, 166, 177, 188, 190, 203, 222, 238, 236, 238, 242, 247, 248, 258
  Lop Nor Nuclear test 192, 203
  Manchurian Incident xvi
  Nixon's policy 190–1, 220, 238, 247
  Tiananmen Square 1989 25
  Treaty of Peace and Friendship 24
  War 1937 xvi, 23
Christianity 216 *see also* religion
'Chrysanthemum Club' xxxii
Chūkakuha 86
Chūō Kōron 87
Chūritsu rōren see National Liaison Council of Independent Unions
civic society 106, 254
class system xxvii–xxviii, 8, 110
  'class society' model xxvii–xxviii
  feudal xiv, 110
  'middle mass' theory of xxvii–xxviii, 110
  unionism and 147
Clean Government Party (CGP) **25–6**, 30, 39, 44, 47, 56, 62, 63, 64, 65, 66, 67, 68, 69, 70, 71, 74, 75, 77, 90, 120, 126, 134, 152, 178, 187, 188–9, 195, 200, 204, 205, 213, 235, 257
  coalition politics 208
  party structure 205
  Sōka Gakkai and 215, 257
clientelism 236
Clinton, Bill 141, 197
Cold War xvii, 100, 123, 141, 142, 166, 178, 191–2, 201, 221, 226, 240, 245, 246, 258
Collick, Martin xxxiv
communications 171–2
communism 27, 61, 122–4, 145–6, 184, 191, 223, 246
Communist Party *see* Japan Communist Party
companies *see* business; industry
conflict theory xxix
conformity, social 240–1 *see also* culture
Confucian inheritance xiii, 234
Congress of Industrial Unions 9, **26–7**, 103, 123, 184
consensus 36
  theory xxix
  based society, Japan as 29–30, 96
conservatism xiii, 70, 188
  creative xxx
conservative parties (1945–55) **27–30**, 161, 204
Conservative Party **30**, 56, 70, 77, 152, 200
Constitution 1889 (Meiji) xiv–xv, 31, 32, 113, 173, 222, 233
Constitution of 1946 xvii, xviii, xix, xxiv, 11, 20, 29, **30–4**, 43, 86, 109, 112, 113, 135, 176, 189, 204, 207, 222, 245
  amendments 31–2, 33
  'GHQ draft' 32, 112
  judicial review 233–4
  peace clause xiii, xviii, xxiv, 30–1, 32–3, 34, 39–40, 41, 47, 96, 209, 221, 244
  Prime Minister's role 211–12
  revision and revisionists xxiv, 31–2, 33–4, 177, 181, 192
  separation of powers 234
  separation of religion from state 215
  Supreme Court and 233–4
Constitution Research Commission (1957–64) 32, 33, 116
construction and building 163–4 *see also*

history, Allied Occupation
consumer groups **34–5**, 209 *see also* interest groups
Co-operative Democratic Party 27, 72
corporatism xix, xxx, 7, 8, 94 *see also* business
corruption, political 16–17, 25, 45, 55, 64, 86, 87, 109–110, 111, 121, 133, 134, 149, 155–6, 165, 176, 218, 237, 239
    construction and building industry 163, 224–5
    shipbuilding scandal 223–4
    'structural' corruption 213
    see also business, government involvement in; scandals
court system **35–6**
cow walking (*gyūho*) **36–7**, 95, 240
Crichton, Michael xxxii
crime 37–8, 175 *see also bōryokudan*; corruption
criminal justice system 35–6, **37–8**, 131, 234
    courts 31, **35–6**, 131, 170
    litigation levels 36, 131
    prosecutors, role of 37
    see also judiciary
culturalist theory xxii–xxiv, xxxiii
culture xii–xiii, 173–6, 227
    conformity 240–1
    education and 48, 49, 110, 164, 178, 180
    family and politics **92–4**, 234
    homogeneity **110–1**
    individual autonomy and 2
    institutional loyalty 186
    litigation and 35
    mutual obligation (*giri-ninjō*) 104–5
    politeness, levels of 243
    religion and 214–6
    samurai ethic 92
    social relationships 89, 199
    submission to authority and 82, 89
    tatemae-honne (public position and real intention) **240–1**
    uniqueness of xxix
    see also political culture, customs and traditions; minorities
Culture Agency 164
Curtis, Gerald L. 155, 242

Dale, Peter N. xxix
Daybreak Club (*Reimeikai*) **39**
decentralisation xviii, 111, 152, 153, 154, 164, 200 *see also* local government
decision-making,
    general process of xxv–xxvi
    Japanese process of xxxvi, 1–5, 186–7, 198
    nemawashi (consultation process) 5, **186–7**, 216
    ringi system (decision-making) **216–7**
    'tribes' parliamentary 241–2
    see also political culture
Defence Agency 5, 17, 22, **41**, 134, 135, 182, 257
defence policy xxiv, 17–18, **39–41**, 42, 44, 97–100, 116, 124, 161, 182, 201, 245–6, 247–8
    Japan-US Mutual Security Treaty (1951) [revised 1960] xix, 40, 41, 138, 180, 189, 190, 192, 202, 219, 220–1, 229, 232, 244, 245, 246, 256, 258
    National Defence Programme Outline 40
    nuclear issues 191–4, 219–20
    relationship with the U.S. 40, 41, 98, 177, 181,182, 192–4, 195, 200, 219–20, 232–3, 244–5, 245–6, 247–8, 258
    'Self-Defence Forces' 32, 39, 41, 87, 97, 99, 100, 105, 119, 160, 176, 180, 189, 232, 245, 249
    Theatre Missile Defence 41
    U.S. military bases 33, 174–5, 189, 193, 196–8, 219, 247
    'Yoshida doctrine' 258
    see also atomic weapons; Constitution (1946), peace clause; pacifism; Security Treaty revision crisis; weapons
democracy x–xi, xxv–xxvi, 81, 122
    education and 49
    post 1945 xxiii, 27–8, 122, 153, 225, 232
    stakeholder democracy 122
    theories of Japanese xxiii–xxiv
Democratic Liberal Party (*Minshu jiyūtō*) xvii, 28, 42, 72, 257
Democratic Party (I) 27–8
Democratic Party (II) **42–3**, 44, 48, 53, 68, 101, 108, 109, 110, 111, 128, 133,

135, 137, 151, 159, 176, 181, 188, 205, 233
  electoral history 60, 61, 69, 70, 72, 76, 77, 256
  party structure 205
Democratic Reform League 42, **43**, 69, 78
Democratic Socialist Party (*Minshatō*) 9, **43–4**, 47, 124, 126, 128, 130, 135, 136, 147, 150, 151, 187, 188, 189, 190, 202, 204, 205
  electoral history 62, 63, 64, 65, 66, 67, 68, 71, 74, 75, 208
  party structure 205
Democratisation Leagues (*Mindō*) 9, 26–7, 184
Den Hideo 225
deregulation 111, 152, 172, 182, 200, 201
disaster relief 106
discrimination
  minorities 173–5, 197
  women 142, 171, 189, 253
Diet *see* Parliament (National Diet)
'Dodge Line' reforms xviii, 27, 116, 257
Doi Takako 44–5, 67, 71, 119, 128, 132, 237, 253
Dōmei see Japan Confederation of Labour
Dore, Ronald P. xxviii, xxxv, xxxvi
Drysdale, Peter 14, 25
Dulles, John Foster 100, 197, 230, 231, 247, 258

earthquakes
  Great Hanshin-Awaji (1995), politics and **105–6**, 180, 186, 256
Economic Deliberation Agency 46
economic development xx, xxiii, xxx–xxxi, xxxii–xxxiii, 17–18, 19, 97, 98, 99, 116, 122, 169, 246–7
  administrative guidance and (*Gyosei shido*) 1–2
  consumer groups and 34–5
  construction and building 163–4
  negative aspects of xxvii
  role of State xxxii–xxxiii, 17–19, 31, 91–2, 165,168–70
  see also Economic Planning Agency; investment; modernisation; trade
'economic miracle' (1960s) xxvi, xxx–xxxi, 1–2, 16, 17, 18, 64, 97, 99–100, 168, 225–6, 246

Economic Planning Agency 5, 22, **46**, 116, 139, 140,196, 212, 254
Economic Stabilisation Board 46, 136
economy x, xxii, 1–2, 97, 118, 126–7, 165, 169–70, 182, 229, 246, 248–9
  Allied Occupation and xvii, xviii, 91, 94, 246
  balance of payments crisis (mid-80s) 157–8, 248
  'bubble economy' 179, 237, 249
  exchange rate 247
  Maekawa Report **157–8**
  oil crises and 91–2, 98, 160–1, 192, 226, 239, 248
  revisionism (1980s) xxxi–xxxii, xxxiii, 248
  stagnation xxxv, 229, 249, 254
  state regulation and 1–2
  see also business; industry; markets; monopoly and anti-monopoly policy; trade; taxation
Eda Saburō 47, 118, 128, 183, 203, 218, 225
Eda Satsuki 47–8, 133, 136, 225
education xxviii, 8, 93, 128–30, 164–5, 178, 181, 182, 215
  Allied Occupation and 48, 128, 164
  Extraordinary Commission on Education (1984) 49
  industry and 94
  policy 3, 48–9, 164–5
  politics and 48–9, 92, 128–9, 161, 181, 254–5
  samurai, role of xiv
Eisenhower, Dwight 220, 221
elections 49–57
  expenditure and 52, 58, 59, 149
  Independent candidates 55, 206
  Prime Ministers and 210
  Supreme Court decisions and 234
  see also electoral systems; opposition parties; parties, political
electoral behaviour xx, 50, **57–60**
  campaigning 58–60, 155
  'inherited seats' 148–9
  jiban (supporters) 58
  kaban (finance) 58
  kanban (reputation) 58
  kōenkai system (personal support groups) 54, 58–9, 148–9
  malpractice 57, 59–60, 155

personality, importance of 50, 52, 54, 56, 58–9, 112
'talent candidates' 55
turnout 57–8
electoral boundaries 50–1, 54, 55, 234
electoral law 57, 59–60
Public Offices Election Law 59
electoral systems xx, xxxiii, **49–57**
d'Hondt system of PR 55, 60, 65, 73
'first past the post' 50, 55
history of 50–2, 57, 60–78
House of Councillors 54–6, 60–70
House of Representatives xx, 50–4, 56, 57, 70–8, 90
Kaifu model 52–3
'negative gerrymander' 54, 55, 234
population distribution and 6
proportional representation 50, 53, 54, 55–6, 60, 65, 112
reform of 188, 189, 200
Emperor (Tennō) iv, xv, **78–80**, 79, 117
Constitution (1946) 30, 32, 33, 79, 215
cult of 48, 80, 110
extremist groups and 86–8, 122–3, 176
national paternalism and 92
obligation to 104
politics and **79–80**, 92, 245, 257
revisionists and 79
role of xv, xvi, xvii, xviii, 20, 33
Taishō xv
war responsibility of 79–80, 87, 104
employers groups 124–5
employment xxviii, 146–7, 167, 173
policy 3, 170–1, 254
Recruit scandal (1988–9) 213
see also unionism
Environment Agency 3, 4, 22, 46, **80–1**, 82, 172, 212, 254
environmental politics 18, 34, 80, **81–3**, 85, 163, 172, 208, 254
international issues and 83
whaling 82
equality, Japanese society and xxvii–xxviii, 152, 254
Europe, relations with 83–4, 166
European Union 83
Asia-Europe Meeting (ASEM) (1996) 83
Hague declaration (1991) 83
Japan-US-Europe triangle 83, 84
exchange rates 247, 248

Bretton-Woods system 247
export see trade
extremist movements
left **84–6**, 208 see also left wing parties; terrorism
right, **86–8**, 176
Ezoe Hiromasa 213

factions and factionalism xix–xx, xxix, 21, 27, 28, 29–30, **89–91**, 105, 199, 199, 210, 227, 257
giri-ninjō and 104–5
'tribes' (Parliament) (zoku giin) 18, 149, 172, **241–2**
uchi-soto (inside-outside) distinction 243–4
see also electoral systems
Fair Trade Commission **91–2**, 161, 212
Fallows, James xxxi
family 92–4, 174, 225–6, 243
obligation and duty 104
oyabun-kobun relationships 89
politics and **92–4**, 188, 199, 234
religion and 214
social control and 93
see also culture
'Family State' myth of 92
Far Eastern Commission 32
farmers and farming see agriculture
Federation of Economic Organisations 19, 87, **94–5**, 122, 124, 125, 207
party relations and 94–5
Federation of Small and Medium Industries 94
feudal system xiv, 6
filibustering 36–7
Financial Services Agency 5, 139
fishing rights and disputes 142, 162, 235
Flanagan Scott C. 59
Food Control Law 7, 162
food production xii, 33–4, 162–3 see also agriculture
foreign aid **96**
foreign policy xiii, 1, 6, 23, **96–100**, 161, 166–7, 178, 227–8
Afghanistan 98, 99, 160
China and 23–5, 97, 98, 99, 100, 116, 161, 228
Indonesia and Malaysia 116, 228, 229
Iraq 160, 232
Middle East **160–1**

U.S. influence in 98–9, 117, 118, 120, 137, 160–1, 166, 227–8, 245–9, 258
foreign pressure **100–1**
Foster-Carter, Aidan 143
France xii
franchise *see* voting
free trade *see* trade
freedom
　political activity and 207
　of press 207
　of speech 207
From Five **101**, 111, 176, 251
Fukuda Takeo 1, 91–2, **101–2**, 105, 134, 139, 148, 150, 161, 189, 195, 196, 210, 211, 235, 237, 238
　'Fukuda doctrine' 228
　Shōwa Denkō scandal 224
　LDP faction 138, 176, 177, 178, 181
Fukui Haruhiro. 148, 204
Fukuyama, Francis xxxii, xxxiii, 99
Fujimori, Alberto 242
Fujiwara Hirotatsu 26
Fujiyama Aiichirō **101**, 139
Fuwa Tetsuzō **102**, 124, 223

G7 and G8 summit meetings 118
GATT 246, 248–9
Genda Minoru 192
General Agreement on Tariffs and Trade (GATT) 117
General Council of Japanese Trade Unions 9, 43, 47, **103–4**, 118, 124, 129, 130, 146, 147, 184, 190, 203, 207, 223
genrō (elders) xv–xvi
George Mulgan, Aurelia xxi, xxxiv, xxxvi, 7, 22, 149, 163
Gilson, Julie 83–4
giri-ninjō (mutual obligation) **104–5**, 198
Goodman Roger 225
Gorbachev, Mikhail 231
Green Breeze Party 61
Green Breeze Society 61, 62, 63, 206
Gulf War 67, 99, 178, 200, 244, 245, 253

habatsu see factions and factionalism
Hashimoto Ryūtarō 22, **106**, 109–10, 133, 140, 150, 180, 210, 211, 242
　government of 193, 195, 197, 231
　resignation of 138, 165
Hara Kei 57, 230
Hata Tsutomu 26, 44, 101, **107–8**, 127, 195, 200, 211
　government 132, 151, 187, 188
Hatoyama Ichirō 23, 27, 28–9, 43, 71, **108–9**, 119, 140, 161, 210, 211, 230, 246, 247, 257, 258
Hatoyama Yukio 42, 52, 108, **109**, 133, 211, 223
health care 125, 167
　insurance system 125, 218
Hendry, Joy 243
Higashikuni 209, 210, 211, 223
Hirano Rikizō 135, 235
Hiroshima xvi, 191–3, 202, 203, 245
history
　Allied Occupation xvii–xx, xxiii, xxiv, 2, 3, 6, 17, 23, 26–7, 28, 29, 32–3, 97, 103, 119, 123, 137, 166, 181–2, 185, 209–10, 215, 222, 245–6, 257–8
　continuity/discontinuity theories of xxiii, xxvii
　Meiji period xiv–xv, xvi, 3, 166, 168, 173, 204, 215
　Tokugawa (Edo) period xiii–xiv, 173
　see also Cold War; Occupation policy
HIV-tainted blood scandal **109–10**, 133, 167
Hokkaidō 6, 51, 171, 174, 230
Hokkaidō Development Agency 4, 163, 171, 172, 184, 189, 196, 212
Home Ministry 17, 152, 153, 167–8
homogeneity **110–1**, 174 *see also* population
Hood, Christopher P. 49
Hook, Glenn D. 40, 41, 118, 229
Horne, James xxxiv
Hosokawa Morihiro 67, 101, **111–2**, 126, 127, 128, 159, 188, 210, 211
　coalition Cabinet (1993) 7–8, 26, 34, 43, 44, 45, 47–8, 52, 59, 71, 108, 111, 130, 133, 134, 140, 147, 154, 165, 179, 187, 200, 208, 225, 226, 253, 254, 256
Hosoya Matsuta 26, 223
House of Councillors xx, 25, 32, 44, 54–6, 60–78, 112–3, 125
　electoral history **60–70**, 148
　electoral system 54–6, 112, 115
　functions and power of 112
　Independents 60, 61, 62, 63, 64
　Liberal Democratic Party and 148
　veto powers of 68

women in 253
see also Parliament (National Diet)
House of Growth 237
House of Peers xv, 32, 54, 60, 112, 113
House of Representatives xv, xix, 21, 25, 27, 35, 44, 50–4, 101, 102, 112, **113–5**
  committee system 114
  change in electoral system for 7
  debate 186
  electoral history 60, **70–8**, 113–4
  electoral system 50–4, 57, 109, 140
  reforms of late 1990s 114
  U.S. Congress model and 114
  Westminster model and xvii, xxi, xxxvi, 47, 114
  women in 253, 254
  see also Parliament (National Diet)
Hughes, Christopher W. 25, 143
human rights 176, 208, 253
  Constitution 1946 and 31, 33
  see also minorities

Ichikawa Fusae 55, 133, 253
identity, Japanese xiii
Ienaga Saburō 164
Ike Nobutaka 58
Ikeda Daisaku 26, 236
Ikeda Hayato xix, 18, 23–4, 33, 101, **116–7**, 136, 140, 177–8, 195, 196, 199, 209, 210, 211, 219, 221, 228, 235, 238, 239
  shipbuilding scandal and 224
immigration xiii, 110–111, 175–6 *see also* minorities
Imperial Household Agency 79, **117**, 212
Imperial Household Ministry 79
Imperial Rule Assistance Association xvi, 136
Inamine Keiichi 198
Independent Association 70
India x, 193, 226, 227
industry xix, 2, 94–5, 126–7, 146–7, 168–9, 179
  computer 2, 169, 248
  government regulation of 1–2, 16–17, 94–5, 149, 168–70, 238
  manufacturing 6, 130, 157, 228
  shipbuilding 223–4
  sunset 2
  textile 246–7
  see also business; corporatism; economic development; trade
information and communication 158–9, 171–2 *see also* media
Inoguchi Takashi xxxiv, 241
Inoki, Antonio 231–2
interest groups x–xi, 157, 206–9
  agricultural sector 6–7, 8, 162–3, 207
  business **19**, 126–7, 207, 209, 224
  Liberal Democratic Party and 242
  lobbying tactics 241
international organisations, Japan and 116, **117–8**, 166, 246
International Metal Workers' Federation-Japan Chapter 117
International Monetary Fund (IMF) 116, 117, 118, 246
'internationalisation' (*kokusaika*) xiii, 49
Inukai Takeru 28
investment xii, 158, 169
  overseas xxxi, 157–8
Iraq 160, 232
Ishibashi Masashi 12, 45, 109, 116, 118–9, 137, 183, 210, 211
Ishibashi Tanzan **119**, 161
Ishida Kōshirō **119–20**
Ishida Takeshi 198
Ishihara Shintarō **120**, 177, 178
Itō Daiichi xxxiv
Itō Hirobumi xv
Itō Masayoshi **120–1**, 235
Iwai, T 241

Jain, Purnendra 193
Japan Chamber of Commerce 19, 94, **121**
Japan Committee for Economic Development 19, **122**
Japan Communist Party (JCP) xviii, xxvi, 8, 26, 27, 47, 56, 102, 103, 119, 122–4, 153, 173, 174, 176, 191, 202, 204, 203, 205, 206, 222, 223, 232, 236, 241
  China and 123, 222
  democratic centralism and 90–1, 205
  electoral history 60, 61, 62, 63, 64, 65, 66, 67, 68, 69, 70, 71, 73, 74, 75, 77, 123–4
  Emperor and 122–3
  factions and suppression of 90–1, 123
  history of 122–3, 204
  Japan-US Security Treaty and 223
  modernisation of 177
  party structure 205–6

women and 253
USSR and 123, 177, 222
Japan Confederation of Labour 43, 118, **124**, 130, 208
Japan Co-Operative Party 27
Japan Democratic Party 11, 29, 101, 108–9
Japan Federation of Economic Organisations 95, **124**, 125, 207
Japan Federation of Employers' Associations 19, 95, **124–5**, 207
Japan Liberal Party (I) 27, 108, 245
Japan Liberal Party (II) 29, 161
Japan Medical Association **125**, 167, 208
Japan New Party 67, 68, 75, 76, 111, 126, 159, 187, 188
Japan Political League of Small and Medium Enterprises **126–7**
Japan Progressive Party (JPP) 27–8
Japan Proletarian Party 235
Japan Renewal Party 75, 108, **127**, 187, 200, 233
Japan Socialist Party (JSP) xix, xxiv, 9, 10–12, 27, 28, 29, 36, 37, 42, 43–4, 45, 47, 116, 123, **127–8**, 136, 151, 153, 173, 174, 177, 183, 202, 203, 204, 205, 218, 224, 237, 256
  coalition with LDP and New Party Harbinger (1994) 140, 179, 188
  decline of 52, 128
  defence policy and 40–1, 226, 252
  education policy 180
  factions in 90, 235, 252
  history 61, 62, 63, 64, 65, 66, 67, 68, 69, 70, 71, 72, 73–74, 75, 119, 127, 135, 190, 204, 216
  New Wave Society 47
  party structure 205
  pacifism of 127, 189
  'positive neutrality' 252
  Security Treaty revision crisis and 87, 128, 137
  Socialism Association 47, 218
  split within 103, 106, 127–8, 130, 235, 252, 253
  unions and 103, 104, 127, 147, 204
  women and 253, 254
  veto power of 127
Japan Times 11
Japan Teachers' Union 8, 48, 49, 88, 103, **128–30**, 137, 164, 208

Japan-US Mutual Security Treaty (1951, revised 1960) xix, 40, 41, 138, 180, 189, 190, 192, 202, 219, 220, 223, 232, 245, 246, 247, 257
  Sunakawa decision (1959) 234
  see also Security Treaty revision crisis
Japan-United States Administrative Agreement 33
Japanese Consumers Association 34
Japanese people xiii, 175
  homogeneity of 110–1
  see also culture; family; minorities; political culture; religion
Japanese Trade Union Council 8, 43, 44, 67, 68, 104, 124, **130–1**, 183, 184
Johnson, Chalmers xxx–xxxi, xxxii, xxxiii, 2, 169
Johnson, Lyndon 219
judges **131**
judicial review 31, 35, 131, 233–4
judicial system xiv-xv, xvi, 35–6, 131 *see also* court system; criminal justice system
judiciary 31, 35–6, 131
  constitution and 31, 35, 113, 170
  separation of powers 170, 234
  Supreme Court 31, 35–6, 131, 170, **233–4**

Kaifu Toshiki 52–5, 99, 107, 108, **132**, 139, 160, 178, 187, 200, 210, 211, 250, 254
Kajiyama Seiroku **132–3**, 138, 198
Kakizawa Kōji 151
Kakumaruha 86
kamikaze 85
Kan Naoto 42, 43, 109–10, **133**, 167, 225
Kanagawa 50, 51
Kanba Michiko 221
Kanbayashiyama Eikichi 16
Kaneko Tokunosuke 51–2
Kanemaru Shin 88, 108, **134**, 142, 200, 238, 218, 237
Kano Michihiko 188, 251
Kanzaki Takenori **134**
Kashmir 227
Kasuga Shōjirō 123
Katayama Tetsu 11, 27, 28, 43, 71, 123, 127, **135**, 161, 170, 190, 210, 211, 216, 224, 235, 252, 257
Katō Kōichi 21, **135–6**, 178, 256, 257

Katsumata Seiichi **136**, 183, 218–9, 252
Kawaguchi Junko 167, 254
Kawakami Jōtarō 10, 11, 47, 87, 116, **136**, 183
Kennedy, John F. 246
Kenseikai 204 *see also Minseitō*
Kishi Nobusuke xix, 1, 11, 14, 18, 23, 24, 33, 43, 87, 95, 101, 113, 116, 119, 128, **137–8**, 140, 148, 182, 190, 199, 209, 210, 211, 219, 220, 238
   Security Treaty revision crisis 221, 246, 256
Kōbe 105–6, 180, 256
Kodama Yoshio 87
kōenkai system (personal support groups) 54, 58, 105, 148–9
Koh Byung Chul 3, 5, 187
Koiso Kuniaki 223
Koizumi Junichirō xxi, 68, 107, 114, 133, 134, 135, **138–9**, 143, 150, 166–7, 172, 179, 209, 211, 231, 239, 256, 257
   government xxxvi, 22, 42, 99, 138–9, 160, 161, 249, 254
Kōmoto Toshio **139–40**, 162, 181, 189
Kon-Chiku-Shō 140
Kōno Ichirō 29, 119, **140**, 161, 182, 209, 220
Kōno Yōhei **140–1**, 187, 210, 253
Konoe Fumimaro 257
Korea, Japanese rule, 141
Korea (ROK South) **141–4**, 219
   Japan and xiv, 25, 36, 97–8, 99, **141–4**, 197
   Treaty on Basic Relations (1965) 142, 219
Korea (DPRK North)
   Declaration of 2002 139, 143–4
   Japan and 36, 139, **141–4**, 238, 247, 248
   nuclear issues and 142–3, 144
Korean war 1950–3 xvii, 28, 41, 97, 141, 192, 223, 257
Korean minority 175
Koseki Shōichi. 32
Krauss, Ellis S. xxxiv
Kume Ikuo. 147
Kuriyama Akira 51, 52
Kuwait 33, 132, 160
Kyōto 138

Labour Farmer Party 61, 73

labour unions *see* unions
Lam Peng Er 229
landlordism 6
language xii, 243
Large, Stephen S. 79
Left Socialist Party 47, 61, 73, 118, 127–8, 136, 183, 235, 252
left-wing parties xviii, 43–4, 47, 61, 123, 233 *see also* Japan Communist Party; Japan Socialist Party; socialism
legislation
   forced passage of **95–6**
   see also Parliament (National Diet)
legitimacy, political xiii
Lesbirel, S. Hayden 192
Levellers' Society 174
Liberal Democratic Party (LDP) xix, xx–xxi, xxiv, xxxiii, xxxiv, xxxvi, 1, 11, 16, 17–18, 20–2, 27–30, 44, 101, 107, 116, 123, **148–51**, 178, 204, 205, 221, 226
   'Black Mist' scandals (1966–7) **16–17**
   coalition politics 113, 130, 148, 149, 199, 215, 253, 256
   constitutional reform and 33, 151
   'construction tribe' 163
   dominance as a single party 17–18, 20–1, 70, 148, 149, 205
   economic crisis and xxxv, 2
   education policy and 49, 161
   elections and electoral system 50, 51, 55–6, 58–9, 61, 102, 114, 120, 125, 148–9, 161, 204
   environmentalism of 81, 82
   ex-bureaucrat members 148
   factions within 20, 21, 23, 26, 89–90, 133, 135, 149–50, 182, 199, 205, 209, 210, 233, 235, 244, 252, 257
   farmer support of 6–7, 149, 162
   funding of 149–50
   history 62, 63, 64, 65, 66, 67, 68, 69, 70, 71, 72, 73, 74, 75, 77, 148–9, 161, 187–8, 204
   industry and 94–5
   'inherited seats' and *koenkai* system 148–9, 205
   interest groups and 242
   Lockheed scandal 64, 140, 155, 162, 183, 187, 239
   opposition, in 52–3, 111
   parliamentary tactics 36–7, 95, 112–3,

240, 241–2
party system 204–5
Policy Affairs Research Council 139, 176, 186, 204, 256
Recruit scandal 44, 120–1, 132, 183, 213, 237
'tribal' parliamentarians (*zoku giin*) 18, 149, 172, 205, **241–2**
see also New Liberal Club
Liberal League 77, **151**
Liberal Party (I) 28, 29, 60, 61, 72, 76, 119, 161, 199
Liberal Party (II) **151**
Liberal Party (III) 30, 43, 76, **151–2**, 200
Liberal Reform League 151
liberalism, 'creative' 152
List, Friedrich xxxii–xxxiii
lobbying 206–7 see also pressure groups
Local Autonomy Agency 153, 168, 212
local government 11, 31, **152–4**, 168, 186, 198, 204
'progressive local authorities' 64, 153–4
Lockheed Scandal 64, 87, **155–6**, 162, 183, 187, 239

MacArthur, Douglas (General) xvii, xviii, 11, 14, 20, 26, 31–2, 33, 41, 79, 129, 141, 182, 222, 245, 257, 258
Maekawa Haruo 157–8
Maekawa Report **157–8**, 182
majoritarianism 96
Malaysia 116, 228, 229
Management and Co-ordination Agency (*Sōmuchō*) 2, 3, 4, 120, **158**, 168, 172, 212
Manchukuo 137
Manchuria xvii
Manchurian Incident xvi, 11
manufacturing industry 6, 130, 157, 228
see also industry
Maoism 233
Maritime Safety Agency 171
market forces 169 see also economy; industry; trade
markets 1–2, 157–8, 226–7
foreign penetration of Japan 1–2, 246, 248–9
Japanese world 1–2, 246, 248–9
political interference in 24, 169
see also economic development; economy; trade

Maruyama Masao xxiv–xxv
Marxism 145, 223, 232, 235, 241
see also extremist movements; left-wing parties; political theory, Marxist; socialism; student political movements
Mashiko Teruhiko 51–2
mass society xxvii–xxxviii
Masumi Junnosuke 168
Matsumoto City 12, 32
Matsumura Kenzō 161
Matsuno Raizō 16
Matsuoka Komakichi 9
Matsushita Institute of Government and Management **159–60**
Matsushita Kōnosuke 159
McCormack, Gavan 106
media
newspapers 158–9
popularisation of 158
role in politics 16–17, 80, 138, **158–9**, 207
television 159
medicine and medical issues 125
Meiji Resoration (Renewal) xiv–xv, xvi, 48
Middle East, relations with **160–1**, 166, 200
oil issues and 160
Miki Bukichi 29, 119, **161**
Miki Takeo 1, 20, 27, 40, 91, 102, 139, 155, **161–2**, 93, 196, 210, 211, 239
Minamata disease 180
ministers, parliamentary see Cabinet; Parliament (National Diet)
Ministry of Agriculture, Forestry and Fisheries 3, 4, 7, 81, **162–3**, 196, 207, 235, 252
Ministry of Communications 171
Ministry of Construction 3, 4, 5, **163–4**, 172, 184, 196, 219
Ministry of Economy, Trade and Industry **164**, 170, 196
Ministry of Education **164**, 208
Ministry of Education, Culture, Sports, Science and Technology 3, 4, 8, 22, 48, 49, 129, **165**, 220
Ministry of Finance 3, 4, 21, 46, 101, 107, 111, 116, **165–6**, 177, 196, 219, 224, 241
Ministry of Foreign Affairs 3, 4, 11, 21, 97, **166–7**, 223

Ministry of Health and Welfare 3, 4, 11, 81, 82, 109, 125, **167**, 172
Ministry of Health, Labour and Welfare 3, 4, **167**, 171
Ministry of Home Affairs 3, 4, 137, 153, 158, 163, **168**, 212
Ministry of International Trade and Industry (MIT) xxxi, 2, 4, 18, 46, 81, 82, 116, 164, **168–70**, 172, 219, 238
Ministry of Justice 3, 4, 35, 37, 82, **170**
Ministry of Labour 3, 4, 135, **171**, 167, 173
Ministry of Land, Infrastructure and Transport 3, 4, 163, **171**, 172, 184
Ministry of Local Autonomy 212
Ministry of Posts and Telecommunications 3, 4, 158,169, **172**, 219
Ministry of Public Management, Home Affairs, Posts and Telecommunications 158, 168, **172**
Ministry of the Environment 4, 81, **165**
Ministry of the Navy 17
Ministry of Transport 3, 4, **173**, 184, 196, 219
Ministry of Transport and Communications 173
Ministry of War 17
Minobe Ryōkichi 11, 120, **173**, 174
Minobe Tatsukichi 173
minorities 111, 158, 173–6, 189
   Ainu 174
   Burakumin 173–4
   Chinese 175
   Korean 175
   Okinawans 174–5, 197
   politics and **173–6**
   see also discrimination; immigration
Minseitō 42, **176**, 204, 233, 251
Mishima Yukio 85, 87, **176**
Mitsuzuka Hiroshi **176–7**, 178
Miyamoto Kenji 102, 123, **177**, 222, 223
Miyamoto Yuriko 177
Miyazawa Kiichi 37, 51, 52, 99, 108, 121, 133, 135, 140, 148, **177–8**, 188, 195, 200, 210, 211, 213, 253
modernisation
   theories of xxv–xxvi
   in post-war Japan xxvi, xxx–xxxi
   see also economic development
Mongolia 98

monopolies and anti-monopoly policies 91–2, 135, 162, 182, 232
   Anti-Monopoly Law (1947) 91, 92, 162
Moore, Ray A. 32
Mori Yoshirō 87, 107, 134, 135–6, **178–9**, 210, 211, 231
   government 138, 178
Morita Akio 120, **179**
Moriyama Mayumi 254
Mouer, Ross xxix
Murakami Yasusuke xxvii
Muramatsu Michio xxxiv, 153, 154
Murayama Tomiichi 40–1, 73, 96, 106, 107, 128, 132, 140, **179–80**, 188, 189, 210, 211, 256
Mutual Security Treaty 95
Myanmar (Burma) 228

Nagasaki xvi, 191–3, 245
Nagoya 6
Nakagawa Ichirō 139, 150, 177, 178, **181**, 196
Nakagawa Yatsuhiro 226
Nakane Chie xxix
Nakano Kansei 43
Nakasone Yasuhiro 1, 2, 25, 39, 40, 41, 44, 49, 66,107, 111, 121, 139, 142, 148, 150, **181–3**, 188, 189, 195, 210, 211, 213, 235, 236, 237, 239, 252
   defence policy 135, 248
   education policy 164
   government 21, 98, 104, 130, 134, 135, 154, 172, 181–3, 196, 253, 257
Nakayama Masa 254
Narita New Tokyo International Airport 86, 140, 208
Narita Tomomi 47, 118, 119, 136, **183**, 218
National Co-operative Party 27, 28, 60, 72, 135, 161
National Democratic Party 28, 161
National Educational Research Institute 164
National Labour Union Alliance 8, 130, **183**, 184
National Labour Union Liaison Council **184**
National Land Agency 4, 46, 134, 163, 172, **184**, 196, 212

National Liaison Council of Independent Unions 118, 130, **184**
National Liaison Council of Labour Unions 130, **184**
National Party 27
National Personnel Authority 17, **185**
National Public Safety Committee 5, 22, **185**
National Public Service Law 185
National Resources and Energy Agency 169
National Science Museum 164
nationalisation 28
nationalism 27, 40, 86
    education policy and 48, 49, 129
    extremist groups and 86–8
nawabari **185–6**
Neary, Ian J. 174, 175
nemawashi (consultation process) 5, **186–7**, 216
Nepal 227
newspapers 158–9
    journalists' clubs 159
    see also media
neutralism xxiv
New Frontier Party (NFP) 26, 42, 44, 48, 67, 68, 69, 73, 76, 91, 96, 101, 108, 111, 120, 126, 127, 132, 134, 151, **187**, **188**, 200, 205, 214, 215, 233, 251
New Liberal Club 64, 65, 66, 71, 74, 75, 140, **187–8**
New Party Amity 42, 44, **188**
New Party Future **188**
New Party Harbinger 42, 67, 69, 70, 73, 75, 76, 77, 109, 126, 132, 133, 140, 187, **188**, 253
New Party Peace 26, 134, **188–9**
New Politics Club 28
New Socialist Party **189**
New Wave Society 47
New Zealand 193
    relations with 13–14
Nikaidō Susumu 26, **189**, 236
Nikkyōso see Japan Teachers' Union
Nishio Suehiro 43–4, **189–90**, 224
Nishioka Takeo 188
Nixon, Richard M. 24, 98, 190–1, 197, 219, 246
'Nixon shocks', 1971 **190–1**, 220, 238, 247
Noda Yoshihiko 43

Nosaka Sanzō 102, 123, **191**
nuclear issues 33, 39, 40, 177, **191–4**, 202–3, 219–20
    anti-nuclear movements 202–4, 208, 247–8
    Non-Proliferation Treaty Research Association 203
    see also atomic weapons; pacifism; weapons
Nuclear Non-Proliferation Treaty 193

Obuchi Keizō 23, 26, 30, 107, 133, 134, 138, 141, 152, 178, **195**, 210, 211
Occupation policy xxiv, 6, 17, 20, 91, 135, 153, 167, 185, 223, 225, 241, 245–6, 257–8
    atomic weapons, discussion of 192, 202
    Economic Stabilisation Board 46
    economy xvii–xviii, 46, 91, 94
    education and 48, 128, 164
    land reform 162
    religion and 215
    see also history, Allied Occupation; Japan-US Mutual Security Treaty
Oda, Hiroshi. 234
OECD 116, 117, 246
Ogata Taketora 29
Ogi Chikage 30
Ohira Masayoshi 40, 65, 96, 98, 102, 105, 107, 135, 139, 148, 150, 162, 178, **195–6**, 181, 210, 211, 216, 235, 237, 238, 239, 248
Ohnuki-Tierney, Emiko. 243
Oka Takashi 201
Okamoto Kōzō 85
Okimoto, Daniel I. 2, 170
Okinawa 25, 174–5, 206
    Japanese politics and 22, 24, 51, 60, 64, 97, 174–5, 193, **196–8**, 219, 230, 246, 247, 248
Okinawa Development Agency 5, 22, 46, 195, **196**, 212
Okuda Hiroshi 124
Olympics 1964 117, 140
Ono Banboku **198–9**, 209, 220
Osaka xii, 6, 50, 105–6, 190
opposition parties xix–xx, xxi, 21, 36, 95–6, 240
    electoral systems and 52
    filibustering and 36–7, 95, 240
    'permanent opposition' mentality 52

see also parties, political
Ota Masahide 198
Ota Seiichi 151
Ouchi Keigo 44
oyabun-kobun relationships 89
Ozawa Ichirō 26, 30, 43, 44, 53, 71, 101, 108, 109, 111, 127, 128, 132, 133, 151, 152, 179, 187, 195, **199–201**, 253, 256
Ozawa Tatsuo 214

pacifism xxiv, 8, 40, 96, 100, 127, 137, 152, 160, 189, 200, **202–4**, 208, 232, 244 *see also* atomic weapons; Constitution of 1946, peace clause; nuclear issues; weapons
Pakistan 193, 226, 227
Parliament (National Diet) xv, xviii–xxi, 36–7, 240, 243–4
　checks and balances xiii, xxi, 100
　committee system 114, 150, 243–4
　debate (*nemawashi*) 186
　disruptive techniques in 36–7, 95
　history of xv–xvi, xvii–xxi, 20–3
　legislation, forced passage of **95–6**
　separation of powers 233–4
　Westminster model and xvii, xxi, xxxvi, 47, 114
　women in 253–5
　working relationships in 240, 241–2, 243–4
　see also Cabinet; Constitution of 1946; House of Councillors; House of Peers; House of Representatives; opposition parties; political culture
parliamentarians, 'tribes' of (*zoku giin*) 18, 149, 172, **241–2**
Parliamentary Management Committees 36, 240, 243–4
parties, political 29, 57–60, **204–6**, 209, 210
　bureaucratic background of members xix, xxxvi, 148, 153, 185, 238, 204, 241
　funding of 149
　history of 204
　Independents 206
　minor/mini 66, 206
　pressure groups and 208
　religious 25–6, 205
　see also factions and factionalism; opposition parties; names of individual parties e.g. Liberal Democratic Party; political culture
party system xv, xviii–xxi, xxiv, 50–56, 113–5, 187
　redistributive regulated party rule xxxvi
　see also electoral systems; factions and factionalism; opposition parties
Passin, Herbert 153
Peace Citizens' Party 69
peace clause *see* Constitution of 1946, peace clause
Peace Comrades Association 47
Peace Keeping Operations bill (1992) 37, 39, 40, 228, 244 *see also* United Nations
Pearl Harbour xvi, 245
Pempel, T. J. xxx, 82, 148
Perry, Matthew Commodore xiv, 245
Peru 242
　Embassy hostage crisis (1996–7) **242**
Plaza Accords (1985) xxxi, 157, 182, 237, 248
pluralist theory xxxiii–xxxiv
police 13, 17, 37, 137, 153, 185 *see also* criminal justice system
policy-making 210–11 *see also* decision-making
Police Reserve Force 41, 141, 257
politeness, levels of 243
political behaviour *see* political culture
political culture, customs and traditions xi, xxiii–xxiv, 57–8, 60, 82, 89, 96, 198, 199
　institutional loyalty 186
　litigation and 35
　giri-ninjō (mutual obligation) **104–5**, 198
　omote-ura (surface-background) **198**
　oyabun-kobun relationships 89, **199**
　ringi (circulation of proposals) **216–7**
　samurai ethic 92
　tatemae-honne (public position and real intention) **240–1**
　uchi-soto (inside-outside) 240, **243–4**
　women in politics 253–5
　see also culture; electoral behaviour
politics, theories of xxii–xxxvii, 246
　authority maintenance model xxxiv
　collective irresponsibility xxiv–xxv
　comparative xxii

consensus versus conflict xxix
cultural xxix
historical continuity/discontinuity xxiii, xxvii
Japan as distinct political economy xxxii–xxxiii, 246
Japan as a model xxviii, xxi
Marxist xxii, xxiv, xxvi, xxvii, 47, 222
New Left xxvii
patterned pluralism xxxiii–xxxiv
rational choice xxxiii, 243
revisionist 246
underlying attitudes in xxii–xxiii
pollution xii, 80–3, 168, 173, 202, 212
   Basic Law on Pollution Policy (1967) 80–1, 82
   Big Four cases 82
   'export of' 82
   Minimata Bay, mercury poisoning 81–2
   see also environmental politics
Pombeni, Paolo xxxvi
Popular Rights Movement xv
population xii, 6, 176
   homogeneity of 110–1, 173
   post war changes 50, 93
   see also culture; family; minorities; women
Post Office Savings Bank 172
Postal Enterprises Agency 172
postal services 171–2
prefectures see local government
pressure groups **206–9**
   access to power 207
   professional groups 208
   see also interest groups
Prestowitz, Clyde V. xxxi
Prime Ministers xxi, 20, 79, 182, **209–12**
   Constitution (1946) and 31, 211–12
   list of 211
   power of xviii, xix, xxi, xxxv, xxxvi, 3, 18–19, 33, 201, 210–11
Prime Minister's Office 2, 5, 22, 41, 46, 80, 117, 184, 195, 196, **212**
   external agencies 212, 220
   internal functions 212
prisons see criminal justice system
privatisation 130, 138, 181
   Post Office 172
Progressive Party 72
protectionism 2, 34–5, 127, 169–70 see also trade

Public Prosecutors Office 37, 170
Public Safety Committee 212
Public Security Agency 41
Public Security Force 41

racial discrimination see discrimination
railways 172, 182
Ramseyer, J. Mark xxxiii, 10
Recruit Scandal (1989) 1, 44, 67, 120–1, 134, 178, 183, **213**, 237
Reagan, Ronald 183
Red Army groups 84–6
Reform Club 69, **214**
Reform Forum 21 108, 127
Reformist Party 28, 29, 61, 72, 108–9, 161, 223
Reischauer, Edwin O. 246
religion xii, 25–6, 173, 203, **214–6**, 227, 233
   freedom of 13
   politics and xii, 25–6, 93–4, 110, 207, **214–6**, 237, 257
   new religions 12, 110, 173, 214–6
   'new new' religions 214, 233
   separation of State from 80, 117, 214, 215
Religious Corporate Body Law (1995) 13
Rengō see Japanese Trade Union Council
representation see electoral systems
resources, natural xii
Return Home Movement (kikyō undō) 232
Right Socialist Party 10–11, 61, 73, 103, 135, 136
ringi **216–7**
Rix, Alan xxxiv
Robinson, Donald L. 32
Roosevelt's New Deal xvii
Rosenbluth, Frances M. xxxiii, 10
Rozman, Gilbert 231
Russia
   Japan and xiv, 179, 229–31, 248 see also Union of Soviet Socialist Republics
Ryūkyū islands 219, 247 see also Okinawa, Japanese politics and

Sagawa Kyūbin scandal 134, **218**, 237
Saionji Kinmochi xvi
Sakisaka Itsurō 47, 218
Salary Man New Party 66, 67, 206

samurai xiv
 ethic of 92
San Francisco Peace Treaty xviii, 97, 220, 230, 234, 245
Sanbetsu kaigi see Congress of Industrial Unions
Sasaki Kōzō 47, 136, 183, **218–9**
Sata Tadataka 136, 252
Satō Eisaku 16, 20, 21, 24, 97, 101, 116, 117, 137, 140, 148, 149, 155, 190, 192, 193, 196, 209, 210, 211, **219–20**, 224, 228, 233, 236, 238
 Nixon's Chinese policy and 190–1, 219–20, 246, 247
 Okinawa and 197, 219, 228
 shipbuilding scandal 224
Satō Tokuo 52
Satō Tsuneharu 52
Sawa Nagayo 86
Scalapino, Robert A. xxiii, xxvi, xxvii
scandals 71, 110, 116, 210
 'Black Mist' **16–17**
 HIV-tainted blood (1980s–90s) **109–10**, 133, 167
 Lockheed 64, 87, 140, 162, 183, 187
 Recruit (1988–9) 1, 44, 67, 120–1, 134, 178, 183, **213**, 237
 Sagawa Kyūbin 134, **218**, 237
 shipbuilding (1954) 219, **223–4**, 258
 Shōwa Denkō (1948) 11, 101, 190, 199, **224–5**
Schaede, Ulrike 10
Schoppa, Leonard J. 49
Schreurs, Miranda A. 82
Science and Technology Agency 22, 164, 182, 189, 212, **220**, 239
Second Chamber Club 66, 67, 68, 69, 70, 206
sects *see* religion, 'new new' religions
security *see* defence policy
Security Treaty revision crisis (1960) 11–12, 41, 43–4, 62, 84, 87, 95, 97, 101, 113–4, 128, 136, 137, 140, 182, 210, 219, **220–1**, 232, 246, 247, 252
Seiyūkai xv, 204
Self-Defence Forces *see* defence policy
Senkaku Islands 25, 198
separation of powers 233–4
Separatists Liberal Party 28, 72, 108, 119, 161

Shidehara Kijūrō 11, 27–8, 32, 210, 211, **222**, 257
Shield Society 87, 176
Shiga Yoshio 123, 177, **222**
Shigemitsu Mamoru 28, **222–3**, 230
Shigenobu Fusako 85–6
Shii Kazuo 124, **223**
Shiina Etsusaburō 161
Shinkansen network 172
Shinkyōren (New Union of Japanese Religious Organisations) 203
Shinsanbetsu (New *Sanbetsu*) 223
Shintō 214, 215, 243
shipbuilding scandal (1954) 219, **223–4**, 258
Shōwa Denkō scandal (1948) 11, 101, 190, 199, **224–5**
social capital 171
Social Democratic League 47, 65, 66, 68, 75, 133, **225**
Social Democratic Party 68, 70, 77 *see also* Japan Socialist Party
social movements 207–8, 232–233 *see also* anti-Americanism; extremist movements; nuclear issues; Security Treaty revision crisis
social welfare xx, xxvii, 47, 124, 125, 165, 166, 173, 190, **225–6**
 family and 92, 225–6
 policy 3, 18, 165, 166, 225–6, 239
 'welfare tax' 226
socialism 43–4, 47, 61, 71, 90, 94, 106, 118–9, 136, 137, 145, 183, 190 *see also* Japan Socialist Party
Socialism Association 47, 218
Socialist Masses Party 136
Sōdōmei see All-Japan Federation of Labour Unions
Sōhyō see General Council of Japanese Trade Unions
Sōka gakkai 25–6, 110, 187, 205, 207–8, 215, 216, 236, 257
Sony Corporation 179
Sports Peace Party 67, 68, 69, 206, **231–2**
Sri Lanka 227
stability, political xiii, xxxv
Steinhoff, Patricia G. 85
Steven, Rob xxvii–xxviii, 147
Stockwin, J.A.A. xxxiv, 227
'structural reform' theory 47, 218 *see also* Japan Socialist Party

student political movements 84, 86, 208, 219, 221, **232–3**
  All-Japan Federation of Student Self-Governing Associations (*Zengaku-ren*) 232
  see also extremist movements
suffrage 204, 253
  women 253–5
  see also electoral systems
Sugimoto Yoshio xxix
Sun Party 101, 108, 176, **233**, 251
Sunakawa decision 234
Supreme Commander *see* history, Allied Occupation
Supreme Court 31, 35–6, 131, 170, **233–4**
  'political question' and 234
  see also judicial review; judiciary
Suzuki Mosaburō 35, 47, 103, 218, **234–5**
Suzuki Muneo 166, 239
Suzuki Zenkō 1, 120, 178, 181, 182, 189, 210, 211, 234, 239, **235**, 252
  U.S. relations and 235
Sweden 147
syndicalism 145

Taishō Democracy xv
Taiwan xvii, 23, 24, 25, 97, 99, 116, 137, 175, 197, 198, 219, 238, 242, 247, 258
Takahashi Sumiko 254
Takano Minoru 9, 103, 146, 223
Takayanagi Kenzō 32
Takeiri Yoshikatsu 26, 236, 256
Takemi Tarō 125
Takemura Masayoshi 71, 111, 126, 188
Takenaka Heizō 139
Takeshita Noboru 21, 23, 51, 88, 107, 120, 121, 127, 134, 149, 150, 183, 195, 200, 210, 211, 213, 218, 233, **236–7**, 250
Takikawa Yukitoki 108
Tamaki Kazuo 215, **237**
Tanabe Makoto 143, **237–8**
Tanaka Kakuei xx, xxx, 20, 24, 52, 97, 101, 105, 107, 134, 149, 155, 161, 184, 191, 200, 210, 211, 224, 228, 235, 236, **238–9**, 247
  government of 184, 189, 196, 199, 195, 226, 237, 241, 250
  China and 238
  Lockheed scandal and 87, 155–6, 183, 210, 239

  Reconstruction plan (1974) 163, 184, 238–9
  resignation 150, 155–6, 161, 239
Tanaka Makiko 139, 166, **239–40**, 254
Tanaka Yasuo 153
tatemae-honne (public position and real intention) **240–1**
taxation xii, 126, 152, 157, 165, 168, 183, 188, 189, 196
  consumption tax 107, 111, 165, 237
  maruyū system 157
  social welfare and 226
Taxation Party 67
Taxpayers' Party 66, 206
telecommunications 171–2, 182
terrorism 160–1, 242, 244–5
  Embassy hostage crisis, Peru **242**
  Narita Airport 86
  national 12–13, 84–6
  Red Army Groups 84–5
  Tokyo-Yokohama Security Treaty Joint Struggle 84–5
  Tupac Amaru Embassy Hostage crisis **242**
  U.S. September 11th 2001 39–40, 41, 42–3, 99, 160–1, 244, 245
  see also Aum shinrikyō
Thatcher, Margaret 183
Tokuda Kyūichi 123, 191, 222, **241**
Tokugawa period xiii–xiv, 173
Tokyo (Edo) xii, xiv, 6, 11, 50, 120, 173
  subway poisoning (1995) **12–13**, 180
Tokyo Municipal Assembly 10, 198
Tokyo-Yokohama Security Treaty Joint Struggle 84–5
Tōjō Hideki 137, 223
trade 2, 6, 8, 91–2, 97, 99, 111, 117, 168–9, 226, 228, 246, 248–9
  balance of 157–8, 248
  friction with US 91–2, 99, 157, 220, 246, 248–9
  foreign pressure (*gaiatsu*) 100–1, 157–8
  restriction 91–2
  Semiconductor Trade Agreement (1986) 248
  Structural Impediments Initiative 248
  see also economic development; markets; trade; protectionism
transparency, political xxviii, 187
transport 172–3
'tribes' of parliamentarians (*zoku*) **241–2**

Tsuji Kiyoaki 154, 185, 216
Tupac Amaru Embassy Hostage crisis (Peru) **242**

unemployment 167, 226
uchi-soto (inside-outside) 240, **243–4**
Union of Soviet Socialist Republics
    China and 203
    fragmentation of 98, 142
    relations with Japan 23, 24, 97, 98, 99, 109, 140, 166, 177, 197, 203, 223, **229–31**, 244, 246, 247
    territorial disputes with 230–1
    World War II and 230
    see also Russia
unions xviii, xx, 8–9, 26–7, 43–4, 49, 86, 103–4, 118, 122, 124, 125, 130–1, **145–8**, 170, 183–4, 207, 220, 237
    Allied Occupation and 145–6
    Congress of Industrial Unions 9, **26–7**, 103, 123, 184, 223
    decline of unionism 147
    enterprise unions 146, 147
    General Council of Japanese Trade Unions 9, 43, 47, **103–4**, 118, 124, 129, 130, 146, 147, 184, 190, 203, 207, 223
    general strike (1947) 26
    Japan Confederation of Labour 9, 43, 103, 118, **124**, 147, 190
    single industry unions 26
    wages and conditions, bargaining 125, 129, 146–7
    Yūaikai (Friendly Society) 9, 145, 188
    see also All-Japan General Federation of Labour Unions (*Sōdōmei*)
United Kingdom xii, 79, 99, 112, 131, 209, 214, 216
    relations with 83, 117
United Nations
    Japan's role 6, 33, 39, 40, 97, 117, 202, 220, 226, 228, **244**, 246, 247
    Security Council 244, 245
United States 234
    China, Nixon and 190–1, 220, 246–7
    foreign policy involving Japan 96, 97, 98–9, 100, 160–1, 192–4, 220–1, 245–9, 258
    Japan, relations with, xiii, xvii, xxiv, xxvii, xxxi, 23, 24, 96, 97, 116, 166, 190–1, 201, 202, 220–1, 229, 232–3, **245–9**, 235, 239, 257–8
    Korean War and 141–2, 247, 248, 257
    Okinawa 196–8, 246, 247–8, 249
    September 11th 2001 39–40, 41, 42–3, 99, 160–1, 244, 245, 249
    trade and investment pressure from 100–1
    see also anti-Americanism; defence policy; history, Allied Occupation; Occupation policy
universalist theory xxii–xxiv, xxvii
universities 48–9, 232–3
Uno Sōsuke 132, 139, 210, 211, **249–50**
urbanisation xx, 57–8

Van Wolferen, K. xxv, xxxi–xxxii
Vietnam War xxvii, xxviii, 62, 97, 128, 190, 192, 219, 228, 232–3, 247, 248
    political activism and 232–3
violence, political 84–7 *see also* extremist movements; terrorism
Vogel, Ezra F. xxviii, xxxi, 226
Voice of Japan Communist Party 222
Voice of the People 188, **251**
voting 57–60
    history of xv, xviii, 57
    women and xviii, 57, 253
    see also elections, electoral behaviour

Wada Hiroo 127, 136, **252**
Watanabe Michio 87, 121, 178, 183, **252–3**, 257
Watanabe Osamu 80
weapons 39, 195, 202–4
    mass destruction 33
    see also atomic weapons; nuclear issues
welfare *see* social welfare
Welfare Party 66, 206
Welfield, John 142
Whitney, Major-General Courtney 32
Williams, David xxxii–xxxiii
women xviii
    employment and 146, 147
    politicians 44–5, 132, 239–40, 253, 254
    politics and 142, 171, 189, **253–5**
    post-war changes 93
    pre-war role of 92–4
    rights of 45, 57, 92, 128
World Bank 117
World Trade Organisation 8, 34, 118, 163, 248

World War II xvi–xvii, 223, 230, 245
  fiftieth anniversary 180, 187
  Okinawa 196–7, 246
  Pearl Harbour xvi, 245
  war crimes trials, Tokyo (1946) 223
  see also history, Allied Occupation;
  Occupation policy

Yamagishi Akira 44, 130, 147
Yamaguchi Jirō 17
Yamahana Hideo 256
Yamahana Sadao, 179, 238, **256**
Yamamoto Kenzō 191
Yamamoto Kōichi 183
Yamamoto Mari 203
Yamasaki Taku 88, 135, **256–7**
Yanagisawa Hakuo 139
Yano Junya 120, 236, **257**
Yatabe Osamu 189
YKK 257
Yokohama 6, 11
Yokomichi Takahiro 43
Yomiuri Shinbun 33, 113
Yosano Akiko 45

Yoshida Liberal Party 72, 135, 137, 235, 238
Yoshida Shigeru xvii, xviii, 20, 23, 27, 28, 29, 61, 71, 90, 97, 100, 101, 108, 119, 140, 148, 155, 161, 181–2, 209, 211, 219, 222, 230, 246, **257–8**
  shipbuilding scandal and 223–4, 258
  Yoshida doctrine 258
Young Storm Association (*Seirankai*) 88, 176, 177, 178, 181, 237, 252, 256

zaibatsu xviii, 91
zaikai (Big Business) 16, 94, 207
Zenmin rōkyō see All-Japan Council of Private Sector Trade Unions
Zenrō kaigi see All-Japan Trade Union Congress
Zenrōkyō see National Liaison Council of Labour Unions
Zenrōren (I) see National Labour Union Liaison Council
Zenrōren (II) see National Labour Union Alliance